VENICE AS THE POLITY OF MERCY

Venice as the Polity of Mercy

Guilds, Confraternities, and the Social Order, c. 1250–c. 1650

RICHARD MACKENNEY

UNIVERSITY OF TORONTO PRESS
Toronto Buffalo London

Toronto Buffalo London
utorontopress.com

ISBN 978-1-4426-4968-2

Toronto Italian Studies

Library and Archives Canada Cataloguing in Publication

Mackenney, Richard, author
Venice as the polity of mercy : guilds, confraternities, and the social order, c. 1250–c. 1650 / Richard Mackenney.

(Toronto Italian studies)
Includes bibliographical references and index.
ISBN 978-1-4426-4968-2 (cloth)

1. Guilds – Italy – Venice – History. 2. Confraternities – Italy – Venice – History. 3. Venice (Italy) – Economic conditions – To 1797. 4. Venice (Italy) – Politics and government. 5. Venice (Italy) – Religious life and customs. I. Title. II. Series: Toronto Italian studies

HD6472.V4M337 2018 945'.311 C2018-903916-7

University of Toronto Press acknowledges the financial assistance to its publishing program of the Canada Council for the Arts and the Ontario Arts Council, an agency of the Government of Ontario.

Funded by the Government of Canada
Financé par le gouvernement du Canada

al miglior fabbro
Brian Pullan
e alla memoria di
Bruno Borsato
(?- 2008)
maestro della vita genuina

Contents

List of Figures ix
List of Tables and Appendices xiii
Acknowledgments xv

Introduction: Economy, Polity, and Religion, c. 1250–c. 1650 3
The Venetian Popolo: Anonymous or Autonomous? 3
The Spectrum of Representation 8
The Sources and Their Scope 17
The Stones of Venice 23

1 Venice as Mercantile System, c. 1250–c. 1300 28
Polity, 1297 28
Polity, 1268 31
Economy, 1271 33
Religion, 1247 36

2 Proliferation and Punctuation, c. 1300–c. 1500 75
The Confraternities of Venice 75
Before the Black Death, 1300–48 81
The Impact of the Plague 86
From the Black Death to the Bianchi, 1348–99 86
The Bianchi, 1399 89
The Franciscan Revival and Social Change, c. 1400–c. 1450 93
Plague and Patronage, c. 1450–c. 1500 98
The Vision of the Polity 101

3 Who Were the Venetians, c. 1500–c. 1600? 113
Metropolis and Cosmopolis 113
Rooms at the Inns, 1530–1 119
L'arte dei fabbri 126
Strands of Identity 133
"Quel ramo del lago di Como" 139
The Tale of "Il Medeghino" 147

4 Officers and Office in the Mercers' Guild, c. 1450–c. 1600 151
A Little Republic? 151
Arte dei marzeri and Scuola di San Teodoro 153
Officers and Members 154
Oligarchs or Plutocrats? A Test Case 162
Official Business 178

5 Monuments to Mercy, c. 1500–c. 1600 189
Arti and Scuole in the Sixteenth Century 189
The Scuole del Venerabile 196
The Sovvegni 206
The Scuole and the Stones of Venice 213
The Wider Network 242

6 The Venetians and the Confessional State, c. 1550–c. 1600 245
The Autonomy of the Venetian Laity 245
The Agencies of the Confessional State 247
The Inquisition and the Venetian Laity 252
The Visitation of 1581 271
Venice and the Defence of Political Absolutism 278
Tintoretto and the Last Fight 280

Conclusion: A Final Realignment of Economy, Polity, and Religion? c. 1600–c. 1700 307
Morbidity in an Age of Decline: The Suffragi 307
Family Ties 318
An Envoi: Decadence or Shift? 326

Maps 341
List of Abbreviations 351
Notes 353
Bibliography 407
Index 459

Figures

1a, b, and c The Polity of Mercy, c. 1250–c. 1700 12–14
2 *The Prayer for the Discovery of the Remains of Saint Mark*, 1260–70, mosaic 45
3 *The Tower of Babel*, c. 1220, mosaic 46
4 *Grainstores*, detail from the *Story of Joseph*, 1260–70, mosaic 47
5 *Vigilance Presiding over Fair and Fraudulent Trade*, early thirteenth century, sculpture 48
6 *Bakers*, later thirteenth century, detail from *Trades beneath the Mystic Lamb*, sculpture 49
7a *Capitello delle arti*, fourteenth century, sculpture 50
7b *Measurer*, detail from *Capitello delle arti*, fourteenth century, sculpture 50
8 *The Three Ages*, mid-thirteenth century, schema of Joachim of Fiore 53
9 Giotto, *Judas*, detail from *The Last Judgement*, 1306–13 56
10 *Madonna della Carità*, fourteenth century, bas-relief sculpture 62
11 *Madonna della Misericordia*, fourteenth century, buildings of the Scuola Grande della Carità 63
12 *Madonna della Misericordia*, no date, high-relief sculpture 64
13 *Saint Mark Blessing*, mid-fifteenth century, sculpture 65
14 *Madonna della Misericordia*, late-fourteenth century, high-relief sculpture 70
15 *Madonna della Misericordia*, sixteenth century, bas-relief sculpture 71
16 Bartolomeo Bon, *Virgin and Child with Kneeling Members of the Scuola della Misericordia*, 1445–50, relief 97
17 Plan of the Mercers' Stalls for the Festa della Sensa, 1586 183
18 Tintoretto (Jacopo Robusti), *The Baptism of Christ*, c. 1580, oil on canvas 217

19 Girolamo da Santa Croce, *Saint Thomas à Becket Enthroned with Saint Francis and Saint John the Baptist*, 1520, oil on panel 218
20 Workshop of Alessandro Vittoria, *Saint James*, 1602, sculpture 220
21 Il Pordenone (Giovanni Antonio de' Sacchis), *Saints Sebastian, Roch, and Catherine*, 1531, oil on canvas 222
22a School of Leonardo Corona, *Archangel Gabriel*, sixteenth to seventeenth centuries, from *Annunciation* 223
22b School of Leonardo Corona, *Virgin Annunciate*, sixteenth to seventeenth centuries, from *Annunciation* 224
23 Domenico Tintoretto, *The Eternal Father in Glory with Doge Marino Grimani and Dogaressa Morosina Morosini, and Members of the Guild of Poulterers*, late sixteenth to seventeenth centuries 225
24 Albrecht Duerer, *Feast of the Rosary*, 1506, oil on panel 226
25 Sante Peranda, *Fall of Manna*, 1602, oil on canvas 227
26 Palma il Giovane (Jacopo Negretti), *Plague of Serpents*, end of the sixteenth century 228
27 Palma il Giovane (Jacopo Negretti), *Saint Bartholomew*, oil on canvas, late sixteenth century 229
28 Marco del Moro, *All Saints*, 1572 230
29 Giovanni Bellini, *The Supper at Emmaus*, 1513, oil on canvas 231
30 Sante Peranda, *Virgin and Child with San Carlo Borromeo and Donors*, 1602? (Bartolomeo Bontempelli, "dal Calice") 232
31 Palma il Giovane (Jacopo Negretti), *Madonna in Glory with Saint Anthony Abbot, Saint John the Baptist, and Saint Francis*, 1600–3 234
32 Bonifazio de' Pitati (now attributed to Stefano dell'Arzere), *Martyrdom of Saint Theodore*, late fifteenth century?, oil on canvas 235
33 The Altar of the Mercers' Guild, Chiesa di San Zulian, 1579–84 (for the arte dei marzeri): [Palma il Giovane, *Assumption of the Virgin* oil on canvas] 237
34 Campo San Zulian, warehouse barbacani 238
35 *Madonna della Misericordia*, relief, Merceria San Zulian 238
36 Lazzaro Bastiani, *Saint Antony of Padua on the Walnut Tree*, oil on panel 240
37 Jacobello and Pierpaolo dale Masegne, *Saint Antony of Padua*, c. 1390–5, sculpture 243
38 Tintoretto (Jacopo Robusti), *The Presentation at the Temple*, c. 1540, oil on canvas 285
39 Tintoretto (Jacopo Robusti), *Last Supper*, 1561–2, oil on canvas 288
40 Tintoretto (Jacopo Robusti), *Last Supper*, 1574–5, oil on canvas 290
41 Tintoretto (Jacopo Robusti), *Last Supper*, 1579–80, oil on canvas 291

42 Tintoretto (Jacopo Robusti), *The Presentation at the Temple*, 1587, oil on canvas 292
43 Tintoretto (Jacopo Robusti), *The Assumption of the Virgin*, 1582, oil on canvas 294
44 Tintoretto (Jacopo Robusti), *Ecce homo*, 1566, oil on canvas 295
45 Tintoretto (Jacopo Robusti), *Crucifixion*, 1565, oil on canvas 296
46 Tintoretto (Jacopo Robusti), *Saint Roch in Glory*, 1564, oil on canvas 298
47 Tintoretto (Jacopo Robusti), *Allegory of the Scuola della Misericordia*, 1564, oil on canvas 298
48 Titian (Tiziano Vecellio), *The Presentation of the Virgin*, 1534–8, oil on canvas 302
49 Titian (Tiziano Vecellio), *Madonna della Misericordia*, 1573, oil on canvas 303
50a and b Domenico Tintoretto, *Members of the Scuola di San Cristoforo dei Mercanti*, 1591, oil on canvas 304–5
51 Tintoretto (Jacopo Robusti) and assistants (or Domenico Tintoretto?), *Madonna della Misericordia*, c. 1550–70, oil on canvas 306
52 Giovanni Battista Cima da Conegliano, *The Annunciation*, 1495, oil on canvas 312
53 Giovanni Battista Cima da Conegliano, *Saint Lanfranc Enthroned between Saint John the Baptist and Saint Liberius*, c. 1515–16, oil on panel 313
54 *Madonna della Misericordia*, 1501, relief 315
55a Giuseppe Sardi, Chiesa di Santa Maria del Giglio, façade, 1683 328
55b Giuseppe Sardi, Chiesa di Santa Maria del Giglio, detail, façade, 1683 329
56 Alessandro Tremignon, Chiesa di San Moise, façade, 1668 330
57 Louis Dorigny, *The Triumph of the Name of Jesus*, 1732, fresco 331
58 Giambattista Tiepolo, *The Institution of the Rosary*, 1737–9, fresco 332
59 Gianmaria Morlaiter, *Aaron the Prophet*, 1750–1, sculpture 333
60 Canaletto (Giovanni Antonio Canal), *The Stonemason's Yard*, c. 1725, oil on canvas 335

Tables and Appendices

Tables

1.1 Chronological Registration of Guild Statutes, 1219–1312 34
1.2 Chronology of Foundations of Scuole in Venice, 1247–99 59
3.1 The Calle dei Fabbri, 1530–1 137
4.1 Elections in the Mercers' Guild, 1577–1609 168
4.2 Elections and Officers in the Mercers' Guild, 1577–1609 169
4.3 Number of Terms of Office in the Mercers' Guild, 1577–1609 173
4.4 Offices and Elections in the Mercers' Guild, 1577–1609 174
4.5 Average Span of Years of Office-Holding, 1577–1609 176
4.6 Allocations of Booths for the Sensa, 1585–1602 185
5.1 Foundations of Scuole in Venice, c. 1500–c. 1600 192
5.2 Foundations of Sovvegni in Venice, 1541–99 208
C.1 Foundations of Confraternities in Venice, c. 1600–c. 1700 317

Appendices

2.1 Chronology of Foundations of Scuole in Venice, c. 1300–c. 1500 103
2.2 Foundations of Scuole, by Church of Location, c. 1250–c. 1500 105
6.1 Commissions of Paintings by the Scuole according to Ridolfi (*Maraviglie dell'arte*), before and after Tintoretto 300
C.1 The Impact of the Plague of 1630 on the Populations of Venice and the Terraferma 336
C.2 Foundations of Confraternities in Venice, c. 1600–1727 337

Acknowledgments

This book reflects a scholarly lifetime's fascination with the city of Venice, the Venetians, and their history. I have incurred a multitude of academic and intellectual debts, the greatest of which reflect the extraordinary blend of knowledge and friendship that holds together the academic republic and renders priceless the privilege of being part of it. In the interests of manageability, I name only those who have had a direct influence on the shape and substance of the completed project. The list remains very long indeed.

My education at Aylesbury Grammar School in England was of a calibre that I continue to treasure thanks to the headship of K.D. Smith. From my years at Queens' College, Cambridge University, I still think and laugh in the memories of the late Jonathan Riley-Smith and of the late Ken and Elizabeth Machin. The University of Edinburgh was the nursery of my career, and I am sorry I had to bid farewell to so many colleagues – far too many to mention – whom I still call friends. I am grateful to have had the opportunity to work at Binghamton University (part of the State University of New York), and I thank all the members of the History Department for their patience during the long process of production.

In pursuing research in Venice itself, I received essential support from the British Academy and the Gladys Krieble Delmas Foundation. More recently, I have been the grateful beneficiary of funding and two semesters of research leave from the Dean's Office in Harpur College at Binghamton University. I thank Peter Milleur, Don Nieman, Anne McCall, and Anna Addonisio for their help in facilitating the program of fieldwork that I hope has made the book distinctive.

The repositories of sources that have granted me access and whose staff have offered endless patience in solving a string of queries are the Archivio di Stato di Venezia, Cambridge University Library, the Library of the Warburg Institute (especially the then director, Charles Hope), the Library of the Courtauld

Institute (especially the deputy book librarian, Vicky Kontou), the Library of Villa i Tatti (especially the then director, Lino Pertile), the British Library, the Moberly Library of Winchester College, the Library of the Fondazione Giorgio Cini, and the Biblioteca Querini-Stampalia. The Glenn G. Bartle Library is a trove of treasures – mostly unsung – at Binghamton University. It has enabled me to use precious research time in the teaching semester to best effect (and, in particular, I thank Beth Kilmarx of Special Collections). Kind and expert help with elusive references at late stages was indispensable, and I record my gratitude to Tim Carapella, Madelynn Cullings, and Elise Thornley.

In experimenting with ideas, I thank those who have found me audiences, and I thank the audiences themselves. Peta Motture arranged a marvelous opportunity for me both to study Bartolomeo Bon's *Madonna della Misericordia* before the opening of the new gallery at the Victoria and Albert Museum and then to present a graduate seminar and deliver a public lecture. Patricia Allerston, deputy director of the National Gallery of Scotland, enabled me to revise what I had read about Ruskin and Venice as part of a superb program in Edinburgh. I am glad to have had the occasion to put various ideas to the test in conferences of the Renaissance Society of America in San Francisco, Venice, and Montreal. At Binghamton University I learned much from an invitation to speak at the Center for Medieval and Renaissance Studies. A presentation to the Department of History elicited much-needed encouragement from Doug Bradburn, Leigh Ann Wheeler, and Rafa't Abu el-Haj. I gave a revised version of this in London, which drew fascinating questions from David Chambers, Filippo di Vivo, and Simone Testa.

As is repeated in the notes, I am very grateful for vital contributions to the text from Martin Chick, Nick Davidson, Gary Dickson, Adam Fox, the late Peter Laven, David Luscombe, John Martin, Lauro Martines, Geoffrey Parker, the late Nick Phillipson, James Shaw, Joe Stanley, and the late Sandro Sticca. For their breathing of life into historical topography, I thank Roberto Schiavon and Simonetta Cabras, proprietors of the Nave de Oro in Venice, and I thank Pierangelo Masciadri for his upholding of traditional skills as well as for his introduction to Carla and Andrea Negrini in Bellagio, who in turn set up a tremendously important meeting with the late Antonio Bellati. Ben Angove provided invaluable human "back-up" for endless drafts of the text in his own extremely hectic schedule.

The extraordinary patience and generosity of historians of the painting, sculpture, and architecture of Venice have been indispensable to any insights that the text may offer to historians of all sorts. I express my deepest thanks to Vicky Avery, Tracy Cooper, Richard Goy, Paul Hills, Charles Hope, Deborah Howard, Peter Humfrey, Lyle Humphrey, Anne Markham-Schulz, Allison Morgan Shearman, and Tom Nichols.

Whole chapters have improved beyond measure thanks to Michael Angold, Stephen Bowd, and Mary Laven. Owen Dudley Edwards took on an even larger bleeding chunk and provided a host of insights for the first five chapters. His gift of A.G. Gardiner's *Prophets, Priests, and Kings* cemented my resolve to use illustrative materials with a quotation from G.K. Chesterton:

Stand up and keep your childishness:
Read all the pedants' screeds and strictures;
But don't believe in anything
That can't be told in coloured pictures.

With regard to reference materials, I am immensely grateful to Connor McCormack for his many hours of work on the text – particularly the notes, diagrams, and maps – for submission to the publisher. Joseph Giovenco and Sonja Zabala generously helped in applying some of the captions to the illustrations. In an important sense, those illustrations became their own project. They could not have appeared but for Marina Cotugno, who showed tireless determination and inexhaustible ingenuity over two full years in assembling illustrations and clearing copyrights; I am very grateful to her and to Pancake Produzioni in Rome. Marcy Sloan brought her very considerable professional expertise to bear on finalizing captions, lay-out, and dust-jacket.

Two scholars agreed to the burdensome undertaking of reading what I had thought would be the final version of the entire text. Rob Bartlett has the most searching and original historical mind I have ever encountered. Chris Black combines a profound expertise in the reading of Venetian materials with a peerless capacity for telling comparisons with other places in Italy. I am still humbled that they took on the task of reading the entire draft. I wonder at their expertise in identifying the need for cuts (especially appendectomies) and reconfigurations. I can never thank them enough. A month at the Jefferson Center in Charlottesville on other business (thanks to the director, Andrew O'Shaughnessy) provided a revitalizing environment in which to absorb and digest the wealth of the meticulous comments, corrections, and suggestions – breathtaking in both detail and range – that these splendid scholars and wonderful friends had so magnanimously provided.

I am also mindful of my great good fortune in finding a place for the book with the University of Toronto Press. William Landon was kind enough to refer me to the late Ron Schoeffel, who had placed the text with two expert and probing readers before his sudden death. Since then, Suzanne Rancourt has proved a two-fold model: a model of ingenuity in keeping a text that did all it needed to do within manageable bounds, and a model of patience through the apparently interminable delays of assembling the illustrations. Angela Wingfield's meticulous work on the text made countless improvements. Christine Robertson was peerless in the patience she gave to the author's terror of technology. They shall obtain mercy. In Milford, Pennsylvania, Hillary Needleman's tutorial on the computer was worth more than I can express.

Breaks from the text, accompanied by the gentlest requests for progress reports, have been the gifts of my dear friends in the United Kingdom: Sarah and Andrew Kemp in Aldeburgh, William and Catherine Leith in Jersey, and Mick Lewis and Alison Barnett in Farnham. Whether in Cambridge or in London, Paul and Wendy Hartle have stayed resiliently in touch. Stephen Lees has been a pattern of expert librarianship and constant friendship, and Rob Wyke has offered refreshment of many kinds and great good cheer on numerous occasions in Winchester and London. My brother, Rob, and his wife, Chin, have been the most generous of hosts for weeks on end in Bushey. Greig Angove has freely given accommodation and much else for similar spells in Marylebone, the perfect base for long days at the Warburg Institute. My wife, Margaret, has devoted herself to looking after me through years and years of uncertainty, of thinking and rethinking, of writing and rewriting – and what must have seemed no thinking and no writing at all. Her love and care have always saved me from despair and have been a source of energy and inspiration for the completion of the project.

The two greatest debts that the book itself owes are recorded in the dedication. I can never repay either of them.

VENICE AS THE POLITY OF MERCY

Introduction: Economy, Polity, and Religion, c. 1250–c. 1650

Like Signiors and rich burghers on the flood,
Or as it were the pageants of the sea,
Do overpeer the petty traffickers
That cur'sy to them (do them reverence)
As they fly by them with their woven wings.

– Shakespeare, *The Merchant of Venice*, 1.1.10–14

The Venetian Popolo: Anonymous or Autonomous?

"The government of an exclusive company of merchants is, perhaps, the worst of all governments for any country whatsoever." Such is Adam Smith's unambiguous conclusion to the type of "political Oeconomy" that he classifies as the "mercantile System" in book IV of *The Wealth of Nations* of 1776.[1] It could scarcely be more dismissive or more damning. Its object also has an uncomfortable resonance with the Republic of Venice. Frederic Lane, that wise authority on the history of Venice, once wrote, "All the merchant nobles of Venice operated as one large regulated company of which the board of directors was the Senate."[2] It is difficult to imagine a more sharply defined picture of "the government of an exclusive company of merchants." Smith's vision of free trade, division of labour, and competition among producers for the custom of the consumer is, apparently, quite antithetical to the political economy of the Venetians. By comparison, that economy appears crimped and mean in a small world left behind by the new global vision of the Age of Enlightenment.[3] This book will question the exclusiveness of the government of Venice, and it will do so with particular reference to the generally recognizable value system of the Venetians, adding a religious dimension to their political economy – a dimension of which Adam Smith the moral philosopher, as opposed to Adam Smith the political economist, might have approved.[4] At the very outset, it is worth taking some time to concentrate on the question of whether the constitution of Venice was exclusive and, if so, in what senses.

The starting point for the history of the Venetian Republic has traditionally been the nature of its constitution and the reflection of it in the social structure. Any reconsideration must take this into account, so pervasive is it in the existing literature. The nature of the constitution has, for centuries, seemed rigidly exclusive. Before this book begins a reinterpretation it is worth recapitulating some basic features of what is under scrutiny. In the traditional view of the constitution, government was in the hands of twenty-five hundred adult males aged over twenty-five years, to the exclusion of their own women and children and of other orders. Society itself was a composite of two orders – the *nobili* and the rest – or three orders – *nobili*, *cittadini*, and the rest, depending upon the interpretation of the observer.[5] The constant in this picture is the exclusion of "the rest," the *popolani*, who remain largely anonymous.

The tripartite social structure would have been recognizable to Shakespeare, and it corresponds conventionally enough to the characterizations of contemporary commentators. The "signiors" represent the patriciate, the "rich burghers" correspond to the citizen class, and the host of "petty traffickers" to artisans, shopkeepers, and their families. Such classifications would operate reasonably well in the census that the Venetian government ordered in 1563.[6] There was some debate as to whether the only true citizens were the patricians, but, like them, the cittadini comprised a legally defined class. Few would argue with the notion that the general population was excluded from any meaningful role in political life.[7] Recent research has revealed the extent of the interaction and especially the intermarriage of patricians and cittadini, most significantly as the patriciate sought to fight off its numerical decline in the plague of 1630 and the War of Candia (1645–69).[8] The "petty traffickers" remain excluded from a political order whose fixity provided first continuity, then rigidity and ossification, and finally decay. When we seek to explain stability through a myth of the constitution, the controlling hand of the patriciate never seems in doubt. That notion of decay or decline in the seventeenth century serves to exaggerate the assumption of stability and continuity in the preceding period.[9] In some respects, such an approach swallows whole the myth of Venice as a source of stability and sets up a unitary notion of demise: a stiff, linear plateau followed by an equally stiff, linear descent.

The persistence of such thinking owes much to Cardinal Gasparo Contarini's work on the Venetian constitution, dating from the early 1530s. His book enjoyed a wide audience in the sixteenth and seventeenth centuries and propagated, throughout Europe, Venice's singular immunity to rebellion from within and its invulnerability to conquest from without. It was translated into English in Shakespeare's time, in 1599.[10] In Contarini's account the stability for which Venice was famed was due to the constitution, which in turn was the design of a wise ruling class.

In this picture the corporations of the city into which the nobility had sagaciously organized the ruled were part of the patrician master plan. According to Contarini, the "Scuole Grandi," the largest of the city's religious confraternities, were patrician prototypes and set a pattern that the smaller guilds and brotherhoods followed. All were part of a hierarchy of corporations, which the patrician state oversaw and regulated. At the time of Contarini's writing, there were five large brotherhoods, strategically scattered through all but one of the *sestieri* (sixths) into which the city was divided.[11] Contarini presented them as the means by which the legally defined citizen class, the cittadini, and, following suit downwards in the hierarchy, the rest of the non-noble population, received compensation for their exclusion from magisterial office and the exercise of genuine political power. "The fellowships," Contarini wrote, "are all restrained under the power of and authoritie of the Councell of Ten, so that they may not in any thing make any alteration, nor assemble together, unlesse it be appointed seasons, without their leave and permission, such honours doe the plebeians of eyther sort attaine unto in this commonwealth of ours, to the end that they should not altogether think themselves deprived of publike authority, and civile offices, but should also in some sort have their ambition satisfied without having occasion either to hate or perturbe the estate of the nobilitie."[12]

Here are the fundamental and enduring features of the myth of Venice concerning the place of the *popolo*. What does it matter whether we speak of two social orders or three? The "plebeians of eyther sort," that is, both the legally defined citizen class and the artisans, shopkeepers, and their families (who made up some three quarters of the population), were excluded from magisterial office and the exercise of real power. Under the vigilant supervision of the Council of Ten, the committee for state security, the "plebeyans of either sort" could involve themselves in office-holding in the corporations and leave the patriciate undisturbed in its wise exercise of political power. Even in the early twentieth century it was possible to characterize Venice as a patrician republic, as though no one else really counted for much.[13] An excellent textbook, first published in 1899, which reached its seventh edition in 1941, was still in print in the 1960s. From one of its very useful appendices, "Venetian Constitution in the Fifteenth and Sixteenth Centuries," a candidate reviewing Venice in expectation of an examination question could learn – and parrot – a recognizable and reasonable explanation for Venice's stability.[14]

In his great study of 1971, Brian Pullan transformed the conventional picture. He showed that the Scuole Grandi fulfilled functions that were much more than a substitute for political power. The research that the book embodied broke out of the constraints of a view of Venetian history that the patriciate dominated and directed. Indeed, Professor Pullan demonstrated that the charitable activities of the Scuole Grandi played a significant part in the day-to-day maintenance of the social order. However, he found "quite plausible" Contarini's presentation of these institutions as "compensation" to the cittadini for their "exclusion."[15] Moreover, even his reconfiguration of approaches to the history of Venice never quite removed a residual neatness that may be somewhat misleading. Monumental as his study was, it treated the Scuole Grandi as discrete entities, largely separate from other, similar institutions in the city. This may not do full justice to the ways in which a larger and untidier network of *scuole* touched the lives of the Venetian popolo – not only touched, but guided and reassured. Even a generation after the publication of Professor Pullan's book, it is still possible to treat the patriciate in relation to its self-image and in isolation from everyone except those who wished to join it.[16]

Pullan's work focused on the largest of the confraternities, the Scuole Grandi. The office-holders in these institutions were, by law, all members of the cittadini, and they collected and allocated resources from members of the scuole who, like themselves, were part of an order of the "rich." They distributed assistance, often accruing from investments, to the "poor." This second order might count among its number the "poveri vergognosi," the shamefaced poor, who included members of the nobility. The majority of the poor who received the charity of the Scuole Grandi were non-nobles, or "popolani." However, the poor people in the Scuole Grandi who formed an order were permanently poor – as the rich were permanently rich. The "structural poor" included widows, orphans, cripples, beggars – people who were poor whatever the fortunes of the economy. According to Reinhold Mueller, it was unlikely that the charity dispensed by the Scuole Grandi could have reached more than about 8 per cent of the general population; he speculated that the figure might double if the contributions and distributions of the guilds, the *scuole piccole*, and the Procurators of San Marco were added.[17]

This current study goes beyond the institutions of the cittadini and the ranks of the structural poor and investigates the history of the people who might be self-sufficient at one point in the economic cycle but might face difficulty at another. The picture that emerges is that the temporarily disadvantaged of the Venetian popolani looked after themselves and each other in a complex of institutions that were complementary and bound together in a principle of reciprocity best characterized in contemporary terms as "Misericordia" or "Mercy." From the outset, this study questions the idea that the Venetian social order was, as a human reality, a series of sealed strata – the nobili, the cittadini, and the great formless mass of the popolo, this last given shape only by the directives of government. However much members of the patriciate and the *cittadinanza* fashioned their exclusiveness, there is plenty of evidence of contact through seepage between all three notional layers. Furthermore, in examining the history of the corporations of the Venetian popolo from the thirteenth century to the seventeenth, this study reveals surprising levels of self-determination in their economic and religious life. Time and again, the evidence evokes a busy and self-confident population engaged in the management of their own institutions, microcosmic cells that formed a greater whole of which they were self-evidently part. The exposition will emphasize again and again the strength and versatility of the value system of the Venetian popolo, its rationale of reciprocity, and its active involvement of small groups of people in a much larger complex of corporate entities.

This is not to say that the reverse of the myth was true, that the guilds somehow excluded the government's intervention. Rather, that intervention was not decisive but could be complementary (approving a statute or a new regulation) or informative (transmitting changes that might affect any or all trades). Moreover, guilds and guildsmen might contest a magisterial decision (in the adjudication of trade disputes, for instance, or by resisting the imposition that would supply oarsmen for the state galleys). There is no suggestion of some permanent dialectic of struggle between guilds and government as between society and state. That remained the case even in the later sixteenth century, when both Church and State sought to impose new forms of political and religious discipline in areas of traditional popolano autonomy; the place of religion always modifies the picture and usually complicates it.

In assessing the fortunes of the republic from a standpoint in the institutions of the popolo, the argument seeks to inject movement into the picture of the social order. In setting aside the idea of the static and the linear, it presents instead the dynamic and the circular. In the evidence presented in the chapters that follow, the energy that circulated between economic, political, and religious life was animated by a set of shared values and convictions, and this combination formed a system of political economy that was remarkable both in its resilience and in its adaptability in the interests of the people who were supposed to have been excluded from power. Although the popolani had no role in the governing councils of the commune or of the Signoria, within their own institutions and within a greater whole they played a highly significant role in the historical destiny of the polity.

The book, then, is a study of the circulation of energy – economic, political, and religious – among the people supposedly shut out of public life.[18]

It examines the Venetian polity from the point of view of those allegedly excluded, and the way in which they sought to protect themselves and each other from a change of condition, a change from some relative prosperity to insecurity and want. This was not so much a fear of misfortune as an expression of confidence in the moral code that animated economic life and governed the course of law. What reduced the likelihood of misfortune becoming catastrophe was a complex of institutions that the popolani formed and ran for themselves. This picture contrasts sharply with Contarini's picture of a hierarchy of social orders, with those excluded from power being carefully compartmentalized in their own containers.

The corporations in question were the guilds and the confraternities. In this book these corporations, not through compartmentalization but through their very overlap and interaction, provided a network whose flexibility and adaptability in changing circumstances – whether of personal condition or of larger historical moment – were themselves an expression of social energy. In other words, the book questions whether the successful survival of the Venetian polity was due to a fixed and rigid social order that a legally defined ruling class conceived and regulated, and suggests instead that Venice's fascinating longevity was dependent on a capacity for movement that for centuries looked inexhaustible.

In some ways, this is hardly surprising. Venice was a commercial metropolis set in water and dependent on the movement of people and goods as its life blood: on immigrants for the replenishment of its population and on imports of grain to sustain them.[19] However, as a characterization of a system of political economy this is difficult to translate into a characterization of the constitution, of the complex of magistracies that made up the sovereignty of the republic. Or, rather, it is difficult if we keep the constitution confined to an Aristotelian typology. Was Venice a mixed constitution that perfectly combined monarchy (the Doge), aristocracy (the Senate), and polity (the Greater Council)? Or was it some species of corrupt collective tyranny?[20] The problem diminishes somewhat if we ask instead what constituted the Venetian Republic. What were the components of its machinery? How did they operate in the world of everyday life? What was the balance of social forces that underpinned it? What were the principles that those who lived within the polity recognized and generally shared?

The Spectrum of Representation

The chapters that follow seek to demonstrate the involvement of the popolo in what constituted the Venetian political economy. The institutions under scrutiny demonstrate a freedom and variety of foundation, function, and organization with frequent overlap and interaction but surprisingly little evidence of mutual exclusion. It may be helpful at this point to provide a working definition of each type of corporation and to suggest their respective importance at different times within the overall chronological framework of the study, as well as to remark on those features that look to be distinctively Venetian in their character or broadly similar to those in other cities of Europe.

Before any attempt to spell out certain definitions of type, it is vital to repeat the importance of interaction, the interaction of different institutions that were at once the expression and the generator of social energy. It is essential to keep in the eyes of the mind the facts of foundation before authorization, the occasional manifestation of the magistrates' lack of awareness of lines of category. For example, the Scuole Grandi were emphatically not, from their origins, a separate type of corporation. All trade guilds had devotional confraternities as part of their organization, confraternities sometimes formed around particular trades. Confraternities devoted to the Holy Sacrament shared altars and other ecclesiastical space; self-help groups were linked to trade guilds but could celebrate the cult of particular saints in particular churches. There was a proliferation within the general network – irrespective of institutional type – of dowries, hospitals, alms and alms housing, and strands of support that extended the family in the training of children as apprentices and offered women their own organizations.

The *arti* were trade guilds. They are familiar from medieval history as corporations of particular professions that attended to matters of quality of product and the control of markets. In the Venetian case there is little evidence of a hierarchy of trades, and there was no single guild of merchants. The arti had no formal role in political representation, a contrast with Florence and with London. Established in the course of the thirteenth century, these institutions were to endure until the suppression of the republic itself in 1797.

The *scuole* were devotional confraternities. The origins of the scuola are not clear. It is customary to disown any connotation of education in this distinctively Venetian term, yet, in the gestation of this study, the recognition dawned that the confraternities played a vital role in the inculcation of those values that formed a self-regulating moral economy for the Venetian popolo, a moral economy that in the fifteenth century was to be taken up by the patriciate.

The confraternities devoted to the cult of the Holy Sacrament, the Scuole del Venerabile, were a phenomenon of the sixteenth century. They displayed certain features that were unquestionably innovative in the context of Venice in that time: the cult of the Sacrament itself, the base of the scuole in the parish, their overt loyalty to the Pope in Rome, and their conveyance of a new awareness of the Devil (rather than Death) and of the humanity of Christ and his suffering. Most striking of all is their precocity. Frequently identified as expressions of a new discipline associated with the Council of Trent and the Counter-Reformation, the clustering of their formation in Venice coincided rather with the Renaissance Papacy, with all its connotations of worldliness and corruption – and with an adaptable and energetic local piety.

The *sovvegni* were a new type of corporation in evidence from about the 1540s. These were mutual aid societies initially grouped around particular trades. They required the regular contribution of members for a scale of benefits that included medical attention.

The latest of the corporations under scrutiny were the *suffragi*, confraternities devoted to the cult of the dead. They appeared in the seventeenth century, particularly in the aftermath of the horrendous plague of 1630. In important ways they mark the rupture of the relationship between everyday working life and the eternal, which had proven one of the most enduring features of Venetian tradition.

That summarizes the spectrum of institutions under scrutiny. In what sense were they representative? In order to answer that question, the study asks its readers to abandon the notions of representative government that were nurtured in the aftermath of the Atlantic revolutions of the late eighteenth century and the romantic nationalism of the nineteenth. The Venetians of this book had no experience or knowledge of parties. They elected to office only in the small worlds of their own institutions; they had no role in the governing councils of the State. However, in important ways and across a very broad spectrum, they were able to identify with a public weal, a commonwealth, a res publica. This may have been microcosmic in the election to guild office, in the collection of dues, in the allocation of those dues, in the maintenance of professional standards, and in the recognition of the responsibilities of the collective towards the misfortunes of its members. Yet, in all these ways the popular corporations of the Venetians were an expression of the recognition of a greater whole in which all had some part to play and in which all might need to tap the resources of reciprocity.

In demonstrating this involvement, the exposition seeks to give some idea of the breadth of Venice's spectrum of representation, a spectrum that ran from the votes cast by the popolani in the election of guild officers to the physical likenesses of these "excluded" human beings in the material fabric of the city. It was through these likenesses that the Venetian popolo could identify with heaven itself and could celebrate their values as transcendent in a fleeting world. The material fabric of Venice preserved monuments – monuments to a system of shared values.These values had their own spectrum, shades that ran from the humble embellishment of a church with banners and the stands for them, to tables and tapestries to honour the sacrament, to altarpieces by masters lesser or greater, and to the exaltation of manual labour in sculptures above the central portal of San Marco itself. These various representations helped ordinary people to identify with a status quo that was far from static, and which gave them plenty of scope – subject to a wide range of negotiation under the law – to make a living and look after each other. Put another way, we might ask whether the Venetian popolani had reason to *feel* excluded from the life of the polity. In respect of such a question, the book is a study of collective mentalities or, more precisely and with the help of Adam Smith, of collective moral sentiments.[21]

No doubt some of the detail in the chapters that follow will face the challenge of specialist knowledge. However, before the history of the Venetian popolo is ground into separate units – not just of guild or confraternity but also of trade, workshop, family, household, parish, and neighbourhood – it seems timely to offer a general view of a pattern of Venetian history as it unfolded from the viewpoint of the popolani.[22] These pages test a general hypothesis relating to the changing configuration of economy, polity, and religion in the lives of ordinary Venetians, and the way in which a value system animated by the principle of Mercy adapted to those changes.

At the outset it is essential to emphasize that Mercy was not a pious abstraction to which it was easy to pay lip-service. As is set out in chapter 1, in a Venetian context, Mercy, or Misericordia, contained within it a strong element of material self-interest that was exceptionally well attuned to Venetian economic life. That self-interest provided both a rationale and an incentive for reciprocity: those who contributed towards the support of the less fortunate at a time when they could afford to do so were investing in their own welfare should there come a time when they themselves stood in need.[23] Misericordia provides a representation of the complex of values that may help to explain the changing relationship of economic, political, and religious life in the city of Venice and of the immigrants it attracted from its own territories and beyond. Amid all the economic, religious, and political uncertainties that the Venetians faced, did they enjoy some consoling fortification in the idea that their equals today might be their inferiors tomorrow and their superiors the day after that? Could charity towards one's brethren translate into the mercy that one might need to extend to those less fortunate than oneself and that one might need in one's own misfortunes?

With those careful provisos and with those questions in mind, the following schema might help to shape the mass of detail in successive chapters:

1a. The Polity of Mercy, c.1250–c.1550

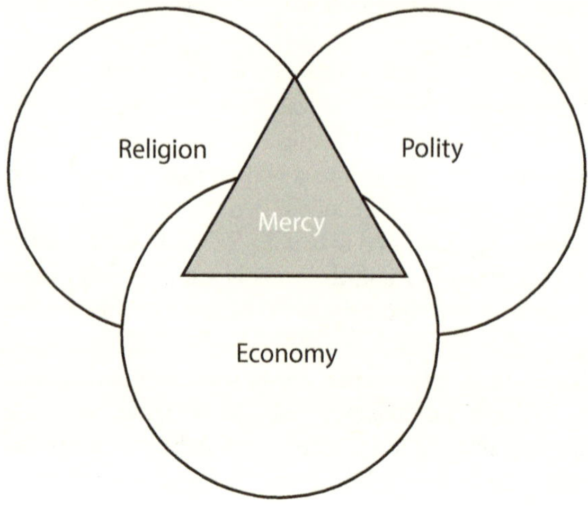

Misericordia appearing as an equilateral triangle amid the three spheres of economic, political, and religious life (see the diagram, The Polity of Mercy).

There is no element in the schema of the constitution springing fully formed from the wise heads of the patricians. Rather, a long period of some three centuries saw first a conjunction in the later thirteenth century and then the slow – and not always steady – development of a working system of economy, politics, and religion down to the middle of the sixteenth century. Thereafter, a protracted realignment of Church and State involved their withdrawal from the working life of the economy, which, left to the devices of the popolo, functioned quite effectively. In the course of the seventeenth century a final realignment was taking place, reconnecting the polity and the economy, while religion moved away from both. The rest of the book will add nuance and qualification to this general picture. Whatever may be the faults of this model in charting a changing configuration from the mid-thirteenth century to the late seventeenth, at least it moves discussion away from a historiography dominated by linear concepts of myth and decline.[24]

In testing the validity of the general pattern against particular evidence, the exposition begins with a formative period in the second half of the thirteenth century (chapter 1). The attention of historians has traditionally focused on the legal definition of the ruling class in the Serrata del Maggior Consiglio (Closing of the Greater Council) in 1297, with the consequent exclusion of the popolo from any political role. This chapter suggests that from the viewpoint

1b. The Polity of Mercy, c.1550–c.1600

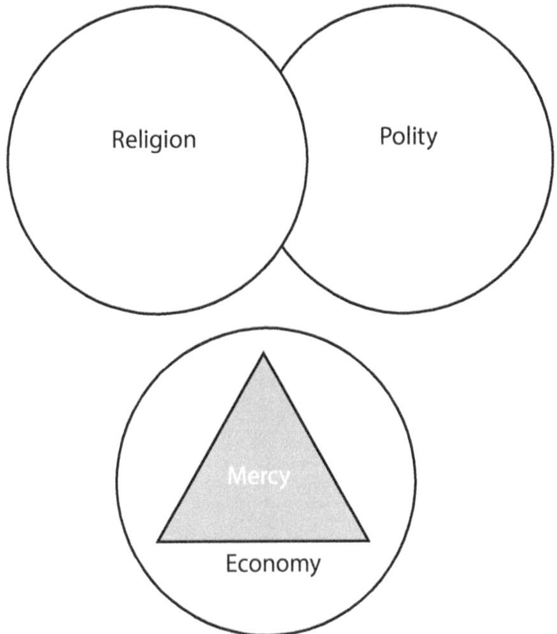

of the popolani themselves the process of definition had a broader base and longer term. Their guilds and confraternities had been in formation for much of the thirteenth century. They celebrated the election of a popular doge, Lorenzo Tiepolo, in 1268, taking an exuberant and extravagant role in the festivities, a public and political occasion of immense solemnity and importance. Very shortly afterwards, in 1271, the magistrates gave the guilds a definitive place in the polity with the ratification of a large number of their statutes. The vexed question of religious change in this period invites a change of perspective on the confraternities. The chapter argues that there is no need for an anachronistic and misleading differentiation between Scuole Grandi and scuole piccole. It suggests instead that the formation of the scuole was an expression of the place of Christian teaching in the medieval urban economy. That is to say, the Scriptures – the Gospel of Matthew and the General Epistle of James in particular – and their spread by the Franciscans, and in Venice perhaps by Saint Antony of Padua, inspired a system founded upon reciprocity in the profit economy. The most fitting contemporary term for that reciprocity was *mercy*, and discussion focuses on how it applied to mercantile activity.

1c. The Polity of Mercy, c.1600–c.1700

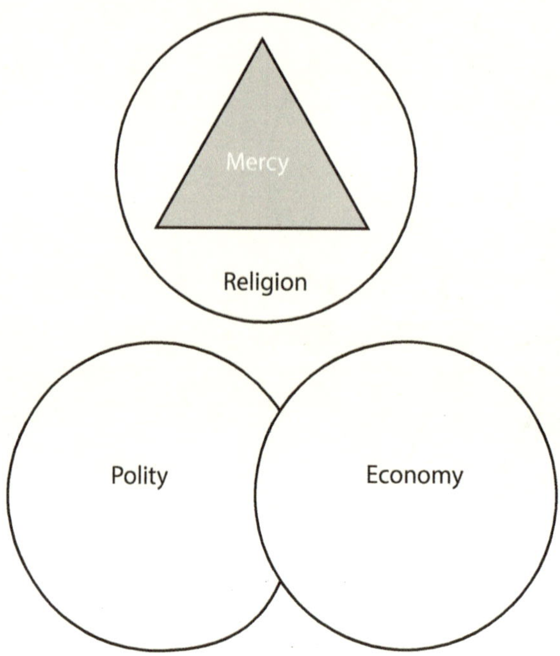

In institutional terms the values that Mercy represented translated into the formation of the Scuola della Misericordia, and the Scuola dei Mercanti, both of which may have had common roots in the Franciscan church of Santa Maria Gloriosa dei Frari.

The political, economic, and religious climate of the fourteenth and fifteenth centuries in Venice and in Europe came under the pressure of catastrophe, especially the Black Death, the Great Schism, and the transformation – or breakdown – of political order in the "age of the despots" in Italy and in popular unrest throughout Europe. Such is the context of chapter 2. This climate of crisis affected the Venetian popolo demonstrably in politics, economic life, and religion, as is clear from the plague in the mid-fourteenth century and from the arrival of the Bianchi, a penitential movement, in 1399. Yet the formation of confraternities continued steadily and strongly throughout the period, perhaps reinforced by the Franciscan revival associated with San Bernardino. However, his influence in Venice may, paradoxically, have made the confraternities more attractive to those above the popolani in social rank. This produced more magnificent and ostentatious artistic patronage, but it also institutionalized a division between lesser and greater confraternities. The distinction between scuole piccole and Scuole Grandi dates clearly from the second half of the fifteenth century, the first signs of a lengthening hierarchy of institutions that was alien to their first principles.

Chapters 3 and 4 shift the focus of attention from the confraternities to the trade guilds – a shift of emphasis rather than of institutional separateness. Each of these chapters examines the history of a different corporation, first the *fabbri* or ironmongers and then the *marzeri* or mercers, who were rivals in the most crowded commercial space of Venice, between Rialto and San Marco. Both chapters concentrate on the meticulousness of the records kept by the guilds themselves. The discussion of the ironmongers attempts to draw the maximum value from the meagre historical records that have survived. Close concentration on lists of members from 1530–1 pushes the implications of these across the western border of the Venetian mainland state into Lombardy. The chapter is a microcosm, a study in very great detail of familiar general themes of Venetian history: Venice was a city of immigrants, and they came to the city in response to forces that pushed them from their homelands and forces that pulled them to the lagoon. The chapter chronicles the push of the piratical tyranny of a gangster on Lake Como and the pull of Venice's need for iron. Despite their efficiency in the absorption of immigrants, however, the ironmongers lost the battle for commercial space to their greatest rivals.

Chapter 4 turns to the records of the guild of mercers, the largest, wealthiest, and most powerful of the arti of Venice. The guild's records contrast with the ironmongers' in their plenty. The guild's relationship with the Scuola di San Teodoro was highly significant. Its membership lists were extensive. Those records also include a list of elections to office within the guild that give particular pause for thought over the spectrum of representation. The chapter includes a test case of whether office was confined to some kind of clique. It goes on to examine the everyday duties of the guild's officers in protecting the mercers' extravagant claims to the monopoly of certain wares, the endlessly tiresome job of assembling the members who were willing to take a stall at the great market following Ascension Day, and the long string of litigation with other guilds and with hawkers who were members of no guild at all.

Chapter 5 steps back from this detail to examine the confraternities in the age of Reformation and Counter-Reformation. The Venetian evidence suggests the need to be cautious in the application of both terms to the popular religion of the city. Once again, the theme of continuity in the history of Venetian confraternities, which contributed greatly to their network in the sixteenth century, is very strong. There were notable accretions to that network in the sixteenth century: the confraternities for the cult of the Holy Sacrament, and the mutual aid societies of certain of the trade guilds. There is no evidence that either of these innovatory institutions caused disruption or diminution to the pre-existing network; rather, they were sources of supplement, reinforcement, and expansion. The demonstration of this comes in an examination of the representative case histories of what the corporations had embedded in the material fabric of Venice by the end of the sixteenth century. The exercise attempts to invoke what a member of the popolo might have seen or experienced in his or her devotional and commercial life between the church and the shop or the marketplace. This is much more than a catalogue of patronage of the arts, and the discussion seeks to demonstrate the closeness – the sheer physical proximity – of religious and economic activity in the lives of the popolani.

Other forces were at work to change that closeness, however, and this is the subject of chapter 6. While economy, religion, and polity offered the people of Venice a practical social harmony that strengthened over time, the conflicts between religious and secular authorities in the sixteenth century generated a major reconfiguration. Again, and emphatically from the viewpoint of the Venetian popolo, the differences between Church and State were less significant than the withdrawal of both from the old social contract, and their attempts to impose from a distance discipline on popolani whom they now asserted were subject to them. The chapter surveys the genesis of the new Confessional State of the age, in particular the Holy Office and the inhibitions it generated in religious and economic life. Discussion then questions whether the Venetian state really defended republican liberty against the Church, or whether both came to share a new authoritarianism. As an illustration of the historical process at work, the chapter interprets the creative fury of Tintoretto as the last great expression of the Venetian tradition in which polity and religion had shared and which, after the mid-sixteenth century, Church and State at once sought to abandon and to control.

With regard to the sources of the Venetian model of interaction in political, religious, and economic life, this is not quite the end of the story and explains the extension of the argument to a conclusion. The seventeenth century in the history of Venice is the experience of "decline." The validity of this generalization is demonstrable in certain obvious ways with regard to power and to prosperity. However, in another sense, it is possible to see a final reconfiguration, driven by historical circumstances and, most importantly, by war and plague, which forced a re-engagement of polity and economy even though the religious preoccupations of the age had soared away from both.

The Sources and Their Scope

In counterpoise to the general features of the study, it is essential to characterize the particular documentation that forms the basis of the investigation, as well as the documentation's problems, limitations, and value.

The principal manuscript sources used in this study are the records of the confraternities (*scuole*) and the guilds (*arti*) of Venice. The confraternities feature throughout the book. The trade guilds receive reference throughout but are in the overwhelming ascendancy in chapters 3 and 4. The scuole piccole have their own index in the Venetian Archivio di Stato, but the most comprehensive collection of their documentation is to be found in the registers of the magistracy responsible for them, the Provveditori di Comun. This was one of the few organs of government that retained a connection to the medieval commune of Venice and may represent some residuum of the old ways. All reference to "the commune of the Venetians" ceased in the fifteenth century. The emergence of the Signoria as its replacement was the prelude to a decisively more authoritarian style of government that would emerge forcefully in the sixteenth century.[25] The documents relating to the scuole have the drawback of being, overwhelmingly, both statutes and copies, the latter a compilation of the eighteenth century. That later compilation is too extensive to be ignored, and it supplements enormously the surviving original documentation in the archival index for "Scuole Piccole." Duplications are extremely rare, but the comparisons that are occasionally possible tend to show some gaps in the records of the Provveditori (see San Cristoforo and then Santi Apostoli).[26] That said, what the copies preserve is consistent, in formulation and expression, with contemporary originals. Professor Ortalli's work on the statutes housed at the Biblioteca Marciana and the Biblioteca Civica in the Museo Correr gives a much broader and firmer basis for this assertion.[27]

In the case of the arti as well as the scuole – and of the typological variations that joined their histories – the records contain a high proportion of statutes. At first sight, this is both distorting and disconcerting. As is well known, a statute setting down rules does not indicate the degree of either their enforcement or their violation. A regulation for fishmongers that prohibited the use of fresh guts to disguise the fact that the fish itself was not of the newest may say either that this was a matter subject to strict policing by the guild or that it was a common violation – or both. In the case of associations of pious layfolk, exhortations to a devout life in the rule books do not tell us how or whether the rules translated into principles and patterns of behaviour.

In mitigation of reliance upon the *mariegole* or rule books of the corporations, especially the scuole, it is worthy of emphasis that, in the case of Venice, they are not rigidly monolithic documents but have an evolutionary, even organic quality that tells their own history.[28] The original regulations, which in some cases go back to the thirteenth century, may be supplemented by pragmatic additions in subsequent generations. Thus, the statute of the mercers' guild, originally in Latin and dating from 1271, was rewritten in the vernacular in 1471, beginning with an extraordinarily extended regulation dating from 1446; it also includes vital information relating to the redefinition of the guild's links to the confraternity of San Teodoro in the middle of the fifteenth century.

The mercers' records are unique in the way in which, despite some significant gaps, they provide corroboration and amplification for each other. In the case of the scuole, the statutes have a richness that derives from a similar developmental character, even though the documents lack the variety of what survives for the mercers. In addition, the statutes of the scuole are preserved in the Venetian Archive in transcriptions made in the eighteenth century, and there are frequent caveats as to the limitations of the copies.[29] The chapters that follow have recourse frequently to records of particular events or problems, sometimes to matters such as the embellishment of a chapel, the addition of liturgical equipment, or even the order and appearance of a procession. In some ways, these materials complement the picture provided by the statutes alone.

While statutes may sometimes express ideals rather than realities, pronouncement rather than enforcement, principle rather than practice, it is also possible to detect certain ways in which practice departed from principle without the reformulation of the principle itself. The documents of the corporations of Venice reflect an outlook generally protective of tradition, though by no means exclusively so. They express, too, a regulation of tradition and a distrust of any innovation that might threaten the collective identity. Such a mentality finds expression in the architecture of the confraternities, as Tracy Cooper has eloquently and incisively demonstrated and as Ruskin would agree.[30] That same outlook also found forthright utterance in a satirical poem by the goldsmith Alessandro Caravia, published in 1541. In criticizing the expense of pompous display and vainglorious building projects among the Scuole Grandi, Caravia remarked on their departure from their first principles:

> You would not find rules better made
> And on the contrary they are badly observed.[31]

In this couplet, Caravia provides both an epigrammatic caveat on the dangers of relying upon statutes as well as an indication of their usefulness.[32]

Whatever the drawbacks of statutes, the historian of Venetian guilds feels the pinch of their absence. The archive of the mercers includes in its wealth of holdings a series of membership lists and a detailed record of elected officers. Their great rivals in the urban space, the ironsmiths, enjoy nothing like the same legacy of documentary survival. However, they too have left some lists of members, in no particular pattern or series, for the years 1530–1. Studied hard and close, and related to extraneous historical circumstance, these lists offer some suggestions of how recent immigrants among the popolo (so, folk *in* Venice rather than *of* Venice) could piece together identities both individual and collective.

It is another symptom of the great energy of popular life that the evidence thwarts any convincing exercise in static quantification. It is well-nigh impossible to assert categorically that there was exactly this number of corporations in such and such a year. A foundation date may be ahead of government approval – or even of a statute. The scuole moved from one church to another, and they amalgamated, reformed, changed, or added to their titles.[33] Therefore, it is vital that this introduction draw readers' attention to Gastone Vio's monumental compilation of evidence concerning the scuole piccole. A work of immense importance, which should be available far more widely and far more readily, it provides the initial data and documentary references for any number of future research projects.[34]

The range of sources that Professor Vio consulted reflects many years of patient accumulation throughout the manuscript collections of Venice, which would have been impossible for any scholar not based in the city. It has proved a huge reassurance to find that, while Professor Vio's findings are more comprehensive than those offered by the sources forming the basis of the current study, they do not undermine the representative character of those materials.

Vio's work consists of a short historical introduction followed by an enormous catalogue that derives from seventy-two documentary sources. In all, he cites 925 references to confraternities from the thirteenth century to the end of the republic in 1797 and a tiny number whose existence is confirmed by evidence from the nineteenth century. Of special significance to the current study is the information that Professor Vio has published that supplements the holdings of the Provveditori di Comun and the scantier archival materials of the arti. Most notable here are the citations that he makes of materials, usually statute books, held in the Civica Biblioteca Correr (hereafter cited as CBC in references) and the Biblioteca Nazionale Marciana (BNM). These sources provide a much more precise picture of how many trade guilds and ferry stations (*traghetti*) had altars and meeting places or were otherwise present in the churches surveyed during the Apostolic Visitation of 1581. Holdings in the Patriarchal Archives and in records that the parishes still hold provided Professor Vio with a further smattering of examples. These I have incorporated with gratitude and with care, and with sorrow in never having had the opportunity to converse with Professor Vio in his lifetime.

Alas, the catalogue itself contains some serious flaws and is baffling in its analytical limitations. The 925 references do not represent 925 separate institutions as he claims.[35] In relation to the materials in this present book, 413 of Vio's 925 references do not appear in the materials that I have consulted, consisting of 245 to the year 1650, and 168 after that date. Of the 245 references, there are 52 to scuole that do not appear in lists deriving from the registers of the Provveditori di Comun. None of these points changes the exposition of the materials presented herein. In addition, and still among those 245 references, there are 115 to arti or trade guilds and 22 to traghetti or ferry stations that did not fall within the remit of the Provveditori di Comun. The data on the trade guilds mark probably the most important contribution of Professor Vio's work to this study, as is clear in the notes to chapter 5. In 39 cases of the 245, the only evidence for the existence of a scuola is the authorization for its foundation, of which more in due course. Included among the 245 are 10 confraternities of priests, which is odd in a listing of lay confraternities, and 7 that Vio judges "*abusive*" (the Italian feminine plural, not an English translation) from eighteenth-century surveys.

Vio's references do not acknowledge obvious overlap. All those who study these data should be aware of the problems of quantification, but Vio's practice inflates his listing without comment or caveat. Thus, in his list of confraternities for the church of San Zanipolo, he has a scuola for San Pietro Martire from 1433 in the church's own records, another for San Vincenzo Ferrer for 1450, a scuola dei Santi Vincenzo Ferrer e Pietro Martire in the records of the Council of Ten from 1565, and a sovvegno for the same saints dating from 1594, along with a scuola for the same two and Catherine of Siena in 1618.[36] He also includes all references that provide only an official authorization for the formation of a scuola with no other evidence that the institution ever came into being; there are fifty-six of these, thirty-nine dating from before 1650. In a handful of cases Professor Vio chose to include applications to found a scuola that the authorities rejected.[37]

This is symptomatic of a broader failure to press the implications of his findings beyond a single listing consecutively numbered from 1 to 925. Unfortunately the historical introduction makes all too clear Professor Vio's adherence to traditional stereotypes of the place of the corporations of the popolo in the Venetian polity. The pattern of formation that he provides assumes the government to have been firmly in control of the process through a downward transmission of its authority and rigorous ongoing oversight. We have already mentioned the inaccuracy of an assumption that official permission alone is an indication that a confraternity came into being. Furthermore, Vio dates the foundation by the date of official permission, even when there is evidence of previous activity – which may run across a number of years. His approach shows the Council of Ten to have supreme control, variously and subordinately assisted by the Provveditori di Comun, the Cinque Savi alle Mariegole, the Milizia da Mar, and others.

In keeping with this picture of neatly defined classification that the authorities decided upon and maintained, Professor Vio deliberately set aside the Scuole Grandi as though they existed as such from their foundation.[38] It is a central contention of this book that these scuole were part of the original institutional flux of the mid-thirteenth century but only became separate in scale and magnificence from the mid-fifteenth century onwards, a process symptomatic of a lengthening hierarchy that was at odds with the traditions of Venetian confraternities and their sense of apostolic equality in brotherhood. Those scuole that became known as "grandi" by 1467 (perhaps only *in* 1467) had several distinctive features. Some of their members, at least in the early stages, practised self-flagellation. This group of scuole was restricted to an all-male membership. They established within their ranks permanent orders of rich and poor.[39] All these distinctive characteristics are noteworthy. However, the assumption of sameness among the hundreds of other scuole sits oddly with the great diversity of Professor Vio's own listing. All of the so-called Scuole Grandi had at some stage a link, either formal or informal, with scuole piccole. It is, by the way, Professor Vio's own catalogue that told this reader that the Scuola di San Rocco was not originally founded as a Scuola Grande.[40] What are we to make of his inclusion of the Scuola della Madonna e di San Francesco dei Mercanti at the church of the Frari? The original rule book for this confraternity dates from 1261 and is in the records of the Scuola "Grande" della Misericordia, and payments for alms were for the "poor of the Misericordia" (poveri della Misericordia). The obligation to flagellation was removed in 1271. The relationship of this organization not just to the Misericordia but also to the Scuola di San Cristoforo dei Mercanti at the church of the Madonna dell'Orto remains elusive.[41]

A further problem presents itself in the large number and proportion of Vio's citations that date from 1650 onwards. This was an important relief to the current study, which closes at mid-century. However, many of Vio's references for this period derive from government surveys of the eighteenth century, notably those of the Provveditori di Comun in 1735 and 1765. In the chapters that follow in this present book, it is clear that there was no exact co-ordination of authorization and foundation.[42] Periods of several years of activity prior to official permission, and similar lengthy periods of no activity at all after such authorization, are quite frequent.[43]

In a further complication, in this case of a rather arbitrary kind, Professor Vio presses upon his references, which are generally from the later period, the classifications "anomalo" and "abusiva," which amount to seventy-nine references in all, seventy-two of which are after 1650. He does not cite evidence to show that these were categories that the magistrates themselves used. Without such citation, we can only assume that on his own initiative he imposed these classifications, and they seem arbitrary. Once again, there seems to be an assumption that an unofficial organization was somehow irregular or even illegal.

The relationship of the compiler's introduction to his catalogue is also strange, for the examples in the latter often contradict or do not substantiate the assertions in the former. There is nothing to suggest that women's organizations were perforce run by male officers.[44] There are no grounds for the assertion that the scuole del Sacramento supplanted pre-existing confraternities.[45] There is no evidence that the guild's chief officer, the *gastaldo*, appointed his own officers.[46] There are errors in the dating of entries in the table for foundations of the thirteenth and fourteenth centuries that in some cases appear to be typographical. The Scuola di San Niccolo dated from 1337, not 1237, and the error makes it appear the oldest of the scuole. The oldest of the confraternities seems rather to have been San Mattio, a foundation of 1247 on the island of Murano, as Vio points out elsewhere, but it is not included in the table.[47]

The catalogue itself follows a continuously numerical pattern consecutively through each of the city's six sestieri and seventy parishes. This has the important usefulness of showing the range of such institutions that might exist within a parish but not necessarily within a parish church. However, the data cry out for other, rather obvious, ways of analysis. A simple chronological list of foundations would be immensely revealing in showing the different dedications across the centuries. It would be most illuminating if researchers were to extend Professor Vio's work into a tabulation that offered a chronological list of foundations within each church, with churches listed alphabetically rather than by sestier. An alphabetical list of the institutions covered by the survey would be of great interest in its own right and, furthermore, would compensate for the lack of an index to them in Vio's study. Astonishingly, the only index that the work contains is of personal names.

In sum, there is much in Professor Vio's work to reinforce the impetus of the argument that this book sets out, and little or nothing to deflect the thrust of that argument. One can only hope that readers agree, and one can only encourage them to make use of Professor Vio's indispensable work.

While statistics are impossible to establish with absolute precision, that problem arises because of the mobility of the institutions under examination.

Their foundations, adaptations, and amalgamations were constant only in their being on the move. That characterization applies not only to the institutions but also to their members. We should pair the mobility and overlap of institutions with the openings for multiple membership of different organizations. For example, Martino Taiamonte – a quarry man, so the name "Martin Cuts-mountain" is nicely appropriate –specified in his will of 1444 that all the six scuole of which he was a member should be present at his funeral, and he listed the scuole of San Marco, Sant'Antonio, San Biagio, Sant'Orsola, and San Cristofalo dei Crociferi, and the guild of stonemasons.[48]

In this study the movement and the multiplicity of the popolo within and between the institutions are paramount. Together they provide a density of cross-reference that, in itself, suggests the different strands of a network of social institutions that might arrest a headlong fall from prosperity to poverty. One might imagine the Venetian constitution as a corporation of corporations, and it was these latter that made up the greater whole. Viewed in this way, the "constitution" was not at all closed; on the contrary, its "constituents" were constantly adjusting, internally to the needs of members and externally to the pressure of changing circumstances – often without any reference to the government.

The Stones of Venice

In the examination and re-examination of the documentary materials, the book attempts to extend its evidential basis through consideration of the material fabric of the city itself. It is a study that derives much of its inspiration from the work of historians who are often referred to, in the manner of philosophers, as a "school," the *école des Annales*.[49] The efforts of some of these historians to broaden the range of historical evidence and to think hard about the minds that created it in the past have sharpened the focus on ideas of "total history" and on the study of "mentalities."[50] The endeavour to come to grips with the insights that these concepts offer, and with the problems that they pose, has been strongly influential in shaping the chapters that follow. On occasion, however, the approach of the Annalistes has been so grandiose in its conviction that the methods and findings of such work are "scientific"; the humans in the past are reduced by it to the status of laboratory rats.[51] In some such work, history dispenses with people altogether; the "gentle rain from heaven" does not even need humans to drop upon.[52]

This study seeks to extend the territory of the historian of Venice to other disciplines in the humanities. In the case of literature, the connection of the writings of an age to the age itself is now a given.[53] The potential of a connection between history and the history of art received the clear and firm endorsement of Erwin Panofsky:

> The art historian will have to check the *intrinsic meaning* of the work, or group of works, to which he devotes his attention, against what he thinks is the *intrinsic meaning* of as many other documents of civilization historically related to that work or group of works, as he can master: of documents bearing witness to the political, poetical, religious, philosophical and social tendencies of the personality, period, or country under investigation. Needless to say that, conversely, the historian of political life, poetry, religion, philosophy and social situations should make an analogous use of works of art. It is in the search for intrinsic meaning or content that the various humanistic disciplines meet on a common plane instead of serving as hand-maidens to each other.[54]

We have already deployed Stephen Greenblatt's concept of the "circulation of social energy." What follows takes up Professor Panofsky's generously open invitation. There are other instances, too, that suggest not merely the compatibility of conventional history and the history of art, even though one must take careful account of opinions that reject such an approach.[55] What this study seeks to offer is a vision of the "total" history of a civilization – which the work of the Annalistes has opened up – that incorporates the evidence and interpretations of historians of the arts.[56] Such an endeavour, in the case of this book at least, does not involve judgments on aesthetic quality, which are very often tied to questions of attribution.[57] Thus, in what follows, the tomb of il Medeghino in Milan appears not because of the qualities of Leone Leoni's sculpture but because of its inclusion of the arms of the Medici of Florence. Mention of Palma il Giovane is not a critical evaluation of his work but the use of it as an index to important changes in the character of Venetian civilization between the late sixteenth and the early seventeenth century.

The justification of such an approach in some ways stems from the many insights that historians of all hues have derived from work on the material fabric of Venice, particularly its architecture, and sometimes from the scholarly work of architects.[58] With concentration, it is possible to set aside the miserable thought of the destruction of more than forty churches (and the six dozen associated confraternities) and to rediscover the presence of the scuole in what survived.[59] And not merely the scuole, but above all their members, for the study seeks to populate the buildings constituted by the stones of Venice, adding a human dimension to the historian's craft and territory. The written records, for all their imperfections, reveal a vast and adaptable infrastructure of mutual assistance and self-interest animated by a pervasive system of shared values.

In this study the lie of the land (and water) has proved immensely important, and so has the engagement with the human types who lived and worked in various locations. Emmanuel Le Roy Ladurie's " territory of the historian" can usefully extend to include topography and ethnography.[60]

The manuscript evidence provides many striking perspectives on and from the viewpoint of the popolani of Venice. Yet the popolani of Venice left their mark on the city far more deeply and emphatically than that, by shaping, building, and embellishing the stones of the city. They were responsible for any number of monuments to the achievements of the great teeming mass of humanity in Venice, some of which still survive.

The deployment of these materials is, of necessity, selective, for even this evidence (evidence at its most concrete) has its inadequacies. The damage and destruction that time and neglect have exacted amount to a terrible toll. All the same, it is still possible to gain some idea of the functioning of the whole criss-cross of institutions that the popolani developed and administered. The survival of such examples under what was, by the middle of the sixteenth century, an onslaught by the authorities of Church and State testifies to the energy that the corporations had generated and channelled. The monuments that the scuole used as an aid to their devotions stood among the remains of the mighty and with no notable sense of inferiority to them. Fire, rats, water, removals, relocations, and restorations have all exacted their toll, but monuments such as San Zanipolo still capture and convey the idea of Venice as an immense collective enterprise. Guild organizations underpinned the training of the masons, house carpenters, and ironsmiths who raised the stones of Venice one upon another, who sculpted the decorations.[61] The imposing tomb of an admiral of the fleet gives pause to recall that it was a guild of merchants who brought timber from Cadore to the Sacca della Misericorida, and guilds of carpenters, caulkers, sawyers, rope twisters, oar makers, and blacksmiths who built the war galleys that made possible his glory.[62]

The history of Venice comprised in many ways the deeds of a collectivity of collectivities. The energies that they generated remain visible but only in indicative examples and not in a quantification of the whole. The monuments and the energy found their representative in the furious creativity of Tintoretto, just as the great synthesis of political, economic, and religious life began to lose its traditional configuration under the pressure of religious and political change, and as inquisitorial procedures began to prevail in the workings of Church and State alike.

Even now, that collectivity of collectivities is discernible in the fabric of the city and in the urban space. The exposition that follows seeks to measure the material impact and to estimate the spiritual contribution of the Venetian popolo to the successful durability of the Venetian Republic. What matters to this book is the capacity of the Venetians for change itself – their energies of adjustment. To these, the stones of Venice, which Ruskin so loved, still bear eloquent witness. The centres that represent the life of the city still stand out: from the bell tower at San Giorgio Maggiore on its eponymous island the eye is drawn to San Marco and the Palazzo Ducale, the visible manifestation of Venice's combination of religious and political life; to the Cathedral of San Pietro di Castello, a reminder that San Marco was not a cathedral but the doge's private chapel. San Pietro stands by the Arsenale, that pre-eminent industrial complex, still breathtaking in its extent. Spanning the wide serpentine Canal Grande, the Ponte di Rialto marks the commercial centre of the city, linked to the piazza by the Mercerie. To the naked and untrained eye, the mendicant churches soar out of the cityscape, the Frari of the Franciscans to the left, the Dominican church of San Zanipolo to the right. (See map 1, "The Sestieri and Parishes of Venice.")

The waters of the lagoon are everywhere present, a reminder of the essential "double viability" of Venice in its streets and canals (map 2, "Venice's 'Double Routeways'"). Giovanni Botero was the clerical author of an early work on the reason of State, a figure in many ways typical of the confessional era. In a book published in Venice in 1589 he suggested that one explanation of Venice's renowned tranquility lay in the shortage of open spaces, which limited opportunities for spontaneous assembly, and in the fragmentation of the urban area by its complex of waterways.[63] It is as though even the topography of the city was in league with the nobility in order to avoid popular unrest. Viewed at the level of the calle or the canal, however, the complex of thoroughfares linked the extensive market spaces of the city, on the nearer side of Rialto, at San Marco, Santi Apostoli, and Santa Maria Formosa, across the bridge at Santa Margherita, San Polo, and San Giacomo dell'Orio (map 3, "The Markets of Venice").

As one walks round the churches of the city, trying to take in the history represented by the stones, only the presence of a few older Venetians at prayer reminds the modern visitor of the spiritual as well as the physical proximity of religious and economic life. Even now, it is here, especially around Rialto, at San Zuan Elemosinario, San Giacometto, San Bartolomeo, or San Salvador, in the horizontal junctions of churches and markets, that one senses the powerful moral purpose that gave conviction and direction to the great human mass of busy diversity that was Venice at the zenith of its wealth and power. It is no wonder that the statutes of one type of social institution, the sovvegno, on occasion used the image of the ant to inspire a work ethic that stayed fixed upon the immediate purposes of making, selling, and buying, but continually set something aside for rough times to come. More important, the examination of what the scuole of Venice did to embellish the churches of the city marked a blend of the everyday and the sacred, a connection that will require much closer attention throughout the book. For the moment, it should suffice to keep in mind that all the market areas of Venice were clearly identified with patron saints and their churches. This relationship was a concrete realization of the close interaction of work and religion in the everyday lives of the Venetians. The connection of work and religion clearly began to assert itself in the mid-thirteenth century, and, far from being harnessed to the exclusive polity, it harnessed the apparently exclusive polity to itself.

1 Venice as Mercantile System, c. 1250–c. 1300

The quality of mercy is not strain'd,
It droppeth as the gentle rain from heaven
Upon the place beneath: it is twice blest,
It blesseth him that gives, and him that takes

– Shakespeare, *The Merchant of Venice*, 4.1.180–3

Polity, 1297

Traditionally, the Serrata del Maggior Consiglio in 1297 is both a centrepiece and a cornerstone. It is the centrepiece of the long chronology of the history of the republic, standing with impressive and beguiling neatness between the elevation of the first Venetian to hold the office of doge in 697 and the final capitulation of the sovereignty of the republic before the armies of Napoleon in 1797.[1] It is the cornerstone of Venetian history in that it seems to define the city's constitutional arrangements and then to sustain them for half a millennium, just as Venice, the home of refugees whom other places rejected, was to become the headstone of the corner.

For Giuseppe Maranini, writing in 1927, the architectural significance of the Serrata within the constitution that he scrutinized so seriously was decisive and led him to moments of uncharacteristic laudatory extravagance, highly revealing of the way in which the detailed study of Venetian history can blend into the celebration of its myth. "A masterpiece of wisdom" for the ruling class, Maranini exclaimed.[2] The patriciate's constitutional stronghold was thenceforth impregnable, for the Serrata stood, "crowning the constitutional edifice, making of it an armed fortress at every point against new forces."[3] Thus, the shutting out, the exclusion, of any "new forces" meant that "the fates of the Venetian constitution had been decided."[4] The history of Venice would thereafter be a history without surprises.

Yet the exclusiveness sits oddly with Maranini's characterization of the building as the product of an organic genesis, a process of "rapid and spontaneous association," and from this "connubio" – a term denoting partnership, deal, marriage, and generation – emerged "a wonderful edifice, logical and juridical, harmonious, symmetrical, as perfect as a human entity can be." For Maranini, the closure was the healing of an emergent factional divide between old families and new.[5] Such an antagonism was to plague other cities of the peninsula and was to play a significant role in the emergence of the Signori – lords or despots – as guarantors of order amid the wreckage of the commune. In Philip Jones's work, the persistence and the prevalence of feudal habits are paramount to an understanding of the politics of the communes. Even he, however, makes of Venice "a totally singular case." Elsewhere in Italy the connection of town and country in the rural *contado* (surrounding area) seemed to ensure the survival of feudal relationships and conflicts. In Venice "there was no landed nobility, and practically no political factions of a conventional type." In short, Venice, "the only society that succeeded in avoiding fracture[,] was the one which had no feudal aristocracy."[6]

According to Frederic Lane, the success of the Serrata lay in the paradox that the apparent closure actually served to broaden the ruling class, to some two hundred families.[7] His pragmatic investigation, however, also blended into myth when he wrote of the "perfection" of the constitution, employing the term in a way that implied far more than mere completion.[8]

Other studies, especially those of Stanley Chojnacki, have greatly extended the range of interpretative possibilities, taking up the relationship of the Serrata to the formulation of the myth, extending the dynamics of reconfiguration into the fourteenth and fifteenth centuries.[9] In the very long term, one may even see a process of atrophy that found surprising sources of renewal throughout the latter half of the seventeenth century.[10]

These characterizations of a process of social adaptation and political survival need to be set against a negative view of the Serrata as the culmination of a protracted struggle that was vividly characterized as *il braccio di ferro* (arm wrestling). For Giorgio Cracco, this occurred not just within the ruling class but between "great and small" and "patricians and plebeians," comprehensible in a model that separated the emergent patrician "state" from popular "society" in a class struggle for control of the sources of wealth in the economy.[11]

These visions of the Serrata all acknowledged its significance, though they differed in scope, some being strictly constitutional, some narrowly political, some socio-political, some expansively socio-economic and political. The variations are worthy of Polonius, but they all identify a process of reconfiguration within the newly defined ruling class and a fundamental exclusion of those who could never fall within that definition.

The events of 1204 had already demonstrated the role of Venice as a supplier of maritime transport for the crusaders. They had requested some two hundred ships, and the Venetians negotiated in addition the provision of a war fleet of fifty galleys.[12] In such an enterprise, private economic interests converged with the public power of the state. The growth of the Arsenale will receive further attention in due course. However, the relationship of the state's shipyards (which in the twelfth and thirteenth centuries occupied only some eight acres of Venice's space) with the private yards that operated throughout the city is an early symbol of the common interests of a wide variety of different groups: the owners of the private yards, the craftsmen who constructed cargo ships, the Lords of the Arsenal, and their gangs of workers who served the state directly and prepared its warships. Even the contract with the crusaders provides an instance of the combination of private enterprise in the transport ships and public funding of the protective war fleet. This is an inchoate coagulation, but within it we may discern an early and significant instance of the furtherance of mercantile interests under the auspices of the state. It was a sign of this sharpening definition that the laws governing the configuration became codified under the auspices of Doge Jacopo Tiepolo in 1242.[13]

It is symptomatic of the collaboration of private capital and the public weal that in 1262 the republic established the funded debt, the Monte Vecchio.[14] It is significant, too, that the invitation to invest in it extended to those soon to be excluded from political life. The fact that two of the principal guilds of the Arsenale, the sawyers and the carpenters, chose to place a portion of their members' money in the Monte is an early and concrete expression of the stake that the Venetians outside the ranks of the nobility had in the maintenance of the state. The 5 per cent annual return went towards members' benefits – including their daughters' dowries – in an early instance of the coincidence of political initiative, economic enterprise, and works of mercy.[15] Many may concur with Maranini's judgment that the corporations became "a magnificent instrument of government, integrating the work of the state with the field of the economy and public assistance."[16] However, it is questionable whether this amounted to "the absolute subordination of the corporations to the state."[17] Indeed, quite the reverse may have been the case, with the government struggling to keep pace with the innovations of the corporations. To consider the popolani's point of view, the legal definition of the ruling class in the Serrata needs a broader contextualization, a contextualization not only political but also economic and religious.

Polity, 1268

In the year 1268 the popolo had occasion for celebration in the election of Lorenzo Tiepolo as doge. According to the chronicler Martino da Canale, the trades greeted the new doge in a great procession. This election marked a further stage in the definition of the polity in that it completed the final elaboration of the famous procedure of nomination and sortition that avoided vote-rigging.[18] Furthermore, the acclamation that Doge Tiepolo received marked a new assertion of regal sovereignty and, in important ways, claimed for Venice the prerogatives of both empire and papacy: "Christ conquers, Christ reigns, Christ commands: to our lord Lorenzo Tiepolo, by the grace of God illustrious doge of Venice, Dalmatia and Croatia, and lord of the quarter part and one half [of a quarter] of the entire empire of Romania, health, honour, life and victory: Saint Mark, give him aid!"[19]

The procession of the guilds, according to the chronicler, followed at once, and Da Canale details each of them: ironmongers, furriers, skinners, weavers, tailors, drapers, doublet makers, masters of cloth of gold, mercers, sausage makers and cheese sellers, fishmongers, barbers, glass makers, comb makers, goldsmiths.[20] All of these "petty traffickers' had undergone incorporation or were to undergo it in the course of the thirteenth century. The absence from the procession of the guilds representing the Arsenale trades is puzzling. However, it is possible that they had been present at the first phase of the celebrations when the galleys about to depart the city had offered their salutation to the new doge.[21] In any event, the procession of 1268 exemplifies the way in which public ceremonial was not only a means of reminding participants – there was no truly separate "audience" – of the attributes of Venetian sovereignty, but also an opportunity for the guilds to display the quality of their wares.[22] Moreover, it is an instance of the ways in which those who were, in three decades' time, to be excluded from the political process were clearly able to enjoy a measure of representation in the celebrations of the state. Provided that we expand the boundaries of this crucial term, *representation*, beyond the idea of party-based politics and popular suffrage, it is possible to identify many ways in which the Venetian popolo found it – and participation – in the business of the state.

What the state represented and who represented the state were also becoming clearer in this period. Towards the end of Da Canale's chronicle he interposed a prayer that one of the most authoritative commentators has characterized as a "credo marciano."[23] Perhaps it is the chronicler's Provençal French that concentrates the attention and spurs the imagination in contemplation of the associations of the term *ducat*. The third stanza of "the prayer that I have made and will make for all my days to my lord Saint Mark for the Venetians" links the

Evangelist's symbol with the *ducado* and with its standard – which is, of course, that of Saint Mark himself:

And you in your Gospel speak of the lion
Of the power of God you made it a symbol
The ducato of Venice carries you on its standard
Wherever water runs people speak of this.[24]

Thus the standard of the republic was identified with both the lion of the Evangelist and a body of territory defined as the Ducato. In 1284 the symbolism would acquire still greater force with the addition of another dimension.

For several reasons it is well to be cautious about the appearance of the ducat as a standardized gold coin. First, the issue was part of a general trend in Italy and Europe in the thirteenth century.[25] Second, the name of the coin merely reflects the title of the ruler; just as *reali* were the coins of a king and *imperiali* of an emperor, so ducats were named for the ducal title.[26] Moreover, the particular circumstances of the ducat's minting remain shadowy rather than blazingly triumphant. The Venetians were well behind the cities of Florence, Genoa, Lucca, and Perugia, which had put out coins – gold in some cases – in the 1250s. The laggardly character of the ducat's standardized issue may well indicate divisions within the government. In the decisive vote in the Council of Forty, only twenty-nine members were present, and seven of those voted against the minting.[27] Perhaps the Venetians had less reason for urgency in declaring their identity by coin than did cities lying between the Hohenstaufen and the papacy, and felt less pressure to assert their independence of either because they had already done so.

Yet, however humdrum the obscure circumstances of the ducat's genesis may be, there is no doubt of the concrete evidence of its stable longevity. The ducat remained as 3.5 grams of almost pure gold (0.997 fine, as close to perfect as is possible) until after 1797. A key feature of Venetian banking was the acceptance of deposits in gold ducats and the making of payments in silver coins, the *grossi*. The price of silver rose in the early fourteenth century. The government intervened and in the 1320s declared one gold ducat to be equal to twenty-four silver grossi. The powerful continuity that was subsequent and consequent was no mere reflection of the constitution but rather a foundation of its strength, providing a precocious instance of the relationship between a stable currency and the secure sovereignty of the state. The *ducato* was the name of the coin and the definition of the territorial state. Both gained recognition "wherever water runs." The relationship of coin and dominion was symbolized by another communal standard, the *confanon*. In turn, the standard of the lion appeared on the coin from the time of its very first issue under Doge Giovanni Dandolo.[28]

In the course of the later thirteenth century the commune was beginning to offer a secure return on investment in the public debt to popolano corporations and their members while guaranteeing its coin with – *pace* Adam Smith – the careful accumulation of reserves of bullion.[29] What, then, did the coin itself guarantee? The issue of the ducat helped the existing trading practices to achieve a new clarity and regularity. At this stage in the city's development, and indeed until a change in the law in 1558, it was quite possible for guild members to engage in the export trades, provided the merchandise involved was of Venetian make.[30] The sharing of risk through ventures defined in contracts of "colleganza" and "fraterna" – and usually based on familial relations – began to take on the character of joint-stock companies. The colleganza certainly had its origins in the twelfth century. It offered investors no percentage on what they provided towards the financing of the venture, but three-quarters of the profit of the voyage.[31] The opportunities for the travelling merchant to conceal the true scale of his profits became subject to greater regulation in this critical period in the latter half of the thirteenth century. The more regulated colleganza became part of the steady system of seasonal voyages or "mude." There was further consolidation of business practice in the development after 1300 of double-entry bookkeeping and marine insurance. The practice of trade, in particular of accurate calculation and the characteristics of high-quality merchandise in a commercial world subject to *fortuna* was, by 1300, acquiring a new sharpness and was to find codification in at least one example of a *prattica della mercatura*.[32]

Economy, 1271

The earliest extant example of a commercial manual from Venice dates from 1311–13.[33] During the period of this part of the study the overseas ventures of the Venetians found their most vivid and eloquent reports in what Marco Polo – another cittadino – recorded of the travels he began in 1271.[34] What travelling merchants might observe and record had a bearing on the development of Venetian political economy. What Marco Polo wrote resonated (suggestions of direct inspiration are undemonstrable) with those invaluable sources for European history, the reports of Venetian ambassadors. At this point, a reminder of Marco's two lives is apposite: not only was he a merchant, but he also served Kublai Khan for twenty years as governor of the province of Quinsai.[35] Intriguingly, in the crowded space of Venice around 1300, we shall encounter Marco again, for he was a member of the devotional confraternity

Table 1.1. Chronological Registration of Guild Statutes, 1219–1312

Year	Guild
1219	tailors
	doublet makers
1222	tile counters
1227	fishmongers
	oil-measurers
1228	kiln-men
1233	ropemakers
	goldsmiths
	sellers of second-hand goods
1243	dyers (revised 1289)
1258	doctors
1259	barrel-hoop makers (revised 1279)
Before 1261?	sellers of linen
	apothecaries
	crossbow makers
	keepers of measures
	makers of weights
1262	sawyers
1263	sellers of oil and fat (revised 1279)
	combmakers
1264–5	traders in second-hand goods
1265	silk weavers
1270	barbers
1271	phial makers
	furriers
	bleachers
	shoemakers
	carpenters
	shipwrights
	caulkers
	wallers
	mercers
	ironmongers
	painters
	corn chandlers
	coopers
1271?	tanners
1275?	linen, fustian, and canvas weavers
1278?	makers of catgut
1278–97	overseers of gold and silver
1279–80	skeiners (revised 1280–8, 1289)
1280	sand merchants
	hatters
1281	cappers
1282	greengrocers
	spindle makers
	bell and basin makers
1283?	tinkers
1284	glass-makers

(*Continued*)

Table 1.1. (Continued)

Year	Guild
1289	overseers of anchors, studs, and sails of foreign provenance
1297?	prow and lantern makers
1300	turners
	makers of earthenware
1301	suppliers of pitch
1307	oar makers
	stonecutters
1311	skinners of dormice*
1312	squirrel furriers

* This designation seems almost comically whimsical, but it is inescapable as a translation of the "arte della pelle del ghiro." The guild-masters were obviously more interested in the quality of the fur than the edibility of the flesh. According to the *Encyclopedia Britannica*, the European dormouse has "a squirrel-like appearance." It is "a grey species with black markings," and its fur is "tawny above and paler beneath, with a white patch on the throat." John Florio's dictionary, *A Worlde of Wordes*, also offers the translation "dormouse' for *ghiro*.

the Scuola della Misericordia, which symbolized the moral adhesive that bound together the polity and the economy of the city. In the life of Marco Polo the circles of merchandise, government, and mercy overlapped and reinforced each other.

Yet, by 1300, so the overwhelming opinion of scholarship would have it, the Venetian patriciate had defined itself and appropriated a monopoly of the political process that excluded non-patricians altogether. However, the year of Marco's departure, 1271, had been, even within the complex of the conjuncture, a defining moment in the history of Venetian political economy.

In 1271 political intervention and the economic activities of those enrolled in the guilds of the city acquired a new and sharpened clarity. The magistracy of the Giustizia Vecchia (Old Justice) approved thirteen statutes, and possibly another one. The figure of thirteen represents more than a fifth of all the fifty-eight arti whose rule books received ratification between 1219 and 1312.[36] This striking instance of energetic activity in turn needs the longer perspective of the earlier thirteenth century, including the emergence of the Giustizia Vecchia upon the formation of a new one, the Giustizia Nova, in 1261.

Do these ratifications embody the imposition of the state's will upon the guilds? Close consideration makes it strenuous to see a neat distinction of patricians and popolani, or a juxtaposition of state and society. In the long period that includes the concentrated action of 1271, every sector of economic activity seemed to find a place: the supply of food, the manufacture and sale of clothing, the building trades for both housing and shipping, metal pots and pans, household wares of wood and leather, luxury goods, and services, as well as the means of supervision and regulation. Then we may add to the picture the obligations of many trades – especially carpenters and caulkers but also makers of oars, crossbows, rope, and canvas, and all those making or dealing in ironware – to work in the Arsenale, the area of which was to expand fourfold in the early fourteenth century. All in all, the guilds of Venice represented the human and material infrastructure of the republic's overseas enterprise.[37] We might extend and elaborate this representative dimension. One of the most striking features of the place of Venetian guilds in the polity was their clearly defined access to courts of law, especially through mechanisms of appeal. It was quite possible for individual guild members to make their voice heard against a decision of the corporation's officers. Moreover, the guilds had regular recourse to the arbitration of a series of magistracies in their disputes with each other. This was also a conduit that enabled the guilds to protest against the decisions of the government itself. The Serrata closed none of these avenues of representation. Documentation from later periods amply demonstrates the ease, speed, and vigour with which the guilds of Venice engaged in litigation.[38]

Furthermore, the guilds themselves were not units of production (that was the function of workshops or shipyards) but representative and regulatory bodies that also tended to the needs of their members. All these organizations of Venetian tradespeople had their own scuola or devotional confraternity, an agency that offered some protection against misfortunes that were not the fault of their members.

Religion, 1247

Before attention turns to the specific institution of the scuola, its development must be set in a larger and more general context of religious change in the later thirteenth century. An arresting indication of the nature and direction of the new religious sensibilities is to be found in the credo marciano of Da Canale. Stanzas 10 and 11 of the prayer are as follows:

> As truly was visible and we well believe it:
> Help the Venetians and make prayer
> To our lord God, in whom we well believe,
> And to his sweet Mother, that God will forgive us
> And keep Venice with no discord!
> Peace, good will, without drawing an evil heart
> Let there be in Venice, beautiful lord, for Mercy's sake!
> As their ancestors did together which this book records ...[39]

Two features of these verses merit special attention, for they indicate the strength, depth, and durability of the values that this book explores. The first is the inclusion of the Virgin with Saint Mark as intercessors before God on behalf of the Venetians. The profound identification of the Madonna with both Mercy and Venice embodied a special translation of devout qualities to the life of the city itself.

The corresponding role of Saint Mark was to act as the symbol of Venice's status as an Evangelist city, which gave its political identity a status especially hopeful of protection. The second is the use of the term *misericorde* in the original. It is the antithesis of *male corde* and *discorde*. There is much more to this than a rhyming convenience. There is a contrast of feelings in the heart (*-corde*): pity and compassion (*misericorde*) as opposed to division (*discorde*) and ill will (*malecorde*).

The modern dictionary definition of *mercy* is twofold – or twice blest. It denotes "forbearance and compassion shown by one person to another who is in his power and who has no claim to receive kindness." Moreover, it is a reflection of the divine, of "God's pitiful forbearance towards His creatures."[40] According to a standard work of reference on Christianity, the distinctive characteristic of Misericordia is its acknowledgment of inequality, "connoting in its object a certain inferiority." The entry continues that Mercy "excludes the idea of equality between giver and receiver."[41] "It droppeth as the gentle rain from heaven," because by a force of spiritual gravity its transmission is eternally downwards. *Charity* is the brotherly love of Christians for each other; it is the love of equals. God does not have charity, for he has no equal. God has mercy, "and earthly justice then shows likest God's, when mercy seasons Justice."

Mercy and Merchants: Scripture and Teaching

In order to grasp the importance of mercy in the city of Venice and in the lives of the Venetians, it is necessary to expand one's thinking beyond the guiding principle of a law court to a principle that informed the behaviour of individuals and groups – with all their human imperfections – towards each other in everyday life. It was also an antidote to *discorde* in that it contained a disavowal of revenge (which Shylock explicitly refuses to forgo) – and the vendetta of factional conflict. Misericordia gave a divine blessing to the insurance that human sentiment, seated in the heart, could provide against the cyclical change from prosperity to misfortune. That was a continual possibility in a city of exchange, and against it Misericordia offered some degree of protection (like the mantle of the Madonna). The rationale of such a system of values was deeply rooted in Scripture, especially in the Gospel of Matthew. This part of the discussion accepts as a given "the primacy of Matthew" among the gospels and seeks to demonstrate the singular importance of its teachings and its adaptability to the medieval urban economy.[42]

Matthew had been a tax-collector. He was to become the patron of bankers and money changers. The exposition of Christ's teaching in his gospel, as translated into the Latin of the Vulgate, constantly resonates with the language of commercial exchange. This in turn had a particularly direct pertinence to the mercantile environment of the cities of medieval Italy. Matthew recorded his own calling in chapter 9 of his gospel, immediately after Jesus's dispensation of forgiveness through the healing of the man sick with the palsy. It was in the full remission of sins that the miracle of healing occurred. Jesus called Matthew, whom "he saw sitting at the receipt of custom."[43] Jesus then sat at meat with "publicans and sinners."[44] According to Luke's account, Matthew held the banquet at his own house.[45] Christ then answered those who criticized his association with such people through a medical analogy, which pointed towards the work of mercy as corporal as well as spiritual: "They that be whole need not a physician, but they that are sick."[46] He then explained remission (another term with resonances of bodily healing) in terms of mercy: "I will have mercy and not sacrifice: for I am not come to call the righteous but sinners to repentance."[47] In the Latin version the tax-gathering sinner was called to join in the works of corporal mercy, held a feast with others of his calling, and heard the Saviour speak of Misericordia. In Matthew's own account, his calling followed the Sermon on the Mount in which one of the Messiah's beatitudes had been: "Blessed are the merciful, for they shall obtain mercy."[48] The Lord's Prayer in that same sermon was a prayer that members of Venetian confraternities constantly recited along with an equal number of aves to the Virgin.

Those who adhered to these teachings (which were learned in an institution called a scuola) would receive a reward in heaven: "merces vestra copiosa est in caelis."[49] This terminology too had a particular relevance to the principles of behaviour of those engaged in commerce. In the Italian derivations of the Latin *merces*, *merce* and *mercede* denote not only grace and pity and, etymologically, mercy, but also recompense, reward, and payment. These are words that link to *mercato*, *mercante*, *merciaio*, and, in the stones of Venice, the city's busiest complex of *botteghe* – the Mercerie. It was one of the great achievements of the Franciscans to have expounded salvation in terms of the profit motive: those who expect a reward in the next life must render an account of the good and the bad that they have done in this one. As the stones still give witness, the sheer number of churches in Venice bore out the connection between religious life and business, a connection that provided a workable value system far, far older than the Protestant ethic.[50] (See map 1, "The Sestieri and Parishes of Venice," and map 3, "The Markets of Venice.")

The combination of works and prayer in the activities of the confraternities of Venice found direct inspiration in the General Epistle of James, Saint James the Less, stepbrother or cousin of Jesus, a text to which many of the statutes refer.[51] The epistle is the work of a Jewish Christian, and its debt to Jewish thought is clear. It follows Christ's ministry in seeking to make Christians of Jews.[52] James's language, however, speaks to its Jewish audience in the language of the Old Testament prophets, and its qualities have led to a comparison with the words of Moses and Elijah.[53] Luther dismissed the apostolic authorship of the epistle on the grounds of its conflict with the teaching of Saint Paul.[54] James's emphasis on the worthlessness of faith without works was a direct counter from Scripture itself to Luther's doctrine of "justification by faith alone."

Luther's scholarly contrivance in order to support his own theological position has overshadowed the general importance of what James wrote.[55] The letter has particular relevance to the local Venetian variety of Christian belief and practice. In certain respects the Epistle of James provides a handbook for the religious life of the scuole that complements the pertinence of Matthew's gospel to the economic activities of the arti. In the epistle there is a clear resonance with the Sermon on the Mount (and a foreshadowing of Adam Smith) in matters such as the dangers of despising the poor and setting store by earthly riches and worldly status.[56] James's chapters are full of references to the transience and corruptibility of material riches, echoing Christ's teaching in the Sermon on the Mount: "Lay not up for yourselves treasures on earth, where moth and rust doth corrupt and where thieves break through and steal." The treasures that the Christian lays up in heaven are not subject to decay – and that is where his or her heart will be.[57] James's most emphatic warning of the dangers of worldly wealth comes at the opening of the epistle's fifth and final chapter:

> 1. Go to now, ye rich men, weep and howl for your miseries that shall come upon you.
> 2. Your riches are corrupted, and your garments are motheaten.
> 3. Your gold and silver is cankered; and the rust of them shall be a witness against you, and shall eat your flesh as it were fire. Ye have heaped treasure together for the last days.

While the exploitations of the poor by the rich are clearly linked to landowners' treatment of reapers, there is also reference to worldly gain in urban commerce.[58]

The letter addresses the twelve tribes of the Jewish diaspora and seeks their spiritual regeneration, though the foreshadowing of the twelve apostles is also clear.[59] That apostolic theme strengthens in the Venetian context with the emphasis on brotherhood.[60] The brotherly obligation to relieve widows, orphans, and the sick likewise offered instruction to members of a scuola.[61] It is possible that such work or works reflected the tradition of a guild, a Jewish "guild for visiting the sick."[62]

From early in the letter, James emphasizes the reversibility of fortunes, and this made works of mercy not empty ritual and doctrine but "proper ethical action."[63] At the end of the epistle, James calls upon the brethren to confess to each other, to pray for each other, and to look after each other. Those in misfortune are not those sick in body but those in any circumstances that cause them distress.[64] This is a vital background to the epistle's great exhortation to prayer: "Confess your faults one to another and pray one for another that ye may be healed. The effectual fervent prayer of a righteous man availeth much."[65] Prayer itself becomes action rather than contemplation. *Orare est laborare*: the natural connection of work and prayer, and the comprehensibility of the value of prayer to the working Christian, was embedded in the statutes of the scuole.[66] God listens to prayer and responds with the infinity of his mercy. In the brotherly reciprocity of active prayer someone in misfortune may be brought to repentance, restored to the collectivity, and saved from death and sin – "returned to mercy," as one statute puts it.[67] You have conformed to the corporation's efforts to support one of its members; one day you may be glad that your brothers and sisters do the same for you. In light of this, the historic breach in the relationship of working life and religion that occurred in the sixteenth century in the formation of the confessional state becomes all the more striking.[68]

James is quite clear on the worthlessness of faith without works in a sustained argument in chapter 2, verses 14–26. The teachings "Ye see then how that by works a man is justified, and not by faith only" and that "faith without works is dead" strike a chord with what one of the Venetian artisans referred to as "una fede operosa." James's example of the efficacy of works is Abraham:

20. But wilt thou know, O vain man, that faith without works is dead?
21. Was not Abraham our father justified by works, when he had offered Isaac his son upon the altar?
22. Seest thou how faith wrought with his works, and by works was faith made perfect?
23. And the scripture was fulfilled which saith Abraham believed God and it was imputed unto him for righteousness: and he was called the Friend of God.
24. Ye see then how that by works a man is justified, and not by faith alone.

Abraham was prepared to make sacrifice of his son.

This teaching follows immediately on the idea that there is no mercy for those who show no mercy: "For he shall have judgment without mercy that hath showed no mercy, and mercy rejoiceth against judgment." According to one commentator, "James resolves the tension between justice and mercy by giving precedence to mercy" – just as Shakespeare would do.[69]

Abraham also features in a moral tale that gave a stern warning against the pursuit of worldly treasures and pleasures and the concomitant neglect of the poor. Abraham, *pater noster*, figures, without mercy, in a frequent subject of Venetian art. *Il ricco Epulone*, the story of Dives, the rich man, and Lazarus, the poor beggar, appears in chapter 16 of the Gospel of Luke. This Lazarus was not the man whom Christ brought back from the dead in Bethany in John, chapter 11, though the confusion appears to have existed in Venice. Perhaps this was in part due to the shared characteristics of sores and shrouds. In this passage of Luke, Dives, who dressed in purple and fine linen and "fared sumptuously every day," ignored the pleas of Lazarus, who sought only the crumbs from the rich man's table, "and no-one gave to him"; he was also afflicted with sores that the dogs licked. When both men died, Lazarus went to Abraham's bosom, and Dives to the fires of hell. The rich man pleaded for mercy ("Pater Abraham, Miserere mei") and asked that Lazarus dip the tip of his finger in water to refresh his tongue as he was tormented in the flames.[70] But Abraham offered no mercy. Dives remained in torment, and Lazarus was comforted. When Dives pleaded that Abraham send him to the rich man's brothers, Abraham answered that they could learn from Moses and the prophets; "neither will they be persuaded, though one rose from the dead"[71] – a teaching that may further have confused Lazarus the poor man with the Lazarus whom Christ brought back to life in Bethany. There can be no confusion about the moral of the tale: earthly riches are worthless, and neglect of the poor brings damnation.

However, the earthly translation of Misericordia brought rewards not only in the life to come but also in the here and now. The kiss of peace, the recitation of the paternoster, and the emphasis on the works of corporal mercy were all embedded in the routine rituals of the scuole by the later part of the thirteenth century. How did these values find their way through the course of many centuries to become part of the lives of Venetians? And why were they acquiring such prominence in the period? One may begin to answer these questions by combining the work of Peter Brown on the cult of the saints in late antiquity with the invaluable compilation of Silvio Tramontin and other contributors on the same subject in Venice.[72] "A sense of the mercy of God lies at the root of the discovery, translation and installation of relics." So writes Professor Brown in his magisterial overview. He cited the example of Saint

Augustine's correspondent, the poet bishop of Nola, Paulinus (353–431), who, prefiguring Shakespeare, described God's mercy as tiny drops "like the gentle dew from heaven."[73] Venetians may have seen its representation in many paintings of "The Miraculous Fall of Manna" to the children of Israel in the wilderness. Manna was the Old Testament prefiguration of the celestial food of the Eucharist, the body of the Son, the Son whom God the Father had sent to redeem the sins of mankind. In another Old Testament prefiguration of the New Testament, Father Abraham obeyed God's will in sacrificing his son Isaac. Of course, Shakespeare also saw the "quality of mercy" – which gives the title to this book and this chapter of it – as heavenly drops.[74] Mercy became the special attribute of the Virgin Mary, and in due course we shall come to the significance of Franciscan teaching in the promotion of her cult. With regard to the configuration of economic, political, and religious life in the later thirteenth century, we must first attend to the new and prominent definition of the cult of Saint Mark.[75]

The role of Saint Mark as patron of the city strengthened and sharpened immeasurably in the later thirteenth century, and it did so in its Venetian variations on general themes identified by Professor Brown. His methodological starting point applies strongly to the mid-thirteenth-century context. The universally comprehensive embrace of Mercy is recalcitrant to the Enlightenment's division of the learned and the vulgar. Just as Adam Smith dismissed the elements of the mercantile system as sustained by mere popular ignorance, so David Hume and Edward Gibbon harped on the lamentable nature of popular superstition.[76] Just as Venice's government of merchants may not have been exclusive, so Venice's religion sheltered all who could identify with the republic, irrespective of wealth or status. In this regard there is a majestic harmony in ideas of mercy, albeit across many centuries.

It was a familiar pattern in the cult of the saints that the discovery of holy relics (*inventio*) would be followed by their removal to a place of installation (*translatio*) where veneration might recall or induce the apparition of the saint in person (*apparitio*). In all aspects of the cult Professor Brown noted the immediacy with which eternity touched the here and now, and how close heaven was to life on earth. (That immediacy was unusually vivid in the middle of the thirteenth century.) In Venice's relationship with Saint Mark there were multiple reinforcements of these elements of the cult of the saints.

The patron saint of a city was the invisible sponsor of the bishop, who exercised the saint's patronage on earth, "the visible *patronus* beneath the invisible *patronus*."[77] The church of Saint Mark in Venice had no bishop. The episcopal seat was San Pietro di Castello. The basilica of San Marco was the doge's private chapel. This made Saint Mark the patron of the doge, which added enormously to the sacral character of the secular ruler.[78] The directness of the relationship became much more prominent in the thirteenth century. The doge's patron had been Saint Teodoro, the Byzantine soldier-saint, and there is uncertainty and indeed confusion as to whether San Theodore had once been the patron of Venice itself.[79] In a listing from the end of the fifteenth century of the foundations of churches in Venice by the Byzantine general, Narses, Marin Sanudo noted "a church under the name of San Teodoro, who was our first protector before the elevation of Saint Mark."[80]

The intensity of the city's dedication to Saint Mark was in many ways increased by the restricted nature of the urban space. In general, an urban community defined itself by pilgrimage to the patron's shrine outside the city walls – that is, until the relics came into the city itself.[81] In Venice the communal identity defined itself by keeping to the familiar paths of the city in the lagoon and, in doing so, invested that space with a sublimation that was immediate and in touch with the everyday, a theme that played in the monuments commissioned by the confraternities of Venice.[82] That sense of the immediacy of heaven's contact with earth redoubled itself in a second inventio.

As is well known, Venetian merchants discovered the body of the saint in Alexandria (inventio). They concealed the remains of the saint under pork, which was abhorrent to Muslim inspectors, and smuggled them to Venice (translatio), reputedly in the year 828. The relics were honoured with a church in the saint's name, but they were lost during the construction work. Miraculously, there was a second inventio, in 1094, in the days of Doge Vitale Falier (1084–96). He was leading the clergy, the nobility, and the people of Venice in prayer for the restoration of the relics when a column of the church opened to reveal them. The second inventio, verifiable in historical time, came to be understood as an apparitio of the saint himself. Both the apparitio and the prayer that had invoked it found their commemoration in the mosaics of the church.

The inventio of 1094 ratified and updated the events of 828. The mosaics recording the second inventio in turn updated the story to the period of their execution in the 1260s. The saint's life, the story of how his relics came to Venice, their loss, and their *reinventio* became the present as it stood in the mid-thirteenth century. In the prayer and apparitio "the performers in both senses are the clergy, the doge and his advisors, the nobility and – perhaps – the people."[83] The beholders of the mosaic could see the pulpits that the Venetians had ripped from Constantinople in 1204; they could test the veracity of the mosaic in the fabric of the church. An episcopal figure leads the *preghiera* – and the response to the *imploratio* was, by the mid-thirteenth century, an expression of divine misericordia. The episcopal figure cannot be a bishop. It could, however, be the chapel's senior priest, the *primicerius*, which was the office of Jacopo Belogno before he became the patriarch of Grado in 1255. Leading the secular congregation in prayer in an event of 1094 is the doge of the time of the mosaics, Ranieri Zen (1253–68). Could the young boy be Philip of Courtenay, only son of the Emperor Baldwin II?[84] (See fig. 2.)

Then there are the members of the popolo depicted at prayer in the very church in which the onlooker stands. Those who do not rank as nobles enjoy *rappresentatio* at a moment in which the miraculous invests the everyday – and vice versa – a reflection of the immediacy of sacred history. The year 828 has its record in 1094, which moves unquestionably to the 1260s, the age of the chronicle history of Martino da Canale and the age of Ranieri Zen's successor as doge, Lorenzo Tiepolo. With regard to the strengthening sense of Venetian identity at this time, it is intriguing to note that leading scholarly authorities agree that the same mosaics are a very early expression of a newly independent Venetian artistic style that owed little to outside influences.[85]

Within that emergent style, representation of the Venetians outside the ranks of the nobility was not confined to the mosaics of the basilica's interior. In the atrium there were and are depictions of Pharaoh's granaries being filled under Joseph's direction and of the Tower of Babel climbing skywards as builders toil on the scaffolding. Once again the remote stories of the scheme of eternity have their immediacy in the grain stores of Venice and in its contemporary building projects – communal enterprises that, unlike Babel, divine judgment would not condemn.[86] (See figs. 3 and 4.)

In the main portal of the principal church of the Venetians there was and is another major scheme of what can be legitimately called popular representation. On the third arch, the largest, from around 1300, Vigilance watches over free and fraudulent trade, a reminder perhaps that all guild members took an oath to conduct their business "bona fide sine fraude," and prefiguring Adam Smith's sentiment that "honesty is the best policy."[87] (See fig. 5.) Beneath the Mystic Lamb on the inner fascia of the doorway there stand examples of those trades. On the left are wall builders, milk sellers, butchers, bakers, warehouse keepers, and shipbuilders (fig. 6). To the right are fishermen – an apostolic trade – blacksmiths, carpenters, coopers, barbers, and shoemakers. Three of the great doors to the basilica are the work of a master goldsmith, Bertuccio, who proclaimed himself on two of them: MCCC MAGISTER BERTUCCIUS AURIFEX VENETUS. Thus the entry to the basilica was defined by the work of a goldsmith, just as at the opposite end of the building, behind the high altar but displayed in all its glory on special feast days, was the Pala d'Oro, the work of four centuries in gold, jewels, and enamel.[88]

2. *The Prayer for the Discovery of the Remains of Saint Mark*, 1260–70, mosaic, Basilica di San Marco, Venice. Courtesy of Procuratia di San Marco – Venezia.

The question remains as to whether this burgeoning exaltation of the humble was a process to which the Serrata put an end. For, in the years after the paradoxical "closure" and in a continuity strikingly similar to the development of Venetian corporations, the representations continued. The closure – which was in many senses an enlargement – necessitated a more ample space in which the Greater Council could assemble. Inseparably from the doge's private chapel, a new palace took shape. In its porticoes, clearly visible in the public space of the piazzetta, beneath the presiding figure of Justice, are sculpted figures that date from around 1400, all announcing their occupation: a stonecutter, a goldsmith, a shoemaker, a carpenter, an official of measures, a peasant, a notary, and a blacksmith.[89] The column has taken the name *capitello delle arti* (figs. 7a and 7b). Moreover, as we shall see, the tendency

3. *The Tower of Babel*, c. 1220, mosaic, Basilica di San Marco, Venice. Courtesy of Procuratia di San Marco - Venezia.

4. *Grainstores*, detail from the *Story of Joseph*, 1260–70, mosaic, Basilica di San Marco, Venice. Courtesy of Procuratia di San Marco – Venezia.

5. *Vigilance Presiding over Fair and Fraudulent Trade*, early thirteenth century, sculpture, first main arch, right side of façade, Basilica di San Marco, Venice. Courtesy of Procuratia di San Marco - Venezia.

received a further infusion of energy during the Franciscan revival of the fifteenth century.

Misericordia and Mercanti: The First Scuole

All of the images noted (figs. 2–7) are solemn with the Misericordia that linked economic activity to the most fundamental principles of the religion of the Venetians and to the public life of the polity. The trades of Venice that were represented in guilds encased within their organization a scuola, or devotional confraternity, membership of which was less compulsory than natural. The scuola of each guild collected and managed the contributions of members in funding a regular mass with candles and music – as agreed with the clergy of the guild's chapel in its chosen church. Further funds were put to pious causes, notably benefits during sickness or injury, and the costs of a funeral for members and their families. Some of these benefits extended to the temporary poor of the guild and to their families, to dowries for girls who might otherwise fall into prostitution, and to relief of the hardship of widows and orphans.[90]

Yet there still remains a strong tendency to separate the *scuole delle arti* from other Venetian confraternities and to elevate the institutions that came to be

6. *Bakers*, later thirteenth century, detail from *Trades beneath the Mystic Lamb*, sculpture, Basilica di San Marco, soffit of third arch. Courtesy of Procuratia di San Marco - Venezia.

7a. *Capitello delle arti*, fourteenth century, sculpture, Palazzo Ducale facing Piazzetta, Venice. Photograph by Emmanuele Lugli.

7b. *Measurer*, detail from *Capitello delle arti*, fourteenth century, sculpture, Palazzo Ducale facing Piazzetta, Venice. Photograph by Emmanuele Lugli.

known as the Scuole Grandi above all of those.[91] This sharpness of division in nature at once reflects the myth of the Venetian constitution and obscures the similarities of function that all the confraternities shared. As already noted, this strict separation owed much to Gasparo Contarini and his propagation of the myth of the Venetian constitution as designed and managed by a wise ruling class. The early history of the scuole disrupts any such pattern.

There was a mysteriously complex relationship between the scuole of Santa Maria and San Francesco at the Frari, Santa Maria and San Cristofalo at the Madonna dell'Orto, and the Scuola Grande della Misericordia. Sometimes, the institutions that in the later fifteenth century became known as the Scuole Grandi are given a separate and distinctive classification as *dei Battudi* (of the beaten) because they practised flagellation. The Scuola di San Teodoro was not a flagellant confraternity but was founded in 1258, even though it did not become a Scuola Grande until 1552, after a hundred years of close association with the *arte dei marzeri*. Even when the designation of the title "Grande" had become a formal classification, at the end of the fifteenth century, the Scuola di San Rocco was not originally to be one of those separated by the title.[92] Like Saint Roch, Saint James (not the author of the General Epistle, but "the Greater," later associated with Spain and the pilgrim church of Compostella) was a pilgrim saint, and the scuola that met under his auspices had a particularly close relationship with the Scuola Grande di San Giovanni Evangelista. Similarly, the Scuola Grande della Carità had its own scuola piccola di Santi Apostoli – to be distinguished, but not decisively, from another organization of that name that met at the church of Santi Apostoli in Cannaregio.[93]

Furthermore, there is evidence to suggest that those excluded from political power – another divide that may be too neat – directed the activities of the scuole with less reference to magistrates (though not necessarily with less regard for them) than Contarini would have us think. In a retrospective on his previous work Professor Pullan noted that the Scuole Grandi assumed that title of distinction in their scale and separateness "no later than" 1467.[94] In his earlier work he set aside detailed consideration of their origins, which this study will examine anew.[95]

There were many scuole delle arti in Venice, duly recognized by the government in the first half of the thirteenth century. There are traces of still earlier foundations of devotional confraternities that were not attached to trades.[96] However, there is a wave of foundations from the mid-thirteenth century onwards, and these appear to relate in various ways to two powerful sources of religious energy that were circulating at the time: the renewed applicability of the apocalyptic vision associated with the twelfth-century prophet Joachim of Fiore, and the appeal to expanding urban populations of the mendicant orders, and especially of the Franciscans.[97]

The developments in Venice in the mid-thirteenth century may seem to denote confident construction, but the period also showed a heightened anxiety. As Professor Pullan emphasized, there was "an unusually vivid sense of standing on the frontiers of eternity."[98] Indeed, there was a widespread fear that the end of the world was impending. The background to such expectations lay in the prophecies of the Calabrian Joachim of Fiore (c. 1135–1202). From the obscure mysticism of his visions, scholars have extracted a basic pattern of prophecy. According to Joachim – of whom the ecclesiastical authorities grew increasingly suspicious – history would unfold in three phases in accordance with a destiny deeply rooted in the Holy Trinity of Father, Son, and Spirit; or Old Testament, New Testament, and "Third Age"; or again Law, Grace, and Love[99] (fig. 8).

That Trinitarian rhythm of prophetic change had a particular resonance for Venice and in Venice. However, the connection of the Joachite revival of the 1260s to the foundation of a whole cluster of confraternities in Venice is resistant to causal proof. The Joachite scheme of eternity in the 1260s appeared in the preaching of Ranier Fasani, first in Perugia and then in other parts of northern Italy, including the Marches of Treviso. By some prophetic calculations based on the number of generations between the birth of Christ and the end of the world, the year 1260 seemed to mark the dissolution of all things.[100] On the threshold of the impending new age, when all humanity would stand before Divine Judgment, Fasani urged repentance, and the most common and passionate of its manifestations was self-flagellation in recollection of the scourging that Christ had suffered during his Passion.[101] In Venice some of the confraternities founded in the 1260s took the title "dei Battuti" because they practised this form of penitence and indeed institutionalized it.

The possible connections between developments in Venice in the 1260s and the flagellant movement are tempting. However, the flagellant "movement' is not synonymous with the regulated and restricted membership of flagellant confraternities. Spontaneous expressions of popular piety that might relate to a movement aroused governmental suspicion in Venice, as the episode of the Bianchi in 1399 bears witness. Moreover, by no means all of the scuole established in Venice in the thirteenth century practised flagellation. Even within the *Scuole dei Battudi*, it is unclear how widespread was the practice of ritual flagellation among the membership. From the middle of the fourteenth century, apparently only sixty brethren in any of the Scuole dei Battudi actually beat themselves, and they were novices rather than full members.[102]

However, it is now pertinent to examine the ways in which the Joachite prophecy that inspired the flagellants could apply to the religious life of the Venetians. The city's churches made manifest the Old Testament as well as

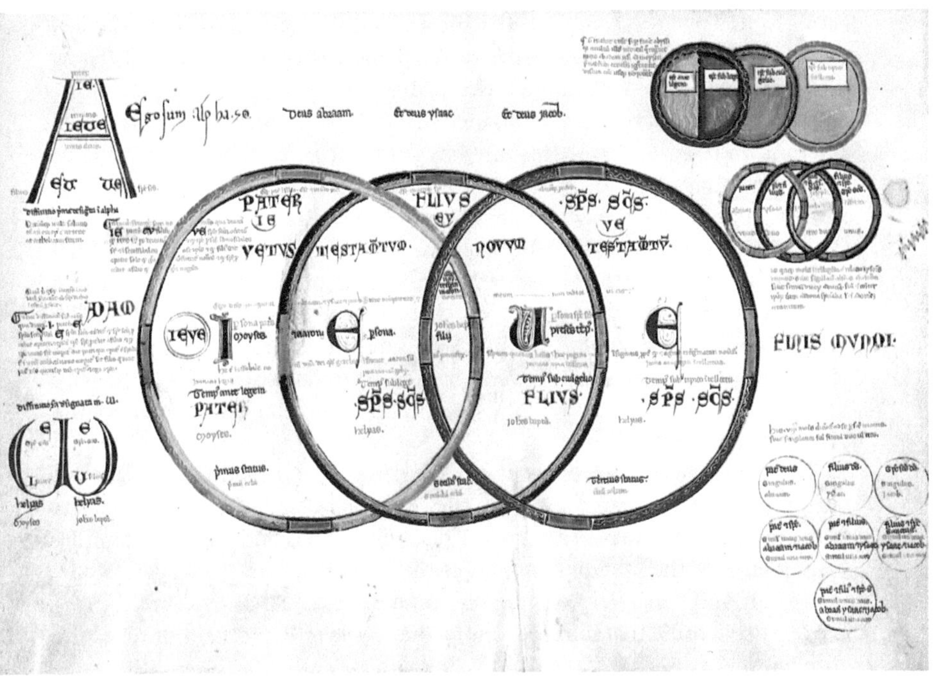

8. *The Three Ages*, mid-thirteenth century, schema of Joachim of Fiore. Courtesy of Curia di Reggio Emilia.

the New, in a pattern suggesting that Venice itself dwelt in the age of the spirit and was the fulfilment of the law – an apocalyptic perfection that was harmonious with what later became known as the myth of Venice.

Unusually in Western Christendom, and deriving from a Byzantine tradition that still stood in the nearby city of Ravenna, some of the most ancient churches of Venice were named for Old Testament prophets, or elders prophesying at the beginning of the New Testament: San Daniele was founded in 820; San Simeon Profeta (Luke 2:25–35) dated back to 967; San Moise (Moses) was founded in the eighth century, and San Zaccaria in the ninth; San Samuele dated from the tenth or eleventh century; San Geremia (Jeremiah) was a foundation of the eleventh century, consecrated in 1292; and San Giobbe (Job) was a foundation of 1395. Many other Old Testament prophets had a feast day in the Venetian liturgical year.[103] There were churches for the archangels Raphael and Michael, who appear in Scripture in the Old Testament or in the Apocrypha. The church of Angelo Raffaele was founded after the archangel appeared to Saint Magnus in the seventh century; the church of Archangel Michael, Sant'Anzolo, now destroyed, dated from 920. There was a further elision of the Old and New Testaments in the cult of the saints who died before Christ rather than in his name: Sant'Anna and San Lazzaro. This last was the resurrected man from Bethany, not the imaginary beggar in the story of Dives and Lazarus. It is possible to see the topography of the city in paintings of heaven itself, identifying the city of Saint Mark with Paradise.[104] In that connection Saint Magnus was a crucial figure. He was possibly the oldest named inhabitant of Venice. In response to a series of visions he founded seven churches in the city: San Pietro di Castello, Santa Maria Formosa, Santa Giustina, San Giovanni in Bragora, San Zaccaria, the Angelo Raffaele, and San Salvador.[105] The material topography of the city thus bore witness to the miracle of its inspiration (see map 4, "Churches of the Visions of Saint Magnus").

While this may be conjecture, there was certainly a legend that a vision of Joachim of Fiore had inspired the mosaics in the basilica of San Marco depicting the founders of the mendicant orders, Saint Francis and Saint Dominic.[106] The influence of the mendicants, and of the Franciscans in particular, is perhaps readily and concretely identifiable and may also help to explain the principle of Misericordia that diffused among the scuole of Venice and suffused the entire network.

As the canon law stated, "man the merchant can hardly ever or never please God."[107] Familiar as the notion may be, it bears repetition that the mendicants played a key part in the stupendous task of accommodating the commercial activities of the towns within the framework of the Catholic Church, an accommodation all but impossible under the strict principles of Augustinianism, which set no store by the city of man.[108] One of the chief means by which the Franciscans did so was to restrain the quest for profit – at its most rampant in the practice of usury – through constant reminders of the Christian's obligations to his fellows. The merchant's "otherhood" was to submerge itself in brotherhood.[109] While that formulation is slightly artificial and forced, it introduces the idea of Christian brotherhood as a crucial annex to merchant activity, and this is a helpful introit to the relationship of commercial and spiritual life in the Venetian scuole.

The Franciscans had revolutionized the Church of Rome with an urban spirituality that acknowledged commercial activity in the very act of rejecting worldly goods. When Dante reported that it pleased God to take Saint Francis to him, it was "to the reward that he deserved" – or "to the payment that he earned."[110] This was a reward for humility. By short extension, humility was the opposite of pride, the sin of Lucifer and the reason for his fall from heaven.

Pride was also the sin of the usurer who, in taking interest over time, presumed to appropriate what belonged to God alone.[111] In 1261, that year of the great flagellant processions, the archbishop of Pisa, Federigo Visconti, exclaimed, "Oh, how much good hope there must be for merchants, who have such a merchant intermediary with God!" As Lester K. Little comments, "Pisa, 1261: Saint Francis of Assisi had become the patron and protector of merchants."[112]

That general connection of Franciscan piety and commercial exchange seems fairly sound. One possibility is that the purveyor of Franciscan values to Venice was Saint Antony of Padua. He had certainly set his stamp on the economy of that city.[113] He had a particularly well-defined view on usury and usurers. On the news of the death of one of that trade, he is said to have broken off from his sermon to say where the dead man's heart would be: "Behold how the word of the Lord is now revealed as true, for He said, 'Where your treasure is, there will your heart be also.' Then Antony said, 'Go to his strongbox and in the largest moneybag his heart will be found.'"[114]

The Franciscans conceived of their own work as a "sacred business."[115] From 1255 there was an altar to Saint Antony in the main Franciscan church in Venice, Santa Maria Gloriosa dei Frari, and the saint's presence is ubiquitous in the church, in the foundation of a confraternity in his name there in 1439, and in Titian's altarpiece for the Pesaro family.[116]

The Franciscans did not offer an endorsement of commercial activity in all its forms. In Giotto's grim representation of the Last Judgment, only a short distance from Venice in the Scrovegni Chapel in Padua, Judas appears among the usurers, who hang by their own purse strings (fig. 9). They had compounded pride with avarice – and received their reward.[117] The Paduan example is instructive. The founding and decoration of the chapel was a conscious act of restitution by Enrico Scrovegni, trying to expiate the ill-gotten gains of his father, Reginaldo, and his own. Saint Antony was somewhat unusual among Franciscans as a "hammer of heretics." He was, however, a key figure in the generation of Franciscan principles within the commercial economy of Venice. He was the first member of the order whom Saint Francis entrusted with the instruction of theology, and in Padua he was associated with the public shaming of debtors – a clear illustration of the involvement of the Church with everyday working life. His emblem was the lily, symbol of the Virgin's purity. He also had a special place among the saintly patrons of Venice, associated with his favouring the republic during the War of Chioggia.[118]

In the context of the city of Venice the most influential teachings of the Franciscans derived from their promotion of the cult of the Virgin Mary and, in very close connection, the role of Mercy in descending from heaven to sweeten and soften relations on earth (Da Canale refers to the Virgin as "douce Mère").

9. Giotto, *Judas*, detail from *The Last Judgement*, 1306–13, Arena Chapel, Padua. Copyright Musei Civici.

The most significant source for these teachings is the writing of Bonaventura (1221–74, canonized in 1482), who became head of the order in 1257. He accepted the doctrine of the Immaculate Conception, which made Mary's birth without sin – an idea that the Dominican Thomas Aquinas rejected – and this immediately elevated the cult of the Madonna. In his teachings Bonaventura also reconfigured the act of prayer into three stages: first, the *deploratio miseriae*; second, the *imploratio misericordiae*; and finally, the *exhibitio latriae*. Begging for mercy became central to any prayer that a Christian might offer. The lamentation of misery preceded it, and the demonstration of sorrowful penitence followed.[119] The Lord's Prayer had already made sorrowful penitence dependent on the Christian's mercy to others (Matthew 18:23–35).

Like Saint Francis, Joachim of Fiore and Bonaventura are celebrated in Dante's *Paradiso*.[120] Their respective influences in giving direction and purpose to the sentiments that helped to inspire the formation of confraternities in Venice in the mid-thirteenth century were not mutually exclusive.[121] However, figures of even their stature in the history of the Church must not obscure this fundamental characteristic of the scuole: they were organizations of the laity. This was to prove a source of strength, albeit a contentious one. It is customary to point out that, despite their name, these organizations were not educational institutions.[122] Yet we may usefully ponder the pedagogical overtones of the term *scuola*, especially since schooling (as opposed to practical training in a place of work) was virtually a clerical monopoly.[123] At the end of the fifteenth century the Milanese ambassador, Battista Sfondrati, referred to members of the scuole as "scholars" (*scholari*).[124] In important ways the scuole inculcated through repetition and practice the values embodied in the term *Misericordia*. Furthermore, the many depictions of Misericordia in Venice and the many agencies that attempted its practical implementation were the combination of contemplation and action that was central to Venetian religion.[125] Having laboured to establish the idea that the scuole were not the creation of the State, it is essential to avoid any notion that they were the imposition of the Church.

This is vital in reconsidering the early pattern of the confraternities' foundations. What prompts the second look is the continuing narrowness of the scholarly perspective on the foundations of the middle years of the duecento. In assessments of the origins of the scuole, those which became known as Scuole Grandi have drawn attention that exaggerates their separateness. Granted, the 1260s saw the probable foundation of four of them: Santa Maria della Carità, San Giovanni Evangelista, San Marco, and the Misericordia. There were later additions to the category in the shape of the Scuole Grandi di San Rocco (1478), San Teodoro (1552), and Santa Maria dei Carmini (1767). Brian Pullan was at pains to point out that the origins of the Scuole Grandi were not a central concern of his study.[126] He cited the sixteenth-century commentary of Francesco Sansovino in making the Scuola Grande di Santa Maria della Carità "the senior Scuola Grande," providing a model for emulation by the Scuola di San Giovanni Evangelista and then the Scuola di Santa Maria della Misericordia.[127] Curiously, Professor Pullan's list did not include the Scuola di San Marco, which did not even appear in his comprehensive index.

Giorgio Cracco included the Scuola di San Marco in a decisive chronological order of the earliest scuole. He begins with the Scuola di San Teodoro, which had a statute dating from May 1258, giving it precedence over the Carità (December 1260), with the Scuola di San Giovanni Evangelista and the Scuola di Santa Maria della Val Verde being founded in 1261.[128] It is implausible that the last named could have taken the title that Cracco uses before its move to Cannaregio in 1308 (which others see as the date of its first foundation). However, the inclusion of San Teodoro marks an important loosening of the separateness and distinctiveness of the institutions that became known as the Scuole Grandi.

Even so, that expansion of parameters can and should go further. The previous discussion of trade guilds pointed to the recognition of twelve arti by 1259 and probably a further five before the institution of the Giustizia Nova in 1261 (see table 1.1). Although the rulebooks of the guilds acquired a new uniformity in 1271, there were seventeen references to the "scola artis" in the statutes that dated before 1261. There were thirty-four further registrations before 1300 (six between 1262 and 1270, thirteen or fourteen in 1271, and a further thirteen or fourteen by 1299), making a total of fifty-one scuole delle arti.[129]

Even if we confine the inquiry to confraternities that functioned independently of a trade (a task that is only possible with careful qualification, as the case of San Teodoro will presently show), then there is a total of ten foundations, which subsumes the four examples from the 1260s that went on to become known as Scuole Grandi. It is not a catalogue that we can compile with references that are exactly contemporary of foundation and statute. However, that very mismatch may inform us of the unregulated and perhaps even spontaneous pattern of formation, a pattern that is certainly not the product of a preemptive blueprint for the future hatched in the minds of a sagacious nobility.

The church of San Bartolomeo at Rialto was founded in the ninth century, apparently in the name of the Greek saint Demetrius. As San Bartolomeo, it became home to a number of confraternities, three of which were associated with an occupation (fustian weavers, quilt makers, oar makers). One of the most important of its confraternities took its name from the Evangelist Matthew, patron of the money changers who congregated around the trading tables near the Ponte di Rialto. The copy of the scuola's mariegola, or rule book, of

Table 1.2. Chronology of Foundations of Scuole in Venice, 1247–99

Year	Title	Church	Sestiere
1247	San Mattia	San Mattia	Murano
1258	San Teodoro	San Salvador	San Marco
1260	Santa Maria della Carità	Santa Maria della Carità	San Nicolo
1261	Santa Maria e San Cristoforo	Frari	San Polo
1261	San Giovanni Evangelista	Sant'Aponal	San Polo
1261	San Marco	San Zanipolo	Castello
1277	San Zulian	San Zulian	San Marco
1277	Santi Lorenzo e Sebastiano	San Lorenzo	Castello*
1280	Angelo Raffaele e San Nicheta	Angelo Raffaele	San Nicolo
1299	San Stefano	San Stefano	San Marco

*Vio 57.108.

1415 recorded that the confraternity had come to the church in 1361. However, it referred in turn to the original foundation of the scuola in the church of San Matteo at Murano in 1247.[130]

Intriguingly, in the thirteenth century, Murano – a miniature Venice of ten islands and a Canal Grande – had experienced its own conjuncture. It had acquired considerable autonomy: its own ducal gastaldo (a title also used for guild wardens), its own councils (both a greater and a lesser, and from 1275 one for its own cittadini), a "Golden Book" of its own patricians, and its own currency. It boasted seventeen churches, of which only three survive. One of its *fondamente* still bears the name of a flagellant confraternity: San Giovanni Evangelista dei Battudi.[131] (Saint John the Evangelist was the only saint who observed the flagellation of Christ.) The autonomy of the island surely served to reinforce the protection of the celebrated glass industry to which it was home from 1291. That insularity served both to shield the city at Rialto from the sparks of the glass furnaces and to limit the possibilities of the migration of its secrets of production.[132] The convent of San Matteo was a Dominican house. Given the compression of so many features of the city itself in this insular setting, it is neither surprising nor unlikely that Murano should be home to so early an example of a devotional confraternity. The transfer from San Matteo on Murano to San Bartolomeo rather than San Matteo di Rialto may be explained in the low life of that latter parish, which drove away at least one other scuola. The Scuola di San Gottardo at Sant'Aponal dates from 1391, but it probably existed before that time. It had evidently located previously at San Matteo di Rialto, which had proved untenable "because of taverns and prostitutes and other dishonest persons who pass by there every day." It was in this area that the public brothel thrived in the fourteenth century.[133]

The second of Venice's scuole from the mid-thirteenth century appears to be San Teodoro, listed by Professor Cracco from 1258 on the basis of its statute of that year. The discussion of the expanding cult of Saint Mark noted Sanudo's identification of the Byzantine soldier-saint Theodore as Venice's first patron. Not only did the saint represent ties to Byzantium, but also he might have become confused with the warrior dragon-slayer Saint George who, inconveniently, was the patron of Venice's enemy and rival, Genoa.[134]

Once Saint Mark was secure as the unmistakable patron of Venice, the cult of Saint Theodore was revived. In 1450 the saint's day, 9 November, became an official feast of the republic. Perhaps the revival was linked to the Venetian pope of that time, Eugenius IV, who was seeking to organize a crusade to relieve Constantinople of the infidel threat. At about that time the confraternity merged with the wealthiest of Venice's trade guilds, the mercers or marzeri. In 1552, enriched with the mercers' resources and status, the confraternity of San Teodoro took the title of Scuola Grande.[135] The example is telling in that it melds dramatically the apparently different categories of scuola – arte, scuola dell'arte, scuola piccola, and Scuola Grande – in the extended history of a single institution. It suggests, moreover, the value of an exercise that reconfigures the early history of the scuole of Venice in the later thirteenth century. Such a reconfiguration may, in addition, suggest the relocation of the Scuola della Misericordia as representative of a complex of religious and moral values that was to give the history of Venice some critical elements of its long-term singularity.

Both these significant examples preceded the foundation of the Scuola di Santa Maria della Carità in 1260. The brethren established themselves at the church of the Santa Maria della Carità. Professor Pullan's source, Francesco Sansovino, wrote that the Scuole Grandi (the legitimate description by his time) "represent also a certain kind of civil government, in which the citizens as in their own Republic, have ranks and honours according to their deserts and qualities."[136] In some ways, the characterization matches that of Contarini, but, coming after the examples of San Matteo and San Teodoro, the idea of a scuola as a commonwealth in microcosm gives a new twist to their autonomy.

The Scuola della Carità currently houses the Gallerie dell'Accademia. Above the doorway to its cloister stands a frieze of the protective Madonna della Carità. There is no question of the importance of Charity, the love of a Christian for his or her fellows, in the history of Venice. This virtue is celebrated as the mother of all virtues in the mosaics of San Marco.[137] However, it is important to note that on the scuola's own building there was a clear differentiation from the Madonna della Misericordia. At the Scuola della Carità the Madonna is not sheltering members beneath her cloak, which is emphatically and tightly closed – a sharp contrast to the protective shield that it offered in depictions of the Madonna della Misericordia, which are by no means confined to the scuola of that name. To illustrate this, one might point to the Madonna della Misericordia that the Scuola della Carità evidently commissioned (figs. 10 and 11).[138] The idea that Sansovino set up and that Brian Pullan followed also suggests a clearer identity for the scuola than do its documents. Some of its members met as the confraternity of the Santi Apostoli, as noted in its statute book of 1288.[139] There appears to be no clear relationship with the Scuola di Santi Apostoli that met in the church of that name from 1350. Nevertheless, the duplication of the name in another institution is an important reminder of the ideal of apostolic brotherhood in the scuole.[140]

There are similarly hazy origins and movements in the early history of what looks to be the fourth foundation, that of San Giovanni Evangelista. It also dates from 1260, and began its meetings in the church of Sant'Aponal. It moved its location to the monastery of its patron in 1301. The ground-floor hall still houses a splendidly impressive Madonna della Misericordia in high relief, sheltering members of the scuola within her mantle[141] (fig. 12).

The Scuola di San Marco of 1261 holds a significant meaning in its title. The city's patron was an almost exclusively political saint, with the exception of his sponsorship of this confraternity. Apart from the basilica of San Marco, the doge's private chapel, which stands in the only piazza of the city, which in turn takes its name from the church, the Scuola di San Marco is the only building or institution in the city that derives its title from the patron saint of Venice. But then, what church or what scuola in Venice does not proclaim at least one feature unique to itself?[142] There is, in any case, an intriguing pairing with the next foundation, that which became known as Santa Maria della Misericordia, for both Saint Mark and the Virgin, in their different ways, in erudition and virginity, were ideal personifications of Venice itself. On the fifteenth-century lintel of the Scuola Grande di San Marco, the saint appears to be dispensing, and radiating, misericordia in the manner of the Virgin herself[143] (fig. 13). The tradition persisted in a work of unknown authorship showing the Madonna of Mercy with Saint Mark, the commission of the Scuola della Misericordia.[144]

The foundation of the Scuola della Misericordia is at once the most perplexing and the most tantalizing, eluding altogether the template of a numerical and chronological ordering of specific institutions. The year 1261 – but after the Scuola di San Giovanni Evangelista – is the conventional consensus for the foundation of the Scuola di Santa Maria della Misericordia, with a revision of its statutes in 1308 when it moved to its new location in Cannaregio. The scuola of 1261 met at the then new Franciscan church of the Frari and took as its title "Madonna e San Francesco," which reflected its location: a church dedicated to the Virgin and tended by the Franciscan order.[145]

10. *Madonna della Carità*, fourteenth century, bas-relief sculpture, Scuola Grande della Carità (Gallerie dell'Accademia), façade. Photograph by Francesco Turio Böhm.

11. *Madonna della Misericordia*, fourteenth century, buildings of the Scuola Grande della Carità. From Silvia Gramigna and Annalisa Perissa, *Scuole di arti mestieri e devozione a Venezia* (Venice: Arsenale Editrice, 1981).

12. *Madonna della Misericordia*, no date, high-relief scuplture, from the Scuola Grande di San Giovanni Evangelista. Courtesy of San Giovanni Evangelista Servizi.

13. *Saint Mark Blessing*, mid-fifteenth century, sculpture, lintel of the Scuola Grande di San Marco, Venice. Photograph by Massimo Bertacchi.

There is a clear possibility that this foundation breaks up the notion of the separateness of the confraternities that became known as Scuole Grandi. There is some circumstantial and suggestive evidence that, without entirely losing its own identity in the Sestier di San Polo, the Scuola della Madonna e San Francesco may have spawned two others. These were to become the Scuola di San Cristoforo dei Mercanti and that of Santa Maria della Val Verde della Misericordia, and they established themselves separately but in close geographical proximity in Cannaregio. The title "della Val Verde" (of the Green Valley) may refer to the area's lack of buildings, and to its orchards, a feature also commemorated in the title of the church of Santa Maria dell'Orto (Saint Mary of the Garden). This realization of the enclosed garden (the *hortus conclusus*), which represented Mary's virginity, marks another blending of the everyday and the sacred in the Venetian cityscape.

The two scuole represented mercantile activity (dei Mercanti) and mercy (della Misericordia) respectively.[146] Saint Christopher, as the man who carried Christ across water, was a saint under whose guidance one would like a ship to sail. The Virgin embodied the quality of Mercy itself. The two institutions that took their names were located in what is still a tranquil area of the city, bounded by wide expanses of water – compared with the rest of Venice – on four sides. Not far to the south is the Canal Grande, and to the north lies the open expanse of the lagoon. Next to the abbey of the Scuola Vecchia flows the Canale della Misericordia, which opens into the Sacca della Misericordia. Here, within a few yards of the scuola, was the mooring place for barges loaded with timber from Cadore, and on a clear day the mountains are visible far away beyond the water. A visit to the Misericordia and then to the merchants' scuola at the church of the Madonna dell'Orto, which stands near the wide Canal di Cannaregio in the west of the city, evokes the combination of the active life of business (*negotium*) and the contemplative life of regular devotions (*otium*), a balance that took various forms in different parts of the city. (See map 5, "The Location of the Scuola di Santa Maria della Val Verde della Misericordia.")

Perhaps such equilibrium steadied itself in Marco Polo's mind as he made his way from his home near the old church of San Zuan Grisostomo to the assemblies of the scuola of which he was a member. He lived in what remains a very quiet area of the bustling city, though the local church was rebuilt at the end of the fifteenth century and shows no sign of its eleventh-century foundation. The nearest bridge to the site of Marco's house is now called Ponte Marco Polo, and the site of his home has a plain commemoration by the Corte Prima and the Corte Seconda, both named "del Milion" after Marco's account of his travels. The *corti* (courtyards) still retain some well-preserved paterae and pilasters in the Venetian-Byzantine style. The relative architectural consistency of the area and the dancing decorative reliefs of plants, birds, and animals give a sense of being in touch with the origins of things. The tranquility of the place tends to belie its location only moments from the commercial heart of Venice at Rialto. The original Fondaco dei Tedeschi would have been visible to Marco as he made his way to his devotions at the Abbazia della Misericordia.

His membership stands in the statute book in a list of 1 August 1319. It is illustrative of the ambiguities of this case of overlap, cross-fertilization, offshoot, and duplication that Gastone Vio – without the slightest question – places the same membership list in the history of the Scuola della Madonna e di San Francesco at the Frari. This is despite the fact that the statute itself is located in the records of the Misericordia.[147] The simple entry "Marco Polo Milion" evokes a world of journey and discovery, both for any specialist and for any general reader. The three words bring to mind the ports and deserts of Arabia, the Old Man of the Mountains and his doped (and duped) assassins, diamonds, Malabar, the pleasure dome of Xanadu, and the decrees of Kublai Khan.[148]

It takes an effort to allow the other 513 names on the list to dispel the reverie. However, what do we know of the other brethren of the Scuola della Misericordia who may have rubbed shoulders (in some cases, shoulders that may have been lacerated by self-flagellation) with the man who became the most famous son of medieval Venice? The immediate impression, startling and intriguing, that the list makes is of the heterogeneity of the names on it. The journey that the mind now makes takes us a world away from a closing of the ranks of the aristocracy in definition of the ruling class and its perpetual defence. Nor is there the slightest suggestion that these are members of a Scuola Grande (why should there be, since contemporaries used no such term?) that was a political exercise yard for the legally defined class of citizens. The full list is available in published and scrupulous transcription.[149] From it the following deductions may readily be made.

First, the list has no alphabetical or chronological order (such as exists in similar lists from other scuole at around the same time). Nor was there any attempt at classification, while in the other lists those enrolled as "nobili' were clearly distinct.[150] The 514 entries provide a name or names for each member. In 207 cases the list gives the name of a parish, which indicates place of residence. In 164 cases, occupation provides another strand of identity. These latter elements sometimes intertwine in the same entry.

From these data stem further observations. A striking proportion of the names stand out in the undifferentiated lists as those of families within the Serrata's charmed circle of nobles. It may be that the list reflects a certain untidiness in the aftermath of the Serrata. Could it be that not all branches bearing a particular name enjoyed incorporation into the patriciate? Might it have been the case that, before the Serrata, there were mere coincidences of family name that did not reflect blood relationships of even a distant kind? Either of those possibilities suggests a social flux that, by 1319, had endured more than twenty years since the doors to the ruling class supposedly slammed shut.

In any case, while the name Trevisan may cause a hesitation over whether this is a native of Treviso or the indication of the membership of a patrician clan, it is much harder to blur other entries into uncertainty. There were four Foscarini, four Contarini, four Morosini, three Venier, and two Sanudo. All in all, up to eighty names on the list have strong suggestions of membership of the patriciate. Perhaps even more surprising in a polity supposedly newly configured by law are the three instances in which the patrician name is sullied (or merely confirmed?) by a distinctly plebeian occupation. "Nicolo Trun caxarol" seems to denote a cheesemaker from the Tron family. The sole member of the Vendramin on the lists, Luca, also bears the milky splashes of this occupation.

Of the three listed with the name da Molin, one is identified as a second-hand dealer: "Bortolomeo da Molin strazzarol."[151]

Admittedly, those three noble tradesmen were a tiny proportion of the 164 names that carry an occupation. However, the list has no obvious exclusions. Of the professions there were fourteen government officials and scribes, sixteen men who identified with banking and brokerage, and six medical men. There was a clear preponderance of luxury trades: twenty-eight goldsmiths and jewellers, ten apothecaries, nine mercers, eight furriers, and eight silk drapers. Yet there were also eight stall keepers and twenty-five who worked in textiles and clothing: including eight tailors, four cloth shearers, two dyers, two dealers in fustian, and three second-hand dealers (including Bortolomeo da Molin). There was a further leavening of nineteen involved in food supply (including two fishmongers, five cheese sellers, three butchers, and four bakers) and eight from the building, wood, and metal trades. In a strangely harmonious way, we find ourselves among the figures of the trades exalted on the façade of San Marco above the main portal or with the popolo rejoicing in mosaic at the *reinventio* of the relics of Saint Mark.

Marco's journey to the Misericordia from his home was by no means exceptional. Other lists show that the scuole did not have a parochial base. The 207 entries naming a parish represented 55 of Venice's *pievi* (parishes). This we may note in other scuole that were never to take the title "Grande": Sant'Agnese, Santa Maria della Celestia, and San Cristofalo dei Mercanti.[152] From the parishes in the vicinity of the Scuola della Misericordia came fifteen members from Santa Maria Formosa, sixteen from San Cassian, nine from San Felise, five from Santi Apostoli, five from San Lio, and three from San Marzilian. The clustering of names listed in the Misericordia in one general area does take the attention, however. A high proportion of members would have had to cross the Canal Grande in order to attend a congregation of the scuola. There were 68 of the 207 who fall into this category. Ten members came from San Giacomo dell'Orio, ten more from San Polo, twelve from San Pantalon, ten from San Trovaso, seven from San Barnaba, five each from Santa Margherita, the Angelo Raffaele, and San Tomà, and four from Sant'Aponal. All of those parishes are in the vicinity of Santa Maria Gloriosa dei Frari, which strengthens the argument that that church had been the scuola's original home. (See map 1, "The Sestieri and Parishes of Venice.")

With its mixes of different social orders, occupations, and parishes, the Scuola della Misericordia can seem to form yet another miniature of Venice. However, Francesco Sansovino's emphasis on the special connection between the cittadini and the Scuole Grandi in the sixteenth century, mentioned herein in relation to the Scuola della Carità, continued in what he had to say about the Misericordia. "It is a common opinion," he wrote, that at the Misericordia "there gathers the greater part of the cittadini originarii, and that therefore, in a certain way, it [the scuola] takes precedence over the others for this reason."[153]

The membership list of 1319 presents no correspondence with a supposed hierarchy of nobles, citizens, and popolani. Sansovino also offered a clue to a different distinctiveness in the Misericordia, in its very origins: "In the sestier of Cannaregio is included the scuola and brotherhood of Santa Maria della Misericordia, and begun by that of the Merchants in ancient times."[154] There was clearly a belief, to which Sansovino gave voice, that the Misericordia and the Scuola dei Mercanti had a shared identity. It bears repetition that what was to become the Scuola della Misericordia was probably founded at the Franciscan heart of Venice, the church of the Frari, in 1261. The records of the Scuola di San Cristofalo dei Mercanti include reference to an indulgence shared with the Misericordia in 1263.[155] The presence of the Scuola dei Mercanti at Santa Maria dell'Orto from no later than 1377, when that church was itself very new, reinforces the idea of common origins with geographical proximity. It is still possible today to walk in a few minutes from the Scuola Vecchia della Misericordia, past the Trecento sculpture of the Misericordia above the confraternity's almshouses in Corte Nova, and on to the Scuola dei Mercanti at Santa Maria dell'Orto, where there are further images of the Madonna della Misericordia, "patroness of the fellowship"[156] (figs. 14 and 15).

The Scuola della Madonna at San Marzilian dates from 1402, according to its statute of 1420.[157] It was not a new foundation but connects to the vexing problem of the Scuola di San Cristoforo. In 1424 a petition to the Council of Ten requesting recognition explains the scuola's origins. At the time, it was the confraternity of Santa Maria Odorifera: "It used to be called of Santa Maria dell'Orto ... But after there arose disorders between those of the scuola, and the brothers of San Cristoforo, the which are brothers of the Mercadanti, the foresaid name of dell'Orto was set aside, and added to the said Scuola di San Cristoforo, the which called itself the Scuola or fraternity of Santa Maria dell'Orto and San Cristoforo." The upshot of this is the request of the petition "that they may take all the things and goods of their Scuola in whatever place they may be and without any contradiction whatsoever and those and these locate with the scuola or fraternity of Santa Maria di Grazia, which is in the parish of San Marzilian."[158]

Within the confusion there is some clarification with regard to the way in which the bifurcation of the foundation at the Frari in 1261 had now further proliferated. The evidence suggests that the Scuola di Santa Maria e San Cristoforo had moved to Cannaregio – perhaps temporarily to the church of Santa Maria Assunta – and transformed into Santa Maria della Val Verde

14. *Madonna della Misericordia*, late-fourteenth century, high-relief scuplture, Corte Nova, Cannaregio. Photograph by Daniel Palleros.

at the Abbazia della Misericordia and a separate Scuola di Santa Maria e San Cristoforo dei Mercanti at the nearby church of Santa Maria dell'Orto. Within the latter, in a dispute over the title, some of the brethren moved the Scuola of the Virgin "Odorifera" (the Fragrant) – presumably a reference to the scents of the garden (Orto) – to join with the Scuola of Santa Maria delle Grazie at San Marzilian, as documented here. San Marzilian was a church with strong Marian connections. According to Sansovino, in 1133 the Bocchi family had brought an image of the Virgin there from Rimini.[159] If this is correct, the arrival of the image pre-dates the naming of the church in 1142, evidently for the Confessor Saint Martial, sometimes seen as a missionary to Gaul under the direction of Saint Peter.[160]

The significance of the connection between mercy and mercantile activity bears further investigation and emphasis. At once, it removes the separateness of the institutions that became known as the Scuole Grandi and emphasizes a key characteristic of all the other confraternities of Venice. In what became the Scuole Grandi the distinction between giver and recipient was gradually institutionalized in separate orders of rich and poor members.[161] In the flagellant confraternities the benevolence of the rich towards the poor was not so much charity between brethren of equal Christian status as mercy from the permanently prosperous to the permanently disadvantaged. A structure of fixed orders of rich and poor channelled the surplus wealth of those who were

15. *Madonna della Misericordia*, sixteenth century, bas-relief sculpture, Scuola dei Mercanti, Santa Maria dell'Orto, Venice. Photograph by Daniel Palleros.

unlikely ever to face poverty to ease the lot of those who were unlikely to face anything but poverty. Such a mechanism placed considerable restrictions on the number of people that such philanthropy might reach.[162]

Such a fixity and permanence of different orders was not typical of the light fabric of netted threads formed by the scuole in the political economy of Venice. In the several hundred confraternities that were never classified as Grandi Misericordia not only acknowledged the inequality of rich and poor but also recognized that the conditions of relative prosperity or relative hardship were reversible. This introduced an important element of self-interest in the relief of misfortune, which is detectable in the link between commercial activity and religious belief and practice that was forming in Venice in the later thirteenth century.[163] As discussed, the sources of such principles lay in the language of commercial exchange in the gospels, especially the Gospel of Matthew, and in particular in the Beatitudes and the paternoster. The teachings of the Franciscans as represented in the work of Bonaventura placed the *imploratio misericordiae* at the centre of the act of prayer, which increasingly became an oration to the Virgin Mary. The enterprise had a singular utility in relating the eternal to the everyday, especially to the activities of commercial exchange.[164]

Misericordia was not so much a check on mercantile activity as its guiding principle. Paying dues to the scuola provided protection against misfortune and placed the giver under the shelter of the Virgin's mantle – which was not the case with the Madonna of the Carità, at least in the image that the scuola dedicated to her and chose to place before Venetian eyes. Mercy was more than a religious injunction or a pious aspiration; it was a principle that linked economic activity and, through the operation of justice in the courts, political life. In Martino da Canale's credo marciano of the mid-thirteenth century, "misericorde" stood in stark juxtaposition to "discorde." In Venetian terms, this is as dramatic a comparison as were the frescoes of the Lorenzetti showing Good and Bad Government on separate walls of the Palazzo Pubblico in Siena or, much more locally, the frescoes of the Palazzo della Ragione in Padua, a sort of vast merchant's manual.[165]

In the later thirteenth century, between the beginning of the Scuola della Misericordia at the church of the Franciscans and the removal of the confraternity to the abbey in Cannaregio, there were several other foundations demonstrating a proliferation of shared principle and aspiration that weakens further any notion of a regulated imitation of those institutions that much later took the designation "Scuole Grandi."

The Scuola di San Giuliano dated from 1277. It took its seat at the eponymous church, a space that offers a density of connection that vividly evokes the network of support offered by the scuole. Saint Julian the Hospitaller was a patron of travellers and the poor, a provider of shelter. The expected zeal of the individual member's commitment resounds from the initiation ceremony. A new brother had to go to the altar of the scuola, where the gastaldo would put before him "those blessed figures which are painted in it, telling him what is contained in them so that he remembers the Passion of Christ. There he must kneel and remove his hood or anything else that he may have on his head, and with every reverence kiss those figures which are painted there and promise to God and to the martyr, Messer San Zulian, to observe that which is contained in our statute."[166] Given the contact of the kiss of peace, it was a practical provision to place among the warden's duties the maintenance and repair of the confraternity's equipment.[167]

On the death of a member the scuola's other brethren took its cross and banner to the home of the deceased, there to recite five paternosters and five aves "or make a charity for the soul." Such provisions applied to both men and women, and membership was not linked to the parish, though servants were excluded. The reference to the scuola's tomb at the nunnery of San Zaccaria shows the permeability of boundaries between monastic and secular religious practice, as well as between religious and lay. The scuola undertook to pay for a vigil for any sick or needy woman. Women were to have their own officers – the deaconesses to be five "good widow women."[168] Women could join as the wives of brethren, or independently if they were residents of the parish.[169]

This was a provision of 1399. Later still, from 1424, comes an example of the confraternity's concern for music. During the procession the priest of San Zulian was to have the organ sound. If he was unable to arrange this, the scuola hired its own organist, deducting his fee from its payment to the church. If the church's organ was out of action, the scuola hired a temporary replacement for its use, again with a deduction. This is an early indication of the importance of music in the life of the scuole, and of their contribution to the musical life of Venice.[170]

Like San Bartolomeo, the church provides a history of the long duration of the scuole that it housed. The church of San Zulian dates back to the ninth century and was directly under the jurisdiction of the patriarch. In 1424, the same year as the provisions of the Scuola di San Zulian for music, the church accepted the scuola of the mercers' guild, which transferred from its seat at San Daniele. The mercers' confraternity in turn connected to the ancient Scuola di San Teodoro. The mercers thus made their religious home in a church on the thoroughfare to which they gave their name, the Mercerie. Eventually, the marzeri could go about their business as mercanti on their way to *mercati* with a reminder of their heavenly *merce* – all without even a detour. They could enter by the main door of the square church and leave through the side exit and still remain in the great complex of mercers' shops. There was a strong presence of mercers in all the confraternities that met at the church, and in the Scuola di San Teodoro at San Salvador.

The church housed a Scuola di San Rocco founded in 1496 – nearly twenty years after the foundation of the Scuola Grande of that name. San Zulian also became the home of the second confraternity of Venice to be dedicated to the Eucharist. That was in 1502 (the first had been in 1395), and it marked the beginning of a remarkable series of foundations in the first half of the sixteenth century. An image of the Madonna della Misericordia stands at the centre of the moulding of the ceiling at the mid-point of the high altar. In the copy of the statute of the Scuola di San Zulian referred to here, the first evidence of government involvement comes in 1559.[171]

In 1280 the Scuola di San Raffaele e Nicheta was founded at the church of the Anzolo Raffaele, an ancient foundation that originally had a link to the convent at San Zaccaria, and which held the body of San Nicheta, the bishop of Antioch.[172] There is a chapel to the saint in the nearby church of San Nicolo dei Mendicoli. The church of the Anzolo Raffaele was a foundation of Saint Magnus, to whom the archangel appeared in the second of his seven visions. (See map 4, "Churches of the Visions of Saint Magnus.) The records of the scuola reveal its origins in an awareness of "la presente vita fragile" and the need to seek a better life with the guidance of Saint John and Saint Augustine.[173]

Augustine greatly admired Saint Stephen as the first martyr for the faith outside the ranks of the Apostles. Augustine's influence was enduringly significant at the church of San Stefano, one of the most beautiful surviving examples of Venetian Gothic architecture. A monastery of the Augustinian order was founded in 1264, and the first stone of the church was laid in 1294. Only five years afterwards, the Scuola di San Stefano drew up its rule book, as recorded in a later copy of it.[174] The church reached completion in 1325. It contains a "ship's keel" ceiling, and the evocation of maritime ventures is again balanced, in the heart of the city, with a secluded cloister for quiet contemplation, a characteristic that gains emphasis from the eremitical calling of the Augustinians there.

There is evidence of a further four confraternities at the church (though the next foundation was not until the late 1520s), and three trade guilds met as confraternities here. They have left their mark on the stones of Venice with some notable commissions. In the mid-fifteenth century the same Bartolomeo Bon who worked at the Misericordia completed a tympanum for the church door. The many other treasures now housed at San Stefano have a variety of provenances.[175] It was at San Stefano in the early sixteenth century that the great preacher Egidio (Giles) of Viterbo delivered his sermons in Venice. He was to become vicar general of the Augustinian order. It seems highly likely that his presence in Venice nurtured, and perhaps even launched, the wave of foundations of Eucharistic brotherhoods (which, as we have just seen, began at San Zulian) in the early sixteenth century. It is curious to note that, unusually, there is no record of such a brotherhood at San Stefano itself. This we may take as yet another token of the independence and diversity of the life of the confraternities of Venice.

The Scuola di San Stefano of 1299 closes the survey of the scuole that were founded in the later thirteenth century. To recapitulate: by 1300 there were at least ten of these, as well as about fifty scuole of the city's trade guilds. It is an anachronistic distortion to impose a distinction between Scuole Grandi and scuole piccole in this period or to present the formations as following the direction of a government strategy. The sense of continuing proliferation, respectful of the state but by no means in thrall to it, strengthened further in the fourteenth and fifteenth centuries.

2 Proliferation and Punctuation, c. 1300–c. 1500

... I do expect return
Of thrice three times the value of this bond.
– Shakespeare, *The Merchant of Venice*, 1.3.154–5

The Confraternities of Venice

In the previous chapter, the earliest foundations of confraternities in Venice were located in a formative conjuncture complementary to the genesis of a mercantile political economy in the years around and after 1250. It is unhelpful to read back the distinction between Scuole Grandi and other scuole from a much later period. This chapter documents and interprets the continuing expansion of the network in the fourteenth and fifteenth centuries. The strength of the proliferation of foundations in this period was tested in the episode of the Bianchi in 1399 and reinforced in its Franciscan character by the revival associated with San Bernardino in the mid-fifteenth century. Thereafter, the needs to cultivate the Virgin and to protect against plague became more pronounced. The steady and ongoing pattern is of particular importance to an understanding of the way in which the scuole came to provide the interwoven strands that Venetians might look to for support in their time of need. Furthermore, the confraternities' provision of material support – potential as well as realized – suggests that they formed the tough fibres of some of the most notable durabilities in the history of the Venetians. This chapter presents a model that suggests the interaction of habits of mercantile exchange with the Christian principle of Misericordia and a reflection of such patterns of thought in the language of the documents.The interpretation has its deficiencies, but they are less marked than the deficiencies of a model that posits a pattern of formation based on the four prototypes of the 1260s that became known two hundred years later for the distinctiveness of their size.

There is a remarkable steadiness to the expansion of the confraternities in Venice between the end of the thirteenth century and the beginning of the sixteenth. Combining the statutes in the registers of the Provveditori di Comun with the most plausible and concrete citations of Gastone Vio's monumental compilation, there were nineteen new foundations in the first half of the fourteenth century, and eighteen more in the second. Between 1400 and 1449 there were twenty-two further foundations, and between 1450 and 1500, there were twenty-one more (see appendix 2.1). Thus, combining these approximations with the ten foundations of the later thirteenth century, we may say that by 1500 there is evidence of at least ninety devotional confraternities in Venice. They were located in nearly seventy different churches throughout the city (see appendix 2.2). On this count, in the majority of cases – fifty in all – a confraternity founded between the middle of the thirteenth century and the end of the fifteenth remained the only one associated with a particular church before the sixteenth century.

Almost immediately after 1500 and on to the middle of the century, the Scuole del Santissimo Sacramento represented major innovation, which demands separate discussion.[1] For now, we may note that after 1501 in these same churches, a Scuola del Venerabile was the next foundation in forty-five cases (see appendix 2.2). In a further seven instances where there had been more than one foundation between 1250 and 1500, a Scuola del Venerabile was the first foundation of the cinquecento. The long duration of steady expansion without intrusive governmental oversight receives reinforcement from Lia Sbriziolo's analysis of the records of the Council of Ten, which also gave attention to petitions from the confraternities of the trade guilds.[2]

It was in the same year as the procession of the Bianchi, 1399, that the Council of Ten sought to regulate the size of the membership of the flagellant confraternities: 550 for three of them, and 600 for the Scuola di San Marco in recognition of the special status of its patron. Yet, in 1446, the membership of the Misericordia, perhaps especially active at this time, stood not at 550 brethren alone but, in addition, 60 novices and no fewer than 850 probationers.[3] It is testimony to the hold of the mythology of the Council of Ten (the Dieci) as all-seeing and omnipotent that scholars argue that the council only attended to the Scuole dei Battuti in matters of state security and that the lack of politically suspicious behaviour in the confraternities "must have" been due to the council's attentions.[4]

The hold of that mythology on the historical imagination leads to some difficult contradictions in Professor Ortalli's otherwise persuasive discussion. She deals briefly with the scuole as, in Brian Pullan's words, "bastions of religious orthodoxy," even though the clergy had only a very limited involvement in their running.[5] She then presents the actions of the Council of Ten against the officers of the Misericordia in 1363 as an "earthquake," involving the removal of one of the officers of the scuola, Francesco Inzegnero, for alleged seditious talk. The council had to insist on the activation of the clause in the statute of the scuola against such words and actions. Inzegnero was banned from holding office in any confraternity again but in 1368 was elected to the committee of the goldsmiths. His appeal against a second removal was rejected by the doge and his council.[6] To some readers it may seem strange that Inzegnero's is but one example of how all the scuole were absolutely bound to the state and formed "a vast security network" that contained thousands of potential informers.[7] If there is no mention of this in some statutes, then we can take it for granted that it applied and that it was unnecessary to put it in writing. In short, "the loyalty of the scuole piccole to the Signoria must have been, however, the rule." By means of "agile political action," the scuole piccole "were becoming useful instruments in guaranteeing the prevailing order."[8] This sits very oddly with "the fact that … the confraternities enjoyed a considerable freedom in the matter of their organization."[9] Moreover, these same "instruments" followed "shared patterns of behavior not forcibly imposed or codified from on high, but sensed as binding, adopted by the scuole according to a course of action similar amongst them, but not compulsory, by way of routes which were independent though parallel."[10] One cites those expansive comments in full in order to demonstrate that Ortalli's eventual conclusion emerges strongly from the evidence despite the previous rehearsal of some stubborn stereotypes.

The evidence from the fifteenth century continues to exhibit a lack of jurisdictional co-ordination between and within different magistracies. Many of the Council of Ten's all-seeing and all-powerful decisions failed to reach the Provveditori di Comun, the magistrates responsible for the scuole from some point after 1277.[11] Lia Sbriziolo compiled an invaluable list of eighty-six instances in the records of the council that involved the regulation of the city's scuole. Some of the quirks and mismatches will appear with reference to specific institutions as this survey proceeds. For the time being, it is worth noting that of the eighty-six decisions twenty-two concern scuole attached to trade guilds. Of the remaining sixty-four entries eleven refer to scuole that do not appear in the registers of the Provveditori. There were a number of brotherhoods that the Council of Ten authorized or acknowledged, of which the Provveditori, formally assuming responsibility for the scuole in 1507, preserve no trace.[12]

These are only the confirmed cases of this kind. The list expands if it includes matches of name but not of date and location. The Council of Ten recorded a Scuola di Santa Maria e San Giovanni Battista at San Zanipolo in 1435, but the Provveditori have this at the Frari in 1443. The council had the Scuola di San

Bernardino at San Francesco della Vigna in 1450, and it amalgamated with the Scuola di San Francesco at the same church in 1456; the Provveditori had the Scuola di San Bernardino at San Giobbe from 1453. The council recorded a Scuola di San Vettor at San Stin in 1469, while the only scuola of that name in the records of the Provveditori di Comun is listed at Santa Margherita. All in all, it seems appropriate to proceed with a survey as presented in what we know of the scuole themselves rather than in the conflicting records of the magistracies responsible for them. In short, one might even ask whether the magistrates' evident lack of control encouraged, or allowed by default, the ongoing strengthening of the scuole in Venetian devotional life. The two magistracies discussed may have sought to intervene in the regulation of the confraternities, but their efforts were separate and uncoordinated. Both could record pronouncement, but neither could guarantee enforcement, and the scuole appear to have enjoyed considerable autonomy.

That process may have made some contribution to what became famous as the stability of Venice itself: a regular active pulse that extended further through the city the network of confraternities that had formed in the later thirteenth century and which the complementary institutions of the trade guilds had accompanied and supplemented. However, the new foundations of the fourteenth and fifteenth centuries, in some ways rather monotonous, had two significant punctuations, both of them potential dislocations, but the pair of them proving instead to be sources of reinvigoration and renewal. The first was the strange and elusive episode of the Bianchi and their assembly in the city in 1399. The second was the fifteenth-century Franciscan revival associated with the presence and preaching of San Bernardino da Siena.[13]

A Context of Adversity

The developments that took place in Venice require broader contextualizations in other parts of Italy and more broadly still in Europe as a whole. The Venetian polity continued to take on a new definition.[14] However, both religious and economic life faced tremendous new pressures. These were not to detach the polity from economy and religion but illustrate instead the continuing interaction of the synthesis that had begun in the mid-thirteenth century. The evidence suggests that the Venetian state did not descend into the crises that afflicted other polities and that the formation of new confraternities also continued unabated, while colossal economic upheaval did not generate anything like the scale of unrest that exploded in other societies.[15] In religious life the removal of the papacy from Rome to Avignon, and the subsequent divisions that culminated in the Great Schism, ended even the pretence of the papal monarchy and gave new emphasis to representative government within the Church. This process was both divisive and inly working. It perforce created in the laity a new spiritual independence and autonomy in the absence of any clear guidance from the Church, whose failure to offer spiritual leadership and comfort would have long-lasting consequences.[16]

The social and economic dislocations of the Black Death and subsequent visitations of the plague brought to a close the general economic expansion that had begun around the year 1000.[17] The collapse of demand and the shortage of labour led to prolonged social conflicts that have attracted the term *revolution*.[18] To such conflicts Venice remained immune. The contrast with Florence and the debates surrounding the Ciompi Revolution of 1378 remain endlessly fascinating. For Florence the polarity of views around such topics as woollen industry (or not), class warfare (or not), and revolution (or not) is a reminder of the possibilities of historical interpretation and argument.[19]

A Resilient Trend

The pattern of formation retained the character of spontaneity without isolation. The developments continued to display consistency and interconnectedness despite associations with particular saintly patrons that were diverse and diffuse. Like the churches in which the scuole were located, each seemed to retain a distinctive individual character while connecting to a greater whole. The problem in expounding the process is that, in order to bring out the diversity and its contribution to the shaping of a greater whole, it would be misleading to resort to the oversimplification of particular "types" of confraternity.[20] After careful consideration of thematic and typological treatment, what follows is loosely organized around chronological divisions of about half a century each. Each of these consists of a set of illustrative case histories. The consolidation of foundations in a single complete listing at appendix 2.1 allows the exposition to move around, where necessary, within the chronology in order to identify certain common themes by cross-reference. The aim is to preserve a sense of the singularity and autonomy of the scuole mentioned, pointing out the connections between certain confraternities while avoiding a mere chronological catalogue.[21]

The prelude to this should be a restatement. Particular events in Venetian religious and social life shifted the emphasis of newly founded confraternities within the steady march of an expanding tradition. The shift became manifest by the middle of the fifteenth century, when the terminology of *Scuole Grandi* and *scuole piccole* first appeared. This in turn reflected the new-found appeal of the scuole to those social orders above and beyond the popolo, who refused to abandon their social distinction. Ironically, this appears to have been a result of the Franciscan revival of the mid-quattrocento associated with San Bernardino of Siena – a revival of the principles of poverty and humility and a distrust of vainglorious display.

Sisters of the Brotherhoods

One subject calls for concentrated attention: the place of women in the scuole. That presence was a given, and the assumption of their inclusion was natural, even automatic, which is especially striking in institutions that assumed the characterization of brotherhoods. This must be recognized and emphasized across the chronological span of the entire chapter.

At the outset, it should be emphasized that the female principle was embedded in the scuole in the widespread association with the Virgin Mary, who often became identified with Venice itself.[22] The first foundation of the fourteenth century, the Scuola di Sant'Orsola, later immortalized by Carpaccio's cycle for the saint, was devoted to the cult of a Virgin Martyr and her eleven thousand women followers of like condition.[23]

The inclusiveness of the confraternities found rich and clear expression in a brotherhood for the Baptist, founded in 1354 at San Giovanni del Tempio. This institution looked to the needs of the poor, the sick, and those in prison – three of the six works of corporal mercy.[24] Revealingly, it specified that there were to be no separate rules for women "in order not to multiply too many words" (per non molteplicar troppe parole).[25] The Scuola di Santi Cosmo e Damiano at San Zuan in Oglio in 1399 used exactly the same formulation.[26] Put differently, language that might appear to certain eyes to limit membership to men in fact was using the plural form that mixed masculine and feminine.

Such instances of separate but parallel organizations for men and women may well have been the norm. The Scuola di Santa Maria della Celestia (1337), which survives in its original fourteenth-century manuscript, planned to recruit seven hundred sisters as well as an equal number of brethren.[27] The Scuola di Santa Marina (1324) aimed at a membership of three hundred women and four hundred men. This example is especially noteworthy since it states unequivocally that the sisters were to elect their own officers.[28]

Other examples suggest that the separation of organizations for men and women may not always have been strict. Two statutes, those of San Francesco at San Francesco della Vigna (dating from 1346) and of the Santissima Croce at San Salvador (1500), specify that it was the duty of the sisters of the scuola to wash corpses in preparation for burial.[29] The foundation of the Scuola della Beata Vergine in 1392 at the church of Sant'Anzolo – another church that no longer exists – is a particularly clear case of the ways in which the brotherhoods could extend to include sisters. This scuola was specifically designated as the brotherhood of cripples, and it appears to have taken a particular interest in women injured at sea.[30] It ran into difficulties in the distribution of large quantities of bread to "our many poor seafaring sisters," a tantalizing reference, the associations and implications of which remain elusive. Perhaps it refers to the wives of sailors injured or lost at sea, but there is no specific exclusion of seafaring women.[31]

Different arrangements were quite possible. The first consorority – that is, a scuola composed entirely of women – was founded in the name of San Gregorio at that church in 1324.[32] Members of the Scuola di Sant'Alberto (founded at the church of the Carmini in 1442), who awaited the conventional "reward for good and for ill," were all women.[33] The exclusion of men from their devotions created a symmetry with the equally unusual example of an all-male scuola, that of San Nicolo di Bari (dei Mercanti), which had held its meetings at the same church since 1319.[34] These examples should be clearly in mind throughout the discussion that follows.

Before the Black Death, 1300–48

By the time the officers of the Scuola di Sant'Orsola had commissioned the famous cycle on its patron's life from Vetor Carpaccio in the 1490s, its title did honour to the Virgin Mary and to Saint Peter Martyr as well. Saint Ursula was probably a mythical figure, perhaps British, perhaps Breton, said to have been martyred along with eleven thousand virgin followers at Cologne at the hands of the Huns sometime during the period between the second and the fourth century. The preamble of the statute succinctly demonstrates the linkage of poor relief with respect for the State and for the Church. No member was to commit "injury, damage or disrespect to Messer the Doge of Venice or his council or to this blessed city which is chosen by God." Venice itself was specially chosen, "elected by God the Father Almighty," a theme of election that gave Venice a special representation in the eyes of God. The purpose of that election, and of the confraternity's place within it, is clear. It was "for recovery and sustenance of all those troubled or fallen and faithful to Holy Mother Church." Tribulation had vivid local reference, the strong dialect of *descazudi* (fallen) had connotations of mercantile exchange ("run out," "fallen due") and of seafaring ("sunk"). The city of God, Venice the chosen city, ruled by the doge and his council, the need to protect against material want – what a range of reference in a few lines, and what a compression of the space between earthly needs and heaven itself![35]

Provision for the poor was systematized in 1454 when the confraternity decided to choose twelve women and eight men as its special beneficiaries. Two features of the "system" stand out. First, there was to be an election of *poveri*, and each needed a minimum of eight votes.[36] Second was the absolute criterion of eligibility. Anyone standing for election as a povero needed to have paid dues to the scuola for a minimum of five years. In other words, it was a requirement that, in order to be eligible to become a povero, the status of the prospective recipient had changed from being able to afford a contribution to that of needing a contribution: an encapsulation of the mechanism of Misericordia.[37]

There was a further mercantile resonance in the next foundation, that of the Concettion della Beata Vergine (1315), a confraternity for the blind that met at San Moise.[38] Among those excluded was anyone who had lost their sight as a judicial punishment. Francesca Ortalli has revealed that when the Giustizia Vecchia sought to foist three judicially maimed members on the confraternity in 1397, the guild appealed to the Avvogadori di Comun, who upheld the statute.[39] There was also a provision, typical of the confraternities, for those who fell sick while away from Venice. Such a clause probably applied in general to those travelling as merchants, but in this case there was also a specific provision for sickness on pilgrimage[40] – as though the quest for a miracle of the restoration of sight might have needed more practical support; this idea is expressed with some roughness in the principle that "he who gives gold buys the kingdom, he who gives money receives eternal life."[41]

The Scuola di San Nicolo di Bari (1319) had the special designation "dei Mercanti." It was usual for merchants and seafarers to seek the protection of this patron.[42] Two features of the scuola are particularly striking. First, the firm exclusion of women, as already noted, is all but unique.[43] Second, the Scuola di San Nicolo shows the independence of the scuola in the classification of its members. The request for the foundation went to both the Provveditori di Comun and, unusually, the Giustizia Vecchia, "at the petition of many noble citizens of Venice." Does this refer to nobles or to citizens? It was not, apparently, possible for any member to buy the status of noble within the scuola itself (a means of scrubbing one's eligibility for office), the statute setting down unambiguously "that it is not possible to take anyone on as a noble unless he is noble and [a member] of the [Greater] Council."[44]

Santa Marina was one of the forty-one Venetian churches that we know to have been destroyed in the nineteenth century.[45] The scuola that met at the church was named after the saint. The limits of membership to four hundred men and three hundred women exceeded those established by the Council of Ten for the flagellant confraternities.[46] Systematic quantitative analysis is not possible, but one wonders what proportion of the population of Venice might have been enrolled in the twenty-six scuole in the city by the mid-fourteenth century if they had by then realized an average of even half such numbers. Equally, losses of members to the plague might have reduced by three-fifths the numbers enrolled as recorded by the Scuola della Carità and at the same time might have served to increase the income from bequests.[47]

There is a contrast in the case of the Scuola di Sant'Agnese, formed in 1325, only four years after the consecration of that saint's church, in that its records were preserved in the original within the holding "Scuole Piccole" in the Venetian Archive, rather than in copies in the documents of the Provveditori di Comun.[48] The original shows that the Scuola di Sant'Agnese had a golden lamp that burned for the souls of its members, living and dead. A funeral cortège bore the confraternity's cross and banner to the home of the deceased, where there was a recitation of twenty-five paternosters and twenty-five aves. There was provision for a member's death outside Venice and for a vigil over the corpse. There are further variations on familiar themes. The scuola made an interesting provision on general attendance: six absences resulted in expulsion.[49] Dice playing and public adultery carried the same penalty – though it is unclear what this tells us about private adultery – and conduct derogatory of the doge and commune was prohibited.[50] The expectation was for a membership of up to 550. Relatives of existing members could join by making a bequest to the scuola to cover their own funeral expenses, a provision that might have increased income during the later visitations of pestilence.[51] In contrast to that of the Scuola di San Nicolo di Bari already discussed, the status of noble in the membership of Sant'Agnese was open to lay people and the clergy for a payment of one ducat and thirty soldi, which exempted that member from consideration for office in the confraternity. Very unusually, the scuola offered apprenticeships to abandoned children, starting at the age of between seven and ten years and continuing until fourteen.[52] This is a direct instance of how a scuola could act as an educational agency, complementing its broader role in the instilling and rehearsing of particular principles that helped to create the identity of the Venetians.

The records of the Scuola di Santa Maria della Celestia (1337) also survive as originals.[53] It is impossible to relate the documents to the stones of Venice that housed the activities recorded in them. Little remains of the convent and church, which were rebuilt after a fire that had started in the Arsenale in 1569.[54] The scuola planned to be enormous, providing seven hundred places for men and a further seven hundred for women. Entry fees were fixed at twenty soldi specifically "to relieve the poor of the scuola."[55] On the basis of the membership projections the potential income for distribution to the disadvantaged was considerable, even allowing for the scuola's other expenses. The statute also offered a significant connection between such good works on earth "where we have no lasting city" and the progression towards an Augustinian "heavenly homeland."[56] The idea of "la celestial patria" surely connects to the very title of the scuola and the church where it met. The link in the records of the confraternity between the relief of material want on earth and the enjoyment of a heavenly reward made a translation from the here and now to the hereafter that suggests much about the realities of life in Venice and its identification as an earthly paradise, half way to a heavenly one. Perhaps the latter was an aspiration wider spread and more devoutly hoped than many commentators have been inclined to think.

The Scuola di San Cristoforo dei Mercanti at Santa Maria Assunta dates from 1346, and its original statute book survives, and, unusually, so does the eighteenth-century copy. In this instance the originals preserved in the archive of the Scuole Piccole readily confirm the accuracy of the copy in the records of the Provveditori di Commun. Moreover, the copy also records the existence of a Scuola di San Cristoforo dei Mercanti at the church of Santa Maria Assunta – which is not mentioned in the original. From 1377 the home of the Scuola di San Cristoforo dei Mercanti was the church of the Madonna dell'Orto – which takes us back to the enigma of the foundations at the Frari beginning in 1261.[57]

Let us restate the problem of the relationship between the principle of Misericordia and its particular appeal to those engaged in commercial activity in Venice, and how this was realized in the scuole. The documents tell of the foundation of a Scuola di Santa Maria e San Cristofalo at the Frari in 1261. The Scuola di San Cristoforo, which met at Santa Maria dell'Orto, identified closely with this initial foundation, recording that the two bodies shared an indulgence in 1263. Some authorities remain unconvinced that this scuola at the Frari became the Scuola di Santa Maria della Val Verde that announced its location in the Abbazia della Misericordia in Cannaregio in 1308.[58] For other commentators the foundation of 1261 may well be the earliest reference to the Scuola di Santa Maria della Misericordia, founded at the Frari in the same year and simultaneously connected to the Scuola di San Cristoforo dei Mercanti. The possibility of a link is much strengthened by the membership list for the Scuola della Misericordia dating from 1319, which shows a high proportion of members drawn from the neighbourhood of the church of the Frari.

The presence of a Scuola di San Cristoforo dei Mercanti at Santa Maria Assunta, also in Cannaregio in 1346, suggests that the confraternity had made a move there from the Frari. Even if there is no mistake in the transcription of the name of the church, then a further move, this time to the Madonna dell'Orto – at some point before we can be sure that the Scuola di San Cristoforo was there in 1377 – is perfectly plausible; Santa Maria dell'Orto was still under construction in 1346. The possibility that San Cristoforo dei Mercanti found a temporary home at Santa Maria Assunta strengthens still further with the reference to the scuola dedicated to Saint Francis at the church of San Francesco della Vigna in 1346.[59] That statute made familiar the provisions for the membership of women, for body washing, and for the recitation of the paternoster and the ave.[60] Members had to be at least fifteen years of age. In return for a fee some of them could assume the intriguing status of "nobeli del puovolo" (nobles of the popolo), acknowledging a "noble" status within the scuola and membership of the popolo outside the confines of the confraternity. There is no necessary link here between the noble title in the scuola and the legal classification of "cittadinanza" outside it. This clear probability further undermines Contarini's assertion that the social and political ambitions of the cittadini were somehow bought off by the status of "noble" (and exemption from office) in the Scuole Grandi.[61]

There was a further twist to the tangle of merchants, their scuole, and the Franciscans in the transfer of the Scuola di San Francesco to (perhaps *back* to) the Frari in 1356.[62] The church of San Francesco della Vigna in fact acquired a tradition of not being able to hold on to scuole that sought to make their home there. A century later there was further to-ing and fro-ing – figurative and physical – over the Scuola di San Bernardino, which eventually established itself at San Giobbe.

That there is no definitive proof of the connection between these different scuole bears repetition. Nevertheless, the very messiness and patchiness of the documentation in the official records of the magistracies responsible for confraternities – not just the Provveditori di Comun but also the Consiglio dei Dieci – may yet reveal something, for the messiness and patchiness relate to a general picture: a picture of the evidently vigorous energies of the scuole in Venice, their apparent freedom of movement and operation, and the lack of a clear-cut magisterial control.

Furthermore, the stones of Venice themselves confirm that by the middle of the fourteenth century there was a necklace of confraternities across the northern part of the city, a necklace of merchants and mercy, at San Cristofalo dei Mercanti (at Santa Maria Assunta and then Santa Maria dell'Orto), at the Celestia, at Sant'Anna, at the Scuola della Misericordia itself. All of them had strong business connections, links to the world of *negotium*, yet all were within view of the expansive still waters of the lagoon and their quiet invitation to contemplation. That picture of centres of strong devotion among laypeople – women and men – is today somewhat weakened by the disappearance of the Celestia and Sant'Anna and the identification of Santa Maria Assunta with the Jesuit order as the church of the Gesuiti, which gave the church its now familiar title only after the society established itself there upon its return to Venice in 1657.[63] The loss to the picture of Santa Maria dei Servi, which Ruskin so lamented, strikes a plaintive note, reminding us of what the stones might have told us until quite recently. As this chapter's selective survey of scuole continues, the realization grows that, but for folly and neglect, cross-reference to the stones might have been much more vivid and emphatic.

The Impact of the Plague

The experience of the Black Death in Venice was severe, and it is possible to illustrate this from the records of the confraternities. Yet there is no real evidence of social unrest. Despite the religious tensions of the age the formation of confraternities among the Venetians continued at a consistent and steady pace. As Reinhold Mueller has pointed out, evidence concerning the impact of the plague in the middle years of the trecento upon the confraternities is scanty. However, he reminds us that two of the scuole left records of their contemporary experience etched in the stones of their buildings. An inscription at San Giovanni Evangelista recording the extension of its property suggests that perhaps the imminence of death led to an acceleration of charitable bequests that may have sustained or even strengthened the continuing process of foundation.[64] The inscription erected by the Scuola della Carità in the entrance hall of its meeting place in 1357 constitutes a veritable chronicle of the city's experience of catastrophe and its mirror in the scuola itself, leaving little doubt of the scale of the epidemic's impact. The disasters began in 1347 with an earthquake, which brought down some of Venice's bell towers and the church of San Biasio, and then came a visitation of pestilence, the symptoms of which were "blood spat from the mouth," "swellings in the groin and armpits," and "the sickness of charcoal black on the skin." It was commonly thought that the visitation of mortality, which lasted six months, carried off two-thirds of the city's people. Of the scuola's thirteen officers ten died, including the *Guardian*, and three hundred of its five hundred brethren were also victims. Even if a papal indulgence for gestures of contrition had increased the flow of benefactions, the fact that the series of foundations of new scuole retained its even pace is testimony to the resilience of the trend and to the strength of spirit that sustained it.[65]

From the Black Death to the Bianchi, 1349–99

The documentation for mid-century is immensely enriched by the records of the Scuola di Santi Apostoli. These provide another significant example of the accuracy of the copy made at a much later date for the Provveditori di Comun.[66]

The statute of 1350 begins with the familiar injunction to keep before one's eyes "the end of this wicked and temporal life." However, the language of exchange in the manuscript is dense and emphatic: "When the soul leaves the body, it goes to give account of the good and the bad and one must receive for good a reward [*guiderdon*] and for the bad one must be punished." The preamble continues the theme of work and acquisition. The salvation of the soul can result from "brotherhood, prayer and alms" – with direct reference to Saint James and to his teaching that "the prayer of a just person [*sic*] counts for much." Like all the mariegole of the scuole examined in this chapter, this one is in strong Venetian dialect. The last reference prompts the reflection that in such documents parts of the Scriptures found a vernacular translation, linguistic and operational, long before the outcries of reformers over the need for a Bible for the common man.[67] A further example of this vernacular devotion comes with the foundation of the Scuola della Santissima Croce at the church of Santa Croce in 1359. The confraternity was founded after a woman at prayer heard the voice of God – speaking good Venetian – asking why there was no scuola in the name of "mio fio Jesu Christo" (my son Jesus Christ).[68]

The beautiful manuscript of the Scuola di Santi Apostoli provides much more detailed regulation than most. Above all, perhaps, these rules reflect how much time the officers and members could expect to invest and expend in the service of the confraternity. In the event of an expulsion a clear reason was to be recorded, leaving open the possibility of readmission, interestingly characterized as "to return to mercy."[69] Bequests were welcome as a means of sustaining poor members. The sale of titles of nobility within the scuola to fifty men and one hundred women served the same purpose.[70]

For the commemoration of a brother or sister who died some way from Venice, "we must place a tapestry with a *palio* on it in the middle of the church and the cushion with the cross and the two candles." Funeral arrangements follow in great detail. There were to be twenty-five paternosters and twenty-five aves: "After the Gospel we must fix all the candles and then, after the credo and after the offering, every brother and sister must set up their candles and hold them firm until the raising of the body of Christ at the Mass. And then everyone having set up their candle with their hands they must leave."[71] This solemn reverence for the Host is an important reminder that the cult of the Eucharist itself was a devotional tradition of the scuole and did not arrive with the foundation of Eucharistic brotherhoods in the sixteenth century. The scuola met at Santi Apostoli, and the hall still survives as a building adjoining the church, marked by a fourteenth-century relief and inscription.

The next year, 1351, saw the foundation of a Scuola di Sant'Anna at the church of that name, which had been founded in 1240 near to San Pietro di Castello and to San Daniele. By the early fourteenth century the Augustinian order had given place to a community of Benedictine nuns. The statute instils the usual preoccupations with the fragility of human life, expressed with reference to Saint John's gospel. The statute warned that it is "fantasy" to deny our sin – and if we do, we deceive ourselves. Then there is a reference to Saint James, pointing out that it is possible to acquire salvation through charity. This elicits divine forgiveness: the expression, rather than the concealment, of the all-embracing extent of heavenly mercy.[72] Outgoing officers celebrated the handover to their successors as a "peace' – that is, a kiss uniting peace with justice, which is in the way with mercy and truth.[73] Mercy was what the gastaldo exercised in his discretionary authority in the admission of women.[74] Dating as it does from 1363, the scuola's decision to commission its own altar is one of the earliest examples of a confraternity's artistic patronage.[75]

The Scuola di Sant'Ambrogio illustrates the importance of combining information from as many sources as possible when discussing the scuole. No magistracy provides a master list. There is no trace of the Scuola di Sant'Ambrogio in either the archives of the Scuole Piccole or the registers of the Provveditori di Comun, or anywhere else in the manuscript documentation that forms the basis of this book. Its initial inclusion in the study derived from the prominent altar of the Scuola of the Milanese in the Frari, and the altarpiece upon it by Alvise Vivarini and Marco Basaiti (1500–10). There is no reason to suppose that the Provveditori excluded scuole for different "nations," since they catalogued both that of the Schiavoni and that of the Albanesi. In fact, the Scuola di Sant'Ambrogio does not even figure in the dealings of the Council of Ten with the confraternities before 1420. Documentation of the decision to permit the foundation appears now to be preserved in the Biblioteca Correr.[76] The entry derives from a later cross-reference in the "Deliberazioni Miste" of the Council of Ten to the missing item.[77] Scholars are indebted to Professor Ortalli, who has tracked down the statute to the records of the Frari itself.[78] The case of the confraternity of the Florentines provides a parallel example from the fifteenth century. The Scuola dei Fiorentini, also at the Frari, appears not at all in the documentary records under examination. Of the scuola's separate building nothing survives, and the first evidence of its existence at the Frari is the wooden statue of the Baptist that Donatello completed for the scuola's altar in 1438. Gastone Vio's references established that in 1443 the Council of Ten granted permission to the Florentines to establish a scuola at the Frari. They did so retrospectively, acknowledging that the confraternity had moved there in 1436 after an original foundation at San Zanipolo the previous year. Once again, Professor Ortalli's research is decisive and refers clearly and emphatically to the statute in the Museo Correr.[79]

The Scuola di San Vettor at Santa Margherita in the Sestier di Dorsoduro (1377) is, on the face of it, the first instance of a sovvegno in the evidence, but it looks as though this is a mistake in the classification made in the eighteenth century.[80] The foundation has the particular feature of a formal approval from the Consiglio dei Dieci, an approval that it granted thirty years later. There is no evidence of a reprimand or penalty or even that such a lapse of time was unusual – no evidence, then, of the all-seeing eye of the Signoria. In 1478 the brotherhood became the preserve of the boatmen at the local ferry station, which was the shape of things to come. The sovvegni were mutual aid schemes of the sixteenth century and were generally attached to the practice of a particular trade.

The Scuola di Corpus Domini, founded in 1395, was the very first of Venice's numerous Eucharistic brotherhoods, though some scholars dismiss any connection between it and those formed in the sixteenth century.[81] The connection is a matter for further discussion. Even so, the scuola had its own significance in its own time. The permission to found it is in the records of the Council of Ten, and it is a vital backdrop to the drama of the Bianchi that was to unfold only four years later.[82]

The Bianchi, 1399

As the name implies, the adherents of the Bianchi, a penitential movement, wore white. They walked in processions lasting nine days, calling for peace and mercy, pleading with the Virgin Mary to answer their prayers. Daniel Bornstein's penetrating and many-sided analysis shows why the devotions of the Bianchi would have appealed to the Venetians. First, there was no sponsorship by the papacy. Indeed, the processions of the Bianchi may represent a kind of popular orthodoxy that reflected the decline of institutional leadership in the age of the Avignon captivity and in the ensuing Great Schism. The attraction and inspiration of the *imploratio* for peace and the emphatic repetition of the cry for mercy would have struck loud and harmonious chords among members of the Venetian scuole. The appeal of the movement was both personal and collective, and it reflected an ease of interaction between clergy and laity that would have been unthinkable at the time of the Council of Trent.[83]

Popular participation in the processions of the Bianchi had already renewed the sense of sacrality in civic life in Siena, Florence, and Perugia. Francesco Datini, merchant of Prato, joined the procession (without, it seems, any intention of undergoing physical hardship). He may have heard and perhaps even joined in the chant of the Bianchi, preserved in the chronicle of Giovanni Sercambi.[84]

The Venetian antiquarian Giuseppe Tassini reported in his *Curiosità veneziane* that the Bianchi also recited the Stabat Mater. He provides a version of the hymn that they chanted in Venice, and the emphasis on the plea for mercy remains to the fore:

Misericordia andiam gridando
Misericordia a Dio clamando
Misericordia al peccator!
Misericordia, o Dio verace
Misericordia e manda pace
Misericordia alto Signor.[85]
(Mercy we go shouting
Mercy to God exclaiming
Mercy to the sinner!
Mercy, O God of truth,
Mercy and send peace
Mercy, Lord on high.)

As in the case of the flagellants of 1260, a connection between a spontaneous movement and pious institutions is by no means automatic, but Professor Bornstein notes that the Bianchi appealed to members of confraternities, offering, as the scuole of Venice did, "a kind of social insurance for the less well off."[86] Since this was the case and since the scuole set such store by Misericordia, why was Venice the only city in which the authorities refused to receive the procession of the Bianchi?

In Venice the Dominican Giovanni Dominici led a procession that included prominent noblemen such as Antonio Soranzo and Leonardo Pisano, and some of the nuns from the convent of Corpus Domini where Dominici was abbot.[87] The procession made its way from San Geremia but halted at San Zanipolo in the face of an order from the Council of Ten, which had not authorized the gathering. This stern agency for the preservation of state security can appear to be the guarantor of peace and order or the grim force of state repression, on the cusp between the myth of Venice and its opposite.[88] Secrecy and ruthlessness, decisive action in the defence of the state – none of this was much in evidence in dealing with the Bianchi in 1399. In managing the episode, the Council of Ten appeared to be caught between insisting upon authorization and not wishing to discourage public expression of piety. In the procession one of the Capi (Heads)of the Council of Ten wrenched the crucifix from Soranzo's hands, and his officers dispersed the crowd. The Council of Ten then had Dominici arrested. The debate on his punishment was unusually protracted, with the council unable to decide on house arrest or exile. Only after twenty-one ballots – in contrast to the usual two or three – did the Council of Ten pronounce banishment.[89]

There was consternation at the convent, and the departure of Dominici had serious consequences for the sisters' relief of the poor. Sister Bartolomea Ricoboni recorded: "After his departure alms seemed to stop coming our way, and from that point we had to scrounge for bread, which had not been necessary before: indeed we used to feed many poor with what we had left over."[90] Soranzo and Pisano were exiled for one year.

The complications of the incident reflected both general considerations and the particular circumstances of Venice. In general terms, processions associated with the Feast of Corpus Christi could frequently lead to disorder.[91] In Venice in 1397, Sister Dorotea recorded that "when the feast of the precious Body of Christ was approaching, the magnificent officers of our confraternity organized a procession."[92] There was a mishap when the sacrament was blown to the ground by wind gusting through an open door. Sister Dorotea, quoting Father Dominici, saw this as a sign of tribulation to come.[93]

Nevertheless, the fact that that procession had been the work of the scuola does not seem to have sounded an alarm with the authorities; there is no documented requirement for official permission. By contrast, the gathering of the crowd in 1399 was spontaneous. Perhaps it was this that aroused the Council of Ten to intervene. Even so, the twenty-one ballots that they took before deciding on Father Dominici's exile cannot reflect a clear-cut response to an obvious threat to public order. It would have been consistent with the emerging pattern of religion, polity, and economy that a celebration of peace through mercy, institutionalized in the pax of the confraternities themselves, was hardly a matter to repress.

There is little evidence that the Council of Ten sought proactive intervention in the activities of the scuole. Perhaps this was an acknowledgment of the essential partnership of the Church, the government, and the rest of the Venetians, in so far as those interest groups were at all distinct. As subsequent chapters will show, the religious life of the Venetians was to draw strength from the widespread cult of the Eucharist in the sixteenth century. In the interim – that is, throughout the entire fifteenth century – the proliferation of the scuole continued its course. There was no new devotion as a result of the penitence of the Bianchi, and no intervention reflecting a governmental concern that religious belief and practice in the scuole might be a source of disorder. There is a strong contrast with Florence here. In that city the authorities were nervous about the formation of confraternities and sought to limit their number as potential nests of political conspiracy.[94]

The response of the Consiglio dei Dieci, the body responsible for the security of the Venetian state, to the devotions of the Bianchi reflects indecisiveness and division at the highest levels of government over the regulation of popular piety. Time and again in this survey of the formation of scuole in Venice, it has proved problematical to fix a date of foundation in relation to a statute or other evidence. This is another example that dispels any notion that the formation of the scuole followed a master plan of the state with the Scuole Grandi as a prototype.

As is well known, the Council of Ten was established to track down conspirators involved in the attempted coup d'état associated with Baiamonte Tiepolo in 1310. The secrecy of the council's proceedings and the absolute inappellability of their sentences made the body a focus of attention in the "anti-myth" of Venice. This last was a vision of an oppressive police state whose tentacles reached as far as the imagination of Charles Dickens in his musings on a "wicked old council" that sent unhappy souls through mouldering hallways to a watery death in the lagoon.[95] The Council of Ten's oversight of the scuole tells a story less lurid and more human.

Suspicion of the spontaneity of the procession of the Bianchi did not engender a more overtly authoritarian approach to the formation of confraternities in the city, for which the Council of Ten held ultimate responsibility. In 1363 the council expressly forbad the formation of any new religious association without its authorization.[96] The government seems to have been perplexed by a need to reconcile the different demands of religion and policy while remaining outwardly pious.[97] The clear acknowledgment that the assembly and procession of the Bianchi were "contrary to the will of God" (contra voluntatem dominii) still preceded the twenty-one inconclusive votes on what to do with the man who led them. After all, the nuns of Corpus Christi prayed for the state. Dominici himself was outraged rather than cowed, as he recorded in his Lettere Spirituali: "Who would believe, finding it written, that so famous a city, free, wise and just as Venice is held to be, in one day should have exiled deliberately and without ire three spiritual men, known for having honoured God and for doing good to the consciences of all, there being no law made to the contrary, at the instigation of those who had blocked so much good and devotion and stirred up in the city and with disregard broken the arms of Christ crucified, beating the bishop's vicar and others who are pure, religious and saintly?"[98]

Here we have the extraordinary spectacle of a respected abbot of Venice accusing the Council of Ten of fomenting sedition (*sedizione*), the very thing that the council was supposed to suppress. Its apparent incapacity to act with a clear rationale in matters of religion did not end with the passing of 1399.

The Franciscan Revival and Social Change, c. 1400–c. 1450

The fifteenth century in Venice witnessed forty-three new foundations of confraternities: twenty-two before 1450 and twenty-one between 1450 and 1500. The list merits a fractional extension of two more foundations to 1502, the year that saw the establishment of the first Eucharistic confraternity since 1395, raising the total to forty-four (see appendix 2.1). There is still no clear pattern of names in the titles of the scuole; for instance, there were eight scuole dedicated to the Virgin in the first half of the century, but only five in the second.

However, even more so than hitherto, it is as well to be cautious with quantifications in relation to dates. Such a correlation may give an impression, but it cannot be statistically precise. This is clear at the outset of the quattrocento. There appear to have been two foundations at the same church, San Barnaba, in 1400, which is a unique occurrence in these records. One was the "Beata Vergine della Nattività," a confraternity that definitely included women and allowed the return of the lapsed after a period of testing, a "prova" (the term also used for the piece of work that an apprentice produced for graduation to master).[99] The trade-based character of the second scuola probably explains the coincident date of the two foundations. The second confraternity was for ironmongers dealing in nails.[100] The organization specified the inclusion of day labourers (*lavoranti*), whose position in guild welfare schemes is always difficult to define, in part because in some trades – notably the stonemasons – the term referred to qualified masters who did not run their own bottega but worked with others who did. That did not apply in all guilds.[101] There is clear acknowledgment that this inclusiveness in turn connected to the diverse origins of members – "because people from various parts of the world come to Venice."[102] The widespread regional provenances of members of the ironmongers' guild are a subject for detailed analysis later. For the moment, we might note this early example of the ways in which a devotional confraternity subject to the Provveditori di Comun could develop from a specific trade subject to the Giustizia Vecchia to accommodate the increasing numbers of immigrants from the expanding mainland state.[103]

The church of San Giacomo dell'Orio remains one of the most evocative measures of the impact that the scuole made upon the surviving fabric of a Venetian church. The scuola of the church's patron saint had moved there by 1422, apparently from the church of San Salvador.[104] It would be fascinating to know more about a confraternity dedicated to Saint James, whose general epistle set down the importance of works and provided the watchwords for the early scuole. However, of all the scuole at the church of San Giacomo this one has not left a record beyond the reference cited here in the late copy of one of its statutes, itself a reference to one of its relocations.

More positively, also in the 1420s, a clustering of foundations of scuole began at the very heart of the city around Rialto and San Marco. The first of these was the Scuola di San Nicolo of 1425, which met at the church of San Salvador. The date is secure. The provisions made by the statute are quite conventional regarding the inclusion of women, their officers, their role at funerals, the election of "good men" (boni homeni), and arrangements in the event of the death of a member away from Venice. There was an approach to the afterlife that we may describe as down to earth. When a poor member died, it was the responsibility of the officers "to make clear to the brothers and sisters that they would have to put their hands in their purses."[105] One notes that the "sisters" are as liable as the brothers to pay up. The enumeration of these familiar principles and the ambition for their practice serves to reinforce continuity with and from the scuole of the fourteenth century.

The church of San Salvador was, unusually, a centre for three further scuole in the fifteenth century. A new confraternity, dedicated to the Blessed Virgin, was founded there in 1439.[106] There is a record of a Scuola di San Lunardo in the same church in 1453. Attention will turn later to the Scuola della Santissima Croce, founded at San Salvador in 1500.

A short way distant, at the church of San Fantin, a scuola came into being in 1440. Associated with the "Buona Morte" (Good Death) and Saint Jerome, the confraternity dedicated itself to comforting those condemned to execution.[107] Nearby, in 1442, a confraternity for Venice's Albanians was founded. Its character as a centre for immigrants who shared a place of birth outside of Venice makes it still more puzzling that those of the Milanesi and the Fiorentini did not register a statute with the Provveditori di Comun.[108] The Scuola degli Albanesi at the church of San Maurizio provided some housing and a hospital, partly in competition with the Armenians. In the documents under scrutiny for this study, we only know of the existence of the Scuola degli Armeni from this reference in the statute of its competitor.[109]

In the vicinity of San Marco, in 1444, came the foundation of a scuola dedicated jointly to San Zaccaria and San Lizaro (which Vio located at San Provolo, the nearby parish).[110] Here again was a scuola at a conventual church. The relics of Saint Zachary, father of John the Baptist, lay at the church of the convent, so an identification with him is not surprising, and nor are provisions to watch and pray through the transience of earthly life. The patronage of Saint Lazarus, the beggar Lazarus in the story of the rich man who showed him no mercy, alludes to the protector of lepers. The scuola survives only as a reference in the statute of the Eucharistic brotherhood at San Provolo, but it provides another routine example to place with Corpus Domini and Sant'Alvise as a lay brotherhood in a monastic church. There is a mention of Doge Francesco Foscari, which is a reminder that his sister Elena was abbess at the convent of San Zaccaria in 1446.[111] The doge himself was a member of the Scuola di San Marco, and its surviving members hoisted the body at his funeral in 1458, when he was honoured by the banners of the other scuole.[112]

The series of foundations around San Marco and Rialto marked a rise in the standing of the scuola to a new prominence in the mental landscape of the powerful. Might this have found expression in the elevation of five scuole to the status of "Grandi' by 1467? Foscari is often associated with the Venetians' turn westward, a deliberate shift in policy from maritime commerce to landed wealth on the Terraferma. This was a policy against which Doge Tomaso Mocenigo had specifically warned in the possible election of Foscari as his successor in 1423. It was feared that the shift would erode the ethic of warlike seamanship and would turn the patriciate into a landowning aristocracy, with its associations of disdain for commerce and of the embrace of soft living.[113]

There may be a reflection of this in the increasing attraction of the scuole to those above the popolo in social rank at mid-century. Members of the patriciate and of the cittadini seem to have recognized the possibilities of the confraternities for pomp and display. At about this time the Scuole Grandi were titularly separated from the scuole piccole, which may reflect the lengthening of the social hierarchy and the emergence of the cittadini as a "parallel but minor aristocracy," like the patriciate, separate from the popolo and superior to it.[114] The suggestive irony in this picture is that the new social status of certain of the scuole was not at all the brainchild of the patriciate but the attractiveness of institutions that were essentially popolano in origin, function, and formation. This is reflected in the fact that Foscari's successor-but-one was to have a key role in the foundation in 1450 of a scuola at San Giobbe in Cannaregio. The confraternity took its name from San Bernardino, the great Franciscan preacher, who had a long association with Venice and, personally, with the future doge Cristoforo Moro.

Thus, in the middle of the fifteenth century, and with the foundation of the Scuola di San Bernardino in 1450, the long-term pattern of the formation of Venice's network of brotherhood reached its second great punctuation. As in the case of the episode of the Bianchi in 1399, the moment was one of pause and renewal, not of fracture or redirection. The Franciscans, through the teachings associated with Bonaventura, and Saint Antony of Padua, and through their presence at the great landmark of the Frari, had already exercised considerable influence on the character of lay confraternities in a great commercial city. That influence was subtly eloquent in its alignment of the language of salvation with the language of exchange: if Venetians were to expect the reward of eternal life in the next world, they should show mercy in this one to those sometimes left behind or cast aside by the mechanisms of trade and profit.

That general point finds particular reference in the density of cross-reference associated with San Bernardino's presence in Venice. His earliest visit appears to have been in 1405, but his influence there began in earnest with his visit in 1422. On that occasion he had preached on trade in the great marketplace in Campo San Polo. He had devoted time to contemplation in the Franciscan community on the island of San Francesco del Deserto, a community founded by Saint Francis himself on his return journey from the Holy Land. At Bernardino's request, Doge Tomaso Mocenigo, Foscari's predecessor, had founded a hospital for plague victims on the island of Santa Maria di Nazaret in the year of his own death, 1423.[115] Bernardino returned to Venice in 1428–9 and, for the last time, in 1442–3.[116] This was at the behest of Pope Eugenius IV, the Venetian Gabriel Gondulmer, who had urged Bernardino to go to Venice and there accept appointment to the bishopric of Siena, his home town. Bernardino refused the elevation, saying, according to Vespasiano da Bisticci, that if he ever wore anything but the Franciscan habit, he would no longer be Bernardino.[117] While in Venice, Bernardino gave much of his preaching to the Christian significance of the Virgin, in particular the way in which her assumption represented a triumph over Death – which drew directly from Bonaventura's teachings.[118] Bernardino's preaching in Venice is suggested in a drawing by Jacopo Bellini.[119] Cristoforo Moro, the future doge on whom such preaching made a profound impression, was a member of the Scuola di San Cristoforo dei Mercanti.[120] It bears repetition that the scuola, at Santa Maria dell'Orto, was only a short distance from the Scuola della Misericordia. In 1442, or certainly by that time, Bartolomeo Bon was at work on his majestic tympanum of the Madonna della Misericordia for the portal of the Abbazia. If Bon had started to sculpt this in 1442, it seems likely that he delayed beginning work on Doge Foscari's great commission for the Porta della Carta in order to do so.[121]

It is a sadness that Bon's Madonna della Misericordia no longer stands above the portal of what is now the Scuola Vecchia, though its preservation and current location are a considerable consolation. However, it was the brethren themselves who were responsible for its removal and relocation in the new scuola. From here it might have gone the way of the treasures of the Servi but for the inspired intervention of a curator from the Victoria and Albert Museum in London, where it is now housed in all its glory[122] (fig. 16). Francesco Sansovino captures something of the impact of the sculpture in its original location above the portal of the Abbazia, which, by his time, was the Scuola Vecchia (Old Scuola) – in contrast with the huge new Renaissance pile,

16. Bartolomeo Bon, *Virgin and Child with Kneeling Members of the Scuola della Misericordia*, 1445–50, relief. Copyright Victoria and Albert Museum, London.

the work of Sansovino's father, Jacopo, which loomed up beside it: "The old building has above its door the statue of the Madonna in marble, with an air of loveliness, beautiful hands, and with drapery very well disposed, and it was sculpted by Bartolomeo [Bon] who made the great gate [Porta della Carta] of the [ducal] palace. Similarly, he sculpted the figures in the frontispiece of the scuola, copiously furnished with silverware, ewers, reliquaries, and other harness necessary for such a meeting place."[123]

The sculpture no longer carries the colours that once adorned it. However, such tiny traces that survive – on the brethren's hoods and habits as they shelter beneath the mantle of the Madonna, which was also richly coloured, and in particular the prominence of a cord worn by one of them at the waist – all suggest Franciscan associations. Given the impact of Bernardino's visits over an extended period of time, dating the piece to 1442 is persuasive but not absolutely necessary to a demonstration of Franciscan influence. Bernardino may have given the whole of the Venetian state some religious unity, for he preached tirelessly throughout the Terraferma, delivering sixty sermons in Padua alone, for instance, perhaps reinforcing the Franciscan principles so closely associated with Saint Antony.[124]

From the Misericordia it is but a short walk or boat ride, passing close to the Madonna dell'Orto where the future doge Moro was inscribed in the merchants' confraternity – Cristoforo as member of San Cristoforo – to the church of San Giobbe. There the Scuola di San Bernardino was founded immediately upon Bernardino's canonization in 1450. Moro had a chapel built at his behest when Moro, "a devotee of the Blessed San Bernardino,"[125] was a procurator of San Marco. The statute of the confraternity enjoins confession and communion on two occasions per year.[126] Most unusually, the original mariegola marks its own end, and the next entry comes only in 1545, though there may be omissions.[127] The foundation suggests swift and decisive action in high places, presumably by Moro, for it overrode a provision of the Council of Ten limiting any scuola dedicated to San Bernardino to the other Franciscan centre, the church of San Francesco della Vigna.[128]

Plague and Patronage, c. 1450–c. 1500

The repercussions of Bernardino's presence in Venice were long lasting. They relate to the scuola and to the Tuscan monuments – including and in particular Doge Moro's tomb, but also the glazed tile decorations of the Martini chapel – that Moro was to commission there. However, the influences were by no means exclusively Tuscan. The Franciscan revival unquestionably inspired two masterpieces by Giovanni Bellini. His *San Francesco del Deserto* – a rocky hermitage in full view of not a desert but a Terraferma landscape, of which every square inch is cultivated – commemorates in its title the island bearing the same name. The altarpiece that he painted for the church of San Giobbe seems likely to invoke the protection of its saints, Francis, Sebastian, and Job, against the plague, a terrible bout of which had swept Venice in 1478.[129] Saint Francis had a recent historical reality in Venice, in contrast to the half-legendary figures of Job and Sebastian, relevant as were Job's boils and Sebastian's arrow wounds to the plague sufferers who were seeing pustules breaking out over their own bodies.

In the mid-fifteenth century, in the aftermath of Bernardino's final visit, the scuole seemed increasingly to enjoy the attention and patronage of several doges, and foundations clustered in the centre of the city. There were also signs that what the scuole came from and what they represented may have made some impact on Venetian humanism. This would be in keeping with a complex of institutions that were the handiwork of a commercially minded laity, institutions that seem to have enjoyed a surprising measure of self-government and did not need the controlling hand of the state.

In 1451 another scuola formed, one that was to become even more famous than the scuola at San Giobbe for its commissions. Perhaps it is consistent with a rise to prominence in association with the rich, well-born, and powerful that the confraternities which, in Daniel Bornstein's arresting formulation, had once been the clients of ecclesiastical patrons, began to become the patrons of ecclesiastical clients.[130] This next confraternity, of San Giorgio and San Trifon, is familiar as San Giorgio degli Schiavoni.[131] It is the first Venetian confraternity to describe itself and others as "scuole piccole" in the documentation studied for this book.[132] The scuola convened originally at the church of San Giovanni del Tempio but is far better known for its own hall and chapel with the unique decorations painted by Carpaccio in 1505–10.[133] The subject of the confraternities' impact on the ecclesiastical fabric of Venice will be considered more expansively in a later chapter.

It is somewhat surprising to find a confraternity for San Rocco and Santa Margherita (1455) at the church of San Samuele. Saint Margaret's association was strongest in the parish and market square of her name in Dorsoduro. Her pairing with San Rocco, who would have his own parish close by Santa Margherita, is a reminder that his cult was wider spread in the city than the overwhelming concentration on the scuola founded in his name in 1478 might suggest – especially since it did not originally take the title "Grande." There was another foundation for him (and San Nicolo) at the church of San Zulian in 1496.[134] Thus, almost three decades after the designation of certain Venetian brotherhoods as "Scuole Grandi," the barrier still seems to have been permeable. Once again there are reinforcing connections: the unifying thread seems to be provided by mercers, who had their own scuola at San Zulian, combined their devotions with those of San Teodoro, and figured prominently in the Scuola Grande di San Rocco itself.[135] In the furtherance of the cult of saints who protected against plague, there were two consecutive foundations for Saint Sebastian, the first in 1463 at the church of San Giacomo dell'Orio, the second in 1470 at the church of San Sebastiano itself. The latter seems to reflect a special urgency, since the construction of the church took place only in 1455–68.[136]

It may well be that provision for the burial of plague victims was a spur to the foundation of scuole at this time, for there were at least eleven visitations of disease that took many lives in the fifteenth century, in 1403, 1411, 1438, 1447, 1456, 1464, 1468, 1478, 1485, 1490, and 1498.[137] If bouts of pestilence did indeed prompt the formation of new confraternities, then the haste was quite indecent at the Scuola di Santa Maria della Visitazione (1474). One of several scuole at the church of San Nicolo dei Mendicoli in Dorsoduro, its officers recorded their complaint in 1498 (another year of plague) "that many say that they are members of the scuola when they are dead and they are not."[138] One takes this to mean that surviving relatives tried to claim funeral expenses from the scuola when the deceased had not been a member or was not up to date with fees.

The last year of the century provides some scent of change. In 1499 the Scuola di San Giuseppe began its devotions. While Death was still the enemy of the brethren, this is the first instance in which a statute promoted the Holy Sacrament as a defence against the Devil.[139] That said, the brotherhood that met from 1500 in the name of the Santissima Croce in the church of San Salvador preserved the traditional formulae of the kiss of peace, the washing of corpses as the duty of women members, and the visitation of the sick – and appears to have been mistaken for a sovvegno in the transcript.[140]

The Scuola di Santa Barbara dei Bombardieri that first met at the church of San Marcuola in 1500 is far better known for its embellishment of its altar at Santa Maria Formosa, a church that housed a Madonna della Misericordia in the Chapel of the Purification.[141] By now, though without a reference in the registers of the Provveditori di Comun, a confraternity in the name of Saint Nicholas was meeting at the church of San Giorgio dei Greci in celebration of the final establishment – after contorted and protracted negotiation – of a scuola for the Greek nation, though a church for it was not completed for nearly half a century.[142]

The very last of this long series of fourteenth- and fifteenth-century foundations stretches the survey to 1501. In that year a confraternity for the Virgin was formed at the church of Santa Maria Maggiore, but paying deference to the pope (Alexander VI) was entirely new. All the enjoinders in the statute – on nobles, on women, on paternosters and aves at funerals, and against blasphemy – were entirely traditional. The long duration of old patterns of devotion serves to emphasize the sudden prominence of the cult of the Eucharist that was to generate a new and predominant type of confraternity from 1502 onwards.[143]

The Vision of the Polity

In 1464, Doge Cristoforo Moro, member of the Scuola di San Cristoforo dei Mercanti and patron of the church of San Giobbe, became the dedicatee of a tripartite work by a Venetian humanist, Giovanni Caldiera, who was a member of the citizen class.[144] His three interrelated books dealt with the moral, economic, and political fields of life. The first was transcendent as *De virtutibus*, and the second and third were specific to Venice, *De oeconomia veneta* and *De praestantia venetae politiae*. Caldiera's works, perhaps with a remote echo of Joachite preoccupations in the threefold division, concentrated on three spheres of human existence that also corresponded to three ages of human development: namely, the life of the monastery, the life of the household, and the life of the polity. The moral order acted to restrain avarice, "a certain insatiable cupidity," which "denies to others when they are in need."[145] Caldiera noted the importance of the scuole in the Venetian polity, and his most authoritative modern commentator summarizes that, for Caldiera, "these are the institutions which bind the men of Venice in civility and charity" and which were at hand to catch those who fell into material want.[146] Caldiera himself commented that the heads of the confraternities were "principes scolarum" (princes of the scuole), which strengthens the opinion that we have now encountered several times, namely that the guilds of Venice were in many ways "little republics."[147] Caldiera's polity acknowledged the mechanical arts as well as the liberal. It was a polity that subsumed private and domestic existence, a polity that seemed to have its own immortality. For Caldiera, it was also a polity in which the Council of Ten exercised a vigilant and all-controlling sovereignty: "So great is the authority and power of these ten men, that they tolerate nothing threatening to the republic, and not only those who act evilly, but also those who speak evilly, and even those who think evil thoughts are severely punished, so that they are in no way allowed to contaminate or infect the republic."[148]

As we have already seen, such a characterization is highly questionable with regard to the relationship of the council with the scuole under its authority. In general terms, Caldiera's picture of a hierarchical and authoritarian political order – which, for him, was an ideal – missed the dynamics of everyday reality in the economic, political, and religious lives of the Venetians. However, in the mid-century Franciscan revival and in the interconnection of economic, political, and religious life that Caldiera made for Doge Moro, we can sense that the understanding of the powerful had begun to awaken to the significance of the scuole. Caldiera makes room for them and the mechanical arts in his picture, and this in itself seems to be some acknowledgment of their role in sustaining the prosperity and stability of Venice. Moreover, Caldiera does so with reference to the main elements of an identifiable pattern that had begun to emerge in the middle of the thirteenth century. It was a pattern that continued to take shape in the latter half of the fifteenth century.

In summary, the origins of the scuole in the middle of the thirteenth century suggest neither a clearly defined typology divided between scuole variously classified as "Grandi," "piccole," or "delle arti," nor a broader government plan for the perfection of the constitution. Rather, the dense complex of circumstances in the restricted space of the city gave the political economy of Venice a permanent dynamic that could become a dynamic of permanence. Even so, the interaction of politics, economics, and religion was neither independent of external forces nor immune to them, as witness the interrelated influences of Franciscan teaching and the Joachite vision. The synthesis may best be understood through the influence of Mercy on patterns of everyday life that moved to the rhythms of commercial exchange. The polity of Mercy was to face many further tests of its adaptability. As the territories of La Serenissima continued to expand, one of the most exacting of those examinations was how the economy, the polity, and religion could absorb and draw strength from the great tide of humanity that brought to the city its life blood, and how the polity and those new to it negotiated their identities as Venetians.

Appendix 2.1. Chronology of Foundations of Scuole in Venice, c. 1300–c. 1500

Year	Title	Church	Sestiere
(i) 1300–49			
1300	Sant'Orsola	San Zanipolo	Castello
1315	Nattività della Beata Vergine (dei Ciechi)	San Moise	San Marco
1319	San Nicolo	Santa Maria dei Carmini	San Nicolo
1322	San Giovanni Battista	San Giovanni in Bragora	Castello
1323	Santa Lucia	Santa Lucia	Cannaregio
1324	Santa Catterina	San Stae	Santa Croce
1324	San Gregorio	San Gregorio	San Nicolo
1324	Santa Marina	Santa Marina	Castello
1325	Santa Maria Annunziata	Santa Maria Zobenigo	San Marco[a]
1325	Sant'Agnese	Sant'Agnese	San Nicolo
1333	Santa Maria dell'Ascensione	Santa Maria del Broglio	San Marco[b]
1335	San Martin	San Martin	Castello
1337	Santa Maria della Celestia	Santa Maria della Celestia	Castello
1337	San Nicolo	San Nicolo	San Nicolo
1340	San Zuan Degolà	San Zuan Degolà	Santa Croce
1346	San Cristoforo	Santa Maria Assunta	Cannaregio
1346	San Francesco	Santa Maria dei Frari	San Polo
1347	Sant'Andrea	Sant'Andrea	Santa Croce
(ii) 1350–99			
1350	Beata Vergine [dell'Umiltà, reg.]	San Lio	Castello
1350	Santi Apostoli	Santi Apostoli	Cannaregio
1351	Sant'Anna	Sant'Anna	Castello
1354	San Giovanni Battista [del Tempio]	San Giovanni del Tempio	Castello
1354	Santissima Annunziata	Santa Maria dei Servi	Cannaregio
1359	Santissima Croce	Santa Croce	Santa Croce
1360	Santa Marta	Santa Marta	San Nicolo
1360	San Biagio	San Biagio	Castello[c]
1360	Santo Volto dei Lucchesi	Santa Maria dei Servi	Cannaregio[d]
1361	Sant'Ambrogio (dei Milanesi)	Santa Maria dei Frari	San Polo[e]
1368	Madonna [Purificazione in cat.]	Santa Maria Formosa	Castello
1377	San Vettor [sovegno]	Santa Margarita	San Nicolo
1392	Beata Vergine Annuntiata (dei Zotti)	Sant'Anzolo	San Marco
1394	San Gottardo	Sant'Aponal	San Polo[f]
1395	San Giobbe	San Giobbe	Cannaregio
1395	San Lunardo	San Lunardo	Cannaregio
1399	Beata Vergine (del Rosario in cat.)	San Polo	San Polo
1399	San Saba	Sant'Antonin	Castello
1399?	Santi Cosmo e Damiano	San Zuan in Oglio	Castello [?]

(*Continued*)

Appendix 2.1. (Continued)

Year	Title	Church	Sestiere
(iii) 1400–49			
1400	Nattività della Beata Vergine	San Barnaba	San Nicolo
1400	San Lorenzo	San Barnaba	San Nicolo
1400	Beata Vergine Assunta	San Stae	Santa Croce
1402	Beata Vergine delle Grazie	San Marzilian	Cannaregio
1402	Sant' Alvise	Sant'Alvise	Cannaregio
1408	Beata Vergine e San Matteo	San Samuele	San Marco
1410	San Vitale (Poveggiotti)	San Trovaso	San Nicolo[g]
1413	San Giovanni Battista	San Marcuola	Cannaregio
1418	Santissima Trinità	Santa Trinità	San Nicolo
1422	San Giacomo	San Giacomo dell'Orio	Santa Croce
1423	Beata Vergine Assunta	Santa Maria Mater Domini	Santa Croce
1423	San Magno	San Geremia	Cannaregio
1425	San Nicolo	San Salvador	San Marco
1436	Santa Cattarina	San Geminiano	San Marco
1439	Beata Vergine (scuola)	San Benetto	San Marco
1439	Beata Vergine	San Salvador	San Marco
1439	Sant'Antonio	Santa Maria dei Frari	San Polo[h]
1439	Nattività della Madonna	San Marcuola	Cannaregio[i]
1440	San Fantin	San Fantin	San Marco
1442	S. Maurizio e S. Gallo	San Maurizio	San Marco
1442	Sant'Alberto	Santa Maria dei Carmini	San Nicolo
1444	San Zaccaria e San Lizier	San Provolo	Castello
(iv) 1450–1501			
1450	San Bernardino	San Giobbe	Cannaregio
1450	San Domenico	San Zanipolo	Castello
1451	San Zorzi Trifon	San Giovanni del Tempio	Castello
1452	San Michiel	Santa Maria dell'Orto	Cannaregio
1453	San Lunardo	San Salvador	San Marco
1455	San Rocco e Santa Margarita	San Samuele	San Marco
1458	San Vincenzo e San Pietro Martire e Santa Catterina	San Zanipolo	Castello
1463	San Sebastiano	San Giacomo dell'Orio	Santa Croce
1470	San Sebastiano	San Sebastiano	San Nicolo
1474	Santa Maria Elisabetta [S. Maria della Visitazione, reg.]	San Nicolo	San Nicolo
1478	San Rocco	San Rocco	San Polo
[1480?	Beata Vergine del Rosario	San Domenico	Castello]
1489	Madonna	Santa Maria Formosa	Castello
1491	Sant'Alessandro [e San Vicenzo dei Bergamaschi]	San Silvestro	San Polo[j]
1492	Spirito Santo [sovvegno in cat.]	Spirito Santo	San Nicolo
1496	San Rocco	San Zulian	San Marco

(*Continued*)

Appendix 2.1. (Continued)

Year	Title	Church	Sestiere
1498	Beata Vergine della Concettion	Santa Maria dei Frari	San Polo
1499	San Giuseppe	San Silvestro	San Polo
1500	Santissima Croce (suffragio)	San Salvador	San Marco
1500	Santa Barbara dei Bombardieri	San Marcuola	Cannaregio
1500?	San Nicolo	San Giorgio dei Greci	Castello
[1501	Beata Vergine	Santa Maria Maggiore	Santa Croce]

a. Vio 291.242, citing archival documentation in the patriarchal records and those of the parish.
b. Vio 279.236, citing Biblioteca Nazionale Marciana.
c. Vio 84.38, citing copy of mariegola in *Archivio Veneto*, which links the foundation to the *arte dei cesteri*.
d. Vio 535.493, citing Inquisitori et Revisori sopra le Scuole Grandi, the records of the Servi itself, and Consiglio dei Dieci, parti miste.
e. Vio, 635.586, citing Civica Biblioteca Correr.
f. Cf. Vio 692.650, which gives the Council of Ten's authorization from 1383.
g. Vio 859.844, citing Scuole Piccole b. 326, Archivio di Stato di Venezia.
h. Vio 737.703 links the scuola to San Chiereghino and locates it at San Simeon Grande, but gives no reference.
i. Vio 488.438, citing Biblioteca Nazionale Marciana.
j. Vio 680.638 provides the link to San Vicenzo and the *bergamaschi*, citing Civica Biblioteca Correr.

Appendix 2.2. Foundations of Scuole, by Church of Location, c. 1250–c. 1500

Church				Sestiere
Sant'Agnese				(San Nicolo)
		1081:	Foundation	
		1321:	Consecration	
	Scuole:			
		1326:	Sant'Agnese	
		(1580:	Venerabile)	
Sant'Alvise				(Cannaregio)
		1388:	Foundation	
	Scuola:			
		1402:	Sant'Alvise	
Sant'Andrea della Zirada				(Santa Croce)
		1329:	Foundation	
	Scuola:			
		1347:	Sant'Andrea	

(*Continued*)

Appendix 2.2. (Continued)

Church				Sestiere
Sant'Anzolo				(San Marco)
		920:	Foundation	
		1800s:	Demolished	
	Scuole:			
		1392:	Beata Vergine dell'Annunziata (Zotti)	
		(1522:	Venerabile)	
Sant'Angelo Raffaele				(San Nicolo)
		600s:	Foundation	
		1193:	Consecration	
	Scuole:			
		1280:	San Raffaele e Nicheta	
		(1542:	Venerabile)	
Sant'Anna				(Castello)
		1240:	Foundation	
		1659:	Consecration	
	Scuola:			
		1351:	Sant'Anna	
Sant'Antonin				(Castello)
		500s–600s:	Foundation	
		1680:	Consecration	
	Scuole:			
		1399:	San Saba	
		(1558:	Venerabile)	
Sant'Aponal				(San Polo)
		1000s:	Foundation	
	Scuole:			
		1394:	San Gottardo	
		(1506:	Venerabile)	
Santi Apostoli				(Cannaregio)
		800s:	Foundation	
		1578:	Consecration	
	Scuole:			
		1350:	Santi Apostoli	
		(1511:	Venerabile)	
San Barnaba				(San Nicolo)
		800s:	Foundation	
		1350:	Consecration	
	Scuole:			
		1400:	Nattività della Beata Vergine	
		1400:	San Lorenzo (fabbri)	
San Benetto				(San Marco)
		1000s:	Foundation	
		1692:	Consecration	
	Scuole:			
		1439:	Beata Vergine	
		(1539:	Venerabile)	

(Continued)

Appendix 2.2. (Continued)

Church			Sestiere
San Bartolomeo			(San Marco)
	1048:	First documentation	
	1771:	Consecration	
Scuole:			
	1368:	San Matteo	
	(1507:	Venerabile)	
San Biagio			(Castello)
Scuola:			
	1360: San Biagio		
Carità (Santa Maria della Carità)			(Dorsoduro)
	1116:	Foundation	
	1471:	Consecration	
Scuola:			
	1260:	Santa Maria della Carità	
Carmini (Santa Maria dei Carmini)			(San Nicolo)
	1286:	Foundation	
	1348:	Consecration	
Scuole:			
	1319:	San Nicolo	
	1442:	Sant'Alberto	
Celestia (Santa Maria della Celestia)			(Castello)
	1237:	Completion	
	1800s:	Demolition	
Scuola:			
	1337:	Santa Maria della Celestia	
Corpus Domini			(Cannaregio)
	1366:	Foundation	
	1800s:	Demolition	
Scuole:			
	1395:	Corpus Domini	
	(1504:	Venerabile)	
Santa Croce			(Santa Croce)
	700s–800s:	Foundation	
	1800s:	Demolition	
Scuole:			
	1359:	Santissima Croce	
	(1538:	Venerabile)	
San Domenico			(Castello)
	1312:	Foundation	
Scuola:			
	1480?:	Beata Vergine del Rosario	
Sant'Eufemia			(Giudecca – San Nicolo)
	952:	Foundation	
	1371:	Consecration	
Scuola:			
	(1508:	Venerabile)	

(*Continued*)

Appendix 2.2. (Continued)

Church			Sestiere
San Fantin			(San Marco)
	1134:	First documentation	
Scuole:			
	1440:	San Fantin [San Gerolamo e Buona Morte]	
	(1544:	Venerabile)	
San Francesco della Vigna			(Castello)
	1253:	Foundation	
Scuole:			
	1451?:	San Bernardino	
Santa Maria Gloriosa dei Frari			(San Polo)
	1250:	Construction	
	1280:	Consecration	
Scuole:			
	1261:	Santa Maria e San Cristoforo	
	1346:	San Francesco	
	1438:	San Giovanni Battista (fiorentini)	
	1439:	Sant'Antonio	
	1498:	Beata Vergine della Concettion	
San Geminiano			(San Marco)
	1098:	First documentation	
Scuole:			
	1436:	Santa Catterina	
	(1504:	Venerabile)	
San Geremia			(Cannaregio)
	1000s:	Foundation	
Scuole:			
	1423:	San Magno	
	(1507:	Venerabile)	
San Giacomo dell'Orio			(Santa Croce: San Nicolo)
	1089:	First documentation	
Scuole:			
	1422:	San Giacomo	
	1463:	San Sebastiano	
	(1507:	Venerabile)	
San Giobbe			(Cannaregio)
	1300s:	Ospizio, i.e., functioning as a hospice	
	1493:	Consecration	
Scuole:			
	1395:	San Giobbe	
	1450:	San Bernardino	
San Giovanni in Bragora			(Castello)
	700s:	Foundation	
	1505:	Consecration	
Scuole:			
	1322:	San Giovanni Battista	
	(1573:	Venerabile)	

(*Continued*)

Appendix 2.2. (Continued)

Church			Sestiere
San Giovanni Evangelista			(San Polo)
	970:	Foundation	
Scuola:			
	1261:	San Giovanni Evangelista	
San Giovanni Grisostomo			(Cannaregio)
	1023:	Foundation	
Scuola:			
	(1531:	Venerabile)	
San Giovanni del Tempio			(Castello)
	1119:	First documentation	
Scuole:			
	1354:	San Giovanni Battista del Tempio	
	1451:	San Zorzi Trifon (Schiavoni)	
San Giovanni Novo			(Castello)
	1142:	Foundation	
Scuole:			
	1399?:	Santi Cosmo e Damiano	
	(1506:	Venerabile)	
Santi Giovanni e Paolo (San Zanipolo)			(Castello)
	1182:	Monastery	
	1430:	Consecration	
Scuole:			
	1261:	San Marco	
	1300:	Sant'Orsola	
	1450:	San Domenico	
	1458:	San Vicenzo, San Pietro Martire e Santa Cattarina	
San Gregorio			(San Nicolo)
	1088:	Foundation	
Scuole:			
	1324:	San Gregorio	
	(1523:	Venerabile)	
San Leonardo (San Lunardo)			(Cannaregio)
	1144:	Foundation	
	1343:	Consecration	
Scuole:			
	1395:	San Lunardo	
	(1581:	Venerabile)	
San Lio			(Castello)
	1108:	Foundation	
	1610:	Consecration	
Scuole:			
	1350:	Beata Vergine dell'Umiltà	
	(1515:	Venerabile)	
San Lorenzo			(Castello)
Scuola:			
	1277:	Santi Lorenzo e Sebastiano	

(Continued)

Appendix 2.2. (Continued)

Church			Sestiere
Santa Lucia			(Cannaregio)
	1028:	Foundation	
	1343:	Consecration	
Scuole:			
	1323:	Santa Lucia	
	(1520:	Venerabile)	
San Marcuola			(Cannaregio)
	1000s:	Foundation	
Scuole:			
	1413:	San Giovanni Battista	
	1500:	Santa Barbara dei Bombardieri	
	(1507:	Venerabile)	
Santa Margherita (Santa Margarita)			(San Nicolo)
	837?:	Foundation	
	853–4:	Consecration	
Scuole:			
	1377:	San Vettor	
	(1503:	Venerabile)	
Santa Maria Assunta			(Castello: in Cannaregio for the Provveditori di Comun)
	1100s:	Foundation	
Scuola:			
	1346:	San Cristoforo	
Santa Maria dell'Orto			(Cannaregio)
	1350:	Foundation	
Scuole:			
	1377:	Beata Vergine e San Cristoforo	
	1452:	San Michiel	
Santa Maria Formosa			(Castello)
	600s:	Foundation	
	1585:	Consecration	
Scuole:			
	1368:	Madonna della Purificazione	
	1489:	Madonna	
	(1506:	Venerabile)	
Santa Maria Mater Domini			(Santa Croce)
	c. 960:	Foundation	
Scuole:			
	1423:	Beata Vergine Assunta	
	(1512:	Venerabile)	
Santa Marina			(Castello)
	878:	Foundation	
Scuola:			
	1324:	Santa Marina	
Santa Marta			(San Nicolo)
	1315:	Foundation	
Scuola:			
	1360:	Santa Marta	

(*Continued*)

Appendix 2.2. (Continued)

Church				Sestiere
San Martin				(Castello)
		600s–700s:	Foundation	
		1653:	Consecration	
	Scuole:			
		1335:	San Martin	
		(1524:	Venerabile)	
San Marzilian				(Cannaregio)
		800s:	Foundation	
		1721:	Consecration	
	Scuole:			
		1402:	Beata Vergine delle Grazie	
		(1512:	Venerabile)	
San Maurizio				(San Marco)
		800s:	Foundation	
	Scuole:			
		1442:	San Maurizio e San Gallo (Albanesi)	
		(1511:	Venerabile)	
Misericordia				(Cannaregio)
		936:	Foundation	
	Scuola:			
		1308:	Santa Maria della Misericorida	
San Moise				(San Marco)
		700s:	Foundation	
	Scuole:			
		1315:	Nattività della Beata Vergine (Ciechi)	
		(1510:	Venerabile)	
San Nicolo dei Mendicoli				(San Nicolo)
		600s:	Foundation	
	Scuole:			
		1337:	San Nicolo	
		1474:	Santa Maria della Visitazione	
		(1506:	Venerabile)	
San Polo				(San Polo)
		800s:	Foundation	
	Scuole:			
		1399:	Beata Vergine (del Rosario)	
		(1507:	Venerabile)	
San Provolo				(Castello)
		800s:	Foundation	
	Scuole:			
		1444:	San Zaccaria e San Lizier	
		(1517:	Venerabile)	
San Salvador				(San Marco)
		1000s:	Foundation	
		1177:	Consecration	
	Scuole:			
		1425:	San Nicolo	
		1439:	Beata Vergine	
		1453:	San Lunardo	

(Continued)

Appendix 2.2. (Continued)

Church				Sestiere
San Samuele				(San Marco)
		900s–1000s:	Foundation	
	Scuole:			
		1408:	Beata Vergine e San Matteo	
		1455:	San Rocco e Santa Margarita	
		(1528:	Venerabile)	
San Sebastiano				(Dorsoduro)
		1007:	Foundation	
	Scuola:			
		1470:	San Sebastiano	
Servi (Santa Maria dei Servi)				(Cannaregio)
		1330:	Foundation	
	Scuole:			
		1354:	Santissima Annunziata	
		1360:	Santo Volto dei Lucchesi	
Spirito Santo				(San Nicolo)
		1483:	Foundation	
	Scuola:			
		1492:	Spirito Santo	
San Stae				(Santa Croce)
		966:	Foundation	
	Scuole:			
		1324:	Santa Cattarina	
		(1504:	Venerabile)	
San Stefano				(San Marco)
		1294:	First stone	
	Scuola:			
		1299:	San Stefano	
Santa Trinità				(San Nicolo)
		1000s–1100s:	Foundation	
	Scuole:			
		1418:	Santissima Trinità	
		(1507:	Venerabile)	
San Zaccaria				(Castello)
	See San Provolo.			
San Zuan Degolà				(Santa Croce)
		700s:	Foundation	
	Scuole:			
		1340:	San Zuan Degola	
		(1514:	Venerabile)	
San Zulian				(San Marco)
		942:	Foundation	
		1580:	Consecration	
	Scuole:			
		1277:	San Zulian	
		1496:	San Rocco	
		(1502:	Venerabile)	

3 Who Were the Venetians, c. 1500–c. 1600?

The duke cannot deny the course of law:
For the commodity that strangers have
With us in Venice, if it be denied,
Will much impeach the justice of the state,
Since that the trade and profit of the city
Consisteth of all nations.

– Shakespeare, *The Merchant of Venice*, 3.3.26–31

Metropolis and Cosmopolis

Up to this point the argument has concerned the inner workings of the Venetian polity as viewed in the history of institutions peculiar to the city, the scuole. The singularity of Venice is a feature that the isolation of the city in the lagoon emphasized in history and which, but for the Tronchetto with its road and railway track, the waters still surround. Despite the city's geographical location, it is essential to understand the paradoxical significance of external influences upon the history of the republic.

At bottom, this was a question of the movement of peoples. For some commentators, the very name of the city reflected the welcome that it offered to immigrants: Venezia or Venetia, deriving from the Latin "veni etiam" or "you come too."[1] Venice was a city of immigrants, many of them refugees. This fundamental process of arrival and integration was not always a regular drip-feed; at times it could become an overpowering flood. One of the most fascinating aspects of Venetian history is the question of how so much movement could contribute to a peerless reputation for stability. An obvious explanation might lie in the successful management and regulation of admission to the city through diligent governmental oversight. The previous chapters have argued that, seen from "below" or, more prosaically, from within the corporations of the popolani who made up the critical mass of the city's inhabitants, such an interpretation is difficult to sustain. The remarkably steady development of the network of scuole was not the result of a patrician master plan but was due to a rationale of self-interest that underpinned schemes of mutual aid, with no systematic managerial control from the magistrates, be they of the Giustizia Vecchia, the Provveditori di Comun, or even the Consiglio dei Dieci.

However, the steadiness of such development between the middle of the thirteenth century and the end of the fifteenth was further strengthened by the limited intrusiveness of events external to Venice that might have threatened the internal stability of the city itself. Even the advance of the Turks and its pressure upon the profitability of long-distance maritime trade in the fifteenth century, though prompting change, did not dictate its pace. Partly as a result of the Ottoman push westward, there were two extraordinary long-term transformations in the character of Venetian political economy. The first of these was the contraction of far-flung mercantile activity and the complementary expansion of metropolitan activity in the city itself.[2] The second was the gradual dilation and consolidation of the republic's territorial dominion on the Italian mainland, the true significance of which has only become apparent in the past three decades, at least to an anglophone audience.[3] (See map 7, "The Growth of the Venetian Dominions.")

In addition, at this point in the late fifteenth century the external forces to which this chapter has already alluded burst into the Venetian state and fractured the harmony of politics, economics, and religion. In 1509, Venice suffered a sudden and comprehensive defeat at the hands of a European coalition at the battle of Agnadello. The effect of an action that may not have lasted more than fifteen minutes and which was over within the hour was territorially, politically, and psychologically shattering.[4] The mainland state was lost, and any broader ambitions in Italy dissolved. It is hard to recognize the Venice of 1494 in the Venice of 1509.

The recovery of the Venetian Republic only really began in 1513, and it owed far more to divisions among the enemies of Venice than to any inherent strengths of its own.[5] It is testimony to the degree of destruction and conquest in the peninsula that, despite defeat and diminution, Venice was alone among the states of Italy in not having to endure the dominion of a foreign power. At about the same time, with less violence but equal drama, the European maritime world had changed forever, and so had the place of Venice within it. The Portuguese establishment of a route to India via the Cape of Good Hope posed a long-term threat to the Venetian monopoly of the European spice trade.[6]

The connection of Venice to a wider world that had changed in such degree generated tremendous strain within the pattern of economic, political, and religious life that had circulated such energy since the middle of the thirteenth century. Consideration of these changing dynamics reconnects discussion to the institutions of the city and how they adjusted to the forces that might have overwhelmed them.

Towards the end of the fifteenth century the French ambassador, Philippe de Commynes, remarked of the Venetians that "most of their people are foreigners" (la pluspart de leur peuple est étranger).[7] This chapter will suggest that rather than the Venetians possessing foreigners, those same foreigners possessed the Venetians, albeit in a relationship of mutual advantage. Venice was both metropolis and cosmopolis.

In Commynes's time the evidence of Venice's capacity to accommodate outsiders probably looked inexhaustible. In his description there are three other striking features that connect to the presence of all the immigrants. The first two are the density of the ecclesiastical landscape, which included "quite seventy two parishes and many a confraternity," and the majestic power that the Arsenale advertised – "the most beautiful thing in all the world today." Third, in discussing the constitution, Commynes noted the exclusion of the popolo from the political process: "the people have no role in it and there is no appeal to it in anything, and all offices are for the nobility."[8] Commynes astutely catalogued these three features as separate items, but this chapter will seek to show the dynamics of their connectedness.

We can take up that theme of connection with the immigrants themselves. Venice's lordship of the Adriatic was obvious from the presence of so many people from the Slav regions. The largest merchant ships docked at the long Riva degli Schiavoni, which stretched from the religious and political centre of Venice at San Marco to its industrial heart at the Arsenale. The Schiavoni (or Dalmati) had their own scuola from 1451, and in the early sixteenth century they established their own place of worship in Castello, not far from the *riva* named after the Slavs. The interior walls of the scuola told the stories of their patron, Saint George, and of Saint Jerome in the exquisite cycles of Vetor Carpaccio of 1505–10.[9] The Armenian presence is documented from the twelfth century, though a scuola was formed later.[10] Albanians (from 1443) also established a confraternity to accommodate temporary visitors and to offer relief to fellow nationals who were in Venice for a longer term and who had fallen into distress. There were several thousand Greeks in the city. They too had their own scuola, though the Venetian government was obdurate over the establishment of a church for the Orthodox faith: negotiations lasted half a century, and the Scuola of San Nicolo dei Greci dates only from 1539. The problems of establishing a Greek Orthodox church, San Giorgio dei Greci, in Venice may well have been tied to Venetian difficulties in overseeing Greek churches in Venice's maritime territories, particularly in Crete.

We know of at least 232 merchants from Nuremberg who were in Venice in 1500. Nuremberg was a city of 25,000 people at most.[11] The proportion of its merchants who were therefore in Venice at the same time as each other testifies to the importance and attractiveness of the city, however arduous the long journey across the Alps. The exact figure derives from the records of the vast Fondaco dei Tedeschi, the warehouse of the Germans, at Venice's commercial centre, the Ponte di Rialto. When the warehouse burned down in 1505, the Venetian government intervened to assist in the construction of a replacement. In extravagant defiance of the elements, its outer walls were decorated with the frescoes of two painters from the Terraferma state, Giorgione (da Castelfranco) and Tiziano (da Cadore).[12]

There were communities of Italians who came from beyond the lands of the republic. The Florentines had their own scuola in the Campo dei Frari. Their altar in that great church displayed the gilded and painted wooden statue of their patron saint, John the Baptist, the work of Donatello. To the other side of the high altar stands the altar of the Scuola dei Milanesi, showing Milan's patron saint, Ambrose, in pride of place among other saints in the altarpiece by Alvise Vivarini, which Marco Basaiti completed.[13] The exiles of Lucca, who had departed their faction-ridden city in 1315, played a key part in the establishment and growth of silk manufacture in Venice. Of the physical presence of their thriving confraternity, centred on a cult of the Holy Visage (Volto Santo), alas, barely a trace survives. Other "nations" – a term deserving careful scrutiny – included those from Poveglia, Bergamo, the Valtellina, and Friuli. Persians and Turks, like the Germans, eventually established their own *fondachi* (warehouses).[14] Much of this suggests that the Ghetto of Venice, the home of the city's Jews, which historians for so long studied in isolation, had a certain typicality. Amid the synagogues there was also a Scuola degli Ebrei. Like so many communities of immigrants in Venice, the Jews of the city expressed a collective identity of their own in the formation of a scuola, that distinctively Venetian form of confraternity.[15]

Caution must season any generalization about immigrants in Venice. Many questions remain. For the time being, we should note the differences of status, wealth, and political influence even within the confines of the legally defined class of citizens, the cittadini. The key criterion for the attainment of this status was a stipulated period of residence in Venice itself: fifteen years in order to trade as a "Venetian" in Venice; twenty-five years to trade as such both in Venice and overseas. There were variations between the standing of those cittadini who worked as secretaries in the chancery (the only non-nobles in government, according to Commynes) and those who traded with the privileges of patricians as merchants in Venice and abroad, or merely in Venice. A legally defined class blurred at the edges into both the patriciate and the popolani.[16]

What, among the immigrants within the popolani, constituted the long and short terms of residence? In this regard, can the evidence establish lines of distinction between the immigrants who arrived in Venice of their own accord, in particular trades – in other words, those who came to earn – and those who came to beg? The pressures that pushed people from their homelands and those that pulled them to Venice were widely different. This chapter investigates a case history involving an established connection between Lombardy and the Venetian iron business that became a startling influx of newcomers in 1530–1. Even a detailed analysis of the lists of those who were in Venice in a particular year cannot give a definitive picture of the exact durability of place of origin as an element of Venetian identity, or of a foreign identity in Venice. Many stonemasons styled themselves "Lombardo." We have already noted Titian and Giorgione as immigrants from Cadore and Castelfranco, respectively. Paolo Caliari is even now more famous as "Veronese."[17] This example raises the puzzling question of family names and their relationship to place of origin. At one level, the names of those families whose adult male members could hold magisterial office formed the most exclusive aspect of the Venetian constitution. A family name was essential for those who were aggregated to the patriciate in the later seventeenth century. In the specific instance of the painter Paolo Caliari, known as il Veronese, it appears that his assumption of that name served, paradoxically, to emphasize the painter's Venetian identity. By contrast, his biological and professional heirs (their term was "haeredes Paulo Caliari Veronesensis") could make no career headway in Verona itself.[18] Another painter from that city, Bonifacio, who was no blood relation to the Caliari, had the perfectly recognizable *cognome* "de' Pitati" but is sometimes confusingly identified as "Bonifacio Veronese." Even a family name associated with the aristocratic lifestyle of the villa, as at Pojano Maggiore in the Veneto, turns out to be the adoption of the place name Poiano as a surname.[19] The *sopranome*, a nickname of sorts, gave a further precision to identity and identification.[20]

The archives have yet to yield answers that might be exact and comprehensive, and those repositories may yet reshape the questions themselves. As an interim assessment, this chapter examines two pieces of documentation. The first gives some idea of the variety of temporary visitors who took accommodation in the city's places of lodging. The second shows how swiftly the corporations of the city could absorb immigrants whose specialized trade could keep them in Venice on an open-ended basis. What gives these contrasting documents a sharp focus is that, by extraordinary coincidence, they are exactly contemporary and have their mass and focus in the years 1530–1.

The coincidence is particularly fortuitous when set in the cluster of changes that hit Europe, Italy, and Venice at about the same time. The Sack of Rome in 1527 proved to be the prelude to a period of imperial hegemony that received acknowledgment in the Treaty of Bologna in 1530 and in the coronation of Charles V as emperor by the pope in the same year.[21] The court was now the place to be – as Charles V's perfect gentleman ("uno des mejores caballeros del mundo"), Baldassare Castiglione, made clear in a work that was to become the literary product of the Italian Renaissance that Europeans sought most avidly and absorbed most attentively.[22] There was not much room in this new Europe, the Europe of princes and courts, for the republican tradition that had revived in the Renaissance but which now survived as uncompromised sovereign liberty only in the Republic of Venice.[23]

The Venetian representative at the negotiations for the Treaty of Bologna was Gasparo Contarini, a figure who could observe both Venice and Europe, both the Church and the world.[24] Contarini's work on the Venetian constitution marked the new place of Venice in the new Europe, a place that was more singular but also smaller than it once had been. The republic had ended its period of expansive influence in far-flung places and was set in a phase of isolation in which it absorbed people from outside who came to the city to appreciate its curiosity and to satisfy their own.[25]

By the end of the 1520s, Venice had also experienced the immediate consequences of the upheaval of Italy, and, in this, its absorption of refugees gives a human and material dimension to its abstract significance. The Sack of Rome had scattered many of that city's inhabitants far and wide. Among the most celebrated to find their way to Venice were the satirist Pietro Aretino (1492–1556) and the architect Jacopo Sansovino (1486–1570). In Venice they were, with Titian (1485?–1576), to form an aesthetic cartel of high exclusiveness. Their careers combined the praise of Venice for its abstract qualities and the realization of those qualities in the material fabric of the city. As the instrument of that most princely doge, Andrea Gritti (r. 1523–38), Sansovino was responsible for the *renovatio urbis* both at Venice's commercial heart at Rialto (one may still dine under the snug vaults of his warehouses) and at San Marco. There his Libreria and Zecca trumpeted the pre-eminence of Venice in books and coin, the only two items that we might describe as mass-produced in the Renaissance economy.[26] The complementary juxtaposition of Venice's commercial centre at Rialto and its political and religious heart at San Marco continued to proclaim the dynamic interaction of politics, economics, and religion, an interaction that was soon to change – and, in some ways, to cease.

Aretino was a ferocious critic of the princely court: "The court, my masters, is hospice of hopes, burial ground of lives, wet nurse of hatreds, breeding ground of envies, mentress of ambitions, market place of lies, harem of suspicions, prison of concords, market of falsehoods, school of frauds, homeland of flattery, paradise of vices, hell of virtues, purgatory of kindnesses and limbo of joys." In the same discourse he wrote that "not going to court is what life's about" (vita è il non andare in corte).[27] In a letter to Doge Andrea Gritti in 1530 he also celebrated the virtues of his new home as a haven for those displaced from their proper abodes.

> O universal fatherland! O freedom common to all! O refuge of displaced peoples! How much greater would be the woes of Italy, if your goodness were less! Here is the refuge of all Italy's peoples, and the stronghold of its riches; here its honour is salvaged. Venice embraces Italy when others despise her, and upholds her when others abase her, feeds her when others starve her; she welcomes her when others hunt her; and in cheering her again in her tribulations, she keeps her in charity and love. So let Italy kneel before Venice and give prayer to God for her, whose majesty by means of her altars and sacrifices, wishes Venice to share the eternity of the world, that world which is astonished that Nature should have miraculously made place for her rise in the most impossible location, and that Heaven should have been so generous in its gifts in nobility, in magnificence and in dominion, in buildings, temples, pious houses, in councils, in benignity, in customs, virtues, riches, fame and glory than any other [city] that ever was.[28]

For Aretino, the security of his new patria appears to have touched a reality beyond the rhetoric. Aretino's encomium spoke for many of the displaced – peoples of Italy who found a "rifugio delle sue nazioni" in Venice, people for whom there was a mundane and vernacular quality to Venice's identity as a safe place in which to go about one's business. There is some important evidence that shows that reality in action. What follows pays particular attention to the plight, and flight, of people involved in the iron trade from the easternmost lands of war-ravaged Lombardy. Tradespeople from that area came to Venice under specific pressures in 1531. First, however, we turn to documentation that provides a glimpse of the great human tide arriving in Venice from all over the Mediterranean world.

Rooms at the Inns, 1530–1

The Giustizia Nova came into being in the mid-thirteenth century. This "New Justice" took a title that distinguished it from the Giustizia Vecchia, which retained its function of supervising the corporate organization and market practices of the city's guilds.[29] The Giustizia Nova was responsible for the oversight of trade in foodstuffs, of taverns (including the irksome *furatole*, hole-in-the-wall drinking haunts that were similar to speakeasies, famous during Prohibition in America), and, by extension, of provision, accommodation, and sustenance in the city's temporary lodgings.[30]

A register of those people who stayed in some of the city's inns survives for 1530–1 as "Registro 12 'Stella'" in the magistracy's records.[31] It seems impossible that the register could constitute a complete record of all those who visited the city and lodged there in the period. Nor is it clear whether certain visitors were supposed to take accommodation licensed by the magistrates. The entries in the register are frequently hurried and vague or incomplete. Moreover, the folios are not numbered. Nevertheless, scrutiny of the information provides some unusually vivid examples, albeit anecdotal, of the staggering variety of people who visited Venice and the purposes for which they might have come. There is no corroboration of who owned the housing that offered accommodation to visitors, of how visitors shared beds, of how the costs of rented rooms may have been divided among guests, and of how the receipts were split between host and proprietor. There is no evidence of any link to the guild of innkeepers.[32] A still larger question poses itself: how could these *locandieri* offer space to several visitors at a time? Artisan households were comfortable but of modest proportions. How did this overcrowded city make room for more crowds?[33]

For all the puzzles, the register offers evidence of the tremendous diversity of humanity in Venice, not only among those who came there but also among those who put them up. The register begins at 3 March 1530 (two days into the Venetian administrative year) and ends on 21 October 1531. Of the 151 hosts, 85 were women and 66 were men – itself an illustration of the possibilities that women had for a working life.[34] The very concentrated picture of the locations of the premises shows how people from all over Italy and the Mediterranean world were funnelled into extraordinarily close proximity with each other. The size of the Venetian parishes that designate these locations varied enormously in area and in population. Moreover, proximity to San Marco itself might involve all three of the city's sestieri that lie on that side of the Canal Grande: San Marco, Castello, and Cannaregio (see map 1, "The Sestieri and Parishes of Venice"). The two parishes with the largest numbers of guesthouses were San Zan Novo (also "dei Furlani," which identified with the people from the subject region of Friuli) with ten *locande*, and Santa Maria Formosa, with fourteen. San Zan Novo connected the cluster of small parishes behind San Marco as viewed from the piazza with six places of lodging at San Filippo Giacomo and one at San Provolo. The parish of Santa Maria Formosa is very large in extent, and the fourteen inns in it connected all the way to Rialto via the parishes of Santa Marina (three lodging houses), Santa Maria della Fava (three), San Lio (six), San Zuan Grisostomo (one), and then to San Bartolomeo (two), and San Luca (four). There was a further clustering behind the government offices to the north side of the piazza, close to the Calle dei Fabbri, with five inns in the Frezzaria, two at San Gallo, two at San Paternian, and one at San Zulian. From the west end of the piazza there were places to stay at San Moise (three), San Fantin (four), and Santa Maria Zobenigo (four). Beyond these limits there were isolated locande at Sant'Anzolo (one) and San Stefano (one). In these records there were only five inns on the other side of the Canal Grande.

For many of the innkeepers the income from letting rooms, even if they shared it with the owner of the dwelling, supplemented what they earned in another trade. Of the sixty-six men who are listed as hosts, twenty-nine designated another occupation. These included minor government office ("sazador al sal," "masser alle acque," "sanser"), two tailors, two shoemakers, a few members of the cloth trades, one or two builders, and Arsenale workers.

It is curious that there should be no representatives of the trades that dominated the principal thoroughfares between San Marco and Rialto: the mercers in the Mercerie and the ironsmiths in the Calle dei Fabbri. This prompts questions about the relationship of dwelling and place of work, questions that may find answers from the stones of Venice themselves. The shops in the Mercerie were probably just too small. They often included storage space ("volta o magazen").[35] Perhaps local innkeepers of modest occupation acted on behalf of the owners of the places in which visitors to Venice stayed, and did not sublet accommodation in their own homes or above their own shops. If so, then the documentation may imply that some women who had a trade of their own also had an independence of domestic circumstances that permitted them to take on work in the administration of lodgings.[36] Such may have been the case for the seven women who listed an occupation for the Giustizia Nova: "Anzola lautera" (lute maker), "Chiara pelizera" (furrier), "Franceschina sartora" (tailor), "Franceschina vantera" (glover –might they be one and the same?), "Menega carbonera" (charcoal carrier), "Paula che canta" (singer), and Polesina, the wife of Bortolomeo the printer.[37]

The domestic and working lives of the other seventy-eight women who were responsible for looking after temporary visitors remain, for the time being, unknown to us. Some may have been prostitutes, given the scale of the profession in Venice. Few would accept Sanudo's claim that there were ten thousand courtesans in the city, but when census records became more sharply classified in 1642, thirteen women in the parish of San Paternian were crudely characterized as whores ("puttane").[38] From one angle, it seems close to incredible that places hosting diplomatic missions, parties, and occasionally families that included apparently respectable women, and lodging arrangements that were clearly for the convenience of commercial transactions, could also have involved a network of prostitution. From another, the vast human thesaurus that barely distinguished residents and visitors in Venice was not contained within a discrete and free-standing sector of regulated hotels; the melting pot may on occasion have been a flesh pot.

The idea of a melting pot gains added force when we review the origins of both the visitors and those who accommodated them. Among the men who were innkeepers originally from the Venetian mainland, there were Alessandro, a shoemaker from Brescia; his compatriot Piero; and Hieronimo from Vicenza. Others with Italian origins were Marco Bellaci, a Florentine; Piero from Rome; and Zan from Parma. Bartolomeo styled himself as Flemish, and Rigo Ener is identifiable as a German. Simon Thodesco also had a German background but was, like Ioseph Navastra, designated as Jewish.

Women who ran lodgings and claimed to be from the Italian mainland included Maddalena from Verona and Maddalena from Vicenza – though one must ask whether this is the same person since the addresses cited are in the adjacent parishes of Sant'Anzolo and San Stefano, where there were no other locande. Margarita and Paula both used the designation "veronese," and there was a Lucia from Vicenza. "Orsa da Noal" came from the Padovano at some point in her family's history. "Lodovica trevisana," "Zuanna furlana," and "Franceschina istriana" were in some way attached to other Venetian possessions (the Trevigiano, Friuli, and Istria, respectively). "Malgarita" and "Angela" each had the designation "greca." One woman, Sara, was described as "ebrea"; "Antonia da Pescara" and "Anzola sarda" came from more distant places in Italy. A certain Luzia claimed a Spanish identity. By contrast, Lugrezia is the only woman of the eighty-five on the list to be described as "veneziana." Even this case does not tantalize as greatly as "Isabetta bressana veronese," an entry that seems to claim two places of origin for the same person. Or perhaps she was born in one place and moved to Venice from another: "the Brescian woman from Verona." That the presence of "Venetians" should be quite so tiny is certainly worthy of note and emphasis, especially since it occurs again in quite different lists from exactly the same period. It is tempting to make a comparison with the immense human diversity of Manhattan.

This gives an impression of Venice's geographical range of attraction in Italy and further afield. It may well be that visitors gravitated towards lodgings run by their compatriots. In March 1530 the apothecary Fabio di Marco Romano lodged with Piero Romano, in the same month four Greeks from

Corfu registered with Maria greca, and so on. However, the Giustizia Nova administered "Houses" (Case) for visitors from certain regions. On 18 March 1530, apparently in an attempt to define "prohibited hotel keeping" (albergaria proibita), the magistrates acknowledged Zuane da Parma as the custodian of the "Casa della patria del friul" (House of the Friulian homeland) in Santa Maria Formosa. Iacomo Filisco ran the "Casa dei visentini" for Vicentines, and a woman called Cassandra was in charge of an establishment for those from Lendinara. The Giustizieri set up a hostelry for the people from Rovigo but did not designate a host.[39] The Fondaco dei Tedeschi could not contain all those who came from Germany and tried to stipulate that Germans lodge only at the Lion Bianco and other listed inns at San Bartolomeo ("et altre deputade per alozamento deli oltramontani a San Bortolomeo").[40]

However, the lack of detail entered for many of the guests frustrates any further quantitative analysis, not least because there is no indication of the duration of any particular stay. All too often the entries offer no more than a few names and the description "forestieri" – which Goldoni's play *La Locandiera* suggests may mean no more than "guests."[41] It is more fruitful to concentrate on particular cases that give some idea of the variety of purposes that might prompt a visit to Venice.

The patchiness and inadequacy of the records may be features that are in themselves revealing. Faced with a vast and rapid influx of outsiders, how could a single magistracy hope to license and regulate their accommodation and record the details of all those who came to stay? By contrast, the corporations of the popolo may have proved more adaptable to the absorption of people from outside Venice; it was in their economic interests to do so, which may have provided focus for their efforts. In any case, the comparison of the government's impossible task of regulation with the guilds' documented management is worth a reference now.

Even in the apparently regulated world of temporary visits, those who attended the corridors of power – literally the corridor in the Palazzo Ducale that led to the Sala dei Scarlatti, the Sala degli Scudi, and on to the Sala degli Stucchi, the antechamber before an audience with the Senate – may have rubbed shoulders the night before with merchants, artisans, or scholars in accommodation nearby.

The registro "Stella" records a dozen visits of ambassadors. Pietro Bissolo, representative of the Bresciano, stayed at the premises of a broker in March 1530. The servants of the imperial ambassador lodged with Paula Veronese at Santa Maria Formosa on the sixteenth of the same month. Other representatives from the Venetian provinces – Asolo, Verona, Cividal di Belluno – may not have held the balance of European power, but the courtiers of Cardinal

Grimani, who stayed with Francesco dallo Thodesco at San Sovero in May, and the courtiers who served the Duke of Ferrara (in lodgings with Isabeta Palazol in November 1530) were in the entourages of a cardinal and a duke, men of some status. Annibale Bentivoglio of the ruling house of Bologna stayed, with his eight servants, in lodgings for which Michiel, a spinner ("filatoyo"), was responsible. "The magnificent Lord Ser Lodovigo di Alifia," the "orator" of the king and queen of Poland, no less, stayed with Anzola Veronese at San Fantin. On 7 October 1530 he had presented his credentials in the collegio, accompanied by six patricians clad in scarlet.[42]

The theme of Venice's exchange and interaction with the rest of the state and with the Mediterranean world beyond it extends from diplomatic dialogue to culture and learning. Greeks from Corfu, or Armenian Christians, might have been present for unspecified business. However, it is quite clear that Ciprian Paluri, a Cypriot scholar, had "come to stay in the city to study and be a scholar in order to go after some time to Padua to the University" (venuto a star in questa terra ad studiar et esser scholaro per andar poi fin qualche tempo a Padoa al studio di Padoa). He was to stay with a tailor, Battista by name. In the other direction, Pierantonio di Gottardo from Brescia, and Zuan Michiel Ventura from Crema, were "scholars come from the Studio di Padova to furnish themselves with books and other materials in this city" (scholari venuti dal studio di Padova per fornirsi di libri et robe in questa Terra), though where they were to stay in Venice remains blank.

In some cases, the lodgers sought or brought medical expertise. Pamphilo, from Spilimbergo, arrived with two servants, but he was already "gravely ill" (amalato gravamente). Simon, a Jewish surgeon, stayed at the Pomo d'Oro, the shop of the Golden Apple. This is an unusual reference since all the other Jews in the lists lodged with their own people in the Ghetto. However, perhaps Simon found lodgings at the shop itself rather than at a separate inn. Another visitor, Zuan Bolognin, was a physician and surgeon based at the Pomo d'Oro, but he stayed with Cabriel Vernaldo at Santa Sofia in the Ruga Do Pozzi. Francesco da Cremona had arrived with his nephew "to practice his art of medicine" (ad esercitar l'arte sua della medicina). Cristato di Cristati from Verona professed "the arts and philosophy and medicine, and is now in the city to practise medicine" (ha facto profession in le arte et phillosofia et medicina et praticar medicina); he was to stay with Piero, who made strings, perhaps for musical instruments. Music was also the business of Giulio da Modena "newly brought here as master organist at the Church of San Marco" (novamente conducto per maistro sonador del'organo de la Giesia di San Marco); he was to stay, initially at least, with Vincenzo, a maker of padding.

A group of Germans (Giusto and Lunardo Relengin, Cristoforo, a boy called Michael, Leonardo and Gasparo Scinger, and Zuan Stelaur) were youngsters "who are learning the language and the merchant's trade" (che imparano la lengua et la mercantia); they stayed with Rigo Ener. Another group of young Germans came "to learn Italian and the abacus and the practices of the city and of merchandising" (ad imparar la lingua italiana et abacho et la pratica dela terra et delle mercadantie). Their entry emphasized that they were "not like foreigners travelling in transit" (non sono como li forestieri viandanti per transito). They were to stay with one Leonardo, who packed bales in the Fondaco dei Tedeschi. It looks as though the great German emporium functioned as a warehouse, a trading post, a place of lodging, and a centre for on-the-job training at one and the same time.[43] Another packer, Iusto, looked after four German merchants in January 1530.

It may have been part of the education of these young Germans to encounter – as would have been unavoidable in the great commercial crossroads that was Venice – merchants from Corfu (who were Venetian subjects) and merchants from the Levant (Jewish merchants who were not *tedeschi* but the subjects of the sultan). For others, the cosmopolitan character of the Venetian market may have been less important than the business to transact there. From Milan and the Bresciano there came a group of half a dozen "carders, discarders and dealers in cloth ... to practise and to work their trades" (garzotti, scantezini et revendadori di panni ... a far et esercitar et lavorar delli soi mestieri).[44]

There is also evidence of a considerable traffic in jewels. Presumably the value of the jeweller's wares and the relative ease of their transportation made the journey to Venice, in order to transact business, less taxing than in other trades. Thodesco Figaruol, and others, lodged with Zorzi, a tailor, on 16 September 1530. Galdin from Milan was "a jeweller and setter of jewels, a maker of rings" (zoielier et ligar zoie et far anelli). Upon arrival he was to work his trade in the shop of one Messer Iacomo and to stay with a dealer in second-hand goods, Isepo.

Piero romano, a goldsmith, appears six times in the register. He was host to visitors from Belgrade, to Turks, and to Fabio di Mario, a fellow Roman, who was an apothecary formerly at the Agnus Dei. Piero took in Pamphilo da Spilimbergo, who was sick. On two occasions, however, his responsibilities as host had a strong business dimension. Both of these entries refine his trade as a goldsmith to a "jewel polisher and jeweller" (che conza zoie zoielier). On 28 February 1530 three jewellers arrived from Milan to stay with him. Not long afterwards, on 1 April, he appears to have provided a temporary base from which immigrant goldsmiths could prepare for a longer-term residence in the city. These newcomers had "come to stay in this city to work in the ruga of silverware and works of gold" (venuti a star in questa terra ad lavorar in ruga dei arzenti et lavori d'oro).

What distinguished a short-term visitor from a foreign diplomat, or a Levantine Jew from a patrician officer of the republic who served on the mainland, is difficult to define and hold fast when they might all be staying in the same part of the city, in the hands of a goldsmith, a woman from Verona (or was it Brescia?), a female charcoal dealer, or a stevedore from the German fondaco (an Arabic word italianized to characterize an institution for Germans in Venice). The fondaco, and indeed the inns in the registro "Stella," all functioned in several roles, combining something of the shop, the hostelry, and the trading post. By a fascinating coincidental twist, a trade that also operated independently of government control and exhibited strikingly similar characteristics, accommodated a particular crowd of immigrants who had been driven from a particular region for particular reasons in the precise years 1530–1. This was the business of Venice's guild of ironsmiths (the *fabbri*), and the "commodity that strangers have" was both the convenience of business in Venice and a thing of use, iron.

L'arte dei fabbri

The multiple uses of iron and its range of employment were among the criteria that Giovanni Botero deployed in his definition of the greatness and magnificence of cities. His words provide a useful back-drop for the importance of ironwork and ironworkers in the economy of Venice: "The revenues from iron mines are not very big, but an infinite number of people make their living from working the iron and trading in it; they mine it, refine it and smelt it, they sell it wholesale and retail, they make it into engines of war and weapons for attack and defence, into endless kinds of tools for farming, building and every craft, and for the everyday needs and necessities of life, for which iron is no less needful than bread."[45]

The guild of ironworkers was one of the most ancient of all the incorporated trades of Venice. Probably the first Venetian artisan whom we can name is the "faber" Giovanni Sagornino who appears in an addition to the *Cronaca* of John the Deacon in an entry for the year 1030. Doge Pietro Barbolano (r. 1026–31) had called him to perform labour service in works at the Palazzo Ducale through the gastaldo of the ironsmiths. Sagornino had refused and had appealed against the obligation, an appeal that Doge Domenico Flabianico (r. 1032–43) upheld.[46] The specific circumstance carries a much broader symbolism, for it was this very access to courts of appeal – both for an individual against the guild and for a member of the guild against the government – that was one of the most distinctive features of the history of Venetian arti. Moreover, the dynamic that linked the individual, the corporation, and the polity is symptomatic of precisely that circulation of energetic movement that underpinned the stability of Venice itself.[47]

Those who worked with iron enjoyed a special status celebrated in the main portal of the basilica of San Marco. They were also prominent in the time-honoured festival of Zuoba Grasso (Fat Thursday), when they combined with the city's butchers to slaughter bulls on the Piazza San Marco and then distributed some of the meat among the poor before having a banquet of their own. This strange sacrificial ceremony commemorated the role of the two trades in defending Venice against the ambitious pretensions of the patriarch of Aquileia in 1162. The donation of the bull (along with twelve pigs and three hundred loaves of bread) was the conditional annual tribute to which the patriarch had had to agree in order to secure the release of those of his adherents whom the Venetians had captured. The bloody mayhem of the ritual continued as part of the carnival season until its abolition by the Consiglio dei Dieci in 1525. The driving force of the ban was probably Doge Andrea Gritti and his vision of a grandiose reordering of the heart of the city.[48]

The statute of the ironworkers' formally incorporated "ars fabrorum" dates from its registration with the Giustizia Vecchia on 4 December 1271, only two days after that of their great rivals, the mercers. As confirmation of the obligation that Sagornino had questioned, the very first regulation reminded the guild of its members' duty to labour on the fabric of the doge's palace.[49] At the time, the guild was to hold its meetings at the church of Santa Maria del Tempio, which was between the Piazza San Marco and the church of San Moise (and is not to be confused with the church of San Giovanni del Tempio).[50]

The statute refers to the guild's trade in locks and keys, and then to that in bolts for naval construction.[51] The iron for use by members of the guild came from Cadore, Wallachia ("Vlach"), Carinthia, and Lombardy, but there is also evidence for imports from Feltre, Belluno, Trento, the Trevisana, Friuli, and Istria.[52] Other finished wares were listed as knives, cobblers' awls, meat cleavers, hatchets, razors, anchors, spearheads, and crossbows – a list that spans supplies to other professions and much larger-scale production for the armouries of the state. Charcoal for the braziers that made the iron workable was available only at Rialto. In a careful avoidance of any move towards cornering the supply of raw materials by a monopolist or a cartel, the guild's members requested a quota from a bulk buy of charcoal, a purchase that the guild itself made and then redistributed.[53] Any quota not claimed and paid for would be redistributed among other members who could afford an extra portion of the unclaimed shares.[54]

One of the most striking features of Venice's guilds was their combination of businesses small and large within the same corporation. There was no clear division between guilds of merchants and guilds of producers – institutionalized in Florence, for instance, in the distinction between the Arti Maggiori and the Arti Minori. In Venice's guild of mercers, retail and wholesale trade were never subject to separate regulation. In the case of the ironsmiths there was an easy coexistence of industrial production in a surprising symbiosis of the botteghe in the Calle dei Fabbri – one of the two thoroughfares (the other was the Mercerie) that linked Rialto and San Marco – and the vast docks, warehouses, and foundries of the Arsenale, the largest industrial complex in pre-industrial Europe.[55]

This is particularly surprising given the flames and sparks that were part of the ironsmiths' everyday work, and the understandable concerns of the Venetians to minimize the risk of fires (such as that which had devastated the city in 1104). The government had ordered the transfer of glass manufacture to the island of Murano in 1291 in order to remove the dangers of the furnaces from the heart of the city. Even the design of chimneys in Venice reflected a need to minimize the emission of sparks and hot cinders.[56] One of the most famous words that the Venetians have given to the world derives from an area in Cannaregio that was surrounded on all sides by water, with the only pedestrian access being a single bridge. This place was apparently the site of iron foundries, whence tradition and etymology derive its name: the Ghetto.[57]

Yet the list of wares – ranging from ship's bolts to razors, from large-scale production for the state through supplies to trades such as barbers and shoemakers, to the domestic hardware of ordinary households – linked the life of the Arsenale and the grand enterprise of the state with the routines of the most modest homes. In reality, no great distinction appears to have existed between something very close to mass production and petty retail. Indeed, the symbiosis may even have proved a source of economic strength. Even now, those who buy fish at the Rialto market for the restaurant business buy at the same stalls as do small-scale domestic purchasers.

Certainly, the Arsenale, the "factory of marvels," was notable both for its expanse and for its concentration: its expanse was over sixty acres of land and water, and its concentration was a workforce that ran into thousands.[58] What a contrast with the cramped botteghe of the Calle dei Fabbri, the shop fronts running to just a few feet each, which represented as many as 250 tiny enterprises in 1531. In characterizing the trade of the fabbri, one must find terminology that can cover the whole range of activities between blacksmith and ironmonger. In the later sixteenth century, ironwork accounted for about one-eighth of the total cost of a galley: 4,350 out of 32,250 ducats. However, if artillery at 5,600 ducats is included, then the proportion rises to almost a third.[59]

How then were these two very different areas, the Arsenale and the Calle dei Fabbri, complementary? The most fundamental answer seems to lie in the overlap of personnel. The example of Sagornino and, more emphatically, the statute of 1271 make clear the requirement of labour service to the state. The shipyards did indeed link to the rest of the city. One prominent symbol is that the great foundries of the Arsenale may well have been used in the production of the bronze "Moors" standing atop the Torre dell'Orologio at San Marco – and still tell us the time – and perhaps of church doors or bells.[60] There were technical similarities as well. The skills involved in making pulleys to hoist and haul great ships into dry dock shared the same principles in the making of miniature pulleys for the washing lines that were so essential in households needing to make full use of the city's limited space.[61] One of the clearest indications of interconnection added light fingers to the skill of the hand. Pilferage of the Arsenale's stock by its own workforce was a persistent problem, and the overseers complained of depletions through handfuls of nails that found their way to the miscreant's retail premises.[62]

What is particularly surprising, however, is the strength of the flow of traffic in the other direction, from Rialto to the Arsenale. In this the fabric of the city remains our surest guide. (See map 6, "Rialto and Calle dei Fabbri.") The basic (not quite raw) materials of the ironsmiths' trade arrived for unloading at two "banks" next to each other and to the Rialto itself: iron at the Riva del Ferro and charcoal at the Riva del Carbon.[63] The iron was semi-finished, in "loaves" (pani) or bars. It is important to remember that one metric ton of such iron came out of three tons of rock and had already consumed six tons of charcoal. In the late fifteenth century the charcoal seems to have been moved in baskets of a regulated and often disputed size by the small guild of fifteen porters, the *carboneri*.[64] While the designations show that the materials arrived here at the commercial centre of the city, redistribution was easiest by water. The canal, wide and straight by Venetian standards, runs from San Luca via the Rio de San Luca, the Rio dei Barcaiuoli, and the Rio San Moise and goes direct to the Bacino, eliminating for heavily laden barges and those who rowed them the huge bend in the Canal Grande, which runs from the Riva del Carbon to San Marco via San Samuele. The stretch from the church of San Luca to that of San Moise runs a short distance away from the Calle dei Fabbri and in roughly parallel direction.

The flow of traffic was clearly much more than the retail complement to the industrial production of the Arsenale. We know that the fabbri stored their supplies of charcoal in the scuola at San Moise. The location in itself is a reminder of the link between profitable economic activity and the religious values that directed it, and with the cult of Moses – the leader of a large following of refugees who were mutually related. Moreover, if attention expands to include the Calle dei Fabbri, then the activities pursued there by the ironsmiths suggest a dynamic equilibrium with the Arsenale itself. This in turn is evoked in the areas that designated particular ironware for naval and military use.

The Calle dei Fabbri begins for those on foot between the churches of San Luca and San Salvador (close to the Riva del Ferro and the Riva del Carbon) and proceeds to San Marco (much more directly than the Mercerie) via the parish of San Geminiano. The Calle del Carbon provides another route to San Marco and specifically to the ironsmiths' warehouse and their scuola at the church of San Moise, via the Calle dei Fuseri, where the makers of anchor shanks and capstan spindles had their workshops. The end of this narrow street marks the beginning of the Frezzaria where the master ironsmiths produced arrows and crossbow bolts. The alley opens near the church of San Moise, by the scuola. Here one stands at the site of a complex once defined by the making of anchors: "anchore" had their own calle, sottoportico, corte, and ponte. According to Tassini, anchors for the fleet were the principal product of these workshops, and he cites legislation from 1332 regulating the quality of iron to be used.[65] A short distance away, turning left out of the Frezzaria – in a brief walk via what was once the church of San Geminiano, onwards via part of the piazza, then over the Ponte dei Dai – lies the Calle dei Fabbri itself. This in turn links by way of "Buckle Alley" (Calle Fiubera) to the church of San Zulian at the end of one section of the Mercerie, and thence to the Spadaria, with its own access to the piazza. That this was the territory of the swordsmiths is emblazoned in a sculpted relief in which the lion of San Marco stands proudly above three blades. The swordsmiths (*spaderi*) combined in the same corporation with cutlers and sheath makers (*vazineri*). Perhaps the latter also made scabbards, which would provide another overlap of warlike preparation and domestic provision in this sector of the economic life of Venice.

In summary: supplies of iron and charcoal arrived at the Rialto. The guild distributed the charcoal among members according to their indents. The guild controlled the quality of the iron. Members could produce a wide variety of goods, including bolts that held together the timbers of ships, capstans, anchors, domestic cutlery, and pots and pans. Other goods in the intense concentration of shops between Rialto and San Marco included arrows (often crossbow bolts) and swords, as well as cutlery.

Who were the buyers? The state surely drew supplies of weaponry from this complex of workshops. From the fabbri, ordinary residents could obtain hardware and certain domestic necessaries for cooking, eating, and laundry (one thinks once again of the market for washing-line pulleys). However, this was surely not a set of botteghe that drew the attention of visitors with money to spare for the luxuries of Venice. These they could seek and find in the shops of each section of the Mercerie. The Calle dei Fabbri was no place for gewgaws or trinkets. One way of understanding the coexistence is perhaps to bear in mind that the shops in the Calle dei Fabbri supplied bulk wares to the organizers of building projects – nails, balconies, bars for windows – wholesale, but on commission and not from stores.[66]

In listing "the notable things that are shown to lords [people of importance] in Venice" (le cosse notabile si mostrano a signori in Veniexia), Sanudo included the Arsenale and the "Marzaria" but does not appear to have given the Calle dei Fabbri a thought. Visitors would have had to request a tour.[67] It is also notable that Sanudo's list provides a subtle template for visitors' descriptions of Venice from the late fifteenth century to the mid-seventeenth. One looks in vain for a reference to the Calle dei Fabbri in the descriptions of Canon Pietro Casola in 1494, the merchant Arnold von Harff in 1497, William Thomas in 1549, Fynes Moryson in 1595, William Lithgow in 1609, Thomas Coryate in about 1610, or John Evelyn in 1646 – despite the fact that the Mercerie impressed them all, and most of them marvelled at the Arsenale. One can only speculate that some of those who saw the Mercerie may have strayed into a street only a few grains of an hour-glass away. If so, they may have contrasted the soft luxuries of the mercers with the warlike preparedness and everyday necessity of the ironsmiths' wares, but none of them was so impressed as to comment for posterity.

However, there is room for the interjection that the shops provided equipment for the Venetian militia. From the fourteenth century weekly training took place on the Lido in the use of the crossbow for men between sixteen and thirty-five years of age as identified by the Capi di Contrada. According to Sanudo, this continued in the sixteenth century with regular bows. Later the Consiglio dei Dieci ordered training with firearms ("schiopeti et archibusi").[68] Machiavelli must have envied the Venetians such a citizen army.

In contrast, the Mercerie were the famous preserve of Venice's luxury trades, providing Venetians and visitors with the opulent temptations of all life's inessentials. Yet in the journey that we have just made from Rialto to San Marco, the mercers and their goods were flanked by walls of iron. The fabbri and the marzeri were constant rivals, and their seemingly incessant litigation can read as a drain on their economic energies. However, there is a revealing symbolism in the character of the main routes between Rialto and San Marco. The one offered wares as hard as iron; the other, goods as soft as silk. Between Venice's commercial heart at Rialto and the city's political and religious centre at

San Marco were hundreds of premises that combined the advertisement of armed power with the richest comforts that prosperity could offer.

There is even a symbolism in the quarrels of ironsmiths and mercers over the goods that each claimed the privilege to sell. The mercer Bartolomeo Bontempelli at once comes to mind. He appears in the records of the mercers in the 1560s as a shopkeeper at the sign of il Calise (the Chalice), and the show of his "divers suits of gold" at Carnival was well known, as were his regular window displays. He also supplied the republic – almost certainly not through the arte dei fabbri – with iron taken from his mines near Agordo in the Venetian territories north of Belluno. He became a cittadino and was a member of several scuole that were to benefit from his wealth. Bontempelli made a bequest of the interest on a sum of 100,000 ducats to the Scuola Grande di San Rocco. He was one of the founders of the Scuola del Rosario at San Zanipolo in 1575. He offered the English ambassador (Sir Dudley Carleton) a refurnishing of his residence, apparently as a gesture of goodwill towards the representative of a Protestant state. Bontempelli also offered the republic 100,000 ducats towards any war effort that it might launch against the papacy. We can still see his likeness in a conventionally devout altarpiece that he commissioned for the church of San Salvador, which was home to several confraternities (see fig. 30). The speculation that he may have moved in the circle of Paolo Sarpi when it assembled at the Nave d'Oro (the shop of a fellow mercer, of Flemish origin, Francesco Zecchini) is tempting. Bontempelli was a man who dealt in raw materials in bulk and in finished products for retail premises and who disposed of considerable capital. He was also a figure who moved from modest premises near the Rialto via membership of arte, scuola dell'arte, scuola piccola, and Scuola Grande to giddying circles at the height of political influence. His career subverts any idea that the Venetian constitution protected the exclusive political monopoly of a merchant patriciate. In light of such an example, rather than representing a bifurcation of the warlike and the luxurious, the Calle dei Fabbri and the Mercerie prompt the idea that a mailed fist could always find a velvet glove and that makers of either or both could wield considerable influence within the political economy of Venice.[69]

For the moment, it is useful to concentrate on the physical space of the ironsmiths in Venice. At San Moise, the southern end of the thoroughfare that proclaimed their trade, stood both the warehouse for their scuola and the meeting place for their devotional confraternity. At some point the scuola had been located at the Frari. It remained at the church of San Moise until 1582, when it began a twenty-year stay at the church of San Vitale. When it returned to San Moise in 1602, it enjoyed the patronage of three saints: Sant'Alo (Saint Eligius), San Liberale (Saint Liberalis), and San Giovanni Battista. The Lombard connection also stamped upon the scuola the imprint of the Catholic revival, and San Carlo Borromeo joined the patrons after his canonization in 1610.[70] The paradox of this elevation will explain itself in due course. The economic life of the fabbri was subject to the regulations contained in their statute, which in turn bore the authorization of the state. The same statute and the same authorization were linked to the religious brotherhood to which members might look if and when they needed the administration of the works of corporal mercy.

Strands of Identity

The physical environment as it now exists is suggestive and evocative of an energetic microcosm of economics, politics, and religion. The records of the guild of ironsmiths provide much more detail on the dynamics of cohesion within the corporation, though from a very different perspective. The records are fairly typical of Venetian guilds in providing evidence of extensive litigation, and the next chapter examines these materials from the perspective of the ironsmiths' principal rivals, the mercers, who sought to dominate not only their own "Marzarie" but also the Calle dei Fabbri of the ironmongers, and thus the two principal thoroughfares between Rialto and San Marco. Otherwise, the documents that survive are disappointingly jejune, except in one important respect. Like those of the mercers, the records of the ironsmiths contain some unusually full lists. One of these gives details of bulk purchases of charcoal, which are published elsewhere.[71] Another is an inventory of the liturgical accoutrements of the scuola, which represent the material impact of the confraternities on Venetian religious life.

Those documents that compel attention in an exposition focused upon the identities of the Venetians are lists of members. There are four such lists in all.[72] Three date from 1530–1 and are the guild's compilation for the Savi sopra le Tansse (ministers over taxes), presumably at their behest. The first list is of the ironsmiths who were enrolled in the scuola. It dates from 6 January 1530 (the Feast of the Three Magi). The second dates from 10 January 1531 and has a pivotal role in explaining the striking differences between the first and third. The third is from only a few days later, on 21 January 1531. This one lists members of the arte and the taxes for which they were liable. It is not entirely clear that a collection took place, but each page gives a total of its number of names and the total sum anticipated. The guild submitted the first list to the Savi sopra le Tanse with a note that an alphabetical book had been lodged with the Cinque Savi sopra le Mariegole (the five ministers over statute books) on 11 January.

These first three lists span barely a year. Given the range of occupational titles displayed by the lists, it is safe to assert that the manual skills of the ironsmiths were of a high order. However, the first and the third lists show a surprising lack of overlap in terms of a continuing recorded membership. It is only upon investigation of the circumstances prevailing at the time of the third compilation that we may understand the kind of forces that could have effected so dramatic a change. The composite of all three lists of 1530–1 is revealing in this regard.

Before embarking on the sea of detail, it is apposite to suggest the significance of people's movements to and from Venice and in or out of such lists. Beneath the calm surface of La Serenissima was a complex of currents that were constant only in their motion. The variations in the composition of a single corporation within a bare twelve months give an intriguing picture of the tidal movements of humanity from which the Venetian political economy drew such energy. Moreover, the documentation demonstrates the flexibility of Venetian guilds in the incorporation and accommodation of newcomers from a wide geographical area.

The nature of their trade, of necessity, took the ironsmiths some distance from the lagoon. This was fundamentally a question of the bulk supplies of the requisite materials, iron and charcoal. As noted, the statute of 1271 sought to regulate the quality of iron by stipulating particular sources of supply. Once again, however, it is essential to be aware of the degree to which the economic life of the guilds operated independently of the government. There was no staple centred on Venice that regulated the market.[73] Given the importance of iron to farms, houses, and the military, the Venetians took their supplies whence they could obtain them. In the thirteenth century such sources included Gorizia and Austria via Friuli. Styria and Carinthia supplied Friuli rather than Venice. The land routes for the iron trade comprised Udine, Cadore (with its links to Zoldano, the Agordino, and Belluno), Trento, Padua, and Vicenza. Ironsmiths in Treviso, Pordenone, and Ceneda gave serious competition to the masters of the trade in Venice. From the fourteenth century the water mills needed in iron processing put the city at further disadvantage. This was the case also in the manufacture of woollen cloth.[74] With the extension of the mainland state in the quattrocento, more sources of supply became available, especially after the Peace of Lodi in 1454, when the Venetian presence in the Bergamasco became much more prominent.[75] Still Venice played no part in redistribution. As late as 1488 the Senate continued to lament its incapacity to control the trade even as far as Padua.[76]

Supply was complicated. Transport costs were much lower by water than by land.[77] Although the river routes did not run continuously in Venetian territory, there was a market in Venice for semi-finished ore from Lombardy, which arrived as bars, wire, or plate at the Riva del Ferro. The suppliers were producers and merchants in Brescia and Bergamo. One can see just how important the Lombard connection was to become. Yet the trade itself eluded any effective government control. Fraud and corruption were endemic, and the needs of the Arsenale were such that the state could not be particular about the routes or means by which the iron reached it. As early as 1419 it became permissible for anyone to bring iron to Venice. The state could not afford to be stiff necked about regulation in the face of the imperatives of defence and the private enterprise that would bring in supplies via trading links with the Terraferma.[78]

The first catalogue of names is the most detailed and sheds some light upon the ways in which the compilers recorded identification, and the subjects thought of their identities. It offers a number of pointers towards an answer to the question "Who were the Venetians?" And it raises further questions which we may ask of all the lists. How did people in Venice make sense of themselves? How did they come to know who they were? How did they communicate this to others? How did observers and compilers identify a particular person as an individual distinguished from others?

To be precise, there were ten elements of identification in all, though no individual entry combines each and every one of them. Such precision is unusual in guild records.[79] It also stands in contrast to the vague records of visitors to the city whose accommodation was the responsibility of the Giustizia Nova. In addition, it prompts the idea that those who were members of a Venetian scuola attached to a trade guild could braid, as it were, some combination of up to ten such strands in order to fashion an individual self, always within the all-embracing eleventh, the collective identity of a particular corporation. It is intriguing to wonder how this might have strengthened a sense of selfhood in a city in which so many people were immigrants or transients. How, if at all, the collective historical identity remained alive in the guild – for example, in traditions passed on by some masters to their apprentices – remains a matter of speculation.[80]

The guild made a general distinction in the subdivision of the list between ironsmiths (*fabbri*) and those who worked with scrap (*strazzaferri*). There are 242 names on the list, comprising 192 fabbri and 50 strazzaferri. The ten elements that provide identification within the collectivity of the guild are as follows. The first three elements occur regularly in that order; the other seven strands are less predictable.

1. Title: *Ser* in each case in this list.
2. Christian name: in alphabetical order.
3. Father's Christian name.

4. Family name: in a very few cases. This category subsumes the occasional nickname, which is often indistinguishable unless preceded by *ditto* (called).
5. Place of origin: only very rarely is this listed as Venice.
6. Occupational title: there are many different and highly specialized trades within the guild.
7. Location: usually by parish.
8. Location: occasionally by street, but this does not exclude category number 7.
9. Shop sign: in fifty-two cases.
10. In receipt of alms: there are a dozen examples of the description "povero alle limosine."

These categories are in many ways artificially precise. Family names or surnames were uncommon, and only became the norm after the Council of Trent's insistence on the keeping of baptismal records in the mid-sixteenth century. The category of "nickname," apparently light-hearted in English, was often a refinement of identity and might involve a precise place of birth. In Premana in Eastern Lombardy at the northern end of the Val Sassina, a place that had a long and steady rhythm of emigration to Venice, there were only a few family names, perhaps ten or twelve, and these were constantly ornamented by "sopranomi." In these lists the designation "dalla Vorcha," which appears to be an unidentifiable shop sign, is in fact Orca, a small suburb of the town of Lecco.[81]

Among the longest entries is "Ser Passin di Zuan da Chiusa Barozi a San Zuminian calder ala Zustitia," which records eight elements (nos. 1, 2, 3, 5, 4, 6, 7, 8). Quite a number deploy seven elements, such as these three in succession: "Ser maino de Iacomo da versass favro a San Zuminian tien l'agate" (nos. 1, 2, 3, 5, 6, 7, 9); "Ser martin de martin da ollin calder a san luca tien san martin" (nos. 1, 2, 3, 4, 6, 7, 9, with the shop sign of the name saint reinforcing the identity of the proprietor); and "Ser matio di piero burrifaldi calderer a san salvador tien la torre" (nos. 1, 2, 3, 4, 6, 7, 9). Most entries seem to record five or six of the possible components. That of "Ser bastian favro a santa margarita" (nos. 1, 2, 6, 8) is most unusual in using only four. The designations used most consistently are title, Christian name, father's name, and parish. Those elements enable a tabulation that shows the overwhelming concentration of business activity between Rialto and San Marco in the neighbourhood of the Calle dei Fabbri (table 3.1).

Thus, 173 members of 242 had their businesses in the area of the Calle dei Fabbri in eleven different parishes plus the Pellizeria and the Frezzaria. By far the highest number of ironsmiths was found in San Luca (sixty-five, of which

Table 3.1. The Calle dei Fabbri, 1530–1

Parish	Fabbri	[Signs]	Strazzaferri	Total
San Luca	39	[18]	26	65
San Geminiano	41	[17]	4	45
San Salvador	17	[9]	6	23
San Zulian	8	[4]	1	9
San Basso	5	–	–	5
San Lio	5	[2]	–	5
Santa Maria Formosa	6	[1]	1	7
Santa Marina	4	–	–	4
San Moise	4	[1]	–	4
San Paternian	2	–	1	3
San Bortolomeo	1	–	–	1
Rialto in Pellizeria	1	–	–	1
Frezzaria	1	–	–	1
Elsewhere in San Marco, Cas-	134	[52]	39	173
tello, Cannaregio (20 parishes)	30	–	1	31
Other side of Canal Grande	23	–	9	32
Unspecified	5	–	1	6
Total	192	[52]	50	242

thirty-nine were fabbri and twenty-six strazzaferri), San Geminiano (forty-five, of which forty-one were fabbri, but only four strazzaferri), with San Salvador a remote third (twenty-three, of which seventeen were fabbri and six strazzaferri). The shop sign was an advertisement requiring some investment. All fifty-two of these on the list in question were found in the Calle dei Fabbri or very nearby. There was a scattering of premises throughout the city, but only twenty-three ironsmiths' shops on the other side of the Canal Grande.

The pattern for the strazzaferri taken separately is much the same; forty listed in the area around San Marco (thirty-six at Rialto), and only nine across the Canal Grande. None of them had a sign. It may well have been the case that scrap iron dealers were itinerant. They appear so in the eighteenth-century collection of Gaetano Zompini depicting street trades. Here the strazzaferri go from door to door offering to repair basins and cooking pots and, in an intriguing diversification, to castrate cats.[82]

The second compilation lists members according to their regional origins. There was certainly a long tradition of immigration to Venice from Lombardy, and the connection was neither new nor sudden. All the same, the circumstances that drove many ironworkers to Venice provide an example of economic migration spurred by the urgency of an immediate situation. The medium- and long-term consequences prompt comparison with the largely short-term visitors who appear in the records of the Giustizia Nova. However, we will defer extensive consideration of the circumstances.

The third list, of just over a year after the first, yields less extensive data and continues the baffling variety of trades. The list contains 213 entries, usually of only four or five strands of identification. The subdivisions are not alphabetical but rather seem to be organized around contiguous addresses, presumably for ease of collecting the specified dues: Spadaria and Curazaria, then Cassellaria and San Lio and Santa Marina, Castello, the Calle dei Fabbri, and then the other side of the Rialto. The sum for collection from the 213 entries is 29 lire 14 soldi. There is no formal recognition of a group of strazzaferri; perhaps they were not included. In ninety-four cases no occupation is specified. Of those occupations that are, by far the most frequent are ironsmiths (twenty-eight) and makers of domestic pots for polenta ("caldera," thirty). There were nine working with vice and file ("da le lime"), nine locksmiths, three clockmakers, a bell maker, and a host of trades: makers of shackles ("maniglie"), of stoves ("fa stuore"), wire ("da le vergole"), hair clips ("fa rize"), locks ("da locheti"), gun barrels ("di schiopi").[83]

The member who was described as a "maker of dolphins" (fa li dolfini) may have fashioned decorations for gondole.[84] The occupational title "fa ferri da denti" probably designates a maker of dental instruments. Even more problematic than the occupational titles is the fact that only thirty-nine names are common to both this compilation and the first one, that of 1530. An explanation of such a startling speed of turnover in the membership lies in the second list of the 1530–1 records, which dates from 10 January 1531.

The composite list, which is too long to include here, shows the speedy rate of change within the membership, a feature we shall see repeated in the guild of mercers. The consolidation of the three lists is based upon scrutiny of each entry and the matching of the ten components set out previously. The variations in the guild's own lists are striking in themselves, which reveals how difficult it was in a pre-statistical age for agencies in authority to identify who was who. The lists remind us of how impossible it was for the Venetian government to be all-seeing and all-knowing, regardless of the reputation it came to acquire. More important still, we should remember that such data as the government gathered and relied upon were the autonomous compilations of the very corporations that the state was assumed to control so closely.

Some cautious general observations are possible, however. A composite of the lists produces 242 entries on the first list from January 1530, with 158 from the second (10 January 1531), and 213 from the third (21 January 1531). The numerical variations reflect the fact that the lists do not form a series and were not compiled with the same scope and purpose. Even so, these 613 entries represent no fewer than 476 different people. Of those, 365 (about 80 per cent) appear only once: 152 on the first list, 70 on the second, and 143 on the third. Only 22 names appear on all three lists (under 5 per cent). Only 39 appear on both the first and the second list (under 8.5 per cent), only 18 on the second and the third (under 4 per cent), and only 16 on the first and the third (barely 3.5 per cent). What explains these extraordinary variations in the membership of a single highly skilled corporation? In order to answer this question, it is necessary to turn attention to the western frontier of the Venetian state and to the eastern lands of the Duchy of Milan.

"Quel ramo del lago di Como"

The opening line of Alessandro Manzoni's great novel, *I Promessi Sposi*, written in the age of the Risorgimento but set in the days of the travails of Spanish Lombardy in the seventeenth century – "Quel ramo del lago di Como" – directs attention to the author's homeland (Manzoni was born in Lecco) on the eastern shore of Lake Como. It was precisely this small region that was to play a fascinating and revealing part in the history of Venice's guild of ironsmiths in 1530–1.[85]

Human and commercial exchange between Venetian territory and Lombardy had been a steady process with a long history. The proximity of the lands of La Serenissima to those of the Duchy of Milan increased throughout the fifteenth century as the republic extended its mainland state. With the acquisition of the Bresciano and the Bergamasco between the 1420s and 1441, the lands of the Venetians came to border on those of the Ambrosian Republic. The Milanese had established a scuola for their nation in Venice itself at the church of the Frari in 1361. Members of the Lombardo family, notably Pietro, Tullio, and Antonio, were among the most skilful of the stonemasons who worked in Venice in the quattrocento, and the handiwork that they fashioned still graces some of the most beautiful places in Venice, such as the church of Santa Maria dei Miracoli (the work of the Lombardi probably dates from the late 1480s). Tullio may have embellished the work of Bartolomeo Bon on the choir screens at the Frari.[86] It was a canon of Milan's cathedral, Pietro Casola, who wrote one of the most laudatory accounts of Venice as he waited to depart on a pilgrimage to the Holy Land in 1494. His description is full of apologies to his own city for the implicit denigration in giving Venice pride of place in the variety of its wares, in the whiteness of its wax, in the quantity of victuals (though not their quality), and in the splendour of its churches.

As noted, Casola did not refer to the Calle dei Fabbri. However, he recorded the marvellous impression that the iron works of the Arsenale left upon him in its production of the wares commemorated in the street names near Rialto: "There are also masters continually occupied in making crossbows, bows and large and small arrows; and all by order of the Signoria. In one great covered place, there are twelve masters each one with his own workmen and his forge apart; and they labour continually making anchors and every other kind of ironwork for the galleys and other ships. There seems to be there all the iron that could be dug out of all the mountains of the world."[87]

He seems unaware that some of the iron may have been dug out of mountains in his homeland. The ironsmiths' guild clearly drew a considerable number of members from the Lombard region. The consolidated list for 1530–1, for instance, names at least thirteen masters who were called after Ambrose or Ambrogio (mangled into dialect as "Ambroxo" or "Ambruoxo"), patron saint of Milan. (By contrast, only seven take the name of Venice's patron saint, Marco.) The connection of the guild to a specific area of Lombardy is manifestly clear in a list of masters that the guild's officers compiled in 1531.

The list is dated 10 January, just ten days before the scuola submitted its list to the Savi sopra le Tanse. The terms of reference are unusual, but unusually clear. "These are all those who are called when we have our general meeting, who vote in the said meeting, copied from the book [that] was sent to the Five Lords Expert on the Statute Books ..." The concluding phrase of the compiler's description appears to be unique for its time in all the documentation left behind by Venetian guilds: "... and of what nation they are as here below distinct one by one annotated appears. And first..."[88]

The subdivisions of the list that then follow show how tiny and how precise the idea of a "nation" (the Venetian word) could be among immigrant groups in Venice: *piccolo mondo antico.* Antonio Fogazzaro's story of love and loss in Lombardy in the age of the Risorgimento offers the historian of sixteenth-century Venice two fascinating insights. The first is the extraordinarily localized dialects. Fogazzaro's imaginary account of the exchanges of a Paduan with a Lombard from Lake Lugano evokes the strange noises that would have characterized the conversations of the Venetian ironsmiths' guild. Second, the author's use of *natio* as an adjective, omitting the *v* of *nativo* – on one occasion quoting Bellini's opera *Maria Stuarda* – offers insight into just how close the identification of birthplace with "nation" could be in that "piccolo mondo antico."[89] In the lists that the fabbri compiled in 1531, certainly, the term *nation* seems to apply to place of birth or homeland rather than to any larger entity, secular or ecclesiastical. The subdivisions are as follows: [90]

Quelli che sono da Ballabio	(there follow 34 names)
Questi sono de Valde saxena	(19)

Questi sono da Mandello	(10)
Questi sono da lecho	(28)
Questi sono li bregamaschi	(17)
Questi sono li Venetiani	(29)
Questi sono di Albania	(1)
Greci	(1)
Furllani	(2)
Schiavoni	(4)
Bressani	(2)
Cremonesi	(1)
Cremaschi	(2)

Several observations are immediately pertinent. First, the reader of these records is struck by their neatness and precision (and legibility). There is a stark contrast to the haphazard and patchy documentation of the Giustizia Nova. Other scholars have noted the inadequacies of the Provveditori di Comun – one of the protagonists of government as far as the scuole were concerned – in their efforts to keep track of immigrants to Venice, especially in the case of those who came from outside the territories of the republic.[91] Second, barely one-fifth of the members describe themselves as Venetians. Third, nearly half of all the names designate an area of mainland Italy between Bergamo and Lake Como. Fourth, of that group, more than three-quarters apparently came from places outside of Venetian territory. Fifth, thanks to the diligence of the compiler, each member bears the title "maestro" (not "ser" as in the other lists). Finally, that formal technical qualification clearly marks the holder as someone who cast a ballot in the guild's deliberations and resolutions ("liqualli balloteno InditoCapitolo"). Each master had a right to participate in the election of the guild's officials and to express a view for or against a proposed resolution or policy. Such information is very striking in the answer it provides to the question "Who were the Venetians?" Moreover, the second list, which is divided according to nation or place of birth, specifies "who cast votes in the said meeting" (also its heading), which adds range to the spectrum of representation, a theme of the book as a whole. Where then had these ironsmiths come from? And why had they come to Venice?

Ballabio, Val Sassina, Mandello, and Lecco – these were the homelands of 91 of the guild's 158 members. Thus, almost three-fifths of the members of the arte dei fabbri in Venice were from places clearly and specifically very near to "quel ramo del lago di Como," the area which Manzoni describes at the start of his epic and romantic novel. This region was not within the territories of the Venetian Republic. Nevertheless, Manzoni himself recognized or knew the historical porosity of the Milanese and Venetian border. The hero of his story, Renzo, aspires to a life of peace under Venetian jurisdiction, away from war-torn Lombardy.[92] Such a contrast and such an aspiration also existed in 1531. The Venetian territory of the Bergamasco virtually blended into the Milanese province of Lecco.

Lecco, Ballabio, Val Sassina, and Mandello all lay in the geographical extension of Venice's westernmost province of Bergamo, beyond its political limit into the most easterly area of the Milanese between the western limit of the Alpi Orobie and the eastern shore of Lake Como. Those same mountains define the northern limit of Venice's Bergamasque province. On both sides of the political border the land is hard and mountainous, though very green. In a few minutes in a motor vehicle one may move from lakeside to mountain top. The Venetians had difficulty securing the Val Brembana, which linked the city of Bergamo to the Valtellina. In geological terms, the area seems a world away from the fertile Lombard plain, which is in fact adjacent to it in the south. (See map 8, "Lake Como and Its Environs.") From this region in a northward direction there were routes (difficult routes) overland to Constance and the cities of Germany and the Swiss Confederation via the Stelvio and Brenner passes and Bolzano.[93] Venice had clearer control of two other northward routes, one via Treviso, Belluno, and Pieve di Cadore, and the other via Trento and Bolzano. To the south there was the less demanding river route from Lecco via the Ghiara d'Adda – recognized by the Venetians as under Milanese jurisdiction – to the River Po, which then runs via Cremona, the Mantovano, and Ferrara to the Adriatic Sea. The area of Lombardy that sent so many ironsmiths to Venice was notorious as a corridor for contraband.[94] The Venetian government's eventual decision to begin the building of new fortifications at Bergamo in the 1580s was perhaps symptomatic of a desire to define a border, but only once it was clear that Lombardy was firmly under Habsburg control. During the episode to which we now devote attention, the lack of clear sovereignty may well have suited all those, including the republic, who stood to gain by the vagueness.[95]

This same small area was typical of the larger region – rocky and chronically short of cereals. There was some stock rearing, and the area offered Alpine pasturage for the summer months to animals from the Lombard plain. The main resource of the area was iron, essential to Venice as a maritime and military power, but not a commodity that came through Venice as its monopoly.[96]

The Venetians had some significant sources of iron within their provinces of Bergamo and the Bresciano, especially in the Val di Sclave.[97] There was an awareness of the connection of the importance of the republic's western provinces as a producer of armour, and of Venice's vulnerability to attack from the westward. In his *Ragguagli di Parnaso* (1610) Traiano Boccalini addressed with some sarcasm Venice's need for not only a breastplate against the Turks but also a backplate against Christian enemies, for "every time that it has confronted the Turk, in all of Brescia it has never been able to find a corselet to cover its back."[98] Venetian interests probably commanded a workforce of 3,000–4,000 people in the mines and furnaces.[99] In 1539, estimates suggest that Venetian territories produced 2,500 metric tons of iron per year, about one-third of the production of Italy as a whole. The Venetian total included 240 tonnes of arms, 190 tonnes of nails, and 470 tonnes of agricultural implements.[100]

The Lecco–Val Sassina region was to become the chief mining area of Spanish Lombardy in the seventeenth century.[101] By that time, the concentration of Venetian interests had shifted to Friuli, especially the area of the Agordino.[102] The mines and blast furnaces of Val Sassina probably produced 1,000 metric tons of pig iron annually. The excavations have proved so extensive that locals know the area as "the Gruyère mountains" because they are so full of holes. Once dug from the hills, the ore was carried in baskets on the backs of women to the furnaces, where it was smelted and then moved by mule to Lecco.[103] There is no evidence here, however, to demonstrate the export of iron from this area to Venice. Moreover, the logistical problems of transportation would have been formidably daunting. In times of peace the iron would probably have gone via Lecco to the armourers of Milan. That said, a region that might prove the source of a commodity vital to Venice's interests, outside Venetian territory but contiguous across a very ill-defined border, at a time of grievous political upheaval in Lombardy and Milan, would have made a substantial supplementary contribution to Venetian supplies.

The people of the Bergamasco–Val Sassina were the product of the region. Matteo Bandello (1485–1561), the storyteller, described his homeland as "mountainous, rugged, wild and stony."[104] Near the river, those who worked at the forges were among other riverbank trades such as millers, fullers, fishermen, ferrymen, and those who provided horses for towage.[105] In Val Sassina itself, perhaps two-thirds of the valley's population worked as miners, lumbermen, muleteers, and refiners.[106]

Alongside such activities in the area itself, emigration must take its paradoxical place: one of the chief characteristics of the region was that its people often left it. There was a natural circulation in the Bergamasco from countryside to town as shortages forced people to leave rural areas. In the village of Olmo in Venetian territory to the east of Val Sassina, a document of 1606 listed 151 people of the population of 375 "absent." The causes of poverty in the area were legion. Aside from infertile land, any combination of oppression, a need for alms, intermittently soaring grain prices, and even low pay could throw locals on to the network of institutions called "Misericordiae." In Venetian territory there were 143 such agencies in 249 localities. Later, in 1575, the Misericordia of Bergamo had seven thousand people on its books, more than a quarter of the city's population. One estimate suggests that five people in eight found emigration a temporary or longer-term necessity.[107]

An eye for commercial advantage found reflection in a tendency for natives of the Bergamasco to advance their fortunes in Venice. Brian Pullan once asserted that the cittadini of Venice formed "a frozen middle class denied the notorious pastime of rising."[108] Some immigrants from Bergamo found ways to avoid becoming frozen in this way and sometimes traversed the full spectrum of the Venetian social order. The Carminati and the Bergonzi made fortunes in the mercers' guild. They were among eighteen families from Bergamo to enter the ranks of the Venetian patriciate from 1646 to 1649. Of the total aggregations (eighty-two families by one calculation) those of Vicentine origin were only seven, and those from Brescia only four.[109] Other prominent entrepreneurial families from Bergamo included the della Vecchia and the Zechinelli from the Valle Brembana Superiore, and the Locatelli may have hailed from the Val Sassina.[110]

To these movements of people from region to region and through the ranks of the social order, the role of the Venetian state seems to have been largely irrelevant, except in so far as the lightness of governmental structures limited its capacity to interfere. As in the development of the constitution, so in the acquisition of the Terraferma, there was no grand design. The acquisitions were piecemeal and empirical. On the mainland the government in Venice depended on reaching accommodations with local power structures and the balance of social forces within them. Additionally, the character of Venetian rule in any of its "dependent" regions was subject to the formative influence of local conditions, both traditional and circumstantial. What can appear pragmatic and flexible might have been incomplete and imprecise, and there is no reason to insist that the one possibility excluded the other. The machinery of government that the Venetians might mobilize was very slight. In 1495 the personnel of the Venetian Republic on the Terraferma numbered about 130 officers. There were advantages to this lightness. La Serenissima had not subjected its new territories to wholesale plunder and had not imposed alien constitutional arrangements. However, this minimalist attention to military, fiscal, and economic matters may have been the outcome of an incapacity for vigorous enforcement rather than of political judgment of the need for restraint.[111] For all that, by the mid-sixteenth century, once the state had reassembled itself after the collapse of 1509, the congeries of Venetian territories sounded a curious harmony. The population of Venice itself was around 150,000 persons, and this appears to have found a rough equivalence in Friuli, the Trevigiano, the Vicentino, the

Veronese, and the Bresciano. The example of the Bergamasco at about 200,000 souls unbalances the symmetry but only slightly.[112] Overall, it seems fair to say that the *dominio* of the *Dominante* was, of necessity, locally sensitive and generally light. Perhaps this was true of all sixteenth-century governments. However, the Republic of Venice was less likely than other states to impose sudden and burdensome expedients in the interests of raising money for war.[113]

These cautious generalizations may be applicable to the mainland in the fifteenth and sixteenth centuries. The intensity of the forces that drove people from their homeland and the complementarity of those that drew them to Venice became especially powerful in the years around 1530. Particularly arresting is the evidence suggesting that, while conditions in the city were quite dreadful at the time, the extent of upheaval and uncertainty on the mainland was even greater and drove emigrants to seek sustenance in Venice.

After the Sack of Rome in 1527, all of the Italian states, bar Venice, seemed to have fallen under the de facto dominion of foreign powers. In Venice itself the conditions of life deteriorated dramatically as famine and disease compounded the horrors of war. Floods in the late 1520s had intensified shortages of grain. The resources available for distribution as alms or food were entirely inadequate for the numbers of the poor. Those numbers swelled drastically with huge influxes of people from the Terraferma. The grimness of Sanudo's account of starving children in the streets of Venice begging for bread dates from 1527, and the gloom deepens when he laments the lack of government action. In February of the following year, beggars from Vicenza and Brescia were swarming all over Venice, and still there was no public provision.[114]

The situation could not ease in isolation, because pressure from the mainland continually added to it. In March 1528 Luigi da Porto wrote from Vicenza to Giovanni Morelli in Venice. He described an outbreak of disease that appears to have been typhus. There was nowhere in Vicenza that one could avoid hundreds of beggars who were so famished that their eye sockets looked like rings without gemstones, nothing but skin and bone. Da Porto attributed the problems in his native city to the influx of people from rural areas, especially from Alpine villages.[115]

The complex of pressures in the emergency forced new initiatives upon the authorities in Venice, if only to maintain some semblance of public order. Again, the innovations did not derive from governmental creativity, but rather relied upon the allocation of new burdens to guilds, parishes and the recently formed Eucharistic confraternities.[116]

It seems all the more remarkable that within a matter of three years the guild of ironsmiths was able to record so neat, orderly, and systematic a list of all its members, some four-fifths of them newcomers in the year 1530–1.

The circumstances of the 1520s and 1530s were dire, but the absorption of newcomers was certainly something that guilds sought to regulate. The stonemasons who had arrived in large numbers from Lombardy at the end of the fifteenth century had been expected to enrol in the guild within eight days, and if any master was away from Venice for more than a year, he was expected to start his membership again upon his return.[117] So, in the crisis conditions at the end of the 1520s, the guilds had a mechanism in place to accommodate immigrants, while the government measures, slow to mobilize, aimed to contain the problems caused by unprecedented numbers of beggars.

It is worth reiteration that the newly arrived ironsmiths were formally enrolled as guild-masters who could anticipate full participation and representation in the corporation's affairs. Perhaps the newcomers had commercial links with Lombards already enrolled as members in the arte dei fabbri.

In the homeland of these ironworkers near Lake Como, trading in iron between the mountains and the lake would never have been easy even in time of peace. There were iron deposits in the Val Sassina, whose geography is something between a valley and a plateau, narrow, flat, and straight, with the convenience of water from the River Pioverna through all its length, as well as plentiful supplies of timber. Now, ironworks (and dairies) line it on both sides, and the imagination can see the advantages that mines and forges in the area would have enjoyed. There was, and remains, a price to pay for close proximity to the town of Lecco on Lake Como. At the southern end of the Val Sassina, the road is precipitously steep, proceeding via Orca and Ballabio. However, at least the descent is swift, which is a sharp contrast to the steep and tortuous route from the north of the Val Sassina to Bellano on Lake Como. Nature has created a resource and an incentive to clear the obstacles to its transportation. The incentives would have deteriorated dramatically when man added obstacles of his own. This happened at the end of the 1520s.

For the years 1530 and 1531, Sanudo's diaries contain almost a hundred references to Lecco and a further ten to Mandello. There is hardly a mention of either place in the years before or after. Sanudo records the reports of Venetian representatives on events around Lecco. The various sources that he quotes combine to give a vivid idea of the degree to which the once mighty Duchy of the Sforza had lost control of its own regions, and its own destiny. The account that follows reconstructs from Sanudo's diaries and other sources the circumstances that made the peaceful conduct of trade in iron between Val Sassina, Lecco, and beyond quite impossible in 1530–1. The historical imagination might try to translate the periods of no news, the uncertainties, changes of fortune, and the military depredations into the enervations, anxieties, and material losses of unprotected people trying to make a living in the local economy in the natural environment just described. Particularly striking in Sanudo's journal of reports and the events that they record is this: however violent the conflict in the eastern territory of the Milanese, and however close the geographical proximity of Venetian lands, there is never a suggestion that the conflict might spread to the territories of the republic – even though refugees could clearly escape to it. Rather than resorting to the usual generalization that immigration to Venice increased as a result of the upheavals of war on the Italian mainland, what follows sets out in detail the specific case history that helps to explain why so many ironsmiths from the eastern shore of Lake Como came to Venice in the years 1530–1.

The Tale of "Il Medeghino"

The ruler of the Duchy of Milan at that time, Francesco Maria Sforza, had proved a political survivor. In the 1520s he had thrown in Milan's lot with the League of Cognac (which included Venice) against the emperor. He had had to capitulate to imperial forces after the league's disastrous defeat at Landriano in 1528, and he was restored to his duchy by the favour of Charles V himself.[118]

In 1530 Sforza was attempting to assert his authority over Lecco and the surrounding areas, both on land and on the waters of Lake Como. He was up against another supporter of the League of Cognac, a scion of a family of Milanese physicians, Gian Giacomo de' Medighini. The family name often appears as "Medici," which was and remains a tenuous connection, for there was no biological relationship whatsoever to the Florentine dynasty. Gian Giacomo was a rapacious adventurer in the style of Cesare Borgia, but without the high-mindedness, and he used any means available in order to advance his own interests. Had Machiavelli lived to learn of his exploits, he might have made Gian Giacomo, instead of the ruthlessly bloodthirsty Agathocles of Syracuse, the subject of chapter 8 of *The Prince*. In the late 1520s, having re-entered the good graces of the emperor, Gian Giacomo made war on the Swiss and then began an improbable piratical campaign on Lake Como from his impregnable fortess at Musso, whence he issued his own coin and where, along with the adjoining valleys, he was absolute. He refused obedience to Sforza in 1529 and then drove his enemies from Bellagio, Varenna, and Bellano.[119]

Duke Sforza's siege of Lecco exerted the force of hunger on those who remained in the city.[120] Gian Giacomo's stronghold at Musso on the west bank of Lake Como gave him access by water to the town of Lecco, and it enabled the crafty gangster to conduct a curious campaign of inland piracy. Sforza could only hope to take Lecco with the military support and diplomatic good graces of mercenary forces from the Grisons and the Swiss Confederation, and they had their own strategic interests in securing the place for themselves.[121] Sforza sought naval support from the Venetians for action on the lake.[122]

Sanudo reported the terms of the eventual treaty on 15 February 1531 (by which time the local ironsmiths had been safely enrolled in the arte dei fabbri in Venice). The Castellano was to receive from the Duke of Milan 35,000 ducats, 10,000 ducats of that sum at once. He would then depart with his troops, guns, and supplies.[123] Sforza's agreement was still conditional upon his separate negotiations with the eight Catholic cantons of the Swiss Confederation and with the Grisons, and Sanudo noted that the continuing conflicts in the lands of the Swiss might cause yet further delay.[124] The Castellano formally handed over his stronghold at Musso on 9 March, and his forces left Lecco on the eighteenth of the same month.[125] Sforza claimed that the "guerra di Musso" had added a cost of 200,000 ducats to his impecuniousness, including the payment of 35,000 ducats to Gian Giacomo himself.[126]

The chronicle of Benedetto Giovio, the brother of the humanist Paolo and an accomplished scholar in his own right, provides a precise account of the changing fortunes of the "guerra di Musso," demonstrating both the resourcefulness and the ruthlessness of "il Medeghino." Gian Giacomo apparently left his stronghold without punishment for his atrocities, "omnium rapinarum et flagitiorum impunitate data." Indeed, Giovio's whole account concludes with the palpable expression of relief at the destruction of the fortress at Musso: "shortly after this, the fortress of Musso, which had been the source of so many woes, by order of Duke Francesco [Sforza], was destroyed" (paulo post arx ipsa Mussi, quae tantorum malorum occasio fuerat, iussu Francisci ducis excise est).[127] Giovio's compatriot Franco Magnacavallo provides evidence of the vertical impregnability of the fortress at Musso and Gian Giacomo's successful sortie against heavy siege guns in its defence. He also offers a graphic account of the horrors of war in the region. In some areas near Lake Como so many people were displaced and so many roads disrupted that, for a period, wolves dominated the countryside, hunting in terrifying packs so that the local inhabitants avoided travelling alone.[128]

Set against this situation in their homeland, the ironsmiths of Lecco, Ballabio, Val Sassina, and Mandello surely found enrolment in one of the guilds of Venice, with the assurance of participation in the guild's proceedings, a comforting and agreeable contrast. There is an acute irony in the contrast between all those ironsmiths who painstakingly braided their strands of identity, and the shameless adventurer Gian Giacomo. A few years after Gian Giacomo's death in 1555, his brother, who had been Pope Pius IV since 1559, asked Michelangelo to design his tomb. Michelangelo declined the commission, and it went instead to Leone Leoni, who had served Charles V. Gian Giacomo's spectacular tomb still stands in the duomo in Milan, surmounted by the *palle* (balls) on a coat of arms that proclaim him as a Medici. This false commemoration has inserted il Medeghino in many indexes in continuous series with members of the Florentine family.[129] The connection seems to have derived from an agreement between Pius IV and the Medici that the pope's family could use the stemma of six "palle" on the grounds of Gian Giacomo's military service to the Florentine dynasty.[130] The link remains feeble and dubious, its advertisement shameless and outrageous. However, Gian Giacomo's memorial inscription is paired with that of the young Gabriele de' Medici, who apparently achieved the astonishing feat of perishing in a naval battle involving the Swiss.[131]

The tale of a soldier of fortune and his brother who climbs as high as the throne of Saint Peter is worthy of the age of the Borgia, but it is surprisingly – and for some, perhaps, uncomfortably – close to an apparently new era. In the best traditions of nepotism in the Renaissance papacy, Pius advanced the career of his sister's son when he was only twenty-one years of age. The nephew in question was one Carlo Borromeo, a leader of what has come to be known as the Counter-Reformation. We must postpone the final twist of this extraordinary tale. However, it is worth reflecting upon the mobility of the borders between the age of the Renaissance papacy and the Italian Wars and the age of the Counter-Reformation. John Addington Symonds provided a delightfully agile summary of il Medeghino's historical achievement as "witnessing and taking part in the dismemberment of the Milanese duchy, playing a game of hazard at high stakes for his own profit with the last two Sforza, the Empire, the French and the Swiss." He succinctly depicted the three close relatives – Gian Giacomo, his brother Pope Pius IV, and his nephew Carlo Borromeo – as, respectively, "the captain of adventure soaked in blood, the churchman unrivalled for intrigue and the saint aflame with holiest enthusiasm."[132]

The story down to 1531 by no means diminishes the crisis in Venice itself. The hardships there prompted initiatives that some may see as a "New Poor Law"; they also left greater scope for purely ecclesiastical initiatives from agencies such as the Compagnia del Divino Amore, the Theatines and the Somaschi, and from the new rigorists who energized such agencies and who were imbuing the Church of Rome with a new spirit: Girolamo Miani, Gaetano Thiene, and Gian Pietro Caraffa.[133] Their initiatives – and soon after those of Ignatius Loyola and the Jesuits – marked what may prove to have been the first stirrings of the reconfiguration of the relations of the Roman Church and the Venetian State, and the withdrawal of both from the concerns of everyday economic life. For the moment, we might note that the Somaschi, emblematic of the new orders and the new spirit in the Catholic Church in the confessional era, take their name from a hamlet on that troubled road between Bergamo and Lecco. As an indication of the work that they had in hand from the outset, it is interesting to note that their date of foundation was the year that has figured so prominently in this discussion: 1531.[134] Their work as clerics in tending the poor might serve as a symbol of the inadequacies of political authorities in dealing with the sorrows that their conflicts had created.

There is a final ironic twist. In 1610, shortly after the canonization of San Carlo Borromeo, the arte dei fabbri in Venice, still conscious, it seems, of their Lombard connections, added him to their patron saints.[135] Could they have known that this model of Tridentine sanctity was the nephew of il Medeghino, the man who had driven their forbears from their homes and, while they toiled to identify themselves in Venice, arrogated and still arrogates, in the duomo of Milan, at the centre of the diocese of his sister's son, an eternal imposture?[136] That question we must set aside. By 1610 the dominance of the commercial space in the heart of Venice, between Rialto and San Marco, had passed to the ironmongers' great rivals, the mercers. Their documentation contains significant lists of members and officers. It also offers a range of insights into the guild's economic and religious life and suggests how the corporation functioned as a miniature polity.

4 Officers and Office in the Mercers' Guild, c. 1450–c. 1600

O that estates, degrees and offices
Were not deriv'd corruptly, and that dear honour
Were purchas'd by the merit of the wearer!

– Shakespeare, *The Merchant of Venice*, 2.9.41–3

A Little Republic?

The discussion of the genesis of the distinctive political economy of Venice in the thirteenth century called into question the idea that the process relegated the guilds to a purely economic role and altogether barred them from political life. Indeed, evidence from the sixteenth century suggests that the corporations of the city played a critical part in enabling those who came to Venice as immigrants from the expanded territorial state to develop a collective sense of Venetian identity. The purpose of this next part of the study is to test such findings in the specific confines of a single guild, to observe its operations from within. The starting point is the machinery of election that made the officers of a guild the representatives of their membership – a sharp focus and an exhaustive exercise, but still concentrating on the idea of representation. Yet this would be to no avail if the offices themselves carried no real responsibilities or were largely superfluous to the economic activities of the members of the guild. In order to test the significance of the work of the guild's officers, the chapter proceeds to investigate the practical burdens of office. Participation and representation in electoral politics, market regulation, and policies in defence of economic interests constantly finding voice in courts of law – it is unusual to associate such characterizations with the day-to-day lives of Venetian popolani who were supposedly excluded by the government of merchants. However, is it possible that a guild could function as a miniature polity all to itself, economically protectionist and politically responsible for those it governed in internal and external affairs, and always attached to religion through its scuola? Where better to gauge the validity of such ideas than in the largest and richest of the guilds of Venice, the arte dei marzeri.

The etymology of *mercer* and its Franciscan connotations of reward, gain, desert, and merchandise were discussed in the first chapter of the study. While in English the term *mercer* denotes a dealer in textiles, especially silk and other costly materials, the variety of goods covered by the term in its Venetian usage is quite extraordinary. Richard Rapp's translation, the trade of "dry goods retailers" is more comprehensive, but it is difficult to find a single term that communicates the diversity of mercers' wares. The marzeri dealt in all sorts of goods and members used more than eighty different occupational titles. This was partly because the guild was an enormous agglomerate of trades, having enveloped hatters, cappers, stringers, glovers, perfumers (who gave scent to gloves), and makers of belts and buttons and what-have-you, but also because the shop fronts of Venice's "Marzarie" between Rialto and San Marco displayed such an abundance and variety of all kinds of small wares, which guild members might offer wholesale, retail, or both.[1] More general impressions of the Mercerie give a vivid picture of an abundance and opulence of wares that visitors found captivating but impossible to take in in detail because of the speed of turnover. Canon Pietro Casola, the Milanese pilgrim, recorded in 1494: "Who could count the many shops so well furnished that they also seem to be warehouses, with so many cloths of every design, tapestries of every sort, camlets of every colour and texture; silks of every kind; so many warehouses full of spices, groceries and drugs, and so much beautiful white wax! These things stupefy the beholder – it cannot be fully described to those who have not seen it."[2]

Mercers did not deal in wax; that was the province of apothecaries.[3] However, Casola's experience of the Mercerie was similar for John Evelyn a century and a half later: "Hence I pass'd thro' the Mercerie, which is one of the most delicious streetes in the world for the sweetnesse of it, and is all the way on both sides tapistred as it were with cloth of gold, rich damaskes and other silks, which the shops expose and hang before their houses from the first floore, and with that variety that for neere half the year spent chiefly in this Citty I hardly remember to have seene the same piece twice exposed."[4]

At this point, the study probes the corpuscular structure of a single cell within the greater body of the commonwealth. Since the focus of attention is shifting from the constitution of Venice to the constituent elements of the republic, the exercise is fundamental to its line of inquiry. Contarini's neat and integrated picture of clearly defined corporate entities within a greater whole might suggest the reflection of the macrocosm in the microcosm. This chapter asks whether the macrocosm was a reflection of the untidy realities of inconsistency, contradiction, and confusion within the microcosm, a microcosm that nevertheless retained a striking autonomy. The chapter begins with an example of representation that is straightforwardly recognizable in the modern world, namely, the electoral process of the mercers' guild. While this did not by any means boil down to "one mercer, one vote," it sheds considerable light on the curious paths along which the popolani of Venice might have understood themselves to be part of a greater whole.

The first stage of the investigation is based upon a list of officers of the mercers' guild for the period 1577–1609.[5] The period coincided with the gradual fading of the euphoria after the victory of the Holy League over the Turks at Lepanto in 1571, with the immediate aftermath of the devastating plague of 1576, with the economic gloom of the 1590s, and with the political crisis of the interdict of 1606 and its aftermath.[6] The guild held annual elections to the positions, the outgoing officers nominating electors who in turn worked with them to nominate candidates for a committee of six that was responsible for administration and discipline, which candidates the enfranchised masters of the guild then voted for and elected by majority.

As in the case of other guilds, the regulation of elections and the duties of those elected occupy a substantial part of the original guild statute, which was a list of numbered "capitoli" (chapters) grouped to form a "capitolare." The mercers' sumptuous mariegola dates from 1471 and translates closely, though not exactly, the Latin original of exactly two hundred years before. As will become apparent in due course, the statutes, along with the rest of the guild's extensive documentation, are evidence of a changing and evolving organization, not of an ancient set of rules modified and outmoded by subsequent generations of practice.[7]

Two particular features of the earliest statute are strikingly durable, and merit careful emphasis. First, while the terms *merchant* (mercator) and *mercer* (merzarius) are interchangeable, the statute makes a distinction between wholesalers and stall-holders only to apply its regulations to them all: "not only for [goods] in warehouses, but also for [goods] on stalls" (tam in voltis quam in stacionibus).[8] Such a distinction persists in the separate classification of wholesalers and retailers in the sixteenth and seventeenth centuries. Second, the capitolare consistently refers to members as men or women; women's place in the guild is formally acknowledged throughout.[9] Wives and mothers of guildsmen, and perhaps their daughters, were enjoined to become members of the scuola and pay their dues: "And moreover, we will that if the aforesaid women wish for their devotion to enter our scuola, those we must accept and inscribe as are inscribed the other women mercers who are in the parishes and go to the markets at San Marco and San Polo and to the fairs, all of whom are subject to our statute and pay dues as is the custom."[10]

Arte dei marzeri and Scuola di San Teodoro

That last quotation from the documents confirms the centrality of the devotional confraternity, the scuola, to the organization of members of the trade guild, the arte. In the context of the criss-cross provided by the scuole and arti between them, we might remember that the mercers' scuola was, from at least 1450, closely partnered with the ancient Scuola di San Teodoro, which was to become a Scuola Grande in the mid-sixteenth century, and to which the women of the mercers' guild were clearly attached. A clear understanding of this dimension of the officers' activities must await examination of the relationship between the arte dei marzeri and the Scuola Grande di San Teodoro, a relationship that shows how the activities of guild and confraternity found physical expression in the city's restricted space. The Scuola di San Teodoro was located near Rialto, opposite the church of San Salvador, which in turn stood at the very beginning of the Mercerie di San Salvador, the Mercers' Row; the row connected Rialto with San Marco via the Mercerie dell'Orologio, which led to the clock tower at Piazza San Marco. We know that the arte dei marzeri and the Scuola di San Teodoro formalized their shared activities in 1450, the year in which Saint Theodore's Day became one of the official feasts of the republic (anticipating the fall of Constantinople to the Turks in 1453 and laying formal claim to its spiritual inheritance with a hint of future Venetian independence of papal Rome).

Members of the mercers' guild and their wives and children enjoyed automatic membership of the Scuola di San Teodoro, paying "only as much as they wish through devotion to pay." These generous terms flew through the mercers' assembly on a vote of sixty-nine to three. The amalgamation was renewed in 1552, when the scuola became a Scuola Grande.[11] Alas, its archive remains uncatalogued.[12] Moreover, the enactment shows the accepted participation of women in every area of the guild's economic activity – as heads of shops, as stall-holders at markets, as street peddlers, and as merchants at fairs, the most important of which evidently took place at Treviso.[13] One notes at once within the guild a model of a political economy bound together with its religious practices. With that in mind, women's lack of formal involvement in guild elections is perhaps a little less stark an exclusion than it might at first appear. Furthermore, within the dense detail some sense of a miniature republic is already apparent.

Officers and Members

The attention that statutes gave to the guild's processes of electing officers to represent the membership – subject to formal approval but otherwise free of state involvement – is worthy of emphasis. Once again, it is legitimate to ask whether the apparent exclusion of non-noble Venetians from the magisterial offices that patricians monopolized was synonymous with the exclusion of the popolo of Venice from the republic's political processes. Membership in a guild was, in itself, exclusive. Just as the cittadini chose a grand chancellor as "the prince of the common people," so guild members elected officers who were to be their "judges" to run the affairs of the corporation, and they did so at the behest of the magistracy to which they were responsible, the Giustizia Vecchia. In 1271 the Giustizia Vecchia's magistrates gave the custodian's assistants the overtly judicial title of "iudices," and the dialect equivalent, "zudesi," persists throughout the list of elections.[14]

Before proceeding with detailed analysis, it is important to establish a working definition of each titular office in relation to its duties and to the terminology that the mercers themselves used in recording their electoral results.[15] The titles of the guild's representatives were as follows. The chief officer was a *gastaldo*, a term that might be translated as "custodian." The equivalent office in the city's Scuole Grandi was the "guardian grande," or "warden." Both titles had clear connotations of protection and conservation. From the very earliest statute it is clear that the "gastaldio" was indeed a judge and was to listen to pleas and to issue sentences.[16] He also had an incentive to be efficient in the collection of the fines that he imposed on members; the guild kept two-thirds of these, and the magistrates took only one-third. This surely indicates a concession of autonomy from the government to the guild.[17] It was the custodian's further obligation to assemble all members of the guild twice a year for a reading of the statute.[18] There is a clear correspondence to the government offices that were responsible for collecting fines on behalf of the Consoli dei Mercanti (Consuls of Merchants), and, indeed, on behalf of those gastaldi who served the doge himself as "gastaldi ducali."[19]

The custodian took advice from three "zudesi," literally "judges," more accurately "adjudicators." One of them was the "zudese de mezz'anno" (adjudicator of mid-year). It seems probable that this office spanned two years by joining two adjudicator colleagues half way through their terms, and they remained in post until half way through the terms of the two who took office after the next election. This would have made for a desirable measure of administrative continuity. The office of zudese indicates that the custodian could refer to a close body of advisers any cases that required the guild's decision, and one of these officers would have been equipped to pass comment on precedents, case law, and discussions from the previous year. The statute of 1271 specifies that the gastaldio is to convene the iudices "for the utility or business of the said guild" (pro utilitate aut negocio huius artis).[20] The office of adjudicator also extended to judgments on whether apprentices or junior assistants ("zoveni") who had taken a test ("prova") might proceed to the rank of master. The only form of the test that the earliest statute specifies was financial. The custodian and the adjudicators appear to have asked for a payment of thirty soldi from men or women "who wished to be master or maestra." The fee doubled to three lire for men or women who had trained somewhere other than Venice.[21]

The compilation of records of proceedings at meetings of the guild's officers was the responsibility of the guild's secretary or "scrivan," a term perhaps best translated in this context as "scribe." Described as "preco" in the statute of 1271, he was also more widely responsible for the guild's records of its membership and the insertion of new capitoli in the guild's statute book. Such additions all required government approval, and many of them originated with the magistrates themselves and applied generally to all guilds.[22]

The guild's enfranchised members also elected a "sindaco." The connotations of "syndication" refer to responsibility for the guild's financial records. In the interests, once more, of sticking as closely as possible to contemporary terminology, the commentary favours *syndic* over *accountant*.

"Di rispetto" (of respect) is a title that the scribe applied to those elected as reserves, to be held in honour as officers but without a specific title. There were only four years in which there were such elections.

The six or so officers appear to have constituted the executive. The nomenclature of the next lamination, of five more offices, is altogether larger and looser and may well have depended on the personal preferences of the scribe who recorded them in any year. Any one of these five changing titles classified six more members of the guild's committee. With the six executive officers already mentioned, these constituted the "dodese," or the twelve who made up the electoral body. The various electoral positions are classified in five column headings in the tables: "degani," "banca," "compagni," "dodese," and "zonta."

The etymology of the terms gives some sense of their function. The title *degani* translates readily as "deacons" and is noteworthy for its ecclesiastical resonance. It may well be a reflection of the traditionally close association of the guild (*arte*) with its devotional counterpart or scuola, which attended to members' spiritual and material welfare.[23] The title *degano* is recorded every year from 1577 to 1584 (except 1578); it disappears almost completely after 1584 (there is one officer called a degano, elected in 1594). The *banca* (bench) is another term for the membership of the guild's electoral committee and refers to the form on which they sat. This title applied only four times: for 1578, 1585, 1586, and 1590. *Compagni* (companions) is another term for those officers chosen for the guild's committee of nominating electors, with evocations of association, not only with each other but with the custodian and adjudicators. That sense of co-operation perhaps strengthens when one notes that companions are elected every year from 1587 to 1609 (with the sole exception of 1590), operating with the Twelve and occasionally the adjunct to form an electoral body. The committee of electors is most frequently recorded in its most neutral description, one that merely refers to the number of its members, "the Twelve." However, the category includes six to eleven names when the scribe chose to apply it. Continuing the analogies between the organization of the guild's officers and the government of the state itself, it is of some importance to remark that a few of the most significant of the republic's component magistracies are also recorded in such terms, particularly "the Ten" for the Council of Ten, and "the Forty" for the three councils of that number each, which were Venice's supreme courts of appeal, and to which non-nobles, including guildsmen and women, had access and recourse. The term *zonta* refers to a supplementary committee of electors, which was six strong. They formed a "zonta," which was the Venetian dialect form of *giunta*, meaning that this group was "joined" to the guild's principal six officers. It is even used as an alternative to the Twelve (in 1577, 1589, 1600, 1602, 1607, and 1609). The term brings out the sense of the committee being an adjunct. In the context of the idea that the guild functioned as a miniature republic, it is worth commenting that the Council of Ten also had its zonta.

The tabulations in this chapter deliberately keep these five titles separate in order to preserve the contemporary record of identification and to avoid too rigid a division between officers and electors. The homogeneity of the relationship between the electors and the other officers, and of them all with the constituency of enfranchised masters, may have been a source of strength rather than a symptom of oligarchy. The discussion that follows investigates the possible elision of the interests of officers, electors, and the guild's general membership rather than setting up the juxtaposition between an inner circle that ran the guild's affairs and a membership of hundreds essentially bereft of representation. However, the commentary amalgamates all the data relating to the nominating electors in order to investigate fully the patterns of multiple office-holding.

The five official titles do not appear in the statute of 1271. Their role in the guilds of Venice – not of the mercers alone – was defined by the Council of Ten in a reform of 1531 that replicated a similar and earlier innovation in the Scuole Grandi. The principal role of the functionaries appears to have been to co-operate with the outgoing executive officers in the election of their successors for the following year. The masters as a body approved the nomination of the twelve electors.[24] An understanding of this apparent restriction of the body of electors is vital to explaining the apparent disparity between membership as a whole, the enfranchised masters, the seemingly small numbers of electors, and the variable size of the assembly that chose the electors themselves. It is essential to grasp the strength and energy of the representative principle, and the clear connection between the electoral process and the two general assemblies of the guild that met every year.

At this point, it is appropriate to make a few general remarks about the work that the six executive officers might be obliged to do. This work will figure in much greater detail in the second half of the chapter, which explores the role of the guild's officers in the day-to-day regulation of its members and their business. For the moment, it is worth pointing out that the responsibilities of officers fell into three broad categories: the management of affairs internal to the guild; negotiation on the guild's behalf with external agencies; and finally the co-ordination of the guild's position in relation to unusual circumstances or in preparation for specific events.

Into the first category came economic matters such as the examinations that earned a member the title of master. It may have been the case that the qualification was a matter of deciding whether a master was a wholesaler or a retailer, a distinction reflected in the scale of fees. For the period of time covered by the detailed electoral records, one of the most time-consuming tasks was the allocation of market stalls for the two-week market in Piazza San Marco that followed the doge's "Marriage of the Sea" on Ascension Day (forty days after Easter).

Members accused of infringing the guild's regulations also came before the bench, literally, to defend themselves, though they were at liberty to appeal against the guild's verdict to the magistrates of the Giustizia Vecchia or other higher authorities. The exclusion of the non-noble population from magisterial office did not amount to exposure to arbitrary rule and may, on the contrary, have helped to reinforce the disinterestedness and objectivity of those adjudicating the conflicts among the popolani.[25] The committee had to oversee the regular payment of membership dues ("benintrade") to the scuola, money for candles for the monthly mass ("luminarie"), allocation of benefits during sickness, and funeral expenses for deceased masters. Decisions on the disposal of alms and dowry funds also figured among these responsibilities.

Financial accounts for the mercers do not survive in their archive. For comparison, one turns to the goldsmiths' accounts of 1540–53.[26] This guild had a smaller membership than the mercers but was of comparable status. The ledger may also help to make sense of the work of the mercers' syndic. Like the mercers' guild, the *arte degli orefici* was exempted from personal service in the galleys in 1596. Its membership was less numerous. In 1541, 91 goldsmiths paid candle money; in 1544, 150 of them did so. In 1595 the goldsmiths were assessed for 109 galleymen from 405 members; the mercers for 147 from 567.[27] About half of the goldsmiths' annual income derived from candle money and dues, and a further 25 per cent from investments. The goldsmiths spent about a third of their income on administration, which included the allocation of market stalls, errand runners, payments to the government, and legal fees. About one-fifth of expenditure took the form of alms to members. The cost of ceremonial amounted to around 45 per cent of all money disbursed, and that included a startlingly high proportion on candle wax and oil – around 22 per cent of all outlays.[28] In a list of 1612 the mercers recorded the names of masters and the dues that they were to pay in candle money, at a rate of either six or three lire. This compilation includes 474 names, 305 at three lire and 169 at six lire. If all the moneys came in, the total would have been 1,929 lire – thus the significance of the payments of luminarie.[29]

However, the exact proportion of dues that the officers actually collected may have been much lower. We know from a register of 1593 that 347 mercers, about a third of all members, owed a debt of some kind to the guild. The delinquency rate was much higher among masters, about 80 per cent of whom had dues or fines outstanding. About half of all debts were carried forward. Since indebtedness to the guild was a disqualification from the electoral process, this too acted to keep the number of electors at an apparently paltry level. Suddenly, the 10 per cent of masters who voted for the electoral committee may represent half of those eligible to participate.[30]

The guild's external dealings were divided between disputes with other guilds before magistrates, and negotiation with agencies of the government itself. Venetian guilds frequently resorted to litigation. They enjoyed ready access to courts of law. It is not at all clear who represented the guild in court proceedings. The speculation that the guild nominated one or more of its own zudesi to represent the guild's decisions to the patrician zudesi would give the relationship of guild and magistracy a rationale, but it remains a speculation. Whatever the reality in that aspect of the guild's official duties, we might see the civil cases of the city's guild disputes as conflicts natural to a state and, rather than threatening a system, as a sign of strength within it.[31] Again, there is a sense of a judicial continuum between guild business and magistrates' court rather than a sense of separation and exclusion, and the connection is quite explicit in the statute of 1271.

In 1446 the mercers defined an empire of goods in which they had the exclusive right to trade, and that list forms capitolo 24 of the guild's statute of 1471.[32] The guild incorporated over eighty occupations apart from mercers; hatters, cappers, sellers of plumes, and sellers of lace all had a place in the arte dei marzeri. Nevertheless, the long list of wares that the guild claimed to monopolize set up endless disputes with other arti about who was entitled to sell what. The statute of 1271 sought to pre-empt conflict with tanners and bleachers.[33] For the later period, one notes in particular the extraordinarily long-running conflict with the fabbri over which metal wares each could sell. The mercers seemed to be striving to lay claim not only to the business of their own street, the Mercerie, between Rialto and San Marco, but also to that of "Ironmongers' Alley" (Calle dei Fabbri), which runs in meandering parallel.[34]

Among their other burdens, the guild's officers took receipt of the government's demands. These might be decrees of the Greater Council, the Senate, or even the Council of Ten, or the more mundane regulations of the Giustizia Vecchia requiring revisions of the statute or general notice to membership. However, the traffic of material was not always or entirely at the government's behest. This is most notably the case in the matter of provision of oarsmen for Venice's reserve fleet of one hundred galleys. The responsible magistracy, the Milizia da Mar, ordered the compilation of membership lists by the guilds on several occasions (1539, 1575, 1586, 1594, 1612), and based its demands for oarsmen upon such lists. However, the mercers, like many other guilds, frequently disputed the government's demands, most notably in the petitions ("suppliche") of 1609–11.[35]

The burden of supplying men for the fleet was long term. However, government demands could also produce immediate administrative problems that required attention at particular times. Guild members who elected not to serve in the galleys in person had been able, individually, to hire substitutes to serve in their stead. In 1594 the drapers' guild, along with the guilds of the wool and silk merchants, gained exemption from personal service for their members and agreed instead to pay as a corporation the sum that would provide substitutes who would enlist. The mercers, together with the goldsmiths, negotiated a similar exemption in 1596.[36] This move quite changed the nature of the imposition and its administration. There were also a number of once-only occasions that required the membership's approval of expenditure and the active mobilization of those enrolled in the guild. Examples here are elaborate ceremonies such as the decoration of a galley to welcome Henri, Duke of Alençon, on his way from Poland to coronation in France in 1574 as Henri III; or the celebration of the coronation of the dogaressa in 1598.[37] The government also called upon the guilds to relax their demands for qualification as master in order to admit immigrants who could replenish the workforce after the dreadful losses to plague in 1575–7.[38]

Before engaging with the dry statistics of office-holding, it is important to emphasize the seriousness with which the guild approached elections of its officers. The mariegola of 1471 contains three specific provisions that indicate practice, principle, and the relationship between the two, which gives lubrication and form to the figures themselves. With regard to practice, the statute records a tangible urgency in the need that the officers have expressed for the translation of deliberation to decision to implementation.[39] In a regulation that shows the way in which dealing with a problem could generate a rule in surprisingly quick time, the officers noted that the guild was to assemble as a body twice a year but that "quite a few times business and matters arise as a result of which on many occasions this trade of ours suffers considerable disadvantage because we the Gastaldo and compagni do not have the liberty to act upon such matters." Accordingly, the board proposed that the gastaldo have the power to assemble fifteen members from among "the most sufficient and expert in our trade" (lo più sufficienti et esperti in el nostro mestier). Their review and determination was to be "valid in the same way as if it were taken in the [general] meeting" (sia cussi valido quello i faranno sucomo fosse prexo in sto capitolo). That motion carried – another vote – by sixty-five to seventeen. However, there was an immediate reaffirmation of the importance of a broad base of representation: "We will that in our meetings each and every one enrolled in our trade may come and stand for election and vote as has been the custom in the past."[40]

The compromise was an intriguing process that gave power of nomination to the guild's committee, with the final electoral choice coming from a general ballot of the whole membership.[41] A word or two is necessary in explanation of the relationship between standing for election and nomination for election. In summary, the guild agreed to hold a general meeting on two occasions each year. The business of such gatherings was to ensure that no one without expertise came to hold office. The sitting committee was to co-opt up to six members from the guild's "most sufficient" members to form the adjunct. These compagni were to meet on the Friday following the Sunday of the Twelve Apostles and to celebrate mass – with the careful provision for "peace, love and charity" (paxe e amor e charità) – at the church of San Zulian. That group then drew up a list of four candidates for the office of gastaldo, six for the zudesi, and twelve for compagni. The following Sunday the guild was to hold a general meeting at which its members were to choose from this list one gastaldo, two zudesi, and six compagni. There was then to be a second election on the first Friday after the second Sunday in September, again after mass. The sitting officers then nominated two members for the post of scribe and two adjudicators of mid-year. In an important incentive for public spiritedness there were to be stiff fines for turning down any office: fifty lire for an elected gastaldo, twenty-five lire for an adjudicator, and eleven lire for any of the companions, and the same again if the electoral re-run produced the same result. Following service, there was to be an interval of time before the former incumbent might once again stand. The period specified was two years for the gastaldo and one year for the other offices. It appears that a candidate could not stand for an office junior to the last that he held.

That was not the end of the matter. Evidently there was a body of opinion that thought the nominating committee too narrowly based in composition, and a later rule ordained that it should be a group of between thirty and forty members present.[42] It is particularly important to observe that these statutory mandates found their execution in the broad basis of the body of office-holders and the high turnover of office-holding.

That sense of the twin needs of representation and implementation forms the background for the elections themselves, to which analysis may now turn. Those features designed in the later fifteenth century are still discernible, with variations, in the guild's electoral processes in the period 1577–1609. For the purpose of being ready for regular and recurrent business, to represent the guild's interests in specific negotiations, and to provide authorization and organization for particular events, the mercers of Venice recorded 634 elections to offices in the period 1577–1609. There were 194 elections to the six executive offices (plus occasional reserves) and 440 nominations as the twelve or so electors. So, the outgoing committee of six combined with an elected group of twelve to form an electorate of about eighteen who chose the committee of six for the following year. The rhythms of the process resonate with those of the election of the doge himself, which was by no means a free vote in the Greater Council.[43]

Oligarchs or Plutocrats? A Test Case

The mercers' listings of individual names provide two or more of four elements (fewer than do the ironsmiths' lists): Christian name, family name, trade, and name of shop. Rarely do the lists specify the member's parish. There are considerable problems of identification, and it is important to offer an explanation as to how the lists reached a rough standardization. How do we identify exactly who was who? The question is, once more, fundamental. How did guild members perceive themselves? And how, if at all, was this reflected in the manner in which they recorded each other's identities? The complexity of the braiding of the four different strands is very striking and tends to frustrate any straightforward exercise in quantification. It requires corroborative reference to the general lists of members compiled over the period, the most comprehensive of which dates from 1586. In that year the franchise applied to 245 masters who dealt wholesale and to 121 master retailers. The membership of that year will receive more detailed scrutiny in due course.[44]

For the elected officers, the rarest of the four components of identity is trade. Despite the four score or so other trades, it looks as though the officers listed were predominantly marzeri. The lists of elected officers tend to be a combination of name, surname, and shop. The mix is not consistent, but the names, surnames, and shops can be cross-referred to the guild's lists of general membership. The recurrent family names among the membership as a whole are readily identifiable. In alphabetical order (with standardized spelling) they are as follows: Bergonzi, Carminati, Locadelli, Negroni, Poleni, Rossi, Rotta, Rubi, and Teseri. These are decisive identifications, and although the family name is not always included in a listing, the Christian name and shop sign can readily connect to it. This contrasts with the ironsmiths' listings and may suggest the mercers' more elevated status. For those families just listed, it is possible to assemble a few details by way of background and future, some of which are suggestive of the way in which the world of the guilds might blend with that of the cittadini and even the nobility.

According to a list of 1567–8, compiled for the Milizia da Mar, Matteo di Antonio Bergonzi at the sign of the Bergamo had a capital estimated between 200 and 400 ducats.[45] In the same compilation Matteo di Bartolomeo Bergonzi, a maker of string in Santa Fosca, had 100 ducats. Yet Anna Maria di Bartolomeo Bergonzi married Francesco di Giovanni Grimani in 1646 and took with her a dowry of 50,000 ducats. The Bergonzi themselves were ennobled in 1665.[46] In the same list Zuanbattista di Francesco Carminati, a mercer at the sign of the Sun was rated at 1,000 ducats. The Carminati, a famously rich family, also from Bergamo, bought their way into the Venetian nobility in 1687.[47] They literally left their mark on the stones of Venice in the form of a Palazzo Carminati and a *salizzada*, *ponte*, *fondamenta*, and *calle* that all still bear the family name.[48]

In 1567–8 Baldissera di Zuan Locadelli at the sign of the Colombina (Little Dove) was rated at no more than 500 ducats. There is a contrast with Zuanpiero di Antonio Rotta, plume seller at the sign of the Ostrich (Struzzo), who may have had 200 ducats but is listed as a "povero." It is conceivable that the family changed its fortune with its profession, for the Rotta family were in the law when they attained patrician status in 1685.[49] Battista di Vielmo Rubi at the sign of the Fortress may have had a capital of 2,000 ducats. Marco di Zanantonio Rubi at the sign of the Squash may have been worth 4,000 ducats. Ambriuoxo di Battista Teseri, plume seller at the sign of the Crown, had a rating of 4,000–5,000 ducats, but his brother Iseppo no more than 200 ducats. Of the elected officers, only Iseppo Negroni stands out as very rich, with a fortune estimated at 25,000 ducats, but he was by no means the wealthiest member of the mercers' guild. That designation falls clearly on Gierolemo Vignale at the sign of the Fountain with an estimated capital of 50,000 ducats, or on Zilio da Ponte, who may even have had 60,000 ducats, and neither of them appears to have held office at all.

Some scholars are emphatic that the guilds of Venice were oligarchic in their practices, and such figures as noted might seem to confirm their opinion.[50] The following discussion tests whether the size of the electorate necessarily made the election of officers unrepresentative of the membership as a whole. Were guild members content to leave the administration of the corporation to those willing to shoulder such burdens, even at the risk of allowing them to promote their own interests? Could the membership as a whole have been indifferent as long as mercers were allowed to pursue freely their own material interests? Might the price of regular contributions as a qualification to vote have deterred those who were content to leave the management of the guild to others? After all, the guild itself was not the unit of production. That unit was the workshop, over which the master presided as an extension of his household. Even that unit was not self-contained, however. The terms of apprenticeship contracts were a matter for negotiation between master and apprentice but were then subject to regulation by both guild and magistrates. The guild's officers appointed examiners to test the qualifications of the apprentice aspiring to become a master.[51] It is both teleological and anachronistic to read back to the 1500s the modern assumptions that representation must be strictly measured by participation. Even if the electorate was small and the elections non-competitive, election was not a formality, and votes in favour and against ("'di si" or "di no") are recorded in all cases.

The strength of any link between family prominence and election to office must be one of the chief priorities of the study. At this point the calculations recombine the categories and include electors as officers. Among the 634 elections, five Bergonzi held office twenty-five times between them. Of fifteen Rossi, only three held office at all (though for a total of fifteen terms). Of the seventeen recorded members of the Rotta family, six held office for a total of seventeen terms. Only two Rubi held office (seven terms), two Locadelli held office (eight terms), and only one Negroni served at all (three terms), as did only one of the Carminati (also three terms). No member of the Teseri family appears to have stood for office.

Of the thirty-eight mercers who held office on five occasions or more, fifteen were identified by family name, and twenty-three by Christian name and shop sign. However, half of those with family names do not connect to families frequently mentioned in other guild records. These are Milan (who held office eleven times), Aguzzi (ten times), Bossello (seven times), Allegri, Gidotti, Mezi, and Panizzi (six times each). Only one member of each of these families appears to have taken office in the mercers' guild in this period. This is an important premonitory rehearsal of the broader point that the data give no evidence of an interconnected structure of oligarchy.

In addition, influential and significant figures whose importance is attested in other sources are only very shadowy as office-holders. Bartolomeo Bontempelli dal Calese appears on the lists of officers only twice: as one of the Twelve in 1579 and as custodian in 1582. In neither instance is his surname recorded, so his identity was defined by Christian name and shop sign. Bernardo Sechini ("Zecchin" in some sources) also had connections with high politics, for his shop, the Nave d'Oro (Golden Ship), was one of the places where Fra Paolo Sarpi's circle met to discuss matters of contemporary religious and political controversy.[52] Sechini was an active member of the guild and held office several times, as an adjudicator in 1579 and 1582 (which is interestingly coincidental with Bontempelli), as one of the Twelve in 1581 and 1586, and as the syndic in 1587. Sechini's surname appears every time that his name is recorded, but, unlike Bontempelli, the name of his shop is never entered. By further contrast, the office-holding record of Jacopo Bergonzi, who served eight times, increases by a further seven if Jacopo dalla Madonna is Jacopo Bergonzi. This seems irrefutable since Jacopo Bergonzi dalla Madonna was the syndic in 1588, while one Jacopo dalla Madonna was the custodian in 1590 and 1599, the syndic in 1601 and 1602, one of the Twelve in 1606, and a member of the adjunct in 1607.

The lists of officers are, it seems, both loose and recalcitrant because identifying an individual on the basis of name, date of office, and shop sign is intrinsically delicate. Zuanmaria Rotta appears as a companion in 1608, but he is alternately Zuan and Zuanmaria in the general membership lists. It seems a fair assumption that this is the same person because the shop sign is always the Due Ancore (Two Anchors), though there is also one Iseppo Rotta at the same shop who was the syndic in 1604. The range of possibilities may even run from *A* to *Z*. Antonio dal Sant'Antonio is recorded as a member of the adjunct in 1609, but Zuanantonio dal Sant'Antonio was a companion in 1598, one of the Twelve in 1601, 1605, and 1606, and a member of the adjunct in 1607. It is possible that the two names are those of father and son, but it is at least equally possible that they are one and the same. There is a definite instance of this being so in the case of Battista dai Tre Zii (of the Three Lilies) who was an adjudicator in 1586 and one of the Twelve in 1596. However, one Zuanbattista dai Tre Zii was an adjudicator in 1593, one of the Twelve in 1597, 1599, 1605, and 1606, and a member of the adjunct in 1609. But then "Battista" was an abbreviation of "Zuan Battista."

How much simpler it would be if the officers had all had family names! Many clearly did. A very few of them – Francesco Gradignan, Lorenzo Gritti, Marco Navagier, and Zuanbattista Querenghi – appear to bear the surnames of noble families (and held nine terms of office between them). One wonders whether these names were indeed of noblemen, and what was the nature of their connection to the guild – at one remove as property owners and landlords of shops, perhaps? There are sixty-six other family names, referring to ninety-three different members who held a total of 248 offices. Many of them were members of the legal class of cittadini (citizens), whom Brian Pullan once described as a "parallel but minor aristocracy."[53] The presence of even a few patrician names and of a large number of the cittadini sets up a further correspondence between the organizations of those supposedly excluded from power and the exclusive state itself.

However, when it comes to identity within the guild of mercers, we are faced with passive malleability rather than family assertiveness. There was clearly no insistence on identification through family name. On the contrary, it would appear that family name was, more often than not, dropped. Lorenzo Aguzzi dal San Piero appears ten times on the lists, but on six of those occasions he is identified by Christian name and shop. Lorenzo Gidotti alla Scala (the Staircase) has his surname listed only once in seven entries. Oracio [*sic*] Milan al Treviso is identified primarily by his unusual first name, and "Milan" appears only three times in eleven listings. Cristofalo dall'Ocha (the Goose) is recorded with his family name, Pizzioli, only once in seven entries.

Perhaps identity was so loosely defined that shop sign was a more precise way of saying who you were or about whom you were talking. Among the surnames that appear in the membership lists, Pollani (or "Polemi") appears frequently. In the case of the officer Andrea Pollani, the inclusion is not helpful, because there are two persons of that name. Andrea Pollani dal Frate (the Friar) was one of the Twelve in 1588, and he appears on five further occasions as "Andrea dal Frate." As such, he is named as a member of the adjunct in 1602. That distinguished him from another Andrea Pollani who, astonishingly, was also a member of the zonta in the same year. But the latter is Andrea Pollani a San Lio (so, the parish is, unusually, invoked to identify him). We can further distinguish the two on the basis of the general membership lists, which include Andrea di Ierolimo Pollani who was "dal Frate" and in the parish of San Zulian, and Andrea di Francesco Pollani who was a "stringher" in San Lio.[54] One of the most prominent names in the membership lists is that of the Locadelli (also listed as "Lucadei"). There is a Corte Lucatello by the Ponte dei Baretteri near Rialto. The complex of alleys there provided cover for wares unloaded in the canal at the bridge, which then went all the way to San Zulian and the large shops nearby such as the Città di Milano (the City of Milan). The latter was the premises of Antonio Valfredo, who set up shop there in 1561, but neither he nor his shop features in the lists of officers. Two members of the Locadelli family are listed among the officers. Zuan Locadelli was the "zudese di mezz'anno" in 1600. The anonymous-sounding Zuan dalla Maddalena was a member of the Twelve in 1597 and 1608 and was part of the zonta in 1602. However, the other membership lists – not the list of officers – establish that the shop of Zuan Locadelli was the Maddalena. His relation Bortolomeo Locadelli was the scribe in 1605, but when he was later on the adjunct (1607 and 1609), he is listed only by forename and shop as "Bortolomeo dal Transilvan." It is tempting to speculate that the only time he used his surname was when he was scribe, and he was therefore quite literally styling himself and asserting both an identity within the family and an identification with the family that other keepers of the guild records generally suppressed. Alas for such an attractive theory, he is also scribe the following year, and he lists himself – or supervises his inscription – only as "Bortolomeo dal Transilvan." (See table 4.1.)

One reason for the absence of standardization may be the apparently very high turnover of the office of scribe. The lists of officers cover thirty-three years. In four cases (1580, 1592, 1598, and 1607) the scribe is not specified separately from the committee. Only two members apart from Bortolomeo Locadelli, namely Beltrame Carminati dal Paradiso and Ierolimo dal Zeneral, held the office more than once and, in each instance, in consecutive years, 1595–6 and 1601–2 respectively. It rather looks as though this was a job that few chased, and perhaps the consecutive years for Beltrame and Ierolimo imply that they had their respective arms twisted to stay on because no one else wanted the office. More positively, the rotation of the office of scribe subverts the idea of a tight clique in control of the guild's business. Put simply, for the twenty-seven occasions (there were three in 1600) in which the name of the scrivan is recorded, we have twenty-five different people. Such a high turnover appears generally valid for all of the guild's offices.

The distribution of the elections by office appears in table 4.2. Before the data are addressed, a question arises concerning the relationship between representation by officers and participation by members. This chapter emphasizes the turnover of office, which is unmistakable, and questions any formulaic notion that the narrowness of the electoral base is in itself a clear sign of oligarchical control. Any such connection is already undermined by the previous discussion of the prominent members and wealthy families that appear to have taken little interest in office-holding. Before elaborating that argument, it is important to set out the apparent disparity between the number of officers and the number of electors.

In 1586 the guild's officers oversaw the compilation of the most comprehensive list of the mercers' "names of brothers." In that year the guild listed 964 members, subdivided into different categories and recorded in different bound booklets. We have already mentioned the masters: 245 wholesalers and 121

Table 4.1. Elections in the Mercers' Guild, 1577–1609

	Officers								Electors			
	G	Z	Z 1/2	S	Sin.	Risp.	D	B	Comp.	12	Zon.	Total
1577	1	1	–	1	1	–	5	–	–	–	9	18
1578	1	2	1	1	–	–	–	4	–	8	–	17
1579	1	2	1	1	1	1	5	–	–	6	–	18
1580	1	2	–	–	2	–	6	–	–	6	–	17
1581	1	2	–	1	1	–	5	–	–	8	–	18
1582	1	2	1	1	2	–	4	–	–	8	–	19
1583	1	2	1	–	1	–	5	–	–	7	–	17
1584	1	2	1	1	1	2	4	–	–	6	–	18
1585	1	–	1	1	1	–	–	5	–	8	–	17
1586	1	2	1	1	2	–	–	4	–	11	–	22
1587	1	2	–	1	2	–	–	–	5	8	–	19
1588	1	2	1	1	1	–	–	–	3	8	–	17
1589	1	2	–	–	2	–	–	–	4	–	11	20
1590	1	2	1	1	1	–	–	4	–	10	–	20
1591	2	2	1	1	2	–	–	–	5	10	–	23
1592	1	–	1	–	1	–	–	–	7	9	–	19
1593	1	1	1	1	1	–	–	–	5	7	–	17
1594	1	2	2	1	1	–	1	–	4	9	–	21
1595	1	2	1	1	1	–	–	–	5	11	–	22
1596	1	2	1	–	3	6	–	–	6	10	–	29
1597	1	2	1	1	1	–	–	–	4	8	–	18
1598	1	2	–	–	3	–	–	–	6	–	–	12
1599	1	1	1	1	1	–	–	–	5	9	–	19
1600	1	1	1	3	–	–	–	–	6	–	9	21
1601	2	2	1	1	1	–	–	–	5	9	–	21
1602	1	1	1	1	1	–	–	–	5	–	9	19
1603	1	1	1	–	2	–	–	–	5	8	–	18
1604	1	2	1	1	1	–	–	–	2	11	–	19
1605	1	2	1	1	1	–	–	–	3	11	–	20
1606	1	1	1	1	–	–	–	–	4	9	–	17
1607	1	2	1	–	1	–	–	–	5	–	10	20
1608	1	2	–	1	–	–	–	–	4	10	–	18
1609	1	2	1	1	–	2	–	–	5	–	12	24
Total	35	55	27	27	39	11	35	17	103	225	60	634

Key: G, gastaldo; Z, zudese; Z ½, zudese di mezz'anno; S, scrivano; Sin, sindaco; Risp., di rispetto (reserve); D, degano; B, banca; Comp., compagno; 12, dodese; Zon., zonta

retailers. In addition, there were 282 apprentices ("zoveni"), and 285 members who were formally classified as poor ("poveri"), along with 31 women in a separate category of "donne."[55] The list was to be submitted to the government in order for the state to determine the level of the mercers' contribution to the crews of the reserve galley fleet. It seems likely that the women were shop holders in their own right and may have employed male assistants who could serve

Table 4.2. Elections and Officers in the Mercers' Guild, 1577–1609

Office	No. of Elections	No. of Members Elected	No. Holding More Than One Term
Officers			
Gastaldo	35	31	2
Zudesi	55	50	3
Zudesi di mezz'anno	27	23	4
Scrivan	27	25	2
Sindaco	39	26	5
Di rispetto	11	11	0
Electors			
Degani	35	31	4
Banca	17	16	1
Compagni	103	100	3
Dodesi	225	122	52
Zonta	60	43	12
Total	634	[478 offices] [275 different people]	88

in the war fleets in person. However, it is important to note that another list compiled by the guild, apparently only for internal record, listed a further 121 women, meaning that the real number of members of the mercers' guild was over a thousand. What a task it must have been to track them all down and then draw up the list.[56]

It is vital to remember that only masters were enfranchised. (In any case, it is difficult to imagine where a thousand members could comfortably have congregated to vote – probably not at a location such as the church of San Zulian, where the mercers' scuola had an altar, or even at the Scuola Grande di San Teodoro.) There is at least one instance when a man listed as "povero" had been an official of the guild: Bortolomeo Archuzio had been a deacon in 1579 but is listed as a povero in 1586. In that year the list of masters, wholesale and retail, comprised 366 names. The number of votes cast in the annual elections shows how small the electorate proved in practice. The largest number of voters was 104 in 1578, but only nineteen were present in 1598 (an occasion that produced only twelve officers, the smallest number in the sequence). At this point, one needs to underscore that many masters, perhaps as many as four-fifths, excluded themselves from the elections because they had debts outstanding to the guild.

It is also worth bearing in mind that that high turnover may have contributed to the variable numbers of masters recorded as enrolled in the guild, which in turn may partly account for the small numbers of voters. Between

1561 and 1568 the Giustizia Vecchia recorded the establishment of 170 new mercers' shops, about one in three of all the new premises for any trade registered in that period. That figure is a minimum and is strictly confined to shop owners described as "mercer." As we know, many other trades listed could have been associated with the mercers' guild.[57] In 1575 the mercers' officers drew up a list of members between the ages of eighteen and forty-five years for the purposes of allocating personal service on the galleys of the reserve fleet. Of the 874 names on this list, no fewer than 332 – about 38 per cent – had joined in the year of the compilation or the previous year. A further 22 per cent had joined between 1570 and 1573. Of the 874 members, 75 per cent had registered in the guild within the previous ten years.[58] This contrasts strongly with the extended span of years over which officers served more than one term. Could it have been that the elections to office from a relatively small pool provided a continuity that at once compensated for and complemented the high turnover of the general membership?

The variability of the number of mercers in any year also requires attention, and it is important not to compare a single static figure for the number of masters with the annually changing list of officers over a period of a third of a century. All the figures for the number of electors look paltry compared with the 366 masters eligible to vote in 1586 or the 446 shops listed in 1594.[59] However, the investigation of the guild's debtors in 1593 brought to light the fact that 79 of the 347 (about 23 per cent) had ceased trading ("non fa più bottega"), that is to say that they had gone out of business or changed trades by the time the guild sought to call in their debts. Moreover, the number of masters seems to have risen in the early seventeenth century: 417 names appear in the list of those who paid candle money to the guild in 1612.[60]

The salient features of the overall pattern of office-holding in table 4.1 are these. The number of committee members (officers and electors) varied between a maximum of twenty-nine in 1596, when the guild was in negotiation with the government over exemption from personal service in the galleys, and a low of twelve in 1598. The overall average was about nineteen (which stays the same if we remove the highest and lowest numbers of officers). In other words, wholesale and retail masters of the mercers' guild who were eligible to vote chose six officers responsible to both members and the state from a list of nominees drawn up by the outgoing officers and nominated electors. That general point about what we may call, without anachronism, "the electoral process" merits emphasis in a discussion of a popolo that supposedly did not participate in the city's politics. There is scarcely any sequence that clusters particular names in a period of a few years, apart from the three consecutive occasions on which Vivian di Panizzi dalle Tre Fontane (the Three Fountains) was custodian (1584–6).

As for the offices themselves, there is a general looseness below the rank of custodian, and this is particularly marked among the dozen electors, whose members are variously recorded. The guild elected a custodian every year, except in 1591 and 1601 when it elected two – perhaps because of the illness or death of the first incumbent (other records do not show any instances of the removal of officers before the end of their term). There were no designated adjudicators in 1592, but in that year the companions and adjunct accounted for sixteen of the total of nineteen posts and probably subsumed the three zudesi. There was no election to the office of adjudicator of mid-year on seven occasions. There was no scribe in eight years, and again one takes it that members of the committee shared the office. Similarly, there was no syndic in each of five separate years. Here the evidence for sharing is more direct since there were two syndics in seven different years, and three in two other years.

Loosest of all were the lines that distinguished the titles of deacons, bench, companions, the Twelve, and the adjunct. In various combinations these titles provided between twelve and fifteen officers every year, except 1598 when the total was only six. The titles of deacon and bench were largely lost after 1586. Thereafter, there are virtually unbroken runs of elections of companions (standard except in 1590) and of the Twelve, except in the five years when the latter were replaced by the adjunct.

The next stage of analysis is the presentation of the numbers of different names entered next to each office (table 4.2). In considering the patterns in this table, it is important to remember the standardization of the names of the office-holders, which sought to eliminate any exaggeration of the number through inconsistent record-keeping. Even with that careful safeguard, table 4.2 shows a wide spread of office among the 275 unique members who were elected to office – or elected to the office of elector. The columns show the number of elections to each office, the number of different names on record as holding each office, and a confirmation of the number of those who held each individual office for more than one term. Thus, more than once, two members became custodian, three became adjudicator, and two became scribe. It is perhaps notable that there were twenty-six different syndics for thirty-nine elections to that office, but any greater frequency here can surely be attributed to expertise in drawing up accounts. Even in a combination of all five different titles that designated membership of the guild's committee of twelve, the average number of terms of office per name never reaches two. Combining the deacons, the bench, the companions, the Twelve, and the adjunct gives the result that the 440 elections to all of these involved the participation of 243 different mercers, of the total number of 275 who served as officers. The final column demonstrates that only 88 names served more than one term in the same office. Differently expressed, fewer than 14 per cent (barely one election in eight of the 634) resulted in the same person holding the same office more than once.

The spread of office-holding among the 275 different mercers is striking, and there is no decisive evidence of particular names exercising a noticeable grip on individual offices. Vivian di Panizzi dalle Tre Fontane, who was custodian four times, and thrice in consecutive years (1584–6) is, again, a notable and still isolated exception. Lorenzo Aguzzi dal San Piero was twice an adjudicator, as were Madernin di Rigo and Bernardo Sechini, but their two terms were several years apart. The three mercers who served twice as adjudicator of mid-year all served in consecutive years, but this may reveal precise record-keeping by the scribe, since, as noted, the office spanned two successive years. One might repeat that only two scribes served twice, both of them in consecutive years. Castello del Noris, "coroner," was a companion in both 1603 and 1604. Those who appear frequently among the Twelve, such as Alvise dal San Todaro, Battista dal Banchetto, Benetto della Riossa, and Jacopo alla Colombina all served over an extended period of years and held other offices in other years.

A possible anomaly in table 4.2 is represented by its total of office-holders, artificially high at 478, since the total number of unique members to hold office was only 275. Table 4.3 eliminates that potential distortion by examining the number of terms of office that each of the 275 held. Jacopo Bergonzi dalla Madonna stands alone in holding fifteen terms of office. He is followed by three who served eleven terms – Jacopo alla Colombina, Madernin di Rigo, and Oracio Milan dal Treviso. One mercer held office ten times (Lorenzo Aguzzi dal San Piero), one served nine terms (Zuan Rossi dal Pero), and two won eight elections (Battista dal Banchetto and Zuanbattista dai Tre Zii). Seven held office seven times, and nine served six times. However, the number of office-holders in any of the numerically descending terms of office only reaches double figures for the number of members at five (there were fourteen of them) – surely not many over thirty-three years and 634 elections. The cumulative percentages in the final column are the most revealing. Fewer than 9 per cent of candidates held office more than five times. That is to say, over 90 per cent – 253 of the 275 office-holders – were elected five times or fewer. Over 86 per cent of those elected served four times or fewer; 80 per cent, three times or fewer; and 70 per cent, once or twice. Those who held office only once account for exactly 56 per cent: 154 of the total number of 275 office-holders.

Table 4.4 relates the number of terms served by each of those who held office to the total of 634 elections held in the period. At first sight, this can seem a different picture, concentrating high proportions of office in small numbers of office-holders. Less than 9 per cent of the office-holders were successful in almost 30 per cent of elections, and fewer than 10 per cent of the officers won

Table 4.3. Number of Terms of Office in the Mercers' Guild, 1577–1609

Terms of Office Held	No. of Office- Holders	% of Office-Holders	Cumulative %
15	1	0.36	0.36 99.64
14	–	–	
13	–	–	
12	–	–	
11	3	1.10	1.46 98.54
10	1	0.36	1.82 98.18
9	1	0.36	2.18 97.82
8	2	0.73	2.91 97.09
7	7	2.55	5.46 94.54
6	9	3.27	8.73 91.27
5	14	5.09	13.82 86.18
4	15	5.45	19.27 80.73
3	28	10.18	29.45 70.55
2	40	14.55	44.00 56.00
1	154	56.00	
Total	275	100.00	100.00

very nearly half of all the elections. All the same, it remains extremely difficult to demonstrate that any of the categories constituted a coherent interest group running the guild's business. Even for a sequence of records spanning thirty-three years, there is an element of distortion due to changing generations. Again, it was evident that rich families were not necessarily prominent as office-holders. Moreover, as is shown by the general catalogue of members for 1575, the turnover of membership itself was very high.[61] In some cases, members listed in the early years of the lists of officers may have been at the end of their careers. Agostino Cegrini al San Cristofalo appears on the list of

Table 4.4. Offices and Elections in the Mercers' Guild, 1577–1609

Terms of Office Held	No. of Office-Holders	No. of Elections	% of Elections	Cumulative %
15	1	15	2.37	2.37 97.63
14	–	–	–	
13	–	–	–	
12	–	–	–	
11	3	33	5.20	7.56 92.44
10	1	10	1.58	9.15 90.85
9	1	9	1.42	10.57 89.43
8	2	16	2.52	13.09 86.91
7	7	49	7.73	20.82 79.18
6	9	54	8.52	29.34 70.71
5	14	70	11.04	40.38 59.62
4	15	60	9.46	49.84 50.16
3	28	84	13.25	63.09 36.91
2	40	80	12.62	75.71 24.29
1	154	154	24.29	
Total	275	634	100.00	100.00

officers as syndic in 1579 and among the Twelve in 1582. From other records we know that he had been custodian in 1574, the year that the guild – with many others – agreed to a government order to participate in the welcome for Henri of France.[62] That instance is of interest in suggesting that becoming custodian was not the apogee of office-holding. The experience of the office seems to have fed into the guild's subsequent management. Cegrini's case is typical. His example implies that there was no cursus honorum in the offices and that none of them was necessarily taken for granted as honorific.

That particular instance typifies a general trend. Of the thirty-five elections for custodian, very nearly half (seventeen) brought to office someone who held or was to hold three offices or fewer including this one. For eight such candidates, there was only one other office, and five custodians in the period held no other office at all. Of twenty-five scribes, twenty-three held five offices or fewer. The amalgamation of those who served as electors – deacons, members of the bench, companions, the Twelve, and the adjunct – gives a total of 440 elections. A little over one-tenth of these (forty-seven) gave the office to people who held a total of eight posts or more. A further 226 of the elections in this category – more than half – were held by men who served a total of three terms or fewer.

More extensively than the implications of the example of Cegrini do, the next quantitative exercise tests whether there was any hierarchy among the offices themselves. The most prolific office-holder, Jacopo Bergonzi dalla Madonna, was custodian on two occasions, drew up the guild's accounts as syndic five times, and served eight times as either one of the Twelve or on the adjunct. At the other end of the scale, of those who held office only once, there were five custodians, five scribes, and four syndics.

If we turn our attention once again to an amalgamated committee of electors, then, of the 275 names we may count 243 who held one or some of the five titles for the posts. This means that there were thirty-two officers who never served as deacons, on the bench, as companions, as members of the Twelve, or as members of the adjunct. The thirty-two members in this category were involved in a total of thirty-six elections that covered the full range of the guild's officers: eight custodians, twelve adjudicators, two adjudicators of mid-year, six scribes, four syndics, and four "di rispetto." Only two of the thirty-two, Mario da Monte (who held four offices) and Cristofalo Rubi (two offices), held office more than once.

Having divided the data in a wide variety of ways, and in an effort to return to a general overview, it is revealing to revisit the idea of the generational snapshot that even the thirty-three years of the lists of officers provide. Table 4.5 summarizes the period of office-holding for each officer who served more than once.

Jacopo Bergonzi's fifteen terms spread over twenty-nine years, nearly nine-tenths of the entire period of the lists. Those who served eleven terms did so, on average, over a period of twenty-eight years – almost as long. Lorenzo Aguzzi dal San Piero, who served ten times, did so over nineteen years. For those who held office nine times, the average period was twenty-four years, and so on. There are numerous examples of very long periods of time between offices for those who served on few occasions. Andrea dal Giesù held six offices over twenty-one years, Michiel di Mezi alla Gatta (the Cat) held six over twenty-four years, and Andrea Pollani six over twenty-five years. The average for this category of six-time office-holders is somewhat reduced by the unusual pattern of Vivian di Panizzi's career, serving six offices in only nine years, including four times as custodian, and three of those tenures occurred in consecutive years (1584–6). Defendi dal Gallo served five times over twenty-four years, and

Table 4.5. Average Span of Years of Office-Holding, 1577–1609

No. of Offices Held	No. of Office-Holders	Average No. of Years
15	1	29
11	3	28
10	1	19
9	1	24
8	2	23
7	7	19
6	9	16
5	14	22
4	15	21
3	28	9
2	40	5

Paolo dal San Rocho served five times over twenty-eight. The figures show that anyone on the list who held office on four occasions or more did so, on average, over a period of more than twenty years. Zuanantonio Bozza held his four offices over thirty years. Even below that category, offices were often spread over many years. Andrea dal Profeta (the Prophet) served three times in fifteen years, Iseppo della Fontana three times in seventeen years, Graziosi Negroni three times in nineteen years, and Zorzi Rotta three times in eighteen years. Of those who held office only twice, we might point to Jacopo Gavazeni alla Campana (the Bell) who was an adjudicator in 1580 and a companion in 1602, and Ierolemo dai Tre Anzolli (the Three Angels) who was a deacon in 1577 but waited twenty years to hold office again, this time as a member of the Twelve.

Office-holding in concentrated periods of years is virtually non-existent, and holding the same office with any regularity is extremely rare. The data suggest that the mercers observed periods of "contumacia," a required interval between periods in office, in keeping with the regulation of 1471. The same data even hint that there may have been a strong ethic of semi-public service. In the statute of 1271 any member who refused office was fined five lire and then made to serve, anyway. That system of penalties persisted in the statute that the guild drew up two hundred years later.[63] In only one case is there evidence that an elected candidate refused the post. The very last name on the alphabetical list, Zuanpiero dal Pozzo (the Cistern), was elected a deacon in 1580, but the entry carries the note "to elect in his place for having paid 15 lire" (far in suo luogo per aver pagato £15). This may be the product of inconsistent documentation, and perhaps other cases are not matters of record. James Shaw has found documentation that has convinced him of the mercers' reluctance to serve, with five refusals of the office of custodian in 1595.[64]

"Far suo logo": that line of unique annotation is the only entry in the list under scrutiny for Zuanpiero. As for the mercer who held office most frequently, Jacopo Bergonzi dalla Madonna may have been a self-seeking schemer, a self-important ass, or a committee-loving bore. It is perhaps most likely that he was a selfless semi-public servant. In the context of the data that this chapter has exhaustively examined, it is perhaps even more likely that he was a selfless semi-public servant. Perhaps opinion of him varied among his fellow mercers, those who did or did not hold office. Against the possible objection that office was a largely irrelevant triviality stands the uniquely rich documentation of the mercers' archive – for which historians owe a debt to the diligence of these same office-holders. The very records that the officers kept illustrate a significant point in respect of guild self-government. The collection of "atti diversi" (various acts) in the mercers' archival holdings stands as evidence of the way in which the day-to-day business fed into alterations and additions to the statute, strongly suggesting that the Venetian designation of a guild statute, the mariegola, was just that: a "madre-regola" or "mother-rule."

In general terms, these conclusions follow. For each office, for each year, for each category of office-holder from multiple to single, all the evidence points to a broad spread and an even share. The data dispel any idea that there was a controlling oligarchy or plutocracy that managed the guild's affairs in its own interests, or a hierarchy of office with some positions exercising pivotal power and others reserved for makeweights. There is also no evidence of the government's controlling hand in the guild's processes, a characteristic that we have already observed in the scuole piccole. The scribe of 1588 was Zuan Zoncha, who kept the sign of the San Sebastiano at San Salvador. He had been condemned by the Holy Office in 1582 to various penalties, including life imprisonment. He was released after a few months to care for his ailing wife, but the Inquisitors attached the condition that he was never to be seen in his shop.[65] In light of such a sentence, it is intriguing that his fellows in the guild of mercers should have seen fit to elect him to such a responsible office.

If there are analogies between the organization of the guilds and the structures of government, then they suggest complementarity rather than conflict, connection rather than exclusion. No systematic or manipulative political control, no conspiracy, no oligarchy, no plutocracy, no hierarchy – it is somewhat frustrating to draw conclusions that seem so often to prove what was not the case rather than what was; however, in itself, this may be instructive and may provide some insight into the workings of the republic. In a general survey of the significance of Venice, Brian Pullan remarked that the study of La Serenissima is often the story of the dog that does not bark, a matter of explaining why things did not happen rather than why they did.[66] Perhaps the mercers' records reflect the macrocosm in the microcosm, the corporations as untidy miniatures of the state as a whole. The water and stone of the city can symbolically reflect its history, the water representing the economy, constantly on the move and seeking new channels, the stone representing the stability of the constitution. That too has its miniature replication in these data. The economic activities of the mercers, in their teeming membership of a thousand, were reflected in high turnover and constant movement. The 275 masters who held office in the guild over the thirty-three years of documentation under scrutiny appear to have provided a longer-term continuity without rigging arrangements in favour of particular factions. The data prompt a contrast with the Republic of Florence. The electoral processes in that restless city, in which guild membership was the criterion of political participation, have been subject to the closest scholarly scrutiny. However, in a characteristically elegant summary John Hale demonstrated that a political population of some five thousand adult males reduced in practice to an inner circle of about seventy-five "men of influence."[67] At this point, the comparison suggests that in Florence the electoral base was apparently broad but in reality narrow, while in Venice the base was apparently narrow but in reality broad.

The central importance of this part of the study, though, is that the motivation of office-holders in the guild of mercers may have covered as wide a spectrum of possibility as it did for the holders of magisterial office in the patrician state. There has long been debate on whether patricians were the selfless and devoted servants of the republic or self-interested draft dodgers who sought to avoid the expense and inconvenience of office. The truth may well have lain in a synthesis, with the former predominating sometimes, and the latter at other times.[68]

Official Business

External Protection: The Mercers' Wares

All of the foregoing returns to dust if it transpires that the work of the officers was of no great significance. If the offices of the guild were of little effect or if they were honorific, if they were marginal to the day-to-day activities of those who dealt in mercery, or if there was no "execution" as the mariegola of 1471 seemed to press for, then all the data become questionable. However, there is substantial evidence in the records of the mercers of just how busy their officers were, not only in matters of routine but also in dealing with complicated and protracted negotiation. In this assessment it is necessary to move well beyond the confines of the lists of officers, but what this loses in chronological exactness it gains in material precision.

Nevertheless, in order to avoid a narrative confusion, it is useful to set some chronological markers, beginning in 1446. A careful reading of what the guild itself described as "the foundation of our trade" (el fundamento del nostro mestier), drawn up in 1446 and inscribed in the beautiful mariegola of 1471, confirms two significant features: first, the exacting detail of what the officers were to regulate and, second, the impulse towards enforcement.[69] The provision was to be read out loud at every one of the guild's general meetings. The range of what the mercers claim as mercery is remarkable and seems close to what we would term *merchandise*. The statute defined *merzeria* as goods imported via the Fondaco dei Tedeschi, with particular reference to basins and copperware, tin-plated iron, burnished mirrors, glass for mirrors, caps, gloves of wool or leather, pie cups, scissors, shears, rosaries, hats, spectacles, weights for scales, razors, blades, belts, combs of horn or wood, and cushions – whether or not subject to duty. Those who bought stolen silk and made from it ribbon, thread, braid, fringes, belts, and household goods were prohibited from doing so. Metalware and textiles were interspersed: basins, chandeliers, copper and brassware, arms and armour such as breastplates, gloves, armguards and accessories for crossbows, felt, pewter from Flanders, thick cord, large bags, hats (wool or straw), playing cards, caps, and draw-strings. Other merchandise included wares imported from Milan and Lombardy. Goods from Florence and Tuscany include tinsel, wedding chests, mirrors framed with bone, small chests for novices, silk, beads or wire for the abacus, and whittling knives. All types of cutlery from the Romagna, Modena, or Ferrara "and anywhere else" were also the mercers' preserve. Mercery made in Venice or elsewhere defined itself as combs, felts, caps, veils of cotton or silk, small boxes, caskets, kerchiefs whether or not embroidered with silk, veils, bonnets, cloth of gold from Cologne, pewter, cushions square and round, bellows, and "all of the aforesaid and those not listed" (tute le cose prenominadi como quelli non son denotadi). The regulations were to apply to men or women, whether they sold from shops, stalls, or benches or were street traders. Anyone who dealt in such goods was to join the mercers' scuola, to which they would be welcomed: "we will accept them all and love them as brothers" (quelli tutti aceteremo e ameremo como fradelli). The metal goods listed set up obvious conflict with the ironmongers, though the statute did not specify their trade, instead making particular reference to dealers in fustians and to spicers, goldsmiths, the silk trades, fruiterers, and second-hand dealers.

There was a clearly and precisely expressed insistence on implementation ("perche le preditte cose habia effecto") that had several constituent elements.

First, the officers had a clear incentive for enforcement since they received one-third of any fine that they collected. The other parts were to go to the scuola and the Giustizia Vecchia. All officers of the guild were empowered, singly or in a body, to stop, search, and confiscate, or they could order such measures ("chadaun che sarà in offitio inquerir e cerchar e far cerchar pignorar e far pignorar"). These considerable powers of policing were carefully refined in co-operation with the officials of the Giustizia. The magistrates could award a licence to street traders as long as their mercery was not above forty soldi in value. If the officials of the magistracy found upon inspection that the value of the wares involved (whether they were carried openly or concealed) exceeded this sum, they could take half of the fines due to the guild's own officers and to the scuola "so that they do not waste their exertion" (per che i ditti officiali non perda la sua fadiga).

There is some proof to this pudding in that membership lists drawn up more than a hundred years later, in 1586 – a comprehensive list, not merely of elections to office – revealed a membership of around a thousand strong, with occupational designations covering eighty trades and all of the wares listed in the statute. To that extent, the polity as represented by the Giustizia, the economy as represented by the guild itself, and religion as represented by the scuola shared a functional interaction. Broadly speaking, the little republic that was the mercers' guild shows the three spheres of polity, economy, and religion overlapping in dynamic microcosm.

Internal Administration: The Festa della Sensa

The officers had to defend the guild's interests and regulate the economic activities of its members and keep both those spheres of activity in contact with the devotional calendar of the scuola. There was the matter of the feast days that the guild observed, for instance. Apart from Sundays – and, as we have seen, at least four Sundays were taken up with electoral business – there were more than twenty other occasions on which the officers had to ensure that shops were shut and, on many of them, organize processions and church services. The guild observed at least two dozen of its own holidays: Christmas and the two days following; the Epiphany; Good Friday; the Day of the Resurrection (Easter Day) and two days after that; Pentecost and the next day; Corpus Christi; Santa Croce; the Feast of the Apostles; four days dedicated to the Virgin; the days of San Marco, San Lorenzo, San Giovanni Battista, Santa Cattarina, San Nicolo, Santa Lucia, and All Saints; and a day honouring the dead (presumably All Souls, the day after All Saints).[70] The equipment that the scuola had to provide for such ritual occasions was often in need of attention. In 1564 the guild had moved its altar in the church of San Zulian in order to give greater accessibility to that of the Venerabile – tended by what was only the second of the city's Eucharistic brotherhoods – placing it by the adjoining wall, between the two windows "where Saint Francis is at present."[71] The new location also involved the officers in ordering the altar's embellishments in major commissions of work by the sculptor Alessandro Vittoria and the painter Palma il Giovane. Yet, even if there were gear to maintain and prepare for specific occasions, there were constant concerns about security. In light of recent thefts ("furti et latrocini") at the Scuole Grandi di San Rocco and San Marco, the mercers' officers decided in 1574 that protection of items of precious holiness needed strong locks ("bone seradure").[72]

Security was also a problem that the officers faced when organizing the allocation of stalls for one of the great occasions of the Venetian year, appropriately combining a celebration of economic prosperity, political power, and religious piety, the three spheres mingling once again. In this example the data combine emphatically with the administrative detail to form the underpinning of a regular opportunity for profit at the solemn religious and political heart of the city. The Feast of the Ascension (the Sensa) was an exaltedly holy day in the Christian year. In Venice the celebration involved the doge "wedding" the sea by throwing into it a ring (or a replica) that had been among the gifts of Pope Alexander III in gratitude for his refuge in 1177 – thus confirming the republic's ancient sovereign independence. That marriage of religion and politics then gave way to a market that lasted for two weeks, a fine opportunity for the Venetians to fleece gullible visitors such as the Brescian in Castiglione's *Cortegiano* who failed to recognize the slide on a Venetian trombone.

> I heard a Brescian speak a joly grosse matter, which, being this year in Venice at the feast of Ascension rehearsed in a place where I was to certaine mates of his the goodly matters he had seene there, what sundrie merchandise, what plate, what sortes of spices and what cloth and silk there was, then how the Signoria issued out with a great pompe in the Bucentoro to wedde the Sea, in which were so many gentlemen well apparayled, so many sortes of instruments and melodies, that a man would have thought it a Paradise.
>
> And when one of his companions demaunded him what kinde of Musicke did please him best of all that he had hearde there, hee saide: All were good, yet among the rest I saw one blow on a straunge Trumpet, which at every push thrust it into his throate more than two handful, and then by and by drew it out againe, and thrust it in a fresh, that you never saw a greater wonder.
>
> Then they all laughed, understanding the fond imagination of him that thought the blower thrust into his throat that part of ye Shagbut that is hid in putting it backe againe.[73]

For the occasion of the fair, market stalls covered Piazza San Marco. The mercers took pride of place, extending their own Mercerie – where their shops were closed – from the clock tower to the Molo, with thirty stalls lining the sides of a lane in front of the church of San Marco. Their records provide a plan of the stalls as the mercers were to provide them for the fair of 1586 (fig. 17). There were to be fifteen booths in each of two lines, each booth probably eleven feet high and ten feet wide, and with a display on a "balcony" that presumably folded away before the stall was locked.[74] The first booth presented its display towards the clock tower, proffering its holder's wares to visitors as soon as they entered the piazza. These stalls looked east with their backs to the church near the palace ("appresso il Pallazo"). Facing them were a further fifteen stalls, similarly arranged, designated as in the vicinity of the bakers' shops ("appresso la Panataria"). (The name persisted despite the fact that there were no longer any bakers' stalls; they had been cleared in order to create the space for the library.)[75] The stalls were to remain in place from the eve of the Ascension until the Sunday before Corpus Christi, Trinity Sunday, which in turn was a week after Whit (Pentecost) Sunday. The arrangements that the officers had to make for storage of the booths for the fifty weeks of the year when the guild did not need them are unclear.

However, there was neither enthusiasm nor neatness in the guild's allocation of places. As we shall see, the guild was beset with litigation from its corporate rivals; the allocation of stations for the Sensa was to generate chronic legal dispute within the guild itself.[76] In the later sixteenth century the responsible officers had to work with the indifference of members, the concerns for security of the booths that they were to set up, and the demands on their own willingness to take a place. In some ways this was scarcely surprising. In 1574 the Council of Ten insisted that the mercers should have new booths made for the piazza,[77] barely a month before the government's demands for a decorated barge that would participate in the celebrations for the visit of the future Henri III of France.[78] As for the reluctance to take up a stall, this was probably due to two considerations. First, it may have been a protest against the council's insistence on the closure of the regular shops in the Mercerie, and, second, there were clear concerns that the booths were not satisfactorily or sufficiently secure against thievery for the two weeks of the market.

In 1581 the guild agreed to have thirty new booths made, to be rented for the Sensa at five ducats each.[79] With no indication that the new booths were ready, the custodian, Michiel dal Re (at The King), presided over a motion that the allocation of stalls for the Sensa would have to be mandatory, without the possibility of a member refusing a place. While the committee voted in favour of this by a unanimous sixteen, the general meeting was not so readily disposed,

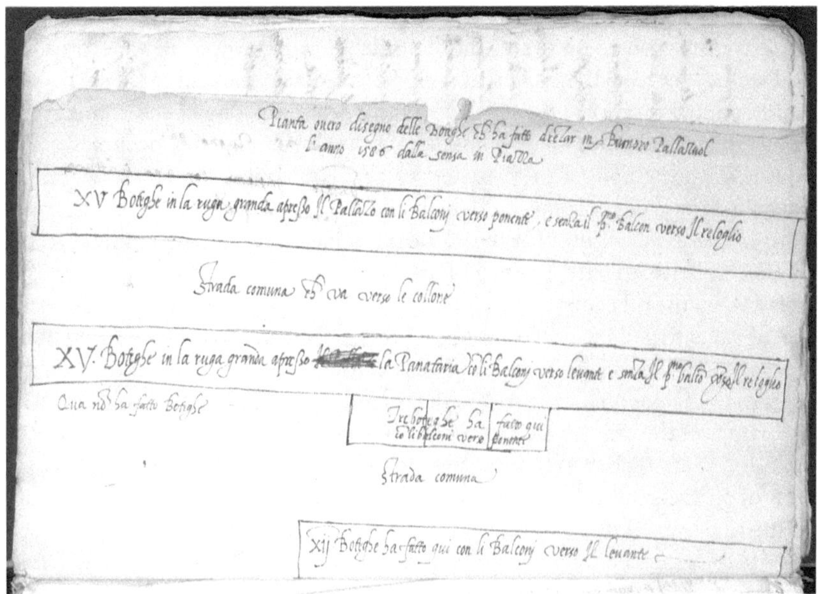

17. Plan of the Mercers' Stalls for the Festa della Sensa, 1586. Copyright Archivio di Stato di Venezia.

and it passed at only sixty-one to fifty-four.[80] The coercion failed completely. In 1585 there were only nine volunteers for the thirty places. The Procuratori di San Marco ordered a compulsory sortition, which appears to have backfired so badly that it made the volunteers think twice. Two of them appear to have backed out, for the guild's committee resolved to allocate twenty-three stalls (meaning that members had taken up only seven places) whose holders must "go to the Sensa by compulsion" (andar in sensa per forza).[81] The following year, the custodian, Francesco Gradignan, made it a matter of record that he could find no one who wanted to take a stall.[82] This example of the failure of government intervention shows a guild's capacity to dispute the government's authority, even that of high-ranking magistrates such as the Procuratori di San Marco. Perhaps it also suggests that lower-level magistrates, who were closer to guild business, may have thought it best to leave well alone.

One of the reasons for this stubborn reluctance may have been the condition of the booths themselves.[83] By now, one of the mercers, Brunoro Palazuol, "marzer alle Tre Pigne," having petitioned the Procuatori three years previously, undertook to provide the thirty new stalls.[84] The stalls were still not ready in

1593 – that is to say, nearly twenty years after the Ten had demanded that the guild commission them – and those available were in need of waterproofing and locks.[85] By 1595 the guild was seeking to replace Palazuol in the task.[86]

The annual bickering over allocations for what was one of the commercial, political, and religious high points of the Venetian calendar occupies a vast swathe of the archive of the arte dei marzeri. This one task, which one might have thought potential stall-holders would have anticipated with an eagerness born of the expectation of profit, appears to have generated an annual round of tension between hard-pressed officers and an ill-disposed membership. The pressure on the officers perhaps found its most eloquent summary in the number of stalls that they ended up taking themselves in those years for which a clear record survives. In an effort to cut through the records and to cut short the story, it is possible to correlate the records of the eventual allocations with the names of the officers elected for any one year (table 4.6).

In the years that the records cover, officers of the guild took about 40 per cent of all the stations available. Given what we have established with regard to the turnover of office-holding, it is possible that such a proportion reflects a sense of responsibility among the elected officials for the guild as a whole. It is perhaps noteworthy that the pressure upon them to take up the slack of the general membership seems to ease. Without a fully documented sequence it is impossible to offer more than a general impression. Nevertheless, in the first five years of the imperfect sequence officers seem to take on around a half of all the places to be allocated, and in the series beginning in 1599 the proportion falls to around one-third. Perhaps the members were unhappy with the arrangement that closed their botteghe on the Mercerie for the duration of the market on the piazza during the Sensa. There seems to be some relief in the record of 1610 that allows those shops to remain open for business, in the clear hope that this will generate more competition with the stalls on the piazza, and more money for the mercers: "And for the honour due to the celebrated festivals of the Church and of the whole city and in order not to remove the opportunity of some gain and competition for the shops of the Sensa, that in order to augment public grandeur they [the shops of the Merceria] must remain open."[87]

Church, city, profit, the three of them in concert for public greatness – all in all, the three circles of mercers' polity, mercers' economic activity, and mercers' devotions still seem to have been holding together the mercers' miniature commonwealth in 1610. The guild received a demand from the government to allocate stalls on the Piazza San Marco for the fair that lasted two weeks after Ascension Day. There was an attached condition, that the shops in the Mercerie would remain closed during that period. The guild's members grumbled and

Table 4.6. Allocations of Booths for the Sensa, 1585–1602

Year	Stalls Allocated		Total	Officers Holding Stalls
	Palazzo	Panataria		
1585	9	21	30	15
1587	15	?	15	8
1595	15	15	30	15
1597	15	15	30	11
1598	–	–	30	16
1599	15	1	16	4
1600	14	14	28	10
1601	13	14	27	9
1602	15	15	30	12
Total			220	100

chafed, objected, and eventually prevailed. This seems a persuasive and entirely human picture of how the mercers' little republic defined its place in "the public grandeur" of the larger commonwealth.

The year 1588 – when Brunello Palazuol was supposed to be renewing the booths, and only two years since the guild had compiled, in response to government demands, what became the most comprehensive membership list in all its records – seems to have been a time of particular tension. On 26 September the custodian, Francesco di Rossi, returned to his shop, the Melon, to find a paper "with words of insolence and dishonour towards our brotherhood" (comparolle de incarzo e dishonor della squolla nostra). A disgruntled member, evidently fined for failing to attend a funeral, had threatened physical violence in menacing terms: "To you gastaldo of the mercers I give warning that blows will not be lacking for you if you hold to this path because I have paid 12 lire for not going to a funeral [and] if this came into your purse for you I would be in the right for the miserable year that you have to stay, I'll make things happen. I beseech you to let this feast go [;] if not you'll get your head smashed in and don't complain that you weren't warned, if it comes from Monte Olivetano[?] you won't know where it's come from."[88]

The threat was not necessarily idle. In a later example, from 1663, Biasio Nadal appeared before the bench and used "improper words threatening our representatives" (parolle inproprie minacciando li detti nostri ministri). One of the officers, Giacomo Baldisera, was threatened with a knife and knocked down by Nadal, or made to beg for mercy by him, in the Mercerie near the clock tower ("fu assalito del sudetto Biasio Nadal in marzaria dal Relogio e posta mano ad un pugnal lo reduse asuoi piedi").[89]

Litigation

While resentments could be fierce within the guild, the officers had to deal with many other disputes, those of a jurisdictional nature, with a large number of other corporations. For a case against the hatters ("capelleri") in 1593, the mercers assembled documentation referring to a dispute with the braidmakers ("passamaneri") of that same year; a dispute against the knitters ("guchiadori") from 1588; a decision of the Collegio delle Arti concerning the mercers' relations with perfumers ("muschieri") and miniature makers ("miniadori") from 1574; and a ruling from the Council of Ten against the mirror makers ("specchieri") of 1569. This was in turn supported by a ruling from the council concerning the carpenters ("marangoni") of 1566, and a previous dispute with the hatters from 1534. The documentation stretched back to 1474 for a case concerning the sawyers, citing the "fondamento del nostro mestier" of 1446 from the mariegola. The Giustizia Vecchia had made a ruling concerning the painters ("depentori") in 1436, and the earliest precedent that the mercers drew to their defence was a Senate ruling of 1430 on a dispute with the ironmongers ("fabbri").[90] When the reader pauses to consider the work of assembling the documentation, and, moreover, the number of disputes represented by such documentation, and then doubles the time, effort, and material by remembering that the mercers are keeping only their side of the argument, then the amount of paperwork, legal work, and legwork is astonishing – even allowing for the involvement of a lawyer.

In the mercers' own list of legal actions, prominent was the idea that anyone who sold more than one type of goods must join each of the scuole for the full range of his or her wares: apothecaries selling pots or glass jars had to join the potters; fruiterers who sold ironware were to join the fabbri or, if they sold cord, the scuola of the mercers; the "pignater" who sold playing cards was to join the stationers; and so on.[91]

The mercers laid claim to such an empire of goods that disputes with other trades were inevitable. Capitolo 24 of the mariegola sets out a claim of imperialistic proportions. There were seemingly endless disputes with the ironmongers. It may be that the mercers were seeking to move into the Calle dei Fabbri as well as their own Mercerie, thus exploiting the two main thoroughfares between Rialto and San Marco. Those two walkways, both crowded with tiny shops, are joined by a street that in its very name symbolizes potential disputes: Calle della Fiubera. This "Buckle Alley" takes its name from an item that the ironmongers could claim as metalware and that would be a component of the belts the mercers claimed as their monopoly.[92] Perhaps the shoemakers could also have claimed the right to use buckles. For their litigation with the ironmongers the mercers assembled file after file of precedents, many of them relating to disputes between the fabbri and other metal trades such as the swordsmiths and the cutlers.[93] These cases tested every avenue of appeal in Venetian courts. In 1613 the arguments of mercers and ironmongers involved the Giustizia Vecchia, the governors of the Fondaco dei Tedeschi (the mercers always claimed the monopoly on ironware that came into Venice via the German warehouse), the Auditori Vecchi, the Council of Forty, the Provveditori alla Giustizia Vecchia, and the Cinque Savi alla Mercanzia, and even decisions from the Maggior Consiglio.[94]

In 1596 the mercers were involved in a case of fantastic contortions with the dealers in second-hand goods ("strazzaruoli"). The strazzaruoli brought a case against Bortolomeo, marzer at the sign of the San Vidal, objecting that he was not entitled to sell tapestries, which they claimed as their own. The dispute went before the Giustizia Vecchia, but the mercers invoked the Auditori Nuovi, who halted the proceedings and absolved Bortolomeo. The mercers then proceeded to insist on their own vast array of wares with a proclamation from the Provveditori di Comun to be read on the Ponte di Rialto, in the Piazza San Marco, at San Salvador, the Ponte dei Baretteri, San Zulian, Santi Apostoli, San Pantalon, San Polo, and San Stefano. It appears that all that the second-hand dealers could do was lament "the greed and avidity of the mercers" (l'ingordigia et avidità dei marzeri).[95] The mercers had rested their argument on a dispute with the drapers from 1572 over whether "fodre gottonate" could be classified as tapestries. The drapers had accused the mercers of trying to persuade the court to recognize black as white ("pensano darci a conoscer il nero per bianco"). The mercers took the case to the Provveditori di Comun, with the stated purpose of shutting up the drapers once and for all ("ricerchiamo di chiuderli la bocca affatto") and throwing out the drapers' case as full of opinions that were contradictory, empty, repugnant, and coloured with absurd reasoning ("opinioni varie, vane, repugnanti in se stesse collorite con ragioni absurde"). Two highly placed lobbyists, Bontempelli and Secchini, represented the mercers before the Council of Forty, but the Avogadori di Comun ruled against the drapers. The drapers had the decision reversed by the Provveditori di Comun, but a second ruling from the Council of Forty found for the mercers.[96] No wonder that the canvas makers ("tellaroli") thought that "it should be enough for the mercers' guild to have so many guilds subjected to it" (doveria bastare all'arte de marzeri d'haver tant'arti a lei sottoposte).[97]

Perhaps the energies that the mercers' expended in litigation derived from the sense of participation in the affairs of the guild that its brethren could share. The guild's elections convey a lively sense of representation. The mercers operated their own miniature political economy, and it met with plenty of resistance to its policies of protection and furtherance. Even in those unfathomable disputes with other guilds of Venice, it was the devotional brotherhood, the scuola, that was invoked by all parties as the focus of participation in any trade. Wrangling in courts never became fighting in the streets, and perhaps the very litigiousness of the Venetians was an expression of vitality in the commonwealth. The whole was held together, however, above all by the Venetians' shared value system that derived from their local version of the Christian religion.

5 Monuments to Mercy, c. 1500–c. 1600

He finds the joys of heaven here on earth,
And if on earth he do not merit it,
In reason, he should never come to heaven!

– Shakespeare, *The Merchant of Venice*, 3.5.70–2

Arti and Scuole in the Sixteenth Century

The previous two chapters moved the focus of this study from corporations that were formed for primarily devotional purposes to others that were associated with particular occupations. While attention to the former may result in an impression of harmony and concord, close study of the latter reveals the extent of motion and rivalry. The history of all Venice's brotherhoods was dominated by movement in the limited and crowded urban space. Both the expansion of the network of confraternities and the dynamics of the trades were symptomatic of the vitality of the relationship between economic, religious, and political life. Both were indications of a steady strengthening of the warp and weft of social institutions that offered an infrastructure of support for their members. Membership itself was not rigidly exclusive, and the capacity of all these corporate entities to absorb people from a parish, a trade, a loose area in the city, or a region outside of it was a key to the cohesiveness of the larger entity that we call Venice. The dynamics of this institutional infrastructure drew purpose and direction from the economic, religious, and indeed political energies of the popolo, who had their own systems of representation – systems that owed surprisingly little to the initiatives of Church or State.

This chapter explores further those themes in an examination of two new types of confraternity that developed in the sixteenth century, the Scuole del Venerabile and the sovvegni. The Scuole del Venerabile were religious confraternities devoted to the cult of the Eucharist. They showed several features quite new to Venetian confraternities, especially the humanity of Christ, the need to be vigilant in the face of the Devil's snares, their connections both to the papacy and the parish, and their spontaneous formation very early in the sixteenth century. The sovvegni were mutual aid societies, the earliest of which were attached to trade guilds, in particular those of the Arsenale. There is no evidence to suggest that these agencies owed anything at all to the initiatives of ecclesiastical or political authorities.

The new types of association fitted into the existing complex of institutions and invigorated the interaction of existing popular corporations. This introductory section sets out some examples of the continuing interaction of arti and scuole and seeks to demonstrate that there was no question of their supersession by the new associations. There follows a detailed examination of the nature and impact of each of the two new types of corporation. The fourth and final part of the discussion offers examples of the interaction of different corporations – the surviving residue of the social energy of the Venetian popolo – in the urban and commercial space and fabric of the city, that is to say in the stones of Venice themselves.

The interaction of trade guilds and devotional confraternities has already featured prominently in this study. Discussion of the mercers noted the overlap of different types of corporation within a single, loosely defined guild.[1] The links between the mercers' guild and other corporations make a useful starting point for a survey of the interactions of trade guilds and devotional confraternities within the urban space and their impact on the fabric of the city by about 1600. It is revealing to extend the connection of the mercers' guild, or complex of guilds, to other corporations. Members of the arte dei marzeri promoted the foundation of the Scuola del Rosario at the church of Santi Giovanni e Paolo in 1575. This confraternity had celebrated the victory of the Holy League over the Turks at Lepanto and was committed to "the extirpation of heretics" (l'esturpazione degli eretici). Among its first officers and electors, who were thirty-three in number, fifteen were mercers, including Bartolomeo Bontempelli.[2] At the Scuola del Venerabile at the church of San Basso in the years between 1568 and 1588, six mercers were prominent among the office-holders. Francesco Sechini ("Cecchini" in this reference) dalla Nave – that is to say, the owner of the shop where Paolo Sarpi's circle sometimes met – was gastaldo and responsible in 1599 for the commissioning of the vault for the burial of members.[3] In these examples we have two mercers, Secchini and Bontempelli, prominent in anti-papal circles, who were closely associated with organizations that took the fight to heretics and promoted the cult of the Eucharist, conventional pieties of the Catholic revival. The paradox, and contradiction, of these instances and others is a theme that will require fuller exposition in due course.

The devotional confraternity of the mercers' guild the "scuola dell'arte dei marzeri," met at the church of San Zulian. Their prominent altar was embellished with work commissioned from those powerful operators the sculptor Alessandro Vittoria and the painter Palma il Giovane.[4] The mercers' confraternity embraced other scuole in the church. The Scuola di San Rocco e Santa Margherita, founded in 1496, used the mercers' meeting place, certainly from 1512.[5] So too did the much more ancient Scuola di San Zulian. In 1574 the general meeting of the confraternity recorded twenty-two members in attendance, at least nine of whom practised a trade controlled by the mercers.[6]

Such connections were by no means peculiar to the mercers; there are many other examples. Moreover, just as trade guilds could move towards a closer association with confraternities that were not based upon a shared occupation (arti and scuole), so too devotional confraternities could acknowledge a link to particular crafts (scuole and arti). It may be significant that this kind of realignment was occurring in the late fifteenth century, when the scuole were attracting members of the patriciate, and the confraternities founded in the mid-thirteenth century for flagellants were acquiring a new prestige as Scuole Grandi. In the course of the sixteenth century these institutions became both celebrated and notorious for their pompous displays and their monumental building projects. It may be that the popolani were drawing closer to each other in the scuole piccole and scuole delle arti in a protection of first principles and in a reassertion of the value system that bound them together.

Under a regulation of 1464 no one could become a master among the *veluderi* (weavers of velvet) unless he had enrolled in the Scuola di San Cristofalo at the church of Santa Maria Assunta.[7] Similarly, the Scuola di San Nicolo, which met at the church of San Nicolo dei Mendicoli, set down in 1469 that all those from the local parishes of San Nicolo and Angelo Raffaele who sold fish in the Pescaria at Rialto were required to be members of the scuola. This was a most unusual mix of parish and occupation among confraternities that, in general, were not based upon either. The association with fishmongers appears to have strengthened, however, for in 1559, the confraternity referred to itself as San Nicolo dei Pescadori.[8] The Scuola di San Vettor in 1478 was associated with local boatmen who met at the church of Santa Margherita.[9] Also in 1478, the Scuola di San Lorenzo at the church of San Barnaba, at the behest of the nail makers ("favri di agudi") made it a requirement for "lavoranti" among the ironsmiths to be members.[10] The Scuola della Nattività della Beata Vergine at the church of Sant'Aponal, in 1532, owed its origins to some sellers of flour ("farineri") who had first met at the church of San Silvestro in 1526 (a confraternity of which there is no other record).[11] The confraternity of San Mattia (which met at the church of that name from 1535) had no overt occupational connection, but it is striking that in a general meeting of fifty-seven members, twenty of the thirty officers and electors listed were goldsmiths or jewellers.[12]

The plain listing of the foundation of new brotherhoods in Venice for the whole of the sixteenth century appears in table 5.1.

Table 5.1. Foundations of Scuole in Venice, c. 1500–c. 1600

Date	Dedication	Church
(i) 1500–49		
1500	Santissima Croce	San Salvador
1500	Santa Barbara dei Bombardieri	San Marcuola
1500	San Nicolo	San Giorgio dei Greci
1501	Beata Vergine	Santa Maria Maggiore
1502	Venerabile	San Zulian
1503	Venerabile	Santa Margherita
1504	Venerabile	Corpus Domini
1504	Venerabile	San Cassian
1504	Venerabile	San Geminiano
1506	San Giovanni Battista	San Giovanni in Bragora
1506	Venerabile	Sant'Aponal
1506	Venerabile	San Giovanni Novo
1506	Venerabile	Santa Maria Formosa
1506	Venerabile	Santa Maria Zobenigo
1506	Venerabile	San Nicolo
1506	Venerabile	San Trovaso
1507	Sant'Eustachio	San Stae
1507	Venerabile	Santa Sofia
1507	Venerabile	San Bartolomeo
1507	Venerabile	San Geremia
1507	Venerabile	San Giacomo dell'Orio
1507	Venerabile	San Marcuola
1507	Venerabile	San Pietro di Castello
1507	Venerabile	Santa Trinità
1507	Venerabile	San Polo
1508	Venerabile	Sant'Eufemia della Giudecca
1510	Venerabile	San Stae
1510?	Venerabile	San Moise
1511	Venerabile	Santi Apostoli
1511	Venerabile	San Luca
1511	Venerabile	San Maurizio
1511	Venerabile	San Severo
1511	Venerabile	Santa Marina[a]
1512	Venerabile	Santa Maria Mater Domini
1512	Venerabile	Santa Maria Nova
1512	Venerabile	San Marzilian

(*Continued*)

Table 5.1. (Continued)

Date	Dedication	Church
1513	Beata Vergine del Terremoto	San Bartolomeo
1514	Beata Vergine delle Grazie[b]	San Baseggio
1514	Venerabile	San Giovanni Decollato
1515	Venerabile	San Lio
1516	Venerabile	San Silvestro
1516	Venerabile	San Basso
1517	Venerabile	San Provolo
1518	Venerabile	San Paternian
1519	Beata Vergine della Concettion	Santa Maria Assunta
1520	Venerabile	San Vidal
1520	Venerabile	Santa Lucia
1521	Venerabile	San Salvador
1521	Venerabile	Sant'Agostino
1522	Santa Cecilia	San Cassian
1522	Venerabile	Sant'Anzolo
1523	Corpo di Cristo	San Gregorio
1524	Venerabile	San Martin
1525?	Beata Vergine Assunta	San Stin
1528	Venerabile	San Samuele
1528	Venerabile	San Vio
1530	Venerabile	San Baseggio
1531	Sant'Iseppo	Sant'Iseppo
1531	Venerabile	San Zuan Grisostomo
1532	Nattività della Beata Vergine	Sant'Aponal
1533	Presentazione della Beata Vergine	Sant'Ubaldo
1533	Venerabile	San Tomà
1535	Beata Vergine	San Simeon Profeta
1535	Concezion della Beata Vergine	San Giacomo dell'Orio
1535	Venerabile	San Pantalon
[1536	Poveri vergognosi	Sant'Antonin][c]
1537	Nome di Dio	San Francesco della Vigna
1537	Passione	San Zulian[d]
1538	Venerabile	San Felise
1538	San Felise	San Felise
1538	Venerabile	Santa Croce
1538	Venerabile	San Simeon Grande
1539	Venerabile	San Canzian
1539?	Venerabile	San Benetto
1541	Marangoni dell'Arsenale	San Filippo Giacomo
1542	Venerabile	Angelo Raffaele
1544	Venerabile	San Biasio
1544	Venerabile	San Fantin
1545	Beata Vergine della Nattvità	San Giovanni Decollato
1545	San Polo	San Polo
1546	Beata Vergine della Pace	San Zanipolo
1546	Nattvità della Beata Vergine	San Trovaso
1546	Assunta	Santa Margherita

(*Continued*)

Table 5.1. (Continued)

Date	Dedication	Church
(ii) 1550–1600		
1550	Venerabile	San Stin
1552	Scuola Grande di San Teodoro	(own building)
1553	Beata Vergine [degli Angeli]	Angelo Raffaele
1553	Venerabile	San Boldo
1554	Crocefisso	Santa Maria Mater Domini
1554	Santa Margherita	Santa Margherita
1556	San Giovanni Battista	Santa Maria dei Frari
1556	Santa Maria Assunta	San Giacomo di Rialto[e]
1558?	Venerabile	Sant'Antonin[f]
1559	Sant'Apollonia	San Barnaba[g]
1559	San Francesco di Paola	San Trovaso
1560	Sant'Antonio degli Orefici	San Silvestro[h]
1560	Venerabile	San Simeon Profeta
1561	Santissima Croce	Sant'Aponal
1562	Santa Maria dell'Umiltà o dell'Annunziata	San Bartolomeo[i]
1563	Santa Maria della Neve	Frari[j]
1566	San Giorgio dei Genovesi	San Zanipolo[k]
1567	San Cristofalo	Santa Maria Assunta
1567	Venerabile	San Matteo
1568	Beata Vergine delle Grazie e San Spiridion	San Samuele[l]
[1568	Compagnia del Divino Amore	Ospedale degli Incurabili][m]
1569	Ascensione	Santa Maria in Broglio[n]
1572	Venerabile	San Simeon e Tadeo
1573	Venerabile	San Giovanni in Bragora[o]
1573	Corona del Salvatore	Sant'Alvise[p]
1575	Beata Vergine del Rosario	San Zanipolo
[1575	dell'Elemosina	Oratorio dei Gesuati][q]
1577	Visitazione/Annunciazione	San Pantalon[r]
1580	Beata Vergine e San Matteo	San Samuele
1580	Beata Vergine della Pietà	San Giobbe
1580	Sant'Iseppo	Santa Fosca
1580	San Lorenzo Giustinian	Santa Sofia[s]
1580	Venerabile	Sant'Agnese
1581	Beata Vergine Annunciata	Sant'Aponal
1581	Beata Vergine della Cintura	San Stefano
1581	Santissima Croce	San Nicola
1581	Santissimo Nome di Dio	San Domenico
1581	Venerabile	San Lunardo
1581	Venerabile	San Maurizio
1582	Beata Vergine [del Rosario]	Sant'Eufemia[t]
1582	Concezione di Maria Vergine	San Francesco della Vigna
1582	Santa Maria Elisabetta	San Cassian[u]
[1584	Adorazione delle 40 ore	Redentore][v]

(*Continued*)

Table 5.1. (Continued)

Date	Dedication	Church
1585	Beata Vergine della Presentazione	San Geremia
1586	Santissima Croce	San Nicolo
1587	Venerabile	Santa Fosca
1588	Beata Vergine del Parto	Sant'Agnese
1588	Santissimo Nome di Dio	San Zanipolo
1589	Beata Vergine Assunta	Santa Sofia
1589	Beata Vergine della Nattività	Santi Apostoli
1590	Beata Vergine Assunta	San Simeon Grande
1592	San Francesco di Paola	San Simeon Grande[w]
1592	San Rocco	San Canzian
1593	Passione	Santa Maria dei Frari
1593	Crocefisso	San Bartolomeo[x]
1594	Beata Vergine del Carmine	Santa Maria dei Carmini
1594	Madonna della Purificazione	Santa Maria Formosa[y]
1594	San Vicenzo	San Zanipolo[z]
1595	San Biasio	San Biasio
1595	San Giacinto	San Domenico
1596	Beata Vergine Assunta	San Giacomo dell'Orio[aa]
1596	Beata Vergine delle Grazie	San Marcuola
1597	Beata Vergine di Pietà	San Canzian
1598	Beata Vergine del Parto	San Lunardo
1599	Figliole dei remeri dell'Arsenale	San Bartolomeo[bb]
1599	Santa Catterina da Siena	Santa Maria dei Servi
1599	dei Cordigeri	San Nicolo dalla Lattuga[cc]

a. Vio, 198.145.

b. Or della Visitazione; Vio 834.812.

c. Vio 128.81, citing CBC: a "congregazione" that met in its own building. Not a conventional *scuola laica*, perhaps, especially in the reduced means of all its members. The "poveri vergognosi" included people of some standing who were too ashamed to admit their poverty, others who were poor and felt the shame of it, and others who needed secrecy; see C.F. Black, *Italian Confraternities*, 147–50, 160, 169–70, 172.

d. Vio 428.380, citing CBC.

e. Vio 844.821, citing SP b. 97. The confraternity was for Bergamasque immigrants from the Val Cedrina.

f. With San Sabba (1399), PC P, fol.101v.

g. With Venerabile, PC Z, fol. 509r.

h. Sovvegno.

i. Vio 414.365, citing CBC. The example is complicated by a reference to a mariegola of 1506 and by Vio's reference to another scuola, citing only the permission of the Council of Ten for 1504 at 413.363. All suggest that this was a confraternity for the Germans in Venice.

j. Vio 646.594, citing CBC.

k. Vio 186.135, citing records held at the church itself.

l. Vio 339.291, citing CBC.

(*Continued*)

Table 5.1. (Continued)

m. Vio 916.898; The Oratorio could scarcely be described as a *scuola laica*, but the reference locates the new institution in the broader context of foundations in the sixteenth century.
n. Vio 286.239, a sovvegno of the scuola of this title, citing BNM.
o. From San Giovanni Battista, 1322, and then 1506.
p. Vio 493.442, compagnia di donne, citing the records of the church.
q. Vio 907.893, citing CXm and AP Gesuati. This compagnia was "riservata ai dirigenti della scuola della congregazione dell'Oratorio," so was scarcely a lay confraternity: included as per table note 14.
r. Vio 851.831/832. The reference is to the *catastico* of the church, but the confraternity lasted until 1684, when it was suppressed and its goods passed to the church.
s. Scuola and sovvegno.
t. Scuola and sovvegno.
u. Scuola and sovvegno.
v. Vio 938.918, a "compagnia dei devoti," with a statute in photostat in the holdings of the church. Since the Redentore did not accept endowments, this is curious, but see table note 14.
w. Scuola and sovvegno.
x. Vio 419.368, citing the parochial *catastico*: unusual as another "fraterna delle prigioni," but it carried the approval of the patriarch from 1597.
y. Sovvegno.
z. Scuola and sovvegno.
aa. Scuola and sovvegno.
bb. Sovvegno.
cc. Vio 653.602, citing the parish archive, founded by the head of the order, Gesualdo da Castrovillari.

In all, there were fifty-four new confraternities dedicated to the Eucharist, Scuole del Venerabile, between 1500 and 1550. However, there were also twenty-five other new confraternities, thirteen of them Marian. That figure of twenty-five in itself and on its own comfortably maintained the momentum of the fifteenth century (twenty-four foundations, 1400–50; sixteen foundations, 1451–99). By about 1500 there were around ninety devotional confraternities in the city of Venice. The total of seventy-nine foundations of all types between 1500 and before 1550 almost doubled the number. It is in this remarkable context that attention should turn to the confraternities devoted to the cult of the Eucharist.

The Scuole del Venerabile

It is all too easy to see the emphasis on the cult of the Eucharist in the sixteenth century in direct relation to the conflicts of the confessional era. That is to say,

Zwinglian and Calvinist questioning of the real presence of the body and blood of Christ generated a Roman reaction that insisted upon the miracle of transubstantiation through the intervention of the priest. Rigorists such as Carlo Borromeo and Gabriele Paleotti wanted every parish to have a confraternity for the "Santissimo Sacramento," and the cult of the Eucharist in confraternities was in the vanguard of the Jesuit missions.[13]

In the sixteenth century, with the triumph in the Church of Rome of a rigorist reaction to Protestant heresies, belief in the celebration of the transformative miracle in the hands of a separate and celibate order of ordained priests became a central test of orthodoxy. After the relaunching of the Holy Office of the Inquisition in 1542, to express other views was dangerous. Not to receive communion from the hands of a Catholic priest was itself ground for suspicion. Solemn recognition of the processions that honoured the Eucharist was the sign of an obedient believer. The inspection of churches by the agents of Rome sought to ensure that the cult was pre-eminent, a rite for the high altar, not a side chapel. Local commitment to the wonder of the faith that the Eucharist represented was, for the papal visitor – and later for historians – a strong sign of the success of the Counter-Reformation. For some commentators, the commitment of a parish or diocese to the cult of the Eucharist became a means of measuring the way in which Tridentine pronouncement itself was made real in local enforcement.[14]

In the age of Reformation and Counter-Reformation the scuole of Venice were not entirely immune to outside influence. However, much more striking is the persistence and adaptability of local religious traditions. The intensification of Eucharistic piety in the city may well have connected to the presence of a highly placed reformer in Venice in the early years of the cinquecento. Egidio (or Giles) of Viterbo, a celebrated preacher and energetic promoter of change, was a papal envoy. His theology emphasized the idea that the Church itself was the body of Christ, a doctrine that would resonate with the confraternities as microcosms of the larger body of the Church in Venice.

In 1504, Sanudo recorded that Egidio did not preach at the church of San Stefano, Venice's great Augustinian centre, as he had done the previous year.[15] He was on a diplomatic mission to warn the Venetians against opposing the new pope, Julius II, in the Romagna.[16] Egidio was in Venice in 1505 and in 1506–7, this time balancing a warning about the Romagna with urging the Venetians to take the cross against the Turk.[17]

When Egidio preached at San Stefano in 1507, he did so after his elevation to the rank of vicar general of the Augustinian order. According to Sanudo, Egidio used the occasion to introduce new regulations in the monastery.[18] On his promotion of the cult of the Eucharist, there is pictorial evidence from papal

Rome. When Julius was campaigning against Bologna in 1506, he venerated a relic in Orvieto that, in the thirteenth century, had mysteriously bled, dispelling the doubts about transubstantiation in the mind of a local priest. Julius had Raphael commemorate his act of worship in one of the frescos in the Vatican stanze, in which series we also find the great outdoor celebration of the mysteries of the sacrament, the *Disputa*. Some authorities also see Egidio's influence in the Neoplatonic scheme of Michelangelo's Sistine ceiling, which includes a dramatic and intensely human representation of a live body nailed to wood, the *Crucifixion of Haman*.[19] This may draw upon medieval traditions of the Virtues "nailing the body of sin," a body that Christ took upon himself. In Professor Wind's magisterial interpretation:

> By contemplating this paradoxical image of Christ crucified by the Virtues, the penitent sinner was meant to learn that he must crucify in himself the body of sin by letting the Virtues kill the Vices – allowing the powers of Haman to be put to death by the joint forces of Esther, Mordecai, and Ahasuerus. If salvation through the agony of the flesh – Augustine's *salubris cruciatus* – can thus be vested in Haman's cross, retributive justice will become one with the mercy of a death in Christ: "For if we have been planted together in the likeness of his death, we shall be also in the likeness of his resurrection: Knowing this that our old man is crucified with him, that the body of sin might be destroyed" (Romans 6:5–6).[20]

Egidio's commitment to reform in a manner that can seem Counter-Reformation *avant la lettre* is more concretely manifest in his role as architect of the Fifth Lateran Council of 1512.[21]

Yet one must perforce return to the absence of any reference to Egidio in the statutes of the scuole. In addition, it seems paradoxical that, although there are many examples of Eucharistic foundations in a period when Egidio was several times in Venice, his preaching evidently did not inspire the formation of such a brotherhood at the Augustinian church of San Stefano, a church that was home to several other scuole.

That said, the Scuole del Venerabile displayed a number of striking features that were quite unfamiliar in the institutions examined so far. In the period between the mid-thirteenth century and the end of the fifteenth century – perhaps in keeping with millennial anticipations and with the advent of the great mortalities from 1348 onwards – the members of confraternities watched and prayed for they knew not the hour of their death. One of the oldest expressions of reciprocal self-interest in the actions of the brotherhoods of Venice was the knowledge that fellow brethren would attend a member's funeral and commemoration. It was a benefit that any member might need. If he or she attended regularly on such occasions, then he or she could expect others to do the same for him or her. In the Scuole del Venerabile, by contrast, the enemy was the Devil, the enemy of mankind, roaring like a lion. In defence against the fiend was the agonizing sacrifice Christ had made – of course, familiar from foundations of earlier date, but now much more human and immediate in terms of rough wood, nails, and torn flesh: body and blood. Christ's suffering was a torment that he bore patiently to save all. The statute of the Scuola del Venerabile that was founded at the church of San Polo in 1507, one of many from that year, expressed with vivid comprehensiveness the new preoccupations.

> To the praise and glory of the Most Holy Trinity, Father, Son, and Holy Spirit. Amen.
>
> Having considered many times we brethren that there is no greater obligation for human nature, which is formed in the image and likeness of God, than that to this Omnipotent Creator and His Redeemer, who wished to redeem us from the hands of the Devil, who He Himself wished Himself to offer in hostage, and sacrifice on the wood of the cross, and with the greatest love, and charity wished to give himself in food, to greater Faith and witness of His Most Holy Passion giving us in the communion of his most holy body and to drink in his most precious blood, as in His Last Supper for his testament charitable He demonstrated to his dear disciples, before he tasted the harsh passion of the most cruel and bitter death on the cross, by means of which we have been recovered from the hands of the Devil, and bought with his most precious blood, as says holy scripture, you are bought for a great price with the most holy blood of the immaculate lamb made obedient for us until death to give us his realm of eternal life. Whence, in memory of so much charity, love and inestimable goodness, which he has used towards us sinners ungrateful for such benefit, deservedly with all our strengths, mental and bodily, we are bound to give him due honour, and give him praise and do him reverence with every devotion and demonstration of gratitude possible for us, so that our redeemer may have mercy upon us in this world, and the next, and give repose with the salvation of our souls. Inspired, therefore, by all the grace of the Holy Spirit, from which every good work proceeds, to give a beginning to this blessed SCUOLA, and union of brothers, and sisters, entitled the Brotherhood [Fraternità] of the most holy sacrament there having been conceded to us by the most excellent lords Heads of the Council of Ten, as in their letters below is clearly contained. We give a beginning to this holy and pious work, as appears here below, chapter by chapter the rules that must be observed.[22]

In its Christian language the statute of 1507 anticipates Aretino's remarkable *L'umanità di Cristo* of 1535. Aretino describes the crucifixion in horrendous human detail. After Christ had been "stretched out on the wood, … his hand was taken with which he created the sun; and, once the palm was opened, one man positioned the point of the nail, and another raising his arm and bringing down the blow pounding the head of the nail with the face of the hammer, heaven thundering its resentment of this; his flesh penetrated he was affixed by this to the wood."[23]

In light of these terrible injustices the reward of Christ's mercy is all the more wondrous.[24]

Given the absence of concrete examples of external influence and given the statutes' anticipation of Aretino's powerful expression of Christian humanism, it appears that the piety of the scuole adapted to reinforce its self-sufficiency rather than looking to outside forces of succour for spiritual want. Indeed, do we need to look for transmissions from outside and, as it were, downwards in order to explain this great addition to the piety of the Venetian popolo? The Scuole del Venerabile had their own internal dynamic that, perhaps indirectly, reaffirmed popolano traditions in the face of their distortion by the Scuole Grandi. In 1541 the guildsman Alessandro Caravia, a goldsmith by trade (and a correspondent of Aretino), launched a satirical attack on the pomposity and condescension of the Scuole Grandi, contrasting them with the Scuole del Sacramento. The cittadini of the Scuole Grandi, he said, were, almost literally, too grand to participate in the devotions of the Scuole del Venerabile. Yet while he embraced the faith and works of the Eucharistic brotherhoods, Caravia also expressed reservations about the superstitions associated with the cult of the saints. This combination of sentiments was in keeping with the generally Erasmian traditions of Venetian piety even though it can seem to foreshadow Tridentine principle in the cult of the Eucharist and evangelical influence in concerns about the cult of the saints.[25]

In short, it is quite possible to find resonances of the piety of the Scuole del Venerabile in virtually any strand of reforming thought in the sixteenth century. After 1500 the Venetian Scuole del Venerabile, the first of which was founded in 1502, offered their members a symbol of Christ's sacrifice without priestly mediation and were an assertion of something not so far removed from the "priesthood of all believers." While they were clearly not the instruments of the Counter-Reformation, they anticipated some of its principles. Then again, they had something in common with the ideas that Erasmus expressed in the *Enchiridion*, and Duerer's *Knight, Death, and the Devil* may also express the need for the militant Christian to concentrate on the humanity of Christ and outstare the spooks of superstition.[26] In order to understand the apparent precocities of the Scuole del Venerabile, it may be most illuminating to examine the resonances with the traditions that the Venetians had developed in the previous three hundred years. It becomes all the more paradoxical to note that the new confraternities in Venice in the early sixteenth century looked to the authority of the pope in Rome, His Holiness Pope Julius II, who was engineering a European coalition against the Venetians.[27] Moreover, in contrast to the generally supraparochial character of Venice's earlier confraternities, the scuola at the church of San Polo was typical of the Scuole del Venerabile in basing itself firmly in the parish and was open to "everyone in the *contrada*" (ciascun della contra).[28]

The Scuola del Venerabile at the church of San Geremia in Cannaregio was also founded in 1507. Its statute provides a rare and open acknowledgment of what had caused it to come into being. "The founder and beginning of which by divine inspiration was the Reverend Father Francesco Colomban of the Order of the Friars Minor Observants, preacher in that time in the said church of San Geremia, however, by means of the help of Messer Antonio Contarini by divine reservation patriarch of Venice."[29]

Whether this was an isolated link between the ecclesiastical authorities and the scuole or whether the influence of the preacher and the patriarch was more general is impossible to demonstrate. The Scuola del Venerabile at San Gieremia was founded amid a gaggle of others, and it certainly did not claim to be the first of its kind. Nor did subsequent foundations refer to Colomban or to Antonio Contarini. Indeed, there is no sense of a strong template to which all the Scuole del Venerabile owed a clear debt. There were no preambles on Man as God's image, or Christ's body on the cross, in the Eucharistic brotherhoods at the church of San Giovanni in Oglio in 1507, of San Pietro di Castello, or of Santa Ternità.[30]

It is impossible to tie the development to the grand controversies of the sixteenth century in any simple or convincing way. Furthermore, the devotion of the Venetian popolo to the celebration of the Eucharistic rite appears to have been a remarkable strengthening of the tradition that linked their faith to their works – not so much reformation as reaffirmation.

The immediate and obvious pattern is the extraordinary concentration of foundations in the first half of the sixteenth century. Before 1502 there had been only one confraternity dedicated to the Eucharist in its title. At the church of Corpus Domini, it dated from 1395, though its statute was not copied in the registers of the Provveditori di Comun.[31] Its earlier appearance in this study was due to the brotherhood's close involvement with the procession of the Bianchi in 1399. However, the cult of the Eucharist was an integral part of Venetian religiosity, not least because of its close association with works. At the end of the fifteenth century Canon Pietro Casola described the richness and solemnity of the Corpus Christi procession that he witnessed on 29 May 1494. He made particular record of the prominence of the Scuole Grandi. The sacrament itself stood upon a golden chalice, "the largest I ever saw." Mercy and Charity preceded even Saint Mark. The Scuola della Misericordia headed the procession, with children dressed as angels, great quantities of candles, and at least five hundred brethren, and there followed the scuole of the Carità, then San Marco, San Giovanni Evangelista, and the more recent foundation of San Rocco.[32] The splendour of the occasion loses nothing in comparison with the procession of 1606, as recorded by Sir Henry Wotton. On that occasion, too, the Eucharist was closely associated with the religious independence of the Venetian state. There is no need to associate Venetian reverence for the Holy Sacrament with Tridentine or even Roman infiltration.[33]

In the sixteenth century as a whole, sixty-six Eucharistic confraternities were founded. There were only a further five in the whole of the seventeenth century and the first part of the eighteenth. It is vital to emphasize that fifty-six of the fraternities came into being before the first session of the Council of Trent in 1545, while only eleven others came into being in the second half of the century. Of a total of sixty-four foundations between 1550 and 1600, that figure of eleven compares with twenty-four Marian foundations. There is no clear pattern of response to any attempted imposition on the part of the ecclesiastical hierarchy.

Indeed, of those fifty-six foundations before 1545, forty-two were in existence by 1525. Narrowing the focus still further, there had been nineteen foundations before 1508, fourteen of these in the years 1506–7. That last figure compares with fourteen for the entire period 1545–1712. It is worth refining the comparison with periods already discussed. In the forty-three years between 1502 and 1545, the fifty-six Eucharistic foundations represented more than five times the corresponding figure for the thirteenth century, well over a third more than the figure for the whole of the fourteenth century, and a little under a third more than for the whole of the fifteenth. Of the total number of scuole in the mid-sixteenth century (about 170, a figure representing a period of three centuries), the Eucharistic foundations of 1502–45 represented about one-third.

Cautiously, one might advance the interpretation that the Scuole del Venerabile provided another source of solidarity in areas somewhat removed from the centre of the city (which was roughly the area between Rialto and San Marco). The data displayed by table 5.1 temper this generalization for the formative years before 1508, with examples from the Sestier di San Polo and two important foundations in the Sestier di San Marco (at the church of San Bartolomeo by Rialto and at the church of San Zulian in the middle of the Mercerie). With documentation from 1502, this last-mentioned was the earliest of all the Eucharistic confraternities of the cinquecento. There were other foundations in the area around Rialto and San Marco (for example at the churches of San Luca and San Salvador) only a little later. All the same, in the first, formative, period, the foundations of Eucharistic confraternities tended to locate in areas in which the culture of the popolo set the local tone. Table 5.1 suffices as a representation of the speed with which the innovation took hold and spread. What it cannot show is the ease with which the new type of scuola joined and fitted with the existing network, despite the unfamiliar features of the Devil, the parish, and the pope. The Eucharistic confraternities gave a new vitality to the existing structure by a process of symbiosis rather than by breathing new life into institutions that had become ossified.

In this regard, a strict attention to the examples of fraternities devoted to the Eucharist in the first half of the sixteenth century may exaggerate the definition of the type. Referring to the preamble of 1507, we may note something of a precedent in the formation of the Scuola di Santa Catterina at the church of San Geminiano in 1436. Its statute contains the traditional maritime imagery of the need for "us dwellers in the world" (noi secolari) to "navigate by ship out of this shadowy and fog-bound world." However, it also refers to "the Enemy" without referring to Death, leaving the possibility that it may refer to the Devil, and it most definitely – and unusually for this early date – spoke of man as made in the image of God. There was also acknowledgment of the pope as "left to us by Messer Jesus Christ on earth as our shepherd."[34] There was a marvellous mix in the statute of the Scuola di San Giuseppe at the church of San Silvestro, which was founded in 1499. It repeated the scriptural injunction to watch and pray, "for death comes without warning." Yet it also promoted the Holy Sacrament as a protection against the Devil.[35]

Of the Eucharistic brotherhoods the first was at San Zulian, and we have already noted that the devotional configuration of this church was firmly linked to the organizations of the mercers' guild. The Eucharistic foundation at the church of Santa Maria Nova had a statute dated 1512 that refers to an earlier Marian confraternity and to taking over the meeting place of this last at the altar of the Pietà.[36] Quite how this arrangement related to a new preamble dated 1544 remains unclear.[37] Problems of dating are even more complicated in the case of confraternities at San Provolo (another church now destroyed). There the Scuola del Venerabile, with a statute of 1517, amalgamated upon its foundation with that of San Zaccaria and San Lizier.[38] Yet other sources say that the latter had moved to the church of San Zaccaria itself in 1507.[39] Such an example may suggest that the new scuole replaced others. As a counterpoise to this interpretation, the Scuola della Beata Vergine del Terremoto in the church of San Bartolomeo came into being in 1513 and shared the altar of the Venerabile for its meetings.[40] It was possible even for an existing confraternity to renew its mariegola in the name of the Holy Sacrament. Thus, the Scuola del Venerabile at San Pantalon dated from 1535: "Noting that this scuola is most ancient, as appears in the old statute book of the scuola of San Pantalon, which was then united with that of Corpus Christi and having made the whole of its statute book, which had disappeared in 1530."[41]

The example has a broader significance. As stated at the outset, the data on the confraternities do not permit any categorical assertion that so many scuole existed in such and such a year. However, lest the reader should think that the institution of the Scuole del Venerabile involved the elimination of pre-existing confraternities, the quotation constitutes the only reference to the Scuola di San Pantalon in these records.

Indeed, it was possible for a new confraternity simultaneously to form and unite with a Scuola del Venerabile. This was the case when the magistrates granted permission for a Marian confraternity at the church of San Biasio in 1560, acknowledging that it would join with the Scuola del Venerabile of 1544. The second institution was apparently an initiative of the officers of the Scuola del Venerabile. This is the sole reference that the registers make to a confraternity dedicated to the Virgin at San Biasio.[42]

Vice versa, the Scuola del Venerabile might come to identify with an existing confraternity of another title. The Eucharistic foundation at Sant'Antonin in 1559 referred to itself in 1609 as the "Scuola del Venerabile e San Saba," thereby announcing its association with the Scuola di San Saba, which dated back to 1399.[43] In 1573 the newly formed Eucharistic confraternity at the church of San Giovanni in Bragora acknowledged its derivation from the confraternity dedicated to the Baptist.[44]

Separate foundations of Scuole del Venerabile in the early years of the sixteenth century already displayed features that, like angels in marble, gradually took on clearer definition as the number of Eucharistic confraternities expanded. This was particularly so in three respects: first, the lack of disruption to existing patterns of confraternal piety; second, the firm identification of the Scuole del Venerabile with the local parish; and, third, the reassertion of the inseparable relationship between faith and works, as set out in the Epistle of James. The Eucharistic foundation at the church of Santa Margherita of 1503 confirmed a traditional commitment to its "brothers and sisters, both living and dead."[45] In the following year the brotherhood at the church of San Cassian referred to itself as the "confraternity of our parish."[46] The same page of the statute also records 109 members, a figure that reflected considerable local interest. The confraternity undertook to visit the sick and to take the Eucharist to them. Whether this involved the ministration of the Eucharist or merely its display is unclear, but there was no provision for the attendance of the parish priest.[47]

The other foundation of 1504, at the church of San Geminiano, also guaranteed the sacrament to the sick.[48]

In the case of the foundation at the church of San Geremia, there is a clear association of the cult of the Eucharist and visits to the sick, a connection of faith and works, the corporal works of mercy. The visit was to be accompanied by torches and candles "in order to communicate the infirm of the parish in accompanying the sacrament" (per il comunicar deli infermi della contrà in accompagnar esso sacramento). The implication of this phraseology may be that the very act of taking the sacrament to the sick ("accompagnar") had the effect of its ministration ("comunicar"). The point to emphasize is that brothers and sisters in the scuole reached such an arrangement through the reworking of their own traditions rather than through external imposition.

In this early part of the sixteenth century, the years 1506–7 witnessed the formation of a notable cluster of Eucharistic brotherhoods. The scuola at the church of San Nicolo dei Mendicoli was severe in its definition of its parochial responsibilities. It stopped its payments of alms to Donna Maria Gritti either because she had left the parish or because she had wrongly claimed to be a resident; "for being outside the parish" (per esser fuori della contra nostra) leaves open both possibilities.[49] The confraternities at the churches of San Zuan in Oglio and Santa Maria Formosa both assured that the brethren would take the Eucharist to the sick.[50]

In 1507 the foundation at the church of Santa Sofia embraced parishioners "of every age and of both sexes" and undertook to take the sacrament to them without distinction, that is to say, "to the home of the poor as to that of the rich."[51] The preamble to statutes became more common but was never formulaic. The Scuola del Venerabile at the church of San Bartolomeo of 1507 emphasized love of God and love of one's neighbour ("amor proximi").[52] The brethren here shared the celebration of Corpus Christi with the German community nearby at the Fondaco and specified the route that their procession took. In this instance we have a solemn celebration of the Eucharist in a Venetian scuola that shared the occasion with the German community, which came to be suspected of Lutheranism.[53]

The rapid and enthusiastic rhythms of 1506–7 subsided into a steady and unspectacular beat in the remainder of the period. However, the connection of the sacrament to the performance of works, particularly taking the sacrament to the sick, grew in emphasis. This principle was reasserted time and time again, at the scuole at the churches of Sant'Eufemia in 1508, San Stae in 1510, Santi Apostoli in 1511, San Severo in the same year, San Lio in 1515, San Silvestro the year after that, San Paternian in 1518, Sant'Anzolo in 1522, and San Benetto in 1539.[54] Within the parish the Scuola del Venerabile was all embracing, summed up in the case of that at the church of San Tomà that "may not say no to anyone" (non si possi dir no ad alcuno).[55]

Perhaps the most striking concentration or restatement of the principles of the Eucharistic brotherhoods was the Scuola del Venerabile at the church of San Samuele, founded in 1528. The preamble was fairly typical, and there was no age limit for entrants from the parish. A connection to the Venetian body politic appeared in praise for Doge Andrea Gritti. Yet the commitment to parishioners without distinction between rich and poor was unmistakable. As a fascinating renewal of tradition in this relatively recent type of institution, the statute extolled visits to the sick that bore the sacrament as "one of the Seven Works of Mercy" (una delle sette opere della Misericordia).[56] The renewed commitment to Mercy, the reinvigoration of the relationship between faith as represented by the Holy Sacrament, and works that demonstrated a commitment to the sick and to the poor – these themes also appeared in the preamble of the statute of the Scuola del Venerabile at the church of San Polo.

The apparently new institutions dedicated to the Eucharist still made a connection between faith as represented by the sacrament and works as represented by Misericordia. The language was still that of commercial exchange. The saved had been bought ("comprati") at a great cost ("empti estis pretio magno"), and the act of redemption (by the "Redemptor") was preventing the loss of eternal life that, by implication, stood in pledge. This articulation of the relationship between faith and works in the language of commercial exchange made widely comprehensible the principles that held the Venetians together in bonds of fraternity. The emergence of another new type of brotherhood, the sovvegno, a charitable agency that began to appear among the scuole in the 1540s as an appendage to certain of the trade guilds, strengthened further those bonds.

The Sovvegni

The sovvegni, self-help societies among the scuole piccole that had been formally diminished by the elevation of the Scuole Grandi, rejuvenated the idea of reciprocity among equals that had been so important in the life of Venice's trade guilds. The shared principles of devotional confraternities and trade-based organizations perhaps sharpened the definition of this new type of association that took a natural and reinforcing place in the network of corporations in Venice in the course of the sixteenth century. Like the scuola, the institution appears to have been peculiar to Venice. Historically speaking, the sovvegni of Venice were manifestly practical organizations with a clear structure of mutual aid funded from members' regular contributions. In these ways they represented a clear historical extension of the reciprocity that had become so marked from the thirteenth century onwards. By the same token, they show that fixed orders of membership consisting of those who were permanently rich and those who were permanently poor in the institutions that became known as Scuole Grandi in the later fifteenth century were not at all typical of the mechanisms that the Venetians deployed in the relief of poverty.[57]

The earliest recorded sovvegni began among the considerable membership of the guilds of workers in the Arsenale. The total number of masters enrolled in the major guilds in the shipyards in the middle of the sixteenth century (caulkers, carpenters, and oar makers) was probably more than two thousand. It is possible, therefore, that the sovvegni for the Arsenale alone may have had aspirations to reach, in different ways, some six thousand Venetians.[58] Second, they proceeded to spread, to an extent that the surviving documentation does not permit us to quantify, in various parts of the city. There is some identification with the less prosperous areas of Venice. In addition to the sovvegni of the Arsenale guilds in Castello, there were three sovvegni in each of the sestieri of Dorsoduro and Santa Croce, and two in San Polo. There was only one each in Cannaregio and San Marco. In their extension the sovvegni transcended and complemented the bounds of trade guild, devotional brotherhood, and parish, and, in the occasional reference to the papacy or the elusion of official record, even the bounds of the Venetian state.

In this regard it is useful to reflect upon the origins of the sovvegni in the guilds of workers in the Arsenale. Once again, the example illustrates the ease of movement of ideas and operations between trade guilds and scuole. The foundation of a sovvegno for Saint Blaise at the saint's named church in 1595 increased the concentration of mutual aid societies in the vicinity of the Arsenale in Castello.[59] Table 5.2 sets out the formation of sovvegni in Venice in the sixteenth century and indicates the location of each in the parishes of the city.

Eligibility

As already noted, the sovvegni began among the trades of the Arsenale. The identification of the membership of a sovvegno and a particular profession continued in the case of Sant'Antonio degli Orefici, founded in 1560 at the church of San Silvestro. The goldsmiths, practitioners of a trade whom we would expect to be prosperous, showed no self-consciousness in acknowledging their debt to other sovvegni as models, such as that at the church of San Polo, and those of the carpenters, caulkers, sawyers, house

Table 5.2. Foundations of Sovvegni in Venice, 1541–99

Date	Title	Church	Membership
1541	Marangoni dell'Arsenale	San Filippo Giacomo	?
1545	San Polo	San Polo	200 (at 1559)
1546	Beata Vergine Assunta	Santa Margherita	–[a]
1553	Beata Vergine degli Angeli	Angelo Raffaele	19 (at 1699)
1560	Sant'Antonio degli Orefici	San Silvestro	114 (at 1560)
1569	Scuola dell'Ascensione	Santa Maria in Broglio	–[b]
1580	Beata Vergine e San Matteo	San Samuele	250 (at 1604)
1580	San Lorenzo Giustinian	Santa Sofia	28 (at 1632)
1582	Beata Vergine	Sant'Eufemia	74 (at 1588)
1582	Santa Maria Elizabetta e La Beata Vergine di Loreto	San Cassian	45 (at 1611)
1586	San Nicolo	San Nicolo	42 (at 1593)
1588	Beata Vergine della Nattività	Sant'Agnese	38 (at 1589)
1592	San Francesco di Paola	San Simeon Grande	32 (at 1592)
1594	Madonna [delle Grazie]	Santa Maria Formosa	46 (at 1610)[c]
1594	San Vincenzo e San Pietro Martire	San Zanipolo	30 (at 1594)
1595	San Biasio	San Biasio	23 (at 1595)
1595	Beata Vergine della Celestia	Santa Maria della Celestia	–[d]
1596	Beata Vergine Annontiata	San Giacomo dell'Orio	21 (at 1618)
1599	Figliole di Remeri dell'Arsenale	San Bartolomeo	30 (at 1599)

a. Vio, 844.821, citing SP b. 97; AP parish records.
b. Vio 286.239, citing BNM.
c. Vio 170.118.
d. Vio 148.101.

carpenters, and others. The regulations excluded treatment for injuries incurred in brawls, a proviso that was quite common. However, the terms of membership in this instance did not cover treatment of plague.[60] There was further elaboration of the criteria of eligibility in the sovvegno dedicated to the saints Vincent Ferrer, Peter Martyr, and Catherine of Siena at the Dominican centre of San Zanipolo (of 1594). Again, membership of the scuola was a prerequisite for membership of the sovvegno. The statute set out a precise pattern of documentation. The physician's certification was to include the name, the family name, and the number of days of sickness involved. The approved medical men were available every day at the premises of Il Mondo (The World) at San Zanipolo, or of L'Abramo (The Abraham) at San Marco.[61] A voucher was necessary to authorize a home visit. The extent of insurance was refined in 1597 to exclude "old fistulated sores, ruptures, the French disease or the like."[62]

Contributions and Benefits

The sovvegno of the Madonna at the church of Santa Maria Formosa had a particularly close relationship with a pre-existing confraternity dating from 1489. The sovvegno launched with a notably energetic promotion. Like other of these organizations, it set an age limit of forty upon those who enrolled. However, in a striking introductory offer, the sovvegno of the Madonna removed that stipulation until after the first Sunday in March 1595.[63] There was a requirement to join the scuola as well as the sovvegno, but the scuola was open to "every sort of person and of any age" (ogni sorta di persona, sia di che età si voglia).[64]

The provisions of this particular sovvegno had considerable nuance. The entry fee (or "benintrada," the same term that the scuole used) was forty soldi, the weekly contribution thereafter was two soldi, and eligibility for benefits began after two years of contributions. Then the entitlement became sixteen soldi per day, excluding Sundays, or four lire and sixteen soldi per week. Although injuries received on occasion of offence ("scandalosi feriti") were not to receive subsidized treatment, there was limited provision for the rehabilitation of former prisoners: they were entitled to a single penny (there were twelve of these to the soldo) one month after release.[65] The statute of the sovvegno at Santa Maria Formosa was copied into a much later part of the register than was that of its sister organization, the scuola.[66] This may suggest that the authorities did not identify the close relationship of the two organizations.

One of the dangers to the thesis of this book might be the accusation that it constructs a myth of Venice "from below," presenting a utopian vision of self-help and prosperity, as though the popolo itself was a single harmonious entity. As a corrective, one should point out that in 1559 the officers at the sovvegno of San Polo claimed that of its two hundred members eighty were not making contributions to the general fund.[67] There were expressions of concern about how to sustain a viable system in the face of a tendency for the well-off to leave the sovvegno out of avarice, and for the poor, out of indigence.[68] All members were to make an initial payment of twelve soldi, and then a further one soldo every Sunday. After two years a member might claim two lire a week in assistance, and the figure rose to four lire after four years of contributions. The organization had five founders, had twenty-one members at the general meeting of 1548, and by 1559 claimed to have two hundred brethren.[69] A master in the building trades in the middle of the sixteenth century could expect to earn thirty soldi a day, therefore, even after four years, the benefit of two lire (forty soldi) per week amounted to only a little more than a day's pay.[70]

In certain other respects, terms appear to have been quite generous. Even plague victims were eligible for relief as long as they were not in isolation in the Lazzareto. The retention of a physician's services in 1572 illustrates a broad general theme ensuring certification of unfitness to work.[71] While a number of these mutual aid societies required claimants to obtain a certificate of sickness from an approved physician, the sovvegno at the church of Sant'Agnese set aside seventeen ducats as a retainer for its "medico" and allowed a further ducat for travelling expenses in visits that the physician might make to the homes of the sick.[72]

Sovvegni, Scuole, Arti, and Parish

The first sovvegno listed in the records of the magistrates responsible for the scuole was that of the carpenters who worked in the state's shipyards, dating from 1541, and was based at the church of San Filippo Giacomo, near San Marco but only a few parishes away from the Arsenale itself.[73] The second, at the church of San Polo (1545), set out regulations deliberately modelled upon those of the carpenters and caulkers in the Arsenale, and of the shoemakers.[74] The statute also describes this sovvegno as a "brotherhood or scuola" (fraternam sive scollam).[75]

All members of the goldsmiths' sovvegno at the church of San Silvestro were also required to be members of the scuola dell'arte of the goldsmiths.[76] Moreover, the organization undertook to provide members with charcoal for their work and to find supplies of the fuel beyond the monopoly of the ironsmiths.[77] In the interlacing of provisions applying to the arte, the scuola dell'arte, and the sovvegno, and in the attempt to keep members working if at all possible, the goldsmiths provided an example of how different initiatives might complement each other in the relief of temporary need. It seems to have been attractive as an organization, for the meeting of 1569 recorded 114 votes.[78]

We find a different emphasis in the sovvegno of the Virgin and Saint Matthew that met at the church of San Samuele in 1580, a date of renewal and foundation ("fu rinovata et fondata") since the sovvegno appears to have grown out of the older Scuola di San Mattio e San Samuele. It was a prerequisite of membership in the mutual aid organization (sovvegno) to enroll in the confraternity (scuola). There was no overt link to any occupation, and the priority was the care of the members who were sick. The organization embraced rich and poor, implying that sickness was a leveller of human hierarchy, "oppressed by illness, wealthy in goods by fortune, be they poor in them, all are understood to be poor" (oppressi d'infermità siino richi di beni di fortuna, siino poveri di essi tutti si intendino poveri), and all could claim "a pious subvention" (un pietoso sussidio). In what looks to be a sign that the organization sought to meet the needs of locals, the officers undertook to seek additional contributions as alms from parishioners, "beating at the doors of nobles, citizens, merchants and artisans alike" (battendo alle porte così de nobili, citadini, mercanti et artesani).[79] While acknowledging the inroads of malingerers, the brotherhood claimed to have 250 members in 1604.[80]

The picture of further generation from existing institutions found clear expression in the mutual aid society of the Virgin Annunciate that met some distance away across the Canal Grande in the Sestier di Santa Croce at the church of San Giacomo dell'Orio from 1596 onwards.[81] Its statute was saturated with the traditions of an ancient confraternity of Saint James, which had moved at an unspecified date from the church of San Salvador. The preamble and successive chapters dated in the register from 1422.[82] The language used was redolent of the trecento, and the singular resonance of the Epistle of James in Venetian dialect in one of the saint's Venetian churches was particularly marked. Members were enjoined to contemplate "the end of this earthly life" (il fin di questa temporal vita), to watch and pray, and to remember the value of a just man's prayer.[83] There was a blend of the old confraternity and the new mutual aid organization that was remarkable in its seamlessness. The sovvegno was strictly for sick brethren, yet any member might fall sick, and the principle was expressed in traditional Augustinian terms of "this miserable and unhappy world" (questo misero et infelice mondo), which in turn was accompanied by the new image of the ant busily storing up foodstuffs.[84] Even if an illness proved crippling, the suffering brother could receive benefits, but there was to be no subsidy for beggars. Perhaps that insistence upon a respectability identified with regular work increased the likelihood of further support for the sovvegno from the people of the parish. It is also worthy of note that in this case the magistrates' approval of the statute of 1596 only appeared in 1618.[85]

The statute of the sovvegno at the church of San Nicolo dei Mendicoli (1586) voiced the traditional concerns over changing times and changing conditions and applied them to the parish, one of the poorer in Venice with its "high number of people in need because of changing times and more so and especially in our parish of San Nicolo," which already had a scuola dedicated to Saint Nicholas (dating back to 1337) and linked to fishmongers.[86] Despite the links to confraternity and occupation, there was no formal amalgamation. In 1592 the Provveditori di Comun decided that the scuola and the sovvegno should keep separate gastaldi.[87]

The sovvegno of the carpenters at the Arsenale was entered in the registers of the Provveditori, but the sovvegni of the caulkers, sawyers, house carpenters, and shoemakers, mentioned in other statutes, were not. These passing mentions, and another to "molti sovegni" (in the statute of an organization dedicated to the Blessed Virgin of the Nativity in Sant'Agnese in 1589), prompt the thought that the sovvegni, in an important sense, had a life of their own.

The final sovvegno to be founded in the sixteenth century – at least among those recorded by this documentation – brings the chronicle full circle from the first, which was for the carpenters of the Arsenale. The last one made provision for the daughters of the oar makers. Here we have a trade-based organization that extended benefits to family members. There was a clear plan, ambitious in its long-term projection, which asked each member for two soldi a week for a period of five years, after which time the accumulated sum would be invested. The interest earned by the deposit would then provide dowries for those young women who could produce valid certification of baptism.[88] There was to be no insinuating admission (behind the door, "driedo la porta"). Anyone who was not enrolled from the start would have to pay the full five-year amount of twenty ducats, which was a considerable sum. Any such late entrant still needed the approval of two-thirds of a general meeting in order to join.[89]

This chapter has endeavoured to present a picture of the self-sufficiency and complementarity of the guilds of Venice in the sixteenth century, a picture that reflects the documentary evidence. The sources suggest the continuing vitality of the institutions that had first taken shape in the late thirteenth century, and the reinforcement that two new types of corporation were to offer. Any sense of rigid restriction to trade, station, or a particular area of the city is difficult to establish, though the records provide a strong sense of the diversity of emphasis and character between different organizations, and of their independence of the control of ecclesiastical or secular authority.

The corporations of the popolo of Venice were self-contained and yet had a route to a broader totality. The statute of the Sovvegno di San Francesco di Paola (1592), which met at the church of San Simeon Piccolo, provides a vivid example of the nature of the sovvegni, emphasizing the importance of setting something aside in times of relative prosperity in order to have something upon which to draw in time of need. The example of the ant, which sounds as though it may derive from an Aesop's fable, animated an idea of setting aside in good times the resources that one might need in bad. The ant "in summer … never ceases to accumulate food for the winter time."[90]

The single ant was also part of a teeming collectivity of self-interested individuals. The individual worshipper might have experienced a similar evocation on emerging from prayer at a guild chapel to the bustling streets of the metropolis. It is still possible to recreate something of such an experience by visiting the church of San Salvador and then emerging from the side portal onto the Mercerie. The following section refers to churches and how they were embellished and maintained by the guilds. It attempts to recapture the landscape of locality in Venice and to set the corporations in it.

The Scuole and the Stones of Venice

Sponsorship and Projects

This chapter has examined two major innovations in the complex of Venetian corporations in the sixteenth century. Both these new types of fraternity reflected the resilience and versatility of a popolo that seemed to have a firmer grasp on Venetian traditions than did the ecclesiastical and political authorities to which they were supposedly subject.

The different types of brotherhood frequently occupied the same ecclesiastical space, and while they did not share all the same feast days, the brethren of one walked past and perhaps admired the decorated space of another. It was the dynamic of interaction that mattered in the sustenance of the greater whole, not the predominance of one type of confraternity over another. Through the piety of brotherhoods grouped round a shared trade, parish, patron saint, or cult the confraternities contributed to the collective identity of the Venetians. Much of the physical evidence of this close coexistence has now vanished, but certain surviving examples still convey a sense of what was once a mesh of institutionalized values that covered the whole city and touched in varying degrees the lives of many of its inhabitants. Following is an attempt to recreate what a member of one of the brotherhoods, whether or not in the company of other brethren (and sisters), could have seen – both beheld and perceived – in some of the churches of Venice around 1600.

The sustained impact of Venetian corporations on their surroundings is a significant but neglected subject. A document in the records of the house carpenters ("marangoni") gives an indication of a handicraft guild's contributions to the decoration of the city. In 1733 the guild drew up an inventory of the pictures that it had commissioned and which adorned their scuola.

> The name[s] of the painters who painted the pictures of the confraternity of the house carpenters.
> First the Visitation of Saint Mary Elizabeth by Baldissera Diana
> 7 lunettes by the same Baldisera Diana
> The Madonna on her way to Egypt by Sante Peranda
> The Adoration of the Magi by Gerolamo Pilotti
> The Massacre of the Innocents [by] Giulio Mauoro
> The Return from Egypt by Santo Peranda

The Lord in dispute with the doctors by Gerolamo Piloti
A procession of a Dogaressa by Giulio Mauoro
All the beautiful portraits by Leonardo Corona
Five paintings above the balconies by the same artists.[91]

One guild, more than twenty pictures: it is worth a pause to reflect on how many of the hundreds of corporations in Venice in this study might have had similar inventories. There is surely more to such a list than a study of artistic patronage. It is illuminating to broaden the field of vision in the mind's eye so that it goes beyond the commissioning of specific works of art into the world of goods produced by the members of the guilds themselves. In other words, it is revealing to connect religious institutions to the world of work, which gives some idea of how a value system could connect to everyday life.

In 1595, for instance, the ironsmiths drew up an inventory of all the possessions of their scuola.[92] The document reflects the ironsmiths' devotions, their elections and decisions, and their economic activities. The list includes a silver cross, banners and chandeliers for processions, a gilded figure of a saint, and a velvet cloth in which to wrap the corpses of dead brethren prior to burial. Entries for a book recording tax levies, another for decisions and new regulations, an alphabetical record of payment of dues, two painted balls and a hundred brass ones silvered over for ballots, and a stamp to mark each of the balls: such items give an idea of the elaborateness of the guild's elections – and the time and expense invested in them. The ironsmiths stored their fuel at their meeting house at the church of San Moise. The inventory shows that they kept a lamp, a step-ladder, a brass measure with which to distribute charcoal, and a slate on which to note who had taken his share. The inventory also registered the handover of this equipment from one guild warden to another, with a note of any additions.

The surviving records of the Eucharistic brotherhoods, the Scuole del Venerabile, likewise reveal the occasional pattern of patronage by the chief officers, sometimes of a quite competitive nature. At the church of Santa Maria Formosa the contribution of the brotherhood to the upkeep of the fabric included furnishings for the chapel of the sacrament in 1562, an altar cloth of crimson damask in 1566, a gilded tabernacle above the altar in 1572, and six gilded candlesticks the next year, all paid for by the gastaldo and his fellow officers.[93] At the church of San Basso, where the mercers were predominant in the Eucharistic brotherhood, successive guild wardens paid for a walnut desk and then a large tapestry. In 1571 the head of the guild commissioned a painting of the Last Supper, which was gilded, and in 1574 he provided a canvas bag in which to conserve it. Ten years later the warden paid for crystal windowpanes with the sacrament emblazoned upon them. In 1588 a "peace" of gilded ivory and ebony followed. In 1602 Antonio Bufeli, a bookseller at the Aquila Negra, commissioned a new Last Supper and an Agony in the Garden "for no other end than zeal for matters divine, and also to give heart to his successors in good works."[94]

The Case of San Silvestro

Unusually in these records, the Scuola del Venerabile that met at San Silvestro left a clear account of its contribution to the material fabric of the church, certainly by the year 1516. "Given the expenditure made in the said church, that is to say on the altar, the balconies, digging out the pulpit, removing it from beside the Most Holy Sacrament to that of Saint Alexander, removing the walls of the small lower choir, thereby making the church spacious and light and also the removal of the sacristy from below up into the choir for our greater convenience, all at our trouble and expense and interest, and this having been carried out by the confraternity of the Most Holy Sacrament."[95] This entry was the prelude to a request that the church's chapter grant the sacristy to the scuola for its use. The application is undated but is followed by an entry that records the purchase of the ciborium, the vessel that housed the sacrament ("tabernacula") of 1543.[96]

The church of San Silvestro was the home of an exceptionally large number of confraternities – a dozen in all.[97] The organizations that were included in the registers of the Provveditori di Comun were the scuole of Sant'Alessandro (1491), San Giuseppe (1499), the Eucharist (1516), and the Beata Vergine della Pietà (1622). The presence of the Sovvegno di Sant'Antonio (1560), a charitable agency of the goldsmiths, has been noted. There were later foundations of a Compagnia della Buona Morte (1707) and a "suffragio" for the Virgin and Saint Oswald (1727).[98] To these we may add four confraternities of trade guilds. The wine merchants had commissioned a polyptych in the later fourteenth century, though their statute dated from 1565;[99] after the painting was lost or destroyed, the guild replaced it with an altarpiece of Saint Helen and other saints (by Damiano Mazza, c. 1577–80). The coopers, whose statute dated from 1468, decorated their meeting place with a painting of Thomas à Becket and other saints (Girolamo da Santa Croce, 1522).[100] The boatmen who rowed a peculiarly Venetian craft, the "peata," who had worshipped at the church since 1451, commissioned a Baptism of Christ from Tintoretto in about 1580.[101] Musicians were also associated with the church.[102] The *campo* outside, now only a shortcut to the bank of the Canal Grande that avoids some of the worst of the crowds, was itself once vibrant with commerce and crafts.[103]

In light of this information, one follows in Ruskin's footsteps and examines the stones of the church. Alas, the church of San Silvestro survives in a form so unrecognizable as to make the exercise chimeric. As the futility of the enterprise dawns, wild fancy gives way to deep melancholy. True, the works of Tintoretto and Santa Croce remain in the church (figs. 18 and 19). However, these are essentially all that survive. San Silvestro was a ninth-century foundation that was rebuilt in the first half of the fifteenth century and consecrated in 1422. There was an architectural and decorative reconstruction two hundred years later. The chief disaster was the reconstruction of 1837–43, when many of the paintings were sold. The project ended only in 1909 with the completion of the façade.[104]

The example of San Silvestro is instructive. Working back from a twentieth-century façade leads to a nineteenth-century reconstruction that goes further back to a reconsecration in the middle of the seventeenth century. Then we find that an earlier consecration of 1422 took place amid a general reconstruction that itself was a gloss on a foundation dating back to the ninth century. It is all very well lamenting how few Venetian monuments remain intact, but exactly when were they ever "intact"? Although San Silvestro and its immediate environs are now devoid of the commercial life that once flowed there, the Rialto area, which is only a few paces further away, still pulses with vitality. It is this area that repays close attention most bountifully. There are a number of other churches in Venice that show how the values of the scuole were realized in the material fabric of the city.

The Scuole and the Rialto Complex

> Around this temple, let the merchant's law be just, his weights true, and his contracts guileless
> (Hoc circa templum sit ius mercantibus aequum
> Pondera nec vergent nec sit conventio prava)

This is the translation and text of an inscription on the exterior wall of the church of San Giacomo di Rialto, also known as San Giacometto. Editors used a letter by Ruskin to reinforce his message to the businessmen of Victorian Manchester that "we have lost faith in common honesty."[105] For the Venetians the inscription stood as an everyday reminder of the principle that should govern everyday commercial practice. The message could scarcely be more firmly embedded in the commercial heart of Venice, near the Rialto food markets, a few steps from the world's first giro bank that had been operating privately since the twelfth century and which came into state ownership in 1585 – an

18. Tintoretto (Jacopo Robusti), *The Baptism of Christ*, c. 1580, oil on canvas, Chiesa di San Silvestro (for the arte dei piateri). Copyright Curia Patriarcale di Venezia.

19. Girolamo da Santa Croce, *Saint Thomas à Becket Enthroned with Saint Francis and Saint John the Baptist*, 1520, oil on panel, Chiesa di San Silvestro (for the arte dei mastellai). Copyright Curia Patriarcale di Venezia.

area that was also the centre of the economy of the Mediterranean.[106] (See map 9, "Churches and Scuole in the Rialto Complex.")

As a microcosm of a greater whole, the interior of the church imitated that of San Marco. The tiny space was packed with reminders of the guilds whose members worshipped there and who worked nearby. To the right of the high altar once stood the devotional focus of the oil decanters ("travasadori di olio") dedicated to Saint Antony of Padua.[107] The chapel housing the high altar, very unusually, served as a meeting place for the cheese sellers ("casaroli"), whose statute dated from 1436. The side entrance of the church by the Rialto Bridge allowed a member of the guild to enter the church, genuflect before the high altar, and then proceed to his stall at the cheese market via the other door. The statue of Saint James was commissioned by the guild in 1602 from the workshop of Vittoria[108] (fig. 20). To the left of the high altar was the altar of the goldsmiths, whose scuola had met at the church since 1382 and who commissioned a statue of Saint Anthony Abbot from Gerolamo Campagna in the early years of the seventeenth century.[109] In line with the inscription that Ruskin cited, the duty official from the city's weights and measures, itself a guild, was to attend mass at the church.[110] It is indicative of the business of the area that each of the confraternities at San Giacometto was linked to a particular occupation. There were no confraternities – not even a Eucharistic foundation – that drew their identities purely from their devotions.

The same general comment applies to the church of San Zuan Elemosinario (Saint John the Almsgiver), commemorated in Titian's great altarpiece. This completely inconspicuous church was part of the fabric of the Rialto complex of shops. The interior perhaps conveys something of what was lost at San Silvestro. The small and concentrated space of the church has a density of cross-reference within the interior that still gives a sense of the warp and weft of the social fabric that features so largely in this study.

At least five trade guilds had a meeting place in the church. The Scuola del Santissimo Sacramento was the only devotional confraternity. However, that is a record we read from the existing tomb slab. Astonishingly, this church did not make an appearance in the registers of scuole compiled by the Provveditori di Comun, and nor did its Scuola del Venerabile.[111] The merchant canvas makers ("mercanti tellaroli," an interesting example of the narrow distinction between manufacturing and marketing in Venice, who had first assembled in 1496) also had a burial chamber to the left of the chancel.[112] The couriers (from 1359) have already appeared in this study. They and their superb altarpiece of Saint Roch and saints by Pordenone, probably from about 1531, merit a further citation.[113] Those Venetians such as the *corrieri*, who travelled frequently and of necessity in their work, increased their risk of contracting or carrying contagion, and

20. Workshop of Alessandro Vittoria, *Saint James*, 1602, sculpture, Chiesa di San Giacometto, Venice (for the arte dei casaroli). Photograph by Vicky Avery.

the altarpiece shows Saint Roch pointing out a plague sore on his leg to Saint Catherine (fig. 21).

From at least 1581 the corn chandlers ("biadaroli") assembled here under the tutelage of the Blessed Virgin of the Annunciation[114] (figs. 22a and 22b). The poulterers ("pollaiuoli"), whose statute is dated 1595, commissioned a Madonna in Glory from the workshop of Bonifazio de' Pitati, which is still in situ.[115] This work evoked once again the connection of the mundane with the divine. Domenico Tintoretto's depiction of the Eternal Father in Glory with Doge Marin Grimani, Dogaressa Morosina Morosini, and seven members of the guild flattened the social and political hierarchy in the sight of heaven itself. The individual poulterers were probably identifiable to contemporaries.[116] Vicar Gianmaria Carnonati is certainly identifiable, as he administers holy water to Doge Leonardo Donà in the presence of Saint Mark, the patron of Venice, and Saint John the Almsgiver, the patron of the church (fig. 23).

A few paces along the Ruga degli Oresi and past more goldsmiths' shops on the Rialto Bridge itself was the only footbridge across the Canal Grande. At the foot of the steps of Rialto on the other side ("al pie del ponte"), immediately to the right, stood the church of San Bartolomeo, home to another cluster of confraternities. Static enough now, the fabric of the church then was subject to generation after generation of change.[117] The interior space has retained the traces of a crowd of scuole, and there remains hardly an inch that does not seem to reflect their bustling presence. The records of the Provveditori di Comun showed at least four devotional confraternities in the church, and five trade guilds also made San Bartolomeo their devotional base.[118]

Pre-eminent in this study is the example of that ancient confraternity of Saint Matthew, which apparently began in Murano in 1247 and linked the church of San Bartolomeo to the German community at the nearby Fondaco dei Tedeschi.[119] The association sponsored the *Feast of the Rosary*, which Albrecht Duerer painted in 1506[120] (fig. 24). The centrality of the rosary may well have reflected the Germans' eagerness to advertise their delicate beads as essential to the cult.[121] The work so enchanted Emperor Rudolf II that he determined to have it carried beyond the Alps for his collection in Prague.[122]

There is also a monument for the Scuola del Venerabile (of 1507). This confraternity commissioned the *Fall of Manna* from Sante Peranda and the *Plague of Serpents* from Peranda's master, Palma il Giovane (figs. 25 and 26). These pictures date from the late sixteenth century. While the two painters were apparently in competition, the subjects were entirely complementary, as both were reminders and celebrations of the works of corporal mercy: feeding the hungry, and healing the sick.[123]

21. Il Pordenone (Giovanni Antonio de' Sacchis), *Saints Sebastian, Roch, and Catherine*, 1531, oil on canvas, Chiesa San Giovanni Elemosinario (for the arte dei corrieri). Copyright Curia Patriarcale di Venezia.

22a. School of Leonardo Corona, *Archangel Gabriel*, sixteenth to seventeenth centuries, from *Annunciation*, Chiesa di San Giovanni Elemosinario (for the arte dei biavaroli). Copyright Curia Patriarcale di Venezia.

22b. School of Leonardo Corona, *Virgin Annunciate*, sixteenth to seventeenth centuries, from *Annunciation*, Chiesa di San Giovanni Elemosinario (for the arte dei biavaroli). Copyright Curia Patriarcale di Venezia.

23. Domenico Tintoretto, *The Eternal Father in Glory with Doge Marino Grimani and Dogaressa Morosina Morosini, and Members of the Guild of Poulterers*, late sixteenth to seventeenth centuries, Chiesa di San Giovanni Elemosinario (for the arte dei pollaiuoli). Copyright Curia Patriarcale di Venezia.

There is no memorial to the confraternity that met under the tutelage of the Virgin who had saved Venice from destruction in the earthquake of 1513,[124] but the charity for the daughters of the oar makers of the Arsenale can be traced to the fabric of the church. However puzzling the presence of the "remeri" may seem in a place so far removed from the shipyards, the guild's own altarpiece was an evident tribute to the church's patron saint, depicting his martyrdom – another commission that went to Palma il Giovane (c. 1593)[125] (fig. 27). The fustian weavers and their merchant bosses (1503) decorated their altar with a painting of Saint Michael and the Demons by Pietro Malombra from around 1600, though it is now lost.[126] The wine porters (1568) hired Marco d'Agnolo (also known as "del Moro") to paint a Paradiso of All Saints for their confraternity, completed in 1572.[127] Appropriately, this is now in the church of Ognissanti (fig. 28).

From the beginning of the Mercerie, the chief thoroughfare between Rialto and San Marco (lined with hundreds of luxurious shopfronts) leads to the great church of San Salvador, the Holy Saviour. San Salvador commemorated the mingling of the mighty with the lowly in Venice's crowded space, and the serenity of contemplation and devotion that stood a few steps away from the mundane and intense business of commercial gain. That connection is in many

24. Albrecht Duerer, *Feast of the Rosary*, 1506, oil on panel (for the Scuola dei Tedeschi). Copyright The National Gallery, Prague.

25. Sante Peranda, *Fall of Manna*, 1602, oil on canvas, Chiesa di San Bartolomeo, Venice (for the Scuola del Venerabile). Photo copyright Francesco Turio Böhm.

26. Palma il Giovane (Jacopo Negretti), *Plague of Serpents*, end of the sixteenth century, Chiesa di San Bartolomeo, Venice (for the Scuola del Venerabile). Copyright Francesco Turio Böhm.

27. Palma il Giovane (Jacopo Negretti), *Saint Bartholomew*, oil on canvas, late sixteenth century, Chiesa di San Bartolomeo, Venice (for the arte dei remeri). Courtesy of Fototeca della Fondazione Federico Zeri, Università di Bologna.

28. Marco del Moro, *All Saints*, 1572, Chiesa di San Bartolomeo, Venice, now in Chiesa Ognissanti, Venice (for the arte dei portadori di vin). Photograph by Massimo Bertacchi.

29. Giovanni Bellini, *The Supper at Emmaus*, 1513, oil on canvas, Chiesa di San Salvador, Venice (for the Scuola del Venerabile). Copyright Curia Patriarcale di Venezia.

ways replicated at the other end of the Mercerie, in Tintoretto's *Paradiso* in the Palazzo Ducale.[128]

Immediately to the left of the high altar of San Salvador was the chapel of the Scuola del Venerabile (founded in 1508), in which was Giovanni Bellini's *Supper at Emmaus*[129] (fig. 29). In the left transept, next to the tomb of three cardinals from the Corner family, stands the altar whose patron was the mercer at the Chalice, Bartolomeo Bontempelli. He and his brother are depicted before a Pietà with San Carlo Borromeo by Sante Peranda[130] (fig. 30). In the left aisle was the altar at which the "luganegheri" (pork butchers) convened. The guild, whose statute dates from 1497, commissioned statues of the plague saints, Sebastian and Roch, from Vittoria.[131] This notorious fixer may have insisted that his business client Palma il Giovane be awarded the commission to paint

30. Sante Peranda, *Virgin and Child with San Carlo Borromeo and Donors*, 1602? (Bartolomeo Bontempelli, "dal Calice"), Chiesa di San Salvador, Venice. Copyright Curia Patriarcale di Venezia.

the altarpiece of the *Madonna in Glory with Saint Anthony Abbot, Saint John the Baptist, and Saint Francis* (Saint Anthony Abbot's pig made him an appropriate patron of pork butchers) (fig. 31). Just above the nearby door was the church's organ, its portals bearing the *Resurrection* and the *Transfiguration* by Francesco Vecellio. In addition to the confraternities of the Eucharist and the pork butchers, there were scuole for Saint Nicholas (1425), the Blessed Virgin (1439), Saint Leonard (1453), and the Holy Cross (1500), all of which the Provveditori di Comun recorded.[132]

Other documentation reveals that a confraternity of Saint Theodore, once perhaps the patron of Venice, existed in the church.[133] The saint's relics were housed here, and this was the confraternity that became associated with the mercers' guild in the mid-fifteenth century and then became a Scuola Grande in 1552.[134] The confraternity left a depiction of the martyrdom of its patron, once thought to be the work of Bonifazio de' Pitati[135] (fig. 32). In this church, too, met the confraternities of charcoal porters (from 1476) and pewterers (from 1477).[136] Thus, in the early seventeenth century, a pork butcher could say a prayer to Saint Anthony Abbot, contemplate the Madonna in Glory, then pass beneath the heavenward trajectories of the Resurrection and the Transfiguration before descending a few steps into the anthill of the Mercerie. Through throngs of visitors, porters, merchants, artisans, and shopkeepers, the Mercerie stretched from San Salvador towards the Piazza San Marco. On the way was the church of the mercers themselves, San Zulian (Saint Julian the Hospitaller).

The church as it now stands was largely the work of Sansovino and Vittoria and was completed in 1553. The lintel of the façade advertised the portrait of one of the church's patrons, Tomaso Rangone, who achieved notoriety for his high-handed commissioning of Tintoretto for a cycle on the life of Saint Mark for the Scuola Grande di San Marco.[137] The oldest of the confraternities in this church was founded in 1277 during the great formative conjuncture and named Saint Julian as its patron. As the hospitaller, Julian was commemorated for offering shelter to travellers and pilgrims, who abounded in Venice. (A branch of the mercers' guild, the "stramasseri," provided pilgrims with bedding, sometimes at considerable profit.)[138] The church of San Zulian housed its own Scuola di San Rocco from 1478. The confraternity possessed a triptych of Saint Roch and others by Antonello da Messina, probably dating from the late 1470s.[139]

As noted, the Scuola del Venerabile in the church dated from 1502, the first such foundation since 1395 and the first of the dozens more before mid-century.[140] The prominent altar of the Holy Sacrament was decorated with another example of the Fall of Manna, this one the work of Leonardo Corona. It was appropriately paired with a Last Supper that some authorities have

31. Palma il Giovane (Jacopo Negretti), *Madonna in Glory with Saint Anthony Abbot, Saint John the Baptist, and Saint Francis*, 1600–3, Chiesa di San Salvador, Venice (for the arte dei luganegheri). Copyright Curia Patriarcale di Venezia.

32. Bonifazio de' Pitati (now attributed to Stefano dell'Arzere), *Martyrdom of Saint Theodore*, late fifteenth century?, oil on canvas, Chiesa di San Salvador, Venice (for the Scuola di San Teodoro). Copyright Curia Patriarcale di Venezia.

attributed to Veronese. It was at this church that the guild of comb makers assembled (1438).[141] So too did the Scuola della Passione, which benefited from a bequest by Adriaan Willaert, the first *maestro di capella* (musical director) at San Marco, in 1559.[142]

The presence of the mercers was everywhere in the interior, and it remains palpable.[143] The rich stuffs that even now swathe the columns of the high altar could well be from the wares of the mercers themselves. The guild's altar was on the right wall. It may once have borne a polyptych of the Madonna and saints by Gentile or Giovanni Bellini, now lost.[144] A later commission, presumably after the loss, was yet another collaboration of the sculptor Vittoria with the painter Palma il Giovane. The mercers' altarpiece showed the Assumption of the Virgin, and Vittoria's statues were of Saint Catherine and the Prophet Daniel, a reference to the mercers' original base in the church of San Daniele (fig. 33). The guild of second-hand dealers ("strazzaruoli"), closely related to the mercers and in frequent dispute with them, also met at San Zulian (from 1419). Its officers commissioned an altarpiece of Saint James – whose epistle was so forcefully eloquent in the promotion of the works of mercy – a predella by Lazzaro Bastiani dating from the later fifteenth century and now lost.[145]

As in the cases of the churches of San Giacometto and San Salvador, the connection between prayer and commercial activity was a spatial continuum. It was possible to enter San Zulian by one door and leave by another, quite literally on the way to work. The door from the left aisle opened on to a small *campo* with the shop sign of the Città di Milano immediately to the front, and the solid *barbacani* of an attic warehouse ("volta") to the right (fig. 34). Rising from a genuflexion before the high altar, a mercer would have seen on the ceiling, immediately above the mid-point of the altar, a panel showing the Misericordia. (A similar centrality for the emblem of the Misericordia appears above Tintoretto's great Crucifixion at the Scuola di San Rocco.) There is another depiction in relief immediately outside the church (fig. 35).

The streets, wharves, and canals in the area of Venice that lay between Rialto and San Marco were the busiest in the city, and can be so even today. The press of people from all over the known world in search of mementoes of Venice, disagreeable as it can be, all the same serves to evoke the mercantile greatness of the Venetian past, even though few among the crowd now would understand the vitality of the connection between the devotional life that thrived in the churches and the manner in which it underpinned the commercial enterprise that flowed not only around them but also through them. However, it is essential to the understanding of that connection and that movement that the mind's eye attempt to envisage such dynamics in operation throughout the city, for these currents, by their very motion, helped to give the republic its reputation for stability.

33. The Altar of the Mercers' Guild, Chiesa di San Zulian, 1579–84 (for the arte dei marzeri): [Palma il Giovane, *Assumption of the Virgin*, oil on canvas; Alessandro Vittoria, *Saint Catherine, The Prophet Daniel*, sculpture]. Montage courtesy of Greig Angove.

34. Campo San Zulian, warehouse barbacani, Venice. Photograph by Massimo Bertacchi.

35. *Madonna della Misericordia*, relief, Merceria San Zulian, Venice. Photograph by Annie Atwell / Churches of Venice: http://www.slowtrav.com/blog/annienc.

Taking account of churches destroyed or unrecognizable from what they were around 1600, several further groupings of significant survivals suggest themselves. The first is the close identification that existed between the city's two chief mendicant churches and their confraternities. Another pairs the churches of Santa Maria Formosa and San Stefano, and the third examines a quartet of examples in the poorer communities in which lived the Castellani and the Nicolotti. These case histories still give insight into the extent and vibrancy that the interwoven strands of devotional confraternities and trade guilds provided in sustaining the aspirations of the people who lived, worked, and prayed in the city. However, discussion now proceeds to an unusual part of the documentation that enables us to follow the movement of a procession of one of the scuole through the *calli* and *campi* of the city between the church of the Frari and the Rialto.

A Procession from the Frari

The confraternity of Saint Antony of Padua was founded in 1439. At first, it met at the church of San Simeon Profeta, on 15 March, but it transferred to the church of the Frari within a matter of weeks, on 12 June.[146] The confraternity entrusted the painting of an altarpiece honouring its patron to Lazzaro Bastiani at some point between 1475 and 1482. This too is in the collection of the Gallerie dell'Accademia in Venice[147] (fig. 36). The complementary innocence of angels and children was prominent in a description of the confraternity's procession that celebrated its patron (presumably on his feast day, 13 June), from 1533.

The exact route of the procession was not specified. However, the documents give a detailed description of who was to participate and what they were to wear. Moreover, the particulars of the floats – stage, costume, and properties – give an unusually strong sense of the theatricality of the ritual and provide a vivid impression of the experience of the onlookers and participants. This is a significant reminder that a survey of the traces left behind by the scuole should always be related to their regular but irrecoverable ephemera and the fleeting role that these played in the life of the Venetians. Again, it is essential to emphasize that this is the record of one confraternity in nearly 150, relating to one church in more than 70, and the imagination should try to picture such a procession replicated in the feast days of many other guilds.

> … the gonfalon with six large candles decorated with greenery, then the miracles of Lord Saint Antony borne by children dressed as angels, and after these the banner of the friars with the young friars properly attired and then those in long

36. Lazzaro Bastiani, *Saint Antony of Padua on the Walnut Tree*, oil on panel (for the Scuola di Sant'Antonio). Copyright Gallerie dell'Accademia, Venice.

vestments with the relics in hand. After these, twelve torches of two or even three pounds weight, hoisted aloft, the golden ceremonial chains dressed with greenery and in the midst of them the portable shrine of Messer Saint Antony decorated as is required with silverware, small candlesticks, and other ornaments ... and then the singers and after these the Eucharist prepared under the umbrella carried by our brethren, then our Warden with one of the reverend friars and so accompanied all the members of the governing body ... and the others of our brethren have to be accompanied and then the officers according to their degree ... and they have to make their way around the Rialto as they used to do in the olden times and then return to our church.

There was a careful note that ensured the public advertisement of the occasion on the eve of the feast. Representing the confraternity, a child dressed as an angel and the shrine on its platform, with the musical accompaniment of trumpets and fifes, were to go to San Marco and Rialto to announce the procession "so that our feast would be visited by the popolo and that our brethren receive a reminder to attend."[148] The advertisement of the procession is particularly notable as another expression of the essentially accessible and open character of the scuole and their practices. All in all, it is possible to picture the procession, in its ceremonial gear and in its ordering, as similar to the occasion that Gentile Bellini recorded indelibly for the Scuola Grande of San Giovanni Evangelista when it paraded in honour of the confraternity's relic of the True Cross, or one of the doge's processions. Still more important, however, is to ask how frequently other confraternities in other churches acted out similar processions, and what part formal public ritual played throughout the Venetian calendar.[149] One might even speculate that such occasions literally slowed the pace of life in the city, the solemn march giving discipline and respite to the energies of everyday enterprise.[150] The deliberate attempt to attract an attendance of the popolo in general as well as the membership is indicative of the permeability of any barrier that existed between "brothers" and "outsiders."[151]

It is worth pursuing this point along the possible processional route. (See map 10, "Processional Route of the Scuola di Sant'Antonio.) Although the details were not set down, a line of people, generally in twos with larger groups around the floats for the shrine and the Eucharist, would probably have assembled at the church of the Frari itself – where there was plenty of room for an audience – and marched to Campo San Polo, one of the largest open spaces in the city. As a physical expression of the institutional network that the confraternities provided, such a column, after the church of Sant'Aponal, would have touched or passed through the complex of churches at the commercial heart of the city, which, as we have seen, housed a host of scuole: San Silvestro,

San Giovanni Elemosinario, and San Giacometto (which was not parochial). In logistical terms, it seems likely that the procession crossed the Rialto in order to turn around in Campo San Bartolomeo. The only space large enough to contain such a manoeuvre on the other side of the Rialto Bridge nearer the Frari was Campo San Silvestro, but that would have been well short of Rialto itself. If that conjecture seems reasonable, then the gowns of the brethren were within touching distance of the churches of San Bartolomeo itself and of San Salvador.

A few points of detail in the description also merit one or two remarks. We may only glimpse the ritual objects – golden chains, silver reliquaries and candlesticks, quantities of white wax, canopies, floats, and statues – but it is important to remember, perhaps by reference to the ironsmiths' inventory, the multiplication of such items in most or even all of the scuole in dozens of parishes, as well as in the confraternities that had their own premises, not merely the Scuole Grandi but also free-standing institutions such as San Giorgio degli Schiavoni. It is arresting, too, to see the cult of the Eucharist so prominently and so naturally allied to the cult of the confraternity's patron saint, for this may contribute to our understanding of the lack of disruption in the accommodation of a large number of Scuole del Venerabile in the complex of confraternities in Venice in the early sixteenth century.

Finally, the reference to the "miracles of Lord Saint Antony" remains tantalizing. The cult of the saint was strong in Venice. The exquisitely fashioned small statue of the saint by the dale Masegne from the late fourteenth century remains a record of humanity and individuality, and the effect of the lily is worthy of Leonardo (fig. 37). It is now located in the small sculpture gallery between the sacristy and the cloister at the church of San Stefano. The literature in the display claims that this work and the accompanying statue of the Baptist clinched for the dale Masegne the prestigious commission that resulted in their chef d'oeuvre in Venice, the iconostasis above the screen between the pulpits and the high altar in the basilica of San Marco.

The Wider Network

This chapter has traced the strengthening of the safety net that the guilds provided for the Venetian popolo in the sixteenth century, a strengthening due to the continuing vitality of the interaction of arti and scuole and to the formation of two new types of brotherhood, the Scuole del Venerabile and the sovvegni. The discussion has also suggested that one can learn much about the developing network from the monuments to the popolani's value system that have survived in some of the churches of Venice. These monuments are particularly evocative in the area around Rialto, but examples from all areas of the

37. Jacobello and Pierpaolo dale Masegne, *Saint Antony of Padua*, c. 1390–5, sculpture, Chiesa di Santo Stefano, Venice. Copyright Curia Patriarcale di Venezia.

city show how widespread were both the value system and its realization in the material fabric of ecclesiastical space. Given the scale and range of destruction that many of these locations have undergone, it is an impressive testimony to the durability of what the Venetians achieved and created that the relationship between religion and work remains so vivid.

However, from the mid-sixteenth century onwards there were clear signs of a tightening strain between the new rigorist trajectory of the papacy and some of its agencies and the religious traditions of the Venetian popolo, which, for generations, the republic had included in (not excluded from) the identity of the polity. The continuing expression of those traditions within the popolo in the glow of renewed conviction was all the more remarkable as the tensions between the Roman Church and the Venetian State tested to the limit the old principles of the Venetians and the institutions that represented them.

6 The Venetians and the Confessional State, c. 1550–c. 1600

I am sorry for thee, – thou art come to answer
A stony adversary, an inhuman wretch,
Uncapable of pity, void, and empty
From any dram of mercy.

– Shakespeare, *The Merchant of Venice*, 4.1.3–6

The Autonomy of the Venetian Laity

This chapter is concerned with the complex of changes that affected Venice and Europe as religious controversy spread and hardened in the middle years of the sixteenth century, as "Wars of Religion" superseded dynastic conflict.[1] In Venice those changes were to impose new pressures, not only from outside upon the synthesis of economic, political, and religious life that had taken shape, but also from inside, in the new internal forces of spiritual disquiet in the individual conscience. Of all the challenges to the independence of the Venetian laity these were the most profound and searching. The result was not just the elimination of the field of force that had, since the thirteenth century, generated such social energy between economy, polity, and religion, but also the transformation of those spheres themselves into Church, State, and Society.

This stage of the analysis suggests that the popolo remained firm in their adherence to their traditions. However, in a gradual but decisive shift from the mid-sixteenth century onwards the agencies of Church and State realigned their own conflicts in paradoxical detachment from the very people whom they seemed so intent upon controlling. At the outset it is important to recognize that the Church and the State were not unitary and integrated interests; they were riven with their own inner conflicts. Nor, in their overlapping formation of what the exposition defines as a Confessional State, were their positions uniform and recognizably shared in their approach to the body of the popolani. However, from the viewpoint of that same self-sufficient laity, both the Church and the government were consciously changing their relationship with the popolo in the assertion of new constraints that marked a rupture, a clearly defined break with traditional ties.

The accommodation of Roman Church and Venetian State seems a strange harmony. In the age of the Counter-Reformation, the Venetian Republic can appear an exceptional case history in that it remained Catholic but resisted the claims of Rome. According to scholarly exposition of this proposition, the Venetian government defended its "republican liberty," which had found new strength and conviction through the humanist investigation of antiquity.[2] In a general confessional context, Venice can seem a decisive exception.[3] The experience of the Venetians even offered a moral for the failures of the policy of "thorough" in seventeenth-century England.[4]

Viewed from the scuole, however, the experience of the Venetians in this confessional era was, in an important sense, typical of many other European societies. This becomes plainer if we set aside the term *Counter-Reformation* with its implication of one unitary entity reacting to another. In many ways, the division between Catholic and Protestant societies, and even between Catholic and Protestant patterns of belief, was less significant than the collaboration – even collusion – of Church and State in their attempts to impose confessional uniformity.[5]

As we have seen, Venetian piety responded enthusiastically to the calls for moral reform voiced by figures such as San Bernardino in the fifteenth century and, perhaps, Egidio da Viterbo in the early sixteenth. However, at no point in the three hundred years that we have so far surveyed has it been possible to identify the downward transmission of a type of institutional structure that the popolani obediently adopted and then operated under the vigilant oversight of the political or ecclesiastical authorities. As an illustration of the way in which the initiatives of the popolo were often ahead of those of Church and State, we might refer to an earlier part of the discussion and ask: Which served better the refugees from the shores of Lake Como in 1530–1, the "New Poor Law" or the absorbent capacities of the arte dei fabbri? Where is the evidence that the Scuole del Venerabile or the sovvegni were the brainchild of political or secular authority?

What is striking about the Venetian case is that the autonomous and self-sufficient traditions of the Venetian laity, in economic, spiritual, or political life, had a working and comprehensible rationale that had no need of the new initiatives of Church and State in the mid-sixteenth century.[6] To what new initiatives should discussion refer? Perhaps the most appropriate characterization of the innovations of Church and State is "social discipline," a complex of attempts to impose new uniformities in belief, speech, and behaviour – and the morals that should animate them.[7]

The Agencies of the Confessional State

The efforts of states to impose their visions of orthodoxy on those whom they ruled often brought a new social discipline to people in local communities that had long managed with their own complex of localized beliefs – beliefs that institutional Christianity had previously barely touched and which now became reclassified as "superstitions." However, that discovery of popular culture was most startling in rural areas. The resistance of local tradition in towns, certainly in the Roman Catholic world, has received less attention.[8] Most important of all, the shared interests of Church and State were more striking than their conflicts. This was particularly true from the point of view of the ruled, and especially so in Venice.[9] In a striking illustration of the new religious and political absolutisms of the mid-sixteenth century, the Venetians were on the receiving end of the Catholic reaction and its agencies of the Inquisition and the new orders of the religious, and of the new initiatives in the policing of morals from the state. This was definitely not some sinister master plan of a new machinery of social control. Rather, the innovations of Church and State showed a disregard for traditional bonds. In other words, the withdrawal of religious and political authorities from the old social model of collaboration preceded an attempt to impose a new pattern of authority and resulted in a new model, one that was unsettling and puzzling for the Venetian popolo precisely because it excluded them and sought to dispense with their social energy.

The Confessionalism of the Church

Viewed from the corporations of the Venetian popolo, the two most richly documented illustrations of the new configuration of the relationship of the Church and the laity were the Inquisition (which was in operation in Venetian territories from 1547 onwards) and the visitation (which took place in 1581). Each of these will receive detailed consideration. However, there was a proliferation of other initiatives that came to insist upon a new and disorientating discipline in the religious and economic life of the laity – disorientating because the paradox of the new impositions was the way in which they cut across the threads of the old networks and sought to impose a parochialism that threatened to destroy the complementarities of self-sufficiency.

We have already made some reference to the emergence of the new orders of the Barnabites and Somaschi in war-torn Lombardy. The Oratory of Divine Love and the Theatines began to exert a tangible influence in Venice from the 1520s. There is also a telling irony in the hostility of the republic to the Society of Jesus. For, though the society was expelled for its unswerving commitment to the papal cause in 1606, the early history of the order was intimately linked to a Venetian context, and Cardinal Gasparo Contarini was one of its most enthusiastic sponsors.[10]

The initiatives of the new orders, in Venice as in Rome and elsewhere, looked to the margins of society and indeed sought to expand them, emphasizing the helplessness of the laity and its dependence on the saintly endurance of those in clerical orders. That dependence was a direct interruption of the ebb and flow of lay reciprocity that had contributed so much to the social dynamics of Venice from the mid-thirteenth century onwards. For an increasing number of lay people in the sixteenth century, the new, static dependence upon the institutions of the Church was to become permanent. Thus the hospital for female syphilitics, the Incurabili, was the state's foundation in 1522, but it took its inspiration from the Oratory of Divine Love at the church of the Carità and from the founder of the Theatine order, Cardinal Gaetano Thiene of Vicenza, who was later canonized. The hospital began to take in orphans in 1524. Another of the major reformers who exercised significant influence in Venice, Gierolamo Miano, inculcated in orphans that they had to pray for the Church.[11] Similarly, the Zitelle came into being at the church of Santa Maria della Presentazione on the Giudecca in 1561. It was founded by Benedetto Palmi, a Jesuit, and came under the auspices of the order. The church of Santa Maria Assunta was originally a shelter for traduced women, founded by the remarkable Venetian woman Veronica Franco, and took the name of the Soccorso; in 1609 it became another institution of the Theatine order.[12]

The records of the ecclesiastical court of the Inquisition are a paradoxical reminder that the secular state "exercised a vigilant censorship on printers and booksellers and crushed religious dissent."[13] There were occasional but probing questions concerning secular politics, and one or two direct references to the reason of State. These point to the shared interests of the ecclesiastical and secular authorities and suggest that Church and State were in pursuit of the same goal of social discipline. Indeed, Tridentine reform "provided a powerful framework for the consolidation of state authority."[14]

The Confessionalism of the State

In some ways, the proliferation of the state's agencies for the policing of society's morals was even more striking than the innovations of the Church.

The Provveditori alle Pompe (Commissioners on Ostentation) had enjoyed a nominal existence since 1476 but became firmly institutionalized in 1514. It was this magistracy that promulgated and sought to enforce the expulsion of prostitutes from Venice in 1523. Following a major reorganization in 1562, the Provveditori issued a code of restrictions on extravagance in dress in 1578. The Provveditori alla Sanità (Commissioners on Health), founded in 1486, became the responsibility of the Maggior Consiglio rather than of the Senate in 1537. The implication that the state was to judge what was healthy and what would benefit the "salus populi" was indicative of a burgeoning intrusiveness. More overtly aimed at the regulation of morals, the Esecutori contro la Bestemmia came into being in that same year, their purpose to impress the state's authority upon those who blasphemed. Direct interference in matters of dress, health, speech, and behaviour all moved in that same direction of policing and discipline.[15] In Venice it was a secular magistracy that peered into the privacies of marital disputes.[16] In 1539 the state confirmed its adoption of inquisitorial procedures with the first Inquisitori di Stato.[17] The move made for greater secrecy in the machinery of government – "a salutary terror," as Maranini put it – and a power so arcane that the denunciations it received were not always known to the Council of Ten, to which the Inquisitors reported. The Inquisitori wielded a truly absolute and arbitrary power of life and death. The delegation of the Council of Ten's powers disturbed critics such as Ranier Zen, who saw the seepage entering the proceedings of the Esecutori contro la Bestemmia and the Provveditori sopra i Monasteri (Magistracy for Houses of the Religious). Given the secret powers of the state's Inquisitors, the curbing of the power of the council (as occurred in 1582) no longer regulated the sole source of arbitrary proceeding, for it did not restrict the power of the Inquisitors of State.[18] By contrast, in German cities, where, to all intents and purposes, no theory of republicanism existed, such powers of secret arrest were the negation of the most basic liberty of the communal polity.[19]

The republic's intention to supervise ecclesiastical institutions was clearly expressed in the formation of the Provveditori sopra i Monasteri in 1521. There were commissioners for Ospedali e Luoghi Pii (Hospitals and Pious Places) from 1561. The government vigorously resisted the visitation's efforts to look into convents, hospitals, and confraternities in 1580 and then promptly gave the Provveditori sopra le Scuole Grandi (Commissioners for the Scuole Grandi) oversight of the hospitals of those institutions in 1594.

The Church's insistence on confession and penitence thus had its balance in the secular authorities' policing of morals. These were announcements of a tremendous shift in the relations of economy, polity, and religion. For the Scuole Grandi the impact was transformative. In John Bossy's summary of what Brian

Pullan's work revealed about the Scuole Grandi, "we find ample evidence of a change they underwent, roughly in the course of the sixteenth century, from artificial kin-groups whose raison d'être was mutual aid to professional welfare organizations which were more useful to the general community in precisely the measure that they became less vigorous an embodiment of reciprocal human relations."[20]

In the case of these organizations, the Scuole Grandi, which were structured round orders of the permanently rich and the permanently poor, the change of character was striking enough. However, the element to which Bossy drew attention, reciprocity, had even greater implications for the rest of the scuole. On this the pressure of the new agencies of confessionalization was to be colossal. Far from defending the popolo from the assertive absolutism of the Church, the State began to exert its own arbitrary rule. This was particularly true in its exploitation of the guilds for taxes to pay for war, and in its retreat into the mysteries of reason of State by the end of the sixteenth century.[21]

In short, at a time when the margins of society expanded, when the dependence of the laity upon the clergy became more pronounced, when a great divide was opening up between the Church and the world of work, the State offered the laity no shelter, and in the case of Venice decisively disregarded mercantile traditions of exchange and self-sufficiency. That gulf between the Church and the world of work broke a connection that the scuole and their artisan members had traditionally forged in Venice.[22] Let us not exaggerate the coherence of this model of the work of ecclesiastical and political authorities. The Church was not a monolithic entity, and its agencies were often short of time, money, and personnel. The Venetian state was suspicious of interventions from Rome, and the ruling class was divided in its sympathies. Yet, let us try to imagine how the Church and the State, whatever their intentions, appeared from the viewpoint of the popolo. The pressure from the Church that was opening the breach with the world of work was at its most asphyxiating – smothering the vitality of the traditional value system – in the work of the Holy Office of the Inquisition. In this the Venetian state seemed an enthusiastic collaborator.

The new policing of morals, couched in the pieties of "protection," was a tangible interference in the value system of the Venetian popolo. The typicality, and the paradox, of this model was that the authorities of Church and State had much more in common with each other, whatever their conflicts, than they did with the ruled.[23]

"La tutela del culto" was a protection of the *culto* from the popolo itself. Enclosure, removal, and a parallel "tutela dello Stato" were also under way. Within the terms of reference of the Confessional State, what were the popolani expected to confess, religious absolutism or political absolutism?[24] Were they to profess their commitment to the new orders, the Inquisition, the visitation, Cardinal Borromeo or Cardinal Bellarmine, and a Church that made a distinction between the religious and the laity as though the laity had no religion without the clergy? Or were they to entrust their destinies to the reason of State, which deliberately and demonstrably excluded them from the arcana of power, arcana that were ever more closely the business of Doge Leonardo Donà, Doge Nicolo Contarini, or Fra Paolo Sarpi? Thus, "the stony adversary" in this chapter's heading was not the authoritarian Church of Rome that was warded off by the zealous republic, but a Confessional State formed of both the rigorist Church and the absolutist State, for it was the both of them – even in their conflicts, and perhaps especially so – that broke with the popolo.[25] From this perspective, the interdict crisis of 1606 was no "defence of republican liberty." Rather, the state's dispute with Rome merely obscured the emergence of more emphatically absolutist principles of political organization. The popolo felt the weight of those principles in demands for tax and galley service.

Among the authorities there was a clear impatience with people getting ideas above their station. "Tailors, wood cutters, fishmongers and the other dregs of the plebeians" had no business meeting in squares, shops, and taverns to discuss the Bible, predestination, justification, grace, free will, works "and other very confused questions and the high dogmata of the faith." Cardinal Aleandro objected to having to make his case to "idiots" (a term that, at its root, means no more than "private"), "for holy doctrine is not something to be taken away and put in the hands of the vulgar and stupid."[26] It was not the place of "artisans and riff-raff" (artegiani et vil canaglia) to discuss matters of the faith.[27] Carafa pronounced the Church's hostility to "sects of artisans and others of base hand" (seta di artesani et altri di bassa mano).[28] For some, Venice made Germany seem a haven of tranquility. The church of San Zanipolo – where the painter Lorenzo Lotto had his lodgings – was a centre of subversion, which enjoyed promotion at the hands of its "true devils of friars."[29] The disdain among the authorities of Church and State that was becoming apparent in the 1540s was accompanied by the assertion of the unquestionable downward transmission of ecclesiastical and political authority.

In the context of the relationship of Church and State and, in turn, the relationship of these to the religious life of the popolo, what had happened to change the nature of the scuola in the confessional era perhaps finds its best summary in the example of the Scuola della Dottrina Cristiana, which met at the Oratory on the Zattere. The operation of this formal and conventional educational establishment was directed by the Cappuchins, the Theatines, and, above all, the Jesuits. It became a forum for the antagonisms of Church and State. In the aftermath of the interdict crisis the Council of Ten set out to destroy every trace of Jesuit influence, which it depicted as covert and subversive. In 1609 the council decreed – in response to a denunciation – that the Congregation's role in the teaching of Christian doctrine was to be altogether reformed, that "that scandalous secret congregation of so many people instituted by the Jesuits without any involvement of this Council be abolished and destroyed" (abbolita et destrutta quella adunanza di tanta gente insieme nella scandalosa congregatione secreta instituita già da Giesuiti senza alcuna participation di questo Consiglio). In a condescending expression of the inevitable dependence of the popolo on higher authority, the Council of Ten pointed to the Society's plan "to draw to itself ... artisans and simple persons" (per attirare a se ... artigiani et persone semplici). The council arrogated the organization to itself.[30] The absolutist tendencies of the state, which had been in gestation since the 1530s, became more marked and, by the time of the so-called Spanish conspiracy of 1618, were unmistakable.

The Inquisition and the Venetian Laity

Under these dual pressures – the one of a new insistence of a separation of clergy and laity, and the other of a separation of the state from its subjects – it was perhaps understandable that the lay popolani of Venice should feel the attraction of new religious ideas that might bolster their traditions. There were many robust expressions of sympathy for the evangelical message and its "priesthood of all believers," its impatience with the external trappings of religion, especially the cult of the saints, and even of the Virgin. Much scholarly work has emphasized that these views owed a considerable debt to the refinements of humanistic intellectualism as well as to the message of the Scriptures that "evangelicals" sought to communicate.[31] Time and again, hearings before the Inquisition in Venice referred to the alleged expression of such views.[32] Lay participation in religious life had traditionally given the laity a "stake in the city's institutions" – another expression of the representation that this book seeks to investigate. In some ways, "evangelicals" can be seen as preserving "the familiar qualities of late medieval religion," and they were less concerned with abuses than with the "barriers and walls that seemed to be under construction around their religious institutions." The sense of a construction of new enclosures set against the flow of tradition seemed "to hem in the sacred and to cut it off from ordinary people."[33] Significant evangelical teachings may have appealed to the Venetian laity, but the gospel message was not merely Protestant. Rather, it appealed to the religious traditions of the Venetian laity and on occasion "combined with endowments for Masses and invoked the saints."[34]

In short, the appeal of evangelicalism was not synonymous with the appeal of Protestantism. It is important to underscore the vibrancy of the lay Venetian collectivity, resistant to both Protestantism and rigorist Catholicism. Much of the evidence concerning patterns of belief among the popolani derives from the responses that they gave to questions from the tribunal of the Inquisition. Consideration of such materials necessitates a methodological caveat. It is vital to be aware of the possible evasiveness of those under interrogation. Contact with Lyons or Geneva was purely in the course of business, ignorance of the religious beliefs of other traders, no knowledge that heretical books were in a bale of merchandise – all such pleas could have been defensive stances, for instance, even as we cite them here. However, such defences also implied the kind of liberty of exchange that had been vital to the commercial greatness of Venice. Dissatisfaction with the idea of transubstantiation might well have reflected the Church's change of emphasis in the cult of the Eucharist, a change from "One of you will betray me" to "This is my body."[35] The theme of individual betrayal of a spiritual collective made much more sense to a brotherhood than did the new message of resistance to Protestant belief and its questions about "the real presence."[36] In such ways, the defence of Venetian traditions may have overlapped with some features of evangelicalism. In two other matters, also, it is the defence of identifiable tradition that is striking, not the attraction of new ideas from the north or the imposition of new doctrines from Rome. The discussion of Venetian merchants and artisans who appeared before the Inquisition will emphasize both of these. The first is the use of a reputation for almsgiving in defence against alleged unorthodoxy, and the second is an impatience with the discipline of the parish as a separate entity of social control rather than as a complementary agency of popular self-sufficiency.

Put another way, the realignment of Church and State in Venice was never able to impose the wholesale abandonment of a popular value system that had developed such an obviously viable relationship between faith and works. What came under scrutiny for the popolani of Venice in the confessional era was less an attachment to new ideas than a committed defence of traditions that had long stood the test of time, traditions in which Church and State had long shared and which they had now chosen both to abandon and to replace. The picture presents both separation and subordination, both distance and interference.

The year 1542 was once seen – most notably in the persuasive arguments of Delio Cantimori – as a critical turning point in the history of the Church of Rome, for in this year new forces redirected its energies with unwavering concentration and resolute conviction. Two prominent champions of moderation, Bernardo Ochino, the Sienese head of the Capuchin order of Franciscans, and

Pietro Martire Vermigli, an Augustinian monk who was also a distinguished humanist scholar, fled to Geneva, either because their hopes of reform in Italy were dashed or because the new atmosphere in the peninsula made it impossible for their Protestantism to remain cryptic – depending on the prejudice of the observer. Contarini's elaborate compromise with the Protestants at Regensburg on transubstantiation was in ruins by the time he died in 1543.[37]

More recent scholarship has questioned the decisiveness of what happened in 1542.[38] The significance of one event, however, still seems incontrovertible. It was in 1542 that the Roman Church mobilized a revamped and reinvigorated inquisition. Certainly, this event had a longer-term gestation. The Inquisition had been active in northern Italy in the late fifteenth century. Michele Ghislieri (later Pope Pius V) was cutting his teeth as an Inquisitor from the late 1520s, and there was a powerful continuity between the Observant Congregation of Lombardy and the rigours that emanated from Milan under Carlo Borromeo, that unwavering formulator and stern enforcer of Tridentine principle – and nephew of the unprincipled gangster il Medeghino.[39] Nevertheless, the reactivation of the Inquisition in the rigorist cause announced a new determination to root out heresy and unbelief; the Church suffering had become the Church militant and was set on becoming the Church triumphant – and this was no mere reaction to Protestantism.[40]

It was to be another five years after this new mobilization that the Holy Office of the Inquisition was established in Venice in 1547. That delay, along with the Venetian government's insistence that it should have its own representatives on the tribunal, has traditionally come forward as evidence of the republic's wariness of Rome's intrusion into its affairs, and its outright resistance to any suggestion that Roman jurisdictions of canon law could challenge the sovereign laws of Venice. With the historical scholarship that portrays the Inquisition as an understanding and fair-minded court, nothing like as severe as its secular counterparts, both the State (as defender of "republican liberty") and the inquisitorial procedures of the Church now have their apologists. As a result, the Confessional State can appear as an explicable progression towards the centralized sovereignty of modern times, perhaps even a necessary one.[41]

However, from the viewpoint of the Venetian laity in their confraternities, their workshops, and their taverns, the overlap in personnel of Church and State was symptomatic of the new collaboration of ecclesiastical and political authorities. It is perhaps revealing that the Roman Inquisition in Venice, in two fine studies – the one of its proceedings against printers and the other of those against Jews – has featured as "the Roman Inquisition" and "the Inquisition of Venice."[42] That interchangeability may in itself suggest that all those who sat on the tribunal were, at one level, operating in the same confessional cause.[43]

The pattern of proceedings against suspects in Venice has received detailed scholarly attention, and the principal features are now uncontroversial. The tribunal was composed of the following personnel: the papal nuncio and the Inquisitor, or their deputies, as the agents of the papacy in Rome; the patriarch or his vicar general; and one or more of the Tre Savi sopra l'Eresia as representatives of the interests of the Venetian state. The more prosaic title of the Tre Savi was "Assistenti," and the implication that they were merely present to assist may be an indication of their role.[44] The Inquisitor was usually a highly experienced judge and could expect a bishopric on the Terraferma at the end of his term of service. After 1560 and until 1578, the Inquisitor was a Dominican and a native of the Venetian Terraferma, though thereafter, to 1630, the Inquisitor was a foreigner.

The tribunal's collective approach varied from one Inquisitor to the next, but figures such as Felice Peretti (later Pope Sixtus V) were especially assertive in the Roman cause. Peretti, the last Franciscan to serve in this office in Venice itself, was the direct appointment of the ferocious Michele Ghislieri (later Pope Pius V). Peretti was relieved of his office for his excessive severity on two occasions. The fact that Peretti's loss of office happened twice may indicate the Venetian government's incapacity to restrain the Inquisition. In the period 1560–90 the patriarch was Giovanni Trevisan, whom Carlo Borromeo notoriously despised. There is no evidence to show that the Assistenti actively frustrated the work of the tribunal, and there are many examples that demonstrate the lack of concern on the part of the Tre Savi for the protection of the Venetian commercial ethic.[45] In the investigations that figure in the research for this chapter there is no evidence that a Venetian member of the tribunal restrained or diverted a line of questioning, no chink of division in the views of Roman churchmen and Venetian patricians. Once again, one wonders whether Paolo Sarpi's disguise of rhetoric as history operated to exaggerate the differences of interest, views, and principle between the Venetian state and the Roman Church. As von Ranke judged it, "the ordinances of Rome were for the most part, and on all essential matters, fully carried into effect." He included the drownings of heretics in the Venetian lagoon on the orders of the Inquisition as part of a list of "dissentient opinion subdued by main force, and annihilated throughout Italy."[46]

The views that anonymous denunciations recorded in the latter half of the sixteenth century were usually identified with those of the "Lupterano" (Lutheran) – which essentially meant anything not Catholic.[47] In a loosening of that specific doctrinal bondage, the more general characterization to which historians have turned is "evangelical." Such a characterization is in keeping with a general tendency for "suspects" to insist that they acknowledged the sole authority of the Scriptures as the source of their beliefs.[48] A comprehensive list of such views appeared in the investigation of Antonio dall'Oio, a weaver of woollens. He was a native of Friuli, and the case derived from denunciations by acquaintances in the town of Porcia in 1557. He began by breaking down, falling to his knees and pleading that any error was due to ignorance. He then collected himself sufficiently to explain that for ten years he had been "delighted to read the Gospel, and to have been mastered by it and to have become instructed" (mi ho dilettato di leger lo evangelio et in quello esser amaestrato et instrutto). He then demonstrated his mastery and instruction by listing all the doctrines that he had not found in Scripture: infant baptism; the real presence in the Eucharist; "real sacrifice is the fulfillment of the law" (ch'el vero sacrificio sia l'adempimento della legge); the cult of the saints (adoration, the keeping of saints' days, praying to images); confession; confirmation; ceremonies at extreme unction ("che debba darsi senza cerimonie"); monasteries; clerical celibacy; Purgatory; indulgences; the authority of the Church. His twenty-strong enumeration of discrepancies flowered into doctrinal dispute: that justification came through faith, not works; that salvation was possible only through the Bible; that free will only achieved its exercise through Christ. He knew of no reference in Scripture to fasts (real abstinence, he said, was abstinence from sin) or to vigils.[49]

Even in the torture chamber Antonio dall'Oio insisted that his faith was in the truth of the gospel, going so far as to challenge that "if in the gospel I shall be made to understand any error I am ready to remit myself and submit to the truth" (se per lo vangelio mi sarà fatto conoscer error alcuno son prompto a rimetterme et sottoponermi alla verità). His judges pressed upon him his obstinacy, insisting that his subterfuge was making him incapable of the truth ("subterfugendo et non se lasciava render capace de la verità").[50] By the end of the month he was ready to abjure, saying that he did so without fear of punishment or death ("non lo dico per paura ne di pene ne di morte"). The phrasing – "no one is forcing me to make this declaration and I do not do so out of fear" – suggests that the Inquisitors, and not just the accused, used a strategy for the fashioning of their records. Antonio was sentenced to do penance in public in Porcia, wearing the habitello, with a candle in hand and a halter around his neck.[51]

In questioning all those features of the institutional church that he could not find in the Bible, in his references to justification by faith, Antonio may have been in contact with some Protestant teachings. The failure of such views to establish a momentum for ecclesiastical reform in Italy in general has long puzzled historians.[52] In the end, the explanation may lie in a combination of intellectual over-refinement (at once reflecting the sophistication of Italian humanist preoccupations and their lack of a broad social base) and the further isolation of such views in the individual prosecutions of the Inquisition itself.[53]

In the specific case of Venice, the spiritual self-sufficiency of the laity may have been resistant both to some of the fundamental tenets of evangelical belief and to the clerical authoritarianism of the Holy Office. On the one hand, that self-sufficiency would have found attractive the notion of a priesthood of all believers. On the other, the long tradition that faith would be manifest through works would make justification by faith alone a doctrine lacking in social efficacy. If, however, works were for show rather than for practical effect, then they might become questionable, as was the case in the writings of the goldsmith Alessandro Caravia. By the same token, any insistence on mechanical ritual on the part of the ecclesiastical authorities would meet sturdy vernacular rebuttal. In his own testimony, that same Caravia argued that he did not abstain from meat on the Church's designated days, because of a delicate digestion, and dismissed questions on predestination with the assertion: "This is about predestination, and I know as much about predestination as that wall" (questo e dela predestinatione et tanto mi so de la predestinatione quanto sa quel muro).[54]

It is notoriously difficult to establish a typology of investigations or to quantify different categories of cases in a convincing manner. Moreover, it is essential to emphasize that the strategies behind recorded questions and the strategies for evading them varied from one case to the next, and continue to do so. Ordinary Venetians may have used the investigations for their own purposes, as part of conflicts within neighbourhoods for instance. In 1590 a denunciation reached the patriarch's curia, informing it of a confraternity at San Polo made up of different "nations" – Venetians, Florentines, Bergamasques, and others – in which members preached, after dark, from a vernacular Bible, imitated Christ's washing of the disciples' feet and practised flagellation. A Jesuit confessor apparently encouraged the complaint, but it nevertheless manifests tensions among the popolani between Venetian and Florentine religious practices.[55] In other cases, proceedings may have halted through lack of resources, or because the tribunal recognized other motivations, or because of evidence of the suspect's good Christian behaviour.[56]

The selection that follows is drawn from investigations in which the professional title of a merchant or artisan is prominent and has significant bearing on the case. The exposition concentrates on the illustration of four categories of cases that are particularly pertinent to the identities of those Venetians who were excluded from the exercise of formal political power. The first involves groups that can be identified as guilds, as the arti and scuole of the Venetian laity. The second concerns the frequent mention of a lack of regularity in the matters of attendance at mass and of auricular confession in the home parish, symptoms of a new and insistent parochialism. The third, a set of examples in which the suspect's defence is a defence of Venetian mercantile traditions of exchange and reciprocity, represents a broader resistance to the intrusions of the Church. The fourth and final category relates to the reason of State and the way in which heretics were sometimes suspected of disrespect towards secular powers. The invocation of "resistance" may suggest a dialectic of conflict. If there was any such thing, then it was complicated by the puzzlement of those under interrogation as to why those in power – whether secular or lay – should first detach themselves from everyday life and then interfere with it.

Investigations of Arti and Scuole

In a case that remains undated but is found in a file with others from 1568, members of the guild of cloth-stretchers, the *chiovaroli*, were accused of working on Sundays and of forcing other trades that were involved in the manufacture of cloth to do the same.[57] The six stretchers so accused made their opening defence on the basis of the exceptional character of their trade. Their need to stretch cloth in order to dry it made them dependent upon the weather, and in this they were similar to sailors, they said, for "in negotiation with the sun and certain of the winds and without that and those you can do nothing" (a negotio con il sole e con certi venti che senza di quello et di quelli non si puol far niente). Recent cold weather had caused the stretched cloths to freeze and break. The six *chiovaroli* pointed out the link between the expansion of woollen cloth production and the vast number of poor people now dependent upon it for work – which, we might remind ourselves, would have included Tintoretto's father, who was a dyer by trade. The stretchers argued that they could not keep the *arte della lana* supplied unless they kept their yards open "liberamente." The implicit argument was that the Sabbath was made for man, and not man for the Sabbath, and making the whole of woollen cloth manufacture idle would cost fifty thousand ducats a month in poor relief of the unemployed, who depended for their livelihood on the industry.[58]

As a dispute between different organizations, one of artisans and one of merchants, this was a case that might rather have gone to the secular magistracy responsible for the wool trade, the Provveditori di Comun.[59] Indeed, part of the contention before the Inquisition was that the Provveditori della Giustizia Vecchia had already pronounced that the stretching yards were to be closed on Sundays and holidays. The yard bosses made the case that the day labourers who had lodged the complaint were doing so in order to spend their money in dancing and drinking and gambling, a sort of "immoral economy": "For we keep those labourers on a salary of so much per year but, rather, they are moved to grab the salary and because they do not wish to do what they are obliged to do, indeed, we can say that motivated by certain of the things that suit them, so that they may on feast days go dancing at the tavern and over-indulge and which is more spend the whole day with cards in hand squandering their pay making their families at home suffer, which previously they did not."[60]

How intriguing that the hearing also included a petition from the dyers' day labourers, who had brought their case to the tribunal because of their religion, complaining that the dyer bosses were making them work on Sundays and holidays without additional payments, which also meant that they had no time to attend mass.[61] The journeymen's petition has the hallmark of a tactical move that placed the Inquisition in a position that gave them no choice but to support attendance at mass. The "patroni," however, seem to have defended a tradition of keeping people in work and keeping them off welfare. It is ironic to find these puritan bosses locked in dispute with their wastrel workers before the Inquisition rather than rationalizing the working year by the removal of holidays in order to improve the capitalist process of production.[62] There is no indication of the result of the case.

In two more complicated instances, it might appear that organizations with a considerable number of German members may have used the muscle of collective action in order to subvert the Church's calendar. These cases show that the authorities' fears of heretical collectives were not always completely unfounded. They also suggest that some popular organizations were fairly brazen in their infringements and by no means intimidated by the threat of punishment by the authorities.

The journeymen of the guild of confectioners ("l'arte dei pistori") had a record of unruliness and a certain amount of violence. In 1543 the guild recorded its concern that the journeymen were seeking to take over the scuola with a view to making it follow "Lutheran ordinances" (ordini lupterani), such as had brought confusion and ruin to Germany as a whole.[63] The masters of the guild feared these workers and carried arms to protect themselves. The guild sought to ban the journeymen from attendance at meetings of the scuola.[64] In 1569 twelve tradesmen, including textile workers, a goldsmith, and a couple of minor government officials, denounced no fewer than thirty-eight confectioners, along with their assistants ("fanti") to the Holy Office for eating meat on prohibited days. It may have been the case that bread prices were high or bread quality poor, for the accused, "not content with committing so many, many falsities and thieveries in [the making of] bread, … moreover show themselves infidels, and Lutherans and dare on the days forbidden by the Sacred Holy Mother Church, that is Friday, and Saturday and all the days of Lent and other vigils, to eat meat, and other things, as we good Christians eat on Sunday, and other days not so prohibited."[65] Subsequent action is not a matter of record, and there is no further information in the records of the guild itself for that date.

Two other investigations involved another essentially German institution, the hospital of the German shoemakers. Was the institution subverted by Lutherans for the deliberate propagation of their faith? But why take over a brotherhood when the beliefs of Lutherans were hostile to such organizations? What is perhaps more striking is that the corporate organizations of the Venetian artisans and shopkeepers simply represented the balance of interests and inclinations of their members, as usual. In 1582 the Inquisition received denunciation of "a hospital that long ago was dedicated to the benefit and comfort of poor German shoemakers," urging that a case be brought against Benedetto, a German cobbler, who was supposed to be in charge of the institution. The hospital had an income of one hundred ducats a year from property that it let. Benedetto stood accused of having sold its beds and furniture, and later its cross and candles; of failing to observe the sacraments or the Virgin Mary's holidays, "on which many people used to come together for devotion and give alms in the strongbox for the benefit of poor people who were sick"; and even of keeping a concubine on the premises. The hospital had once been an integral part of the network of scuole. A certain Fra Lionardo attested: "For a time it was well governed, while there was a scuola of Germans who were good Christians. Then there came into it to govern it the Venetian shoemakers, which is the company of San Tomà, joined with that of this hospital."[66]

The confraternity was the subject of a further investigation six years later. The denunciation named "Versemon Giovanni e compagni," who appear to have been the officers of the scuola. It was alleged that they had not enforced the obligation that members had to confess and communicate annually and to attend a weekly mass. According to the regulations of the institution, any absence needed a certificate from the member's confessor, and delinquents were "expelled with the utmost disgrace" (scacciati vergognosissimamente). There were, in Venice, "countless German shoemakers who had left from Lutheran regions"; however, they could not exercise their trade unless they joined the scuola dell'arte. It is quite intriguing to note that these newcomers had been elected to the guild's offices and in that sense were the representatives of the body of brothers. Nearly all Lutherans, they had begun to exploit the possessions of the scuola and to arrogate to themselves its jurisdictions. Only the efforts of Antonio Strave from the fondaco and of Benetto Erle, "padre et prior," had kept the confraternity going.

The "infiniti" (infinite) were nine in number. Four of these were caught by the authorities and punished, and three were "fugitive impenitents" (fuziti impenitenti). Erle himself was denounced for stealing the confraternity's cross from its altar at San Samuele. He answered allegations of eating meat, ignoring the rule book, and working on feast days with the assertion that "we have our very beautiful Catholic statute." The most searching investigation was reserved for a shoemaker named Martin, who appears to have been the gastaldo of the confraternity. In the event, he was able to summon three testimonies on his behalf – one from his confessor, another from the sacristan of the Scuola del Santissimo Sacramento at San Samuele, which reported that Martin had attended at due times, and the third from the Scuola della Madonna, also at San Samuele. The secretary of the confraternity, Tedaldo, a mercer from San Silvestro, bore witness that Martin was "our brother of the confraternity and he is much loved by the confraternity and he gives alms, and in particular these days past he has given a ducat on his behalf to make a bronze base for the silver cross of our confraternity."[67]

In this case, then, there was an element of division within the confraternity itself (which was linked to a particular trade), and the acquittal was the result of the self-regulation of traditional bodies rather than the policing agencies of the Inquisition itself.

Artisans and Parochial Discipline

Other prosecutions involved groups that were more loosely organized than the trades and confraternities just discussed. In 1548 a circle of some twenty artisans, including two of their wives and an unspecified number of children, came under investigation. One of them, a goldsmith named Iseppo, in whose house the group met, was reported to have mocked the saints and the doctrine of Purgatory. (This is clear dissent rather than religious laxity.) Apparently, Iseppo thought it better to give alms than to keep lamps and candles burning to honour saints ("meglio dar per l'amor di Dio che tenir impezato le cesendole et candelle dinanzi alli santi et imagini di santi").[68] In 1565 an apothecary named Marcantonio allegedly went further, turning the commercial theme against the clergy themselves, particularly in the matter of indulgences and saying "that indulgences are the wares of priests and friars and that it would be better to give those monies that people give to priests and friars or monks to the poor for the love of God."[69]

There was a resonance here with a couplet from Caravia's poem *Il Sogno dil Caravia*, which remarked that the friars ran a market in burials and treated human bodies as though they were sacks of merchandise.[70] Francesco Cagnola, a silk worker from Milan, was similarly forthright in the matter of moneys that went on devotions to the saints and might instead have been paid as alms ("che li denari che si spendino in impizzar candele et far ornamenti a santi sarà meglio darli per elemosine"). It was less judicious of him to suggest that the pope, cardinals, and bishops should be sent to the galleys and that the clergy were "fat pigs" (porci grassi) with no care for the poor. As far as Francesco was concerned, giving alms to someone poor was worth the celebration of a Jubilee ("il far limosina ad un povero e come un Giubileo").[71] In general terms, the anticlerical character of the lay and vernacular culture of Venice may have had roots as deep as Boccaccio's stories of lecherous lapses by monks and friars. However, even Boccaccio – perhaps even Caravia – might have blushed at the rhyme that Domenico Longino, a flour porter, regularly recited:

> Turn the page, and look on the missal
> There you'll find the pope, who is up the arssal
> Of the Cardinal, the Cardinal from Ca' Colonna
> He who lapses up the arse, the Pope pardona
>
> (Volta carta, e varda su'l missal
> Che trovare il Papa, che buzera
> Il Gardenal, il Gardenal da Cà Colonna
> Chi cazza in il Culo il Papa ghe perdona)

The punishment to fit the rhyme was very mild. Lorenzo was released with a warning that any further repetition would result in a year in the galleys.[72]

There were many instances of rejections of wasteful and meaningless ceremony, views to which Alessandro Caravia gave still more strident voice. The apothecary Francesco came before the tribunal after a denunciation from some tailors, a shoemaker, a tanner, and the warden of the Scuola della Misericordia. He had heard a preacher at the Frari who had spoken of Purgatory and told the story of Dives and Lazarus (inaccurately recorded as "Rico et Pulone," rather than "Il ricco Epulone"), after which, Francesco admitted having said, "it was better to fry fish than to use oil in torches and lamps" (meglio frizer del pesce che consumar l'oglio in le sendendoli et lampade).[73] In some ways, Giacopo Saliceti proved a representative voice of the Venetian religious tradition when he opined that salvation came by faith alone, but, he went on (in another phrase that defies translation), that this faith had to be a faith combined with works: "una fede operosa." The case also illustrates the new insecurities of workshop or tavern, for Francesco went on record as saying, "Had I known anyone [present] that was not of my opinions, I would not have opened up" (se io non havesse conosciuto che alcuno fusse stato delle opinioni mie non mi haverei slargato).[74]

The previous chapter suggested that the parochial base of the Scuole del Santissimo Sacramento was an extension and reinforcement of the safety net of institutions that might catch a Venetian in the event of a fall from the relative securities of being healthy enough to subsist through reasonably regular work. The second group of examples suggests that the Inquisition and its Assistenti sought to impose conformity within the confines of the parish as a sign of religious orthodoxy rather than acknowledging the parish as a helpful but permeable supplement to a broader network. In 1553, Vicenzo, a witness for Tomaso, a silk throwster, asserted that the suspect attended mass at the churches of Santa Maria della Fava, the Frari, and San Rocco. There was another testimony on Tomaso's confessional habits, and Battista di Anzolo said that he did so at the churches of the Frari and San Zanipolo and "in Cannaregio."[75] A goldsmith called Iseppo – perhaps the same man investigated for the circle that he convened at San Moise – was seen at mass at the churches of San Lio, San Benetto, and San Moise.[76] In an appearance before the tribunal in 1561, Girolamo de Luca, a silk worker at San Geremia, said, "I have confessed here and there and I have never had a regular confessor and likewise I have taken the Eucharist here and there" (mi son confessato di qua et di la et non ho havuto confessor fermo et mi son communicato similmente de qua et de la).[77]

Such practice was by no means confined to suspects. A witness in the case of Gaspare Dugate in 1575, one Bortolomeo, informed the court: "I don't have a regular confessor but sometimes at San Zanipolo, sometimes at San Francesco [della Vigna], sometimes at the Frari, and this year I confessed myself at the Carmeni" (io non tengo fermo confessore ma hora a San Zanipolo, hora a San Francesco, hora ai frari et quest'anno mi son confessato ai carmeni).[78] Given that this information was provided by a witness, it might be an indication that such practice spread beyond those who were denounced as heretics – in keeping with a tradition that went back to the time of Marco Polo.

In 1560, Domenego Gottardo, an apothecary, whose shop was at San Fantin, told the tribunal that he attended mass "now at San Zanipolo, now here, now there" (hora vado a San Zanipolo, hora de qua, hora de la). He had, apparently, attracted others to readings of the vernacular Bible, in what was a kind of alternative scuola. The testimony of Anzolo Moderno, that Gottardo had ceased to attend the Scuola del Sacramento, counted against him: "For some time now he has ceased to embrace his devotions and no longer comes to the Fraternity of the Sacrament" (da un pezzo in qua el si ha sbrazzato delle devozioni et non viene più alla schola del sacramento).[79] This was perhaps symptomatic of a new parochial discipline, isolated – in some ways insulated – as the business of the Church, no longer complementary to the other institutions of the laity but nonetheless set on regulating them.[80]

The Inquisition and Commercial Practice

The third set of examples gives some idea of the general pressure that the tribunal of the Holy Office exerted upon Venetian commercial practice.

The bookseller Vincenzo Valgrisio, a French immigrant who had been based in Venice since 1531, faced accusations of stocking heretical books that spread the "pestiferous contagion of heresy" (pestifera contagione della heresia). In 1570, when upbraiding him for the books that he held in his shop, the Holy Office invoked that decree of the Council of Ten from 1542 that required printers and sellers of books to be licensed. Valgrisio argued that the composition of his stock was explicable by "a certain pardonable thought of mine not to lose my merchandise" (qualche mio escusabile pensiero di non perdere la mia mercantia). In a nice conjuncture of the commercial and the religious he pointed out to his judges, "I have also been gastaldo or warden of the Brotherhood of the Holy Sacrament" (et ancho son stato Gastaldo overo Guardiano della Schuola del Sant.mo Sacramento), which the brotherhood's secretary, a mercer, Zuane at the San Francesco, confirmed.[81]

There were some revealing exchanges in the interrogation faced by Nicolo di Battista Pellizari in 1563 that reveal the tension between the new discipline and the commercial traditions of the Venetians. A Vicentine merchant, Pellizari had surrendered to the Inquisition in Venice, by the sound of it in order to clear his name as swiftly as possible and return, undistracted, to his business: "But really I beg you, it being now that payments are due in Lyons and Besançon, and for silks, that Your Lordships keep this under consideration, so that I may attend to these dealings, on which depends the whole business of the aforesaid Nicolo, and from the failure of that business in these present days and times of year may stem his total ruin and bankruptcy."[82]

Against the accusation that he had received a letter containing heretical opinions he pleaded, "I only pay attention to those parts and those letters that pertain to my business dealings" (non mi curo se non de quelle parti et di quelle lettere che spettano alli mei negocii).[83] One of his correspondents may have inclined to the Huguenot cause, but Nicolo only received a communication from him in order to monitor his business interests ("per lo interesse della mia mercantia").[84] He insisted, "But as I have said at other times, dealing in the course of business as do many other merchants with different sorts of people; I couldn't prevent them from writing to me what occurred to them and what they heard." Even though he pledged to do as the tribunal advised him in future, he repeated that his dealings with others were only "in respect of merchandise and not knowing that I was doing wrong" (per rispetto delle mie mercantie et non sapendo di far male).[85]

In 1568, Paolo Avanzi had, like Pellizzari, given himself up in order to demonstrate his innocence. His testimony reveals another ecclesiological barrier, this one infusing the term *prattica* with religious impropriety, a severe tightening of the layman's terminology of *dealing* or *contact* into religious practices:

"If in the course of business it appears that I have had dealings with persons who are found to be of bad opinions, I did not know them for such, nor did I have dealings with them as being like this, but exclusively in business terms, as also Jews, Turks, and every type of nation."

His use of the phrase *tutto mercantilmente* provides a marvellously untranslatable adverb, to which both "completely as merchants do" and "all in the course of business" might do some feeble justice. Paolo extended the argument as a matter of business not only to infidels and every other type of people but still more generally to all who were engaged in commercial exchange: "Nor can merchants do any less than negotiate with everybody. And if anyone wishes to become involved with this and prohibit it you will find the majority of business people in the same position."[86]

The exchanges of merchants could indeed extend to giving unto others. Among the acts of Tomaso the silk throwster that put him under suspicion – and surely this seems absurd not only to the practising Christian of any hue but to anyone of reason and compassion – was that he had given food to someone who came from Geneva. He had done so for a man who was a travelling merchant ("mercadante viandante"): "I didn't know he was a heretic, and there are many merchants who go here and there to make a living" (io non lo conosceva heretico, et ne sono molti mercanti che vanno di qua et di là per vivere).[87]

The merchant Alessandro Bonanome was interrupted in transit in Venice in 1571. He sold wares, which he had collected in Venice, in a region that this study has identified in a different connection, namely Lecco, Como, Lugano, and Chiavenna: "silks, spices, soaps, currants, camlets and various other stuff in the bales which I don't know about, because I don't know what they put inside" (sede, spicciarie, saoni, uve passà, zambellotti et diverse altre robbe quali mi non so quel che siano nelle balle perche non so quello che li mettino dentro). (While it was the case that he travelled to Lombardy, that region was not necessarily his homeland, for the transcript suggests that he spoke a strong Venetian dialect.) His defence against the accusation that his beliefs were suspect was that "when I go to mass every day I give alms, as much as I feel [that I can] and as I see need, as good Christians should do and as God and the Virgin inspire me."[88] One is bound to ask what would have been the fate of refugees from Lecco to Venice in 1530 or 1531 had they too been subject to this kind of interference.

Other cases readily add to the theme of confessional interference in everyday economics – that of Giovanni Zonca, a merchant of Venice with commercial interests in the city of Antwerp, is notable for the preservation of his letters, and the case has received considerable scholarly attention.[89] The investigation of "Zuan Sffoger marcadante alemano," however, is perhaps deserving of closer scrutiny than it has so far received. "Sfogger" or "Sfulgher" has been identified clearly by John Martin as denoting the great Augsburg banking house of Fugger.[90] The case is of special interest in that it concerns a representative of a type whom Venetian tradition would have welcomed to the city: an immigrant, a merchant well-connected in Germany and at the Fondaco dei Tedeschi. Moreover, as a merchant and as a property owner in Venice and on the mainland, this was an individual of some means. He practised his own type of piety, which found expression in works, especially in almsgiving. In the new climate of the later sixteenth century his German background and business connections immediately tied him to suspicions of Lutheran practices. The proceedings also offer some insight into the sturdy self-awareness of the Venetian (and Venetan) popolo: lay, vernacular, and resistant to intimidation and condescension. Fugger apparently had a house on the Canal Grande at San Zuan Grisostomo, but it was rather his way of life in his property in Mestre that aroused suspicion. His accusers maintained that he had warned the peasants on his land not to keep images of saints, "telling them and threatening them, that if he knew they kept [images of saints] at home, he would make it his business to ruin them" (digandoli et manazandoli che sel sapesse che ditti contadini ne tegnisse in casa chel cercheria de mandarli in esterminio).[91] Moreover, so ran the allegation, he did not attend mass, he read forbidden books, and he had expressed the intention to destroy a chapel on the property.

First to appear to give testimony was his parish priest from the church of San Zuan Grisostomo, Giacomo di Stefano, who described Fugger as follows: "He is a man who gives plenty of alms for the poor of the parish, for the Scuola of the Sacrament and for other of the church's needs, and he often comes to take up a child at christening." The priest had visited the home, "pretending to want some of his tapestries to decorate the church in honour of the Most Holy Sacrament" (fingendo di voler delle sue Tapezzarie commodar la Chiesa per honorar il S.mo Sacramento).[92] "Fingendo": the deposition provides a fleeting whiff of that general tendency of the age towards self-fashioning, dissimulation, and the necessity of hypocrisy.[93]

This clergyman of the parish then listed in Fugger's house a painted crucifix, a small unframed picture of Saint John baptizing Christ in the River Jordan, a picture of Saint John, and one of the Madonna and Child. There was a further example of this last picture in the bedroom, with a lamp before it, a lamp that was not new because the cord on it had become blackened with oil. Also in the bedroom were two pictures of the Annunciation and one of the Holy Family. That made a total of eight devotional images. The priest went on to recall that in the study was a golden chain, attached to a drawer handle on the writing desk, with a golden figure of Christ on the cross. Fugger had told the priest that he had laid the chain on the Holy Sepulchre when he made a pilgrimage to Jerusalem.[94]

There was gruff, ready, and even more supportive testimony from some of the workers on the estate at Mestre. The first of these was made by Mio the ploughman: "I don't get worked up about anything except going behind the oxen" (non mi inpazzo in altro se non ghe vado drio i buo). He refused to admit to any accusation of Lutheranism: "I don't know that I said he was a Lutheran because I don't know what Lutheran means" (non so di haver ditto chel sia Lutheran perche non so che vogia dir Lutheran). On his reading habits, Mio said that he had never seen Fugger peruse anything but the household accounts, and, on the decoration in the property: "have a look if you like, I'll show you what a beautiful Madonna and what beautiful things he's had painted in the downstairs, and in the bedroom and everywhere."[95] Mio knew of those who wished ill of his master, but, as in the case of the parish priest, Fugger's generosity as an almsgiver was clear to all. He gave to convents in Venice, and, when anyone left his employ, Fugger would give him something beyond the salary. He had also made a kind of spiritual adoption of a young girl, the daughter of a very poor mother. Fugger clothed her "superbly, like the daughter of a gentlewoman."[96]

The interrogators pressed the point and asked how he knew all this, and Mio's response was to quote the witness of his own eyes and to inform the tribunal that Fugger was in Mestre only rarely, which made for a clear memory of each visit: "I've already told you that he's not here much, and when he is here one day the next day he leaves; he stays in Venice, and nearly all the time he's at the Fondaco dei Tedeschi, because he's a rich German merchant and he does a fair amount of business."[97]

After the ox manager came the man who looked after the horses, Domenico q. Michiel. Like Mio, he said, "I only attend to looking after my horses" (mi attendo a governar li mei cavalli). Like Mio, he knew Fugger's reputation as an almsgiver and a man of his word ("tutti dise ben de ello che l'è lemosinario et tutto quel che'l promette l'attende"). Domenico insisted that he had no knowledge of heresies but knew that when anyone came to the estate, Fugger would say, "Be in God's grace, be in God's grace, and if God wishes you well, then I will wish you well too" (Sta in gratia di Dio, sta in gratia di Dio per che se Dio te vorrà ben te vorrò ben anchora io). Fugger was always offering praise to the Madonna and had had a painting produced, "which I'll show you" (che ve la mostrerò). In concluding his testimony, Domenico repeated that, to tell the truth, he took little account of anything other than looking after the horses ("non so altro, et a dir el vero non tengo troppo conto del altro che de governar li cavalli").[98]

The next testimony was even more forthright in vouching for Fugger's good faith, though in other respects it corroborated what Mio and Domenico had already deposed. Pietro Busato q. Angelo was asked whether he knew of "anything" about Fugger that did not correspond to the character of a good Christian. He answered: "Good God, no! I'll tell you that there are few gentlemen who are of this charity in almsgiving, and he's a person who would not keep back a penny of what he promises for all the gold in the world." He had not seen Fugger at mass, but then his master was in Mestre only rarely.[99]

The proceedings concluded with a detailed but anonymous report on the chapel itself. It looks as though this was the result of a stealthy visit to Fugger's "palace," for its concluding note recorded that the visitor could not gain entrance to some of the rooms because Fugger kept the keys with him at all times. Evidently, the intruder did not wish to break and enter. The strong indication is that whoever made the reconnaissance did so as an agent of the Holy Office. There was some kind of vestibule, which, according to the report, had room for barely six people, with a locked door through which it was possible to see into the chapel itself. From there one could observe the altar, with cloths and adornments that were usual, as well as some naked angels, each of which held a symbol of Christ's Passion. There was some suggestion that another image between the angels had been deliberately obscured: "And it appears that these little angels are in a shaded mist, and I could not easily discern if that said mist had been made to overshadow or conceal the image that appears to be or had been in the midst of the said little angels." There was some quasi-pagan imagery as well, for on each side of the chapel there were nymphs or sirens, and they spread foliage with their tails. These were (in a strange resonance with Veronese's defence of his work at the monastery of San Zanipolo) "fantasies of the painter" (bizarie del pittore). Yet Christian convention was much to the fore in letters that made "a Jesus, yellow in colour in large old-style letters, abbreviated" (un Jesus di color giallo in lettere grande antiche breviato). There was a painted figure of Christ between two kneeling angels who also bowed to him, and a little chalk on the Saviour's body "does it no deformity" (non li fa niente di disformità). Another painting just outside the chapel showed a Madonna and Child between saints Roch and Sebastian and beneath the Holy Spirit in the form of God the Father. These external figures seemed to have been painted long ago, while those in the chapel appeared more recent.

In the portico through which one entered the palace were stories from the Old Testament and the New, and to the left of the staircase was "a most devout image of the Madonna with her son in her arms, and Saint John in the form of a boy nearby, and a small angel that is presenting to the Madonna and her son a little basket of graceful flowers and most beautiful fruits." The observer then noted a Last Supper. The locked rooms, according to other witnesses, contained "fine pictures of the Madonna and other lovely and devout things" (belli quadri della Madonna et altre belle cose devote).[100]

There are no records of proceedings after this, and it would appear that the Inquisition saw no reason for taking matters further. It remains tantalizing to think what Fugger himself might have said to his interrogators. Some commentators might point to the scrupulous mildness of the file as indicative of the temperance and restraint of the Inquisition's work. Others may see a co-ordination of the defending testimonies provided by the workers from Fugger's estate as covering any deviation from the orthodox.

The lack of dated evidence precludes an assessment of how long the case lasted. Yet it is interesting to think of the human resources and the time consumed by such an investigation. The accusations bore six names. There were eight recorded testimonies (including the previous owner of the property in Mestre) from secular witnesses, in addition the pretence of the parish priest, and then the final surreptitious report – in all, thirty-five sides of written evidence of the proceedings, none of which refers in any detail to the nub of the accusation: that Fugger wanted to smash images of saints and destroy the chapel in his property in Mestre. The fascinating words of the merchant's workers, and the intriguing descriptions of the devotional objects that he had both in Venice and Mestre, suggest a conventionally pious individual for whom, as for Adam Smith, honesty was the best policy, and almsgiving was the natural extension of profit-making.

Some kind of association with a company as well known as the Fugger was no special protection in Giovanni's (or Johann's) case. But then views as innocuous as Fugger's did not always disperse the clouds of suspicion. In 1566, Lorenzo Vex, a maker of small clocks, made a defence of reading the Bible that was comfortably within the bounds of many evangelical testimonies. He dissociated himself from the works of Luther and Zwingli and believed only what he read in the Old and New Testaments. He admitted that he did not abstain from meat and that he did not pray to the saints. He had had dealings with a factor of the Krafter, and one Christopher, a factor of the Fugger, now deceased, who had supplied him with a German Bible from Zurich. Perhaps he offended his judges by asking them, "Do you want me to believe in anything else?" (Volete che credo in altro?). He was executed in 1577, and his body disposed of on the seashore in unconsecrated ground ("in littore maris in loco non consecrato").[101]

Guildsmen and Reason of State

In the fourth category of examples on which this part of the analysis concentrates are two unusual instances of the way the tribunal could turn its attention to secular politics and reason of State. The case of Zuangiacomo, a swordsmith, who was investigated in 1551, illustrates how suspicions of religious belief could shade into a questioning of secular power – at least in the minds of the authorities. Zuangiacomo's case brought in the heads of the Council of Ten, who interrogated him about his association with those "inspired by the truth." Zuangiacomo acknowledged only four associates – very few for such inspiration, said one of the investigators. "I don't know what to say, what do you want me to say[?], there aren't any more of them, and if there were more, I would tell you more … if there were a hundred or ten thousand, I would tell you."[102]

Zuangiacomo's circle met in the church of San Marcuola, and one witness was asked whether "they said nothing of dearths, complained of governments, spoke of the state" (dicevano niente delle carestie, si lamentavano di governi, parlavano di stato). Zuangiacomo was brought back before the tribunal for the question, "You said nothing of government or of the secular power and of princes?" (Parlavi niente del governo della potentia temporal et de principi?) Zuangiacomo admitted, "Indeed we said that princes are constituted by God and are blessed" (Anzi havemo ditto che li principi sono constituti di dio et sono benedetti). It is interesting to note that shortly after these grand questions of political power, the suspect faced a question about alms and replied in the simple terms of reciprocity that any guildsman might have used: "whoever had something gave to someone who did not" (chi ne avea dava a chi non havea). The line of interrogation on secular power pressed him, and he answered that, where princes (not republics, we might note) were concerned, it was important and necessary "to give them all appropriate obedience, unless [they offended] the honour of God, and to be obedient to them" (di darli tutta quella obedientia che si convien, salvo l'honor di Dio et di esserli obedienti). That was not the end of it. Just prior to his abjuration, he affirmed: "I desire that we all be Christians, princes as well as others … in all our meetings we pray that God give peace to all powerful princes and lords … so that we live quietly and peacefully in all humility and chastity."[103]

Half a century later Francesco Faggioni from Padua was accused of making a link between Church and State that was intellectually far more serious in that it connected to clear doubts concerning the existence of God. The list of his errors included "that there is no God, nor saints, nor Paradise, nor Hell, nor pains of hell" (che non vi sia Dio ne santi ne Paradiso ne inferno, ne penne dell'inferno); and "that the Christian religion was instituted for reason of state" (che la religion Christiana sia stata instituta per raggion di stato). Everything came from nature, which governed men as it did the animal kingdom. Francesco elaborated the idea that man was like a watch; when the spring broke and it ceased to chime, "that's how man dies: breath leaves him, and there's nothing else."[104] Francesco appears to have been a doctor of philosophy in Padua. While it may seem curious to include his example when seeking to characterize patterns of belief among the working laity of Venice, there is a twofold justification for doing so. First, the witnesses to his pronouncements who appeared before the Inquisition were not his learned peers but included a tailor, two goldsmiths, and a fruiterer at the Rialto. Second, that collection of lay tradespeople might just as easily have gathered at the shop of Francesco Secchini, the Nave d'Oro, where the circle of Paolo Sarpi assembled.[105] The atheistic implications of the ideas charged to Francesco were not typical of the lay vernacular culture of Venice, but the freedom of speculation perhaps was.[106] The charge was Lutheranism but could just as easily have been Machiavellianism. The state was becoming increasingly jealous of its "reason" and took pains to conceal it from the likes of shopkeepers, especially when it came to matters of religion.[107] One final piece of information that connects Faggioni to this study is that he had once been chaplain at the church of Santa Maria della Misericordia.[108]

The Visitation of 1581

Materials that relate to the beliefs of tradesmen as they themselves testified before the Inquisition very largely – with some exceptions such as the cloth-stretchers and the confectioners – concerned the individual. There was a comprehensive review of the collective religious life of the Venetians in 1581, when the Church made a formal and extensive visitation. Such machinery is readily identifiable with the enforcement of the decrees of the Council of Trent and, in particular, with the forceful initiatives of Cardinal Carlo Borromeo. Once more, the general assertiveness of the Church needs to be set against practical problems of implementation. Few visitations appear to have been thorough, and what they reported was haphazard. It is important not to read too much into silences and omissions.[109] The visitation to Venice in 1581 was no exception.

In the context of this study the value of the visitation's documentation is that it gave some attention to the number of confraternities in any particular church, and its officials were especially concerned to ensure the careful maintenance of the cult of the Eucharist. However, the visitation's emphasis upon the condition of the clergy was a tactic that the papal nuncio used to persuade the Venetian government to accept the visitation in the first place. The attempts of both ecclesiastical and secular authorities to outflank each other provide insight into the internal wrangling of the Confessional State that the Venetian popolo faced.

However, those same negotiations revealed the representatives of the Church to be both agile and determined. Carlo Borromeo had indeed been insistent with Pope Gregory XIII that the agency of the visitation was to check upon the enforcement of the decrees of the Council of Trent. Borromeo himself had conducted the inspection in Venetian territory in the dioceses of Bergamo and Brescia. Inspections in the dioceses of Dalmatia and Istria had been entrusted to Agostino Valier, the reforming bishop of Verona. The choice of Cardinal Alberto Bolognetti as nunzio in 1578 may well have been at the behest of Borromeo himself, and Bolognetti began at once to probe ways of mobilizing a general visitation, actively seeking the participation of Valier and of Federigo Corner, the bishop of Padua. In Rome the Venetians were notorious for their lack of discipline, and the purpose of the visitation was to go among them and bring them to order.[110] The admission of the visitation had been the result of protracted negotiation and some clever manoeuvring by Bolognetti in the face of reluctance and resistance on the part of the Venetian authorities. Indeed, the Venetians managed to have nunneries excluded from the agenda, such as the conventual churches of the Frari and San Zanipolo.[111]

Bolognetti was aware of the need to outflank objections to the visitation's jurisdictional competence in dealing with lay institutions. He proposed to persuade the Venetian authorities by pointing out that the visitation would remove incompetent priests from the parishes. Accordingly, he sought authorization for visiting convents in the first instance and planned to use them as a foothold for a general investigation of the entire city. By appearing to connive in the concealment of certain errors in the monastic houses, he might disarm the protectiveness of the Venetians in other institutions: "It would be better to hide rather than reveal through visits and investigations some errors which occur in the monasteries, which, being made open may not only offend the honour of noble personages, but also cause conflicts and discords between them."[112]

Only a churchman could make the point that such procedure was merely politic: "and this consideration goes almost side by side with reason of state" (et questo rispetto s'accosta quasi alla ragion di stato). The sticking point was that hospitals, procuracies, and confraternities were matters for the secular power: hospitals for the Senate, procuracies for procurators, and confraternities for the Council of Ten. All in all, Bolognetti wrote, "it was necessary to leave the hope that one of these three organs would never consent to the visit unless these three things had to be left untouched."[113]

In this complex of calculation it is a slightly whimsical thought that Borromeo objected vehemently to the way in which the clergy in Venice wore the biretta as the laity did ("secondo il costume dei laici," in Borromeo's own words). Even in an item of dress the separateness of the celibate clerical order was a matter of concern. The detail reveals a very imposing generality, a new separateness of the clergy – and a new subordination of the laity.[114] According to Valier himself, when the visitors began their inspection of the church of San

Bartolomeo, they discussed with the local clergy the importance of ecclesiastical discipline. We may condense the programme of visits, as follows.

Summary of the Visitation

26–31 May	6 days	4 working	4 churches
June	30 days	20 working	56 churches
July	31 days	9 working	9 churches
August	7 days	2 working	2 churches
Total	74 days	35 days of visits	71 churches

It is unclear how far in advance the visitors planned their excursions. In May, July, and August they only managed to survey one church a day: fifteen working days and fifteen parishes. The critical mass of their work was in June, when on the twenty days of visitation they managed about three churches per day. In some instances the information garnered was surprisingly thin. To discover so little in a full day at the church of Santa Maria Formosa remains startling. Who planned their itineraries? The schedule for 3 June was wasteful, and it is curious that visits to the churches of San Samuele and San Vitale (reasonably near each other) were followed by the hike to the church of Sant'Aponal (not directly accessible by boat).

Overall, in its inspections of seventy-one Venetian churches, the Visitation noted 527 altars and 59 scuole, some of them associated with trade guilds. Evidence in large part from the records of the Provveditori di Comun suggests that there were approximately 180 such institutions. The addition of the visitation's figures for the parochial populations of Venice results in a total figure of about 150,000. Their figure of 59 confraternities represents, in very approximate terms, one confraternity for every 2,500 people in the parishes. The figure that we may compile from the records of the Provveditori di Comun, about 180, applied to the same total population, suggests one confraternity for every 825 people. Since the visitors recorded 59 confraternities, and the records of the magistrates suggest 180, then it seems quite possible that the visitation recorded only one confraternity in three of those that may have existed in 1581.

Then, as we have already noted, the visitation was to impose "ecclesiastical discipline," in Valier's phrase, and its chief object was the condition of the clergy, not the compilation of a statistically accurate survey of lay religious institutions. Nevertheless, the unit of such discipline was the parish, and one of the principal expressions of such discipline was devotion that honoured the Eucharist. This was a matter of the utmost priority for Borromeo, who wished to see the sacrament universally transferred to the high altar.[115]

The visitation of 1581 recorded eighteen Scuole del Santissimo Sacramento.[116] Of these, only one (that at Santi Ubaldo e Agata) was an addition to those listed in the records of the Provveditori. Of the churches surveyed by the visitation, nine did not have either an altar to the Most Holy Sacrament or a Eucharistic confraternity in 1581, and the registers of the Provveditori di Comun do not contradict any of those instances.[117] This tally is an unusual harmony. Those same registers of the secular magistrates suggest that by 1581 there were sixty-four Eucharistic brotherhoods in the city. In addition to the nineteen scuole that they noted, the visitors recorded thirty altars to the Holy Sacrament without linking them to scuole.[118] There are seventeen instances in which the visitors noted an altar and a confraternity that correspond to the Provveditori's ledgers for the same church. In nine instances the visitors did not record confraternities that had a statute with the Provveditori.[119] There were only three instances in which the visitation's compilation and the records of the Provveditori di Comun corresponded without the visitors' noting the presence of an altar for the Most Holy Sacrament.[120]

The statistics may be complicated, but the conclusion to be drawn from them is clear. In the matter of Eucharistic piety in the confraternities of Venice in the later sixteenth century, there was neither a definite pattern of response to the attempted imposition of discipline on the part of the ecclesiastical hierarchy, nor an obvious expression of the teachings of the Council of Trent. When an example of new principles and new precepts seems to offer itself, it proves difficult to demonstrate any Tridentine connection. The Scuola del Venerabile in the church of San Lunardo was a foundation of 1581, but there is no suggestion of a new discipline in the parish in the year of the visitation or in its immediate aftermath. The visitation recorded the presence of an altar but not of a confraternity. The year dated the first entry in the copy of the statute held by the magistrates. It lamented the absence of a statute, not the sudden need for a new foundation, and this suggests that some kind of organization had been in existence before that date. The Provveditori only approved the eventual statute in 1594.[121]

The visitors missed or did not bother to record some two-thirds of the confraternities based in the seventy-one churches that they inspected. However, the tabulations do not permit a precise compilation in all seventy-one cases of the instances in which the visitors recorded an altar that represented a scuola as the Provveditori recorded it.

Two cases offer extensive and detailed evidence of a clear and rare correspondence between the records of the visitation and other documentation, even though the matches owe comparatively little to the records of the Provveditori. These were the churches of San Bartolomeo and San Silvestro. In these churches large numbers of confraternities were certainly active, even though the damage of restoration at San Silvestro has left few signs of the reality of the interior in the late sixteenth century. At San Bartolomeo the visitors provided an accurate catalogue of scuole. However, they did so much more systematically for the trade guilds (which were not, in the main, subject to the Provveditori) than for the devotional confraternities (which were). Of the nine altars that they listed, they identified five quite clearly with separate trades (those of the oarsmen, the German porters, the fustian weavers, the wine porters, and the cotton-cloth makers). They had a separate entry for the Scuola del Rosario, which was identified with the German nation. In all those cases the altar, scuola, and trade took separate entries for the single institution. For the confraternities the record was not so comprehensive. The visitors recorded the altar for the Beata Vergine del Terremoto, founded after the earthquake of 1513, but they made no mention of a confraternity. Had the church received specific attention because it was the home of the patriarchal chancery, and the patriarch was himself one of the visitors?

At the church of San Silvestro the visitors listed ten altars in all, seven of them tended by specific confraternities: for example, the altar of Saint Antony for the goldsmiths, the crucifix for the wine merchants, the altar of Saint John the Baptist for the boatmen, and the altar of Saint Thomas for the coopers. The scuola of the Bergamasque nation identified with Saint Alexander. There had been a confraternity in the name of Saint Joseph in the church since 1499. The seventh of the confraternities – again, the entry distinguished between scuola and altar – was the Venerabile, which the Provveditori had recorded as at the church from 1516.

The two examples of the churches of San Bartolomeo and San Silvestro are outstanding and atypical. The visitation passed through the Rialto complex as though it were a ghost town. What had happened to "the fervid world of artisans and merchants which met around the Rialto," of which Lotto and Caravia were part?[122] What the evidence evoked for the area in the previous chapter is almost entirely wanting. It is difficult to imagine that the two sets of documentation came into being to describe the same places.

Away from the commercial centre of the city there are two further examples of how little the visitation recorded of the religious life of the laity in the parish. The first – not so far from San Marco or Rialto if one knows the by-ways – is the great popular centre of Santa Maria Formosa. In the case of this church, the comparison of entries made during the visitation with other records produces only one match, that of the Venerabile. Of all seventy-one churches that the visitors examined, this is one of only three examples of a scuola that both the visitors and the Provveditori registered in which the visitors did not also record an altar for the sacrament – but then, there are no matches for altars since the visitors listed no altars at Santa Maria Formosa. We have noted the significance of the church as one of those inspired by a vision of Saint Magnus, and also the geographical extent of the parish. From the Provveditori we have evidence of a scuola for the Madonna of the Purification in 1368, and the church was the centre for confraternities of several trades: bombardiers, fruiterers, and cabinet-makers. The Venerabile itself had been at the church since 1506.

The second example is also an oddity but for very different reasons. The church of San Giacomo dell'Orio was a flourishing centre of deep-rooted popolano religious tradition and has an interior that provides arresting examples of what might be seen as "Tridentine" teachings. The cult of the Eucharist was particularly prominent in San Giacomo; the sixteenth-century pulpit takes the form of a chalice. The Chapel of the Holy Sacrament was an extension of 1549. Zanetti listed three works of Palma il Giovane that were there: the *Road to Calvary*, *Christ in the Tomb*, and the *Miracle of the Loaves and Fishes.*[123] There is a strong suggestion of the involvement of the Theatine order in the Chapel of Saint Laurence, in which Palma showed both the saint's martyrdom and his distribution of his riches to the poor.

Yet it was in the Old Sacristy that Palma's work apparently carried the burden of new teaching. This was not, we should stress, the commission of a scuola, but, along with the particular emphasis on the Eucharist and the coincidence of the painter's work with the Apostolic Visitation of 1581, it gives a striking indication of the changing environment in which the scuole now gathered. In a cycle that made multiple references to food and to spiritual nourishment, to the Eucharist as both sacrifice and sacrament and as the culminating message of the Old Testament and the New, Palma followed "the new direction of the post-Tridentine Church."[124] Among the scenes most relevant to such a characterization were *Elijah Fed by an Angel*, *The Miraculous Fall of Manna*, *The Passover*, and *The Easter Lamb*. The parish priest, Giovanni Maria da Ponte, in supplication to the Virgin and Child, with saints James, Silvester (in papal tiara), and Mark, appeared in the altarpiece. Immediately beneath, Palma placed a glowing chalice surrounded by the four evangelists, as though the Eucharist itself represented the combined message of all four gospels.

The extension of Tridentine influence through an expansion of Eucharistic piety in accordance with the Church's teachings may seem a clear model of the new dogmata of the confessional era. However, we cannot yet generalize on the basis of the single example of San Giacomo dell'Orio. The church was home to a number of confraternities – San Giacomo (1422), San Sebastiano (1463), the Venerabile (1507), and the Concezion della Beata Vergine (1535). None of these did the visitation see fit to record, and that in itself may suggest the continuing vigour of the religious traditions of the local popolo. The "model" of Counter-Reformation piety apparently made little impression on the representatives of central ecclesiastical authority, though one passing reference in modern scholarship (of a slightly vague and cosy character) asserts that the visitors approved of Palma's "beautiful" pictures.[125] Here, the inadequacies of the visitation's records are overlain with the stark divisions of art historians over the influence of the Counter-Reformation on pictorial content and style, a further justification for avoiding the term altogether.[126]

In the year of the visitation, 1581, the Venetian government sent an instruction to its ambassador in Rome. In a strangely paradoxical way the document provides a final element in this examination of the visitation itself. It was certainly an insistent defence by the Venetians themselves of what the most important modern authority has described as "sana laicità" that gives some indication of the change under way. The document has obvious flaws in its face value, most notably that it was a means by which the government could limit the intrusions of the Roman Church into the institutions of the republic. Yet it has certain impressive repetitions that reflected what was under threat.

First, while the sense of a rhetorical stance is inescapable, the document was no exercise in classical eloquence. The language was the dialect of everyday life, of *la vita genuina*. Second, and still more important, the vernacular language expressed a single fundamental theme. The institutions of the Venetians were emphatically lay in character. In this regard the document provides evidence of the overlap of the lay and ecclesiastical spheres as something that the representatives of the state were aware of and knew they should defend. Whatever the tactical dimension, much of what the document stated was unexceptionable and, in that same language of the streets that buzzed with commercial exchange, would have been quite recognizable to the members of the guilds and confraternities. From the outset, the instruction pointed out that many institutions were "adjoined to and dependent upon these churches, but instituted, maintained, and governed by lay people" (annexe et dependenti da esse chiese, ma instituite, mantenute, et governate da laici). It was the membership whose money kept the Scuole del Venerabile in wax in every parish in the city. The "innumerable" trade guilds all had a confraternity "governed and maintained by their own lay people" (governate et mantenute dalli proprii laici). Those guilds applied alms to the relief of their poor and sick and to other pious works. There had never been a need for supervision, even of the accounts ("nel qual maneggio di danaro, ne meno nel governo non ha mai alcuno posto mano per rivedere conti"). Any interference would place confusion in the souls of the whole popolo and would generate an inexpressible "mala soddisfatione." In the context of this study the document even suggests, therefore, that meddling in the administration of the scuole would be a source of unrest, and that avoiding such interference was a source of stability.

Another overlap of the lay and ecclesiastical spheres was the election of priests by the people of the parish. Those who tended to the fabric of the parish churches and the distribution of alms were also "all lay persons" (tutti laici). These funds, and those applied to dowries, were "contributed readily by lay persons, because they were managed by lay persons" (tutti maneggiati da laici) who did not need to explain their actions to anyone else ("maneggiano il tutto ne di cosa alcuna rendono conto ad altri"). The Scuole Grandi were "all governed by laypersons" (tutte governate da laici). In this part of the document the reason of State made an appearance, for the instruction acknowledged that the government obliged the Scuole Grandi to make contributions towards manning the fleet. The state was still a voice for Venetian tradition even though the expression of tradition was becoming a convenience rather than a commitment. The scuole and procuracies were "lay places always governed by laypersons" (lochi laici sempre governati da laici). This part of the argument drew emphasis in its contribution to social stability through the care of the poor. Hospitals too, from their ancient "constitutione" were "governed by laypersons" (governati da laici).[127] Even the houses of female religious were subject to the jurisdiction of the patriarch and three senators, as the popes themselves had acknowledged.[128]

The independence and self-sufficiency of the laity in their religious values, their traditional combination of faith and works, and particularly their proven faith in the efficacy of the works of mercy seem in the instruction to have received acknowledgment from the state and perhaps caused the visitors some perplexity. The representatives of the Church of Rome were already hearing such assertions from individual Venetian popolani in their supple and sturdy responses to questioning from the tribunal of the Holy Office. The idea that such independence of thought and the behaviour that it animated might be pervasive could have tested the machinery of religious repression to breaking point and driven the Venetian state into a politic defiance on the same side as its own people. The priorities of the state itself put such an alignment in common cause out of the question.

Venice and the Defence of Political Absolutism

In earlier chapters, time and again the argument has drawn attention to the initiative and enterprise of the Venetians who were excluded from power, and to the pace that they set the government to keep up with them. In the later sixteenth century, and in the build-up to the interdict crisis in particular, the government was not in a position to bide its time and wait for an opportunity to align with its subjects in a united front against Rome. The ideological divisions within the patriciate itself made such a strategy impossible. Moreover, the international preoccupations of the republic went beyond even the struggle with Rome. The state was desperately short of manpower and money for defence against the Turk at sea in the Mediterranean, which necessitated its own downward pressure upon the economy – the economy that the popolo sustained – in order to squeeze from it further resources. This in turn came in the age of the reason of State, when the word *politican* first entered the language and when politic men were withdrawing into the corridors of power in order to savour its exercise in secret and away from the public view. The similarities to what was under way in the ecclesiastical sphere are inescapable.

From the 1530s onwards the state sought to enclose and impose in the matter of the policing of morals.[129] After mid-century the government created magistracies that were designed to maximize the revenues of the fisc, beginning in 1551 with the Provveditori sopra oro e monete (Commissioners on Gold and Coin). In 1556 the Provveditori sopra beni inculti (Commissioners on Uncultivated Property) became a permanent institution, and in 1574 it was supplemented by the Provveditori sopra beni comunali (Commissioners on Communal Property). There was a general reform of taxes in 1579, and the Banco di Rialto passed to the state's management in 1584. That same year saw the institution of the Revisori e regolatori delle entrate. The Provveditori sopra feudi (Commissioners on Feudal Domains) and the Sopraintendenti alle decime del clero (Commissioners on Clerical Tithes) both came into being in 1586. War was transforming Venetian policy and, with it, the institutional structure of the Venetian state. All these agencies of revenue raising were to prove vital to the effort in the War of Candia, 1645–69.[130] From the 1590s onwards the government's burdens upon the trade guilds caused the latter to push back against what were essentially the impositions of arbitrary rule. This story is reasonably well known, but it is worth recalling that the struggle of the guilds with government reached a climax in 1611. In response to the hard-hitting petitions of the arti, the government reduced its demands for the provision of oarsmen for the fleet by 28 per cent.[131]

By that stage, the government had defied Rome's interdict and, through Paolo Sarpi in particular, had launched an intense propaganda campaign articulating the principle of the inviolability of secular sovereignty, making the cause of Venice the cause of all states.[132] By the time of the so-called Spanish conspiracy of 1618, the state's concern to be a law unto itself (quite literally) was clear from its own documentation of the crisis.[133]

In the early seventeenth century the state's intention to obscure its machinations from its subjects put Venice firmly in the age of the reason of State.[134]

In fact, the cause of all states was the cause of all princes. Sarpi's attack on the Inquisition's powers was apparently a defence of lay independence.[135] It was much more emphatically a defence of the power of the secular state.

Recent scholarship has convincingly ascribed a tract on "the power of princes" to Sarpi. Advancing cautiously with the attribution, the work, though fragmentary, sends up some flares that may illuminate the politics of the age. In it, the term *repubblica* was interchangeable with *stato*, and "whoever governs a state does so by divine right" (qualunque governa lo Stato lo governa iure divino): a principle that applied to the doge as much as it did to the king of France.[136] While, on the one hand, the state defended its subjects against the intrusions of clerical authority, on the other, it was to be the authority of the prince that punished offences against religion.[137] Just as the laity were "incapable in spiritual matters," the prince had to defend certain "parts of government" in secret because of "the incapacity of the commonalty."[138] There was, in short, no distinction between the sovereignty of the prince and the sovereignty of the republic: both governed "subjects," while the "citizens" were nowhere to be seen.[139]

Within the tiny microcosm of the Venetian Republic this marked a momentous change. Walter Ullmann made much of the contribution of medieval political thought, especially that of Aquinas, in promoting a move away from the vision of man in society as a *sub-ditus* (sub-ject), as he had been under the Roman imperial constitutions and remained under the principles of medieval kingship, to the *civis* (citizen), as he was to become in the thought of the twelfth and more emphatically the thirteenth centuries. That shift marked a return to the *lex lata* of the Roman Republic from the *lex data* of the Empire. Ullmann made a powerful case for the influence of such ideas during the late eighteenth century.[140] The suggestion in this present study of Venice is that before the rebirth of the citizen in the Atlantic Revolutions, he had undergone, in the age of reason of State, a reversal of status from *civis* to *sub-ditus*.[141]

However, the institutions and agencies of Church and State did not create a model of confessional and political absolutism by mere sleight of hand, and even less did they do so by dint of their own intelligence. The defiance of the popolo in defence of the traditions of Venice was to give the culture of the city its most glorious expression, even though the glow of that expression was not that of the dawn but that of the twilight.

Tintoretto and the Last Fight

"Then Tintoret ... stands up for a last fight, for Venice and the old time." It is somewhat disingenuous to quote these words of Ruskin at this point, since the "last fight" to which he referred was Tintoretto against Michelangelo, Raphael, and Titian.[142] However, with regard to the corporations of the Venetian popolo and all that they achieved, there is an important sense in which the life and work of Tintoretto stood for "Venice and the old time." Tintoretto completes our story as the supreme representative of the great synthesis of economy, polity, and religion that is the centrepiece of this study. The works of Tintoretto that figure most prominently in this discussion have appropriately attracted the characterization of a "theatre of piety."[143] The comparison of his works to mystery plays that broke down "the barrier between spectacle and observer" is entirely apposite.[144] Tintoretto was the Shakespeare of the Venetian popolo in the tremendous range of his sympathies and in the way in which he represented the universal through small vernacular details – a similar kind of anachronistic topicality and topical anachronism that we may find in the sleeve, hats, clock, and pulpit of *Julius Caesar*, a kind of permanent re-enactment of an eternal scene for future generations as in "How many ages hence shall this our lofty scene be acted o'er?"[145]

In what sense was Tintoretto representative? In using the word *supreme* to describe him and his art, it is vital not to imply any elevation or isolation, for his life was integral with the life of the popolo, and his was the last, greatest, and most articulate voice of the institutions and attitudes that bound the Venetians together. He was the artisan in the workshop, and he wove his identity through *mistro*, *ser*, parish, trade, and nickname, just as the ironsmiths did.[146] This study can confirm from the standpoint of the confraternities the conclusions of art historians: that Tintoretto is "a maverick individualist who identifies with the nameless majority" and that his paintings are "open and popular, common in the sense of shared convictions."[147]

His position as a representative of the history of the Venetian popolo is both lineal and lateral. It is lineal in reaching back into the past, deep into the past, into the dark tangle of roots that made the great complex of what we have characterized as tradition.[148] It is lateral in that he was embedded in that tradition as it lived, breathed, and expressed itself in the second half of the sixteenth century.

The lineal aspect of the tradition that Tintoretto represented found consistent expression in the record of his life made by Carlo Ridolfi, which was first published in 1642. Ridolfi, often characterized somewhat misleadingly as the Venetian Vasari, was not perhaps a penetrating guide to style and never thought of himself as a writer. However, he was diligent and accurate in his descriptions of works of art, a quality that has helped immeasurably in the work of identification and in the attribution of paintings to Venetian artists.[149] In particular, his life of Tintoretto has the singular advantage of deriving its information from people who knew the artist at close quarters, especially members of his family. (He also wrote the lives of Tintoretto's son, Domenico, and of his daughter, Marietta, both of them painters.)[150] Moreover, it is not necessary to rely solely upon Ridolfi, for it is possible to corroborate what he had to say about the Venetian context both with the frothy poetic encomium of Marco Boschini (1660) and with some of Tintoretto's more severe critics. The broadening corrective that emerges is, once again, the need to avoid an over-concentration upon the Scuole Grandi as separate, or even separable, from the larger complex of institutions that offered some prospects of security to the artisans and shopkeepers and their families who constituted three-quarters of the metropolitan population. Indeed, we might see Tintoretto's work as a reconnection of the Scuole Grandi with the broader institutional network.

The artists and the commissions listed in appendix 6.1 did not operate in vacuo, but, by Tintoretto's time, the Venetian context of artistic creativity was itself in the process of changing. The process that reshaped the relationship between economic, political, and religious life had begun in the later fifteenth century. In some ways it is symbolized by the practice of referring to the flagellant confraternities as "Scuole Grandi."[151] That separation and elevation of a handful of confraternities may well have been part of a more general tendency to emphasize the social hierarchy through gradations of ostentatious display.[152] Then, in the early sixteenth century, the popolo strengthened the role of the parish in its network of the social fabric in the proliferation of confraternities named for the Eucharist. At the same time, the upheavals of war in Italy intensified the religious uncertainties of the age. The pressures of change began to reshape everyday economics, the political life of the republic, and the place of the Church within it to contours generally recognizable in the confessional era. Venice, always a crossroads of European commerce, likewise absorbed the cross-currents of religious sentiments. While, on the one hand, the popolo nurtured many parish-based confraternities of the Eucharist that clearly proclaimed their allegiance to the papacy in Rome, on the other hand, some of its members found attractive the spiritual sentiments that were gaining expression in the north of Europe.

There was no particular contradiction in this reinforcement of tradition with innovation, and there should be no assumption that the Venetians were responding to conflicting fields of force, at least in their own minds. The attractions of ideas that found their expression in Luther's "priesthood of all believers" were obvious in a city in which the commercial laity traditionally enjoyed a certain autonomy of a generally Erasmian character.[153] As the questions concerning empty display and mechanical ritual gained currency, the emergence of a hierarchy among Venetian corporations that gave new status to a handful of them also tended to emphasize the pomposity and vanity of their displays. The disquieting thought that such ostentation wasted moneys that might more usefully have gone to the poor as alms was natural enough in a system of values that had established a clear complementarity between works and faith. In that fundamental way, the professions of belief by individual Venetian artisans before the tribunal of the Holy Office can be seen as representative of the traditional values that they collectively embraced.

Some scholars have suggested that Caravia may have been Tintoretto's link to a wider literary culture, a culture not as elevated as that of Aretino, Bembo, and the *poligrafi*, but instead much closer to the artisan world of work and workshop. Unlike Titian, Tintoretto never aspired to become a court painter – but then Venice did not have a court. Nor did he operate the kind of connections cultivated first by Sansovino, Aretino, and Titian, and which had the smack of imitation in the contractual pressures that Vittoria later exercised on behalf of his protégé Palma il Giovane. The workshop of Tintoretto was a unit of production and may have underpinned the painter's prodigious output at inexpensive prices. The "prestezza" of completion of some 650 works at ten or twelve per year perhaps offset the low fees charged by Tintoretto.[154] Of the importance of his workshop, suffice it to say that only the work at the Scuola di San Rocco after 1570 is known to have been that of the master himself. His assistants appear to have been his children Domenico (c. 1560–1635), Marco (d. 1637), and Marietta (c. 1556–c. 1590), and, from outside the family, l'Aliense (Antonio Vassilacchi, 1556–1629), Vicentino (Andrea di Michieli, 1542–1617), Paolo Fiammengo (1540–96), and Lodovico Pozzoserrato (c. 1550–c. 1604). As a jeweller with a workshop of his own, Caravia shared a similar background, and his satire on the pretensions of institutions that existed to advance and to advertise their own status resonates with Tintoretto, who appears to have cherished fame but had little regard for money, certainly in comparison with Titian, Veronese, and Palma.[155]

That identification with the vernacular world of everyday commerce was a connection that Marco Boschini made in general terms in his paean to Venetian painting.[156] However, it was a connection that in Tintoretto's particular case made of him a genuinely representative figure: *Tintor retto* – "A dyer, right enough," said Boschini. We might see Jacopo Robusti as following his father's trade in providing materials with colour. His father's occupation was itself a reminder that Venice was a marketplace for colours. Tintoretto and his contemporaries, it was said, displayed their wares for sale in the Mercerie, as would any aspiring seller. Veronese, according to Boschini, used colour in ways that the dye-stuffs of a rich mercer could not match.[157]

Although Tintoretto did not apparently seek great fortune from his work – he painted no opulent self-portrait in fine clothes as Titian had and as Palma would – low pricing appears to have been part of a coherent market strategy that undercut his competitors.[158] There is even some suggestion that this practice helps to explain the furious pace at which he and his bottega had to work. Needing a large number of commissions in order to make a living, Tintoretto left many of his works apparently unfinished, sometimes little more than sketches, which earned him the disapproval of Vasari, Aretino, and Dolce.[159]

In the context of Tintoretto's relationship to the artisan world of work, there is little doubt that his prices enabled the full range of popular corporations to bid for his services. His work is recorded in at least forty-one churches of Venice. Some twenty-seven confraternities availed themselves of his services, making him, according to Professor Rosand, "the voice of the Venetian scuole and the society they represent."[160] There were several trade guilds in this number, and eight Scuole del Venerabile.[161] As a young man, Tintoretto painted a Saint Barbara for the tailors, now apparently lost. The altar of the fishmongers in the church of Santa Maria dei Carmini still bears *The Presentation at the Temple* (also the occasion of circumcision), which Tintoretto painted for them in about 1540. The painting is an early example of the connection between the vernacular and the sacred. The subject may celebrate the fishmonger's skills of neat and accurate cutting, and on the steps to the altar lie the languishing poor in need of alms (fig. 38). Sometime before 1548 Tintoretto also worked for the guild of glassblowers. His work did not necessarily become more costly as his reputation waxed. The boatmen at San Silvestro used Tintoretto's services for an altarpiece depicting the Baptism of Christ, one of the few surviving monuments to the many confraternities that met at the church (See fig. 17). As late as the mid-1580s he worked on *The Adoration of the Cross* for the linen makers' guild for a fee of only twenty ducats.

His work for the Scuole del Sacramento inspires reflection on continuity and change in the traditions of Venetian guilds and suggests quite forcefully that the tradition generated its own changes but was resistant to innovation from outside authority. Let us consider the basic matter of the arrangement of church furnishings around the cult of the sacrament. It is clear that this was an area in which Carlo Borromeo had set his rigorous sense of purpose upon conformity to a precise vision for church interiors. There was to be no mingling of clergy and laity. The clergy were to enter singing and were to be separated from the laity by balustrades. Every baptismal font was to bear an image of Saint John, and the christening was to proceed by infusion, not immersion. There were further regulations to ensure that the church organ would be fixed and immovable and that the positioning of the pulpit was appropriate. The Eucharist itself should be placed upon the high altar, not in a side chapel. Within columns on

38. Tintoretto (Jacopo Robusti), *The Presentation at the Temple*, c. 1540, oil on canvas, Chiesa di Santa Maria dei Carmini, Venice (for the arte dei pescivendoli). Copyright Curia Patriarcale di Venezia.

the altar the sacrament was to occupy a splendid tabernacle, multisided like the Holy Sepulchre, and this would replace the traditional plain ciborium.[162]

Tintoretto's depictions of the Last Supper at the churches of San Marcuola, San Simeon Grande, and San Polo related overtly to church furnishings (the brocade back rest, the tapestry on the *banco*, the wooden crucifix) and the ecclesiastical space – which extended into the picture itself.[163] An explanation for this may lie in the dynamics of the old tradition that Tintoretto brought to a new intensity of vernacular expression. The work that he executed for the Scuole del Venerabile did not always involve a Last Supper. He was responsible, however, for at least six versions of the subject, one of which, at the church of San Giorgio Maggiore, was not the commission of a confraternity. There were also a half-dozen versions of the Washing of the Feet, and the same number of paintings of Lazarus, the patron saint of beggars. The relationship between equality in Christ and a general sense of social levelling is unmistakable.[164] Some of Tintoretto's depictions of the Last Supper preserved the tradition of capturing the announcement of betrayal, not the institution of the Eucharist. In an important sense he represented the Scuole del Venerabile as "typical units in the pious fabric of society."[165]

That last comment applies also to his work for the Scuole Grandi, and there is a sense in which his work for them sought a return to first principles. The tension within such work was reflected in the commissions of the confraternities of San Marco and San Rocco. The Scuola di San Marco's current function as Venice's principal hospital makes difficult any attempt to reconstruct the cycle of paintings that Tintoretto produced for the halls in 1547–8.[166] The scene of Saint Mark freeing the slave marked a breakthrough for the young painter with regard to its combination of *disegno* and *colorito*. Its theatricality has also led to the fascinating comparison with a passion play.[167] It was a controversial piece, which many members did not wish to accept, but the stubborn persistence of that relentless self-publicist Tomaso Rangone, whose portrait bust already swelled in pride above the main door to the church of San Zulian, was to prevail. Zanetti noted the connection between Tintoretto's depiction of identifiable members of the confraternity and the miraculous appearance of Venice's patron. Even in this, Rangone in his ducal robes stood out.[168] The eventual acceptance of Tintoretto's work was grudging, though he worked at the scuola again from 1562 to 1566. At the Scuola di San Rocco there are no such problems of reconstruction. Tintoretto first worked there in 1564. He changed the rules of the commission by placing his competition piece, *The Glory of Saint Roch*, in situ, offering it to the confraternity at no charge if they chose not to accept it.

Those details are well known and have been the subject of meticulous scrutiny by scholars of art history.[169] In this study of the corporations of the popolo of Venice the appropriate questions have a slightly different emphasis. With specific reference to Tintoretto's works, what is it that makes them representative of the social world of the scuole? What are the qualities of his paintings that are revealing in historical terms? There are two essential components to both answers. First, Tintoretto's work for the confraternities, and his oeuvre in general, was vernacular. It presented the familiar objects of everyday life but raised them to a level of exaltation that we may refer to as sublime. This quality is entirely in keeping with the tradition that placed depictions of artisans above the main doorway to the doge's chapel at San Marco and that referred to "everyday miracles." The second element for consideration, which a mere historian addresses with trepidation, is stylistic. And it is revolutionary. Tintoretto's style complemented the everyday quality of his paintings by attaching them seamlessly to the space that the viewer occupied (and still can occupy). Tintoretto's summation of the life of the Venetian popolo was to provide a direct and natural continuity from the vernacular to the sublime. This was made possible by a change from the representation of depth by a succession of planes to the quite different effect achieved through a single and powerful receding axis. Wölfflin's strictly aesthetic approach to the history of style provided an unwitting contextualization. "As a destroyer of renaissance requirements, nobody is more important than Tintoretto." The axial rather than planar composition meant that figures never settled into a row, and it provided a "new stage setting." The move from the tangible to the intangible was possible because so many of Tintoretto's pictures were "like a piece cut haphazard out of the visible world."[170] We have already noted the way in which *Saint Mark Freeing the Slave* embraces the observer's participation. *The Presentation of the Virgin* at the artist's local church, Santa Maria dell'Orto, "violently pulls the viewer into the picture space." In the Last Supper for the Scuola del Venerabile at the church of San Trovaso, the apostle in the foreground, reaching back for a flagon of wine, "becomes the primary means of visual entry into the painting"[171] (fig. 39). In *The Washing of the Feet* for the same organization, the ordinary Venetian onlooker becomes involved in the action as the Apostles help each other to remove their Venetian leggings, "an illustration of the kind of active Christian charity (amor proximi) to which the commissioning confraternity was expressly committed."[172] By such means the pictures demanded direct participation, "a kind of active devotion."[173]

Other means of connection between the vernacular and the sublime were real and concrete, celebrating precisely the kind of *fede operosa* that the scuole practised and which members of the Venetian laity, including Caravia, defended and extolled. Tables, chairs, and settings, including glassware, were recognizably Venetian. They served to contextualize the last and first, the Last

39. Tintoretto (Jacopo Robusti), *Last Supper*, 1561–2, oil on canvas, Chiesa di San Trovaso, Venice (for the Scuola del Venerabile). Copyright Curia Patriarcale di Venezia.

Supper and the first celebration of the Eucharist, a combination that generates its own sense of eternity, a sense of timeless values, which in turn translated into active and practical help for the needy: for the mother and child by the table in the example at the church of San Polo, and for the helpless beggar at the church of Santa Margherita (figs. 40 and 41).

The beggar in *The Last Supper* from Santa Margherita lies on steps. The sense of spatial and architectural continuity is striking even though the painting is no longer in situ. Such an effect is immeasurably more noticeable, and consistently so, in Tintoretto's series of paintings at the Scuola di San Rocco. The omission of "Grande" from the title here is deliberate. One estimate has suggested that nearly a quarter of its members were engaged in the same trade as that of Tintoretto's father. The deacon at the scuola for the commission that began in 1564 was Zuan Piero Mazzoleno, who had been Guardian Grande at San Cassiano when Tintoretto worked for the church's Scuola del Venerabile.[174] The commission may even have been part of an attempt to reform the scuola "along Caravian lines."[175]

Whether there was such conscious intent in the program is debatable. However, the coherence of the cycle for that confraternity depended upon the dynamic interaction of the vernacular and the eternal. The visitor progresses, like the brethren themselves, through a series of rooms decorated with sacred stories that functioned as meeting places for the conduct of everyday business: the Sala dell'Androne for assembly; then, upstairs, the Salone for general meetings; and a smaller room to the side of that, the Sala dell'Albergo, for sessions of the committee.[176]

In the great downstairs hall, in *The Annunciation*, the Virgin receives news from the Angel Gabriel as she sits in a room that opens on to a workshop full of the tools of a Venetian carpenter's trade.[177] In *The Presentation at the Temple* a matter-of-fact group of Venetians, quite possibly brethren of the scuola, still return the viewer's gaze (fig. 42). In the *Last Supper* in this cycle the viewer's involvement is ensured by the extension of the guild-hall itself via the beggars in the foreground.[178] The column base in the *Nativity* – it is difficult to think of this as other than real, according to Boschini – aligns with the hall itself, giving the brethren "an overlap between their Meeting House and the sacred abode of the Holy Family."[179] Axial depth also allows a movement out towards the viewer, as well as drawing one in. In *The Flight into Egypt* the Holy Family moves out of the painted surface rather than across it and seems poised to arrive in the space of the hall.[180] Even more marked is the manner in which *The Assumption of the Virgin* takes the lintel of the actual door space and adds to it a threshold to Paradise. The reality of the effect is enhanced by the cherub's leg that protrudes over the lintel, a lintel that is no more than the pictorial extension of the

40. Tintoretto (Jacopo Robusti), *Last Supper*, 1574–5, oil on canvas, Chiesa di San Polo, Venice (for the Scuola del Venerabile). Public domain.

41. Tintoretto (Jacopo Robusti), *Last Supper*, 1579–80, oil on canvas, Chiesa di Santa Margherita, Venice, now in Santo Stefano, Venice (for the Scuola del Venerabile). Copyright Cameraphoto Arte.

42. Tintoretto (Jacopo Robusti), *The Presentation at the Temple*, 1587, oil on canvas. Courtesy of Scuola Grande di San Rocco, Venice.

tangible portal of the doorway below.[181] In an extraordinary process that is at once physical and psychological, the threshold to heaven takes what is below the lintel, the subliminal, and elevates it to the sublime. However, in the process of so doing, the scene returns to familiarity by crossing the threshold onto a floor space and into a representation of the space of the identifiably everyday world (fig. 43).

On its ceiling the Upper Hall houses what remains almost certainly the greatest monument to the works of corporal mercy in Venice: Tintoretto's depictions of water for the thirsty (*Moses Strikes the Rock*), food for the hungry (*The Miraculous Fall of Manna*), and succour for the sick (*The Plague of Serpents*), which had resonance for stricken Venetians.[182] On the wall at the end of the hall are the saintly protectors against plague, Sebastian and Roch. The cycle expressed the "founding principles" of the Scuola.[183]

From the hall a doorway leads to the Sala dell'Albergo. It was here that the officers of the scuola took their decisions on the allocation of alms, housing, and dowries and on pompous display and building projects – in short, on the balance of faith and works that was a source of such strain from around 1540 onwards, a strain that found expression in Caravia's "Dream." In the Sala dell'Albergo, in a painting that reacts to the order "Behold the Man!" and passes it on to the beholder, Tintoretto placed the scourged and mocked Redeemer on steps "which appear to descend directly into the realm of the viewer below"[184] (fig. 44). In *Christ before Pilate* "the architectural frontage of Pilate's praetorium is also a direct continuation of the adjacent wall of the albergo itself."[185] Given the decisions that the elected officers took on practical matters of everyday subsistence amid such mighty reminders of the moral and social weight that they and their deliberations carried, the interconnection of the sacred and the secular, the everyday and the eternal, finds its supreme concentration. In this room where a committee met, the ideal of communal devotion in a lay confraternity found its broadest and most profound expression in "sheer visual power and moral conviction."[186] Above the long tribunal around which the officers sat is Tintoretto's *Crucifixion* of 1565 (fig. 45). The painting left Ruskin lost for words in *The Stones of Venice*: "I must leave this picture to work its will on the spectator; for it is beyond all analysis, and above all praise."[187] However, one brilliant aperçu, which he expressed in *Modern Painters*, is worthy of note. In the shadow of the cross an ass eats palm leaves that were strewn in his path only a few days earlier, a melancholy reminder of how quickly the crowd's cries turned from "Hosanna!" to "Crucify him!"[188]

Elsewhere in the scene Venetian armour gleams on a Venetian horseman. The Venetian rope that has hoisted the Redeemer to a jolting agony has its twists taken up in the musculature of his crucified arms.[189] Carpenters who might

43. Tintorettc (Jacopo Robusti), *The Assumption of the Virgin*, 1582, oil on canvas. Courtesy of Scuola Grande di San

44. Tintoretto (Jacopo Robusti), *Ecce homo*, 1566, oil on canvas. Courtesy of Scuola Grande di San Rocco, Venice.

45. Tintoretto (Jacopo Robusti), *Crucifixion*, 1565, oil on canvas. Courtesy of Scuola Grande di San Rocco, Venice.

be working at the Arsenale prepare the cross piece for one of the thieves, one tradesman boring a hole to ease the iron nail's passage once it has penetrated the man's hand, just as it might have helped to hold together the planks of a galley of the republic. Both of the thieves are dressed in contemporary Venetian clothes.[190] The cruel mockery of the scourging of the "King" is played out, literally, in a game of dice that might have been recognizable from the Ponte dei Dai near San Marco, the stakes a piece of Venetian cloth. The heartlessness of the action is intensified by its everyday details: axes, wedges, a crossbow, a quiver full of arrows, pliers, the sponge, a packed lunch – all in a day's work. Ridolfi's summary made the implicit connection: "In short, Tintoretto did not omit anything at all that could seem to be real in that event, and that could move the emotions of pity in those who see it as though they had seen and observed that tragic scene. And in truth, in representing the mysteries of our holy religion, one would have to bring it about to make it in a manner that produced devotion, not ridicule, as one now sees it."[191]

Once more, the theatrical element is astounding.[192] The viewer can enter the space of the picture from either of the lower corners. Christ's words of forgiveness to the good thief sound a harmonious resonance in the call to the works of mercy at the very beginning of the statute of the scuola. Some of the brethren are present to Christ's right. The inscription and the artist's signature form a combination that "explicitly locates the picture in the world of sixteenth-century Venice."[193]

The oval in the ceiling that Tintoretto put in place to outdo his competitors draws attention only with difficulty, and *Saint Roch in Glory* cannot match the intensity of the scenes of the Passion on the lower walls (fig. 46). One feature of the upper compositions is particularly striking in the context of this study, however. In the soffit, Tintoretto incorporated allegories for each of the Scuole Grandi. Directly above the head of the crucified Saviour, here in the Scuola di San Rocco, flanked deferentially by the allegories for the scuole of San Giovanni Evangelista and of San Marco, is the emblem of the Misericordia, with members of the scuola sheltering beneath the cloak of the Virgin (fig. 47).

The Crucifixion at the Scuola di San Rocco has a counterpart in *The Paradiso* in the Sala del Maggior Consiglio in the Palazzo Ducale, a late work, but "a kind of throwback to an earlier age."[194] This view of heaven, some four hundred figures arranged in one of the largest oil paintings in the world, has some striking topographical resonances with the city of Venice. The placing of San Teodoro corresponds to his column on the piazzetta, the Lion of Saint Mark marks the piazza of the city's patron, and a little to the left stands the figure of San Moise, in rough similarity to where the church of that name stands in the city. The axis from San Marco brings the eye to the figure of the Saviour, San Salvador, who is in the act of crowning his Virgin Mother, who was often identified with Venice itself.[195] Ridolfi

46. Tintoretto (Jacopo Robusti), *Saint Roch in Glory*, 1564, oil on canvas. Courtesy of Scuola Grande di San Rocco, Venice.

47. Tintoretto (Jacopo Robusti), *Allegory of the Scuola della Misericordia*, 1564, oil on canvas. Courtesy of Scuola Grande di San Rocco, Venice.

purveys an arresting anecdote of the mechanics of the composition. The canvases were so large that Tintoretto needed an enormous hall in which to complete them, and he did so by "spreading [the work] out in various parts of the old Scuola of the Misericordia, a place spacious enough for so vast an enterprise."[196]

In 1604, in a snooty academic lament for the condition of painting in Venice, Federico Zuccaro condemned the picture as not like Paradise at all. He advised aspiring artists not to follow Tintoretto:

> Do not do as he who painted a Paradise
> So confused amid these waters
> That he understands it less who fixes his eye on it
> He makes those citizens of up above
> Like common people in the market place.
> For which he is deservedly derided.[197]

Zuccaro's dismissive condescension fails to note its own implicit vice versa. That is to say, in the Paradise of Tintoretto, common people in the marketplace may sometimes have thought themselves citizens of heaven. The irony of a meaning opposite to that alleged by a critic would have given Tintoretto, and Caravia, reason to smile. Indeed, even the unquestioning eulogy of Boschini, in comparing the skill of Venetian painters in their use of the brush with the gondolier's skill with the oar, suggests how painters mediated between the everyday life of the city and the sublime.[198] The very criticism that commentators levelled at Tintoretto – that his work was rushed and incomplete – overlooked the energy and urgency with which he asked for the viewer's participation, and it was that participation which provided completeness. Hippolyte Taine found the ferocity and the lack of finish complementary.[199] As Henry James put it, a picture by Tintoretto is "a great fragment wrenched out of life and history, with all its natural details clinging to it and testifying to its reality."[200] This characteristic expressed "the social action of a working Christian morality." It made Tintoretto's work "open and popular" and, yes, common "in the sense of shared convictions"; it made the work humble rather than vulgar. The painter was "clearly most at home in the world of the scuole," and, "in every respect, Tintoretto's is the voice of the Venetian scuole and the society they represent."[201] By contrast, he was not at ease in the "somewhat vulgar region of ceremonial grandeur" or in the accompanying waste that so infuriated Caravia.[202] In his evocations of "the joys of heaven here on earth" Tintoretto may have overcome the "stony adversary" of this chapter's epigraph. Moving from the words of Shakespeare back to the words of Ruskin, perhaps, after all, Tintoretto triumphed in his last fight, triumphed "for Venice and the old time."

Appendix 6.1. Commissions of Paintings by the Scuole according to Ridolfi (*Maraviglie dell'arte*), before and after Tintoretto

Artist	Scuola	Location
Carpaccio (1465–1525)	San Giovanni Evangelista	San Giovanni Evangelista
	Sant'Orsola	San Zanipolo
	San Giorgio degli Schiavoni	San Giorgio degli Schiavoni
Gentile Bellini (1429–1507)	San Giovanni Evangelista	San Giovanni Evangelista
Giovanni Bellini (1430–1516)	Centurieri	San Salvador
	Venerabile	San Salvador
Cima da Conegliano (c. 1459–c. 1518)	Varoteri	Crociferi
	Mercanti	Madonna dell'Orto
Pordenone (1484–1539)	Corrieri	San Giovanni Elemosinario
	San Francesco	Frari
Palma Vecchio (1480–1528)	Bombardieri	Santa Maria Formosa
Titian (1488/90–1576)	Carità	Carità[a]
Paris Bordone (1500–71)	San Marco	San Marco (Scuola)
Andrea Schiavone (1522–63)	Taiapiera	Sant'Aponal
Bonifazio de' Pitati (1487–1553)	Sartori	San Giovanni Elemosinario
	Pollaiuoli	San Giovanni Elemosinario
Paolo Veronese (1530–88)	Lanaioli	San Pantalon
	Mercanti	Madonna dell'Orto
Carlo Veronese (1570–96)	Varotai	–
Tintoretto (1518–94)	(see text)	
Domenico Tintoretto (1560–1635)	Mercanti	Madonna dell'Orto[b]
Sante Peranda (1566–1638)	Rosario	San Zanipolo
	San Giovanni Evangelista	San Giovanni Evangelista
	Venerabile	San Bartolomeo
Leonardo Corona (1561–1605)	Cintura	San Stefano
	Venerabile	Santa Maria Nova
	Rosario	San Zanipolo
	Tintori	Santa Maria dei Servi
	Venerabile	San Paternian
	Marangoni	?
Antonio da Ferrari "il Foler" (c. 1529–1616)	Venerabile	San Zuan Novo
Maffeo Verona (1574–1618)	Tintori	Celestia
	Carità	Carità
	Mercanti	Madonna dell'Orto
	Ciechi	?
	San Stefano	San Stefano
Palma il Giovane (1544–1628)	Venerabile	San Zuan in Bragora
	Giustizia	San Fantin

(*Continued*)

Appendix 6.1. (Continued)

Artist	Scuola	Location
(with Vittoria) Luganegheri	San Salvador	"
(with Vittoria) Marzeri	San Zulian	"
	Varoteri	Crociferi
	San Giovanni Evangelista	San Giovanni Evangelista
	San Teodoro	San Teodoro
	Rosario	San Zanipolo
	Venerabile	Santa Chiara
	Venerabile	San Polo
	Calegheri	San Tomà
	San Lazaro	San Zaccaria
	Mercanti	Madonna dell'Orto?
	Tintori	?[c]
	Friulani	San Giovanni del Tempio

a. As a further connection of Titian's work to the value system of the popolo, it is intriguing to note that, in a late work, Titian painted portraits of members of his family in the shelter of the mantle of a Madonna della Misericordia. (See figs. 48 and 49.)

b. The sense of completing a full circle in returning to the Scuola dei Mercanti is reinforced by Domenico's depiction of the Madonna della Misericordia. Ruskin followed the attribution to Domenico's father and, in so doing, described the work as "purest work of his art and fairest of his faculty." Note that the copyright office of the Gallerie dell'Accademia also attributes the work to Jacopo Tintoretto (See figs. 50a, 50b, 51).

c. Note that Ridolfi does not provide a location but also lists both Leonardo Corona and Maffeo Verona as completing commissions for the *tintori*, at the churches of Santa Maria dei Servi and the Celestia respectively.

48. Titian (Tiziano Vecellio), *The Presentation of the Virgin*, 1534–8, oil on canvas (for the Scuola Grande della Carità).

49. Titian (Tiziano Vecellio), *Madonna della Misericordia*, 1573, oil on canvas. Copyright Galleria Palatina, Palazzo Pitti, Florence.

50a. Domenico Tintoretto, *Members of the Scuola di San Cristoforo dei Mercanti*, 1591, oil on canvas (for the Scuola dei Mercanti). Copyright Gallerie dell'Accademia, Venice.

50b. Domenico Tintoretto, *Members of the Scuola di San Cristoforo dei Mercanti*, 1591, oil on canvas (for the Scuola dei Mercanti). Copyright Gallerie dell'Accademia, Venice.

51. Tintoretto (Jacopo Robusti) and assistants (or Domenico Tintoretto?), *Madonna della Misericordia,* c. 1550–70, oil on canvas (for the Scuola dei Mercanti). Copyright Gallerie dell'Accademia, Venice.

Conclusion

A Final Realignment of Economy, Polity, and Religion? c. 1600–c. 1700

Let music sound while he doth make his choice,
Then if he lose he makes a swan-like end,
Fading in music.

– Shakespeare, *The Merchant of Venice*, 3.2.43–5

Morbidity in an Age of Decline: The Suffragi

The idea of decline has dominated the study of Venetian seventeenth-century history and may generally apply to the republic's political economy. The economic horizons of Venice shrank as the Atlantic opened up a world that seemed ever to widen. Its political weight also diminished in the changing configuration of European states. The commercial and imperial future was to lie with the mercantilism of the English and the Dutch, who in many ways followed the pattern of Venice and thus extended the history of government by merchants.[1] A debate persists as to whether the decline of Venice was relative or absolute, and in comparative context, in certain spheres of activity, there is no clear evidence of decline at all.[2] However, there can be little doubt that the wealth and power of the republic had ebbed between the interdict crisis of 1606, in which Venice still figured as a European power of weight and moment, and the Treaty of Karlowitz in 1699, by which time even its pre-eminence in Italy came into question – and that in comparison with the Duchy of Savoy.[3]

Two features of the history of Venice in the seventeenth century illuminate the republic's changing place in a changing world:[4] the plague of 1630 and the wars against the Turk – the War of Crete, which lasted from 1645 to 1669 and two wars in the Morea (1684–99 and 1714–16).[5]

After previous visitations of pestilence the population of the city and its territories had shown a strong capacity for recovery. After the losses of 1630, while the population of Venice itself returned to its former level and even surpassed it, the demographic infrastructure of the Terraferma, on which the city depended for the replenishment of its population, was all but destroyed. Those healthy units of dependent territories – the Padovano, the Veronese, the Vicentino, the Bresciano, the Bergamasco – which had in earlier periods proved so fertile in sending a surplus population to their provincial capitals and to the Dominante itself were exhausted. The data that Karl Beloch meticulously assembled illustrate the impact of the pestilence. Even though some of the figures may be open to question, it is appropriate to present them at appendix C.1, adding the minor refinement of percentages of population losses.[6]

Always bearing in mind the inadequacies of the statistics, the general picture is clear enough. The plague of 1630 probably carried off at least one person in three. The population of the Dominante and its mainland territories may well have declined from about a million souls to around 650,000. For a single small state, the number of losses was enormous – roughly the equivalent, perhaps, of the whole of the population of contemporary London.[7] The human losses were greater in the cities, running at about 40 per cent, and perhaps 30 per cent in rural areas. The loss of almost 45,000 lives in Venice, horrifying in itself, is below the 40 per cent average for the urban centres of the state as a whole. That overall proportion is raised by the dreadful number of deaths in Verona, which may have lost more than 40,000 people, or more than 60 per cent of the number of inhabitants in the city. The Veronese as a whole appears to have lost around half of its population. By Beloch's figures, losses in the city of Padua may have been more than 45 per cent, and the losses in the Padovano could have been about 35 per cent.[8] It is hardly surprising that the visual and visible culture of the age took on a new morbidity,[9] which in turn had its effects on the practice of charity in the city, on the relationship of religion and work, and on the general pattern of political, economic, and religious life.

These data merit attention and absorption, for they make it plain that, as a result of the plague's apparently relentless depredations, the mobilization of human and material resources for protracted international conflict became immeasurably more strenuous.[10] During the War of Crete direct taxes on the Terraferma ran at about 366,000 ducats annually but could go as high as 700,000 ducats in a single year. The decline in the number of able-bodied men in the guilds – perhaps both a reflection of the aging of the workforce and an acceleration of it – was also a source of difficulty.[11] In 1603 the government required the guilds to supply 5,787 galleymen, or to hire substitutes to serve instead of members, from a guild labour force of 20,253. In 1660 the government demanded 5,855 oarsmen from a workforce that, remarkably, had risen to 21,051. However, in 1603 those classified as able bodied (and therefore eligible to serve or be substituted) stood at 17,570, while in 1660 the figure was only 13,314. The government's demands for men for the galleys thus rose from almost exactly 33 per cent of the able-bodied workforce enrolled in guilds in 1603 to 44 per cent in 1660.[12] Even more starkly, in terms of the Arsenale's productive capacity in time of war, the labour force there had lost some 600 of its 1,500 members (about 40 per cent) to the plague of 1630.[13] While the city of Venice itself may have made up its losses of people by 1655 (when a census calculated the population to be almost 160,000), the population structures of the mainland state had been wrecked. It appears the city itself could not sustain the recovery, for the population of Venice may have fallen to below 140,000 by the end of the century.[14] The need to raise fighting men for service on land and sea, the diminution of the skilled workforce needed to build the galleys, the shortage of oarsmen fit and trained to row them, and, in addition, the need to raise the money with which to pay for it all, played a role in matters as contrasting as the renewal of the ranks of the patriciate and the readmission of the Society of Jesus.[15]

The Jesuits, whom the republic had expelled in 1606, were the most recalcitrant of the religious orders in Venice, not only in their defiance of the state but also in their insistence upon the separateness of the order of the clergy. As we have seen, the origins of the society had strong Venetian attachments: the visit of Ignatius as a pilgrim in 1523, his return in 1535, the arrival of his first followers the next year, and Gasparo Contarini's sponsorship of the order's establishment as an instrument for the renewal of the ruling class through religious reform. In 1583, according to one source, confessors from the order had seemed to "own" some of the most influential of Venetian senators.[16] Whatever the influence of the Jesuits among patricians, their fervour in the Tridentine enterprise that set out to separate the clergy from the laity and then to reassert the superiority of the former over the latter set them at odds with the lay spirituality of Venetian tradition.[17] Their expulsion for refusing to comply with the state's orders in the interdict of 1606 was a dramatic uprooting. The Council of Ten pronounced a perpetual ban from Venice and all its territories. According to the decree, the society "has been the first to show itself disobedient to the orders of this Council, having, by insidious ways, both in this City, and in others of our State, seduced the religious to follow its wicked example." At this point, the council clearly sought to make the ban irrevocable. The Jesuits were to return only with the unanimity of the Council of Ten and the support of five-sixths of the votes in a meeting of the Senate, that is to say, a minimum of 150 favourable votes with the quorum set at 180.[18]

By 1657 matters had changed. The negotiations were protracted, but the republic needed the support of the papacy, desperately so, for the War of Crete, which had broken out in 1645, and there were candidates for election to the patriciate who favoured the Jesuits. A Senate vote of 93 in favour, 44 against, and 42 undecided – in which those most hostile outnumbered those most favourable – transformed into a readmission on the basis of a vote of 116 in favour, 53 against, and 19 abstentions ("non sinceri").[19] In a measured rationalization of what should happen, which shows him a creature of the age of reason of State (and a precursor of the Ecole des Annales), Giovanni Pesaro argued that despite the stipulations of their "most prudent ancestors" the Senate should understand that, "with conjunctures, interests change, and with interests, maxims must change" (con le congiunture si mutano gli interessi, e con gli interessi devono mutarsi le massime).[20] Obligingly, in 1656, the Venetian government closed fifty-nine convents in its territories, including, in the city itself, Santo Spirito and the Crociferi. Those two institutions accounted for 92 per cent of the wealth of all fifty-nine.[21] The order of the Crociferi was suppressed, its members vacated Santa Maria Assunta, and the Jesuits moved in, buying the church at a price of 50,000 ducats.[22]

All in all, the Crociferi had provided an effective example of a centre for the aspirations of autonomous organizations often linked to particular occupations – a vivid and tight encapsulation of the traditions of Venetian confraternities. From 1657 Santa Maria Assunta was the Jesuits' church, and a rebuilding in the eighteenth century essentially obliterated its past, a past that embodied the interaction of productive, gainful work and a system of values that regulated and animated such work. The stones of the area still have much to tell us.

The church of Santa Maria Assunta had long been an embodiment of the close relationship of work and religion that had taken shape in Venice from the thirteenth century onwards. In this place the confraternities of various trades had enjoyed a particular concentration. The church itself was located in the Sestier di Cannaregio. That sixth of the city was home to those microcosms of the Venetian republic, the Scuola della Misericordia on its own site and the Scuola di San Cristoforo dei Mercanti at the church of Santa Maria dell'Orto – places of negotium and otium, of business and contemplation, the Venice of intense commercial exchange and the Venice of mental serenity, the Venice that engaged and the Venice that rose above. Santa Maria Assunta was a conventual church that did not have its own parish. Even now, the area around the church is marked with the names of trades: mirror makers (Salizzada dei Spechieri), chains (Calle delle Cadene), woodwork (Calle del Legname), barrels (Calle della Scuola dei Bottai), candles (Corte delle Candelle), and tailors (Calle dei Sartori).

Here, then, stood the church of Santa Maria dei Crosichieri, or the Crociferi, of those who were devoted to the Virgin and who took the sign of the cross.[23] The earliest of the confraternities here was that of the Visitation, which was of the guild of furriers, the *varoteri*, and dated from 1312, though its statute was renewed in 1446.[24] The Scuola di San Cristoforo dei Mercanti may have been here in 1346 before its move to the church of Madonna dell'Orto nearby.[25] The makers of velvet established a base at the church in 1347, very unusually taking Saint Mark as their patron.[26] The guild of tailors operated under the protection of Saint Barbara and of Saint Homobonus; they made their spiritual home at the church in 1392 and established a hospital nearby in 1515.[27] A religious confraternity in the name of Saint Michael existed from 1452, and the guild of the Purification sought to meet the needs of the coopers ("botteri," or "bottai") from 1483.[28] The interaction and co-existence of organizations for work and welfare continued throughout the sixteenth century. A confraternity of the Conception was founded in 1518. Then came a sovvegno for weavers, in the name of Saint Christopher, in 1567; a confraternity for makers of mirrors in 1569; and one for braid makers in 1593.[29]

The return of the Jesuit order to the church of Santa Maria Assunta in 1657 symbolized the new accommodation of Church and State that had taken shape in the sixteenth century, and which had been accompanied by the simultaneous separation of the clergy from the laity, at the insistence of the former and – as some cases before the Inquisition suggest – to the bewilderment of the latter.[30] In some ways this marked a transformation of the idea of the scuola, which had traditionally played a formative and practical role in the education, broadly defined, of the Venetian laity. The Somaschi and the Jesuits now exerted a monopoly of education at all levels, representing the papacy even more emphatically than did the nunzio.[31]

It was to be a further half a century after their return that the Jesuits built their own church, and they certainly set their stamp on the surrounding area. Domenico Rossi's design for the project that began in 1710 looked to the examples of both Palladio and Longhena, but the interior was unusually elaborate (fussy, even) for a Venetian church: extravagant altars, rich materials, a complex though unitary pattern of ornamentation. Heaven was open to the worshipper, and the world of work was nowhere to be seen.[32] Just as the patriciate could not be tainted with the degradation of manual labour, so "the new religious art did not understand that work is, for the Christian, a prayer that brings him closer to a God who was man."[33]

Inside, some of the church's most significant paintings have dispersed. A general catalogue is unnecessary, but, in drawing this study to a close, we note that one guild commission, an *Annunciation* that the silk makers had ordered from Cima da Conegliano in 1495, is now in Saint Petersburg (fig. 52). Its two wings, of Saint Mark and Saint Sebastian respectively, are in the National Gallery in London. The guild of furriers had also patronized Cima, and in 1515 or 1516 he produced an altarpiece of Saint Lanfranc and saints, now in Cambridge (fig. 53).[34]

52. Giovanni Battista Cima da Conegliano, *The Annunciation*, 1495, oil on canvas (for the arte dei veluderi). Copyright The State Hermitage Museum, Saint Petersburg. Photograph by Natalia Antonova, Inna Regentova.

53. Giovanni Battista Cima da Conegliano, *Saint Lanfranc Enthroned between Saint John the Baptist and Saint Liberius*, c. 1515–16, oil on panel (for the arte dei varoteri). Copyright The Fitzwilliam Museum, Cambridge.

Many of the paintings produced by Palma il Giovane for the Crociferi remained in the church when it passed to the Jesuits. A number of these had strong connections to the cult of the Eucharist, such as *The Fall of Manna* and *Elijah Fed by an Angel*, and they bring to mind a comparison with the same artist's works in the church of San Giacomo dell'Orio. The Jesuits also retained Palma's *Beheading of John the Baptist*. They had removed it from the furriers' guild-hall, the Scuola dei Varoteri, where it had replaced the work of Cima mentioned above. These examples suggest that the Jesuits did not particularly prize monuments to the religiosity of trades and tradespeople, and, if they retained such paintings (as in the case of the *John the Baptist*), then they wanted no advertisement of a connection with the trade. In the case of the work of Palma, the reinforcement of the Eucharistic message seems readily explicable. However, we should remember that this followed the suppression of the order that had commissioned the work in the first place.[35]

In the area near the church of the Gesuiti, apart from the names of the thoroughfares listed above, little survives to provide historical witness to the little republics of social energy that had thrived in the area. In 1723 the confraternity of the furriers was dismantled, stone of Venice by stone of Venice, and some of it was removed to the Campo Santa Margherita, where it still stands, with an image of the Madonna della Misericordia on its wall. It is still integrated with everyday life, serving as a back-drop for a fishmonger's stall and a back-stop for youngsters kicking a football (fig. 54). The removal of the scuola from its original home was, curiously enough, accompanied by a ban on playing football near the Gesuiti. That this was by decree of the Council of Ten, once so hostile to the Jesuits, exemplifies the new gulf between religion and work that had opened in the confessional era, as well as the collaboration of religious and secular authority.[36]

The history of the Jesuits in Venice, and out of it, in the seventeenth century suggests the introversion of religious and secular authorities in their own quarrels and resolutions and, in turn, the distancing of both from the everyday life of the working popolo. This final part of the study asks how changes in the latter half of the seventeenth century might illuminate the significance of the corporate institutions of the Venetian popolo in the period that this book has attempted to cover. The evidence suggests the following. In the confraternities there were signs of a break in the relationship of the everyday and the eternal. Among the trade guilds there were indications of ossification due to a strengthening of family ties, which may reflect a general tendency throughout Venetian society. These two developments, taken together, not merely as viewed from the corporations of the popolo but also within them, perhaps provide a new picture of decline. In suggesting the demise of a traditional pattern of economic and

54. *Madonna della Misericordia*, 1501, relief, at the Scuola dei Varoteri, Campo Santa Margherita, Venice. Photograph by Daniel Palleros.

religious life, it seems apposite to reinstate the concept from the point of view of the city's corporations.[37]

The scuole piccole, unlike the Scuole Grandi – the categories were hardened for the government's tax purposes – did not figure in the government's demands for manning the fleet.[38] However, their history offers some suggestive guidance with regard to the impact of the plague on the culture of the popolani.

The rich data assembled by Professor Vio should make possible a detailed study in due course, but the conclusion of a history book that ends its own detailed story in the middle of the seventeenth century is not the place to launch it. In Vio's catalogue 293 of the 925 entries date from the period after 1650, which gives an indication of the scale of the task that he has set. There are important technicalities in the materials presented by Professor Vio that lead on naturally to the fall of the republic at the end of the eighteenth century, and even a little beyond. Government catalogues from the eighteenth century would be vital to such a study, which would need at least and at once to engage in tasks like the comparison of the workings of the Council of Ten and the Provveditori di Comun, the investigation of Vio's categories of institutions that he designated "abusive" or "anomalo," the quantification and characterization of the place of confraternities of priests in the network, the examination of the curious phenomenon of confraternities of Sant'Adriano, and some assessment of how active the confraternities then were.[39] Moreover, such a project would need to provide the statistics refined in such exercises with a proper context of eighteenth-century Venetian history.

Accordingly, the following table summarizes what is contained in the copies of statutes compiled by the Provveditori di Comun in 1727 for the period 1600–1700. It suggests significant change after mid-century.

The magistrates began their compilation of the registers that were to contain copies of the mariegole of confraternities in 1728.[40] If we look at the year before that, 1727, which is the latest date in the registers, then we may note, in addition to the figures in the table, five Marian foundations, three for other dedications, one instance of a scuola and sovvegno combined, twenty-two sovvegni, and seven suffragi: thirty-eight in all. The detail from which these figures derive is presented in appendix C.2.

The general data in the table display plenty of evidence of continuities. The plain number of foundations compares with the patterns of previous periods, or indeed surpasses them. Moreover, in terms of overall numbers, far from fading, the momentum seems to gather. A figure of exactly one hundred new foundations in the span of the seventeenth century, forty-four before 1650 and fifty-six afterwards, suggests the vitality of traditions in terms of a continuing

Table C.1. Foundations of Confraternities in Venice, c. 1600–c. 1700

Dates	Marian Scuole	Other Scuole	Scuole and Sovvegni	Sovvegni	Suffragi	Total
1600–50	17	21	2	4	–	44
1651–1700	9	8	1	20	18	56
Total	26	29	3	24	18	100

dynamic of formation. A further thirty-eight foundations between 1701 and 1727 shows an even speedier rate of generation.

However, the bare figures prompt further observations. First, in the second half of the century, the combined total of dedications to the Virgin and to the saints dropped by more than half, from thirty-eight to seventeen. Second, sovvegni only constituted one-eleventh of the foundations before 1650 (four of forty-four). The sovvegni were a major innovation of the sixteenth century in their function as mutual aid societies, which, in a number of instances, were attached to particular occupations. The reduction to only four foundations of this type of organization in the first half of the seventeenth century and then a strong revival suggests some sort of break in continuity. The suffragi, however, were a new type of confraternity, and the designation appears only after 1650, and rather meekly at that. By the end of the century, there were eighteen such organizations. That number constitutes nearly a third of the total for the period 1651–1700, and 18 per cent of the figure for the whole century.

To repeat, the sovvegni were agencies that functioned to provide material aid for temporary misfortune, and the suffragi existed for the commemoration of the dead. This separation of organizations for the material aid of the living, from organizations for the commemoration of the dead, was a striking innovation, at least in the deliberately general and speculative context of this conclusion. In keeping with the diverse and diversifying traditions of the web of confraternities in Venice, the evidence points to a certain complementarity of different institutions.

The suffragi did not burst onto the scene as the Scuole del Sacramento had done at the beginning of the sixteenth century, and there was no pattern of formation that predominated over other types of foundation for a half a century as the Eucharistic brotherhoods had done. There was no innovatory statement as to the nature and purpose of the suffragi beyond the clear but incidental statement that they functioned "in relief of the souls in Purgatory" (in sollevo dell'anime in Purgatorio).[41]

The scribes of the Provveditori di Comun did not recognize a new type of confraternity when they made the compilation in 1727, though the familiarity of the institution by that time seems to have created the occasional misnomer. In one of the registers for the Sestier di Santa Croce, there is an entry headed "Suffragio della S.ma Croce in Santa Maria Mater Domini" for a mariegola of 1554. There is no mention of a suffragio in the statute, and the organization clearly referred to itself as a scuola.[42] There was a similar problem of designation at the church of San Moise for 1616, where the brotherhood dedicated to the Santissima Croce was a scuola.[43] The first suffragio dated from 1656, barely a year before the return to Venice of the Society of Jesus. This problem of categorization, in showing how difficult it is to prise the confraternities apart as separate types, is itself illustrative of the overlap and complementarity of different types of organization in the general corporate network. Furthermore, the suffragi in some ways extended this book's spectrum of representation in their very designation, with the term's overtones of "suffrage," and "vote," and the etymologies that link "vote" in turn to religious devotion, such as "votary" and "votive."

The distinction between help for the living and prayer for the dead did not emerge suddenly, and it did not involve striking typological innovations of the kind that occurred in the sixteenth century. However, in the life of the scuole the continuum between the portal of this life and the threshold of the next had been a most durable tradition. That continuum had once been both concrete and abstract: on the one hand, institutional and practical, and, on the other, spiritual and cultural. It was a continuum best understood in relation to the applicability of the Christian principle of Misericordia to everyday life. It constituted a meaningful link between the here and now and eternal values in a visible complex of trading and religious corporations, of churches and markets. As the argument has set out repeatedly, it formed a strongly woven cable between altruism and self-interest, a nexus that found reminders and memorials in the material fabric of the city, the expressions of a quintessentially vernacular culture. The rupture of this network in the confessional era and its aftermath may reflect the new morbidity of the Baroque age.[44] It may also relate to changes in the larger picture of the Venetian social and political structure.

Family Ties

The most obvious change in the ordering of Venetian society in the later seventeenth century was the opening of the ranks of the nobility to admit new members. There are indications that this was a reflection not merely of the aspirations of wealthy families outside the patriciate but of a strengthening of kinship ties throughout the social order. This development may have been at the expense of those institutions that had traditionally complemented, supplemented, and even substituted the ties of family.

In 1646 the legal definition of the patriciate modified in order to accommodate the wealth of families that did not belong to clan groups named as noble in and after the Serrata of 1297.[45] In a single isolated instance, during the crisis of the War of Chioggia in 1381, some new families had advanced to patrician status, but the principle of a fixed and unchanging ruling class defined by the family names of its members had seemingly provided one of the most enduring continuities in the history of Venice and one of the most mesmeric qualities of the city's myth.

In reality there were many gradations of wealth and status within the patrician order.[46] In light of this it should hardly come as a surprise that the second order of Venetian society, the cittadinanza, was no single entity but crossed a range of wealth and status. Even in its legal definition it was itself a tripartite model. Despite the precedents of the patriciate's intermarriage with the cittadini, co-operation with some of them in the chancellery, and privilege granted to them, the decision of the ruling class to open its ranks in 1646 – not long after the dreadful visitation of the plague in 1630, and during the first year of the War of Candia – was a dramatic step, as Alexander Cowan has shown.[47] Between 1646 and 1718, 128 new families joined the ranks of the Venetian patriciate. The Venetian government carried out examinations of the credentials of applicants, but the fundamental criterion was a capacity to pay 100,000 ducats for the privilege of admission, of which 60,000 ducats was an entry fee and 40,000 ducats went to the mint. The connection between the sale of nobility and the government's need to meet the costs of war was clear. In the course of the wars themselves there were five admissions in 1646 in the first year of the War of Crete, no fewer than thirty-eight during the first war in the Morea (1684–99), and eight during the second (1714–16). The Cretan campaigns alone had cost the lives of some 280 adult male patricians.[48] The newcomers came from five general groups of people. Non-noble Venetians (both cittadini and popolani) provided two-thirds of the new admissions (84 of the 128). Members of the nobilities of the Terraferma accounted for just over one-fifth of the families raised to patrician status in Venice, and there was a smattering of foreigners and illegitimate sons of Venetian nobles. The process of replenishing the ranks of the nobility expanded in intermarriage as well. Of a sample of 695 patrician marriages for the period 1660–1700, Dr Cowan identified 103 instances (15 per cent of the total) of marriage between a patrician groom and a bride from a newly ennobled family. Moreover, the sample contained 139 examples (20 per cent) of brides who came from outside the patriciate altogether. In another perspective on the changing patterns of intermarriage with outsiders,

Dorit Raines has calculated that, in the fifteenth century, one in eleven patrician males took a non-noble wife, while in the seventeenth century that figure was one in six.[49]

There was much rhetorical humbug in resistance to the new admissions. In the course of trying to block new aggregations, patrician objections included the following: that the Martinelli "knew nothing of anything except their merchandise," that the Corregio "by their dealings and customs do not know how to take their place among gentlemen," that the Laghidi "were by nature given over to money and barely fit for society."[50] These condescensions, however, demonstrate an ignorance of the commercial origins of the patriciate itself. After all, there was little to justify the rulers of Venice as a "noblesse d'epée."[51]

Any elevation to the nobility precluded the taint of manual trade. That principle had reinforcement in its application to admission to the ranks of the cittadini as well.[52] In keeping with the process that lengthened and strengthened the Venetian social hierarchy from the fifteenth century onwards, certain measures gave privileges to the cittadini, enabling their closer association with the patriciate. The cittadini gained a monopoly of office in the originally flagellant scuole (later known as the "Scuole Grandi") in 1410. From 1506 the cittadini were enrolled in a "libro d'argento," just as the patricians had their "libro d'oro." From 1478 the *cittadini originarii* alone could take the seventy-six posts in the chancellery (fifty-two of these were permanent positions), and in 1568 they even enjoyed something of a serrata of their own.[53]

One of the most revealing exclusions came in 1558, in other words around the time of Caravia and Tintoretto. From the thirteenth and fourteenth centuries it had been perfectly possible for Venetian artisans to engage in the export trade, provided that the goods were of Venetian make.[54] That is to say, de facto, a Venetian artisan could operate with the same trading status as a "cittadino de intus tantum." This seems to have been unexceptionable and became *de iure* in 1385. In 1558 that law was revoked.[55] However, just as sumptuary laws, in Venice and elsewhere, could not stop the display of wealth, so such attempts to block social ascent by law were doomed to failure.[56] In some ways it was the good fortune of the Venetian patriciate that new money aspired to noble status – a common feature of the sixteenth and seventeenth centuries that Braudel famously labelled "the betrayal of the bourgeoisie."[57] What renewed the patriciate was new money, and in more than half the ennoblements that money was of mercantile origin.[58] We might usefully relate that statistic to another of Dr Cowan's calculations. As stated, of the 128 ennoblements between 1646 and 1718, no fewer than 84 were of families that came from cittadino and popolano stock, by far the largest category of aggregations.

The absence of a clear distinction between the cittadini and the popolani is, in itself, revealing. How precise was the line between manual labour and petty commerce? On a similar measure, where did petty commerce end and large-scale merchandising begin? After all, there was no separate category of "merchants" in the census of 1563; the critical mass of the population below the rank of the cittadini were "artisans and shopkeepers." In general terms, the very absence of distinctions between different types of commerce was one of Venice's great sources of economic vitality. In the specific case of the mercers' guild, which became the largest of the arti in the seventeenth century, it is virtually impossible to make clear identifications between occupation, wealth, and status; any or all of them could change. Based on the analysis of a 1568 survey – admittedly a rather impressionistic set of estimates by third parties – members of the mercers' guild might have resources of fifty thousand, or even sixty thousand, ducats. The steadying influence was a large, and always mobile, stratum of the middling sort.[59] As we have seen, a number of family names among the mercers rose into the citizenry, and sometimes into the nobility itself.

Much the same seems to have been the case when the guild is examined from outside. Anna Bellavitis cites the examples of Gerolamo Vignola at the sign of the Fontana, and Paolo Ciceri al Compaso at San Salvador, as practitioners of the mercers' trade who became citizens.[60] Thus, in assessing the make-up of the cittadinanza in the sixteenth century, Professor Bellavitis described the mercers as merchants, but merchants who operated "in a semi-artisanal environment." She found members of the guild based in the Mercerie in the parishes of San Zulian and San Salvador "in full social ascent" in the sixteenth century: "while defining themselves as 'mercers,' and continuing to be part of the corporation, they were asking for the privilege of citizenship in order to trade with the Levant, or even a 'cittadinanza originaria' at the Avogaria di Comun."[61]

There were apparent limits on social mobility: while half of all male artisans in her sample married daughters of merchants, all daughters of artisans married artisans. But what are we to make of the marriage in 1565 between the son of a poulterer and the daughter of a glover (one of the mercers' trades) who brought with her a dowry of four thousand ducats?[62] With regard to the problems of aligning wealth, occupation, and status (and literacy), it is not necessary to confine the examples to the mercers' guild. Professor Bellavitis's research brings to the fore the example of the Balbi, shopkeepers near the church of San Salvador at the sign of the Colombina, who dealt in canvas. In their application for citizenship they described themselves as selling both wholesale and retail ("in grosso et a mendudo"). Lest being a shopkeeper should be seen as inferior, the application made the point that Sebastiano "stayed seated in the shop as great merchants do" (el stava in botega senta come fano li mercadanti grossi); that is to say, he did not work with his hands.[63]

Such examples also offer the reminder that tracing the rise of particular families is a hazardous task because of both the small numbers of family names and the infrequency of their use by those who had them. However, we might recall the example of the Bergonzi as a family whose fortunes make the point about mobility of status, since we have considerable detail on their ascent, which should be viewed as an example of the possible rather than the typical. Immigrants to Venice from Bergamo, the Bergonzi were involved in mercery and silk and enjoyed parentele with the Bontempelli, Rubbi, Gozzi, and Tasca families. Bartolomeo Bergonzi, an elector in the mercers' guild in 1596, gave dowries of fifty thousand ducats to each of his two daughters.[64] Francesco Bergonzi, who became a citizen in 1637 and thereafter a benefactor of the Mendicanti, exported to Constantinople, developing links with the bailo there, Giovanni Soranzo. This proved fruitful, for Soranzo was an active promoter of Bergonzi's application for ennoblement in 1665. He seems to have been effective in this role, since the application received levels of support of more than 80 per cent of the votes cast in both the Senate and the Maggior Consiglio.[65] That story shows an ascent into the nobility by an immigrant family from Bergamo with a shop in the Mercerie. Just as family ties strengthened in the ascent from *botteghieri* to cittadini to nobili (shopkeepers to citizens to nobles), so family ties appear to have begun to strengthen amongst the *artigiani* themselves.

The role of the arti in the management of economic decline has received superlative treatment in the work of Richard Tilden Rapp. He has shown how the Venetian guild system fostered a great adjustment that in many ways warded off economic decline, especially in assisting the migration of an aging workforce from one economic sector to another, in particular from manufacturing to retail, despite the ever-increasing burdens of government demands for galley men and taxes. It is notable that the guild that expanded most in this process was the arte dei marzeri.[66]

As the cittadini and some of the popolani tightened their identities as families by joining the ranks of the nobility, there were signs that within the broader group of the popolani themselves the family relations were strengthening in organizations that had formerly supplemented, complemented, or even substituted a domestic unit of blood relations. It is as though, in drawing the energies and resources of non-nobles to itself, the patriciate drained away some of the adaptability of the popolo and in return passed on some of the ossification of its own identity in the ties of kinship. In an astute analysis of the *status animarum* in compilations for forty-seven parishes in the 1590s and in 1607 – a total of some twenty thousand households and ninety-five thousand people – Monica

Chojnacka showed that 25 per cent of the households involved only one person and that half of these people were women. She was also able to assert that "single adult Venetians rarely turned to their parents for lodgings." This provides intriguing comment on the variety of domestic arrangements among the popolo and gives a pioneering insight into the much neglected subject of working women in Venice. Her findings correlate with comments in this book on independent female members of the mercers' guild and women who worked as landladies.[67]

By the end of the seventeenth century, that variety of economic and social possibilities appears to have narrowed and stiffened, at least in the evidence provided by one guild. In 1698 Pietro Francesco Ravi complained to the Cinque Savi alla Mercanzia of the fact that the guild of mirror makers ("l'arte dei specchieri"), a trade with a long tradition of highly skilled labour, had become exclusive and dominated by family interests to such a degree that sons of masters were no longer obliged to take a "prova," that is, to submit a masterpiece, in order to assume the title of "master." It is useful to bear in mind that in the late sixteenth and early seventeenth centuries apprenticeship was a careful contractual arrangement that imposed considerable responsibilities of health and welfare upon the master. There were instances of trainees who ran away, but a sample of several thousand of these contracts suggests a retention and completion rate of about 80 per cent. Apprenticeship of son to father was the tiny exception, not the general rule.[68] According to Ravi, the practice of automatic ascent to a mastership for the sons of masters had reduced the quality of Venetian mirrors and had given free rein to competition in other countries. Ravi was complaining not about the ossifying effects of traditional practices but about the failure to maintain traditional standards: "In this work, in contrast with other manufacturing [where you have] strong and robust young people, the ones in place, because of the toll of the toils they have borne and because of the natural decline of aging that advances day by day, are not up to this demanding work."[69]

Sons of masters did not gain experience as they aged, because they had not had a proper training, and each of them "turns out less than completely trained, while by contrast all the others passing through a long training, within the limits set out by the law, to the prescribed stages of apprentice, day labourer, and master with the tests that they were previously obliged to do, may come to the necessary understanding and practical skill with such formal training, qualifying as fully trained masters."[70]

Ravi imparted that, in his view, other places were now manufacturing mirrors that were nowhere near the quality of the traditional Venetian model: "however much it has been introduced in other states, this particular manufacture of the

City has never turned out in the condition of perfect finish equal to this one of ours" (quantunque introdotta in altri stati questa particulare manifattura della Città non sia già mai in stato di perfettione uguale a questa).

He addressed the problem of imperfections, having cited the improper use of gesso in the process of manufacture. Now that Venetian techniques were in operation in other centres, then they should at least be the best ones, in the interests of commercial exchange: "… there where they are made with the well-known style of the industry, to which are added the necessary applications so that they will always come out in future with the signs and features desirable under the contract in all nations, with that ebb and flow of reciprocal negotiation that brings with it trade and the commutation of the market." This was important in the continuance of the trade in Venice itself: "… no less for the preservation of a product that in other times was thriving, but also to the increase of trade and of laws, to the end that we cut out irregularities and remove at source the cause so that there follows from this a good outcome in order that profit may result."[71]

The Senate decreed corrective action in accordance with Ravi's petition, ordering the reinstitution of the traditional training and restoration of the progression from apprenticeship to journeyman to master: "… it being the guild itself that is the cause of the small number of workers that operate in it much in decline and perhaps conspiring to its own annihilation … having given their service and completed the period of five years, they have to pass according to traditional practice to the position of journeymen and, from there in two years, with the experience and knowledge that they will have learned, to advance to the rank of master."[72]

It seems that Ravi's complaints, and the Senate's decree, had little effect. In 1701 the guild itself complained to the Cinque Savi alla Mercanzia and blamed its woes on the obligation to take on apprentices. Their misery "derives from the number of apprentices that every day are taken on by masters" (proviene dalla quantità di Garzoni, che quotidianamente sono ricevuti da Cappi Maestri). The complaint begs the question as to whether the masters themselves were qualified to train, or whether they had advanced to this level as the sons of masters without qualification. In 1710 the *arte dei specchieri* classified its membership (to which have been added translation and percentages) as follows:

Maestri [Masters] 403 [35.70%]
Lavoranti [Journeymen] 114 [10.10%]
Moglie di maestri [Wives of masters] 222 [19.66%]
Moglie di lavoranti [Wives of journeymen] 40 [3.54%]

Figlie e figlioli di maestri e lavoranti che lavorano [Daughters and sons of masters who work] 113 [10.01%]
Figlie e figlioli di maestri e lavoranti che non lavorano [Daughters and sons of masters who do not work] 237 [20.99%]

Total 1,129 [100.00%]

The records of the tailors in the sixteenth century emphasized that all sons of masters were obliged to produce a masterpiece, and there were separate tests for doublets and stockings. Furthermore, any candidate for the office of gastaldo was to have completed successfully at least two such "prove." It was not permissible to open a shop without having passed a test for all types of wares that were to be on sale there.[73] By striking contrast, the categories of guild membership for the mirror makers are defined by categories of family membership. There is no category that allows for the presence in the guild of anyone who was not a blood relative of a member. In a note the guild recorded that its list did not include some sixty of the trade's practitioners who had left for the Levant and about a hundred dependents of deceased journeymen.[74] It will take a far deeper and wider exploration of guild records to establish whether or not the example may be typical. However, as a sample the list is by no means negligible. The list of members runs to a total of 1,129 (and it rises to around 1,300 if we include the 60 or so absentees and the approximately 100 dependents of dead journeymen). In light of Ravi's petition and the Senate's decree, it is striking that there is no category of apprentices, and the number of journeymen is proportionately small – just over one for every four masters. It is difficult to tell from the bare listing whether the wives of masters and journeymen were working members or whether they were dependents, or, indeed, whether the wives of all the masters and journeymen were enrolled. It is a tempting speculation that the *lavoranti* in low numbers were masters who did not have their own shops, and even more tempting to suggest that they were placed in the workshops of their fathers without proper qualifications.

It seems likely then that the corporation governing a highly skilled manufacture, with secrets to quality that the Venetians traditionally guarded with jealousy, had apparently shrivelled into a social agglomeration of families. If we accept the information from Ravi as having some grounds, then those members left in the corporation may have lacked the demonstrable know-how and experience dependent upon a clear program of training that the guild controlled. In these concluding reflections it is intriguing to think upon Ravi's attempt to reinvent tradition ("flusso e reflusso" and "reciproca negotiation," as he put it in his vivid evocation of custom). This, he argued, would restore movement to the wheels of commerce that a strengthening of family privileges had caused to seize.

An Envoi: Decadence or Shift?

In the course of the seventeenth century a system of political economy with notable similarities to that developed by the Venetians from the thirteenth century onwards began to take shape in England and the Netherlands.[75] This was not a question of systematic imitation but of an ascendancy of mercantile interests in the life of the state, and of a miscellany of circumstantial resonances. In the aftermath of a century of religious wars neither the English nor the Dutch engaged readily in wars for abstract causes; they looked to store bullion, to import raw materials, and to export finished goods. They looked for economic gain within a fixed, rather than an expanding, economy. An increased share would have to be "upon the foreigner," as Francis Bacon put it.[76] Armed force protected or furthered material interest; it did not and should not mobilize in the name of religion. And the English and the Dutch went to war with each other in that spirit. When General George Monck was asked the reason for war with the Netherlands in 1653, a conflict to enforce the Navigation Acts, he replied: "What matters this or that reason? What we want is more of the trade the Dutch now have."[77] Like the Venetians, the imperial ambitions of the English and the Dutch did not stretch to huge territories; command of the seas and a few strategically placed fortified ports would suffice.

As a monarchy, albeit of a constitutional kind, England could not be compared exactly with the Venetian Republic.[78] The more direct similarities, as Shakespeare seems to have perceived, were not between the two states but between two cities: London and Venice.[79] Sometimes the play *The Merchant of Venice* appears to be an allegory of contemporary London rather than a depiction of Venice.[80]

In the case of the Netherlands there is more evidence of direct influence, especially in the model that the Ghetto of Venice provided for the Jews of Amsterdam.[81] The suspicions of the English towards Catholicism, which intensified after the Glorious Revolution, also mark something of a difference from the Dutch Republic. Andrew Marvell's poem "The Character of Holland" mixed sarcasm and envy in its brilliant rhymes. It was written in 1653, the same year as General Monck set out to enforce the Navigation Acts. However, Marvell hit upon one formula that not only showed the connection between religious toleration and economic prosperity but also calls to mind the preceding achievements of the Venetians:

> Hence Amsterdam, Turk-Christian-Pagan-Jew,
> Staple of sects and mint of schism grew,
> That bank of conscience, where not one so strange
> Opinion but finds credit and exchange.[82]

This conclusion has tried to show that by the time Marvell wrote these lines the pattern of Venetian political economy had changed and had begun to lose the social energy that had still been in evidence at the opening of the seventeenth century. There was still enough life in the relationship between economy, polity, and religion to enable the republic to avoid conquest from outside or collapse from within, but the creative fury that Tintoretto had represented was stilled, not least by the impact of the disastrous plague of 1630.

In cultural terms, the most obvious monument to the impact of the plague was the dedication of a votive church to the Madonna of Health, Santa Maria della Salute, in thanks for the city's eventual deliverance from pestilence. Unquestionably, after its confrontation with the great mortality of 1630, the culture of the Venetians attained a new morbidity. The high altar of the church, by Giuseppe Sardi, shows the Madonna driving away a hideous personification of the plague.[83] Later in the century the façade of the church of Santa Maria del Giglio and that of San Moise were reconstructed as funerary monuments. The former was to the glorification of a commander in the Cretan campaign, Antonio Barbaro, and included depictions of Venetian forces on sea and land, designed by Giuseppe Sardi in 1679. The façade at the church of San Moise was the work of Alessandro Tremignon and celebrated the elevation to the ranks of the nobility of the Cypriot Fini clan, and in particular its two scions, the brothers Vincenzo (who paid for it) and Girolamo (whom it celebrated)[84] (figs. 55a, 55b, and 56). Those two façades symbolize the connection of the costs of the War of Candia and the sale of nobility, and they are symbolic of the parity of new nobles and the old ruling class. However, in both cases the deceased supplanted prophets, saints, and even divinity in the decoration. The figure of Barbaro has been compared to a risen Christ.[85] It is also important to emphasize that these funerary monuments – lugubriously confronting the living as they went about their business – were another sign of the break-down of that integration of everyday and eternal life that was so notable in Venetian tradition.

In relation to the moving spheres of economic, political, and religious life on which this study has focused, we might postulate the following for the later seventeenth century. Increasingly, there developed a detachment of the spiritual realm from earthly life as the polity drew at least a reprieve from the wealth that some parts of the economy continued to generate, which certain of the cittadini and popolani had succeeded in nurturing and which they brought to the ranks of the nobility. This change still comes to mind in certain of the churches of Venice, in which the believer, and even the spectator, are drawn ever upwards to the heavenly sphere and in which all earthly things fall away. In either case, the effect is of dissolution, even though that may be a melting into the sublime.

55a. Giuseppe Sardi, Chiesa di Santa Maria del Giglio, façade, 1683. Photograph by Richard Goy.

55b. Giuseppe Sardi, Chiesa di Santa Maria del Giglio, detail, façade, 1683. Photograph by Richard Goy.

The church of the Gesuiti figured prominently in the later stages of this study. There is a certain symmetry as well as a nominal similarity in comparing it with the church of the Gesuati. At Santa Maria Assunta, the Jesuit church, high, high above the person and the thoughts of the beholder, is the centerpiece by Louis Dorigny: *The Triumph of the Name of Jesus*. In three radiant, shimmering letters the body of the Saviour has become spirit (fig. 57). At the Gesuati, the church of Santa Maria del Rosario, Giambattista Tiepolo's energetic images swirl above the spectator's contemplation, and above a steepling staircase the heavenly host celebrates *The Institution of the Rosary* (fig. 58). Heavenly music bears the spirit aloft in both milieux. At the Gesuiti, in another ceiling painting, Dorigny depicted angel musicians, their own harmonies ascending ever higher. At the Gesuati, Morlaiter's statues seem the intense characters of some stern heavenly opera, about to burst into voice[86] (fig. 59). No wonder that, when Rousseau was

56. Alessandro Tremignon, Chiesa di San Moise, façade, 1668. Photograph by Richard Goy.

57. Louis Dorigny, *The Triumph of the Name of Jesus*, 1732, fresco, Chiesa di Santa Maria Assunta, known as dai Gesuiti, Venice. Photograph by Branislav L. Slantchev.

58. Giambattista Tiepolo, *The Institution of the Rosary*, 1737–9, fresco, Chiesa di Santa Maria del Rosario, known as dai Gesuati, Venice. Copyright Curia Patriarcale di Venezia.

59. Gianmaria Morlaiter, *Aaron the Prophet*, 1750–1, sculpture, Chiesa di Santa Maria del Rosario, known as dai Gesuati, Venice. Copyright Curia Patriarcale di Venezia.

in the city in the 1740s and wanted to see the beautiful girls – "those beauties I so much sighed to see" – who made such celestial sounds at the Pietà, he learned to forget their physical appearance – "scarcely one of them was without some striking defect" – and concentrate instead on the abstract exquisiteness of the harmonies that they sang.[87]

Reference to Rousseau brings us full circle and back to the Enlightenment where we began. The ideas of Adam Smith that resonate most harmoniously with the political economy of the Venetians are found in book 1, section 3, of *The Theory of Moral Sentiments* (sixth edition, 1790). An admiration for the rich and a concomitant neglect of the poor is "the great and most universal cause of the corruption of our moral sentiments." Smith would surely have admired with warmth the means by which the Venetians had sought in their institutions to restrain such sentiments and to embed and advance their opposite. The guild regulations that required all the members of every trade to operate "bona fide sine fraude" are at one with Smith's simple assertion of "the good old proverb" that "honesty is the best policy."[88]

We have already come upon that principle in Venice, at the centre of everyday economic life, enshrined at the church of San Giacometto at Rialto and celebrated by Ruskin. The harmony of the moral philosophy of Ruskin with that of Adam Smith is a suitable point at which to quote him again, this time in a more general assessment of the Venetians. "Great nations write their autobiographies in three manuscripts: the book of their deeds, the book of their words, and the book of their art. Not one of these books can be understood unless we read the two others; but of the three, the only quite trustworthy one is the last."

These words will be familiar to many as the opening lines spoken by Kenneth Clark in his pioneering television series *Civilisation* in 1969.[89] However, Ruskin wrote them as the prefatory opening of his final study of Venice, "St Mark's Rest."[90] The first three parts were published in 1877, and the completed version only in 1884.[91] In Ruskin's study, dismissed by his modern biographer as the "detritus of Ruskin's work towards a new *Stones of Venice*," the opening statement's particular applicability to the history of Venice has a singular resonance for this current work.[92] Ruskin continued: "The evidence, therefore, of the third book is the most vital to our knowledge of any nation's life, and the history of Venice is chiefly written in such manuscript." His reference to the book of art as a reflection of the "general gifts and common sympathies" of a people (he says "race") reinforces the continuing relevance of Ruskin's approach.[93]

We might usefully expand the content of Ruskin's book of art to include music. When we look for the influence of the Venetians in the world and the

60. Canaletto (Giovanni Antonio Canal), *The Stonemason's Yard*, c. 1725, oil on canvas. Copyright The National Gallery, London.

significance of their achievements, the great abstract diffusion can seem inseparable from music, a shift in cultural energies in the seventeenth century that contrasted with a certain decadence in the visual arts. Helmut Koenigsberger's model for Italy has a particular applicability to Venice, as a wealth of scholarship has confirmed.[94] The contribution of the scuole to the Venetian musical tradition has received some attention here but is a formidable subject in its own right.[95] The liturgical music of Venice in the seventeenth century was an expression of independence from Tridentine regulation. Antonio Vivaldi was the "Red Priest" of San Zuan in Bragora, the parish church of so many workers in the Arsenale, and his *Four Seasons* – so debased in saccharin familiarity – brings to mind the images that Tintoretto placed in his glorification of San Rocco. The great vernacular dramatist Carlo Goldoni was also a librettist.

Lorenzo da Ponte, the Jewish immigrant from Treviso who went on to become the first professor of Italian at Columbia University, the master who gave us the unforgettable mordancy of *Così fan tutte*, *Don Giovanni*, and, above all, *Le Nozze di Figaro*, remains "the Librettist of Venice."[96] However, wherever one finds Venetian influence, and in whatever manner it finds expression, it will always be grounded in the vernacular culture of the city itself, in the energies and endeavours of popular life. Canaletto reminds us of this in his *Stonemason's Yard* (fig. 60).[97] In its depiction of some stones of Venice with a scuola across the Canal Grande in the background, it is a fitting envoi to a study of the Venetian popolo, their energies in work, the values that their scuole inculcated, and all that they contributed to the polity of Mercy – and thereby to the greatness of Venice.

Appendix C.1. The Impact of the Plague of 1630 on the Populations of Venice and the Terraferma

In the Cities	Before the Plague	After the Plague	Losses (%)
Venice	142,804 (1624)	98,244 (1633)	44,560 (31.20)
Verona	55,533 (1627)	20,738 (1631)	34,795 (62.66)
Padua	40,000 (1611)	21,331 (1634)	18,669 (46.67)
Brescia (without the Chiusure)	37,885	20,010 (1632)	17,875 (47.18)
Vicenza	31,897 (1629)	19,000 (1634)	12,897 (40.43)
Bergamo	25,000 (1627)	[15,450] (?)	9,550 (38.20)
Crema	13,000 (1607)	5,708 (1631)	7,292 (56.09)
Treviso	10,683 (1612)	7,304 (1632)	3,379 (31.63)
Total	356,802	207,785	149,017 (41.76)
In the Regions	**Before the Plague**	**After the Plague**	**Losses (%)**
Verona (without Legnago, Peschiera)	94,324 (1627)	50,469 (1631)	43,855 (46.49)
Padovano	127,373 (1615)	87,393 (1633)	39,980 (31.39)
Brescia and Alpine valleys	76,276 (1601)	56,010 (1650)	20,266 (26.57)
Brescia, Ebene	150,000	108,680 (1650)	41,320 (27.55)
Vicentino (vicariates only)	132,845 (1629)	97,000 (1634)	35,845 (26.98)
Crema	20,000 (1607)	17, 054 (1631)	2,946 (14.73)
Total	600,818	416,606	184,212 (30.66)

Appendix C.2. Foundations of Confraternities in Venice, c. 1600–1727

Date	Type	Dedication	Church
1601	scuola	San Valentin	San Simeon Profeta
1602	scuola	Beata Vergine Assunta	San Geremia
1602	scuola	Venerabile	Santa Giustina
1603	scuola	Santa Maria Elisabetta	San Tomà
1604	sovvegno	San Liberale	Santa Maria dei Carmini[a]
1605	sovvegno	San Francesco di Paola	Santa Sofia
1606	scuola	Beata Vergine della Neve	San Lucca
1607	scuola	Beata Vergine del Carmine	Sant'Anzolo della Concordia
1609	scuola	Purificazione di Maria Vergine	Sant'Anzolo
1610	scuola	San Diego	San Giobbe
1611	scuola	San Carlo Borromeo	San Lunardo
1613	scuola	Nattività della Beata Vergine	San Benetto
1615	scuola	Beata Vergine Annuntiata	San Cassian
1616	suffragio	Santissima Croce	San Moise
1616	scuola	San Giovanni Elemosinario	San Giovanni in Bragora
1616	scuola and then sovvegno	Santissimo Crocefisso	San Geremia
1616	scuola and sovvegno	Santa Maria Elisabetta	San Simeon Profeta
1617	scuola	San Liberale	San Paternian
1619	scuola	Beata Vergine del Rosario	San Domenico
1619	scuola	Inventione della Santissima Croce	San Moise
1620	scuola	Purificazione di Maria Vergine	San Giovanni Novo
1621	scuola	Beata Vergine degli Angeli	Santa Trinita
1622	scuola	Beata Vergine dei Sette Dolori	Sant'Alvise
1622	scuola	Beata Vergine di Pietà	San Silvestro
1622	sovvegno	Santa Maria Elisabetta	Santa Maria Maddalena
1624	scuola	Madonna	Santa Fosca
1624	suffragio	Morti	San Geremia
1624	scuola	Santa Maria Elisabetta dei Voltolini	San Zulian
1626	scuola and sovvegno	Sant'Ermolao	San Simeon Profeta
1628	scuola	Beata Vergine degli Angeli	Angelo Raffaele
1634	scuola	Beata Chiara	San Stefano
1634	suffragio	Santissimo Crocefisso Centurato	Santa Croce
1635	scuola	Santissimo Crocefisso	San Giacomo alla Giudecca
1635	sovvegno	San Bellino	San Gregorio
1635	scuola	Santa Dorotea	San Simeon Profeta
1636	scuola	Nattività di Maria Vergine	San Maurizio
1636	scuola	San Domenico	San Domenico

(*Continued*)

Appendix C.2. (Continued)

Date	Type	Dedication	Church
1637	scuola	Sant'Antonio	San Giovanni Grisostomo
1638	scuola	Beata Vergine dell'Annunciata	San Giovanni in Bragora
1638	scuola	Beata Vergine della Salute	Spirito Santo
1641	scuola	Venerabile	Santa Maria Maddalena
1643	scuola	San Pio Papa	San Basso
1644	scuola	Veneranda	Corpus Domini
1645	scuola	Sant'Antonio	Sant'Anzolo
1648	scuola	Beata Vergine del Rosario	Angelo Raffaele
1649	scuola	San Domenico	San Zanipolo
1652	scuola	San Nicola	San Stefano
1653	scuola	Beata Vergine di Lonigo	San Giobbe
1653	sovvegno	San Filippo Neri	San Gregorio
1654	suffragio	Santissimo Crocefisso	Santa Trinità
1654	scuola	Beata Vergine della Consolazione	San Felise
1655	scuola	Beata Vergine di Loreto	San Giacomo dell'Orio
1656	suffragio	Santissimo Crocefisso	San Giovanni Novo
1657	suffragio	Angelo Custode	Santi Apostoli
1657	sovvegno	Santissimo Croce e San Giacomo	San Fantin
1657	suffragio	Santissimo Crocefisso	San Marcuola
1659	sovvegno	San Liberale	Santa Maria Maddalena
1660	sovvegno	Beata Vergine della Concettion dei lavoranti pistori	San Mattia
1660	scuola	Beata Vergine del Rosario	San Mattia
1660	suffragio	Santissima Croce	San Pietro
1660	suffragio	Santa Maria della Morte	San Basso
1660	scuola	Sant'Alipio	San Baseggio
1660	sovvegno	Sant'Antonio	San Nicolo
1661	sovvegno	Sant'Antonio	San Vio
1661	suffragio	Morti della Beata Vergine del Pianto	Sant'Eufemia
1661	suffragio	Agonizzanti del Santo Nome di Gesù	Santa Maria dei Frari[b]
1661	scuola	Beata Vergine di Costantinopoli	Sant'Iseppo di Castello[c]
1662	suffragio	Morti	San Vio
1662	suffragio	Beata Vergine della Pietà	San Giovanni in Bragora
1662	scuola	Sant'Antonio	Sant'Eufemia della Giudecca
1663	scuola	Beata Vergine del Parto	San Gregorio
1663	suffragio	Morti	Sant'Agnese
1663	scuola	San Cristofalo	Sant'Agostin

(*Continued*)

Appendix C.2. (Continued)

Date	Type	Dedication	Church
1663	suffragio	San Pasquale	San Francesco della Vigna
1664	scuola	Beata Vergine della Neve	San Girolamo
1666	scuola	Santissimo Nome di Gesù	Santa Maria dei Frari
1669	scuola, then sovvegno	Beata Vergine del Rosario	San Paternian
1674	suffragio	Beata Vergine del Parto	San Lunardo
1675	suffraggio	Morti	San Mattia
1677	sovvegno	Santa Caterina	San Stae
1678	scuola	San Valentin	San Samuele
1679	sovvegno	Beata Vergine Assunta	Santa Fosca
1679	sovvegno	Beata Vergine Assunta	San Vidal
1679	sovvegno	Sant'Antonio	San Trovaso
1679	sovvegno	San Giovanni	San Giovanni alla Giudecca
1679	sovvegno	San Girolamo	San Girolamo
1681	suffragio	Santissimo Crocefisso	San Gregorio
1683	sovvegno	Santissimo Crocefisso	San Tomà
1685	scuola	San Giovanni Battista	Santa Sofia
1687	scuola	Santa Cecilia	San Martin
1689	scuola	Beata Vergine dei Sette Dolori	Sant'Antonin
1690	suffragio	San Gaetano	San Fantin
1691	sovvegno	Sant'Antonio da Padova	San Severo
1692	scuola	Beata Vergine delle Grazie	Santa Marina
1693	sovvegno	Santissimo Redentore	San Severo
1694	sovvegno	Santissima Croce	San Biasio
1695	sovvegno	Beata Vergine del Rosario	Santa Maria dell'Umiltà
1696	sovvegno	Beata Vergine delle Grazie	San Paternian
1696	sovvegno	San Nichetta	San Nicolo
1697	sovvegno	Santissima Trinità	San Vidal
1701	sovvegno	Santissima Croce	Sant'Anzolo
1702	scuola	Beata Vergine del Rosario	Sant'Anzolo
1704	sovvegno	Beata Vergine delle Grazie	San Trovaso
1705	suffragio	Buona Morte	San Geminiano
1705	suffragio	Santissimo Crocefisso	Sant'Andrea
1705	sovvegno	San Giuseppe	Corpus Domini
1705	sovvegno	Santa Lucia	Santa Lucia
1706	sovvegno	Beata Vergine del Parto	Spirito Santo
1706	scuola and sovvegno	Beata Vergine del Rosario	Sant'Antonin
1706	sovvegno	Sant'Antonio	Santa Maria dell'Orto
1707	suffragio	Buona Morte	San Silvestro
1707	sovvegno	Beata Vergine della Celestia	Santa Maria della Celestia
1707	sovvegno	Santi Antonio e Gaetano	San Giovanni Decollato
1707	sovvegno	San Gaetano	Santa Maria Maddalena
1708	sovvegno	Beata Vergine dei Sette Dolori	San Stin

(*Continued*)

Appendix C.2. (Continued)

Date	Type	Dedication	Church
1708	suffragio	San Giiuseppe degli Agonizzanti	San Baseggio
1708	sovvegno	San Pietro d'Alcantara	Santa Maria Maddalena
1708	sovvegno	Santissima Trinita	San Lunardo
1710	scuola	Beata Vergine Annuntiata, Sant'Iseppo e Santa Caterina	Santa Maria del Giglio
1710	suffragio	Beata Vergine del Carmine	Sant'Aponal
1710	sovvegno	Santissima Spina	Sant'Alvise
1711	sovvegno	Sant'Erasmo	San Barnaba
1712	suffragio	Buona Morte	Sant'Antonin
1713	sovvegno	Beata Vergine Assunta	San Giacomo dell'Orio
1713	sovvegno	Beata Vergine del Parto	Santa Maria Mater Domini
1713	scuola	Beata Vergine della Pace	Santa Croce
1714	sovvegno	San Michiel	Santa Maria dell'Orto
1714	scuola	Beata Vergine dei Sette Dolori	San Biagio
1716	sovvegno	Santi Apostoli	San Giovanni Grisostomo[d]
1717	sovvegno	Santissimo Crocefisso	Santa Maria Maggiore
1720	sovvegno	Beata Vergine degli Angeli	Santa Trinità
1720	scuola	Sant'Osvaldo	San Baseggio
1721	scuola	Sant'Antonio	San Benetto
1723	sovvegno	Beata Vergine di Loreto	Sant'Anna
1725	scuola	Beata Vergine del Carmine	San Pietro
1725	sovvegno	Santissimo Crocefisso	San Giovanni in Bragora
1726	scuola	San Giovanni Battista	San Tomà
1727	suffragio	Beata Vergine e Sant'Osvaldo	San Silvestro

a. Vio 830.808, citing SP b. 395.
b. Vio 649.599.
c. Vio 62.18.
d. Vio 603.560.

Maps

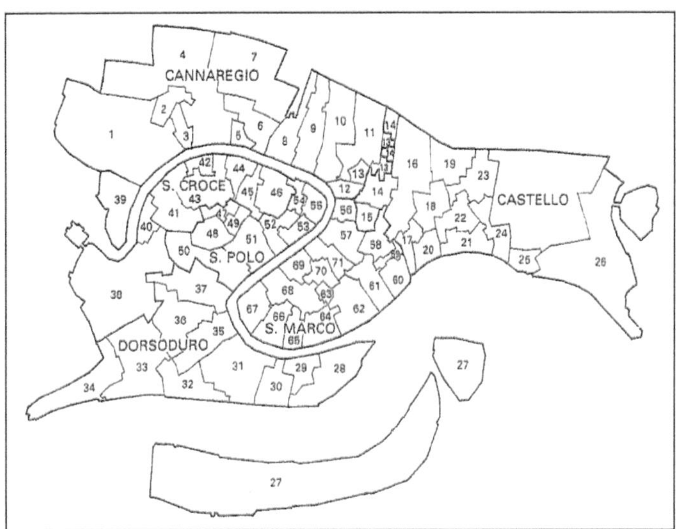

Key

Cannaregio
1. San Geremia; 2. Ghetto; 3. San Leonardo; 4. San Marcuola; 5. Santa Maria Maddalena; 6. Santa Fosca; 7. San Marzilian; 8. San Felice; 9. Santa Sofia; 10. Santi Apostoli; 11. San Canciano; 12. San Zuan Grisostomo; 13. Santa Maria Nova

Castello
14. Santa Marina; 15. San Lio; 16. Santa Maria Formosa; 17. San Zuan Novo; 18. San Severo; 19. Santa Giustina; 20. San Provolo; 21. San Zuan in Bragora; 22. Sant'Antonin; 23. Santa Ternità; 24. San Martin; 25. San Biagio; 26. San Pietro di Castello

Dorsoduro
27. Sant'Eufemia; 28. San Gregorio; 29. San Vio; 30. Sant'Agnese; 31. San Trovaso; 32. San Basegio; 33. Anzolo Raffaele; 34. San Nicolo dei Mendicoli; 35. San Barnaba; 36. Santa Margherita; 37. San Pantalon

Santa Croce
38. Santa Croce; 39. Santa Lucia; 40. San Simeon Piccolo; 41. San Simeon Grande; 42. San Zuan Degolà; 43. San Giacomo dall'Orio; 44. San Stae; 45. Santa Maria Mater Domini; 46. San Cassiano

San Polo
47. San Boldo; 48. San Stin; 49. Sant'Agostin; 50. San Tomà; 51. San Polo; 52. Sant'Aponal; 53. San Silvestro; 54. San Mattio; 55. San Giovanni Elemosinario

San Marco
56. San Bartolomeo; 57. San Salvador; 58. San Zulian; 59. San Basso; 60. San Marco; 61. San Geminiano; 62. San Moise; 63. San Fantin; 64. Santa Maria Zobenigo; 65. San Maurizio; 66. San Vidal; 67. San Samuele; 68. Sant'Anzolo; 69. San Beneto; 70. San Paternian; 71. San Luca

1. The Sestieri and Parishes of Venice
Cozzi, Knapton, Scarabello, *Repubblica di Venezia*, p. XVIII

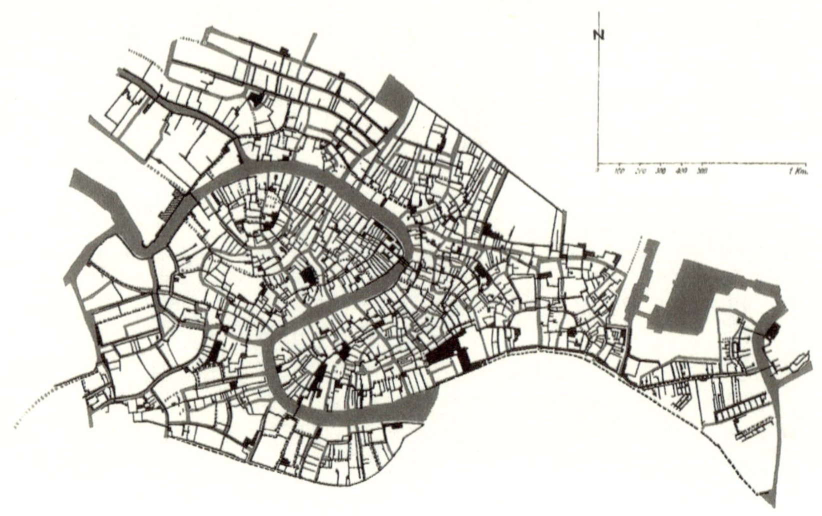

2. Venice's "Double Routeways"
Perocco and Salvadori, *Civiltà di Venezia*, vol. 1, p. 235

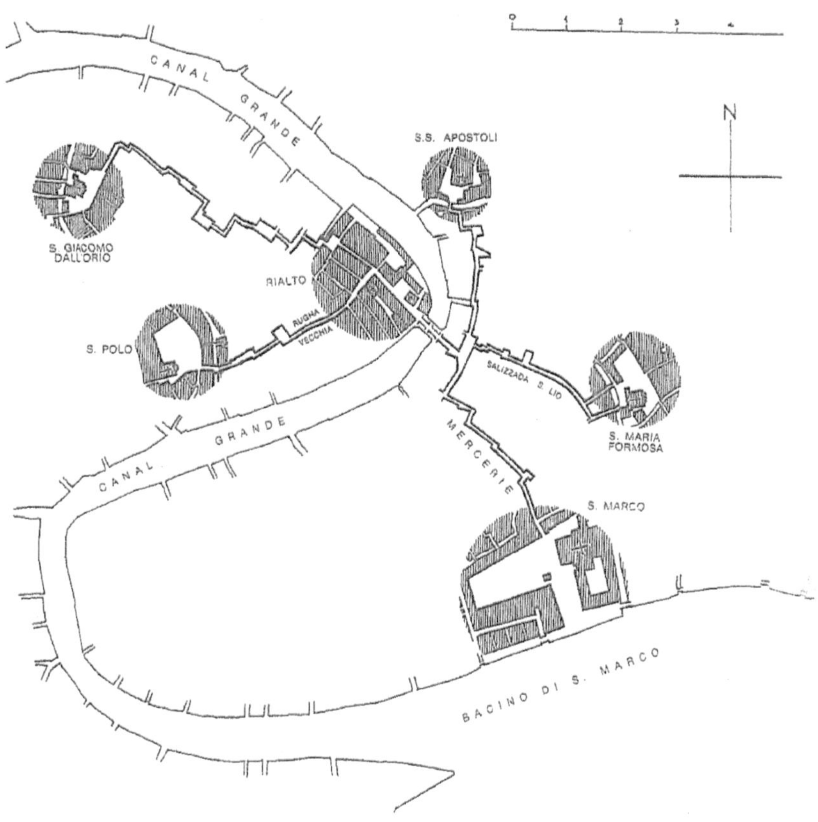

3. The Markets of Venice
Perocco and Salvadori, *Civiltà di Venezia*, vol. 2, p. 610

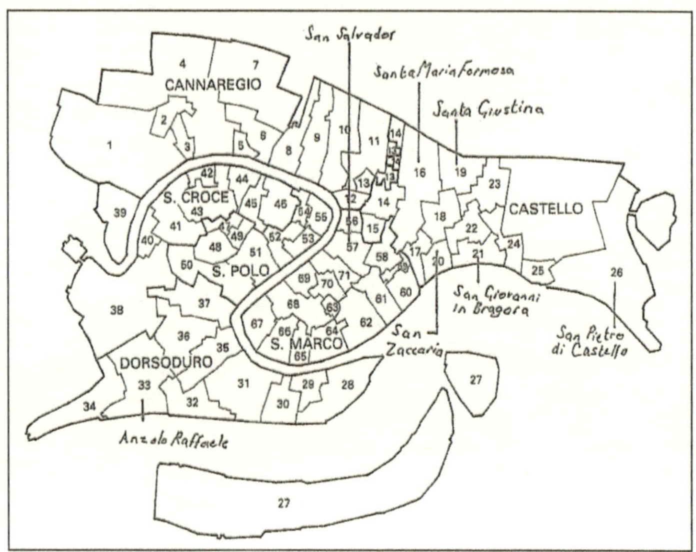

Key

Cannaregio
1. San Geremia; 2. Ghetto; 3. San Leonardo; 4. San Marcuola; 5. Santa Maria Maddalena; 6. Santa Fosca; 7. San Marzilian; 8. San Felice; 9. Santa Sofia; 10. Santi Apostoli; 11. San Canciano; 12. San Zuan Grisostomo; 13. Santa Maria Nova

Castello
14. Santa Marina; 15. San Lio; 16. Santa Maria Formosa; 17. San Zuan Novo; 18. San Severo; 19. Santa Giustina; 20. San Provolo; 21. San Zuan in Bragora; 22. Sant'Antonin; 23. Santa Ternità; 24. San Martin; 25. San Biagio; 26. San Pietro di Castello

Dorsoduro
27. Sant'Eufemia; 28. San Gregorio; 29. San Vio; 30. Sant'Agnese; 31. San Trovaso; 32. San Basegio; 33. Anzolo Raffaele; 34. San Nicolo dei Mendicoli; 35. San Barnaba; 36. Santa Margherita; 37. San Pantalon

Santa Croce
38. Santa Croce; 39. Santa Lucia; 40. San Simeon Piccolo; 41. San Simeon Grande; 42. San Zuan Degolà; 43. San Giacomo dall'Orio; 44. San Stae; 45. Santa Maria Mater Domini; 46. San Cassiano

San Polo
47. San Boldo; 48. San Stin; 49. Sant'Agostin; 50. San Tomà; 51. San Polo; 52. Sant'Aponal; 53. San Silvestro; 54. San Mattio; 55. San Giovanni Elemosinario

San Marco
56. San Bartolomeo; 57. San Salvador; 58. San Zulian; 59. San Basso; 60. San Marco; 61. San Geminiano; 62. San Moise; 63. San Fantin; 64. Santa Maria Zobenigo; 65. San Maurizio; 66. San Vidal; 67. San Samuele; 68. Sant'Anzolo; 69. San Beneto; 70. San Paternian; 71. San Luca

4. Churches of the Visions of Saint Magnus

Cozzi, Knapton, Scarabello, *Repubblica di Venezia*, p. XVIII

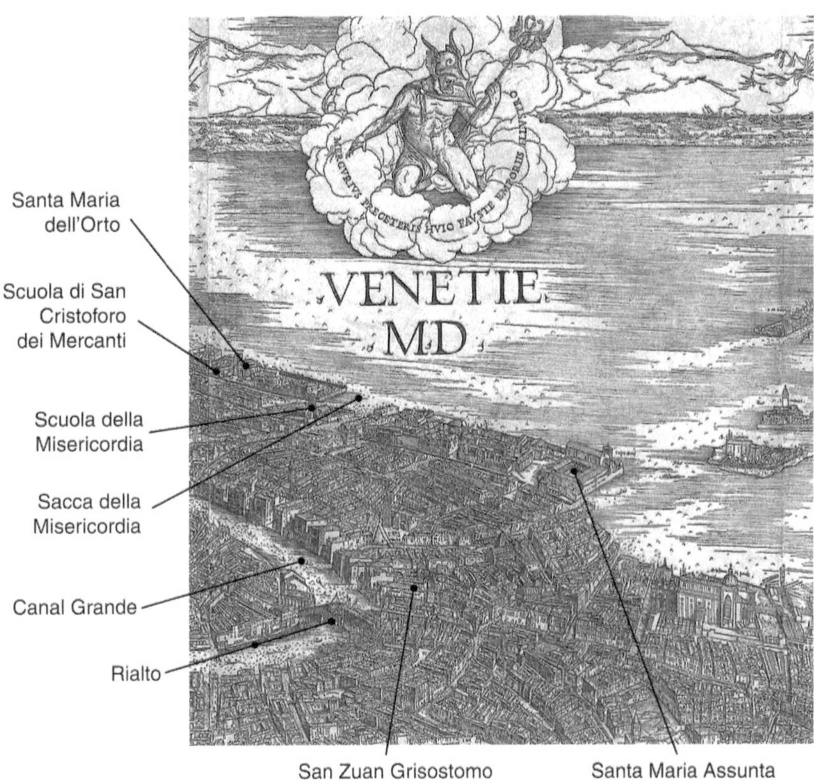

5. The Location of the Scuola di Santa Maria della Val Verde della Misericordia

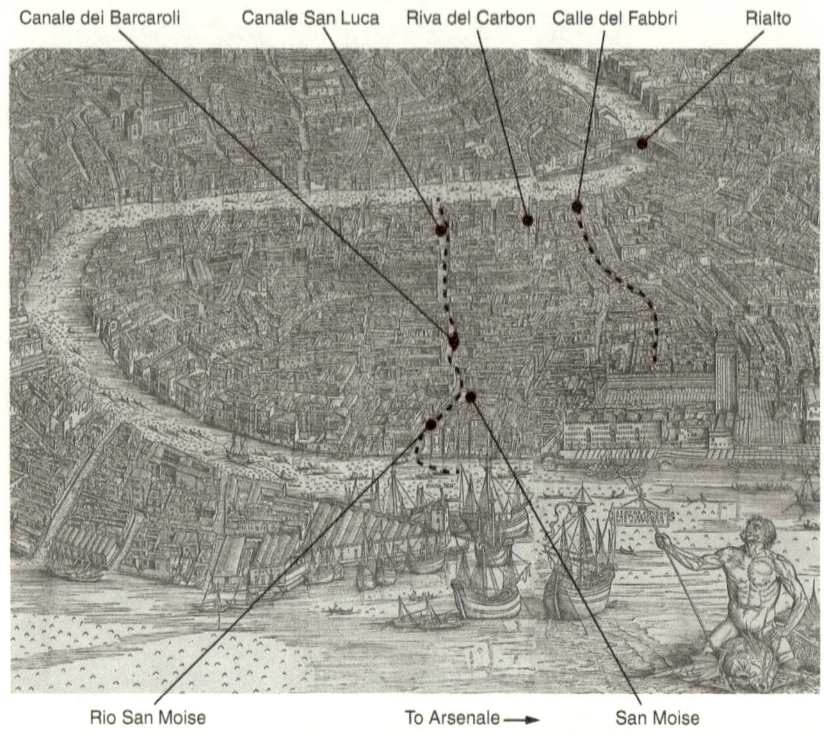

6. Rialto and Calle dei Fabbri

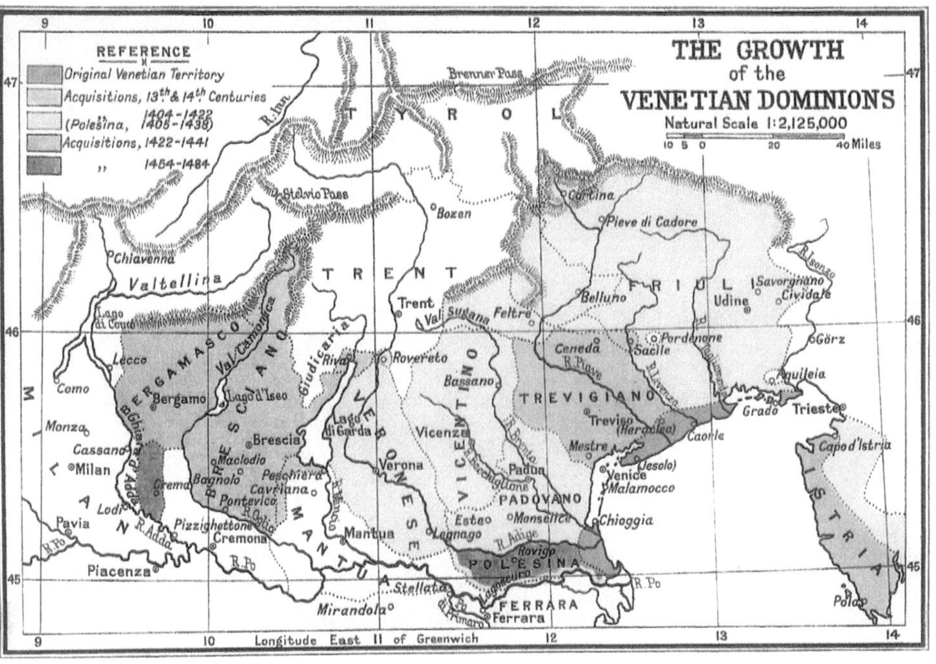

7. The Growth of the Venetian Dominions
Cambridge Medieval History, vol. VIII, no. 81 (b)

8. Lake Como and Its Environs

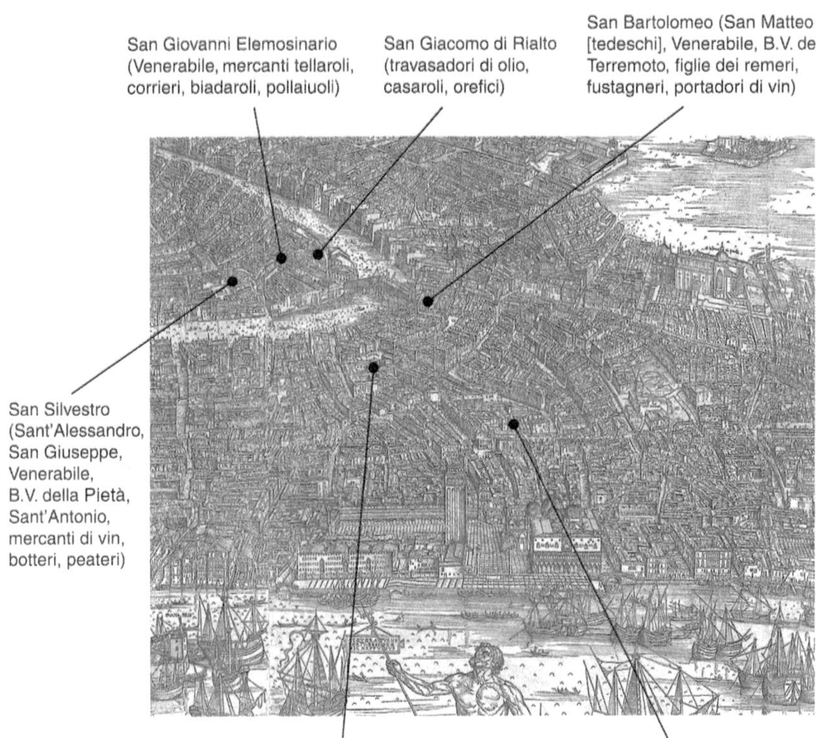

9. Churches and Scuole in the Rialto Complex

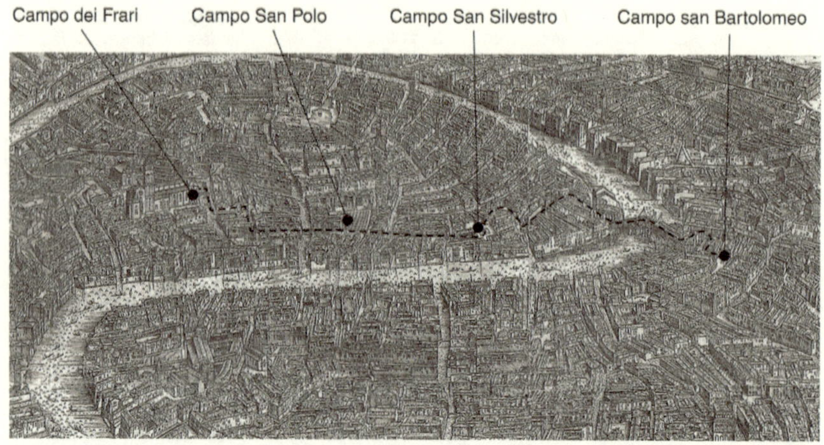

10. Processional Route of the Scuola di Sant'Antonio

Abbreviations

Manuscript Sources

All references to documentary materials refer to the holdings of the Archivio di Stato di Venezia (ASV) unless otherwise stated:

GN	Giustizia Nova
MM	Milizia da Mar
PC	Provveditori di Comun
SP	Scuole Piccole
SU	Santo Uffizio
b.	busta
reg.	registro
fol.	folio
r.	recto
v.	verso
Vio	Gastone Vio, *Le Scuole Piccole nella Venezia dei Dogi: Note d'archivio per la storia delle confraternite veneziane*; *Cultura popolare veneta; Collana di studi e di ricerche della cultura popolare veneta realizzata su iniziativa della Regione del Veneto* (Costabissara (VI): A. Colla, 2004). Citations within Vio are abbreviated as follows.
AP	archivio parrochiale
ASCP	archivio storico della curia patriarcale di Venezia
BCC	Biblioteca Civica Correr
BNM	Biblioteca Nazionale Marciana
BSP	Biblioteca del Seminario Patriarcale
CBC	Civica Biblioteca Correr
CXc	Consiglio dei Dieci, registri comuni

CXm	Consiglio dei Dieci, parti miste
FGC	Fondazione Giorgio Cini

Printed Primary Sources

CAV	*I capitolari delle arti veneziane sottoposte alla Giustizia e poi alla Giustizia Vecchia dalle origini al MCCCXXX*. Edited by G. Monticolo. 3 vols. *Fonti per la Storia d'Italia*, 26–8. Rome: Istituto Storico Italiano, 1896–1914.
CSPV	*Calendar of State Papers and Manuscripts Relating to English Affairs, Existing in the Archives and Collections of Venice, and in Other Libraries of Northern Italy*. Edited by Rawdon Brown et al. London, 1864–.
DMS	Marin Sanudo, *I diarii*. Edited by Rinaldo Fulin et al. 58 vols. Venice, 1879–1903. Reprint, Bologna: Forni, 1969–70.

Secondary Sources

AESC	*Annales, Economies, Societés, Civilisations*
AV	*Archivio Veneto*
BISSSV	*Bolletino dell'Istituto per la Storia della Societa e dello Stato Veneziano*
BSRS	*Bulletin of the Society for Renaissance Studies*
CHC	*Cambridge History of Christianity*
EcHR	*Economic History Review*
EHR	*English Historical Review*
J. Ecc. Hist.	*Journal of Ecclesiastical History*
J. Econ. Hist.	*Journal of Economic History*
JMH	*Journal of Modern History*
JWCI	*Journal of the Warburg and Courtauld Institutes*
NAV	*Nuovo Archivio Veneto*
PP	*Past and Present*
RenQ	*Renaissance Quarterly*
Ren. Studs.	*Renaissance Studies*
RSI	*Rivista Storica Italiana*
SCH	*Studies in Church History*
SV	*Studi Veneziani*
TRHS	*Transactions of the Royal Historical Society*

Notes

Introduction

1 A. Smith, *Wealth of Nations*, vol. 2, 570.
2 Lane, *Andrea Barbarigo*, 48. See also Lopez, "Venezia e le grandi linee dell'espansione commerciale nel secolo xiii," 40; "se taluno ha potuto asserire che i Signori del rinascimento concepivano lo stato come un'opera d'arte, sarebbe ancora più giusto affermare che le associazioni comunali del Medio Evo lo concepivano come un'impresa commerciale." See also Spufford, *Power and Profit*.
3 As an illustration of this transformation, see van der Wee, "Structural Changes," the first essay in Tracy, *Rise of Merchant Empires*, 14–33, and especially 18–23, in which Venice is a central example of "a spirit of aggressive state mercantilism "avant la lettre,"" reaching its zenith in the fifteenth century (23); and Chaudhuri, "Reflections," the final essay in Tracy, *Political Economy of Merchant Empires*, 421–42, and especially 428–9. See also Braudel, "The City-Centred Economies of the European Past: Before and after Venice" in *Perspective of the World*, 92–174.
4 On the importance of Smith's moral philosophy, see Phillipson, *Adam Smith*.
5 Pullan, *Rich and Poor*, 99–101; Pullan, "'Three Orders of Inhabitants,'" 147–68.
6 Beloch, "Popolazione di Venezia," *NAV*, n.s. vol. 3, part 1 (1902), 14; Contento, "Il censimento della popolazione," *NAV*, 19, part 2 (1900), 180; Beltrami, *Storia della popolazione di Venezia*, 80–2.
7 Pullan, "'Three Orders of Inhabitants,'" has a much more decisive characterization than his earlier and more equivocal discussion of the subject in Pullan, *Rich and Poor*, 99–100, on the contrasting views of Gasparo Contarini and Donato Gianotti. On the exclusion of the popolo, see for example, Mackenney, *Tradesmen and Traders*, 3.
8 Cowan, *Marriage, Manners, and Mobility*; Cowan, "New Families"; Bellavitis, *Identité, mariage, mobilité sociale*; Zannini, *Burocrazia e burocrati*; Zannini, "Un ceto di funzionari amministrativi"; Raines, "Strategie d'ascesa sociale."

9 See for example Tenenti, *Piracy and the Decline of Venice*, trans. Brian and Janet Pullan from the Italian; the Italian title, *Venezia e i corsari*, contains no mention of "decline."

10 Gilbert, "The Date of the Composition," 177. According to Gilbert, Contarini's book was "the primary literary work through which the myth [of Venice] gained acceptance" (183). See also Gleason, *Gasparo Contarini*; Bowd, *Reform before the Reformation*; Bowd, "'The Tune Is Marred'"; Pullan, *Rich and Poor*, 103–7.

11 Thus, the Scuola Grande of San Marco was in the sestier di Castello, the Misericordia in Cannaregio, the Carità in Dorsoduro, San Giovanni Evangelista in Santa Croce, and San Rocco in San Polo. With the elevation of the Scuola di San Teodoro in 1552, the sestier di San Marco obligingly completed the neat picture.

12 Contarini [G. Contareno], *Commonwealth and Government of Venice*, 146.

13 Diehl, *Venise: Une république patricienne.*

14 As may already be apparent, the passage is written in note form. I have added my own indicative notes in brackets.

> Reasons for stability of Venetian Government [note the equation of "Constitution" and "Government"] –
>
> 1. Coincidence of theoretical and practical Sovereignty in the same hands [i.e., those of the ruling class as defined in the Serrata].
> 2. Adaptability of the Constitution, e.g. gradual assumption of power by Senate and then by the Ten [i.e., adaptation by narrowing the basis of power].
> 3. Strength of the Executive which excited no jealousy [wise ruling class].
> 4. Impartiality of Justice [ditto].
> 5. Provision made for nobles in Government of Dependencies, for the middle class in civil service and commerce, for the lower classes in the fleet [three social orders neatly compartmentalized].
>
> Large alien population who did not want political power, but to be judged fairly, taxed lightly, and find employment [contentment of those excluded from politics].

Johnson, *Europe in the Sixteenth Century*, appendix 3, 467–71; these "reasons for stability" are set out on page 471. See also the contrasts in appendix 2, "Constitution of Florence in the Fifteenth and Sixteenth Centuries," which concludes with "Causes of instability of Florentine Government," 467. The comparison remains stimulating and perhaps draws upon Jacob Burckhardt's arresting contrast between Florence, "the city of incessant movement which has left us a record of the thoughts and aspirations of each and all who, for three centuries, took part in this movement, and Venice, the city of apparent stagnation and political secrecy." See Burckhardt, *Civilization of the Renaissance in Italy*, 40. See also Stendhal, *Histoire de la peinture en Italie*, for example, "Venice too was rich and powerful; but its government, a stern aristocracy, was a long way away from the stormy democracy of the Florentines" (63).

15 Pullan, *Rich and Poor*, 106.

16 See the major study by Raines, *L'invention du mythe aristocratique*, in particular vol. 1, 13–24, 631–68.

17 Mueller, "Charitable Institutions," 78; "If to a rather hypothetical figure of 8 per cent one could add the poor aided by the guilds, the *scuole piccole* and the Procuratori di San Marco, the totals of poor Venetians aided by various kinds of poor relief would certainly rise and perhaps even double."

18 The book applies, to the Venetian case, the concept articulated by Greenblatt, "Circulation of Social Energy."

19 On the uniqueness of Venice's situation, the lack of a rural *contado*, and the lack therefore of a feudal nobility, see Jones, "Economia e società," 340; Crouzet-Pavan, *Sopra le acque salse*; on grain supplies, see Aymard, *Venise, Raguse et le commerce du blé.*

20 Lane, "Medieval Political Ideas."

21 A. Smith, *Theory of Moral Sentiments*; Phillipson, *Adam Smith*. On the history of mentalities, see Burke, *French Historical Revolution*, 114; Febvre, *Problem of Unbelief*; Febvre, *A New Kind of History*; Yates, *Art of Memory*; Bossy, *Christianity in the West*. For some fascinating insights, see Ortalli, *Scuole piccole*, 79, speaking of the "ampia libertà di organizzazione" and the "comportamenti comuni non imposti forzatamente ne codificato dall'alto, ma sentiti come vincolanti, adottati dale scuole seguendo un percorso simile fra loro ma non obbligato attraverso strade independenti seppur paralleli." This characterization sits oddly with some of Professor Ortalli's other interpretations, for which see chapter 1, note 91.

22 D. Romano, *Patricians and* Popolani; D. Romano, *Housecraft and Statecraft*; D. Romano, "Charity and Community"; D. Romano, "The Gondola as a Marker of Station"; Wheeler, "Neighbourhoods and Local Loyalties"; Favalier, "Le attività lavorative"; Chojnacka, *Working Women*.

23 Ortalli, *Scuole piccole*, 88–91.

24 For two fine surveys of the myth, see Finlay, *Politics in Renaissance Venice*, 14–43, and Muir, *Civic Ritual*, 15–61; the unsettling aspect of these two comprehensive pieces is that the introductions are virtually interchangeable. See also Grubb, "When Myths Lose Their Power." Of the earlier literature, always of interest remain Fasoli, "Venezia: Nascita di un mito," and Gaeta, "Alcune considerazioni sul mito di Venezia." More recent interpretations include Benzoni, "Venezia, ossia il mito modulato"; Benzoni, "Venezia: Tra mito e realtà"; and Crouzet-Pavan, *Venice Triumphant*. On the historiography of the "decline" of Venice, see my conclusion herein.

25 On the Provveditori di Comun and the Avvogaria di Comun, see da Mosto, *L'Archivio di Stato di Venezia*, 178 and 68–9 respectively. In 1423 the Maggior Consiglio put an end to popular approval of its decrees, and the phrase "and it please you" was omitted from the ceremony that presented a new doge to the popolo. From 1462 the ducal *promissio* cut any reference to the Commune of the Venetians, and thereafter the government usually referred to itself as "La Serenissima"; see Lane, *Venice*, 252. On the growth of authoritarianism in Venetian government, see Cozzi, "Authority and the Law."

26 See the examples of Sant'Agnese, Santi Apostoli, and San Cristoforo in chapter 2.
27 Ortalli, *Scuole piccole*, 3–6 includes six examples of originals in these collections and cross-references to the duplicates in the Archivio di Stato: the Scuola di San Gallo e San Maurizio degli Albanesi in San Maurizio; the Scuola di San Giacomo in San Salvador; the Scuola di San Leonardo in San Salvador, the Scuola della Madonna della Grazia, poi Santa Maria Odorifera alla Madonna dell'Orto; the Scuola di Santa Marina in Santa Marina; and the Scuola di San Zaccaria e San Lazzaro in San Zaccaria.
28 Ortalli, *Scuole piccole*, 33, on the mariegola as a matriculation list, i.e., varying according to the dispositions of its members.
29 Ortalli, *Scuole piccole*, 3–6.
30 T.E. Cooper, *Palladio's Venice*, 205.
31 "Non troveria ordini piu ben fatti / Et al contrario son mal osservati." See the facsimile of the poem that immediately follows Gentili, "*Il Sogno dil Caravia*", 139ff (the facsimile is not foliated).
32 I owe a special debt to Professor Lauro Martines for his vigorous advice on this matter. See also Ortalli, *Scuole piccole*, 11.
33 Mackenney, "Formations and Transformations." Ortalli, in *Scuole piccole*, 80, posits a notional figure of twenty thousand members of about two hundred devotional confraternities in the mid-fifteenth century, but she is properly cautious about the problems of being more exact (73).
34 Vio, *Le Scuole Piccole* (hereafter cited as Vio).
35 Vio, p. 15.
36 Vio, p. 179. nos.129, 131; 180.132; 191.139.
37 For example, Vio 505.459, Suffragio della Beata Vergine, rejected by the Council of Ten, 5 March 1682.
38 Vio, p. 19.
39 Pullan, *Rich and Poor*, 33–131.
40 Vio 654.604; T.E. Cooper, *Palladio's Venice*, 267.
41 Vio 624–630.583; T.E. Cooper, *Palladio's Venice*, 268.
42 Vio, pp. 27, 32.
43 Mackenney, "Formations and Transformations."
44 Vio, p. 23.
45 Vio, p. 21.
46 Vio, p. 18.
47 Vio, p. 20, cf. 405.357.
48 Connell, "Employment of Sculptors," 31. Taiamonte also specified a Scuola di Santa Maria dei Miracoli, at which church there is no record of any confraternities. See also Ortalli, *Scuole piccole*, 31.
49 Burke, *French Historical Revolution.*

50 Burke, *French Historical Revolution*, 114, 115; Febvre, *Problem of Unbelief*; Febvre, "History and Psychology"; Febvre, "Sensibility and History"; Bloch, *The Historian's Craft*.

51 See the anonymous review of Le Roy Ladurie, *Montaillou*, in *The Economist*, 3 June 1978, 133–4: "the fact that these people lived cosy private lives in houses, sometimes sunning themselves outdoors or delousing each other, is dwelt on so obsessively that the people of Montaillou often seem like animals in a controlled experiment rather than human beings." I owe an immense debt to Owen Dudley Edwards, whose expertise on Sherlock Holmes was no doubt instrumental in his tracking down for me this barely half-remembered reference. For another review of *Montaillou* that did not bow with the general adulation, see David Luscombe, in *The Listener*, 6 July 1978. I am grateful to Professor Luscombe for his provision of this reference, the text of a talk that he delivered during a concert interval on BBC Radio 3, which I heard when it was broadcast.

52 Le Roy Ladurie, *Le territoire de l'historien*, part 4, 419, defines the history of climate as "L'histoire sans les hommes: le climat, nouvelle domaine de Clio," and goes on to discuss "L'histoire de la pluie et du beau temps," 511–37.

53 Roskill, *What Is Art History?*; Ivan Gaskell, "History of Images"; Gombrich, "In Search of Cultural History"; Gombrich, "Art History and the Social Sciences." For the "new historicism" in English Literature see the pioneering work of Greenblatt, *Renaissance Self-Fashioning*.

54 Panofsky, *Studies in Iconology*, 16.

55 Clark, *The Study of Art History*, delivered as a lecture to the Historical Association and not to an audience of art historians; Huizinga, "The Problem of the Renaissance"; Huizinga, "The Task of Cultural History"; Huizinga, "The Aesthetic Element in Historical Thought"; Geyl, "Huizinga as Accuser of His Age"; cf. Haskell, "Huizinga and the 'Flemish Renaissance,'" in his *History and Its Images*, 433–95. For interpretations of the autonomy of the discipline of history see Southern, *Shape and Substance*; Leff, *History and Social Theory*; Elton, *Return to Essentials*.

56 Burckhardt, *The Civilisation of the Renaissance in Italy* (1990), but note that the German original spoke not of "Civilisation" but of "Kultur"; see Burke, Introduction, 5–6.

57 The trend in the history of art to list works according to named artist began in 1550 with the founder of the subject, Vasari, *Le vite*; on the continuation of the pre-eminence of the High Renaissance, against which Ruskin reacted so fiercely, see Reynolds, *Discourses on Art*; on the development of art history and aesthetic response see Stendhal [Henri Beyle], *Stendhal and the Arts*, and, for the original, Stendhal, *Histoire de la peinture en Italie*; on Bernard Berenson and attribution see Pope-Hennesy, "Portrait of an Art Historian"; Calo, *Bernard Berenson*.

58 Among the works in this category that have proved invaluable to this book are Perocco and Salvadori, *Civilta di Venezia*; Howard, *Architectural History of Venice*; Howard, *Jacopo Sansovino*; Howard and Moretti, *Sound and Space in Renaissance Venice*; Goy, *House of Gold*; Goy, *Building Renaissance Venice*; T.E. Cooper, *Palladio's Venice*; Concina, *History of Venetian Architecture*; Gianighian and Pavanini, *Dietro i palazzi*; Tafuri, *Venice and the Renaissance*; Calabi and Morachiello, *Rialto*; Bassi, *Tracce di chiese*.

59 Bassi, *Tracce di chiese*. According to Professor Bassi's compilation, thirteen Venetian parish churches, nine monasteries, and twelve conventual churches have been lost. The records under scrutiny in the current study suggest that forty-five scuole have therefore disappeared without material trace in the parishes, and twenty-four more perished with their monastic and conventual homes. Professor Bassi also lists four scuole that are no more: the Scuola dei Nobili dello Spirito Santo at Corpus Domini, the Scuola della Dottrina Cristiana at the Punto della Dogana, the Spirito Santo at the salt warehouse nearby, and a scuola at the Pieta. That produces a total of seventy-one lost scuole. The figure for those that perished with their parochial homes is by far the most significant – and the most indicative of the concentrations of scuole in the churches of Venice.

60 I owe a particular debt to Architetto Andrea Negrini and his generosity in arranging for me to meet Ragioniere Antonio Bellati in Premana in the Val Sassina, the results of which appear in chapter 3.

61 Wyrobisz, "L'attività edilizia"; Goy, *House of Gold*; Goy, *Building Renaissance Venice*; Connell, "Employment of Sculptors."

62 Arti, Archivio di Stato di Venezia (hereafter cited as Arti), b. 405, mercanti di legname da Cadore, capitolare secondo, 1586–1604; Lane, *Venetian Ships*; Robert C. Davis, *Shipbuilders of the Venetian Arsenal*.

63 Botero, *Reason of State*, 109; Perocco and Salvadori, *Civiltà di Venezia*, vol. 1, 234–5, 610; see also Chabod, "Giovanni Botero."

1 Venice as Mercantile System, c. 1250–c. 1300

1 See for example the general account by Zorzi, *Venice*.

2 Maranini, *La costituzione*, vol. 1, 348.

3 Maranini, *La costituzione*, vol. 1, 349.

4 Maranini, *La costituzione*, vol. 1, 350.

5 Maranini, *La costituzione*, vol. 1, 361–2.

6 Jones, "Economia e società," 340; Jones, "Communes and Despots"; Jones, *The Italian City-State*; Law, *The Lords of Renaissance Italy*. For the significance of Jones's work, see Law and Paton, *Communes and Despots*; the article with the same title is reprinted there, 3–26.

7 Lane, "Enlargement." On the composition of the ruling class in "case vecchie" and "case nuove," see da Mosto, *L'Archivio di Stato*, 70.
8 Lane, *Venice*, 251–73. Note that these pages are headed "The Corruption and Perfection of the Constitution" and that Lane's ideas do not form a eulogistic teleology. However, the juxtaposition of *corruption* and *perfection* still leaves the analysis in the bind of anti-myth and myth. See for example on page 252: "Many distinctive practices, such as the secrecy of the ballot, for which Venice was in that age distinctive [*sic*], were perfected as measures against corruption."
9 Lane, "Enlargement"; Chojnacki, "Identity and Ideology"; Chojnacki, *Women and Men*; Ruggiero, "Modernization and the Mythic State"; Rosch, "The *Serrata* of the Great Council"; Queller, *Venetian Patriciate.*
10 J. Davis, *Decline of the Venetian Nobility*; Davis, *A Venetian Family and Its Fortune*; Cowan, "New Families"; Cowan, *Urban Patriciate*; Cowan, *Marriage, Manners and Mobility.*
11 Cracco, *Società e stato*; see also Rutenburg, "Arti e corporazioni."
12 Lane, *Venice*, 36.
13 Lane, *Venetian Ships*; Cessi, "Politica ed economia veneziana nel Trecento"; Cessi, "L''officium de navigantibus'"; Cessi, *Gli statuti veneziani.*
14 Lane, "Funded Debt"; Cessi, "Prestiti pubblici."
15 Lane, *Venice*, 150.
16 Maranini, *La costituzione*, vol. 1, 328.
17 Maranini, *La costituzione*, vol. 1, 326.
18 Canale, *Les estoires*, ii, CVIII–CXII, 270–80; Fasoli, "'La Chronique des Veniciens' de Martin da Canale"; Lane, *Venice*, 111.
19 Canale, *Les estoires*, ii, CXV, 284. See also Kantorowicz, *The King's Two Bodies*, 181–2n280.
20 Canale, *Les estoires*, ii, CXIII–CXXXIV, 282–305.
21 Canale, ii, CXV, 284.
22 Mackenney, *Tradesmen and Traders*, 135.
23 Tramontin, "San Marco," 63.
24 Canale, *Les estoires*, ii, CCCXVII, 340.
25 Stahl, *Zecca*, 29–30.
26 Lane and Mueller, *Coins and Moneys*, 7.
27 Stahl, *Zecca*, 31.
28 Lane, *Venice*, 148–50; Stahl, *Zecca*, 28–33 (the vote on p. 31) and 308.
29 Lane and Mueller, *Coins and Moneys*, 105–256.
30 Bellavitis, *Identité, mariage, mobilité sociale*, 21.
31 Lane, *Venice*, 52.
32 Lane, "Fleets and Fairs"; see also Lopez, "Le grandi linee," and Renouard, "Mercati e mercanti"; Cortelazzo, "La cultura mercantile."

33 The text of the merchant manual is published as *Zibaldone da Canale*, available in an anglophone edition as *Merchant Culture in Fourteenth Century Venice.* For the dating of the manual see Stanley, "From Medieval Corporatism to Civic Humanism," 26.

34 Larner, *Marco Polo*; Zorzi, *Vita di Marco Polo Veneziano.*

35 Renouard, "Mercati e mercanti," 94–6. For an astringent corrective to the meretricious efforts to deny that Marco Polo even visited the East, see Tucci, "Il libro di Marco Polo."

36 *I capitolari delle arti veneziane* (hereafter cited as *CAV*). The number of trades is smaller than the number of statutes because some of the latter are revised versions of regulations for the same trade.

37 Lane, *Venetian Ships*, 72–3; Renouard, "Mercati e mercanti," 108; Luzzatto, *Storia economica*, 65–80, noting "il predominio del commercio," 72–80. For the place of such activities in general European development, see Spufford, *Power and Profit*, 228–342.

38 Mackenney, *Tradesmen and Traders*; Shaw, *Justice of Venice*; and chapter 4 herein.

39 Canale, *Les estoires*, ii, CLXIX, 342.

40 *Oxford English Dictionary.*

41 Mackintosh, "Mercy"; quoted in Bossy, *Peace in the Post-Reformation*, 10.

42 The case rests upon the remarkable book by Enoch Powell, *The Evolution of the Gospel.* On the primacy of Matthew see xii–xvi. Powell offers the translation for the lilies of the field that "they card not neither do they spin," attaching the idea more directly to the process of textile production (xii).

43 Matthew 9:9.

44 It is an intriguing aesthetic judgment that Bernard Berenson saw, in Caravaggio's depiction of the *Calling*, stylistic evidence that the artist was by instinct a Venetian painter of the early cinquecento: "If Caravaggio had predecessors in Italy, they were Venetians" (Berenson, *Caravaggio*, 16).

45 Luke 5:27.

46 Matthew 9:12.

47 Matthew 9:13.

48 Matthew 5:7. This in turn recalls Proverbs 14:21: "He that hath mercy on the poor, happy is he."

49 Matthew 6:12.

50 Tawney, *Religion and the Rise of Capitalism*; Weber, *Protestant Ethic*; Trevor-Roper, "The Gentry"; Hexter, "Storm over the Gentry."

51 See chapter 2.

52 Adamson, *Epistle of James*, 57, 119.

53 Adamson, *Epistle of James*, 187; Davids, *Epistle of James*, 19.

54 James 2:24. See Luther, "Preface to the Epistle of St James and Jude," 306.

55 Davids, *Epistle of James*, pp. 1 and 40 on "Luther's hostility, both notorious and unfounded."
56 Moo, *Letter of James*, 174, compares James 5:12 with Matthew 5:34–7.
57 Matthew 6:19–21.
58 James 5:4 and 4:13.
59 Vermes, introduction to *Dead Sea Scrolls*, 18.
60 James 1:16, 1:19, 2:5, 3:1, 5:9, and 5:19; on the "adelphoi," see Davids, *Epistle of James*, 200, which comments that "It is this Apostolic goal he urges on his readers."
61 James 1:27.
62 Adamson, *Epistle of James*, p. 199 on James 5:16–18.
63 Davids, *Epistle of James*, p. 102 on James 1:27.
64 Davids, *Epistle of James*, p. 191 on James 5:13.
65 James 5:16.
66 James 5:19–20; Adamson, *Epistle of James*, 200.
67 Davids, *Epistle of James*, p. 199 on James 5:19–20; see chapter 2.
68 See chapter 6.
69 James 2:13; Adamson, *Epistle of James*, 98.
70 John 16:24.
71 Luke 16:31.
72 P. Brown, *Cult of the Saints*; Tramontin, Niro, Musolino, and Candiani, *Culto dei santi*. See also Vauchez, *Les laics au Moyen Age*; Webb, *Patrons and Defenders*.
73 Quoted in Brown, *Cult of the Saints*, 79.
74 See Shakespeare, *Merchant of Venice*, ed. Drakakis , act 4, scene 1, lines 181–2, and citing Ecclesiasticus 35:19.
75 Tramontin, "San Marco."
76 Brown, *Cult of the Saints*, 15–20.
77 Brown, *Cult of the Saints*, 38–9.
78 Muir, *Civic Ritual*; Ortalli, "Quando il doge diventa santo"; Pertusi, "La presunta concessione"; Benzoni, "Devozioni dogali."
79 Tramontin, "San Marco," 56–8.
80 Sanudo, *De origine*, 14.
81 Brown, *Cult of the Saints*, 42.
82 Muir, *Civic Ritual*.
83 Demus, *Mosaic Decoration*, 110.
84 Demus, *Mosaic Decoration*, 110.
85 Demus, *Mosaic Decoration*, 113; Muraro and Grabar, *Treasures of Venice*, 38–46; Bettini, *Venezia*; Ettore Vio, *St Mark's Basilica*, 190–281.
86 These mosaics are much restored, but their iconography probably remains genuine; Demus, *Mosaic Decoration*, 129.
87 A. Smith, *Theory of Moral Sentiments*, I.iii.63.

88 Muraro and Grabar, *Treasures of Venice*, 46–52.

89 Ruskin, *Stones of Venice*, vol. 2, 330–1; Lorenzetti, *Venice*, 241.

90 Lane, *Ships and Shipbuilders*, 72–3.

91 For example, Mackenney, *Tradesmen and Traders*, 47. Ortalli, *Scuole piccole*, 11, sets aside the scuole delle arti. In a startling oddity she goes along with the traditional misconception of the Scuole Grandi: see *Scuole piccole*, 12n6, "Useremo qui anche la formula 'scuole grandi' pure per il periodo tre-quattrocentesco in cui il termine, dal punto di vista formale, sarebbe improprio, si fa in coerenza con la tradizione storiografica corrente."

92 Vio 654–5.604: note the links with the Scuole di San Rocco e Santa Margherita at San Samuele (1455) and with San Rocco e San Niccolo at San Zulian (1496).

93 Vio, 526.486; 390.345; 428.379; 868.858.

94 Pullan, "The *Scuole Grandi*," 274.

95 Pullan, *Rich and Poor*, 37: "In a study concentrated on the sixteenth century, it is impossible to discuss in detail the origins of the Scuole Grandi."

96 Glixon, *Honoring God and the City*, 3–4; Ortalli, *Scuole piccole*, 10.

97 On the connection of Franciscans and Joachites see Ozment, *Age of Reform*, 103.

98 Pullan, *Rich and Poor*, 35; Pullan, *History of Early Renaissance Italy*, 73.

99 Reeves, *Joachim*; Reeves, *Influence of Prophecy*. On the general mood of apocalyptic expectation see Cohn, *Pursuit of the Millennium*, and on Joachim's place in forming that mood, see pp. 108–13, 129–30 therein.

100 Manselli, "L'anno 1260."

101 Meersseman, *Dossier de l'Ordre de la Pénitence*; Morghen, "Ranieri Fasani." One wonders whether in the cities this self-infliction may have been a pre-emptive acknowledgment that those whose Pride and Avarice led them in search of profit deserved the punishment that, according to Saint John 2:14–17, Christ had meted out with a scourge to the money changers and those selling animals for sacrifice in the Temple: "And when he had made a scourge of small cords, he drove them all out of the temple, and the sheep and the oxen; and poured out the changers' money, and overthrew the tables." The sellers of doves he dismissed with the command "Make not my Father's house an house of merchandise." On the connection of the *Expulsion of the Merchants* and usury see Derbes and Sandona, *The Usurer's Heart*, 52–4, which emphasizes not only that this is an unusual scene in contemporary painting but that Giotto's composition includes the Piazza San Marco in Venice, a public space for usury, in the background (54).

102 Wurthmann, "Council of Ten," 21.

103 Niero, "Culto dei santi dell'antico testamento."

104 Mackenney, "Public and Private," 123–5.

105 Concina, *Le chiese di Venezia*, 24.

106 Reeves, *Joachim*, 97.

107 Quoted in Little, *Religious Poverty*, 38.
108 Poggio Bracciolini, "De avaritia," 266–8; available in English as "On Avarice," in Kohl and Witt, *Earthly Republic*, 260–1.
109 Nelson, *Idea of Usury*; Nelson, "The Usurer." See also Little, *Religious Poverty*; Noonan, *Scholastic Analysis of Usury*; Le Goff, *Your Money or Your Life*.
110 Dante Alighieri, *Paradiso*, XI, 110.
111 Le Goff, *Your Money or Your Life*, 39.
112 Little, *Religious Poverty*, 216–17.
113 Derbes and Sandona, *The Usurer's Heart*, 22–3, 39–40.
114 Anonymous hagiographic narrative in the Vatican Library, quoted in Derbes and Sandona, *The Usurer's Heart*, frontispiece.
115 Little, *Religious Poverty*, 200; see also 202 for a summary of how the mendicants helped to inspire "a revised moral theology that approved of money-making in certain, carefully defined circumstances." See *Sacrum commercium sancti Francisci cum Domina Paupertate*. The editors suggest the authorship of Saint Antony, but cf. Vauchez, *Francis of Assisi*, 165–6. On the cult of Saint Antony at the Frari see chapter 5 herein.
116 Niero, "Santi patroni," 80–2. For further instances see chapter 5 herein.
117 Derbes and Sandona, *The Usurer's Heart*, 39–43, 45–52.
118 Niero, "Santi patroni," 77; Mackenney, *Renaissances*, 113–16; Hyde, *Padua in the Age of Dante*, 188–90. On the cult of Saint Antony in Venice see chapter 5 herein.
119 Derbes and Sandona, *The Usurer's Heart*, 199–200n44; Bury, "*Gonfaloni*," and, on Bonaventura's teachings, 86n51. I am very grateful to both Michael Bury and Gary Dickson for their assistance on this point. On Bonaventura's "brilliant organizational work" see Ozment, *Age of Reform*, 103.
120 *Paradiso*, XXI, 7–18, on Joachim; XII, 127–9, on Bonaventura. On Joachim's influence on Dante see d'Entrèves, *Dante as Political Thinker*, 74; Dronke, "The Conclusion," 174.
121 Cf. Pullan, *Rich and Poor*, 35, which deals only with Joachim.
122 E.g., Glixon, *Honoring God and the City*, 15–16.
123 Little, *Religious Poverty*, 185.
124 Quoted in Ortalli, *Scuole piccole*, 87.
125 Bowd, *Reform before the Reformation*, 27–60: "The Contemplative in Action." On the continuation of the tradition see Alberigo, "Vita attiva e vita contemplativa."
126 Pullan, *Rich and Poor*, 34.
127 Pullan, *Rich and Poor*, 37; Sansovino, *Venetia*, fol. 99r–v.
128 Cracco, *Stato e società*, 226–7 and 227n1.
129 Mackenney, "Trade Guilds and Devotional Confraternities," 16–23 and notes.
130 Provveditori di Comun (hereafter cited as PC) V, fols. 389r–432r. This case provides a useful example of the inadequacies of Vio's work. In his introduction

he asserts that the Scuola di San Mattia was founded in 1247 at San Bartolomeo. While he puts this right in his entry on the scuole at San Bartolomeo by recording that the foundation was in Murano, he fails to correct the error that dates the Scuola di San Nicolo dei Mendicoli as 1237 (p. 20) rather than 1337, thus giving the impression that San Nicolo was the earliest of the scuole. See also Ortalli, *Scuole piccole*, 10. Curiously, she asserts (15n3) that the date of the transfer of the Scuola di San Mattia from Murano is unknown.

131 Lorenzetti, *Venice*, 815.

132 Trivellato, *Fondamenta dei vetrai*, 25–50, 85–110; McCray, *Glassmaking in Renaissance Venice*, 25.

133 “propter tabernas et meretrices et alias inhonestas personas quae transeunt inde quotidie,” quoted in Scarabello, “Per una storia della prostituzione,” 21.

134 Tramontin, “San Marco,” 56–8; Muir, *Civic Ritual*, 78–102.

135 Gallo, “La Scuola Grande di San Teodoro,” and chapter 4 herein.

136 Sansovino, *Venetia*, fol. 99v.

137 Demus, *Mosaic Decoration*, 66, and plate 20a.

138 Gramigna and Perissa, *Scuole*, plate 51, p. 59, and plate 56, p. 61.

139 Scuole Piccole, Archivio di Stato di Venezia (hereafter cited as SP), b. 60, which is Santa Maria della Carità; SP b. 1bis, Santi Apostoli (in Santa Maria della Carità), mariegola, 1288; see also the emphatic clarification offered in Vio, 868.858.

140 On the Scuola di Santi Apostoli at Santi Apostoli see PC O, fols. 257r–286r; and SP, b. 57bis, Santi Apostoli, mariegola 1350–1708.

141 Vazzoler, *Scuola Grande di San Giovanni Evangelista*, 28.

142 See also Ortalli, *Scuole piccole*, 17.

143 Gramigna and Perissa, *Scuole*, 103; Tramontin, “San Marco”; Muir, *Civic Ritual*; Mackenney, “Public and Private,” 123–5; Goffen, *Piety and Patronage*, 94–106.

144 This is now apparently in the Pinacoteca di Brera: Gramigna and Perissa, *Scuole*, 119.

145 Gramigna and Perissa, *Scuole*, 118–19, especially plate 160, p. 119.

146 SP, b. 407, San Cristofalo dei mercanti, catastici, b. 408, pergamene, 1215–1319. Buste 408, 409, and 410 contain manuscripts for the period 1320–1571.

147 Vio 624–27.502–3.

148 Zorzi, *Vita di Marco Polo*; Larner, *Marco Polo*; Tucci, “Il libro di Marco Polo.”

149 Pozza, “Marco Polo Milion.”

150 Mackenney, *Tradesmen and Traders*, 54; Ortalli, *Scuole piccole*, 38.

151 On the second-hand trades see Allerston, “Market in Second-Hand Clothes and Furnishings.”

152 Mackenney, *Tradesmen and Traders*, 51–61; Ortalli, *Scuole piccole*, 35.

153 Sansovino, *Venetia*, fol. 101v.

154 Sansovino, *Venetia*, fol. 101v.

155 SP, b. 408, Scuola di San Cristoforo dei Mercanti, pergamene, 1215–1319, parchment of 1263.
156 Gramigna and Perissa, *Scuole*, 118–19.
157 PC N, fols. 413r–476r.
158 "Se clamava de Santa Maria dell'horto ... ma dapou nascita alguna Discordia intra quelli della scuola, over fradai de San Christofalo la qual se fradai de marcadanti, fu remesso el dicto prenome dell'Orto, e azonta alla dicta scuola de San Christofalo, che la se clamasse scola, over fraternitade de Sancthi Maria dall'Horto, e de San Cristofalo"; "Che i possa tuor tutte cose, et beni della soa schola in cadaun logo i sia e sia senza contradizion alguna, e quelle, e quelli metter e conzegnasse cum la scuola over fraternitade de Santa Maria de gratia, la qual se in la Contrada de San Marzilian." PC N, fol. 441r.
159 Sansovino, *Venetia*, fol. 54r; Candiani, "Antichi titoli delle chiese," and, on San Marziale among the "santi confessori," 120.
160 PC N, fol. 598r. The puzzle that still remains is why there should have been a removal of a scuola called San Cristoforo dei Mercanti from the Frari to Santa Maria dell'Orto in the 1570s; Gramigna and Perissa, *Scuole*, 118–19.
161 Pullan, *Rich and Poor*, 63–83.
162 This limitation is mentioned by Mueller, "Charitable Institutions," 78, though he does not investigate the ways in which the other scuole of Venice may have differed in their approach to the problem of poverty or made a difference to its relief.
163 Ortalli, *Scuole piccole*, 78–9.
164 Bury, "*Gonfaloni*," 85n51.
165 Rubinstein, "Political Ideas in Sienese Art"; Wierusowski, "Art and the Commune"; Hyde, *Padua in the Age of Dante*, 304–5; and, on the Palazzo della Ragione in the complex of the city's religious and civic buildings and markets, Kohl, *Padua under the Carrara, 1318–1405*, 4–6.
166 "Mostrandoli quelle benedette figure le qual e pente in esse e digandoli di quello che si contien in quello azo che li se arecordi della Passion de Christo ivi se deba inzenochiar, e tuore el capuzzo, o altro che li havesse in Cavo e con ogni riverentia basar quelle figure le quali e impente in essa imprometta a Dio e al martire meser San Zulian de osservar quello che in la nostra mariegola se contien." PC U fol. 576r; Ortalli, *Scuole piccole*, 32.
167 PC U fol. 579r.
168 PC U, fol. 580r. This example contradicts Vio's assertion (23) that the officers of the women's organizations were all male.
169 PC U, fol. 581v.
170 PC U, fol. 582r; Glixon, *Honoring God and the City*. For a beautiful depiction of hand-held and manually operated organs see Paolo and Giovanni Veneziano,

The Coronation of the Virgin (1358) in the Frick Collection in New York; Ryskamp et al., *Art in the Frick Collection*, 38. It is a measure of the changes of the confessional era that Carlo Borromeo insisted that all church organs were to be fixed and permanent. See chapter 6 herein.

171 PC U, fol. 584r.

172 PC AA, fols. 320r–331r; Sansovino, *Venetia*, fols. 87v–88r.

173 PC AA, fol. 320r–v.

174 PC T, fols. 503r–533r.

175 The church's holdings and exhibits include, in the small gallery in the cloister, Jacobello and Pierpaolo dalle Masegne's *San Giovanni Battista* and *Sant'Antonino*, of unidentified provenance, though asserting that the quality of these works won the brothers the commission for the great iconostasis in San Marco itself; and, in the sacristy, Tintoretto's *Last Supper* and *Agony in the Garden*, both of which were commissions from the Scuola del Venerabile at the church of Santa Margherita.

2 Proliferation and Punctuation, c. 1300–c. 1500

1 See chapter 5.

2 Sbriziolo, "Scolae comunes"; Sbriziolo, "Scuole dei Battuti"; Ortalli, *Scuole piccole*, 73.

3 Wurthmann, "Council of Ten," 26–8.

4 Wurthmann, "Council of Ten," 41.

5 Ortalli, *Scuole piccole*, 57, 61–4.

6 Ibid., 70.

7 Ibid., 65–6.

8 Ibid., 72.

9 Ibid., 78.

10 Ibid., 79.

11 Da Mosto, *L'Archivio di Stato di Venezia*, vol. 1, 178.

12 According to Sbriziolo, "Scolae communes," the scuole known to the Council of Ten but which do not appear in the records of Provveditori di Comun, were Sant'Ambrogio (authorized in 1361 at the church of the Frari); Visitazione (1399, Santa Maria delle Vergini); San Geminiano (1400, San Geminiano); San Lodovico (1401, the church of San Lodovico was never built); San [*sic*] Simeon e Tadeo (1407, San Simeon Piccolo); Sant'Apollonia (1417, Santa Maria dei Servi); San Vitale (1432, San Trovaso); Santi Michele, Gabriele e Raffaele (1433, Sant'Eufemia); San Pietro Martire (1434, San Giovanni di Murano); Santi Sebastiano e Flaviano (1449, San Zuan Degolà); and San Niccolo dei Tolentini (1475, San Silvestro).

13 Ortalli, *Scuole piccole*, 69–73, concentrates on 1363 and an apparent assertion of the Council of Ten's power over the Scuola della Misericordia. Some readers may

not be convinced that this was the "earthquake" presented by Professor Ortalli on p. 71.

14 Chojnacki, "Identity and Ideology in Renaissance Venice."

15 On the general European situation see for example Lerner, *Age of Adversity*; Holmes, *Europe*.

16 Ozment, *Age of Reform*; Renouard, *Avignon Papacy*, e.g., p. 21 on the war between Clement V and Venice over the succession in Ferrara; Ullmann, *Origins of the Great Schism*; Jacob, "Conciliar Thought"; Hay, *The Church in Italy*.

17 Duby, *Rural Economy*; Lopez, *Commercial Revolution*; Miskimin, *Economy of Early Renaissance Europe*; Cohn, *Black Death Transformed*.

18 E.g., Mollat and Wolff, *Popular Revolutions*.

19 See for example Goldthwaite, *Economy of Renaissance Florence*, 363–4, 547–50; Hoshino, *L'arte della lana*; La Roncière, *Prix et salaires*, esp. 771–92; *Il Tumulto dei Ciompi*; Rutenburg, *Popolo e movimenti popolari*; Rodolico, *I Ciompi* (note the subtitle "Una pagina di storia del proletario operaio"); De Roover, "Labour Conditions"; Brucker, "The Ciompi Revolution."

20 Ortalli, *Scuole piccole*, 17.

21 For the scuole listed in the tables but not discussed in the text, there are precise archival references in the list of manuscript sources at the end of the book.

22 Mackenney, "Public and Private."

23 SP b. 597, fol. 1r.

24 PC P, fols. 546v–579v.

25 PC P, fol. 550r.

26 PC Q, fol. 689r.

27 SP b. 726, Santa Maria della Celestia, mariegola, unnumbered fol., cap. xxx.

28 PC Q, fols. 220v, 217v.

29 PC BB, fol. 269r; PC U, fol. 110r.

30 PC T, fols. 364r–439r.

31 "molti et infiniti pani"; "a molte nostre povere sorelle marinare": PC T, fol. 374v.

32 PC Z, fols. 161r–181r; the restriction is at fol. 164v. See PC AA, fols. 271r–288v on the all-female Scuola di Sant'Alberto.

33 "mercede del ben e del male." PC AA, fols. 271r–289r; quotation from fol. 271v; for the exclusion of men see fol. 271r; Ortalli, *Scuole piccole*, 119–28.

34 PC AA, fols. 91r–127v; see fol. 97v on the exclusion of women.

35 "… inzuria, danno o desprizia de miser lo doxe de veniesia odel so conseio … questa benedeta citade la que sie eleta da dio … per recovramento e sostegnimento de tutti li triboladi descazudi e fedel de la santa mare gliesia." SP b. 597, fol. 3r, cap. xii; cf. Ortalli, *Scuole piccole*, 65–6.

36 SP b. 597, fol. 10r.

37 SP b. 597, fol. 10v; Ortalli, *Scuole piccole*, 88–91.

38 PC U, fols. 462r–573r.
39 PC U, fol. 475r; Ortalli, *Scuole piccole*, 95–9.
40 PC U, fol. 467r.
41 "chi da oro compra regno chi dona pecunia receve vita eternal," PC U, fol. 463r.
42 Niero, "Reliquie e corpi di santi," 195.
43 The first all-female foundation was the Scuola di San Gregorio at the eponymous church in 1324: PC Z, fols. 161r–181r; the restriction is at fol. 164v. See PC AA, fols. 271r–288v on the all-female Scuola di Sant'Alberto; Franzoi and di Stefano, *Le chiese di Venezia* (hereafter cited as FDS), pp. li, 177–9; Ortalli, *Scuole piccole*, 119–41.
44 "a petition de molti nobeli cittadini de Venetia"; "chel non se possi recever per nobele sel non e nobile e de consilio." PC AA, fol. 91r, 97r.
45 Bassi, *Tracce di chiese.*
46 PC Q, fols. 220v, 217v.
47 On projected membership figures see the excellent discussion in Ortalli, *Scuole piccole*, 42–3.
48 SP b. 1, Sant'Agnese, "Catastico dal 1325 in avanti"; b. 3, Sant'Agnese, "Registro parti della scuola, 1576–1620."
49 SP b. 1, Sant'Agnese, catastico, fol. 17r–v.
50 SP b. 1, Sant'Agnese, catastico, fol. 19r, cap. xxii.
51 SP b. 1, Sant'Agnese, catastico, fol. 20r, cap. xxxi.
52 SP b. 1, Sant'Agnese, catastico, 21 October 1376, fol. 22r–v.
53 SP b. 726, Santa Maria della Celestia, mariegola, 1337–1764.
54 All trace of the church disappeared following its conversion to secular purposes in 1810. Only a little of the convent's cloister survives. FDS, 463–4.
55 "per sovegnir li puoveri della scuola." SP b. 726, Santa Maria della Celestia, mariegola, unnumbered folio, cap. xxx.
56 "che nu non avemo citade permanevole"; "la celestial patria." SP b. 726, Santa Maria della Celestia, mariegola, unnumbered fol., preamble.
57 Ortalli, *Scuole piccole*, 4, takes the scuola's separate identity as a given, yet describes it as "San Cristofalo ai Gesuiti," a title that the church took only after its acquisition by the Society of Jesus in 1657; see chapter 6 herein.
58 E.g., Pullan, *Rich and Poor*, 38; Glixon, *Honoring God and the City*, 4, which dates the foundation of the Misericordia to 1308 without further discussion.
59 PC BB, fol. 293r; Ortalli, *Scuole piccole*, 4–5.
60 PC BB, fol. 296r.
61 PC BB, fol. 297v.
62 PC BB, fol. 298r.
63 See chapter 6 and the conclusion.
64 Mueller, "Aspetti sociali," 81. In general, see Brunetti, "Venezia durante la peste del 1348" and, still more generally, Cecchetti, *La vita dei veneziani nel '300.*

65 The inscription is published in its entirety in Mueller, "Aspetti sociali," 96.
66 "la fin di questa cativa e temporal vita"; "E che quando l'anima se parte dal corpo, ella va arender raxon del ben edel mal esi de recever del bene bon guiderdon edel mal de esere ponida"; "per fraternitade e per oracione e per lemosene"; "che molto vale la oration de la zusta persona." SP, b. 57bis, Santi Apostoli, mariegola, 30 marzo 1350–14 maggio 1708, which may be compared with PC O, fols. 257r–286r. This unusual opportunity to make a brisk comparison reveals no notable errors or inconsistencies, an assertion that will surely make a hostage of this note.
67 SP b. 57bis, Santi Apostoli, mariegola, fols. 1r–2r. On the dialect see the vital contribution of Ferguson, *Linguistic History*.
68 PC R, fols. 235r–258r; quotation on fol. 235r.
69 "tornar amisericordia," SP, b. 57bis, Santi Apostoli, mariegola, fol. 4r.
70 SP, b. 57bis, Santi Apostoli, mariegola, fol. 8r; Ortalli, *Scuole piccole*, 38.
71 "E ditto lo vangelio debia studar tute le candele epuo ditto locredo e tolta la oferta cascun frar o suor dela scuola debia impiar le suo candele e tegnirle imprese infina chel sera levado lo corpo di cristo ala messa. Epuo tuti studa le suo candele manose debia partir." SP, b. 57bis, Santi Apostoli, mariegola, fol. 6v.
72 The closing reference to the "multitude of sins" refers to the "extent of forgiveness" rather than "the state of the sinner." Davids, *Epistle of James*, 200.
73 SP, b. 57bis, Santi Apostoli, mariegola, fol. 6v; Psalm 85:10; Vulgate Psalmos 84:11.
74 SP, b. 57bis, Santi Apostoli, mariegola, fol. 11r.
75 SP, b. 24, Sant'Anna di Castello, mariegola, 1351–1425, fol. 12v records the decision to acquire "un oltar fornido de piere de pala e de tuto altro fornimento delo ben della scuola."
76 Vio, 635.586, citing Civica Biblioteca Correr (hereafter cited as CBC).
77 Sbriziolo, "Scolae communes," 427n29.
78 Humfrey, "Competitive Devotions," 412 and 420n18; Ortalli, *Scuole piccole*, 6, referring to ASV SMGloFr, b. 100.
79 Humfrey, "Competitive Devotions," 420n2; Vio 636.587; Ortalli, *Scuole piccole*, 4, with a date of 1435 on 14.
80 PC AA, fol. 17v; and see the conclusion herein.
81 E.g., Worthen, "Tintoretto's Paintings," 711n20. Professor Worthen discounts any historical connection, because Sant'Alvise was a conventual church, not a parochial one. As we have already seen, one of the chief strengths of the network of scuole was its capacity to traverse the boundaries of parish and profession as well as the active life and the contemplative.
82 Sbriziolo, "Scolae communes," 422; Bornstein, *The Bianchi*, 177–86; Ortalli, *Scuole piccole*, 75.
83 Bornstein, *The Bianchi*, 6.
84 Quoted in Origo, *The Merchant of Prato*, 322.

85 Quoted in Tassini, *Curiosità veneziane*, 300.
86 Bornstein, *The Bianchi*, 23–36; quotation from 27–8.
87 Bornstein, *The Bianchi*, 180–2.
88 See for example the responsibility of the Council of Ten for exterminating the Carrara of Padua, in Kohl, *Padua under the Carrara*, 335–6.
89 Bornstein, *The Bianchi*, 184.
90 Riccoboni, *Life and Death*, 42.
91 Galpern, "Late Medieval Piety," 171; Galpern, *Religions of the People*, 52, 60–2, 70–7, 188; Rubin, *Mother of God*, 164–85; Rubin, *Corpus Christi*.
92 Riccoboni, *Life and Death*, 40.
93 Riccoboni, *Life and Death*, 41.
94 Mackenney, *Tradesmen and Traders*, 70; Henderson, *Piety and Charity*, 36; Weissman, *Ritual Brotherhood*, 167.
95 Charles Dickens, *Pictures from Italy*, 273–85; on the "old wicked council," see 279; and see King, "Personal, Domestic and Republican Values," 567.
96 Bornstein, "Conseil des Dix," 187.
97 Bornstein, "Conseil des Dix," 188.
98 Bornstein, "Conseil des Dix," 195–6; quoted text at 196n25.
99 PC AA, fols. 45r–61v; examples from fols. 45r and 48r.
100 PC Z, fols. 125r–142r.
101 Connell, "Employment of Sculptors," 54.
102 "perche el veneno zente de diverse parte del mondo a Venetia"; PC Z, fol. 130v.
103 For a recent general summary see O'Connell, *Men of Empire*.
104 PC R, fol. 323r. It is another error, revealing of the problems of using Vio's work, that he dates the scuola – almost certainly by uncorrected typographical error – to 1322 (Vio, 20).
105 "far saver alli fratelli et alle sorelle che ciascheduna metta man alle sue proprie borse"; PC U, fol. 231r.
106 PC T, fols. 289v–344r.
107 Sansovino, *Venetia*, fol. 46r; Gramigna and Perissa, *Scuole*, 49–51. Ortalli, *Scuole piccole*, 193–9, publishes the confraternity's copy of its patron's *Vita*.
108 See the excellent discussion in Ortalli, *Scuole piccole*, 102–10.
109 PC U, fols. 33r–105v; the need to compete with the Armenians is at fol. 60v; Ortalli, *Scuole piccole*, 103.
110 PC Q, fols. 248r–270v; Vio 245.197.
111 PC Q, fol. 253r. On Doge Foscari's sister see Romano, *Likeness of Venice*, 137.
112 Romano, *Likeness of Venice*, 311.
113 On the turn westward see Lane, *Venice*, 202–73, esp. 225–30; and cf. Crouzet-Pavan, *Venice Triumphant*, 97–137. On Mocenigo see Luzzatto, *Storia economica*, 164–8; cf. Romano, *Likeness of Venice*, 28–34, 83–4, 314–15. On the

aristocratization of the patriciate in the fifteenth century see the cultural criteria deployed by King, *Venetian Humanism*. On the decline of maritime commerce in any case see Doumerc and Judde de la Rivière, "Le role du patriciat."

114 Pullan, *Rich and Poor*, 107.

115 Origo, *World of San Bernardino*, 32–3.

116 Goffen, *Piety and Patronage*, 157.

117 Vespasiano, "Santo Bernardino," 166. There is nice resonance with a similar humility in Bonaventura. It is said that when he was presented with his cardinal's hat, he asked its bearers to hang it on a tree until he had finished washing the dishes; Attwater, *Dictionary of Saints*, 71.

118 Goffen, *Piety and Patronage*, 147.

119 Goffen, *Piety and Patronage*, 157, 249n3; for the drawings see Eisler, *Genius of Jacopo Bellini*, p. 390 and plates 242 and 243. Eisler does not make a precise location for either, but the setting of plate 243 seems less probable as Venetian because of the horse distinctly visible in the background, whereas the architectural detail of plate 242 is clearly Venetian.

120 Mackenney, *Tradesmen and Traders*, 64.

121 Romano, *Likeness of Venice*, 147–52; on the chronology of the contracts see Connell, "Employment of Sculptors," 13.

122 Motture and Lopez Borges, "Venetian Tympanum."

123 "Ha la fabbrica vecchia sopra il portone la statua di nostra Donna di marmo, con bell'aria, belle mani, & con panni molto ben intesi, & fu scolpita da Bortolomeo che fece il portone del palazzo. Scolpi similmente figure che sono nel frontispizio d'essa Scuola, fornita copiosamente di argenterie, di vasi, di reliquie, & d'altri arnesi necessarii a tanto ridotto"; Sansovino, *Venetia*, fol. 101v. See also Markham Schulz, "L'altare maggiore."

124 Origo, *San Bernardino*, 33.

125 "devoto del Beato San Bernardino"; PC O, fol. 124v.

126 PC O, fol. 125r.

127 PC O, fol. 127r.

128 Sbriziolo, "Scolae communes," 436n64.

129 Goffen, *Piety and Patronage*, 188n25.

130 Bornstein, *The Bianchi*, 30–1.

131 PC P, fols. 579v–647r.

132 PC P, fol. 580r; the petition to found a scuola, dated 19 March 1451, asks that its rules be "secondo le conditioni delle altre scuole picciole."

133 Humfrey, "Competitive Devotions"; P.F. Brown, *Venetian Narrative Painting*.

134 PC U, fols. 421r–462r; PC U, fols. 209r–227r.

135 Mackenney, *Tradesmen and Traders*, 91.

136 PC R, fols. 161r–202r; PC Z, fols. 1r–25r.

137 Pullan, *Rich and Poor*, 219.
138 "molti diseno esser in la ditta scuola quando sono morti, e loro non sono"; PC Z, fol. 50r.
139 PC BB, fol. 70v.
140 PC U, fol. 110r.
141 SP b. 257, Santa Barbara dei bombardieri, mariegola, 1500–1762; Humfrey and Mackenney, "Venetian Trade Guilds," 322 and 326 (fig. 6 and table 22).
142 Gramigna and Perissa, *Scuole*, 40.
143 PC S, fols. 327r–337r.
144 King, "Personal, Domestic and Republican Values," 535–74.
145 King, "Personal, Domestic and Republican Values," 545–6 and 546n32.
146 King, "Personal, Domestic and Republican Values," 559–60 and 560n68.
147 King, "Personal, Domestic and Republican Values," 563.
148 Quoted in King, "Personal, Domestic and Republican Values," 567 and 567n86.

3 Who Were the Venetians, c. 1500–c. 1600?

1 Quoted in Lorenzetti, *Venice*, 13, as "return again," which seems wrong.
2 Lane, *Venice*, 224–39; Mackenney, *Tradesmen and Traders*, 82–5.
3 Ventura, *Nobiltà e popolo*; Cozzi and Knapton, *Storia della Repubblica di Venezia*, 3–98; Cozzi, Knapton, and Scarabello, *La Repubblica di Venezia*, 203–552; Mallett and Hale, *Military Organisation*, passim; Law, *Venice and the Veneto*; Grubb, *Firstborn of Venice*; Grubb, *Provincial Families*; Ferraro, *Family and Public Life*; Bowd, *Venice's Most Loyal City*; Carlsmith, *Renaissance Education*; Crouzet-Pavan, *Venice Triumphant*.
4 Gilbert, "Venice in the Crisis of the League of Cambrai"; Mallet and Hale, *Military Organisation*, 212–26; Finlay, *Politics in Renaissance Venice*, 222–4; Cervelli, *Machiavelli e la crisi dello stato veneziano*.
5 Finlay, "Venice, the Po Expedition."
6 Godinho, "Venise"; Lane, "Mediterranean Spice Trade"; Finlay, "Crisis and Crusade."
7 Commynes, *Mémoires*, vol. 1, 591.
8 Commynes, *Mémoires*, vol. 1, 587, 590. As chapter 1 pointed out, there were, in fact, plenty of opportunities for appeal.
9 On Carpaccio's representations of cosmopolitan Venice see P.F. Brown, *Venetian Narrative Painting*, 156–64; and R. Smith, "Carpaccio's African Gondolier."
10 Vio 429.389 gives a foundation date of 1497 for the Scuola di Santa Croce degli Armeni, but the only source is the statute of the Scuola degli Albanesi. On the Scuola di San Nicolo dei Greci see Gramigna and Perissa, *Scuole*, 40–1, and Lorenzetti, *Venice*, 321; on the church of San Giorgio dei Greci see Lorenzetti, *Venice*, 322.

11 Pullan, *Rich and Poor*, 254; Simonsfeld, *Der Fondaco dei Tedeschi*; Strauss, *Nuremberg*, 35.
12 Howard, *Architectural History of Venice*, 56.
13 The merchants of Milan and of Monza had received the approval of the Consiglio dei Dieci for the formation of a scuola in 1361; Sbriziolo, "Scolae communes," 427.
14 Sbriziolo, "Scolae communes," 419; Molà, *La comunità dei lucchesi*, 87–105; Ruskin, *Stones of Venice*, vol. 3, 310; FDS, lvii, 124–6; Vio, 23. The city of Lucca was home to a crucifix said to be sculpted by the hand of Nicodemus himself.
15 Calimani, *Ghetto of Venice*. I am grateful to Rob Bartlett and to Chris Black for questioning whether the scuola was distinctive to Venice. The institution also existed in Padua, but it was never widespread as in Venice, and its presence there seems almost certain to be the result of Venetian influence. I am grateful to the custode of the Scuola del Santo in Padua for this clarification.
16 Commynes, *Mémoires*, vol. 1, 591; Romano, *Patricians and* Popolani; Zannini, *Burocrazia e burocrati*; Neff, "Chancellery Secretaries"; Grubb, "Elite Citizens"; Bellavitis, *Identité, mariage, mobilité*; Cowan, "New Families"; Raines, "Strategie d'ascesa sociale."
17 Mackenney, "Venice," 59–60.
18 Marinelli, "Intorno a Veronese," 51; Rigoni, "La bottega dei Caliari a Verona," 85.
19 Muraro, *Venetian Villas*, 182.
20 A famous local of the Campo Santa Margherita, whom I grew to know during research visits, was always known as Gianni "Pistola." He and his wife had a large number of children. I knew him by no other name and never heard anyone else call him otherwise.
21 Gleason, "Confronting New Realities."
22 Castiglione, *Il libro del Cortegiano*; Castiglione, *The Book of the Courtier*; Burke, *Fortunes of "The Courtier,"* quotation from p. 23; Martines, "The Gentleman in Renaissance Italy"; Burke, *European Renaissance*.
23 Bouwsma, *Republican Liberty*; Muir, "Was There Republicanism?"
24 Contarini, *De magistratibus*; Contarini, *Commonwealth and Gouernement*; Gleason, *Gasparo Contarini*; Bowd, *Reform before the Reformation*; Gilbert, "Religion and Politics"; Libby, "Venetian History and Political Thought."
25 Burke, "Early Modern Venice."
26 Howard, *Jacopo Sansovino*; Tafuri, *Venice and the Renaissance*; Tafuri, "*Renovatio urbis*."
27 See Mackenney, "Venice," 58, quoting Labalme, "Pietro Aretino," 121; and, the most accessible source, Pietro Aretino, *Ragionamento delle corti*, 61.
28 Aretino, *Il primo libro delle lettere*, 27; see also Aretino, *Selected Letters*, 66.
29 J. Shaw, *Justice of Venice*; da Mosto, *L'Archivio di Stato di Venezia*, vol. 1, 194.
30 Biblioteca Marciana, MS, cl. VII, It, 76842, Capitolare Antico contains much information on attempts to regulate the furatole; see also Giustizia Nova, Archivio

di Stato di Venezia (hereafter cited as GN), b. 12, reg. 35, "Registro processi contra furatole (frigipesce) e altri contraventi al commercio del vino," 1509–11.

31 GN, b. 12, reg. 35 simile [parti ed altri atti del collegio dei vii savi alla G.N. sopra vari argomenti] "Stella," 1530–2.

32 Arti, b. 430, osti, mariegola sec. xvi.

33 On the living area in a poplano home see Schulz, "The Houses of Titian, Aretino and Sansovino," 45; on popolano housing in general see Gianighian and Pavanini, *Dietro i palazzi*, and, in particular, 45.

34 Chojnacka, *Working Women*, esp. 47–87.

35 A traditional structure survives in the bottega of Fabris at the beginning of the Merceria di San Salvador.

36 See Chojnacka, *Working Women*, 83, on women as innkeepers.

37 Burke, "Classifying the People," esp. 37–9 on prostitutes; Chojnacka, *Working Women*, 50–73, on neighbourhoods and the prominence of women within them; and, 120, "women's networks – familial, social, occupational, all of which often overlapped – could extend across the city and even beyond."

38 Burke, "Classifying the People," 38.

39 GN b. 5, reg. 12, "Stella," fol. 25r.

40 GN b. 5, reg. 12, "Stella," fol. 150v, 6 February 1530.

41 Carlo Goldoni, *La Locandiera*, 2.2.15, p. 50: commenting on Mirandolina's excellent food, the Cavaliere remarks, "Se Mirandolina farà così, avrà sempre de' forestieri."

42 Sanuto, *I diarii* (hereafter cited as *DMS*), vol. 54, col. 17, 1530, 7 October.

43 Burke, "Early Modern Venice," 400.

44 The translation of *scantizini* is based on a connection with the wool trade and an etymological proximity, in Garzoni, *La Piazza Universale*, 319: wool on combs "si scardassa da scartezzini." *Scardassini* are associated with both the wool and the linen trades; Garzoni, 317.

45 Botero, *Greatness and Magnificence of Cities*, 44.

46 "Aggiunte alla Cronaca di Giovanni Diacono," I. "Notizia del Ricorso del Fabbro Giovanni Sagornino ai Dogi Pietro Barbolano e Domenico Flabianico contro il Gastaldo," in *Cronache veneziane antichissime*, 175–6.

47 Mackenney, *Tradesmen and Traders*, 23–8.

48 Muir, *Civic Ritual*, 160–3.

49 *CAV*, vol. 2, 329, cap. 1, "Imprimis igitur statuimus quod tota ars fabrorum facere teneatur domino duci et pallacio integre omnes fabricationes pertinentie sue artis"; and 329n2, "Quest'obbligo dell'Arte e di origine molto antico; anzi e molto anteriore alla costituzione del libero sodalizio dei fabbri."

50 *CAV*, vol. 2, 333, cap. xii and note 5; Lorenzetti, *Venice*, 524.

51 *CAV*, vol. 2, 339, cap. xxviiii.

52 *CAV*, vol. 2, 340n7, 341n2.
53 *CAV*, vol. 2, 348, cap. lvi; 360, cap. lxxvii.
54 Mackenney, *Tradesmen and Traders*, 16–17.
55 Lane, *Venetian Ships*; Forsellini, "L'organizzazione economica dell'Arsenale"; Perocco and Salvadori, *Civiltà di Venezia*, vol. 2, 564–607; Concina, *L'Arsenale*.
56 I am grateful to Richard Goy for his masterful assistance on this point.
57 Tassini, *Curiosità veneziane*, 285–7; Calimani, *Ghetto of Venice*, 129–32; Lorenzetti, *Venice*, 416.
58 Lane, *Venetian Ships*, 146; Lorenzetti, *Venice*, 15.
59 Lane, *Venetian Ships*, 264–5. Lane's figures make it even more incomprehensible that Caniato's "L'Arsenale" should make only one fleeting reference to the fabbri, merely likening them to the sail makers (*veleri*) as "corporazioni minori," on 661.
60 Muraro, "The Moors of the Clock Tower."
61 See Carpaccio's *The Healing of the Possessed Man* for a Venetian laundry pole, e.g., in P.F. Brown, *Venetian Narrative Painting*, plate 21, p. 160.
62 Lane, *Venetian Ships*, 194.
63 Perocco and Salvadori, *Civiltà di Venezia*, vol. 2, 610–11.
64 Arti, b. 61, carboneri, mariegola, 1476–1781; see the translated extract from their rule book in Chambers and Pullan, *Documentary History*, 285–6.
65 Tassini, *Curiosità veneziane*, 19.
66 Goy, *House of Gold*, 187, 222, 240, 276, 278, 290–2.
67 Sanudo, *De origine*, 62.
68 *DMS*, vol. 18, col. 245, June 1514; Tassini, *Curiosità veneziane*, 264–5; Mallett and Hale, *Military Organisation*, 350–66.
69 For further references to Bontempelli see chapters 4 and 5 herein.
70 Gramigna and Perissa, *Scuole*, 47.
71 Mackenney, *Tradesmen and Traders*, 101–2. For the inventory of 1595 see the first document in Arti, b. 110, fabbri, inventarii, 1595–1600.
72 Arti, b. 109, fabbri, capitoli sciolti, 1531–1734. The unbound lists are from 6 January 1530, 10 January 1531, 21 January 1531, and 16 August 1603. This chapter sets aside the last of these.
73 Braunstein, "Le commerce du fer," 267.
74 The absence of fresh water stunted the trade in the Middle Ages, but the disruptions of war in the rest of Italy made the manufacture of woollen cloth thrive in the sixteenth century; see Fano, "Ricerche sull'arte della lana"; D. Sella, "Venetian Woollen Industry."
75 Hay and Law, *Italy in the Age of the Renaissance*, 150–9.
76 Braunstein, "Le commerce du fer," 278.
77 P. Laven, "Venetian Rivers."
78 Braunstein, "Le commerce du fer," 281–6, 290.

79 I am grateful to Dr James Shaw for this confirmation, which is based on his own extensive research in both Venice and Florence.

80 Natalie Zemon Davis introduced this concept to the audience in the lecture marking the award of her honorary degree in the University of Edinburgh. She rather buries it in her book *Trickster Travels*.

81 Bellati, *Dizionario*, 1387–90, s.v. "sopranomi."

82 Zompini, *Le arti che vanno per via*, no. 20, p. 61.

83 Garzoni, *Piazza Universale*, sheds no light on these terms. I owe the identifications entirely to a conversation with Ragioniere Antonio Bellati.

84 As Sanudo says of the boats, "sempre li bisogna conzieri, o dolfini o altro," in *De origine*, 22; translated as "ornaments are always required, either dolphins or other things," in Chambers and Pullan, *Documentary History*, 6.

85 There are three Manzoni on the lists, and they appear to be brothers: "iacomo de piero manzon da balabio"; "bernardo di piero manzon da balabio"; and "zanmaria de piero manzon da balabio."

86 On immigrant sculptors see Connell, "Employment of Sculptors," 72–80; for the suggestion that Tullio Lombardo continued the work of Bartolomeo Bon at the Frari, see Lorenzetti, *Venice*, 600.

87 Casola, *Pilgrimage to Jerusalem*, 140. In extolling Venetian power in book 7 of his *Della ragion di stato*, Giovanni Botero attributes to the Marquis del Vasto the fascinating remark that "he would rather have the arsenal of Venice than four good cities of Lombardy"; Botero, *Reason of State*, 131–2.

88 "Questi sono Tuti Colloro liqualli sono chiamadi Quando se fa el Capitollo Zeneral liqualli balloteno Inditto Capitolo Copiadi del libro fo mandato ali Signori Cinque Savii sopra le maregolle e de che nation loro sono Como qui sotto distinto auno per uno annotadi appar Et prima ..."

89 Fogazzaro, *Piccolo mondo antico*: my thanks for this reference to the maestro from Ballabio who oversaw service in the wine bar at Fortnum and Mason's in June 2008. I regret that his card did not carry his name. For an indication of the scale of change that the Risorgimento brought about, there is a supplement to Fogazzaro in Namier, "Nationality and Liberty"; see esp. p. 53. Page 46 quotes Mazzini: "The nation is the universality of the citizens speaking the same tongue." What a tidal wave this was for so regionalized a world. For further valuable reflection on the complexities of regional identities in Italy in the sixteenth century, see also Chabod, "Alcune questioni"; Bellati, *Dizionario dialettale*. Rag. Bellati has also translated *I Promessi Sposi* into the Premanese dialect.

90 This is in many ways an act of pietas on the author's part. The list is dealt with in a hasty sketch in Mackenney, *Tradesmen and Traders*, 112–13, which includes an error of addition and the misidentification of Lecco at the insistence of an examiner of the doctoral thesis on which the book was based.

91 Law, "Relations," ch. 4, p. 79v, citing the work of Stephen R. Ell, "Citizenship and Immigration in Venice, 1305–1500" (PhD diss., University of Chicago, 1976), and Mueller, "Aspetti sociali."
92 Manzoni, *I Promessi Sposi*, ed. Michele Messina, 2nd ed. (Messina-Firenze: Casa Editrice G. D'Anna, 1964). I shall always be grateful to Francesco Selandari for his kind gift of this magnificent edition. For discussion of Renzo's ambition to live in Venetian territory, see Benzoni, "Venezia e Bergamo," 19.
93 Lane, *Venice*, 227; Braudel, *The Mediterranean*, vol. 1, 215. On the general logistical problems of transport, see Spufford, *Power and Profit*, 174–228.
94 Cozzi and Knapton, *Storia della Repubblica di Venezia*, 401.
95 Mallett and Hale, *Military Organisation*, 416–17.
96 Braunstein, "Le commerce du fer," 290.
97 Pullan, "Town Poor," 224.
98 Boccalini, *I ragguagli di Parnaso*, vol. 3, rag. lxxi, 219.
99 Cozzi and Knapton, *Storia della Repubblica di Venezia*, 462–4.
100 D. Sella, "Iron Industry," 94–5.
101 D. Sella, *Crisis and Continuity*, 39.
102 Cozzi and Knapton, *Storia della Repubblica di Venezia*, 462–3.
103 D. Sella, *Crisis and Continuity*, 38–9.
104 Quoted in Pullan, "Town Poor," 216.
105 P. Laven, "Venetian Rivers," 215.
106 Sella, *Crisis and Continuity*, 112.
107 D. Pullan, "Town Poor," 226–8, 216.
108 Pullan, "Poverty, Charity and the Reason of State," 28.
109 Benzoni, "Venezia e Bergamo," 38.
110 Pullan, "Town Poor," 218.
111 Law, "Relations"; Law, "Venetian Mainland State"; Ventura, *Nobiltà e popolo*. For studies of individual cities and provinces see Grubb, *Firstborn of Venice*; Bowd, *Venice's Most Loyal City*; Ferraro, *Family and Public Life*.
112 Cozzi, Knapton, and Scarabello, *La Reppublica di Venezia*, 203–14.
113 Mackenney, *Sixteenth Century Europe*, 57, 70–81.
114 Pullan, *Rich and Poor*, 240–1nn3–8.
115 Luigi da Porto to Giovanni Morello in Venice, 26 March 1528, in his *Lettere storiche*, 326–8.
116 Pullan, "Famine in Venice."
117 Connell, "Employment of Sculptors," 72–7.
118 Johnson, *Europe in the Sixteenth Century*, 184–94.
119 See the brilliantly evocative essay by John Addington Symonds, "Como and il Medeghino."
120 *DMS*, vol. 54, col. 540, 1531, 22 July.

121 *DMS*, vol. 54, col. 417, 1531, May.

122 *DMS*, vol. 54, col. 413, 1531, 3 February.

123 *DMS*, vol. 55, col. 500, 1531, 15 February.

124 *DMS*, vol. 55, cols. 541–4, 1531, 19 February; vol. 55, col. 617, 1531, 5 March.

125 *DMS*, vol. 55, col. 665, 1531, 18 March.

126 See the photographic reproduction of the document of Sforza's financial account in the brilliant survey by Chabod, "L'epoca di Carlo V," 288.

127 On the "guerra di Musso" see Franceschini, "Le dominazioni francesi," 317–20; Giovio, *Historiae patriae*.

128 Magnocavallo, *Memorie antiche di Como*, 45–64; 54–5 on the plague of wolves.

129 With regard to il Medeghino's recognition as a Medici, see Nicodemo, "La scultura Milanese," 808. Perhaps still more notably, see Pope-Hennesy, *Italian High Renaissance*, plate 159 (note that this does not show the "palle"), and pp. 504–5, which discuss the documentation concerning the "Medici Tomb" in the "Medici Chapel" without mentioning that the subject had taken an assumed name. In an extremely learned analysis of the background of patronage for the tomb, Pope-Hennesy refers to the "Medici Tomb" passim, with no indication that Gian Giacomo did not belong to the Florentine dynasty. However, the adventurer proves devilish both in his elusiveness and in his persistency. Pius IV and his brother and sister came from a Milanese family of notaries and physicians who had no biological connection whatsoever to the Medici of Florence. Leopold von Ranke makes it plain that Pius was "of mean birth" and notes that his brother was "naturally reckless and enterprising," but does not explain the cognomen; Ranke, *History of the Popes*, vol. 1, 241–9. The most decisive clarification comes in Setton, *The Papacy and the Levant*, vol. 4, 738n60 (there is continuous pagination throughout the four volumes). The internet erroneously transposes the reference to p. 378 with no reference to the note or to the volume, and so it eludes the researcher – that is, until he or she checks Setton's index and finds Gian Giacomo listed as though he were among the scions of the Medici in Florence. See also Beretta, "Gian Giacomo de' Medici."

130 Prosperi, *Dizionario Storico dell'Inquisizione*, s.v. "Pio IV, papa (Giovanni Angelo de'Medici)," in vol. 3, 1212–13. I am very grateful to Chris Black for this vital reference.

131 There is no statue to the unfortunate Gabriele, but the inscription forms an assertive symmetry of the Medici name with the plaque to Gian Giacomo. The rhetorical nonsense of each is as follows: (*to the statue's right*) "IO. IACOBO MEDICI MARCH. MEREGNANI EX/IMII ANIMI ET CONSILII/ VIRO MVLTIS VICTORIIS/ PER TOTAM FERE EVROPAM/ PARTIS APUD OMNES GEN/TIS CLARISSIMO CUM AD/ EXITVM VITAE ANNO AE/ TATIS LX PERVENISSET"; (*to the statue's left*) "GABRIELI MEDICI/ INGENII

ET FORTITUDINIS/ EXIMIAE ADOLESCENTI/ POST CLADEM RHETIS/ ET FRANCISCO II SFORTIAE/ ILLATAM NAVALI PRAELIO/ DVM VINCIT CVM INVICTI/ ANIMI GLORIA INTERFECTO." Il Medeghino appears to have deserved his disreputable sculptor; see Margot and Rudolf Wittkower, *Born under Saturn*, 190–2.

132 Symonds, "Como and il Medeghino," quotations from pp. 216 and 220. One cannot resist speculating about what one might think of this pope had his brother been a Counter-Reformation saint and his nephew a marauding, godless prince. See also Burke, "How to Be a Counter-Reformation Saint." As Feste puts it in *Twelfth Night*, "To see this age! – A sentence is but a cheverel glove to a good wit, how quickly the wrong side may be turned outward" (act 3, scene 1, lines 10–12). Gian Giacomo, wherever his soul may be, must be enjoying the hoax that he has played on posterity. He has the last laugh even in this footnote. After the painstaking accumulation of all the materials cited here, I found it all summarized in Palmisani, *Il Medeghino.* I am grateful to Pierangelo Masciadri for this reference.

133 Pullan, *Rich and Poor*, 263, 273–4; Pullan, "Le Scuole Grandi e la loro opera"; and, more generally, Outram Evenett, *Spirit of the Counter-Reformation*; Delumeau, *Catholicism between Luther and Voltaire.*

134 Mullett, *Catholic Reformation*, 71–2; the order only received papal confirmation in 1537. For the emergence of the new orders and their transformation into the instruments of the Counter-Reformation, see Outram Evenett, *Spirit of the Counter-Reformation*, 74.

135 Gramigna and Perissa, *Scuole*, 47.

136 As Owen Dudley Edwards has pointed out to me, the rhetorical question is somewhat naive. What the gossip of Roman clerics and Venetian diplomats was or might have been is a separate subject.

4 Officers and Office in the Mercers' Guild, c. 1450–c. 1600

1 Rapp, *Industry and Economic Decline*, 20n11, but cf. p. 102, which places the marzeri in a general and expanding sector of "cloth retailers" in the economy of the city as a whole; Mackenney, *Tradesmen and Traders*, 90–111.

2 Casola, *Pilgrimage to Jerusalem*, 129.

3 Mackenney, *Tradesmen and Traders*, 88–90.

4 Evelyn, *Diary*, vol.1, 195.

5 The list derives from Archivio di Stato di Venezia, indice Arti, b. 314, marzeri, capitoli e parti, 1508–1608. I made the compilation before computer-based analysis was common. The general impressions of the evidence figured in the resultant doctoral thesis but seemed altogether too bland for the book that was based upon it.

The omission in the book drew a rebuke in a review by Professor John Najemy. Mackenney, "Trade Guilds and Devotional Confraternities," 303–7; Mackenney, *Tradesmen and Traders*, reviewed by John M. Najemy, *JMH* 3 (1989), 623–6. On Florentine guilds and electoral politics see Najemy, *Corporatism and Consensus.*

6 On these subjects see in particular Fenlon, *Ceremonial City*; Preto, *Peste e società a Venezia*; Davidson, "Northern Italy in the 1590s"; Pullan, "Occupations and Investments"; Bouwsma, *Republican Liberty.*

7 *CAV*, vol. 2, 307–27; Arti, b. 312, marzeri, mariegola, 1471–1787; Mackenney, *Tradesmen and Traders*, 90–110.

8 *CAV*, vol. 2, 308, cap. i and n. 1; 309, cap. iii; 326, cap. lv.

9 *CAV*, vol. 2, 309, cap. iv; 312, caps. xii, xiv, xv; 325–6, cap. xxxxviiii.

10 "E de zonte volemo se le preditte done volesse intrar per soa devotion la nostra scuola, quelle dovemo azetar e scriver como son scrite le altre done marcere e stano per contrada e vano ai merchadi a San marco e a San polo e ale fiere le qual tute siano sotoposte ala nostra mariegola e far fation secondo l'usanza"; Arti, b. 312, marzeri, mariegola, fol. 12v, cap. xxiv.

11 "salvo tanto quanto per sua devotion volesse dar"; Arti, marzeri, mariegola, b. 312, fols. 27–35, caps. xvi–xx.

12 Lorenzetti, *Venice*, 394–7; ASV, Arti, b. 312, marzeri, mariegola, fol. 16r–v, caps. xxvii–xxviiii. Francesco Sansovino clearly separates the Scuole Grandi from other institutions, but describes that of San Teodoro as "prima picciola & fatta dai Merciari"; Sansovino, *Venetia*, fol. 103r.

13 Arti, b. 312, marzeri, mariegola, fol. 8v, cap. xxii; see also Chojnacka, *Working Women.*

14 *CAV*, vol. 2, 309, cap. iv.

15 For a comparable exercise on office in the scuole piccole, see Ortalli, *Scuole piccole*, 18–24.

16 *CAV*, vol. 2, 311, cap. xi; 313, cap. xviiii.

17 *CAV*, vol. 2, 321, cap. xxxxi; 322, cap. xxxxiii.

18 *CAV*, vol. 2, 315, cap. xxvii.

19 Lane, "Maritime Law and Administration," 241.

20 *CAV*, vol. 2, 310, cap. vii.

21 *CAV*, vol. 2, 309, cap. iv; 312, cap. xii.

22 *CAV*, vol. 2, 311, cap. x; 318, cap. xxxiv. See also Ortalli, *Scuole piccole*, 44, for a requirement of literacy among the officers of the Scuola dei Milanesi, and p. 149 on the office of *scrivano.*

23 Mackenney, *Tradesmen and Traders*, 4–7.

24 Shaw, *Justice of Venice*, 115.

25 *CAV*, vol. 2, 314, cap. xxii; 316, cap. xxvii. For an example of the extension of the process of appeal from the guild to the courts of the republic, see the case of

Pancrazio the furnace man in Arti, b. 152, forneri, atti diversi, 1447–1797, a case of 1 February 1503 involving one "Pancratius," who appealed against a verdict of the Giustizia Vecchia to the Auditori Vecchi, apparently winning his case on 18 April 1504.

26 Mackenney, *Tradesmen and Traders*, 171–3.

27 Figures from Rapp, *Industry and Economic Decline*, 60 and 72.

28 Mackenney, *Tradesmen and Traders*, 171–3.

29 Arti, b. 397, marzeri, nomi di fratelli, 1586–1692.

30 Mackenney, *Tradesmen and Traders*, 102–3; Shaw, *Justice of Venice*, 116.

31 Mackenney, *Tradesmen and Traders*, 28; and the fine recent study by Shaw, *Justice of Venice.*

32 The original is at Arti, b. 312, marzeri, mariegola, fol. 10r, cap. xxiv. Something of the range of wares involved is captured in translated form in "The Craft and Wares of the Mercers," in Chambers and Pullan, *Documentary History*, 281–5.

33 *CAV*, vol. 2, 317, caps. xxviiii, xxx; 325–6, cap. liii.

34 Arti, b. 352, marzeri, processi; cf. Arti b. 117, fabbri, processi.

35 Rapp, *Industry and Economic Decline*, 49–54; Mackenney, *Tradesmen and Traders*, 218–32.

36 On the logistics of both hiring and training, see Lane, "Wages and Recruitment."

37 Mackenney, "Trade Guilds," 223–44; Muir, *Civic Ritual*, 235, 237.

38 Preto, *Peste e società a Venezia.*

39 Arti, b. 312, marzeri, mariegola, fol. 8r–v, cap. xxi.

40 "Assaissime volte intrano facende e cose per le qual molte fiate el mestier nostro patisse gran senestro per non haver libertà nui gastaldi e compagni de mandar quelle tal facende ad execution"; "Volemo che in capitoli cadauno scritto nel nostro mestier possa vegnir e andar in election e ballodar como estado uxitado per lo passado"; Arti, b. 312, marzeri, mariegola, fol. 6v, cap. xviii.

41 Arti, b. 312, marzeri, mariegola, fol. 8r, cap. xxi.

42 Arti, b. 312, marzeri, mariegola, fol. 30r, cap. xxxxv.

43 Lane, *Venice*, 111.

44 Mackenney, *Tradesmen and Traders*, 103–6, deriving from Arti, b. 397, marzeri, nomi di fratelli, 1586–1692.

45 For the figures from Milizia da Mar, b. 446, see Mackenney, "Trade Guilds," 260–5.

46 Cowan, *Urban Patriciate*, 170n606.

47 Cowan, *Urban Patriciate*, appendix 3, 225.

48 Lorenzetti, *Venice*, 333, 479.

49 Cowan, *Urban Patriciate*, 69n240, 225.

50 Romano, *Patricians and* Popolani; Shaw, *Justice of Venice*.

51 *CAV*, vol. 2, 312–13, caps. xiiii, xv, xvi; on apprentices see Mackenney, "Guilds of Renaissance Venice," 37–9; also Chambers and Pullan, *Documentary History*, 147, "Two Mercers Make a Tax Return," on the relationship of household and shop.

52 Cowan, *Urban Patriciate,* 196.
53 Pullan, *Rich and Poor*, 107; see also 131.
54 Having reached this triumphant conclusion, I discovered that the "master" list still had them confused.
55 Mackenney, *Tradesmen and Traders*, 103.
56 Mackenney, "Guilds of Renaissance Venice," 40–1 and references. On the lists in general see Rapp, *Industry and Economic Decline*, 48–54; Mackenney, *Tradesmen and Traders*, 219–32.
57 Mackenney, *Tradesmen and Traders*, 92–4.
58 Ibid., 96–7.
59 Ibid., 106.
60 Mackenney, "Trade Guilds," 299–303.
61 Mackenney, *Tradesmen and Traders*, 96–7.
62 Mackenney, "Trade Guilds," 224.
63 *CAV*, vol. 2, 310, cap. vi.
64 Shaw, *Justice of Venice*, 117.
65 Mackenney, *Tradesmen and Traders*, 193–5. On the Inquisition, see chapter 6 herein.
66 Pullan, "Significance of Venice," 452.
67 Rubinstein, *Government of Florence*; Najemy, *Corporatism and Consensus*; Hale, *Florence and the Medici*, 15–19.
68 See for example Queller, *Venetian Patriciate*; Davis, *Decline of the Venetian Nobility*; Burke, *Venice and Amsterdam*; Cowan, *Urban Patriciate.*
69 Arti, b. 312, marzeri, mariegola, fol. 8r–v, cap. xxi.
70 Arti, b. 312, marzeri, mariegola, fol. 5v, cap. xvi; Padoan Urban, "La festa della Sensa."
71 Arti, b. 314, marzeri, parti, 1508–1608, fol. 14v.
72 Arti, b. 314, marzeri, parti, 1508–1608, fol. 83v.
73 Castiglione, *The Book of the Courtier*, bk. 2, pp. 145–6; Castiglione, *Il libro del Cortegiano*, bk.2, LIII, p. 162; Mackenney, *Tradesmen and Traders*, 142–3.
74 Arti, b. 354, marzeri, processi per botteghe in festa della Sensa, fol. 30r, a reference dating from 1608.
75 Lorenzetti, *Venice*, 151.
76 Arti, b. 354, marzeri, processi per botteghe in festa della Sensa.
77 Arti, b. 314, marzeri, capitoli e parti, fol. 77r for 2 June 1574.
78 Arti, b. 312, marzeri, mariegola, fol. 79v.
79 Arti, b. 354, marzeri, processi per botteghe in festa della Sensa, filza A, fol. 3v.
80 Ibid., fol. 4r.
81 Ibid., fols. 22r, 35r.
82 Ibid., fol. 16r.

83 Arti, b. 354, marzeri, processi per botteghe in festa della Sensa, filza 136, no. 4, fol. 15r.
84 Arti, b. 354, marzeri, processi per botteghe in festa della Sensa, filza O, Giuditii e terminationi, fol. 3r.
85 Arti, b. 354, marzeri, processi per botteghe in festa della Sensa, filza Z, fol. 1r.
86 Ibid., fol. 41r.
87 "Et per l'honor che si deve alle festività della chiesa, della Città tutta tanto celebrate e per non levar l'occasione de qualche guadagno et concorso alle botteghe della sensa, che per servir alla grandezza publica devono star aperte"; Arti, b. 354, marzeri, processi per botteghe in festa della sensa, filza Z, fol. 31r.
88 "A ti gastaldo di marzeri te fazzo avisa che bastonae no ti mancherà se sta strada ti tegnirà per che mi o pagà L12 per non esser andà a corrpo se questo ten e vegnisse in borsa per ti averessi rason ma per uno gramo anno che ti a da star, to vol farte naser, te prego lassar andar questa festa se non cheti sara rotta la testa e non te lamenter che ti non sia gavisao le se farà vegnir dal monte olivetto eti non saverà dove le vegan." Arti, b. 314, marzeri, capitoli e parti, 1508–1608, fol. 166v. I am most grateful to Professor Sandro Sticca for his help with translating this text.
89 Arti, b. 352, marzeri, processi, contro Niccolo Bassin, fol. 4r.
90 Arti, b. 358, marzeri, processi, contro capelleri.
91 Arti, b. 313, marzeri, catastico processi, fol. 9r.
92 Arti, b. 117, fabbri, processi, garzoni dell'arte per privilegi.
93 Arti, b. 362, marzeri, processi, contro cortelleri.
94 Arti, b. 365, marzeri, processi, contro fabbri.
95 Arti, b. 313, marzeri, processi, contro strazzaroli, fols. 3r–8r
96 Arti, b. 313, marzeri, processi, contro drappieri, fols. 17r–29v.
97 Arti, b. 313, marzeri, processi, contro tellaruoli, fol. 45r.

5 Monuments to Mercy, c. 1500–c. 1600

1 See chapter 4 herein; Gallo, "La Scuola Grande di San Teodoro."
2 PC Q, fol. 38r.
3 PC O, fols. 200r, 203r.
4 Humfrey and Mackenney, "Venetian Trade Guilds," 323.
5 PC U, fol. 213v.
6 PC U, fol. 587r.
7 PC N, fol. 686v.
8 PC Z, fols. 148v, 149v.
9 PC AA, fol. 21r. The boatmen themselves contested the regulation and lost; fol. 22r.
10 In this case the registers of the Provveditori di Comun recorded the approval of a measure that the magistrates of the Giustizia Vecchia had made; PC Z, fol. 130v.

11 PC BB, fol. 361r.
12 PC V, fol. 407r.
13 E.g., Mackenney, *Tradesmen and Traders*, 170, 171, 198, 199; Cope, *The Venetian Chapel of the Sacrament.*
14 Mackenney, *Sixteenth Century Europe*, 192–4.
15 *DMS*, V, col. 796, February 1504.
16 *DMS*, V, col. 839, 6 February 1504.
17 *DMS*, VI, col. 146, 31 [*sic*] April 1505; *DMS*, VI, col. 427, September 1506; *DMS*, VI, col. 528, January 1507.
18 *DMS*, VII, col. 24, 2 March 1507.
19 C. Shaw, *Julius II*, 196; Bull, "Iconography of the Sistine Chapel Ceiling"; Dotson, "An Augustinian Interpretation"; Wind, "Crucifixion of Haman." I thank Roger Tarr for his kind advice on this matter.
20 Wind, *Religious Symbolism of Michelangelo*, 40.
21 Olin, *Catholic Reform*, 47–60; O'Malley, "Religious and Theological Culture."
22 "A laude et Gloria della Santissima Trinitade Padre, Fiolo, et Spiritio Santo."

> Amen.
>
> Havendo considerato più volte noi Fratelli che nessuna mazor obligation ha la humana natura la qual è formata alla imagine, e similitiudine de Dio, quanto ha ad esso Omnipotente Creatore, et Redemptore suo, el qual se volesse redimere dale man del Demonio, che se instesso se volle offerir in hostia, et sacrificio suso el Legno dalla Crose, et ancora con grandissimo amore, e Carità volesse donarsi a noi in cibo, a mazor fede, et Testimonianza della sua santissima Passione dandone a sumere il suo santissimo Corpo et a bevere el suo preciosissimo sangue, come nella ultima sua cena per suo Testamento caritativamente dimostrò alli suoi cari discipuli, Avanti che el gustasse el duro passo della crudelissima, et acerba morte della Crose, mediante la quale nui semo sta recuperate delle man del Demonio, e comprati con el suo preciosissimo sangue, come dice la santa scriptura: empti estis pretio magno cioè con lo santissimo sangue dello mmaculate agnello fatto obbediente per noi fin alla morte per donarci el suo reame de vita eternal. Onde veramente in memoria di tanta Carità, Amore et inestimabile bontà, che usata a noi peccatori ingrate de tanto beneficio, meritamente con tutte le nostre forze mentale e corporale noi siemo obligati a renderlo el debito honore, e darli laude, et farli reverentia cum ogni devotione, et demonstration di gratuitade a noi è possible, accioche esso Redemptor nostro habbi misericordia di noi in questo mundo, et nell'altro, ne dia riposo cum salvation delle anime nostre. Inspiradi adunque della gratia del Spritio Santo, dal qual procede ogni bona operatione, dovere dare principio a questa benedetta scuola, et unione di fratelli, et sorelle, intitulata Fraternita del Santissimo Sacramento essendone sta concesso dalli eccelentissimi Signori Capi dello eccelso consegio di diese quanto per sue lettere qui sotto chiaramente se contiene. Daremo principio a questa santa, et pietosa opera, come qui sotto per ordene appare di Capitulo in capitulo li ordeni che se debbiano observar. (PC, reg. BB, fol. 398r–v)

23 Aretino, *L'umanità di Cristo*, 198.
24 Aretino, *L'umanità di Cristo*, 204.

25 Gentili, "*Il Sogno dil Caravia*," 139ff.
26 Panofsky, *Albrecht Dürer*, 151–2; Erasmus, "Handbook of the Christian Soldier," with extensive reference to Ephesians 6:10–18. The frontispiece of the volume containing this edition is Duerer's *Knight, Death, and the Devil.*
27 Seneca, *Venezia e Papa Giulio II*, 93.
28 PC BB, fol. 399r.
29 "Il fondator et principia per divina inspirazione dell'ordene di Minori Observanti predicator in quel tempo in detta Giesia di San Jeremia mediante però l'aiuto de Miser Antonio Contarini per divina reservatione patriarca di Venezia"; PC N, fol. 1r–v.
30 PC P, fol. 479r; PC P, fol. 6r; PC P, fol. 51r.
31 Sbriziolo, "Scolae communes," 422n10.
32 Casola, *Pilgrimage to Jerusalem*, 146–50.
33 Smith, *Life and Letters*, vol. 1, 350.
34 "volendo noi secolari navegar nella nave da questo tenebroso et caligionoso secolo"; "lassado a noi da missier Gesù Christo in terra per nostro pastor"; PC T, fol. 52r–v.
35 PC BB, fol. 72v. It is a melancholy reflection that the churches that housed these examples are no more: San Geminiano was destroyed by Napoleon, and San Silvestro by fire and then by rebuilding.
36 PC O, fol. 286r–v.
37 PC O, fol. 294r.
38 PC Q, fol. 248r.
39 Gramigna and Perissa, *Scuole*, 41.
40 PC V, fol. 103r.
41 "Dinotando questa scuola esser antiquissima come appar per la mariegola vecchia della scola di S. Pantalon, la qual fo poi unita a quella del Corpo di Christo fatta tutta sua mariegola la qual fo smarita del 1530"; PC Z, fol. 438r.
42 PC Q, fol. 463r.
43 PC P, fols. 101r, 102r.
44 PC P, fol. 81r.
45 "fradelli e sorelle così vivi come morti"; PC Z, fol. 86v,
46 "la scuola della parocchia nostra"; PC R, fol. 281r.
47 Bossy, "Social History of Confession."
48 PC T, fol. 81r.
49 PC AA, fol. 19r.
50 PC P, fol. 480r; PC P, fol. 164r.
51 "d'ogni età d'ogni sesso … a casa degli poveri come a quella degli ricchi"; PC O, fol. 232v.
52 PC U, fol. 132r.

53 PC U, fol. 140r; Mackenney, "Public and Private," 116.
54 PC Z, fol. 464v; PC R, fol. 77v; PC N, fol. 491r; PC Q, fol. 184r; PC Q, fol. 502r; PC BB, fol. 489v; PC U, fol. 259r; PC T, fol. 110v; PC T, fol. 43r; PC AA, fol. 161r.
55 PC BB, fol. 149v.
56 PC V, fols. 281r–323v; fol. 282r (any parishioner of any age); 281v (praise of Doge Gritti); 283r (visits to the sick as one of the "opere della Misericordia").
57 Pullan, *Rich and Poor*, 63–83; Mueller, "Charitable Institutions."
58 R.C. Davis, *Shipbuilders of the Venetian Arsenal*, p. 13, gives figures of 1,013 caulkers, 1,024 carpenters, and 150 oar makers but does not include sawyers. The numbers of these who worked at any one time were, he suggests, much smaller: 300, 600, and 60, respectively. Rapp, *Industry and Economic Decline*, p. 149, suggests that around 1,500 people worked in the Arsenale daily on the eve of the plague of 1630. The census of 1563 recorded a population of 168,627. This included 41,244 adult male artisans, with women and children adding 86,502 people to the category of "artisans, shopkeepers, and their families," a ratio of almost exactly one adult male artisan to two women and children (not necessarily both of them dependents).
59 PC Q, fols. 385r–401r.
60 PC BB, fols. 653v–654r.
61 PC P, fol. 220r
62 "piaghe vechie infistolade, roture, morbo gallico et simil sorte"; PC P, fol. 220v.
63 PC P, fol. 665r.
64 PC P, fol. 665r.
65 PC P, fol. 667v.
66 PC P, fols. 664r–680v.
67 PC BB, fol. 3v.
68 "il ricco non resti per avaricia, et il povero per povertà"; PC BB, fol. 3r.
69 PC BB, fols. 2r, 5v, 3v.
70 Pullan, "Wage-Earners," 157.
71 PC BB, fol. 15r–v.
72 PC Z, fol. 560r.
73 PC P, fols. 312r–347r.
74 PC BB, fols. 1r–44r.
75 PC BB, fol. 1r.
76 PC BB, fol. 653r.
77 PC BB, fol. 656v.
78 PC BB, fol. 659r.
79 The phrase resonates with Shakespeare's "Signiors, rich burghers … petty traffickers"; see the introduction herein.
80 PC U, fols. 368r, 402r.

81 PC S, fols. 431r–451r.
82 PC R, fols. 323r–333r.
83 PC S, fol. 431v, and chapter 1 herein.
84 PC S, fol. 439r.
85 PC S, fol. 441v. Vio's reference (758.739) dubiously dates the foundation of the scuola from the date of the magistrates' approval, nearly a quarter of a century after the date on the original statute.
86 "tal numero di bisognosi per la mutatione de' tempi e assai maggiore et specialmente nella nostra contrata di San Nicolo"; PC Z, fols. 142r, 148v, and see chapter 2 herein.
87 PC AA, fol. 259r. The magistrates recorded the statute twice, in copies that were not consistent with each other.
88 PC Q, fol. 331r.
89 PC Q, fol. 335r.
90 "d'estate … mai resta d'accumular vittuaglia per il tempo d'inverno"; PC S, fol. 302v.
91 Il nome deli pitori che depensero li quadri dela scuola dei marangoni

> primo la Visitazione di S. Maria Elisabetta di Baldissera Diana
> Sovraporte no. 7 del medema Baldisera Diana
> La Madona che va in egitto de Santo Peranda
> La Adoratione delli Magi de Gierolamo Pilotti
> Le stragie dellinosenti de giulio Mauoro
> Il ritorno degitto de Santo Peranda
> Il Sig. quando disputa alli dotori de gierolemo piloti
> Una prosesione di Una Dogaressa de Giulio Mauoro
> Tutti li ritratti belissimi di Lunardo Corona
> Sinque sovrabalconi delli medesmi autori.

The inventory is in a register marked "Libro di Credito" and dates from 13 May 1733, in Arti, b. 296, marangoni, alfabeto leggi, 1532–1715.

92 Arti, b. 110, fabbri, inventarii, 1595–1600.
93 PC P, fols. 178v–181r.
94 "non ad altro fine che per zelo delle cose divine, et anco per dar anima a tutti gli altri Guardiani suoi successori nelle buone opera"; PC V, fols. 50r–53r; fols. 54r–v list further additions for 1607–26.
95 "Visto la spesa fatta nella Chiesa prefatta cioè dell'altar, di balcone, casar il pergolo, riportarlo dalla banda del Santissimo Sacramento a quello di Santo Alessandro, levar la muretta del coreto da basso, facendone la giesia spaziosa e lucida et anco avendone reporta la sagrestia quella era abasso suso in coro per nostra mazor commodità tutto a suo danno, spese, et interesse et questo essendo sta fatto dalla Scuola del Santissimo Sacramento"; PC BB, fol. 492v.
96 PC BB, fol. 493r.

97 Vio 676–90.634–48, but exaggerating the distinction between 644, 645, and 646.

98 PC BB, fols. 346r–361r; PC BB, fols. 70r–103r; PC BB, fols. 485r–520r; PC BB, fols. 225r–241r; PC BB, fols. 651r–674r; PC BB, fols. 554r–572r; PC BB, fols. 472r–485r.

99 Humfrey and Mackenney, "Venetian Trade Guilds," 325, table, no. 1; Vio 684.642, citing CBC.

100 Humfrey and Mackenney, "Venetian Trade Guilds," 326, table, no. 21; Vio 676.635.

101 Vio 684.641, citing CBC, and arti, b. 7.

102 Vio 676.636, citing a parochial source for a confraternity of "sonadori" from before 1450.

103 FDS, 19.

104 FDS, 19.

105 "Unto This Last," in *Works*, vol. 17, 20, quoting a letter of 18 March 1877.

106 Perocco and Salvadori, *Civilità di Venezia*, vol. 2, 610–11, 614–15.

107 Vio 717.681.

108 Vio 711.670, citing CBC; Humfrey and Mackenney, "Venetian Trade Guilds," 330, table, no. 51.

109 Vio 708.668, citing CBC and Arti b. 425; Humfrey and Mackenney, "Venetian Trade Guilds," 329, table, no. 52.

110 Vio 714.674, citing CBC. The regulation is from 1557.

111 Vio 698.657.

112 Vio 699.658, citing PC M.

113 Vio 700.659; Humfrey and Mackenney, "Venetian Trade Guilds," 326, table, no. 25.

114 Vio 706.664; Miani and Baldin, *Churches of Venice*, 36.

115 Vio 705.663; Humfrey and Mackenney, "Venetian Trade Guilds," 326, table, no. 31; Perocco and Salvadori, *Civilità di Venezia*, vol. 2, 741, table, no. 46.

116 This was even more emphatically so for the members of the shoemakers' guild who appeared in a picture commemorating their visit to meet that same Doge Grimani in the Palazzo Ducale itself, their names recorded on the composition; Wolters, *Storia e politica*, 152–7.

117 FDS, p. LI. On the Rialto see Calabi and Morachiello, *Rialto*; Lorenzetti, *Venice*, 467–8.

118 Vio 404–20.356–73.

119 Vio 405.357.

120 Humfrey, "Competitive Devotions," 420, table, no. 19.

121 Simonsfeld, *Der Fondaco dei Tedeschi*, vol. 2, 134; Mackenney, "Public and Private," 130; Panofsky, *Albrecht Dürer*, 109–13. On the rosary in general, see Winston-Allen, *Stories of the Rose.*

122 Evans, *Rudolf II*, 182; Trevor-Roper, *Princes and Artists*, 113.
123 Vio 404.356; Lorenzetti, *Venice*, 171.
124 Vio 414.364.
125 Vio 410.360, citing CBC to show that the guild had been at the church since 1307. As an illustration of the close ties of arte and scuola, the permission for the confraternity came from both the Provveditori di Comun and the Giustizia Vecchia. Humfrey and Mackenney, "Venetian Trade Guilds," 329, table, no. 38.
126 Vio 408.358 and a duplicate at 413.362; Humfrey and Mackenney, "Venetian Trade Guilds," 329, table, no. 47.
127 Vio 418.367; Humfrey and Mackenney, "Venetian Trade Guilds," 326, table, no. 32.
128 Mackenney, "Public and Private," 123.
129 Vio 389.344.
130 According to Zanetti, *Descrizione*, 185, this was "una tavola con la Madonna di Pietà ed abbasso il ritratto di Bartolomeo dal Calice padrone dell'altare, ed è opera di Santo Peranda."
131 Vio 399.352, citing CBC.
132 PC T, fols. 230v–248r; PC T, fols. 289v–344r; PC U, fols. 105v–132r.
133 Vio 390.345.
134 Gallo, "La Scuola Grande di San Teodoro."
135 Humfrey, "Competitive Devotions," 421, table, no. 32.
136 Vio 396.350, citing Arti b. 61; Vio 397.351, citing Arti b. 436.
137 D. Howard, *Jacopo Sansovino*, 193; T. Nichols, *Tintoretto*, 137–44.
138 Casola, *Pilgrimage*, 153–154; Mackenney, *Tradesmen and Traders*, 142.
139 Vio 428.379; Humfrey, "Competitive Devotions," 420, table, no. 10.
140 Vio 422.374.
141 Vio 425.377. On the attribution to Veronese see Lorenzetti, *Venice*, 369.
142 Vio 428.380.
143 Vio 426.378.
144 Humfrey and Mackenney, "Venetian Trade Guilds," 325, table, no. 12; Perocco and Salvadori, *Civiltà di Venezia*, vol. 2, 741. Zanetti, *Descrizione*, 191; "nella vicina scola de' merciari evvi la tavola dell'altare in sei comparti opera di Gentile Bellini."
145 Vio 425.376; Humfrey and Mackenney, "Venetian Trade Guilds," 325, table, no. 7; Allerston, "Market in Second-Hand Clothes and Furnishings," 37–53.
146 PC BB, fol. 52v.
147 Humfrey, "Competitive Devotions," 420, table, no. 13; Gramigna and Perissa, *Scuole*, 82.
148 "el penello cum sei doppieri adornadi de verdure, poi li miracoli de Messer Santo Antonio portadi da puti vestidi da anzoli, et dapo questi el penello de li frati cum li fratini aparadi et poi quelli da li pluviali cum le reliquie in mano. Driedo

questi dodese torzi di lire do ovvero tre inastadi in brazaleti doro adornati cun verdure et in mezzo de lor el solereto de Meser Santo Antonio ornado come se richiede de arzenti candeliereti et altri ornamenti … et poi li cantadori dapo questi la messa aparada soto la umbrella portada da nostri fradeli poi el Guardian nostro con uno de li reverendi frati insieme et cusì tuti quelli da la bancha siano acompagnadi … et cusì li altri nostri fradelli se habbino a compagnar da poi la bancha segondo li soi gradi … et andar atorno Rialto como anticamente se soleva far poi tornar ala Giesia nostra … mandar se dieba uno solareto adornado et con uno puto vestido da anzolo a trombe e pifari a San Marco et a Rialto et per il ditto anzolo annonciar al populo la Festa … acciò la festa nostra sia visitada dal populo et alli fratelli nostri si arrecorda de venir." PC BB, fol. 63r.

149 See the invaluable primary research of Muir, "Ritual of Rulership."

150 Muir, *Civic Ritual*; Muir, "Ritual of Rulership," 259–62; Glixon, "A Calendar of Religious Occasions Celebrated by the Scuole," in *Honoring God and the City*, 261–81; Tramontin, "'Calendarium' veneziano."

151 Cf. Pullan, *Rich and Poor*, 63–83.

6 The Venetians and the Confessional State, c. 1550–c. 1600

1 Bonney, *Dynastic States*; Elton, *Reformation Europe*; Elliott, *Europe Divided*; Mackenney, *Sixteenth Century Europe*, 219–42, 268–96.

2 Bouwsma, *Republican Liberty*.

3 "The mercantile aristocracy of Venice, preserving inviolate their republican constitution, were able to keep their old character, neither Papist nor Protestant"; "The Catholic merchant aristocracy of Venice fought with surprising solidarity against successive attempts to introduce the social forms of the Counter-Reformation." Trevor-Roper, "Religion, the Reformation and Social Change," 26, 29.

4 "Whether a Catholic system is compatible with an expanding commercial society, except as a deposit in its interstices, is questionable. When the yoke was light and formal, as in Venice, it was not broken, because it could be ignored." Trevor-Roper, *Archbishop Laud*, 436.

5 See Schilling, "Confessional Europe." On the difficult subject of the Counter-Reformation see Davidson, *Counter Reformation*; Janelle, *Catholic Reformation*; Mullett, *Catholic Reformation*. For some attempts to redefine the problems see Reinhard, "Reformation, Counter-Reformation and the Early Modern State"; O'Malley, *Trent and All That*; Birely, *Refashioning of Catholicism*; Bireley, "Redefining Catholicism"; Hsia, *World of Catholic Renewal*. For the high politics of the Church see A.D. Wright, *Early Modern Papacy*; for changing spirituality see Evennett, *Spirit of the Counter-Reformation*; for the social and psychological

context of religious change see Delumeau, *Catholicism between Luther and Voltaire*. The most significant contribution examines collective sentiment and remains at once an overview and a provocation: Bossy, *Christianity in the West*.

6 Trevor-Roper, "Religion, the Reformation and Social Change," 26–7.

7 Reinhard, "Disciplinamento sociale"; Schilling, "Chiese confessionali"; Schilling, "Confessionalisation in the Empire"; Schilling, "Die Konfessionalisierung im Reich"; Schilling, "Territorial State and Urban Liberty"; Schilling, "Civic Republicanism"; Hsia, *Social Discipline*.

8 Delumeau, *Catholicism between Luther and Voltaire*, 154–74; J.E.C. Hill, "Puritans and the 'Dark Corners of the Land'"; Hsia, *Catholic Renewal*, 54–5; O'Malley, *Trent and All That*, 77–8, 86–7; Cozzi, "La Compagnia di Gesù," 308; Del Torre, "La politica ecclesiastica," 403, 413, 415.

9 See Cozzi, "Stato e Chiesa."

10 Mackenney, *Sixteenth Century Europe*, 182; Cozzi, "Fortuna e sfortuna," 60.

11 Niero, "Riforma cattolica," 71; see also 83.

12 Scarabello, "Per una storia della prostituzione," 43–4; Goy, *Venice: An Architectural Guide*, 424–5.

13 Hsia, *Catholic Renewal*, 55; A.D. Wright, *Early Modern Papacy*, 109; Grendler, *Roman Inquisition*.

14 Hsia, *Catholic Renewal*, 55; Gullino, "Il rientro dei gesuiti," 426. On the emergence of the absolutist State and the mental world behind it see Mousnier, "Exponents and Critics."

15 See the magisterial study, with implications far beyond a single magistracy, by Derosas, "Moralità e giustizia."

16 Wright, *Early Modern Papacy*, 119; Hacke, *Women, Sex and Marriage*, 177–229.

17 Cozzi, "Authority and the Law," 334.

18 Maranini, *La costituzione*, vol. 2, 482, 485; Cozzi, *Il Doge Nicolo Contarini*, 215; Derosas, "Moralità e giustizia"; Lowry, "Reform of the Council of Ten." These references make James Fenimore Cooper's tale of baroque Venice, *The Bravo* (1831), altogether less lurid. For the continuing fictional possibilities of the secrets of the Venetian state see Phillips, *The Rossetti Letter*.

19 Schilling, "Civic Republicanism," 7.

20 Bossy, introduction to Delumeau, *Catholicism between Luther and Voltaire*, unnumbered xvii.

21 On taxation see Rapp, *Industry and Economic Decline*, 138–67; Mackenney, *Tradesmen and Traders*, 218–32. On the reason of State see Mackenney, "'A Plot Discover'd?,'" 185–216 and references, in particular Viroli, *From Politics to Reason of State*; Donaldson, *Machiavelli and Mystery of State*.

22 Delumeau, *Vie économique et sociale de Rome*, vol. 1, 501–17, and esp. 516: "nous croyons en effet que c'est au xvie siècle que le fosse a commencé a se creuser

entre l'Eglise et le monde du travail"; and 824–43; Trevor-Roper, "Religion, the Reformation and Social Change," 23.

23 Schilling, "Confessionalisation in the Empire," 232–40.

24 I take this model from Geoffrey Parker, *Europe in Crisis*, 29–47, and I thank Professor Parker for his advice on the nature of the Confessional State.

25 Davidson, "La tutela del culto," which clearly sees a process of the extension of the protection of public morals to the protection of religious faith; Viroli, *From Politics to Reason of State*; Wootton, *Paolo Sarpi*; Chabod, *La politica di Paolo Sarpi*; Cozzi, *Il Doge Nicolo Contarini*. On the overlapping interests of Church and State see de Franceschi, *Raison d'état et raison d'église*; Cozzi, "Fortuna e sfortuna"; Gullino, "Il rientro dei gesuiti."

26 M. Firpo, *Artisti, gioiellieri, eretici*, 48.

27 Quoted in M. Firpo, *Artisti, gioiellieri, eretici*, 123.

28 Quoted in M. Firpo, *Artisti, gioiellieri, eretici*, 119.

29 M. Firpo, *Artisti, gioiellieri, eretici*, 68, 71; quotation from 83.

30 Vio 907–10.893.

31 Cantimori, *Eretici italiani*; Cantimori, "Problem of Heresy"; Enno van Gelder, *The Two Reformations*; J.J. Martin, *Venice's Hidden Enemies*; Jacobsen Schutte, "Periodization."

32 Mackenney, *Tradesmen and Traders*, 174–96.

33 J.J. Martin, *Venice's Hidden Enemies*, 168.

34 Mullett, *Catholic Reformation*, 148.

35 Janelle, *Catholic Reformation*, 168; no reference, but probably deriving from Mâle, *L'art religieux*, 73; Weissman, *Ritual Brotherhood*.

36 Rosand, *Painting in '500 Venice*, 155.

37 Cantimori, *Eretici italiani*; Matheson, *Cardinal Contarini*, 181.

38 Jacobsen Schutte, "Periodization."

39 Tavuzzi, *Renaissance Inquisitors*, 210; Feci, "Pio V, papa (Michiele Antonio Ghislieri)." On the angry crowd that forced the inquisitorial commissioner Ghislieri to flee from Como in 1550, see C.F. Black, *Italian Inquisition*, 109. I am grateful to Professor Black for this reference to the biter bit.

40 I am grateful to Dermot Fenlon for this explanation of the Church's vision, which he offered me many years ago. On the changing religious preoccupations that took a single career from within one vote of the papal throne to the suspect of the Inquisition, see Fenlon, *Heresy and Obedience*; and on the high purpose of the Church, which looked a long way beyond how to respond to Protestantism, see Olin, *Catholic Reform*, 1–37.

41 See for example Bouwsma, *Republican Liberty*; Tedeschi, "Organisation"; and, with more caution, Prosperi, "L'inquisitore come confessore," 222; Seidel Menchi, "The Inquisitor as Mediator," 173, 178, 182, 190.

42 Grendler, *Roman Inquisition*; Pullan, *Jews of Europe*.
43 Pullan, *Jews of Europe*, 15–20.
44 "With the institution of the *Tre Savi sopra eresia* in 1547, co-operation between Church and State in the suppression of heresy entered a new phase"; Fahy, "The *Index Librorum Prohibitorum*," 54.
45 Tedeschi, "Organisation"; Pullan, *Jews of Europe*, 26–44; Jacobsen Schutte, *Aspiring Saints*, 26–41.
46 Pullan, *Jews of Europe*, 38; Wright, *Early Modern Papacy*, 137; Mullett, *Catholic Reformation*, 146; cf. Trevor-Roper, "Religion, the Reformation and Social Change," 42, which characterizes Sarpi as "the theorist of the one genuine mercantile republic which sought to remain within the Catholic Church"; Ranke, *History of the Popes*, vol. 1, 162. For a fascinating review of a different translation of the same work, see Macaulay, "Ranke's *History of the Popes*."
47 This is the suggestion of Klaassen, *Michael Gaismair*, 117.
48 Stella, "Ricerche sul socinianismo"; and, more expansively, Stella, *Dall'anabattesimo veneto al "Sozialevangelismus."*
49 Santo Uffizio, Archivio di Stato di Venezia (hereafter cited as SU), Processi, b. 14, Antonio dall'Oio, 26 October 1557. For a comparable list in the case of a carpenter named Antonio, who was part of the circle of both Lorenzo Lotto and Alessandro Caravia, see Firpo, *Artisti, gioiellieri, eretici*, 79–81.
50 SU, Processi, b. 14, Antonio dall'Oio, 3 March 1557.
51 SU, Processi, b. 14, Antonio dall'Oio, 26 and 28 March 1557.
52 Gordon, "Italy"; Seidel Menchi, "Italy"; Greengrass, *European Reformation*, 145–50.
53 See the magnificent and courageous synthesis by Christopher Black, *Italian Inquisition*.
54 SU, b. 13, Alessandro Caravia, 31 January 1558.
55 Black, *Italian Confraternities*, 62. I am grateful to Professor Black for pointing out this example.
56 For the many-sidedness of proceedings see Black, *Italian Inquisition*, passim.
57 In all references to the *processi* of the Holy Office I have followed Professor Black's strict injunction to avoid the term *trial* since the *processo* did not involve direct accusation. Instead, I have used the looser terms *proceedings*, *case*, *hearing*, or *investigation*.
58 SU, b. 24, Tentori Chiovaroli; "al presente se ne lavora da 20–22 fino a 24 milia alano inelquale ne vive uno grandissimo et infinito numero di poverissimi operarii che per sovention de quelli si spendano a Venetia oggi dì ducati 50,000 dicemo ducati 50,000 al mese et ogni mese che calano tutti male più poverissime et calamitosi persone di questa città si credemo ch'el sumo et grande iddio ne godda de tanto numero di poverissime persone si pascono si viveno dital arte." I am grateful to Nick Davidson for this reference.

59 The manufacture of wool was unusual in not coming under the jurisdiction of the Giustizia Vecchia. See Mackenney, *Tradesmen and Traders*, 14–15.

60 SU, b. 24; "Per che teniamo quelli lavoranti a salario a un tanto alanno ma anci più tosto mosi per usurpare il salario et per non voler far quel tanto quanto esi siano obligati anci ancor possiamo dire mosi per certi suoi comodi per poter la festa andar a balli a taverna a crapulare et più star tutto il giorno con le carte in mano adecipar ogni loro guadagno facendo poi patir le sue fameie di caxe che per avanti non pativano."

61 SU, b. 24; "sono ancor sforciati dalli tintori patroni se vogliono consegnare quel tanto che con tanti lor sudori hanno guadagnato in capo della settimana sono sforciati dico di lavorare ancor le dominiche S.me et altre feste solenne ... senza premio alcuno che non hanno pur tempo di udire le p.e feste le sacratissime messe."

62 Hill, "Uses of Sabbatarianism"; see also Duplessis and Howell, "Cases of Leiden and Lille."

63 Arti, b. 445, Pistori, fol. 59r, cap. 168.

64 Arti, b. 445, Pistori, fol. 60r.

65 SU, b. 28, Querela contra li pistori, che mangiano carne indeferentemente ... 1569, 18 Junii; "Non contenti del fare tante, e tante falsità, e ladrarie nel pane, che per più scovrirse infedeli, e luterani ardiscono li giorni della sacra santa madre chiesa vietati, cioè il venere, e sabbato, e tutti li giorni della quadragesima e altre vigilie, mangiar della carne, e dell'altre cose, come noi buoni christiani mangiamo la Domenica, e altri giorni non prohibiti."

66 SU, b. 49, Benedetto calzolaio Germania, 1582: 6 September, "uno hospital anticamente destinato per benefitio et comodo delli poveri calegari alemani"; 15 September, "nelle quali vi concorrevano multe persone alla devotione et facevano elemosine nella cassella a beneficio delli poveri amalati"; 20 October, "Per un tempo le stato governato bene mentre ci era una schola di alemani boni christiani. Doppoi ci introrno a governarlo li calegari venitiani che è la compagnia di S. Thomaso unita con questa di questo hospital."

67 SU, b. 61, Versemon Giovanni e compagni, not foliated: "scacciati vergognosissimamente"; then 31 May 1588, "infiniti chalegeri Todeschi partidi di Paesi luterani"; 25 August 1588, "sono sta li detti elletti in d.a scolla"; 18v, "per esser tutti squasi lutherani"; 22r, "hanno scominciato a depredar molti beni et giurisditioni di detta scolla"; and following documents: "fuziti impenitenti"; "havemmo la nostra maregula bellissima catholica"; "Nostro fradelo de schola et sia molto afecionado da nostra schola chon far dele lemosene specialmente sti zorni pasadi a dado un duchato in sua parte per far un pie de bronzo ala chroce d'arzento dela nostra schola."

68 SU, b. 7, Girolamo, lavoratore di perle et all., 11 October 1548; that the group met at Iseppo's house is alleged, 18 October 1548. See also Martin, *Venice's Hidden Enemies*, 91–3.

69 SU, b. 20, Gio. Batt. e Marcantonio speziali, 1565, fol. 10v; "che le indulgentie sono mercantie di preti et di frati et che sarebbe meglio quelli denari che si danno a preti e frati over monaci a darli a poveretti per amor di Dio."

70 Quoted in Firpo, *Artisti, gioiellieri, eretici*, 196; "mercato fanno di sepelir morti / come d'un sacco di lana o di pevere."

71 SU, b. 24, Cagnola, Francesco, Milanese, ormesiner, 1568, fols. 1r, 1v, 5v, 8v; Martin, *Hidden Enemies*, 91–2, 167, 214.

72 SU, b. 33, Domenico Longino, portador di farina, 14 and 16 November 1573.

73 SU, b. 16, Francesco speziale alla Duchessa, 13 July 1561.

74 SU, b. 26, Giacopo Saliceti, 1568, testimony of 14 October 1568, fol. 6r.

75 SU, b. 11, Tomaso bavelaro, testimonies of 15 September 1553 and 4 January 1553 (Venetian style).

76 SU, b. 12, Iseppo orese, testimony of 31 October 1555.

77 SU, b. 17, Girolamo de Luca samiter a S. Geremia, 20 March 1561.

78 SU, b. 39, Dugati Gaspare, testimony of Bortolomeo, 9 August 1575.

79 SU, b. 15, Domenego Gotardo spicier, fols. 1r–v, 8r.

80 Bossy, "Social History of Confession."

81 Bellavitis, *Identité, mariage, mobilité sociale*, 44; SU, b. 14, Valgrisio Vincenzio libraio, 1570, 60–1.

82 SU, b. 19, no. 8, Nicolai di Battista de Peliperiis, 1563, fol. 2r–v; "Ma ben le prego, essendo adesso il tempo delli pagamenti di Lione, et Bisanzone et delle sede, Le Sig.e Vostre habbino in consideratione questo et lasciarmi in libertà accioche io possa attendere a questi negocii donde depende tutto il traffego delle mercadantie del prefato Nicolo et dal mancar del qual traffico in questi presenti giorni et stagioni potrebbe nascere la total ruina sua et falimento."

83 SU, b. 19, no. 8, Nicolai di Battista de Peliperiis, 1563, fol. 5r.

84 SU, b. 19, no. 8, Nicolai di Battista de Peliperiis, 1563, fol. 14r.

85 SU, b. 19, no. 8, Nicolai di Battista de Peliperiis, 1563, fol. 15r; "ma come ho ditto altre volte trattando io di negocii come fanno molti altri mercadanti con diverse sorte di persone, non ho potuto impeder che non mi habbino scritto quel che è parso a loro et quel che sentivano loro."

86 SU, b. 29, Paulo Avanzi, fol. 31r; "Se con negocii par che habbia havuto prattiche di persone, che sono scoperte di cattive opinioni, io non li conoscevo per tali, ne li ho pratticato come simili, ma tutto mercantilmente, come anche hanno pratticato hebrei, Turchi et d'ogni sorte natione ... Ne i mercadanti può far di manco di negociare con ogn'uno. Et quando questo si volesse occupar e prohibire nel medesimo grado trovarete la maggior parte di negociatori."

87 SU, b. 24, Tomaso baveler, 1568, a deposition of 12 October 1569.

88 SU, b. 30, Alessandro Bonanome, fols. 1v, 2r; "quando vado alla messa ogni dì fazzo delle limosine quel tanto che mi sento et come vedo il bisogno, come die far i buoni christiani et si come Dio et la Madonna m'ispira."

89 Mackenney, *Tradesmen and Traders*, 193–5; Ambrosini, *Storie di patrizi*, 225; Rossato, "Religione e moralità."

90 Martin, *Hidden Enemies*, 131; 132n1 does not substantiate the identification, and there is no "Johan" Fugger identified in the index of Ehrenberg, *Capital and Finance*.

91 SU, b. 29, Giovanni Sfulgher, fol. 12r, 27 November 1571.

92 SU, b. 29, Giovanni Sfulgher, fol. 12r, 27 November 1571; "e huomo che fa molte elemosine per poveri della parochia, per la schuola del sacramento et per altri bisogni della Chiesa, et viene spesso a levar fanciullo del Battesimo."

93 Mackenney, "'A Plot Discover'd?'" and references; Greenblatt, *Renaissance Self-Fashioning*; Villari, *Baroque Personae*; Huxley, *Grey Eminence*, 249; and in the specific context of Inquisition investigations, Jacobsen Schutte, *Aspiring Saints*.

94 SU, b. 29, Giovanni Sfulgher, fol. 12r, 1571, 27 November 1571.

95 SU, b. 29, fols. 13r–14r, 10 November 1571; "ma vegi se vi piase, che ve mostrerò che bella Madonna et che belle cose l'ha fatto depenzer da basso, et in camera, et per tutto."

96 SU, b. 29, fol. 14r–v; "so ben che l'è limosinario, et fa delle limosine a monesterii de muneghe a Venetia, et a assai poveretti et quando qualche famegio o lavorator se parte, sempre oltra il suo salario e'l ghe dona una piastra et l'ha tolto per fia de anima una puttina fia de poverissima donna che li domandava limosina et la veste superbamente come fia de un signor."

97 SU, b. 29, fol. 14v; "Ve ho ditto anchora che lui sta poco qua et quando el vi è el dì drio si parte lui sta a Venetia, et quasi de continuo e'l sta in fontego di Thodeschi perche l'è mercadante Thodesco ricco et fa assai mercantie."

98 SU, b. 29, fols. 15v–16r.

99 SU, b. 29, fols. 16v–17r; "Per dio No. Ve dirò che sia puochi signori che sia de questa carità de far elemosine, et è persona che non teneria un bezzo de quel chel promette per tutto l'oro del mondo."

100 SU, b. 29, fols. 17r–18r; "Et par che questi angioletti siano in una nebbia adombrata, et non ho potuto ben discernere se detta nebbia sia stata fatta per adombrar o asconder la imagine che par che sia o fusse stato in mezzo di detti Angioletti"; "una devotissima Imagine della Madonna con il figliuolo in braccio, et S. Giovanni in forma di fanciullo appresso, et un Angioletto qual le appresenta alla Madonna et al figlio un cestello di fiori vaghi et di bellissimi frutti." See also Benzoni, *Venezia nell'età della controriforma*, 46–7.

101 SU, b. 31, Lorenzo Vex, 27 July 1566, fols. 3r–6r.

102 SU, b. 11, Zuangiacomo spader, 19 December 1551; "io non so che dire, che volete che dica[?], non c'è ne più, et più se fosse, più vi direi ... se fossero 10m vi li diria."

103 SU, b. 11, Zuangiacomo spader, fols. 19v, 25v, 27r; "Desidero che tutti siamo Christiani così li principi come li altri … in tutte le riunioni nostre pregamo che dio dia pace a tutti li principi potenti et signori … acciò che viviamo quietamente et pacificamente in ogni humiltà et castità."

104 SU, b. 70, Francesco Faggioni Padovano, 17 April 1610, in Padua; "Che il tutto vien dalla natura, la quale come produce gli animali, così produce et governa ancora noi"; "Che l'uomo è simile ad un orologio, che quando si rompe quel spaccio tiene il martellato non si sente più sonar, cosi anco morto l'huomo gli esce il fiato, ne più altro vi è."

105 For a clear affirmation of the significance of these conversations as history moved towards a Machiavellian moment, see Pecchioli, *Dal "mito" di Venezia all'"ideologia Americana,"* 3.

106 SU, b. 70, 1610–24, Francesco Faggioni Padovano per Luteranismo, 8 August 1628, "Petrus Nasus de Simone Francisci Bonzuarius strazzaruol seu sartore," "Zuan Battista Coltrezzus q. Christofori Venetus aurifex ad signum Persicarum in Rivoalto"; 13 August 1624, "Bartolomeus Barbetta Fructarolus in Rivoalto"; 22 August 1624, "Stefano Diana Orefice alle Tre Stelle."

107 Mousnier, "Exponents and Critics," 101.

108 SU, b. 70, 1610–24, Francesco Faggioni, 17 April 1610.

109 Black, *Church, Religion and Society*, 77–81.

110 Tramontin, "La Visita."

111 Chambers and Pullan, *Documentary History*, 206–8, 224.

112 Quoted in Tramontin, "La Visita," 466.

113 Ibid.

114 Prosperi, "Clerics and Laymen," 113, 130, 135.

115 Tramontin, "La Visita," 523.

116 The locations were the churches of Sant'Aponal, San Bartolomeo, San Benedetto, San Biagio, Sant'Eufemia, San Felise, Santa Fosca, San Giovanni Decollato, Santa Margherita, Santa Maria Mater Domini, Santa Maria Zobenigo, San Matteo e San Samuele, San Pantalon, San Raffaele Arcangelo, San Severo, San Silvestro, San Stae, and Santissima Trinità.

117 The churches surveyed were those of San Barnaba, San Bartolomeo di Castello (a case referred to the patriarch), San Cassiano, San Giacomo di Rialto (which was not a parish church), San Giovanni Elemosinario, San Giovanni del Tempio (a church that the visitors noted as a "Priorato"), Santa Giustina (where the Scuola del Venerabile dated from 1602), San Luca, and San Simeon e Giuda.

118 The altars were at the churches of Sant'Agnese, Sant'Agostino, Sant'Antonino, San Canciano, Santissima Croce, San Fantin, San Geminiano, San Giacomo dell'Orio,

San Giovanni in Bragora, San Giovanni Grisostomo, San Giovanni Novo, San Giuliano, San Gregorio, San Leonardo, San Lio, San Marcuola, Santa Maria Nova, San Martin, San Moise, San Niccolo dei Mendicoli, San Paternian, San Pietro di Castello, San Polo, San Provolo, Santa Sofia, San Stin, San Tomà, San Trovaso, San Vitale, and Santi Vito e Modesto.

119 The confraternitiies were at the churches of Santi Apostoli, San Baseggio, San Basso, Santa Lucia, Santa Maria della Trinità, San Marziale, San Matteo Apostolo, San Maurizio, and San Simeon Profeta.

120 These were the churches of Sant'Angelo, San Geremia, and Santa Maria Formosa.

121 PC O, fols. 339r–368r. The approval is registered at fol. 345r.

122 Firpo, *Artisti, gioiellieri, eretici*, 180.

123 Zanetti, *Descrizione*, 437.

124 Miani and Baldin, *Churches of Venice*, 61.

125 Mason Rinaldi, "Convenzioni," 216, 216n21.

126 In the camp of those who see the influence of the Council of Trent in directing artistic change see the bibliography herein for the works of Rodolfo Pallucchini, Stefania Mason Rinaldi, and Madlyn Kahr. Those who see no simple connection between a new assertiveness of the Church and artistic change are Paolo Prodi, Anna Palluchini, Tom Nichols, and David Rosand. For contrasting conclusions in the scholarship, and arguments for clear Tridentine influence, see Mason Rinaldi, "Palma il Giovane all'Ospedaletto dei Crociferi"; Mason Rinaldi, *Palma il Giovane*, 35. Cf. Rosand, *Painting in '500 Venice*, 159: "Tintoretto's piety can be considered Counter-Reformatory only in the most general way, if at all, and to discuss it with specific reference to the decrees of the Council of Trent may be somewhat misleading." The arguments of the sceptics seem far more persuasive in historical context and predominate in the exposition of this chapter. As a model for a study that stands on the cusp between unitary ideas of Reformation and Counter-Reformation this chapter draws encouragement from the method and conceptual framework of Firpo, *Artisti, gioiellieri, eretici*.

127 Tramontin, "La Visita," 477–81. See also Davidson, "Rome and the Venetian Inquisition"; Logan, "Ideal of the Bishop."

128 See Seneca, *Il doge Leonardo Donà*, 252, 252n1.

129 See also the fascinating insights on enclosure in Chojnacka, *Working Women*, 123, 135, 165n11.

130 Gullino, "Il rientro dei gesuiti," 422.

131 Details in Mackenney, *Tradesmen and Traders*, 218–32; Rapp, *Industry and Economic Decline*, 138–67, especially on the damage that taxation inflicted upon the economy; and, more generally, Wilson, "Taxation and the Decline of Empires."

132 Cozzi, "Paolo Sarpi tra Venezia e l'Europa"; Wootton, *Paolo Sarpi*; cf. Bouwsma, *Republican Liberty*; Bouwsma, "Venice, Spain, and the Papacy."

133 Mackenney, "'A Plot Discover'd'?," 204–7.
134 Viroli, *From Politics to Reason of State*; Wootton, *Paolo Sarpi*; Seneca, *Il doge Leonardo Donà*; Sarpi, *Potestà de' prencipi.*
135 Sarpi, "Sopra l'Officio dell'Inquisizione," 128.
136 Sarpi, *Potestà de' prencipi*, 47, 62.
137 Sarpi, *Potestà de' prencipi*, 17.
138 Sarpi, *Potestà de' prencipi*, 75–88; Sarpi, "Sulla publicazione di scritture malediche contra il governo," in *Scritti giurisdizionalistici*, 224.
139 De Vivo, "'Il vero termine.'"
140 Ullmann, *Political Thought*, 29, 87, 176; Ullmann, *Principles of Government*, 125, 157, 253–4; De Vivo, "'Il vero termine.'"
141 Seneca, *Il doge Leonardo Donà*, 253. On the absolutist thinking of Sarpi, see in particular Wootton, *Paolo Sarpi*, 113–17.
142 Ruskin, "The Relation between Michael Angelo and Tintoret," 83.
143 Rosand, *Painting in '500 Venice*, 130.
144 Rosand, *Painting in '500 Venice*, 140.
145 In a letter to his brother, Henry James also made a comparison of Shakespeare and Tintoretto. It is quoted in Lepschy, *Tintoretto Observed*, 125.
146 T. Nichols, *Tintoretto*, 18.
147 T. Nichols, *Tintoretto*, 22; Rosand, *Painting in '500 Venice*, 159. Penny, "John Ruskin and Tintoretto," 270, suggests the appeal of this quality to Tintoretto with reference to the San Rocco *Annunciation*.
148 T. Nichols, *Tintoretto*.
149 Ridolfi, *Le maraviglie d'arte*.
150 Ridolfi, *Life of Tintoretto*, esp. the introduction, 1–9; Humfrey, *Painting in Renaissance Venice*, 33.
151 Pullan, "Some Further Thoughts"; Wurthmann, "Council of Ten."
152 Pullan, "Some Further Thoughts," 274; Pullan, *Rich and Poor*, 99–131, "Pomp and Office"; Romano, *The Likeness of Venice*, 314.
153 Trevor-Roper, "Religion, the Reformation and Social Change," 24.
154 T. Nichols, *Tintoretto*, 104.
155 T. Nichols, *Tintoretto*, 101; Hope, "Titian as Court Painter."
156 Boschini, *La carta*.
157 Boschini, *La carta*, 343.
158 T. Nichols, *Tintoretto*, 103.
159 T. Nichols, *Tintoretto*, 95–6, 105.
160 Rosand, *Painting in '500 Venice*, 161.
161 The trade guilds were the tailors, fishmongers, boatmen, glassblowers, and linen sellers; the Scuole del Venerabile were those at the churches of San Cassiano, San Felice, San Marcuola, Santa Margherita, San Polo, San Severo,

San Simeon Grande, and San Trovaso; T. Nichols, *Tintoretto*, 145, 257, and note 68.

162 Niero, "Riforma Cattolica," 90–1; Prosperi, "Clerics and Laymen," 113, 130, and note 33 on confraternities.

163 Rosand, *Painting in '500 Venice*, 159; Worthen, "Tintoretto's Paintings"; Hills, "Piety and Patronage."

164 T. Nichols, *Tintoretto*, 80.

165 Rosand, *Painting in '500 Venice*, 155, 157.

166 This makes all the more remarkable the re-creative work on an earlier cycle; Humfrey, "The Bellinesque Life of St Mark Cycle." On Tintoretto's work at the Scuola di San Marco see Rosand, *Painting in '500 Venice*, 134–9.

167 Rosand, *Painting in '500 Venice*, 140.

168 Zanetti, *Descrizione*, 252.

169 T. Nichols, *Tintoretto*, 149–232; Rosand, *Painting in '500 Venice*, 145–52.

170 Wölfflin, *Principles of Art History*, 210, 211, 75, 43, 126; T. Nichols, *Tintoretto*, 31, 121; Rosand, *Painting in '500 Venice*, 139–59, esp. 153; for comparable qualities in another series by Tintoretto see Anna Pallucchini, "Considerazioni."

171 T. Nichols, *Tintoretto*, 84.

172 Ibid., 80.

173 Ibid., 214.

174 Ibid., 170.

175 Ibid., 162.

176 On the configurative rationale of the different chambers in a Venetian scuola see T.E. Cooper, *Palladio's Venice*, 264.

177 T. Nichols, *Tintoretto*, 219; Penny, "John Ruskin and Tintoretto," 270.

178 T. Nichols, *Tintoretto*, 204.

179 Ibid., 270.

180 Ibid., 223.

181 Ibid., 229.

182 Ibid., 182.

183 Ibid., 175.

184 Ibid., 170.

185 Ibid., 172.

186 Ibid., 168.

187 Ruskin, *Stones of Venice*, vol. 3, 306.

188 Ruskin, "Of Imagination Penetrative," in *Modern Painters*, part 3, section 2, chapter 3, 262: "In the shadow behind the cross, a man, riding on an ass colt, looks back to the multitude, while he points with a rod to the Christ crucified. The ass is feeding on the *remnants of withered palm-leaves*." See also Ruskin, *Modern Painters*, 263–5, 270–8; also quoted in Lepschy, *Tintoretto Observed*, 99.

189 I owe this insight to a marvellous lecture by Paul Hills, which, he tells me, remains unpublished. It is an evocative exercise to think of this picture when one hears the sound that the ropes make when a vaporetto ties up at a stop, and one feels the jolt of the boat against the floating wooden platform.
190 T. Nichols, *Tintoretto*, 73.
191 Ridolfi, *Maraviglie dell'arte*, 196–7; trans. 32–3.
192 Aretino's account of the Crucifixion had the crowd "shouting as they would shout in a theatre" (gridando come si grida nel teatro), *L'umanità di Cristo*, 198; Rosand, *Painting in '500 Venice*, 142–3.
193 Rosand, *Painting in '500 Venice*, 147–9; quotation from 149.
194 T. Nichols, *Tintoretto*, 132.
195 Mackenney, "Public and Private," 122–8; Sinding-Larsen, *Christ in the Council Hall*, plate 106.
196 Ridolfi, *Life of Tintoretto*, 67; Ridolfi, *Maraviglie dell'arte*, vol. 2, 242.
197 Zuccaro, *Il lamento della pittura*, 128. See also Lepschy, *Tintoretto Observed*, 33.
198 Boschini, *La carta*, 72.
199 Quoted in Lepschy, *Tintoretto Observed*, 113.
200 Quoted in Lepschy, *Tintoretto Observed*, 166.
201 Rosand, *Painting in '500 Venice*, 154, 159, 160, 161.
202 Symonds, *Renaissance in Italy*, vol. 3, 25, 274–8, quoted in Lepschy, *Tintoretto Observed*, 122.

Conclusion

1 *Aspetti e cause*, esp. Kellenbenz, "Le déclin de Venise"; Pullan, *Crisis and Change*; and the splendid synthesis in Rapp, *Industry and Economic Decline*; see also Rapp's other important reflections in "Real Estate and Rational Investment" and "Unmaking of Mediterranean Trade Hegemony." On developments in England and the Netherlands see Davis, *A Commercial Revolution*; Boxer, *Dutch Seaborne Empire*. On mercantilism see Wallerstein, *European World System*; Coleman, *Revisions in Mercantilism*; Coleman, editor's introduction to *Revisions in Mercantilism*; Coleman, "Eli Heckscher and the Idea of Mercantilism"; Heckscher, "Mercantilism"; Judges, "Idea of a Mercantile State"; van Klaveres, "Fiscalism, Mercantilism and Corruption"; Wilson, *Mercantilism*; Wilson, "The Other Face of Mercantilism"; Wilson, "'Mercantilism'"; Wilson, "Treasure and Trade Balances." The Venetian specialist Frederic C. Lane drew a persuasive general picture; see his essays "Economic Consequences" and "Heirs of Gustav von Schmoller." For the stirrings of some important rethinking of the problem, which loosens the identification of mercantile interests with the state, see Mauro, "Merchant Communities," esp. 259–60 on the "extreme case" of Venice.

2 Pullan, review of Rapp, *Industry and Economic Decline*. England's trade with Italy in general was in deficit until late in the eighteenth century; the deficit with Venice was some 100,000 pounds in 1696: see Pagano de Divitiis, *English Merchants*, 126–7, and Mackenney, review.
3 Cozzi, Knapton, and Scarabello, *La Repubblica di Venezia*, 87–147.
4 Rapp, *Industry and Economic Decline*, 167.
5 Cozzi, Knapton, and Scarabello, *La Repubblica di Venezia*, 117–28, 136–42, 556–9.
6 Beloch, *Bevölkerungsgeschichte Italiens*, vol. 3, 166. I am immensely grateful to Elise Thornley for tracking down this reference. Beloch, "Popolazione di Venezia"; Contento, "Il censimento della popolazione"; Beltrami, *Storia della popolazione di Venezia*. See also the concise summary in Rapp, *Industry and Economic Decline*, 32–42. For the relationship of population and economy see Zannini, "Un censimento." For a bracing caveat on statistics from a prestatistical era see Burke, "Classifying the People."
7 Finlay and Shearer, "Population Growth and Suburban Expansion," 40. For a more general set of comparisons of the populations of Europe's cities see Mols, "Population in Europe," 42–3.
8 On the epidemic in Padua see Cipolla, *Cristofano and the Plague*. The human horror requires a leap of the historical imagination and is even now evoked most vividly in Manzoni's literary recreation of Milan in *I Promessi Sposi*: the dying and the dead, the corpses and the wagons, the full repertoire of characters good and evil in the human drama of history.
9 Favilla and Rugolo, *Baroque Venice*.
10 Rapp, *Industry and Economic Decline*, 22–39.
11 Rapp, *Industry and Economic Decline*, 84.
12 Figures from Rapp, *Industry and Economic Decline*, 63 and 74.
13 Rapp, *Industry and Economic Decline*, 52–4, 149–54.
14 Rapp, *Industry and Economic Decline*, 22.
15 Cozzi, "Fortuna, e sfortuna"; Gullino, "Il rientro dei Gesuiti."
16 Cozzi, "Fortuna e sfortuna," 60–1.
17 Pirri, *L'Interdetto*, 3.
18 "… è stata la prima a mostrarsi disobediente a gl'ordini di questo Consiglio, havendo con insidiose maniere sedotto, così in questa Città, come in altre dello Stato nostro, altri Religiosi a seguitar il suo cattivo esempio"; quoted in Pirri, *L'Interdetto*, 26. Cozzi, "Fortuna e sfortuna," 77, asserts that the authorization could only come from a unanimous vote in the Senate.
19 Cozzi, "Fortuna e sfortuna," 87.
20 Quoted in Signorotto, "Il rientro dei Gesuiti," 419.
21 Gullino, "Il rientro dei Gesuiti," 426.
22 Pignatti, "Le pitture," 723.

23 Vio 578–88.528–38.
24 Vio 578.528 citing CBC and Arti, b. 719.
25 Vio 581.531.
26 Vio 579.529, citing CBC.
27 Vio 581.530, citing Arti b. 501. Pullan, *Rich and Poor*, 208; Mackenney, *Tradesmen and Traders*, 64–5.
28 Vio 583.532 and 583.533, citing CBC.
29 Vio 585.535, 587.536, 588.537, and 588.538, the latter two citing CBC.
30 Pirri, *L'Interdetto*, 3; Prosperi, "Clerics and Laymen," 135.
31 Sangalli, *Cultura, politica e religione*, 439–45.
32 Dalla Costa, "La chiesa di Santa Maria Assunta," 715, 721, 720; Bosel, "La chiesa dei Gesuiti," 689; Favilla and Rugolo, *Baroque Venice*, 239–49; Mâle, *L'art religieux*, 511.
33 Delumeau, *Vie économique et sociale de Rome*, vol. 1, 365–520, quotation from 516.
34 Pignatti, "Le pitture," 723–4.
35 Sherman, "Lost Venetian Church"; Pignatti, "Le pitture," 724–5; Mâle, *L'art religieux*, 3–4, 9–10, 510–12; Prodi, *Ricerca sulla teorica*, 7–9, 18.
36 FDS, 154–5; Delumeau, *Vie économique et sociale de Rome*, vol. 1, 824–43.
37 Cf. Rapp, *Industry and Economic Decline*.
38 Mackenney, *Tradesmen and Traders*, 219.
39 Vio, pp. 1–23.
40 Vio, p. 22.
41 The example comes from the Suffragio della Santissima Croce at San Geremia, PC N, fol. 19r.
42 PC S, fol. 106r.
43 PC V, fol. 324r.
44 Favilla and Rugolo, *Baroque Venice*.
45 Cowan, "New Families."
46 Pullan, "'Three Orders of Inhabitants"; Pullan, *Rich and Poor*, 268–9, 372–3; Pullan, "Occupations and Investments"; Pullan, "Service to the Venetian State." On the definition of the Venetian elite see the fascinating exercise by Burke, *Venice and Amsterdam*.
47 Cowan, "New Families."
48 Cozzi, Knapton, and Scarabello, *La Repubblica di Venezia*, 127.
49 Raines, "Strategie d'ascesa sociale," 305.
50 Quoted in Cowan, "New Families," 68.
51 Raines, "Strategie d'ascesa sociale," 283.
52 Pullan, *Rich and Poor*, 103.
53 Zannini, *Burocrazia e burocrati*, 12.
54 Bellavitis, *Identité, mariage, mobilité sociale*, 21.

55 Bellavitis, *Identité, mariage, mobilité sociale*, 39.
56 Ibid., 154; see also Newett, "Sumptuary Laws"; Bistort, *Il Magistrato alle Pompe*.
57 Braudel, *The Mediterranean*, vol. 2, 729–34.
58 Cowan, "New Families," 69.
59 Mackenney, *Tradesmen and Traders*, 94–6.
60 Bellavitis, *Identité, mariage, mobilité sociale*, 60–1.
61 Ibid., 243.
62 Ibid., 244.
63 Ibid., 258 and 258n23.
64 Cowan, *Marriage, Manners and Mobility*, 86–7.
65 Raines, "Strategie d'ascesa sociale," 299–302 and 302n51.
66 Rapp, *Industry and Economic Decline*, 102.
67 Chojnacka, *Working Women*, 11, 14, and appendix, 141.
68 Mackenney, "Guilds of Renaissance Venice," 37–9.
69 Cinque Savi alla Mercantia, b. 164, specchi-stallaggio, document of 17 December 1698; "In questo lavoro a differenza dell'altre manifatture giovini d'età forti e robusti che gli attuali per l'incomodo delle sofferte fatiche e per la natural declinatione dell'età che si va giornalmente avanzando vienano insuficienti al laborioso impiego."
70 Cinque Savi alla Mercantia, b. 164, specchi-stallaggio, document of 17 December 1698; "riuscisse in meno perfetti, là dove all'incontro gli altri tutti passando con lunga servitù di tempo limitato dale leggi ai gradi prescritti di garzone, lavorante e di cappo maestro con le prove che previe sono tenuti fare vengono ad apprendere la cognitione e prattica necessaria riuscendo con tali formalità maestri di perfettion."
71 Cinque Savi alla Mercantia, b. 164, specchi-stallaggio, document of 17 December 1698; "… non meno alla preservatione d'una fabrica in altri tempi florida, et abbondante, ma all'aumento del negotio e de diritti ad oggetto che recisi dalla radice i disordini e rimove dalla sua sorgente la causa, ne susseguiti poi il buon effetto, che sarà risultare con profitto …
72 Cinque Savi alla Mercantia, b. 164, specchi-stallaggio, document of 17 December 1698; "… trovandosi l'arte stessa a causa del scarso numero di Operarii che in essa s'esercitano assai declinante, et potendo sempre più conspirare alla sua annichilatione … prestato il loro servitio et terminato il periodo degl'anni cinque habbino a passare secondo l'antica pratica all'impiego di lavoranti et di là a due anni con l'esperienza e cognitione che haverano appreso avanzarsi al grado di Cappi Maestri."
73 Arti, b. 501, sartori, capitoli e parti, 1492–1683, fols. 3v–4r, 13 September 1520, on obligatory "prove" for sons of masters, and the separate test for "zupponi" and "calze"; fol. 10v, 20 September 1543[?], on the "seconda prova" that any gastaldo

had to have taken; fol. 79r, 22 August 1557, on separate "prove" for each type of clothing.

74 Cinque Savi alla Mercanzia, b. 164, specchi-stallaggio, document of 15 July 1710.

75 Brewer, *Sinews of Power*; Wilson, *England's Apprenticeship*; Wilson, *The Dutch Republic*; Boxer, *Dutch Seaborne Empire*. It is perhaps no accident that the earliest English joint-stock venture, the Muscovy Company of 1552, was the brainchild of John Cabot, a Venetian (albeit of Genoese origin) and a member of the class of cittadini; K.R. Andrews, *Trade, Plunder and Settlement*, 68–9; Benzoni, "Venezia ai tempi dei Caboto."

76 Bacon, "Of Seditions and Troubles," 45, or in his *Works*, vol. 3, 322.

77 Quoted in Howard, *War in European History*, 47, but note the caution of the attribution of these words to Monck in Howard, *War in European History*, 145n8.

78 The contrast has something of a penumbra: see Collinson, "Monarchical Republic." Sir Thomas Smith, *De Republica Anglorum*, reminds in its title page of 1582 that "respublica" could be identified with any type of state: "De Republica Anglorum. The maner of Gouernement or Policie of the Realme of England." See also Fink, *Classical Republicans*.

79 On Shakespeare and the mentalities of the era see Bate, *Soul of the Age*, which makes a strong case in its title, and Kermode, *Age of Shakespeare*. On Shakespeare's general Italian connections see especially Yates, *Occult Philosophy*; also Marrapodi, Hoenslaars, Cappuzzo, and Franzon Santucci, *Shakespeare's Italy*; R. Andrews, "Shakespeare and Italian Comedy"; Clubb, "Italian Stories on the Stage"; Clubb, "Il teatro manieristico italiano"; Holderness, *Shakespeare and Venice*; H. Brown, "Shakespeare and Venice"; Lombardo, "The Veneto"; Mullini, "Streets, Squares and Courts"; Salingar, "The Idea of Venice"; Matheson, "Venetian Culture"; Clough, "Love and War in the Veneto." On *The Merchant of Venice* see Pullan, *Shakespeare's Venice*; Mulryne, "History and Myth"; Roth, "The Background of Shylock."

80 Tretiak, "*The Merchant of Venice* and the 'Alien Question'"; Cerasano, *William Shakespeare's "The Merchant of Venice"*; Kaplan, *Texts and Contexts*; McDonald, *Bedford Companion*; Shakespeare, *The Merchant of Venice*, ed. Drakakis; Hill, "Definition of a Puritan."

81 As a complement to the introduction to this book see Braudel, "Amsterdam," in his *Perspective of the World*, 175–276. On the connection of Venetian Jews to Amsterdam (and Haarlem) see Israel, *European Jewry*, 63, and also Trevor Roper, "General Crisis," 81, 89; Haitsma Mulier, *Myth of Venice*. For contrasts in the structures of the two cities' elites see also Burke, *Venice and Amsterdam*.

82 Marvell, "The Character of Holland" (1653), in *Poems*, 253, lines 71–4; also quoted in Wilson, *Dutch Republic*, 32. On the continuing importance of the tradition that had linked commerce and religion since the thirteenth century, see Margaret

Spufford, "Literacy, Trade and Religion." I thank Adam Fox for this important reference.

83 Favilla and Rugolo, *Baroque Venice*, 12–15, 16–29.

84 Ibid., 30–4.

85 Ibid., 37.

86 Ibid., 239–55.

87 Rousseau, *Les confessions*, vol. 2, 122–4, quoted in English in *Blue Guide Literary Companion*, 167. See also Ellis, *Rousseau's Venetian Story*, 119–20; Rousseau's apparent indifference to painting and architecture may exaggerate the abstraction of his musical experience, 125–6.

88 A. Smith, *Theory of Moral Sentiments*, 63.

89 Clark, *Civilisation*, program 1, "By the Skin of our Teeth"; Clark, *Civilisation*, 1. Clark's justification remains persuasive: "If I had to say which was telling the truth about a society, a speech by a Minister of Housing or the actual buildings put up in his time, I should believe the buildings."

90 Ruskin, "St Mark's Rest."

91 Ruskin, "St Mark's Rest," 197.

92 Hilton, *John Ruskin*, 632.

93 Ruskin, "St Mark's Rest," 203.

94 For cultural change in the period see Koenigsberger, "Decadence or Shift?"; Trevor-Roper, "General Crisis," 50; G.N. Clark, *Seventeenth Century*, 1; Muir, *Culture Wars*; Selfridge-Field, *Venetian Instrumental Music*; Redondi, *Galileo*; de Santillana, *Crime of Galileo*; D. Wootton, *Galileo*; Bouwsma, *Waning of the Renaissance*; Sypher, *Four Stages of Renaissance Style*; Haydn, *Counter-Renaissance*.

95 Glixon, *Honoring God and the City*; Arnold, *God, Caesar and Mammon*; Constable, "'Figlie del Coro'"; Giovanni Gabrieli, *Music for San Rocco, 1608*, dir. Paul McCreesh, 1996, Archiv 449, 180–2, disc and DVD.

96 Bolt, *Librettist of Venice*.

97 See Levey, *Painting in Eighteenth-Century Venice*, 110–13.

Bibliography

Manuscript Sources

Archivio di Stato di Venezia

INDEX: PROVVEDITORI DI COMUN

b. 272–83, Matricule scuole e sovegni, registri n–z; aa; bb

Registro N. Sestiere di Cannaregio, vol.I
Registro O. Sestiere di Cannaregio, vol. II
Registro P. Sestiere di Castello, vol. I
Registro Q. Sestiere di Castello, vol. II
Registro R. Sestier di S. Croce, vol. I
Registro S. Sestier di S. Croce, vol. II
Registro T. Sestier di San Marco, vol. I
Registro U. Sestier di San Marco, vol. II
Registro V. Sestier di San Marco, vol. III
Registro Z. Sestiere di San Nicolo [Dorsoduro], vol. I
Registro AA. Sestiere di San Nicolo [Dorsoduro], vol. II
Registro BB. Sestiere di San Polo

STATUTES OF THE SCUOLE PICCOLE IN THE REGISTERS OF THE PROVVEDITORI DI COMUN

Note: The statues are alphabetical by title (type of scuola) and indicate parish (sestier) and date of foundation or of statute, followed by folios. In cases where there is imprecision regarding exact details of a confraternity, especially with regard to date of foundation, a note of explanation is included.

Abbreviations:

Cann.	Cannaregio
Cast.	Castello
S. Croce	Santa Croce
SM	San Marco
S. Nic.	San Nicolo [Dorsoduro]
S. Polo	San Polo

Angelo Custo (scuola). Santi Apostoli (Cann.). 1657 [Gramigna and Perissa, *Scuole*, 112–13, gives foundation date as a suffraggio as 1557]. N 287r–303r.

Beata Chiara da Montefalco (scuola). San Stefano (SM). 1635. ["Instituta novamente" after expressing fear of extinction in 1634. T 224r]. T 224r–230v.

Beata Vergine (scuola). Angelo Raffaele (S. Nic.). 1553? [refers to "mariegola vecchia," Z 191v, and is followed by a vote recorded in 1553, Z 193v]. Z 191v–228r.

Beata Vergine (scuola). San Basilio [San Baseggio] (S. Nic.). 1514. AA 73r–84r.

Beata Vergine (scuola). San Giuliano [San Zulian] (SM). 1626. T 209r–224r.

Beata Vergine (scuola). San Polo (S. Polo). 1399. BB 103r–136r.

Beata Vergine (scuola). San Salvador [San Salvatore] (SM). 1439. T 289v–344r.

Beata Vergine (sovvegno). Sant'Eufemia della Giudecca (S. Nic.). 1582. AA 455r–467r.

Beata Vergine (scuola). Santa Maria Maggiore (S. Croce). 1501. S 327r–367r. [Gramigna and Perissa, *Scuole*, 66–7, give this as the Scuola della Beata Vergine Assunta from 1507 and confuse it with the *scuola degli strazzaroli*.]

Beata Vergine Annuntiata (scuola). San Cassiano (S. Croce). 1615. S 185r–207r.

Beata Vergine Annunciata (scuola). Sant'Aponal [Sant'Apollinare] (S. Polo). 1581. BB 679r–690r.

Beata Vergine Annuntiata (scuola). Santa Maria dei Servi (Cann.). 1354. O 156r–182r.

Beata Vergine Annunciata (sovvegno). San Vitale [San Vidal] (SM). 1679. U 411r–421r.

Beata Vergine Annunciata [Annunciatione della Beata Vergine Maria] (scuola). San Giovanni in Bragora [San Zuan in Bragora] (Cast.). 1638. Q 322r–331r.

Beata Vergine Annuntiata [or Assunta?] (scuola). Santa Maria Mater Domini (S. Croce). 1423 [renewed 1532] S 207r–226r.

Beata Vergine Annuntiata de' Zotti (scuola). Sant'Angelo [Sant'Anzolo] (SM). 1392. T 364r–439r.

Beata Vergine Assunta (scuola). San Gieremia (Cann.). 1602. N 372r–386r.

Beata Vergine Assunta (scuola). San Stefano Confessor [San Stin] (S. Polo). 1530. ["principiada," 1525]. BB 331r–346.

Beata Vergine Assunta (scuola). Sant'Eustachio [San Stae] (S. Croce). 1400. ["et ristaurata," 1726]. R101r–135r.

Beata Vergine Assunta (scuola). Santi Simeon e Tadeo [San Simeon Piccolo] (S. Croce). 1590. R 202r–218r.
Beata Vergine Assunta (sovvegno). San Giacomo dell'Orio (S. Croce). 1713. S 257r– 273r.
Beata Vergine Assunta (sovvegno). Santa Fosca (Cann.). 1679. O 628r–630r.
Beata Vergine Assunta [Assuntione della BV] (scuola). Santa Sofia (Cann.). 1589. [Statute refers to an earlier scuola.] O 442r–469r.
Beata Vergine Concetione de Lavoranti Pistori (sovvegno). San Mattio [San Mattia] (S. Polo). 1660. BB 273r–293r.
Beata Vergine d'Humiltà (scuola). San Leone [San Lio] (Cast.). 1350. Q 535r–565r.
Beata Vergine da Lonigo (scuola). San Giobbe (Cann.). 1653. O 541r–553r.
Beata Vergine de Schiavi (scuola). Sant'Antonino (Cast.). 1689. P 695v–end.
Beata Vergine degli Angeli (scuola). Santa Trinità (Cast.). 1621. Q 69r–79r.
Beata Vergine degli Angeli (sovvegno). Santa Trinità (Cast.). 1720. [Records show that the Council of Ten gave permission in 1620, Q 411r.] Q 411r– 423r.
Beata Vergine dei Sette Dolori (scuola). San Paternian (SM). 1617. T 344r–364r
Beata Vergine dei Sette Dolori (sovvegno [also referred to as "confraternità sive suffragio"]). San Stefano Confessor [San Stin] (S. Polo). 1708. BB 616r–637r.
Beata Vergine del Carmine (sovvegno). San Pietro (Cast.). 1725. P 680v–691r.
Beata Vergine del Carmine (suffragio). Sant'Apollinare [Sant'Aponal] (S. Polo). 1710. BB 520r–554r.
Beata Vergine del Parto (scuola). San Gregorio (S. Nic.). 1663. Z 295r–300r.
Beata Vergine del Parto (scuola). San Leonardo [San Lunardo] (Cann.). 1615 [meetings from 1598, N 49r]. N 49r–60r.
Beata Vergine del Parto (sovvegno). San Leonardo [San Lunardo] (Cann.). 1674. O 1v– 19r.
Beata Vergine del Parto (sovvegno). Santa Maria Mater Domini (S. Croce). 1713. S 91r– 105r.
Beata Vergine del Parto [Adorante il Suo Divin Parto] (sovvegno). Spirito Santo (S. Nic.). 1707. Z 328r–335r.
Beata Vergine del Rosario (scuola). San Mattio [San Mattia] (S. Polo). 1660. BB 241r– 251r.
Beata Vergine del Rosario (scuola). Sant'Angelo [Sant'Anzolo] (SM). 1702. V 97v–103r.
Beata Vergine del Rosario [Santissimo Rosario] (scuola). San Domenico (Cast.). 1619. Q 428r–453r.
Beata Vergine del Rosario [Santissimo Rosario] (scuola [became a Scuola Grande in 1765; Gramigna and Perissa, *Scuole*, 100]). San Zanipolo (Cast.). 1575. Q 32r– 53r.
Beata Vergine del Rosario [Santissimo Rosario] (scuola [became a sovvegno in 1698, V 250v]). San Paternian (SM). 1669. V 244r–281r.
Beata Vergine del Rosario [Santissimo Rosario] (scuola and sovvegno). Sant'Antonin (Cast.). 1706. P 378r–384r.

Beata Vergine del Terremoto (scuola). San Bartolomeo [San Bortolomeo] (SM). 1513 [renewal and amalgamation, 1605, V 104v]. V 103r–128r.

Beata Vergine della Celestia (scuola). Santa Maria della Celestia (Cast.). 1337. Q 478r– 501r.

Beata Vergine della Centura (scuola). San Stefano (SM). 1581. V 432r–466r. [See also Gramigna and Perissa, *Scuole*, 55.]

Beata Vergine della Natività (scuola). San Giovanni Decollato [San Zuan Degolà] (S. Croce). 1545. S 247r–257r.

Beata Vergine della Nattività (scuola). San Trovaso [Santi Gervasio e Protasio] (S. Nic.). 1546. Z 61v–85r.

Beata Vergine della Neve (scuola). San Girolamo (Cann.). 1664. O 396r–408r.

Beata Vergine della Neve (scuola). San Luca (SM). 1606. T 1r–15r.

Beata Vergine della Pace (scuola). San Zanipolo [Santi Giovanni e Paolo] (Cast.). 1546. Q 79r–98r. [See also SP b. 177, mariegola 1546–1801; Gramigna and Perissa, *Scuole*, 103.]

Beata Vergine della Pace (scuola). Santa Croce (S. Croce). 1713. S 407r–421v.

Beata Vergine della Presentazione (scuola). San Gieremia (Cann.). 1585. N 339r–352r.

Beata Vergine della Purificazione (scuola). Sant'Angelo [Sant'Anzolo] (SM). 1609. T 551r– end.

Beata Vergine della Purificazione [Purification della Beata Vergine] (scuola). San Giovanni in Oglio [San Zuan Novo] (Cast.). 1620. Q 172r–184r.

Beata Vergine della Salute (scuola). Spirito Santo (S. Nic.). 1638. Z 181r–191v.

Beata Vergine delle Gratie (sovvegno). San Paternian (SM). 1696. T 533r–551r.

Beata Vergine delle Grazie (scuola). San Marcuola [Santi Ermagora e Fortunato] (Cann.). 1607 [but claims a foundation of 1596, O 19v]. O 19r–30v.

Beata Vergine delle Grazie (scuola). Santa Marina (Cast.). 1692. P 647r–656r.

Beata Vergine delle Grazie (sovvegno). San Trovaso [Santi Gervasio e Protasio] (S. Nic.). 1704. Z 263r–288r.

Beata Vergine di Loreto (scuola). San Giacomo dall'Orio (S. Croce). 1655. R 218r–224r.

Beata Vergine di Loreto (sovvegno). Sant'Anna (Cast.). 1723. P 691r–695v.

Beata Vergine di Pietà (scuola). San Cancian (Cann.). 1597. O 598r–614r.

Beata Vergine di Pietà (scuola). San Giobbe (Cann.). 1580. O 553r–564r. [See also Gramigna and Perissa, *Scuole*, 124.]

Beata Vergine di Pietà (scuola). San Silvestro (S. Polo). 1622. BB 225r–241r.

Beata Vergine di Pietà (scuola). Sant'Alvise (Cann.). 1622? [date of first meeting]. O 408r–426r.

Beata Vergine e San Cristoforo de Mercanti (scuola). Santa Maria dell'Orto (Cann.). 1261. N 561r–676r. [See also SP bb. 406–13, 420, 436; Gramigna and Perissa, *Scuole*, 118–19.]

Beata Vergine e San Matteo (sovvegno). San Samuele (SM). 1408 ["rinovata e fondata," 1580]. U 368r–411r.

Beata Vergine e Sant'Osvaldo (sovvegno). San Silvestro (S. Polo). 1727. BB 472r–485r.
Beata Vergine e Santa Maria Elisabetta (scuola). San Severo (Cast.). 1635. Q 343v–353r.
Beata Vergine Maria (scuola). San Simeon Profeta [San Simeon Grande] (S. Croce). 1535. S 72r–91r.
Beata Vergine Maria della Celestia (sovvegno). Santa Maria della Celestia [?] (Cast.). 1707. Q 25r–32r.
Beata Vergine Maria di Pietà (suffragio). San Zuan in Bragora [San Giovanni in Bragora] (Cast.). 1662? [date of first entry]. Q 121r–141r.
Beata Vergine Nattività (scuola). San Barnaba (S. Nic.). 1400. AA 45r–61v.
Beata Vergine Nattività (sovvegno). Sant'Agnese (S. Nic.). 1588. Z 545r–end.
Beata Vergine, Sant'Iseppo, e Santa Cattarina da Siena (suffragio). Santa Maria Zobenigo [Santa Maria del Giglio] (SM). 1710. V 150r–175r.
Buona Morte (compagnia). San Silvestro (S. Polo). 1707. BB 554r–572r.
Buona Morte (scuola). San Giminiano (SM). 1705. T 494r–503r.
Buona Morte (scuola). Sant'Antonino (Cast.). 1712. Q 271r–278r.
Concet[t]ion della Beata Vergine (scuola). San Giacomo dell'Orio (S. Croce). 1535. S 16r– 51r.
Concet[t]ion della Beata Vergine (scuola). Santa Maria Assunta [Gesuiti] (Cann.). 1519. O 309r–339r. [See also Gramigna and Perissa, *Scuole*, 108–9.]
Concettion della Beata Vergine (scuola). Santa Maria dei Frari [Frari] (S. Polo). 1498. [Statute from 1513, BB 136v.] BB 136r–149r.
Concet[t]ion della Beata Vergine de Ciechi (scuola). San Moise (SM). 1315. U 462r– 573r.
Concet[t]ion della Beata Vergine Maria (scuola). San Francesco della Vigna (Cast.). 1582. Q 590r–627r.
Corpo di Cristo (scuola). San Gregorio (S. Nic.). 1523. AA 381r–416r.
Corpo di Cristo (scuola). San Lucca (SM). 1511. T 149r–191r.
Figliole de remeri dell'Arsenal (sovvegno). San Bartolomeo [San Bortolomeo] (SM). 1599. Q 331r–343v.
Inventione della Santissima Croce (scuola). San Moise (SM). 1619 [founded 1616, Q 334v, but the statute dates from 1619]. V 324r–351r.
Madonna (scuola). San Felice [San Felise] (Cann.). 1654. O 572r–582r.
Madonna (scuola). San Marzilian [San Marziale] (Cann.). 1420 [date of statute; scuola claimed to date from 1402]. N 413r–476r. [See also Gramigna and Perissa, *Scuole*, 114.]
Madonna (scuola). Santa Fosca (Cann.). 1624. O 42r–51r.
Madonna (scuola). Santa Maria Formosa (Cast.). 1523 [date of new mariegola, which claimed that scuola had existed since 1439, P 136v]. P 131r–160r.
Madonna (sovvegno). Santa Maria Formosa (Cast.). 1594. P 664r–680v.
Madonna degli Angeli (scuola). Angelo Raffaele (S. Nic.). 1628. AA 348r–363v.

Marangoni dell'Arsenale (sovvegno). San Filippo Giacomo (Cast.). 1541. P 312r–347r.
Morti (suffragio). San Mattio [San Mattia] (S. Polo). 1675. BB 430r–450r.
Morti (suffragio). Sant'Agnese (S. Nic.). 1663 [permission granted in 1656, AA 1r]. AA 1r–18r.
Morti (suffragio). Santi Vito e Modesto [San Vio] (S. Nic.). 1661. Z 111r–125r.
Morti sotto la invocazione di Maria Vergine del Pianto (suffragio). Sant'Eufemia della Giudecca (S. Nic.). 1661. AA 437r–455r.
Nattività della Beata Vergine (confraternità). San Maurizio (SM). 1636. V 172r–191r.
Nattività della Beata Vergine (scuola). San Benetto [San Benedetto] (SM). 1613. T 258r- 268r.
Natt[ivi]tà della Beata Vergine (scuola). Sant'Apollinare [Sant'Aponal] (S. Polo). 1532 [but founded in 1526 and came to this church in 1528]. BB 361r–376r.
Nat[t]ività della Beata Vergine (scuola). Santi Apostoli (Cann.). 1589. N 237r–277r.
Presentazione della Beata Vergine (scuola). Sant'Ubaldo [San Boldo] (S. Polo). 1533. BB 572r–592r.
Redentor (sovvegno). San Severo (Cast.). 1693. Q 278r–312v.
San Bellino (sovvegno). San Gregorio (S. Nic.). 1635. Z 288r–295r.
San Bernardino (scuola). San Giobbe (Cann.). 1450. O 124r–156r.
San Biaggio (sovvegno). San Biasio [San Biagio] (Cast.). 1595. Q 385r–401r.
San Carlo (scuola). San Lunardo [San Leonardo] (Cann.). 1611. N 139r–151r.
San Cristoforo (scuola). Sant'Agostin (S. Polo). 1663. BB 44r–52r.
San Cristoforo (scuola). Santa Maria Assunta [Giesuiti] (Cann.). 1346. N 676r–699r.
San Cristoforo (sovvegno). Santa Maria Assunta [Giesuiti] (Cann.). 1709 [statute describes the sovvegno as "ravivato" in 1705, and "fondato" in 1567 as "fratellanza e sovegno," N 321r]. N 318r–325r.
San Diego (scuola). San Giobbe (Cann.). 1610. N 151r–168r.
San Domenico (scuola). San Domenico (Cast.). 1636. Q 565r–590r.
San Domenico (scuola). San Zanipolo [Santi Giovanni e Paolo] (Cast.). 1649. Q 53r–69r.
San Felice (scuola). San Felice [San Felise] (Cann.). 1541 [statute drawn up in 1538, O 185r]. O 182r–193r.
San Filippo Neri (suffragio). San Gregorio (S. Nic.). 1653. AA 416r–437r.
San Francesco (scuola). Santa Maria dei Frari [Frari] (S. Polo). 1346 [in 1437 the general of the Franciscan order gave permission for the establishment of a scuola "in campo iuxta scola sancti ambrosii" (in the square next to the scuola of Saint Ambrose), BB 293r–v]. BB 293r–331r.
San Francesco di Paola (scuola). San Trovaso [Santi Gervasio e Protasio] (S. Nic.). 1559. Z 300r–309r.
San Francesco di Paola (sovvegno). Santa Sofia (Cann.). 1605. N 219r–237r.
San Francesco di Paola (sovvegno). Santi Simeon e Tadeo [San Simeon Piccolo] (S. Croce). 1592. S 293r–313r.

San Gaetano (sovvegno). Santa Maria Maddalena (Cann.). 1707. N 201r–219r.
San Gaetano (suffragio). San Fantin (SM). 1690. U 346r–368r.
San Giacomo (scuola). San Giacomo dell'Orio [moving there at an unspecified date from San Salvador] (S. Croce). 1422. R 323r–333r.
San Giobbe (scuola). San Giobbe (Cann.). 1395. N 124r–139r.
San Giovanni Battista (scuola). San Giovanni Decolato [San Zuan Degolà] (S. Croce). 1340. R 333r–350r.
San Giovanni Battista (scuola). San Giovanni del Tempio [dei Cavalieri di Malta] [dei Furlani] (Cast.). 1354. P 546v–579v.
San Giovanni Battista (scuola). San Marcuola [Santi Ermagora e Fortunato] (Cann.). 1413. N 352r–372r.
San Giovanni Battista (sovvegno). San Tomaso [San Tomà] (S. Polo). 1726. BB 674r– 679r.
San Giovanni Battista (sovvegno). Santa Sofia (Cann.). 1685. N 303r–318r.
San Giovanni Battista [S. Zuanne] (sovvegno della scuola). San Giovanni alla Giudecca (S. Nic.). 1679. AA 490r–515v.
San Giovanni Elemosinario (scuola). San Giovanni in Bragora [San Zuan in Bragora] (Cast.). 1616. Q 662r–671r.
San Girolamo (scuola). San Girolamo (Cann.). 1504 [first date in statute, O 385r]. O 380r–396r.
San Girolamo (sovvegno). San Girolamo (Cann.). 1679. O 564r–572r.
San Giuseppe (scuola). San Silvestro (San Polo). 1499 [approval came only in 1515, BB 80r]. BB 70r–103r.
San Giuseppe (scuola). Santa Fosca (Cann.). 1642 [referring back to a "rinovata devotione" of 1580, O 517v]. O 517r–527r.
San Giuseppe (sovvegno). Corpus Domini (Cann.). 1705. N 386r–396r.
San Giuseppe degli Agonizanti (suffragio). San Basilio [San Baseggio] (S. Nic.). 1708. AA 61v–73r.
San Gottardo (scuola). Sant'Aponal [Sant'Apollinare] (S. Polo). Before 1394 [date of removal from San Mattio di Rialto, BB 690r]. BB 690r–end.
San Gregorio (scuola). San Gregorio (S. Nic.). 1324. Z 161r–181r.
San Leonardo (scuola). San Leonardo [San Lunardo] (Cann.). Trecento? [based on the language of the statute]. N 699r–713r.
San Liberal (sovvegno). Santa Maria Maddalena (Cann.). 1665. N 713r ff.
San Lorenzo (scuola). San Barnaba (S. Nic.). 1400. Z 125r–142r.
San Lorenzo Giustinian (sovvegno). Santa Sofia (Cann.). 1580. N 476r–491r.
San Lunardo (scuola). San Salvador [San Salvatore] (SM). 1423? [Vio 461,408]. U 1r– 33r.
San Magno (scuola). San Gieremia (Cann.). 1598 [but refers to an old statute of 1423, O 32r]. O 31r–41v.
San Martin (scuola and sovvegno). San Martin (Cast.). 1335. Q 353r–385r.

San Mattia (scuola). San Bartolomeo [San Bortolomeo] (SM). 1247. V 389r–432r.

San Maurizio e San Gallo degli Albanesi (scuola). San Maurizio (SM). 1442 [newly revised 1552, U 33r]. U 33r–105v.

San Michiel Arcangelo (scuola). Santa Maria dell'Orto (Cann.). 1452. O 582r–598r.

San Michiel Arcangelo (sovvegno). Santa Maria dell'Orto (Cann.). 1706. O 227r–257r. [See also Venerabile, Santa Sofia.]

San Nicheta Martire (sovvegno). San Nicolo [dei Mendicoli] (S. Nic.). 1696. AA 289r- 304r.

San Nicola (scuola e sovvegno). San Stefano (SM). 1652. V 134r–150r.

San Nicolo (scuola). San Nicolo [dei Mendicoli] (S. Nic.). 1337. Z 142r–161r.

San Nicolo (scuola). San Salvador [San Salvatore] (SM). 1425. T 230v–248r.

San Nicolo (scuola). Santa Maria dei Carmini (S. Nic.). 1319. AA 91r–128r. [See also Gramigna and Perissa, *Scuole*, 70.]

San Nicolo (sovvegno). San Nicolo [dei Mendicoli] (S. Nic.). 1586. AA 256r–271r.

San Pasqual (suffragio). San Francesco della Vigna (Cast.). 1663. Q 141r–162r.

San Pietro d'Alcantara (sovvegno). Santa Maria Maddalena (Cann.). 1708. O 64r–79r.

San Pio Papa (scuola). San Provolo (Cast.). 1643 [until 1646, then to San Basso, Q 314v]. Q 312v–322r.

San Polo (sovvegno [also desribed as "fraternam sive scollam," BB 1r]). San Polo (S. Polo). 1545. BB 1r–44r.

San Raffaele e Nicheta (scuola). Angelo Raffaele (S. Nic.). 1580 [other references suggest a foundation of 1280 (AA 320r), 1351 (AA 323v), and 1470 (AA 324r)]. AA 320r–331r.

San Rocco (scuola). San Cancian (Cann.). 1592. O 493r–507r.

San Rocco [e San Nicolo] (scuola). San Giuliano [San Zulian] (SM). 1496. U 209r–227r.

San Sebastiano (scuola). San Giacomo dell'Orio (S. Croce). 1463 [new mariegola 1553, R 161r]. R 161r–202r.

San Sebastiano (scuola and sovvegno [also "sovegno" only, Z 9v]). San Sebastiano (S. Nic.). 1470. Z 1r–25r. [See also Gramigna and Perissa, *Scuole*, 65–6.]

San Stefano (scuola). San Stefano (SM). 1299. T 503r–533r.

San Valentin (scuola). San Samuele (SM). 1678. T 268r–289v.

San Valentin (scuola). San Simeon Profeta [San Simeon Grande] (S. Croce). 1601 [at this date a beginning was given, though the mariegola dates from 1613, R 350v]. R 350r–371r.

San Vettor (sovvegno). Santa Margherita (S. Nic.). 1377? [the Council of Ten gave permission in 1407; mariegola renewed 1548, AA 17v]. AA 17v–40r.

San Vicenzo, Pietro Martire e Santa Caterina [da Siena] (sovvegno). San Zanipolo [Santi Giovanni e Paolo] (Cast.). 1594 [cf. Gramigna and Perissa, *Scuole*, 100–1, which puts the foundation at 1458]. P 214r–242r.

Sant'Alberto (scuola). Santa Maria dei Carmini (S. Nic.). 1442. AA 271r–289r. [See also Gramigna and Perissa, *Scuole*, 70–1.]
Sant'Alessandro (scuola). San Silvestro (S. Polo). 1491. BB 346r–361r.
Sant'Alipio (scuola). San Basilio [San Baseggio] (S. Nic.). 1660. AA 84r–91r.
Sant'Alvise (scuola). Sant'Alvise (Cann.). 1723 [but dated from 1402 with a renewal at 1608, N 326v]. N 325r–339r. [See also Gramigna and Perissa, *Scuole*, 123.]
Sant'Andrea (scuola). Sant'Andrea (S. Croce). 1347. R 258r–281r.
Sant'Anna (scuola). Sant'Anna (Cast.). 1620. Q 401r–411r. [See also SP b. 24, mariegola, dating from 1351.]
Sant'Antonio (scuola). San Benetto [San Benedetto] (SM). 1721. T 476r–494r.
Sant'Antonio (scuola). San Giovanni Grisostomo [San Zuan Grisostomo] (Cann.). 1637. O 614r–628v.
Sant'Antonio (scuola). Sant'Angelo [Sant'Anzolo] (SM). 1645. T 191r–209r.
Sant'Antonio (scuola). Sant'Eufemia (S. Nic.). 1662. AA 486v–490r.
Sant'Antonio (sovvegno). Santa Maria dell'Orto (Cann). 1706. O 426r–442r.
Sant'Antonio (sovvegno [described in 1661 as a "scuola di devotione," Z 228r]). Santi Vito e Modesto [San Vio] (S. Nic.). 1679. Z 228r–246r.
Sant'Antonio [da Padova] (scuola). Santa Maria dei Frari [Frari] (S. Polo). 1439. BB 52r–70r. [See also Gramigna and Perissa, *Scuole*, 84.]
Sant'Antonio da Padova (sovvegno). San Nicolo [dei Mendicoli] (S. Nic.). 1660. AA 331r–348r.
Sant'Antonio da Padova (sovvegno). San Severo (Cast.). 1691. Q 671r–683r.
Sant'Antonio degl'Orefici (sovvegno). San Silvestro [not stated, but see BB 657r] (S. Polo). 1560. BB 651r–674r.
Sant'Apollonia (scuola). San Barnaba (S. Nic.). 1559 [not stated, but for the date of the approval of the capitoli, see Z 506v–507r]. Z 505r–529r.
Sant'Erasmo (sovvegno). San Barnaba (S. Nic.). 1711. Z 427r–438r.
Sant'Ermolao (sovvegno). San Simeon Grande [San Simeon Profeta] (S. Croce). 1692 ["fu anco da nostri antenati erretto l'anno 1626 a 27 marzo un sovvegno nella scola di San Provolo" (there was also established by our forbears in the year 1626 on 27 March a sovvegno in the scuola of San Provolo), S 421v]. S 421v–431r.
Sant'Eustachio (sovvegno). Sant'Eustachio [San Stae] (S. Croce). 1507. S 1r–16r.
Sant'Iseppo (scuola). Sant'Iseppo (Cast.). 1531. Q 198r–210r.
Sant'Osvaldo (sovvegno). San Basilio [San Baseggio] (S. Nic.). 1720. AA 40r–45r.
Santa Catterina (scuola). San Geminiano (SM). 1436. T 62r–79r.
Santa Catterina (scuola). Sant'Eustachio [San Stae] (S. Croce). 1324. R 40r–77r.
Santa Catterina (sovvegno). Sant'Eustachio [San Stae] (S. Croce). 1677. R 417r–end.
Santa Catterina da Siena (scuola [became a sovvegno in 1686, N 186r]). Santa Maria dei Servi (Cann.). 1599. N 186r–201r.

Santa Catterina da Siena (sovvegno). Santa Maria dei Servi (Cann.). 1686. N 186r–201r. [Consecutive to the previous entry for the scuola of the same title, but clearly distinct from it.]

Santa Cecilia (scuola). San Cassiano (S. Croce). 1522. S 451r–459r.

Santa Cecilia (sovvegno). San Martin (Cast.). 1687. Q 98r–111r.

Santa Dorotea (sovvegno). Santi Simeon e Tadeo [San Simeon Piccolo] (S. Croce). 1635. R 224r–235r.

Santa Lucia (scuola). Santa Lucia (Cann.). 1323. N 396r–413r.

Santa Lucia (sovvegno). Santa Lucia (Cann.). 1705. O 356r–368r.

Santa Maria del Carmine (scuola). Sant'Angelo di Concordia alla Giudecca (S. Nic.). 1635 ["fu dato principio alla devotion" (a beginning was given to devotion) in 1607, AA 467r]. AA 467r–476r.

Santa Maria del Rosario (sovvegno). Santa Maria dell'Umiltà (S. Nic.). 1695. AA 363v–381r.

Santa Maria della Morte (suffragio). San Basso (SM). 1660. V 1r–45r.

Santa Maria Elisabet[t]a (scuola). San Tomaso [San Tomà] (S. Polo). 1603. BB 208r–225r.

Santa Maria Elisabet[t]a (scuola). Santa Maria Maddalena (Cann.). 1622. O 507r–517r.

Santa Maria Elisabet[t]a (sovvegno). San Simeon Profeta [San Simeon Grande] (S. Croce). 1616. S 237r–247r.

Santa Maria Elisabet[t]a et Beata Vergine di Loreto (scuola e sovvegno). San Cassiano (S. Croce). 1582. S 131r–168r.

Santa Marina (scuola and sovvegno). Santa Marina (Cast.). 1324. Q 210r–248r.

Santa Marta (scuola). Santa Marta (S. Nic.). 1360. Z 25r–46r.

Santi Antonio e Gaetano (sovvegno). San Giovanni Decollato [San Zuan Degolà] (S. Croce). 1707. S 168r–185r.

Santi Apostoli [XII Apostoli] (scuola). Santi Apostoli (Cann.). 1350. O 257r–286r. [See also SP b. 57 bis; Gramigna and Perissa, *Scuole*, 111.]

Santi Cosmo e Damiano (scuola). [No parish church] (S. Nic.). 1594. AA 515v–530r.

Santi Cosmo e Damiano (scuola). San Giovanni in Oglio [San Zuan Novo] (Cast.). Trecento? [based on the language of the statute]. Q 683r–end.

Santi Giorgio e Trifon (scuola). San Giovanni del Tempio [dei Cavalieri di Malta] [dei Furlani] (Cast.). 1451. P 579v–647r.

Santi Giuliano e Carlo (scuola). San Giuliano [San Zulian] (SM). 1277. U 573r–end.

Santi Rocco e Margarita (scuola). San Samuele (SM). 1455. U 421r–462r.

Santi Vicenzo e Pietro Martiri e Santa Caterina da Siena (scuola). San Zanipolo [Santi Giovanni e Paolo] (Cast.). 1450 [first meeting, as "San Vicenzo"]. Q 627r–662r.

Santissima Annontiata (scuola and sovvegno). San Giacomo dell'Orio (S. Croce). 1596. S 431r–451r.

Santissima Croce (scuola). San Biasio [San Biagio] (Cast.). 1694. Q 428r–453r.

Santissima Croce (scuola). San Fantin (SM). 1657 [scuola claimed that mariegola of 1707 was a "nova erettione della devota, e pia confraternità sive sovvegno" (a new beginning was given to the devout and pious confraternity or sovvegno) from this earlier date, T 23v]. T 23r–40r.

Santissima Croce (scuola). San Nicolo [dei Mendicoli] (S. Nic.). 1581? [earliest date in statute, AA 246r–v]. AA 245r–256r.

Santissima Croce (scuola). Sant'Apollinare [Sant'Aponal] (S. Polo). 1561. BB 175r–192r.

Santissima Croce (scuola). Santa Croce (S. Croce). 1359. R 235r–258r.

Santissima Croce (sovvegno). Sant'Angelo [Sant'Anzolo] (SM). 1701. T 15r–23r.

Santissima Croce (suffragio). San Pietro (Cast.). 1660. Q 1r–25r.

Santissima Croce (suffragio). San Salvador [San Salvatore] (SM). 1500. U 105v–132r.

Santissima Croce (suffragio [also "scuola" at S 106r]). Santa Maria Mater Domini (S. Croce). 1554. S 105r–131r.

Santissima Spina (sovvegno). Sant'Alvise (Cann.). 1710. N 277r–287r.

Santissima Trinità (scuola). Santa Trinità (S. Nic.). 1418. AA 530r–end. [See also Gramigna and Perissa, *Scuole*, 59–61.]

Santissima Trinità (sovvegno). San Lunardo [San Leonardo] (Cann.). 1708. N 32r–39r.

Santissima Trinità (sovvegno). San Vitale [San Vidal] (SM). 1697. V 128r–134r.

Santissima Veneranda (scuola). Corpus Domini (Cann.). 1644 [first meeting with authorization from the Provveditori; formal foundation could be 1698 or 1714, O 368r]. O 368r–396r.

Santissimo Abito della Beata Vergine del Carmine (scuola). Santa Maria dei Carmini (S. Nic.). 1594 ["fu eretta" (was established), but the mariegola dates from 1597, AA 128r]. AA 128r–161r. [Later, the Scuola Grande dei Carmini; see Perissa and Gramigna, *Scuole*, 68–9.]

Santissimo Crocefisso [see also Gramigna and Perissa, *Scuole*, 121–2, naming the scuola "del Cristo" or "della Buona Morte"] (scuola). San Marcuola [Santi Ermagora e Fortunato] (Cann.). 1657 [date of new mariegola, which itself suggests a foundation of 1623; cf. Gramigna and Perissa, *Scuole*, 121, which states 1635]. N 93r–124r.

Santissimo Crocefisso (sovvegno). San Giovanni in Bragora [San Zuan in Bragora] (Cast.). 1725. Q 162r–172r.

Santissimo Crocefisso (sovvegno). San Tomà [San Tomaso] (S. Nic.). 1683. Z 529r–545r.

Santissimo Crocefisso (sovvegno). San Tomà [San Tomaso] (S. Polo). 1706. BB 592r– 616r. [The relation of this statute to the previous entry is entirely unclear.]

Santissimo Crocefisso (sovvegno). Santa Maria Maggiore (S. Croce). 1711 [first meeting; approval of the Council of Ten, 1707; statute dated 1717, S 367r]. S 367r–377r.

Santissimo Crocefisso (suffragio). San Giacomo alla Giudecca (S. Nic.). 1635. AA 476r–486v.

Santissimo Crocefisso (suffragio). San Gieremia (Cann.). 1659 [claiming a foundation of 1615, N 18v]. N 16r–31v.

Santissimo Crocefisso (suffragio). San Giovanni in Oglio [San Zuan Novo] (Cast.). 1656. P 439r–479r.

Santissimo Crocefisso (suffragio). San Gregorio (S. Nic.). 1681. Z 101v–111r.

Santissimo Crocefisso (suffragio). Sant'Andrea (S. Croce). 1705. S 313r–327r.

Santissimo Crocefisso (suffragio). Santa Trinità (Cast.). 1654. P 242r–260r.

Santissimo Crocefisso Centurato (confraternità). Santa Croce (S. Croce). 1634. S 377r– 407r.

Santissimo Nome di Dio (scuola). San Domenico (Cast.). 1581. P 260r–312r.

Santissimo Nome di Dio (scuola). San Zanipolo [Santi Giovanni e Paolo] (Cast.). 1588. P 347r–378r. [See also Gramigna and Perissa, *Scuole*, 102–3.]

Santissimo Nome di Giesù (scuola). San Francesco della Vigna (Cast.). 1537. P 384r– 439r.

Santissimo Nome di Giesù (scuola). Santa Maria dei Frari [Frari] (S. Polo). 1666. BB 637r–651r.

Santissimo Rosario (scuola). Angelo Raffaele (S. Nic.). 1648 [approval granted in 1653, AA 304r]. AA 304r–320r.

Spirito Santo (scuola). Spirito Santo (S. Nic.). 1492. Z 382v–427r. [See also, SP, bb. 669, 681; Gramigna and Perissa, *Scuole*, 63–4.]

Venerabile (scuola). Angelo Raffaele (S. Nic.). 1542. AA 161r–193r.

Venerabile (scuola). San Bartolomeo [San Bortolomeo] (SM). 1507. U 132r–209r.

Venerabile (scuola). San Basilio [San Baseggio] (S. Nic.). 1530. Z 335r–349r.

Venerabile (scuola). San Basso (SM). 1516 [date of a complaint that the "arche" (tombs) are leaking, fol. V 49r]. V 45r–97v.

Venerabile (scuola). San Benedetto (SM). 1539? [date of first "capitolo generale" (general meeting), T 44v]. T 40r–62r.

Venerabile (scuola). San Biasio [San Biagio] (Cast.). 1544. Q 453r–478r.

Venerabile (scuola). San Cancian (Cann.). 1539? [earliest date in statute (O 471v); *capitoli* not confirmed until 1558 (O 472v)]. O 469r–493r.

Venerabile (scuola). San Cassiano (S. Croce). 1504. R 281r–323r.

Venerabile (scuola). San Fantin (SM). 1544. U 227r–258r.

Venerabile (scuola). San Felise [San Felice] (Cann.). 1538? [date of *capitoli*; statute of 1541, but the scuola was "zà molti anni principata" (already founded many years), O 193v]. O 193r–227r.

Venerabile (scuola). San Geminiano (SM). 1504. T 79r–110r

Venerabile (scuola). San Giacomo dell'Orio (S. Croce). 1507. R 1r–40r.

Venerabile (scuola). San Gieremia (Cann.). 1507. N 1r–16r.

Venerabile (scuola). San Giovanni Decolato [San Zuan Degolà] (S. Croce). 1514. S 226r– 237r.

Venerabile (scuola). San Giovanni Grisostomo [San Zuan Grisostomo] (Cann.). 1531. N 519r–561r.

Venerabile (scuola). San Giovanni in Oglio [San Zuan Novo] (Cast.). 1506. P 479r–506r.

Venerabile (scuola). San Giuliano [San Zulian] (SM). 1502. U 280r–346r.

Venerabile (scuola). San Leonardo [San Lunardo] (Cann.). 1581 [records lament lack of a statute; this scuola was registered with the Provveditori only in 1594, O 345r]. O 339r–368r.

Venerabile (scuola). San Leone [San Lio] (Cast.). 1515. Q 501r–535r.

Venerabile (scuola). San Marcuola [Santi Ermagora e Fortunato] (Cann.). 1507. N 60r–93r.

Venerabile (scuola). San Martin (Cast.). 1524. P 506r–546v.

Venerabile (scuola). San Marzilian [San Marziale] (Cann.). 1512? [date of agreement with chapter of church, O 85r]. O 79r–124r.

Venerabile (scuola). San Mattio [San Mattia] (S. Polo). 1567. BB 450r–472r.

Venerabile (scuola). San Maurizio (SM). 1581. T 462r–476r.

Venerabile (scuola). San Moise (SM). 1510 [date of first *capitolo generale*, 203v]. V 191r–244r.

Venerabile (scuola). San Nicolo [dei Mendicoli] (S. Nic.). 1506. AA 193r–245r.

Venerabile (scuola). San Pantalon (S. Nic.). 1535. Z 438r–464r.

Venerabile (scuola). San Paternian (SM). 1518. U 258r–280r.

Venerabile (scuola). San Pietro (Cast.) 1507. P 6r–51r.

Venerabile (scuola). San Polo (S. Polo). 1507. BB 398r–430r.

Venerabile (scuola). San Provolo (Cast.). 1517. Q 248r–271r.

Venerabile (scuola). San Salvatore [San Salvador] (SM). 1501–21 [no date, but preamble refers to Doge Leonardo Loredan; these are the dates of his rule]. V 351r–389r.

Venerabile (scuola). San Samuele (SM). 1528. V 281r–324r.

Venerabile (scuola). San Severo (Cast.). 1511. Q 184r–198r.

Venerabile (scuola). San Silvestro (S. Polo). 1516? [first meeting of *capitolo generale*, BB 496r]. BB 485r–520r.

Venerabile (scuola). San Simeon Profeta [San Simeon Grande] (S. Croce) 1560. S 51r–72r.

Venerabile (scuola). San Stin [San Stefano Confessor] (S. Polo). 1550. BB 251r–293r.

Venerabile (scuola). San Tomaso [San Tomà] (S. Polo). 1533. BB 149r–175r.

Venerabile (scuola). San Trovaso [Santi Gervasio e Protasio] (S. Nic.). 1506 [date of permission from the Council of Ten; Provveditori did not confirm statute until 1536, Z 313r]. Z 309r–328r.

Venerabile (scuola). San Vitale [San Vidal] (SM). 1520 [statute includes an agreement with the clergy of the church of this year, V 469v; refers to foundation in second year of the dogeship of Francesco Donà (r. 1545–53); also asserts scuola has existed "za molti anni," in 1546 (V 466r); statute contains no government authorization]. V 466r–end.

Venerabile (scuola). San Zuan in Bragora [San Giovanni in Bragora] (Cast.). 1573 [P 91v, though scuola derives from Scuola di San Zuan Battista of 1322, P 81r]. P 81r–101r.

Venerabile (scuola). Sant'Agnese (S. Nic.). 1580. Z 349r–382v.

Venerabile (scuola). Sant'Agostin (S. Polo). 1521–3 [dogeship of Antonio Grimani who is referred to in preamble, BB 192r]. BB 192r–208r.

Venerabile (scuola). Sant'Angelo [Sant'Anzolo] (SM). 1522 [but "gia molti anni" (already many years), T 110r]. T 110r–148v.

Venerabile (scuola). Sant'Antonin (Cast.). 1558 [year of a recorded vote; first reference to the scuola is 1609, but linked to Scuola di San Sabba, founded 1399]. P 101r–131r.

Venerabile (scuola). Sant'Apollinare [Sant'Aponal] (S. Polo). 1506. BB 376r–398r.

Venerabile (scuola). Sant'Eufemia della Zuecca [alla Giudecca] (S. Nic.). 1508. Z 464r–505r.

Venerabile (scuola). Sant'Eustachio [San Stae] (S. Croce). 1510. R 77r–101r.

Venerabile (scuola). Santa Croce (S. Croce) 1538. R 371r–417r.

Venerabile (scuola). Santa Fosca (Cann.). 1587. O 51r–64r.

Venerabile (scuola). Santa Giustina (Cast.). 1602? [first recorded date, Q 113v]. Q 111v– 121r.

Venerabile (scuola). Santa Lucia (Cann.). 1520. O 527r–541r.

Venerabile (scuola). Santa Margarita (S. Nic.). 1503. Z 85r–101v.

Venerabile (scuola). Santa Maria Formosa (Cast.). 1506. P 160r–214r.

Venerabile (scuola). Santa Maria Maddalena (Cann.). 1641. N 39r–49r.

Venerabile (scuola). Santa Maria Mater Domini (S. Croce). 1512. R 135r–161r.

Venerabile (scuola). Santa Maria Nova (Cann.). 1512. O 286r–309r.

Venerabile (scuola). Santa Maria Zobenigo [Santa Maria del Giglio] (SM). 1506. T 439r– 462r.

Venerabile (scuola). Santa Marina (Cast.). 1712. P 656r–664r.

Venerabile (scuola). Santa Sofia (Cann.). 1507 [clearly operating, O 231v; statute 1548, O 231r; in statute of San Michiel Arcangelo (sovvegno), Santa Maria dell'Orto (Cann.), 1706. See above.].

Venerabile (scuola). Santa Trinità (Cast.). 1507. P 51r–81r.

Venerabile (scuola). Santi Apostoli (Cann.). 1511. N 491r–519r. [See also Gramigna and Perissa, *Scuole*, 111–12.]

Venerabile (scuola). Santi Simeon e Tadeo [San Simeon Piccolo] (S. Croce). 1572 [date of approval by the Provveditori (S 278v); a year when a *capitolo* met (S 278r); statute dated 1623 refers to scuola as "gia molti anni principata" (already begun many years), but "senza regola" (without rule); prays for "perpetua vitoria" (perpetual victory) of the state, "gloria del Nostro Ser.mo Prencipe Misser Alvise Mocenigo" (the glory of our Most Serene Prince Alvise Mocenigo), doge 1570–7]. S 273r–293r.

Venerabile (scuola). Santi Vito e Modesto [San Vio] (S. Nic.). 1528. Z 246r–263r.

Visitazione della Beata Vergine (scuola). San Nicolo [dei Mendicoli] (S. Nic.). 1474. Z 46r–61v.

b. 61. Filza di terminationi ed altri atti risguardanti scuole, sovvegni e suffraggi, 1690–1763, including Cattalogo delle scuole, suffraggi et sovegni tutti sottoposti Al Mag.to Ecc.mo de Prov. Di Comun.

The *cattalogo*, of 1763, gives notice of the following institutions that do not appear in the registers:

Beata Vergine del Carmine e San Spiridion (scuola). San Samuele (SM).
Beata Vergine del Rosario (scuola). Santa Cattarina (Cast).
Beata Vergine del Rosario (scuola). Spirito Santo (S. Nic.).
Beata Vergine della Purificazione (scuola). S. Boldo [Sant'Ubaldo] (S. Croce).
Beata Vergine delle Grazie (sovvegno). Santa Maria Formosa (Cast.).
Beata Vergine di Arsenati (scuola). Sant'Antonio (Cast.).
Beata Vergine di Costantinopoli (scuola). S. Iseppo [San Giuseppe] (Cast.).
Crocefisso (sovvegno). Angelo Raffaele (S. Nic.).
Crocefisso (sovvegno). Santa Margarita [Santa Margherita] (S. Nic.).
San Francesco (scuola). San Zanipolo [Santi Giovanni e Paolo] (Cast.).
San Giuseppe e Maria (sovvegno). San Simeon Grande [San Simeon Profeta] (S. Croce).
San Liberale (sovvegno). Santa Maria dei Carmini (S. Nic.).
San Spiridion (scuola). Sant'Antonin (Cast.).
Sant'Orsola (scuola). San Zanipolo [Santi Giovanni e Paolo] (Cast.). [See also SP bb. 597–8, 1300–1805.]
Santa Catterina (scuola e sovvegno). Santa Maria Mater Domini (S. Croce).
Santa Maria Elisabet[t]a (scuola e sovvegno). San Baseggio [San Basilio] (S. Nic.).
Santissimo Crocefisso e San Gaetano (sovvegno). San Baseggio [San Basilio] (S. Nic.).
Venerabile (scuola). San Boldo (S. Croce).

Index: Scuole Piccole

b. 1, Sant'Agnese, catastico dal 1325 in avanti
b. 1 bis, Santi Apostoli in Santa Maria della Carità, mariegola, 1288
b. 24, Sant'Anna di Castello, mariegola, 1351–1425
b. 57 bis, Santi Apostoli, mariegola, 1350–1708
b. 257, Santa Barbara dei Bombardieri, mariegola, 1500–1762
b. 406, Santa Maria e San Cristofalo dei Mercanti, mariegola, 1377–1545
b. 408, Santa Maria e San Cristofalo dei Mercanti, pergamene, 1215–1319
b. 597, Sant'Orsola, mariegola, 1300–1785
b. 726, Santa Maria della Celestia, mariegola, 1337–1764

Index: Arti

b. 61, carboneri, mariegola, 1476–1781
b. 110, fabbri, inventarii, 1595–1600
b. 112, fabbri, processi

b. 152, forneri, atti diversi, 1447–1797
b. 296, marangoni, alfabeto leggi, 1532–1715
b. 309, marangoni, iscrizioni marangoni, 1603
b. 312, marzeri, mariegola, 1471–1787
b. 314, marzeri, capitoli e parti, 1508–1608
b. 397, marzeri, nomi di fratelli, 1586–1692
b. 405, mercanti di legname da Cador, capitolare secondo, 1586–1604
b. 421, orefici, cassa amministrazione, 1541–54
b. 430, osti, mariegola, sec. xvi
b. 445, pistori, mariegola, 1333–1691
b. 501, sartori, capitoli e parti, 1492–1683

Index: Giustizia Nova
b. 5, reg. 12, simile [parti ed altri atti del collegio dei vii savi alla G.N. sopra vari argomenti] contenente specialmente licenze di alloggiamento, "stella," 1530–2
b. 12, reg. 35, registro processi contra furatole (frigipesce) e altri conraventi al commercio del vino, 1509–11

Index: Sant'Uffizio
Processi (Hearings)
b. 7, Girolamo, lavoratore di perle, et al. 1548
b. 7, Casizio, Gio. Pietro, fachino
b. 11, Tomaso bavelaro, 1553
b. 11, Zuangiacomo spader, 1551
b. 12, Iseppo orese, 1555
b. 13, Alessandro Caravia, 1556
b. 14, Da Loio, Antonio, 1557
b. 14, Valgrisio Vincenzo libraio, 1570
b. 15, Domenego Gotardo specier
b. 16, Francesco speziale alla Duchessa, 1560
b. 17, Girolamo de Luca samiter a San Geremia, 1561
b. 19, no. 8, Nicolai de Battista Peliperiis, 1563
b. 20, Gio. Batt. e Marcantonio speziali, 1565
b. 24, Cagnola, Francesco, Milanese, ormesiner, 1568
b. 24, tentori/chiovaroli [1568?]
b. 26, Giacopo Saliceti, 1568
b. 28, Valgrisio Vincentium librarium et al., 1559
b. 28, Querela contro li pistori, che mangiano carne indeferentemente ... 1569, 18 Junii
b. 29, Giovanni Sfulgher, 1571
b. 29, Paulo Avanzi, 1568
b. 30, Alessandro Bonanome, 1571

b. 31, Lorenzo Vex, 1566
b. 33, Domenico Longino, portador di farina, 1573
b. 39, Dugati, Gaspare, 1575
b. 48, Zonca Giovanni
b. 49, Benedetto calzolaio Germania, 1582
b. 61, Versemon, Giovanni e compagni, 1548
b. 70, Francesco Faggioni Padovano, 1610

Index: Cinque Savi alla Mercanzia
b. 164, specchi-stallaggio

Primary Sources

Adamson, James B. *The Epistle of James*. In *The New International Commentary on the New Testament*. Grand Rapids, MI: William B. Eermans, 1976.

Aretino, Pietro. *Il primo libro delle lettere*. Edited by Fausto Niccolini. Bari: Laterza, 1913.

— *Ragionamento delle corti*. Edited by Fulvio Pevere. Milan: Mursia, 1995.

— "Ragionamento delle corti." In *Opere di Pietro Aretino e di Anton Francesco Doni*, edited by Carlo Cordie (Milan-Naples: R. Ricciardi, 1976). Letteratura italiana: Storia e testi, 26. Vol. 2, *Folengo-Aretino-Doni*, 436–57.

— *Selected Letters*. Edited and translated by George Bull. Harmondsworth, UK: Penguin, 1976.

— *L'umanità di Cristo*. Rome: Colombo Editore, 1945.

Bacon, Francis, "Of Seditions and Troubles." In *Essays*, with an introduction by Oliphant Smeaton, 42–8. London: Dent & Sons, 1968.

— *The Works of Francis Bacon, Baron of Verulam, Viscount of St Alban and Lord High Chancellor of England*. 4 vols. London: A. Millar, 1740.

Bandello, Matteo. *Tutte le opere*. 3rd edn., edited by Francesco Flora. 2 vols. Verona: A. Mondadori, 1952.

[Benedetto da Mantova]. *Il beneficio di Cristo: Con le versioni del sec. XVI, documenti e testimonianze*. Edited by Salvatore Caponetto. De Kalb and Chicago: N. Illinois Press and the Newberry Library, 1972.

Boccalini, Traiano, *De' ragguagli di Parnaso del Signor Traiano Boccalini romano Centuria Prima aggiuntasi Cinquanta Ragguagli Del Signor Girolamo Briani Modanese, intitolati Parte Terza. All'Illustriss. e Reverendiss. Sig. Cardinale Borghese*. Venice: Michiel'Angelo Barboni, 1669.

Boschini, Marco. *La carta del navegar pittoresco: Dialogo tra un senator venetian dilettante, e un professor de Pitura, soto nome d'Ecelenza, a de Compare* [...]. In Venetia, per li Baba: MDCLX. Facsimile edition, Venice: Filippi, 1965.

Botero, Giovanni. *Della ragion di stato libri dieci con tre libri delle cause della grandezza e magnificienza delle città*. Venice: 1589.

— *On the Causes of the Greatness and Magnificence of Cities.* Translated and introduced by Geoffrey Symcox. Toronto and London: University of Toronto Press, 2012.

— *The Reason of State.* Translated by P.J. Waley and D.P. Waley, with an introduction by D.P. Waley, and *The Greatness of Cities*, trans. Robert Peterson, 1606. New Haven, CT: Yale University Press, 1956.

Bracciolini, Poggio. "De avaritia." In *Prosatori latini del Quattrocento*, edited by Eugenio Garin. Letteratura Italiana, Storia e Testi, 13. Milan: R. Ricciardi, 1952. Translated as "On Avarice," in *The Earthly Republic: Italian Humanists on Government and Society*, edited by Benjamin Kohl and Ronald G. Witt, 241–89. Manchester, UK: Manchester University Press, 1978).

Canale, Martino da. *Les estoires de Venise: Cronaca veneziana in lingua francese dalle origini al 1275.* Edited by Alberto Limentani. Civiltà di Venezia, Fonti e Testi, XII, Serie Terza, 3. Florence: Olschki, 1972.

I capitolari delle arti veneziane sottoposte alla Giustizia e poi alla Giustizia Vecchia dalle origini al MCCCXXX. Edited by G. Monticolo. 3 vols. Fonti per la Storia d'Italia, 26–8. Rome: Istituto Storico Italiano, 1896–1914.

Caravia, Alessandro. *Il Sogno dil Caravia.* Venice: Giovan'Antonio di Nicolini da Sabbio, 1541. BMV Misc. 2477.4. Facsimile edition, pres. Augusto Gentili, *Venezia Cinquecento*, 1 (1991), following p. 139.

Carleton, Dudley. *Dudley Carleton to John Chamberlain, 1603–1624: Jacobean Letters.* Edited by Maurice Lee, Jr. Brunswick, NJ: Rutgers University Press, 1972.

Casola, Canon Pietro. *Canon Pietro Casola's Pilgrimage to Jerusalem in the Year 1494.* Edited and translated by M.M. Newett. Manchester, UK: Manchester University Press, 1907.

Castiglione, Baldassare. *The Book of the Courtier.* Translated by Sir Thomas Hoby. With an introduction by W.H.D. Rouse, notes by Drayton Henderson. London: Dent & Sons, 1561. Everyman's Library, 1928.

— *Il libro del Cortegiano.* Edited by Ettore Bonora, comment by Paolo Zoccola. Varese: University of Mursia, 1976.

Cerasano, S.P., ed. *William Shakespeare's "The Merchant of Venice": A Sourcebook.* London: Routledge, 2004.

Cessi, Roberto, ed. *Gli statuti veneziani di Jacopo Tiepolo del 1242 e le loro glosse.* Venice: C. Ferrari, 1938.

Chambers, David, and Brian Pullan, eds. *Venice: A Documentary History, 1450–1650.* With Jennifer Fletcher. Oxford: Basil Blackwell, 1992.

Commynes, Philippe de. *Mémoires.* Edited by Joel Blanchard. 2 vols. Geneva: Droz, 2007.

Contarini, Gasparo. *The Commonwealth and Government of Venice, Written by the Cardinall Gasper Contareno and Translated Out of Italian into English.* Translated by Lewes Lewkenor. London: John Windet, 1599. Facs. edn. *The English Experience*, no. 101. Amsterdam: Theatrum Orbis Terrarum; New York: Da Capo, 1969.

— *De magistratibus et Republica Venetorum libri quinque, authore Gaspare Contareno Patricio Veneto.* Venetias apud Baldum Sabinum, 1551.

Cronache veneziane antichissime. Edited by G. Monticolo. Istituto Storico Italiano, Fonti per la Storia d'Italia, no. 9. Rome: Istituto Storico Italiano, 1890.

Dante Alighieri. *La Divina Commedia.* Vol.1, *Inferno.* Comment by Attilio Momigliano. Florence: Sansoni, 1968. Vol.2, *Purgatorio*, ed. Natalino Sapegno. Florence: La Nuova Italia, 1956; Vol.3, *Paradiso.* Comment by Tommaso Casini, 6th edn., edited by S.A. Balbi. Florence: Sansoni, 1968.

Davids, Peter H. *The Epistle of James: A Commentary on the Greek Text.* New International Greek Testament Commentary. Grand Rapids, MI: William B. Eerdmans, 1982.

Erasmus, Desiderius. "The Handbook of the Christian Soldier (*Enchiridion militis christiani*)," translated and annotated by Charles Fantazzi. In *Collected Works of Erasmus*, vol. 66, edited by John W. O'Malley, 1–128. Toronto: Toronto University Press, 1988.

Evelyn, John. *Diary.* Edited by William Bray. 2 vols. London: Dent & Sons, 1907.

Florio, John. *A Worlde of Wordes.* Reprint of 1598 edition. Hildesheim and New York: Georg Olms Verlag, 1972.

Garzoni, Tomaso. *La Piazza Universale di tutte le professioni del mondo.* Venice: Tomaso Baglioni, 1610. Edited by Paolo Cherchi and Beatrice Collina. 2 vols. Turin: Einaudi, 1996.

Giovio, Benedetto. *Historiae patriae, libri dui, Storia di Como dalle origini al 1532.* Como: New Press, 1982. Reprinted from *Opere scelte di Benedetto Giovio.* Como, 1887.

Guicciardini, Francesco. *Storia d'Italia.* Edited by Giovanni Rosiari, preface by Carlo Botta. 7 vols. Capolago: Tipografia Elvetica, 1833.

Kaplan, M. Lindsay, ed. "*The Merchant of Venice*": *Texts and Contexts.* Boston-New York: Bedford/St Martin's, 2002.

Lepschy, Anna Laura. *Tintoretto Observed: A Documentary Survey of Critical Reactions from the Sixteenth to the Twentieth Century.* Ravenna: Longo, 1983.

Luther, Martin. "Preface to the Epistle of St James and Jude." In *Reformation Writings of Martin Luther*, edited by Bertram L. Woolf, vol. 2. London: Lutterworth Press, 1955.

Magnocavallo, Francesco. *Memorie antiche di Como, 1518–1559.* Edited by Elena Riva with Antonio Battaglia. Como: A. Dominiani, 1999.

Marvell, Andrew. "The Character of Holland." In *The Poems of Andrew Marvell*, edited by Nigel Smith, 246–56. London: Longman, 2003.

McDonald, Russ, ed. *The Bedford Companion to Shakespeare: An Introduction with Documents.* Boston-New York: Bedford/St Martin's, 2001.

Merchant Culture in Fourteenth-Century Venice: The Zibaldone da Canale. Edited by John E. Dotson. Binghamton, NY: Medieval and Renaissance Texts and Studies, 1994.

Moo, Douglas J. *The Letter of James: An Introduction and Commentary*. The Tyndale New Testament Commentaries. Leicester, UK, and Grand Rapids, MI: Inter-Varsity Press and William B. Eerdmans, 1985.

Porto, Luigi da. *Lettere storiche dall'anno 1509 al 1528 con la novella di Giulietta e Romeo*. Edited by Bartolomeo Bressan. Florence: Le Monnier, 1857.

Powell, J. Enoch. *The Evolution of the Gospel: A New Translation of the First Gospel with Commentary and Introductory Essay*. New Haven, CT, and London: Yale University Press, 1994.

Riccoboni, Sister Bianca Maria. *Life and Death in a Venetian Convent: The Chronology and Necrology of Corpus Domini, 1395–1436*. Edited and translated by Daniel Bornstein. Chicago and London: Chicago University Press, 2000.

Ridolfi, Carlo. *The Life of Tintoretto and of His Children Domenico and Marietta*. Translated by Catherine Enggass and Robert Enggass. University Park: Pennsylvania University Press, 1984.

— *Le maraviglie dell'arte, ovvero le vite degli illustri pittori veneti e dello stato*. 2 vols. Padua: Cartallier, 1835.

Roskill, Mark. *Dolce's "Aretino" and Venetian Art Theory of the Cinquecento*. New York: New York University Press, 1968.

Sacrum commercium sancti Francisci cum Domina Paupertate. In *The Saint*, vol. 1 of *Francis of Assisi: Early Documents*, edited by Regis J. Armstrong, J.A. Wayne Halligan, and William J. Short, 521–54. New York: New York City Press, 1999.

Sansovino, Francesco. *Venetia città nobilissima et singolare. Descritta in XIIII. Libri*. Venice: Jacopo Sansovino, 1581. Facs. reprint, Bergamo: Leading Edizioni, 2002.

Sanudo, Marin, il giovane. *De origine, situ et magistratibus urbis Venetae, ovvero la Città di Venezia (1493–1530)*. Edited by Angela Carricciolo Arico. Milan: Cisalpina-La Goliardica, 1980.

Sanuto, Marino [Marin Sanudo]. *I diarii di Marino Sanuto*. Edited by Rinaldo Fulin et al. 58 vols. Venice, 1879–1903. Reprint, Bologna: Forni, 1969–70.

Sarpi, Paolo, *Della potestà de' prencipi*. Edited by Nina Cannizzaro; introduction by Corrado Pin. Venice: Marsilio, 2006.

— "Sopra l'Offitio dell'Inquisizione." In *Scritti giurisdizionalistici*, edited by Giovanni Gambarin, 119–212. Vol. 8 of *Opere*. Bari: G. Laterza, 1958.

— "Sulla publicazione di scritture malediche il governo." In *Scritti giurisdizionalistici*, edited by Giovanni Gambarin, 221–31. Vol. 8 of *Opere*. Bari: G. Laterza, 1958.

Shakespeare, William. *The Merchant of Venice*. Edited by John Drakakis. The Arden Shakespeare, 3rd series. London: A. & C. Black, 2010.

— *The Merchant of Venice*. Edited by John Russell Brown. The Arden Shakespeare, 2nd series. London: Methuen, 1961.

Simonsfeld, Henry. *Der Fondaco dei Tedeschi in Venedig und die deutsch-venetianisches Handelsbeziehungen*. 2 vols. Stuttgart: Cotta, 1887.

Smith, Logan Pearsall, ed. *The Life and Letters of Sir Henry Wotton*. 2 vols. Oxford: Oxford University Press, 1907.

Smith, Sir Thomas. *De Republica Anglorum*. Edited by Mary Dewar. Cambridge: Cambridge University Press, 1982.

Vasari, Giorgio. *Le vite de' più eccelenti pittori, scultori ed architettori*. In *Opere*, edited by Gaetano Milanesi, 9 vols. Florence: Sansoni, 1906.

Vermes, Geza. *The Dead Sea Scrolls in English*. Harmondsworth, UK: Penguin, 1966.

Vespasiano da Bisticci. "Santo Bernardino da Massa, 1380–1444." In *Renaissance Princes, Popes and Prelates: The Vespasiano Memoirs; Lives of Illustrious Men of the Fifteenth Century*, translated by William George and Emily Waters, with introduction by Myron P. Gilmore, 163–8. New York: Harper & Row, 1963.

Zanetti, Antonio Maria. *Descrizione di tutte le pubbliche pitture della città di Venezia e isole circonvicine o sia Rinnovazione delle Ricche Minere di Marco Boschini, colle aggiunte di tutte le opera, che uscirono dal 1674, sino al presente 1733 con un compendio delle vita e maniere de' principali pittori*. Venice: P. Bassaglia, 1733. Facsimile reprint, Bologna: A Forni, 1980.

Zompini, Gaetano. *Le arti che vanno per via nella città di Venezia*. Venice, 1785. Reprint, Venice: Filippi, 2009.

Zuccaro, Federico. *Il lamento della pittura su l'onde venete (1605), nel quale si come si duole d'essere al presente mal trattata* (Mantua, 1605). Facsimile edition, Scritti d'arte di Federico Zuccaro, a.c. di Detlef Heikamp, Fonti per lo Studio della Storia dell'Arte Inedite o Rare, I. Florence: Olschki, 1961.

Secondary Sources

Alberigo, Giuseppe. "Vita attiva e vita contemplativa in un'esperienza cristiana del xvi secolo." *SV*, 16 (1974), 177–225.

Allerston, Patricia Anne. "The Market in Second-Hand Clothes and Furnishings in Venice, c. 1500–c. 1650." PhD diss., European University Institute, Fiesole, 1996.

Ambrosini, Federica. "Between Heresy and Free Thought, between the Mediterranean and the North: Heterodox Women in Seventeenth-Century Venice." In Cowan, *Mediterranean Urban Culture*, 83–96.

— *Storie di patrizi e di eresia nella Venezia del '500*. Milan: Francoangeli, 1999.

Andrews, K.R. *Trade, Plunder and Settlement: Maritime Enterprise and the Genesis of the British Empire, 1480–1630*. Cambridge: Cambridge University Press, 1984.

Andrews, Richard. "Shakespeare and Italian Comedy." In *Shakespeare and Renaissance Europe*, edited by Andrew Hadfield and Paul Hammond, 123–49. London: Thomson, 2005.

Arnold, Dennis. *God, Caesar and Mammon: A Study of Musical Patronage in Venice, 1550–1750*. Inaugural lecture, University of Nottingham, 1970.

Aspetti e cause della decadenza economica veneziana nel secolo xvii. Civiltà Veneziana, Studi, 9. Venice-Rome: Istituto per la Collaborazione Culturale, 1961.

Attwater, Donald, ed. *A Dictionary of Saints*. Harmondsworth, UK: Penguin, 1965.

Aymard, Maurice. *Venise, Raguse et le commerce du blé pendant la seconde moitié du 16e siècle*. Paris: SEVPEN, 1966.

Bassi, Elena. *Tracce di chiese veneziane distrutte: Ricostruzioni dai disegni di Antonio Visentini*. Venice: Istituto Veneto di Scienze, Lettere ed Arti, 1997.

Bate, Jonathan. *Soul of the Age: A Biography of the Mind of William Shakespeare*. New York: Random House, 2009.

Bellati, Antonio. *Dizionario Dialettale Etnografico di Premana*. Madonna di Tirana: IDEVV, 2007.

Bellavitis, Anna. *Identité, mariage, mobilité sociale: Citoyennes et citoyens a Venise au xvie siècle*. Rome: Ecole Française de Rome, 2001.

Beloch, Karl J. *Bevölkerungsgeschichte Italiens*. Vol. 3, *Die Bevölkerung der Republik Venedig: Des Herzogens Mailand, Piemonts, Genuas, Corsicas und Sardiniens; Die Gesamtbevölkerung Italiens*. Berlin: W. de Gruyter, 1961.

Beloch, K.J. "La popolazione di Venezia nei sec. 16 e 17." *NAV*, n.s. vol. 3, part 1 (1902), 5–49.

Beltrami, Daniele. *Storia della popolazione di Venezia dalla fine del sec. xvi alla caduta della Repubblica*. Padua: CEDAM, 1954.

Benzoni, Gino. "Devozioni dogali." *SV*, n.s. 31 (1996), 15–25.

— "Venezia: Tra mito e realtà." *SV*, n.s. 45 (2003), 15–26.

— "Venezia ai tempi di Caboto." *SV*, n.s. 23 (1992), 109–30.

— "Venezia e Bergamo: Implicanze di un dominio." *SV*, n.s. 20 (1990), 15–59.

— *Venezia nell'età della controriforma*. Milan: Mursia, 1973.

— "Venezia, ossia il mito modulato." *SV*, n.s. 19 (1990), 15–34.

Berenson, Bernard. *Caravaggio: His Incongruity and His Fame*. London: Chapman & Hall, 1953.

Beretta, R. "Gian Giacomo de' Medici in Brianza (1527–31)." *Archivio Storico Lombardo*, 5th series, 43, no. 1 (1916), 53–120.

Bettini, Sergio. *Venezia: Nascita di una città*. Milan: Electa, 1978.

Bireley, Robert, S.J. "Redefining Catholicism: Trent and Beyond." In *CHC*, vol. 6, 145–61.

— *The Refashioning of Catholicism, 1450–1700: A Reassessment of the Counter-Reformation*. Basingstoke, UK: Macmillan, 1999.

Bistort, G. *Il Magistrato alle Pompe nella repubblica di Venezia*. Venice: Deputazione Veneto-Tridentina di Storia Patria, 1912.

Black, Christopher F. *Church, Religion and Society in Early Modern Italy*. Basingstoke, UK: Palgrave Macmillan, 2004.

— *Italian Confraternities in the Sixteenth Century*. Cambridge: Cambridge University Press, 1989.

— *The Italian Inquisition*. New Haven, CT, and London: Yale University Press, 2009.
Bloch, Marc. *The Historian's Craft*. Translated by Peter Putnam, with an introduction by Joseph R. Strayer. Manchester, UK: Manchester University Press, 1954.
Bolt, Roderick. *Librettist of Venice: The Remarkable Life of Lorenzo da Ponte; Mozart's Poet, Casanova's Friend, and Italian Opera's Impresario in America*. New York and London: Bloomsbury, 2006.
Bonney, Richard. *The European Dynastic States, 1494–1660*. Oxford: Oxford University Press, 1991.
Bornstein, Daniel. *The Bianchi of 1399: Popular Devotion in Late Medieval Italy*. Ithaca, NY: Cornell University Press, 1993.
— "Le Conseil des Dix et le controle de la vie religieuse à Venise à la fin du Moyen Age." *La religion civique a l'époque medievale et moderne, Collection de l'Ecole Francaise de Rome*, 213 (1995), 187–200.
Bosel, Richard. "La chiesa dei Gesuiti a Venezia: Un'ipotesi di interpretazione tipologica." In Zanardi, *I Gesuiti e Venezia*, 689–703.
Bossy, John. *Christianity in the West, 1400–1700*. Oxford: Oxford University Press, 1985.
— Introduction to *Catholicism between Luther and Voltaire*, by Jean Delumeau. Translated by Jeremy Moiser. London: Burnes and Oates, 1977.
— *Peace in the Post-Reformation*. Cambridge: Cambridge University Press, 1998.
— "The Social History of Confession." *TRHS*, ser. 5, 25 (1975), 21–38.
Bouwsma, William J. *Venice and the Defense of Republican Liberty: Renaissance Values in the Age of the Counter Reformation*. Berkeley and Los Angeles: University of California Press, 1968.
— "Venice, Spain, and the Papacy: Paolo Sarpi and the Renaissance Tradition." In *A Usable Past: Essays in European Cultural History*, 247–65. Berkeley and Los Angeles: University of Califormia Press, 1990.
— *The Waning of the Renaissance, 1550–1640*. New Haven, CT, and London: Yale University Press, 2000.
Bowd, Stephen D., *Reform before the Reformation: Vincenzo Querini and the Religious Renaissance in Italy*. Studies in Medieval and Reformation Thought, LXXXVII. Leiden, Boston, and Cologne: E.J. Brill, 2002.
— "'The Tune Is Marred': Citizens and People in Gasparo Contarini's Venice." *European Review of History*, 7 (2000), 83–97.
— *Venice's Most Loyal City: Civic Identity in Renaissance Brescia*. Cambridge, MA, and London: Harvard University Press, 2010.
Boxer, C.R. *The Dutch Seaborne Empire, 1600–1800*. London: Penguin, 1973.
Braudel, Fernand. *The Mediterranean and the Mediterranean World in the Age of Philip II*. Translated by Sian Reynolds. 2 vols. London and New York: Collins and Harper & Row, 1972.

— *The Perspective of the World*. Translated by Sian Reynolds. Vol. 3 of *Civilisation and Capitalism, 15th-18th Centuries*. London: Collins, 1984.

Braunstein, Philippe. "Le commerce du fer à Venise au xve siècle." *SV*, 8 (1966), 267–302.

Brewer, John. *The Sinews of Power: War and the English State, 1688–1783*. London: Unwin Hyman, 1989.

Brown, Horatio. "Paolo Sarpi, the Man." In *Studies*, vol. 2, 208–44.

— "Shakespeare and Venice." In *Studies*, vol. 2, 159–80.

— *Studies in Venetian History*. 2 vols. London: John Murray, 1907.

Brown, Patricia Fortini. *Venetian Narrative Painting in the Age of Carpaccio*. New Haven, CT, and London: Yale University Press, 1989.

Brown, Peter. *The Cult of the Saints: Its Rise and Function in Latin Christianity*. Chicago: Chicago University Press, 1981.

Brucker, Gene A. "The Ciompi Revolution." In Rubinstein, *Florentine Studies*, 314–56.

Brunetti, Mario. "Venezia durante la peste del 1348." *Ateneo Veneto*, vol. 32, part i, fasc. 3 (1909), 289–311; part ii, fasc. 1, 5–42.

Bull, Malcolm. "The Iconography of the Sistine Chapel Ceiling." In *Prophetic Rome in the High Renaissance Period*, edited by Marjorie Reeves, 307–19. Oxford: Oxford University Press, 1992.

Burckhardt, Jacob. *The Civilization of the Renaissance in Italy* (1860). Translated by S.G.C. Middlemore (1945), with a new introduction by Peter Burke and notes by Peter Murray. London: Penguin, 1990.

Burke, Peter. "Classifying the People: The Census as Collective Representation." In *Historical Anthropology*, 27–39.

— "Early Modern Venice as a Center of Information and Communication." In Martin and Romano, *Venice Reconsidered*, 389–419.

— *The European Renaissance: Centres and Peripheries*. Oxford: Basil Blackwell, 1998.

— *The Fortunes of "The Courtier": The European Reception of Castiglione's "Cortegiano."* Cambridge: Polity Press, 1995.

— *The French Historical Revolution: The Annales School, 1929–89*. Cambridge: Polity Press, 1990.

— *The Historical Anthropology of Early Modern Italy: Essays on Perception and Communication*. Cambridge: Cambridge University Press, 1987.

— "How to Be a Counter-Reformation Saint." In *Historical Anthropology*, 48–62.

— *Venice and Amsterdam: A Study of Seventeenth-Century Elites*. 2nd. edn. Cambridge: Polity Press, 1994.

Bury, Michael. "The Fifteenth- and Early Sixteenth-Century *gonfaloni* of Perugia." *Ren. Studs.*, 12, no. 1 (1998), 67–86.

Calabi, Donatella, and Paolo Morachiello. *Rialto: Le fabbriche e il Ponte 1514–1591*. Turin: Einaudi, 1987.

Calimani, Riccardo. *The Ghetto of Venice*. Translated by Katherine Silberblatt Wolfthal. New York: Barnes & Noble, 1987.

Calo, Mary Ann. *Bernard Berenson and the Twentieth Century*. Philadelphia: Temple University Press, 1994.

Cameron, Euan. "Italy." In *The Early Reformation in Europe*, edited by Andrew Pettegree, 188–213. Cambridge: Cambridge University Press, 1992.

Canaletto: The Complete Paintings. Introduction by David Bindman, notes and catalogue by Lionello Puppi. London: Weidenfeld & Nicholson, 1968.

Candiani, C. "Antichi titoli delle chiese." In Tramontin et al., *Culto dei santi*, 99–132.

Caniato, Giovanni. "L'Arsenale: Maestranze e organizzazione del lavoro." In *Storia di Venezia*, vol.5, *Il rinascimento: Società ed economia*. Edited by Alberto Tenenti and Ugo Tucci, 641–789. Rome: Istituto dell'Enciclopedia Italiana, 1996.

Cantimori, Delio. *Eretici italiani del '500: Ricerche storiche*. Florence: Sansoni, 1939.

— "The Problem of Heresy: The History of the Reformation and of Italian Heresies in the History of Religious Life in the First Half of the Sixteeenth Century - the Relation between Two Kinds of Research." In Cochrane, *Late Italian Renaissance*, 211–25.

Carlsmith, Christopher. *A Renaissance Education; Schooling in Bergamo and the Venetian Republic, 1500–1650*. Toronto: University of Toronto Press, 2010.

Cecchetti, Bartolomeo. *La vita dei veneziani nel '300*. Bologna: A. Forni, 1980. Reprint of *La città* and *La laguna*, 1885; *Le vesti*, 1886.

Cervelli, Innocenzo. *Machiavelli e la crisi dello stato veneziano*. Naples: Guida, 1974.

Cessi, Roberto. "L''officium de navigantibus' e i sistemi della politica commerciale veneziana nel sec. XIV." In *Politica ed economia*, 23–61.

— *Politica ed economia di Venezia nel trecento: Saggi*. Rome: Edizioni di Storia e Letteratura, 1952.

— "Politica ed economia veneziana del Trecento." In *Politica ed economia*, 7–22.

— "Prestiti pubblici e imposta diretta nell'antica Repubblica veneta." In *Politica ed economia*, 173–8.

Chabod, Federico. "Alcune questioni di terminologia: Stato, nazione, patria nel linguaggio del Cinquecento." In *Scritti sul rinascimento*, 625–61.

— "L'epoca di Carlo V." In *L'epoca di Carlo V*, edited by Edoardo Arslan et al., 1–506. Vol. 9 of *Storia di Milano*. Milan: Treccani, 1961.

— "Giovanni Botero." In *Scritti sul rinascimento*, 271–458.

— *La politica di Paolo Sarpi*. Venice-Rome: Istituto per la Collaborazione Culturale, 1962.

— *Scritti sul rinascimento*. Turin: Einaudi, 1967.

Chaudhuri, K.N. "Reflections on the Organizing Principle of Pre-Modern Trade." In Tracy, *Political Economy*, 421–42.

Chojnacka, Monica. *Working Women of Early Modern Venice*. Baltimore, MD, and London: Johns Hopkins University Press, 2001.

Chojnacki, Stanley. "Identity and Ideology in Renaissance Venice: The Third *Serrata*." In Martin and Romano, *Venice Reconsidered*, 263–94.

— *Women and Men in Renaissance Venice: Twelve Essays on Patrician Society*. Baltimore and London: Johns Hopkins University Press, 2000.

Cipolla, Carlo M. *Cristofano and the Plague: A Study in the History of Public Health in the Age of Galileo*. London: Collins, 1973.

Clark, G.N. *The Seventeenth Century*. 2nd ed. Oxford: Oxford University Press, 1950.

Clark, Kenneth. *Civilisation: A Personal View*. London: BBC Books, 1969.

— *The Study of Art History*. London: The Historical Association, 1956. Reprinted from *Universities Quarterly* 10, no. 3 (1956).

Clough, Cecil H. "Love and War in the Veneto: Luigi da Porto and the True Story of *Giulietta e Romeo*." In, *War, Culture and Society in Renaissance Venice: Essays in Honour of John Hale*, edited by D.S. Chambers, Cecil H. Clough, and Michael Mallett, 99–128. London and Rio Grande, OH: Hambledon Press, 1993.

Clubb, Louise G. "Italian Stories on the Stage." In *The Cambridge Companion to Shakespearean Comedy*, edited by Alexander Leggatt, 32–46. Cambridge: Cambridge University Press, 2002.

— "Il teatro manieristico italiano e Shakespeare." In *Cultura e società nel rinascimento tra riforma e manierismo*, edited by Vittore Branca and Carlo Ossola, 427–48. Florence: Olschki, 1985.

Cochrane, Eric, ed. *The Late Italian Renaissance, 1525–1630*. London: Macmillan, 1970.

Cohn, Norman. *The Pursuit of the Millennium: Revolutionary Millenarians and Mystical Anarchists of the Middle Ages*. Oxford: Oxford University Press, 1970.

Cohn, Samuel K. *The Black Death Transformed: Disease and Culture in Early Renaissance Europe*. London: Arnold, 2002.

Coleman, D.C. "Eli Heckscher and the Idea of Mercantilism." In *Revisions in Mercantilism*, 92–117.

—, ed. *Revisions in Mercantilism*. Bungay, UK: Methuen, 1969.

Collinson, Patrick. "The Monarchical Republic of Queen Elizabeth I." *Bulletin of the John Rylands University Library of Manchester*, 69 (1986–7), 394–424. Also in *The Tudor Monarchy*, edited by John Guy, 110–34. London: Arnold, 1997.

Concina, Ennio. *L'Arsenale della repubblica di Venezia: Tecniche e istituzioni dal Medioevo all'età moderna*. Milan: Electa, 1988.

— *Le chiese di Venezia: L'arte e la storia*. Udine: Magnus Edizioni, 1995.

— *A History of Venetian Architecture*. Translated by Judith Landry. Cambridge: Cambridge University Press, 1998.

Connell, Susan Mary. "The Employment of Sculptors and Stonemasons in Venice in the Fifteenth Century." PhD diss., Warburg Institute, London, 1976.

Constable, M.V. "The Venetian 'Figlie del Coro': Their Environment and Achievement." *Music & Letters* 63, nos. 3–4 (1982), 181–212.

Contento, Aldo. "Il censimento della popolazione sotto la Repubblica veneta." *NAV*, 19 (1900) part i, 5–42; *NAV*, 20 (1900), part i, 5–96; part ii, 171–235.

Cooper, James Fenimore. *The Bravo* (1831). Reprint, Amsterdam, Netherlands: Fredonia Books, 2002.

Cooper, Tracy E. *Palladio's Venice: Architecture and Society in a Renaissance Republic.* New Haven, CT, and London: Yale University Press, 2005.

— "Patricians and Citizens." In Humfrey, *Venice and the Veneto*, 151–203.

Cope, Maurice E. *The Venetian Chapel of the Sacrament in the Sixteenth Century.* New York and London: Garland, 1979.

Cortelazzo, Manlio. "La cultura mercantile e marinaresca." In *Dalle origini al trecento*, edited by Gianfranco Folena, 671–91. Vol. 1 of *Storia della Cultura Veneta.* Vicenza: Neri Pozza, 1976.

Cowan, Alexander. *Marriage, Manners and Mobility in Early Modern Venice.* Aldershot, UK: Ashgate, 2007.

—, ed. *Mediterranean Urban Culture.* Exeter, UK: Exeter University Press, 2000.

-—"New Families in the Venetian Patriciate, 1646–1718." *Ateneo Veneto* 23, nos.1–2 (1985), 55–73.

— *The Urban Patriciate: Lübeck and Venice, 1580–1700.* Vienna: Bohlau, 1986.

Cox, Virginia. "The Single Self: Feminist Thought and the Marriage Market in Early Modern Venice." *RenQ*, 48 (1995), 513–81.

Cozzi, Gaetano. "Authority and the Law in Renaissance Venice." In Hale, *Renaissance Venice*, 293–345.

— "La Compagnia di Gesù a Venezia (1550–1657)." In *Venezia barocca*, 289–323.

— *Il Doge Nicolo Contarini: Ricerche sul patriziato veneziano agli inizi del seicento.* Florence: Olschki, 1958–9. Republished in *Venezia barocca*, 1–246.

— "Fortuna, e sfortuna della Compagnia di Gesù a Venezia." In Zanardi, *I Gesuiti e Venezia*, 59–88.

— *Paolo Sarpi tra Venezia e l'Europa.* Turin: Einaudi, 1979.

— "Paolo Sarpi tra Venezia e l'Europa." In *Paolo Sarpi tra Venezia e l'Europa*, 235–82.

— *Repubblica di Venezia e stati italiani: Politica e giustizia dal secolo XVI al secolo XVIII.* Turin: Einaudi 1982.

— "Stato e Chiesa." In *Venezia barocca*, 261–85.

— *Venezia barocca: Conflitti di uomini e idee nella crisi del Seicento veneziano.* Venice: Il Cardo, 1995.

Cozzi, Gaetano, and Michael Knapton. *Storia della Repubblica di Venezia dalla Guerra di Chioggia alla riconquista della Terraferma. Storia d'Italia*, vol. 12, tome 1. Turin: UTET, 1986.

Cozzi, Gaetano, Michael Knapton, and Giovanni Scarabello. *La Repubblica di Venezia nell'età moderna: Dal 1517 alla fine della Repubblica. Storia d'Italia*, vol. 12, tome 2. Turin: UTET, 1992.

Cracco, Giorgio. *Società e stato nel medioevo veneziano*. Florence: Olschki, 1967.

Crouzet-Pavan, Elisabeth. *"Sopra le acque salse": Espaces, pouvoirs et société à Venise à la fin du moyen age*. 2 vols. Collection de l'Ecole Française de Rome, 156. Rome: Ecole Française de Rome, 1992.

— *Venice Triumphant: The Horizons of a Myth*. Translated by Lydia G. Cochrane. Baltimore, MD, and London: Johns Hopkins University Press, 2002.

Dalla Costa, Mario. "La chiesa di Santa Maria Assunta di Gesuiti e la concezione palladiana." In Zanardi, *I Gesuiti e Venezia*, 713–21.

Da Mosto, Andrea. *L'Archivio di Stato di Venezia, Indice Generale, Storico, Descrittivo ed Analitico*. 2 vols. Rome: Biblioteca d'Arte Editrice, 1937–40. See also the digital edition, edited by Giuliano Granati and Antonio Romano.

Davidson, N.S. *The Counter-Reformation*. Historical Association Studies. Oxford: Basil Blackwell, 1987.

— "Northern Italy in the 1590s." In *The European Crisis of the 1590s: Essays in Comparative History*, edited by Peter Clark, 157–76. London: George Allen & Unwin, 1985.

— "Rome and the Venetian Inquisition in the Sixteenth Century." *JEcclH*, 39 (1988), 16–36.

— "La tutela del culto a Venezia nel '500." *SV*, n.s. 6 (1982), 87–101.

Davis, James Cushman. *The Decline of the Venetian Nobility as a Ruling Class*. Baltimore, MD: Johns Hopkins University Press, 1962.

— *A Venetian Family and Its Fortune, 1500–1900: The Donà and the Conservation of Their Wealth*. Philadelphia: American Philosophical Society, 1975.

Davis, Natalie Zemon. *Trickster Travels: A Sixteenth-Century Muslim between Worlds*. New York: Hill & Wang, 2006.

Davis, Ralph. *A Commercial Revolution: English Overseas Trade in the Seventeenth and Eighteenth Centuries*. Historical Association Pamphlet, 64. London: Historical Association, 1967.

Davis, Robert C. *Shipbuilders of the Venetian Arsenal: Workers and Workplace in the Preindustrial City*. Baltimore, MD, and London: Johns Hopkins University Press, 1991.

De Franceschi, Sylvio Hermann. *Raison d'état et raison d'église: La France et l'Interdit venitien (1606–1607), aspects diplomatiques et doctrinaux*. Paris: Champion, 2009.

Del Torre, Giuseppe. "La politica ecclesiastica della Repubblica di Venezia nell'età moderna: La fiscalità." In Kellenbenz and Prodi, *Fisco religione Stato*, 387–426.

Delumeau, Jean. *Catholicism between Luther and Voltaire: A New View of the Counter-Reformation*. Translated by Jeremy Moiser, introduction by John Bossy. London: Burns & Oates, 1977.

— *Vie économique et sociale de Rome dans la seconde moitié du 16e siècle*. 2 vols. Paris: E. de Boccard, 1957–9.
Demus, Otto. *The Mosaic Decoration of San Marco, Venice*. Edited by Herbert L. Kessler. Chicago: University of Chicago Press, 1988.
D'Entrèves, A.P. *Dante as a Political Thinker*. Oxford: Oxford University Press, 1952.
Derbes, Anne, and Mark Sandona. *The Usurer's Heart: Giotto, Enrico Scrovegni, and the Arena Chapel in Padua*. University Park: Pennsylvania State University Press, 2008.
De Roover, Raymond. "Labour Conditions in Florence around 1400: Theory, Policy and Reality." In Rubinstein, *Florentine Studies*, 277–313.
Derosas, Renzo. "Moralità e giustizia a Venezia nel '500–'600: Gli Esecutori contra la Bestemmia." In *Stato, società e giustizia nella Repubblica veneta (sec.xv–xviii)*, vol.1, edited by Gaetano Cozzi, 431–529. Rome: Jouvence, 1984–5.
De Santillana, Giorgio. *The Crime of Galileo*. Chicago: Chicago University Press, 1955.
De Vivo, Filippo. "'Il vero termine di reggere il suddito': Paolo Sarpi e l'informazione." In *Ripensando Paolo Sarpi: Atti del Convegno internazionale di studi nel 450o anniversario della nascita*, edited by C. Pin, 237–70. Venice: Ateneo Veneto, 2006.
Dickens, Charles. *Pictures from Italy* (1846). In *Master Humphrey's Clock and Italian Hours*, illustrated by W.H.C. Groome. London and Glasgow: Collins, n.d.
Diehl, Charles. *Venise: Une république patricienne*. Paris: Flammarion, 1915.
Donaldson, Peter S. *Machiavelli and Mystery of State*. Cambridge: Cambridge University Press, 1988.
Dotson, Esther Gordon. "An Augustinian Interpretation of Michelangelo's Sistine Ceiling." *The Art Bulletin*, 61 (1979), 250–5 (part 1), 405–29 (part 2).
Doumerc, Bernard, and Claire Judde de la Rivière. "Le rôle du patriciat dans la gestion des galères marchandes à Venise au début du seizième siècle." *SV*, n.s. 36 (1998), 57–84.
Dronke, Peter. "The Conclusion." In *Dante*, edited by Jeremy Tambling, 160–82. London: Longman, 1999.
Duby, Georges. *Rural Economy and Country Life in the Medieval West*. Translated by Cynthia Postan. Columbia: University of South Carolina Press, 1976.
Duplessis, Robert C., and Martha C. Howell. "Reconsidering the Early Modern Economy: The Cases of Leiden and Lille." *PP*, 94 (1982), 49–84.
The Economist. Unsigned review of *Montaillou: Cathars and Catholics in a French Village, 1294–1324*, by Emmanuel Le Roy Ladurie, translated by Barbara Bray (Harmondsworth, UK: Penguin, 1978). 3 June 1978, 133–4.
Ehrenberg, Richard. *Capital and Finance in the Age of the Renaissance: A Study of the Fuggers and their Connections*. Translated by H.M. Lucas. London: Jonathan Cape, 1928.
Eisler, Colin T. *The Genius of Jacopo Bellini: The Complete Paintings and Drawings*. New York: H.N. Abrams, 1989.

Elliott, J.H. *Europe Divided, 1559–1598*. London: Collins, 1968.

Ellis, Madeleine B. *Rousseau's Venetian Story: An Essay upon Art and Truth in "Les Confessions."* Baltimore, MD: Johns Hopkins University Press, 1966.

Elton, G.R. *Reformation Europe, 1517–1559*. London and Glasgow: Collins, 1964.

— *Return to Essentials: Some Reflections on the Present State of Historical Study*. Cambridge: Cambridge University Press, 1991.

Enno van Gelder, H.A. *The Two Reformations in the Sixteenth Century: A Study of the Religious Aspects and Consequences of Renaissance and Humanism*. The Hague: Martinus Nijhoff, 1964.

Evans, R.J.W. *Rudolf II and His World: A Study in Intellectual History, 1576–1612*. Oxford: Oxford University Press, 1973.

Evennett, H. Outram. *The Spirit of the Counter-Reformation*. Edited with a postscript by John Bossy. Notre Dame, IN, and London: University of Notre Dame Press, 1968.

Fahy, Conor. "The *Index Librorum Prohibitorum* and the Venetian Printing Industry in the Sixteenth Century." *Italian Studies*, 35 (1980), 52–61.

Fano, N. "Ricerche sull'arte della lana a Venezia nei sec. 13 e 14." *AV*, 18 (1936), 73–213.

Fasoli, Gina. "La 'Chronique des Veniciens' de Martin da Canale." *Studi Medievali*, ser. 3, 2, fasc. i (1961), 42–74.

— "Venezia: Nascita di un mito." In *Studi storici in onore di Gioacchino Volpe*, vol. 1, 445–79. Florence: Sansoni, 1958.

Favalier, Sylvie. "Le attività lavorative in una parrocchia del centro di Venezia (San Polo - secolo xvi)." *SV*, n.s. 9 (1985), 187–99.

Favilla, Massimo, and Ruggiero Rugolo. *Baroque Venice: Splendour and Illusion in a "Decadent" World*. Introduction by Filippo Pedrocco. Translated by Simon Turner. Vicenza: Sassi, 2009.

Febvre, Lucien. "History and Psychology." In *A New Kind of History*, 1–11.

— *A New Kind of History*. Edited by Peter Burke, translated by K. Folca. London: Routledge and Kegan Paul, 1973.

— *The Problem of Unbelief in the Sixteenth Century: The Religion of Rabelais*. Translated by Beatrice Gottlieb. Cambridge, MA, and London: Harvard University Press, 1982.

— "Sensibility and History: How to Reconstitute the Emotional Life of the Past." In *A New Kind of History*, 12–26.

Feci, S. "Pio V, papa (Michiele Antonio Ghislieri)." In Prosperi, *Dizionario Storico dell'Inquisizione*, vol. 3, 1213–15.

Fenlon, Dermot. *Heresy and Obedience in Tridentine Italy: Cardinal Pole and the Counter Reformation*. Cambridge: Cambridge University Press, 1972.

Fenlon, Iain. *The Ceremonial City: History, Memory and Myth in Renaissance Venice*. New Haven, CT: Yale University Press, 2007.

Ferguson, Ronnie. *A Linguistic History of Venice*. Florence: Olschki, 2006.

Ferraro, Joanne M. *Family and Public Life in Brescia: The Foundations of Power in the Venetian State, 1580–1650*. Cambridge: Cambridge University Press, 1993.

Fink, Zera S. *The Classical Republicans: An Essay in the Recovery of a Pattern of Thought in Seventeenth-Century England*. Evanston, IL: Northwestern University Press, 1945.

Finlay, Robert. "Crisis and Crusade in the Mediterranean: Venice, Portugal, and the Cape Route to India (1498–1509)." *SV*, n.s. 28 (1994), 45–90.

— *Politics in Renaissance Venice*. London: Ernest Benn, 1980.

— "Venice, the Po Expedition and the End of the League of Cambrai, 1509–1510." *Studies in Modern European History and Culture* 2 (1974), 37–72.

Finlay, Roger, and Beatrice Shearer. "Population Growth and Suburban Expansion." In *London, 1500–1700: The Making of the Metropolis*, edited by A.L. Beier and Roger Finlay, 37–59. London: Longman, 1986.

Firpo, Massimo. *Artisti, gioiellieri, eretici: Il mondo di Lorenzo Lotto tra Riforma e Controriforma*. Roma-Bari: Laterza, 2001.

Fogazzaro, Antonio. *Piccolo mondo antico* (1931). Edited by Anna Maria Moroni, with a note by Riccardo Barchielli. Milan: Arnaldo Mondadori, 1984.

Forsellini, Marco. "L'organizzazione economica dell'Arsenale di Venezia nella prima metà del '600." *AV*, ser. 5, 7 (1930), 54–117.

Franceschini, Gino. "Le dominazioni francesi e le restaurazioni sforzesche." In *Tra Francia e Spagna*, 83–336. Vol. 8 of *Storia di Milano*, edited by Edoardo Arslan et al. Milan: Treccani, 1957.

Franzoi, Umberto, and Dina Di Stefano. *Le chiese di Venezia*. Venice: Alfieri, 1976.

Gaeta, Franco. "Alcune considerazioni sul mito di Venezia." *Bibliothèque d'Humanisme et Renaissance*, 23 (1961), 58–76.

Gallo, Rodolfo. "La Scuola Grande di San Teodoro di Venezia." *Atti dell'Istituto Veneto di Scienze, Lettere ed Arti*, 120 (*Classe di Scienze Morali e Lettere*) (1961–2), 461–95.

Galpern, A.N. "Late Medieval Piety in Sixteenth-Century Champagne." In *The Pursuit of Holiness in Late Medieval and Renaissance Religion*, edited by Charles E. Trinkaus and Heiko A. Oberman. Vol. 10 of *Studies in Medieval and Reformation Thought*. 141–76. Leiden, Netherlands: E.J. Brill, 1974.

— *The Religions of the People in Sixteenth-Century Champagne*. Cambridge, MA: Harvard University Press, 1976.

Gaskell, Ivan. "History of Images." In Burke, *New Perspectives*, 168–92.

Gentili, A. ""*Il Sogno dil Caravia*."" *Venezia Cinquecento*, 1 (1999), 139ff.

Geyl, Peter. "Huizinga as Accuser of His Age." In *Encounters in History*, 188–238. London and Glasgow: Collins, 1967.

Gianighian, Giorgio, and Paola Pavanini. *Dietro i palazzi: Tre secoli di architettura minore a Venezia 1492–1803*. Venice: Arsenale Editrice, 1984.

Gilbert, Felix. "The Date of the Composition of Contarini's and Giannotti's Books on Venice." *Studies in the Renaissance*, 14 (1967), 172–84.

— "Venice in the Crisis of the League of Cambrai." In Hale, *Renaissance Venice*, 274–93.

— "Religion and Politics in the Thought of Gasparo Contarini." In *Action and Conviction in Early Modern Europe: Essays in Honor of E.H. Harbison*, edited by Theodore K. Rabb and Jerrold E. Seigel, 90–116. Princeton, NJ: Princeton University Press, 1969.

Gilchrist, J. *The Church and Economic Activity in the Middle Ages*. London: Macmillan, 1969.

Gilmore, Myron. "Myth and Reality in Venetian Political Thought." In Hale, *Renaissance Venice*, 431–44.

Gleason, Elisabeth G. "Confronting New Realities: Venice and the Peace of Bologna, 1530." In Martin and Romano, *Venice Reconsidered*, 168–84.

— *Gasparo Contarini: Venice, Rome and Reform*. Berkeley and Los Angeles: University of California Press, 1993.

Glixon, Jonathan E. *Honoring God and the City: Music at the Venetian Confraternities, 1260–1807*. Oxford: Oxford University Press, 2003.

Godinho, Vittorino Magalhães. "Venise: Les dimensions d'une présence face à un monde tellement changé - XVe–XVIe siècles." In *Venezia: Centro di mediazione tra oriente e occidente (secoli XV–XVI); Aspetti e problemi*, edited by Hans-Georg Beck, Manoussos Manousacas, and Agostino Pertusi, vol. 1, 11–50. Florence: Olschki, 1977.

Goffen, Rhona. *Piety and Patronage in Renaissance Venice: Bellini, Titian, and the Franciscans*. New Haven, CT: Yale University Press, 1986.

Goldoni, Carlo. *La Locandiera* (1753). Edited by Guido Davico Bonino, with a note by Giorgio Strehler. Milan: Oscar Mondadori, 1983.

Goldthwaite, Richard A. *The Economy of Renaissance Florence*. Baltimore, MD, and London: Johns Hopkins University Press, 2009.

Gombrich, E.H. "Art History and the Social Sciences." In *Ideals and Idols*, 131–65.

— *Ideals and Idols: Essays on Values in History and in Art*. London: Phaidon, 1979.

— "In Search of Cultural History." In *Ideals and Idols*, 24–59.

Gordon, Bruce. "Italy." In *The Reformation World*, edited by Andrew Pettegree, 277–95. London: Routledge, 2000.

Goy, Richard J. *Building Renaissance Venice: Patrons, Architects and Builders, c.1430–1500*. New Haven, CT: Yale University Press, 2006.

— *The House of Gold: Building a Palace in Medieval Venice*. Cambridge: Cambridge University Press, 1992.

— *Venice: An Architectural Guide*. New Haven, CT, and London: Yale University Press, 2010.

Gramigna, Silvia, and Annalisa Perissa. *Scuole di arti mestieri e devozione a Venezia*. Venice: Arsenale Editrice, 1981.

Greenblatt, Stephen. "The Circulation of Social Energy." In *Shakespearean Negotiations: The Circulation of Social Energy in Renaissance England*, 1–20. Oxford: Oxford University Press 1988.

— *Renaissance Self-Fashioning: From More to Shakespeare*. Chicago: Chicago University Press, 1980.

Greengrass, Mark. *The Longman Companion to the European Reformation, c. 1500–1618*. London and New York: Longman, 1997.

Grendler, Paul F. *The Roman Inquisition and the Venetian Press, 1540–1605*. Princeton, NJ: Princeton University Press, 1977.

Grubb, James S. "Elite Citizens." In Martin and Romano, *Venice Reconsidered*, 339–64.

— *Firstborn of Venice: Vicenza in the Early Renaissance State*. Baltimore, MD, and London: Johns Hopkins University Press, 1988.

— *Provincial Families of the Renaissance: Private and Public Life in the Veneto*. Baltimore, MD: Johns Hopkins University Press, 1996.

— "When Myths Lose Their Power: Four Decades of Venetian Historiography." *JMH*, 58 (1986), 43–94.

Gullino, Giuseppe. "Il rientro dei gesuiti a Venezia nel 1657: Le ragioni della politica e dell'economia." In Zanardi, *I Gesuiti e Venezia*, 421–33.

Hacke, Daniela. *Women, Sex and Marriage in Early Modern Venice*. Aldershot, UK: Ashgate, 2004.

Haitsma Mulier, Eco O.G. *The Myth of Venice and Dutch Republican Thought in the Seventeenth Century*. Translated by Gerard T. Moran. Assen, Netherlands: Van Gorcum, 1980.

Hale, John R. *Florence and the Medici: The Pattern of Control*. London: Thames & Hudson, 1977.

—, ed. *Renaissance Venice*. London: Faber & Faber, 1974.

Haskell, Francis. "Huizinga and the 'Flemish Renaissance.'" In *History and its Images: Art and the Interpretation of the Past*, 433–95. New Haven, CT, and London: Yale University Press, 1993.

Hay, Denys. *The Church in Italy in the Fifteenth Century*. Cambridge: Cambridge University Press, 1977.

Hay, Denys, and John Law. *Italy in the Age of the Renaissance, 1380–1530*. London: Longman, 1989.

Haydn, Hiram. *The Counter-Renaissance*. New York: Harcourt, Brace & World, 1950.

Heckscher, Eli F. "Mercantilism." In Coleman, *Revisions*, 19–34.

Henderson, John. *Piety and Charity in Late Medieval Florence*. Oxford: Oxford University Press, 1994.

Hexter, J.H. "Storm over the Gentry." In *Reappraisals in History*, 117–62. London: Longmans, 1961.

Hill, Christopher. "The Definition of a Puritan." In *Society and Puritanism*, 15–30.

— "Puritans and the 'Dark Corners of the Land.'" *TRHS*, ser. 5, 13 (1963), 77–102.

— *Society and Puritanism in Pre-Revolutionary England*. London: Panther, 1969.

— "The Uses of Sabbatarianism." In *Society and Puritanism*, 141–211.

Hills, Paul. "Piety and Patronage in Cinquecento Venice: Tintoretto and the Scuole del Sacramento." *Art History* 6, no. 1 (1983), 30–43.

Hilton, Tim. *John Ruskin*. New Haven, CT, and London: Yale University Press, 2002.

Holderness, Graham. *Shakespeare and Venice*. Andover, UK: Ashgate, 2010.

Holmes, George. *Europe: Hierarchy and Revolt, 1320–1450*. London: Fontana, 1975.

Hope, Charles. "Titian as Court Painter." *Oxford Art Journal*, 2 (1979), 7–10.

Hoshino, Hidetoshi. *L'arte della lana nel basso medioevo: Il commercio della lana e il mercato dei panni nei secoli XIII–XV*. Florence: Leo S. Olschki, 1981.

Howard, Deborah. *The Architectural History of Venice*. London: Batsford, 1980.

— *Jacopo Sansovino: Architecture and Patronage in Renaissance Venice*. New Haven, CT, and London: Yale University Press, 1987.

Howard, Deborah, and Laura Moretti. *Sound and Space in Renaissance Venice: Architecture, Music, Acoustics*. New Haven, CT, and London: Yale University Press, 2009.

Howard, Michael. *War in European History*. Oxford: Oxford University Press, 1976.

Hsia, R. Po-Chia. *Social Discipline in the Reformation: Central Europe, 1550–1750*. London: Routledge, 1989.

— *The World of Catholic Renewal, 1540–1770*. Cambridge: Cambridge University Press, 1998.

Huizinga, Johan. "The Aesthetic Element in Historical Thought." In *Dutch Civilisation in the Seventeenth Century and Other Essays*, selected by Pieter Geyl and F.W.N. Hugenholtz, translated by Arnold J. Pomerans, 219–43. London: Collins, 1968.

— *Men and Ideas: Essays on History, the Middle Ages, the Renaissance*. Translated by James S. Holmes and Hans van Marle. New York: Harper & Row, 1970.

— "The Problem of the Renaissance." In *Men and Ideas*, 243–87.

— "The Task of Cultural History." In *Men and Ideas*, 17–76.

Humfrey, Peter. "The Bellinesque Life of St. Mark Cycle for the Scuola Grande di San Marco in Venice in Its Original Arrangement." *Zeitschrift für Kunstgeschichte*, 48 (1985), 225–42.

— "Competitive Devotions: The Venetian *Scuole Piccole* as Donors of Altarpieces in the Years around 1500." *Art Bulletin* 70, no. 3 (1988), 401–22.

— *Painting in Renaissance Venice*. New Haven, CT, and London: Yale University Press, 1995.

Humfrey, Peter, and Richard Mackenney. "The Venetian Trade Guilds as Patrons of Art in the Renaissance." *Burlington Magazine* 128, no. 998 (1986), 317–30.

Huxley, Aldous. *Grey Eminence: A Study in Religion and Politics*. London: Chatto & Windus, 1949.

Hyde, J.K. *Padua in the Age of Danta: A Social History of an Italian City-State.* Manchester: Manchester University Press, 1966.

Israel, Jonathan. *European Jewry in the Age of Mercantilism, 1550–1750.* Revised edition. Oxford: Oxford University Press, 1989.

Jacob, E.F. "Conciliar Thought." In *Essays in the Conciliar Epoch*, 1–23. Manchester: Manchester University Press, 1953.

Jacobsen Schutte, Anne. *Aspiring Saints, Pretence of Holiness, Inquisition and Gender in the Republic of Venice, 1618–1750.* Baltimore, MD, and London: Johns Hopkins University Press, 2001.

— "Periodization of Sixteenth-Century Italian Religious History: The Post-Cantimori Paradigm Shift." *JMH*, 61 (1989), 269–84.

Janelle, Pierre. *The Catholic Reformation.* London: Collier Macmillan, 1963.

Johnson, A.H. *Europe in the Sixteenth Century, 1494–1598.* 7th edn. London: Rivingtons, 1941.

Jones, P.J. "Communes and Despots: The City-State in Late Medieval Italy." *TRHS*, 15 (1965), 71–96. Also in *Communes and Despots in Medieval and Renaissance Italy*, edited by John E. Law and Bernadette Paton, 3–26. Farnham, UK: Ashgate, 2010.

— "Economia e società nell'Italia medievale: La leggenda della borghesia." In *Storia d'Italia, Annali 1: Dal feudalesimo al capitalismo*, 185–372. Turin: Einaudi, 1978.

— *The Italian City-State, 1000–1300: From Commune to Signoria.* Oxford: Oxford University Press, 1997.

Judges, A.V. "The Idea of a Mercantile State." In Coleman, *Revisions*, 35–60.

Kahr, Madlyn. "The Meaning of Veronese's Paintings in the Church of San Sebastiano in Venice." *JWCI*, 33 (1970), 235–47.

Kantorowicz, Ernst H. *The King's Two Bodies: A Study in Medieval Political Theology.* Princeton, NJ: Princeton University Press, 1957.

Kellenbenz, Hermann. "Le déclin de Venise et les relations économiques de Venise avec les marchés au nord des Alpes." In *Aspetti e cause*, 109–83.

Kermode, Frank. *The Age of Shakespeare.* New York: Modern Library, 2004.

King, Margaret L. "Personal, Domestic and Republican Values in the Moral Philosophy of Giovanni Caldiera." *RenQ*, 28 (1975), 535–74.

— *Venetian Humanism in an Age of Patrician Dominance.* Princeton, NJ: Princeton University Press, 1986.

Klaassen, Walter. *Michael Gaismair: Revolutionary and Reformer.* Vol. 23 of *Studies in Medieval and Reformation Thought.* Leyden: E.J. Brill, 1978.

Koenigsberger, Helmut G. "Decadence or Shift?" In *Estates and Revolutions: Essays in Early Modern History*, 278–98. Ithaca, NY, and London: Cornell University Press: 1971.

Kohl, Benjamin G. *Padua under the Carrara, 1318–1405.* Baltimore and London: Johns Hopkins University Press, 1998.

Labalme, Patricia H. "Personality and Politics: Pietro Aretino." In Rosand, *Titian, His World and His Legacy*, 119–32.

Lane, Frederic C. *Andrea Barbarigo, Merchant of Venice, 1418–1449*. Baltimore, MD: Johns Hopkins University Press, 1966.

— "Economic Consequences of Organized Violence." In *Venice and History*, 412–30.

— "The Enlargement of the Great Council of Venice." In "*Florilegium Historiale*": *Essays Presented to Wallace K. Ferguson*, edited by J.G. Rowe and W.H. Stockdale, 236–74. Toronto: University of Toronto Press, 1971.

— "Family Partnerships and Joint Ventures." In *Venice and History*, 36–55.

— "Fleets and Fairs." In *Venice and History*, 128–42.

— "The Funded Debt of the Venetian Republic, 1262–1482." In *Venice and History*, 87–98.

— "Maritime Law and Administration, 1250–1350." In *Venice and History*, 227–52.

— "Medieval Political Ideas and the Venetian Constitution." In *Venice and History*, 285–310.

— "The Mediterranean Spice Trade: Its Revival in the Sixteenth Century." In *Venice and History*, 25–35.

— "Some Heirs of Gustav von Schmoller." In *Venice and History*, 462–95.

— *Venetian Ships and Shipbuilders of the Renaissance*. Baltimore, MD: Johns Hopkins University Press, 1934. Reprint, 1993.

— *Venice: A Maritime Republic*. Baltimore, MD: Johns Hopkins University Press, 1975.

— *Venice and History: The Collected Papers of Frederic C. Lane*. Baltimore, MD: Johns Hopkins University Press, 1966.

— "Wages and Recruitment of Venetian *galeotti*, 1470–1580." *SV*, n.s. 6 (1982), 15–43.

Lane, Frederic C., and Reinhold C. Mueller. *Money and Banking in Medieval and Renaissance Venice*. Vol.1, *Coins and Moneys of Account*. Baltimore, MD, and London: Johns Hopkins University Press, 1985.

Larner, John. *Marco Polo and the Discovery of the World*. New Haven, CT, and London: Yale University Press, 1999.

La Roncière, Charles M. de. *Prix et salaires à Florence au xive siècle, 1280–1380*. Rome: Ecole Française de Rome, 1982.

Laven, Peter. "The Venetian Rivers in the Sixteenth Century." In *Montagnes, fleuves, forêts dans l'histoire: Barrieres ou lignes de convergence? Berge, Flüsse, Wälder in der Geschichte. Hindernisse oder Begegnungsraühme?*, edited by Jean-François Bergier, 198–217. St Katherinen: Scripta Mercatura Verlag, 1989.

Law, John Easton. *The Lords of Renaissance Italy: The Signori, 1250–1500*. London: The Historical Association, 1981.

— "Relations between Venice and the Provinces of the Mainland." In *Venice and the Veneto*, ch. 4, 77–85.

— "The Venetian Mainland State in the Fifteenth Century." *TRHS*, 2, 5th ser. (1992), 153–74. Also in *Venice and the Veneto*, ch. 1, 153–74.

— *Venice and the Veneto in the Early Renaissance*. Aldershot, UK: Ashgate, 2000.

Leff, Gordon. *History and Social Theory*. University, AL: University of Alabama Press, 1969.

Le Goff, Jacques. *Your Money or Your Life: Economy and Religion in the Middle Ages*. Translated by Patricia Ranum. New York: Zone Books, 1988.

Lepschy, Anna Laura. *Tintoretto Observed: A Documentary Survey of Critical Reactions from the Sixteenth to the Twentieth Century*. Ravenna: Longo, 1983.

Lerner, Robert E. *The Age of Adversity: The Fourteenth Century*. Ithaca, NY: Cornell University Press, 1968.

Le Roy Ladurie, Emmanuel. *Le territoire de l'historien*. Paris: Gallimard, 1973.

Levey, Michael. *Painting in Eighteenth-Century Venice*. 2nd edn. London: Phaidon, 1980.

Libby, Lester J., Jr. "Venetian History and Political Thought after 1509." *Studies in the Renaissance*, 20 (1973), 7–45.

Little, Lester K. *Religious Poverty and the Profit Economy in Medieval Europe*. London: Elek, 1978.

Logan, Oliver. "The Ideal of the Bishop and the Venetian Patriciate." *JEccHist*, 29 (1978), 415–50.

Lombardo, Agostino. "The Veneto, Metatheatre and Shakespeare." In Marrapodi et al., *Shakespeare's Italy*, 143–57.

Lopez, Robert S. *The Commercial Revolution of the Middle Ages, 950–1350*. Cambridge: Cambridge University Press, 1976.

Lopez, Robert Sabatino. "Venezia e le grandi linee dell'espansione commerciale nel secolo xiii." In *La civiltà veneziana del secolo di Marco Polo*, 37–82. Florence, 1955.

Lorenzetti, Giulio. *Venice and Its Lagoon: Historical-Artistic Guide*. Translated by John Guthrie. Trieste: Edizioni Lint, 1961.

Lowry, Martin J.C. "The Reform of the Council of Ten, 1582–3: An Unsettled Problem?" *SV*, 13 (1975), 275–310.

Luscombe, David. "The Sins of Montaillou" [A review of *Montaillou*, by Le Roy Ladurie]. *The Listener*, 6 July 1978, 26–8.

Luzzatto, Gino. "Capitoli e lavoro nel commercio veneziano dei secoli XI e XII." In *Studi di storia economica veneziana*, 89–116. Padua: CEDAM, 1954.

— *Storia economica di Venezia dal XI al XVI secolo*. Venice: Centro Internazionale delle Arti e del Costume, 1961.

Macaulay, Thomas Babington. "Ranke's *History of the Popes*." In *Critical and Historical Essays*, vol. 2, 1–37. London: Dent, 1907.

Mackenney, Richard. "The Guilds of Renaissance Venice: State and Society in the *longue durée*." *SV*, n.s. 34 (1997), 15–43.

— "'A Plot Discover'd?' Myth, Legend and the 'Spanish" Conspiracy against Venice in 1618." In Martin and Romano, *Venice Reconsidered*, 185–216.

— "Public and Private in Renaissance Venice." *Ren. Studs.* 12, no. 1 (1998), 109–30.

— *Renaissances: The Cultures of Italy, c. 1300–c. 1600.* Basingstoke, UK: Palgrave Macmillan, 2005.

— Review of *English Merchants in Seventeenth-Century Italy*, by Gigliola Pagano de Divitiis. *EHR*, 463 (2000), 968–9.

— "The *Scuole Piccole* of Venice: Formations and Transformations." In *The Politics of Ritual Kinship: Confraternities and Social Order in Early Modern Italy*, edited by Nicholas Terpstra, 172–89. Cambridge: Cambridge University Press, 2000.

— *Sixteenth Century Europe: Expansion and Conflict.* Basingstoke, UK: Macmillan, 1993.

— "Trade Guilds and Devotional Confraternities in the State and Society of Venice to 1620." PhD diss., University of Cambridge, 1982.

— *Tradesmen and Traders: The World of the Guilds in Venice and Europe, c. 1250–c. 1650.* London: Croom Helm, 1987.

— "Venice." In *The Renaissance in National Context*, edited by Roy Porter and Mikulas Teich, 53–67. Cambridge: Cambridge University Press, 1992.

Mackintosh, H.P. "Mercy." In *Encyclopedia of Religion and Ethics*, vol. 8, edited by James Hastings. New York: Charles Scribners, 1951.

Mâle, Emile. *L'art religieux après le Concile de Trente: Etude sur l'iconographie de la fin du xvie siècle, du xviie, du xviiie siècle; Italie-France-Espagne-Flandres.* Paris: Armand Colin, 1932.

Mallett, Michael, and J.R. Hale. *The Military Organisation of a Renaissance State: Venice, c. 1400–1617.* Cambridge: Cambridge University Press, 1984.

Manselli, Raoul. "L'anno 1260 fu anno Gioachimitico?" In *Movimento dei Disciplinati*, 99–108.

Manzoni, Alessandro. *I Promessi Sposi: Storia Milanese del secolo XVII.* Edited by Michele Messina. 2nd edn. Messina-Firenze: Casa Editrice G. d'Anna, 1964.

Maranini, Giuseppe. *La costituzione di Venezia* (1927). 2 vols. Florence: La Nuova Italia, 1974.

Marinelli, Sergio. "Intorno a Veronese." In *Veronese e Verona: Catalogo della Mostra – Veronese e Verona*, edited by Marinelli, 31–51. Verona: Federigoni, 1988.

Markham Schulz, Anne. "L'altare maggiore della chiesa veneziana della Misericordia e le sculture di Giovanni e Bartolomeo Bon per la Scuola Vecchia della Misericordia." *Arte Veneta*, 62 (2005), 26–39.

Marrapodi, Michele, A.J. Hoenselaars, Marcello Cappuzzo, and L. Fanzon Santucci, eds. *Shakespeare's Italy: Functions of Italian Locations in Renaissance Drama.* Rev. edn. Manchester, UK: Manchester University Press, 1997.

Martin, John Jeffries. *Venice's Hidden Enemies: Italian Heretics in a Renaissance City.* Berkeley, Los Angeles, and London: University of California Press, 1993.

Martin, John Jeffries, and Dennis Romano, eds. *Venice Reconsidered: The History and Civilisation of an Italian City-State, 1297–1797*. Baltimore, MD, and London: Johns Hopkins University Press, 2000.

Martines, Lauro. "The Gentleman in Renaissance Italy: Strains of Isolation in the Body Politic." In *The Darker Vision of the Renaissance: Beyond the Fields of Reason*, edited by Robert S. Kinsman, 77–94. Berkeley and Los Angeles: University of California Press, 1974.

Mason Rinaldi, Stefania. "Convenzioni della 'maniera' e istanze di rinnovamento in Jacopo Palma il Giovane." In *Cultura e società nel rinascimento tra riforme e manierismo*, edited by Vittore Branca and Carlo Ossola, 207–28. Florence: Olschki, 1985.

— *Palma il Giovane: L'opera completa*. Milan: Electa, 1984.

Matheson, Mark. "Venetian Culture and the Politics of *Othello*." In *Shakespeare and Politics*, edited by Catherine M.S. Alexander, 169–84. Cambridge: Cambridge University Press, 2004.

Matheson, Peter. *Cardinal Contarini at Regensburg*. Oxford: Oxford University Press, 1972.

Mauro, Frederic. "Merchant Communities, 1350–1750." In Tracy, *Rise of Merchant Empires*, 255–86.

McCray, W. Patrick. *Glassmaking in Renaissance Venice: The Fragile Craft*. Aldershot, UK: Ashgate, 1999.

Meersseman, Giles-Gerard. *Dossier de l'ordre de la Pénitence au xiiie siècle*. Freibourg: Editions Universitaires, 1961.

Miani, Martina, and Luca Baldin. *Churches of Venice: The Museum in the City*. Translated by David Graham. Venice: Marsilio, 2002.

Miskimin, Harry A. *The Economy of Early Renaissance Europe, 1300–1460*. Cambridge: Cambridge University Press, 1975.

Molà, Luca. *La comunità dei lucchesi a Venezia: Immigrazione e industria della seta nel tardo medioevo*. Venice: Istituto Veneto di Scienze, Lettere ed Arti, 1994.

Mollat, Michel, and Philippe Wolff, *The Popular Revolutions of the Late Middle Ages*. Translated by A.L. Lytton-Sells. London: George Allen & Unwin, 1973.

Mols, Roger, S.J. "Population in Europe, 1500–1700." In *The Sixteenth and Seventeenth Centuries*, vol. 2 of *The Fontana Economic History of* Europe, edited by Carlo M. Cipolla, 15–82. Glasgow: William Collins Sons, 1976.

Morghen, R. "Ranieri Fasani e il Movimento dei Disciplinati del 1260." In *Movimento dei Disciplinati*, 29–42.

Motture, Peta, and Victor Hugo Lopez Borges. "A Venetian Tympanum of the 'Madonna della Misericordia' by Bartolomeo Bon." *Burlington Magazine*, CLI, no. 1280 (2009), 746–54.

Mousnier, Roland. "The Exponents and Critics of Absolutism." In *The Decline of Spain and the Thirty Years' War, 1610–1648/59*, edited by J.P. Cooper, 104–31. Vol. 5 of *New Cambridge Modern History*. Cambridge: Cambridge University Press, 1970.

Movimento dei disciplinati nel settimo centenario dal suo inizio (Perugia-1260). Appendice 9 to *Bolletino della Deputazione di Storia Patria per l'Umbria.* Perugia: Deputazione di Storia Patria per l'Umbria, 1962.

Mueller, Reinhold C. "Aspetti sociali ed economici della peste a Venezia nel Medioevo." In *Venezia e la peste*, 71–96. Venice: Marsilio, 1979.

— "Charitable Institutions, the Jewish Community and Venetian Society: A Discussion of the Recent Volume by Brian Pullan." *SV*, 14 (1972), 38–78.

Muir, Edward. *Civic Ritual in Renaissance Venice.* Princeton, NJ: Princeton University Press, 1981.

— *The Culture Wars of the Late Renaissance: Skeptics, Libertines and Opera.* Cambridge, MA, and London: Harvard University Press, 2007.

— "The Ritual of Rulership in Sixteenth-Century Venice: A Study in the Construction and Promulgation of Myth and Ideology." PhD diss., Rutgers University, NJ, 1975.

— "Was there Republicanism in the Renaissance Republics?" In Martin and Romano, *Venice Reconsidered*, 137–67.

Mullett, Michael A. *The Catholic Reformation.* London: Routledge, 1999.

Mullini, Roberta. "Streets, Squares and Courts: Venice as a Stage in Shakespeare and Ben Jonson." In Marrapodi et al., *Shakespeare's Italy*, 158–70.

Mulryne, J.R. "History and Myth in *The Merchant of Venice.*" In Marrapodi et al., *Shakespeare's Italy*, 87–99.

Muraro, Michelangelo. "The Moors of the Clock Tower of Venice and Their Sculptor." *Art Bulletin*, 66 (1984), 603–9.

Muraro, Michelangelo, and André Grabar. *Treasures of Venice: The Church of St. Mark's, the Treasure of St. Mark's, the Ducal Palace, the Gallerie dell'Accademia, the Architecture and Monuments of Venice.* Translated by James Emmons. Geneva: Skira, 1963.

Muraro, Michelangelo, and Paolo Marton. *Venetian Villas.* Trans. Peter Lauritzen, John Harper, and Stephen Santarelli. Introduction by James Ackerman. Cologne: Könemann, 1986.

Najemy, John M. *Corporatism and Consensus in Florentine Electoral Politics, 1280–1400.* Chapel Hill: North Carolina University Press, 1982.

— Review of *Tradesmen and Traders: The World of the Guilds in Venice and Europe, c.1250-c.1650*, by Richard Mackenney. *JMH*, 3 (1989), 623–6.

Namier, Sir Lewis. "Nationality and Liberty." In *Vanished Supremacies*, 46–72. Harmondsworth, UK: Penguin, 1962.

Neff, Mary. "Chancellery Secretaries in Venetian Politics and Society, 1480–1533." PhD diss., University of California at Los Angeles, 1985.

Nelson, Benjamin N. *The Idea of Usury: From Tribal Brotherhood to Universal Otherhood.* Princeton, NJ: Princeton University Press, 1949.

— "The Usurer and the Merchant Prince: Italian Businessmen and the Ecclesiastical Law of Restitution." *J. Econ. Hist.*, 7 (1947), Supplement 7.

Newett, Margaret M. "The Sumptuary Laws of Venice." In *Historical Essays*, edited by T.F. Tout and J. Tait, 245–77. Manchester, UK: Manchester University Press, 1907.

Nichols, Tom. *Tintoretto: Tradition and Identity*. London: Reaktion Books, 1999.

Nicodemo, Giorgio. "La scultura milanese dal 1530 al 1630." In *L'età dei Borromei, 1559–1630*, edited by Edoardo Arslan et al., 783–808. Vol. 10 of *Storia di Milano*. Milan: Treccani, 1957.

Niero, Antonio. "Culto dei santi dell'antico testamento." In Tramontin et al., *Culto dei santi*, 155–80.

— "Reliquie e corpi di santi." In Tramontin et al., *Culto dei santi*, 181–208.

— "Riforma cattolica e Concilio di Trento a Venezia." In Branca and Ossola, *Cultura e società*, 77–96.

— "I santi patroni." In Tramontin et al., *Culto dei santi*, 75–98.

Noonan, John Thomas, Jr. *The Scholastic Analysis of Usury*. Cambridge, MA: Harvard University Press, 1957.

O'Connell, Monique. *Men of Empire: Power and Negotiation in Venice's Maritime State* (Baltimore, MD: Johns Hopkins University Press, 2009.

Olin, John C. *Catholic Reform: From Cardinal Ximenes to the Council of Trent, 1495–1563*. (New York: Fordham University Press, 1990.

O'Malley, John W., S.J. "The Religious and Theological Culture of Michelangelo's Rome, 1508–1512." In Wind, *Religious Symbolism*, xli–lii.

— *Trent and All That: Renaming Catholicism in the Early Modern Era*. Cambridge, MA: Harvard University Press, 2000.

Origo, Iris. *The Merchant of Prato*. Harmondsworth, UK: Penguin, 1963.

— *The World of San Bernardino*. London: Jonathan Cape, 1963.

Ortalli, Francesca. *"Per salute delle anime e delli corpi": Scuole piccole a Venezia nel tardo medioevo*. Venice: Marsilio-Fondazione Giorgio Cini, 2001.

Ortalli, Gherardo. "Quando il doge diventa santo: Fede e politica nell'esperienza di Pietro I Orseolo." *SV*, n.s. 41 (2001), 15-48.

Ozment, Steven. *The Age of Reform (1250–1550): An Intellectual and Religious History of Late Medieval and Reformation Europe*. New Haven, CT: Yale University Press, 1980.

Padoan Urban, Lina. "La festa della Sensa nelle arti e nell'iconografia." *SV*, 10 (1968), 291–356.

Pagano de Divitiis, Gigliola. *English Merchants in Seventeenth-Century Italy*. Translated by Stephen Parkin. Cambridge: Cambridge University Press, 1997.

Pallucchini, Anna. "Considerazioni sui grandi teleri del Tintoretto della Madonna dell'Orto." *Arte Veneta*, 23 (1969), 54–68.

— "Venezia religiosa nella pittura del Cinquecento." *SV*, 14 (1973), 159–84.

Pallucchini, Rodolfo. *La pittura veneziana del Seicento*. 2 vols. Venice: Alfieri, 1981.

Palmisani, Vitantonio. *Il Medeghino: Storia e leggende, personaggi e luoghi del "Gran Diavolo" di Musso*. Melegnano: Gemini Grafica Editore, 2012.

Panofsky, Erwin. *The Life and Art of Albrecht Dürer*. 4th edn. Princeton, NJ: Princeton University Press, 1971.

— *Studies in Iconology: Humanistic Themes in the Art of the Renaissance* (1939). Boulder, CO: Westview Press, 1972.

Parker, Geoffrey. *Europe in Crisis, 1598–1648*. London: Fontana, 1979.

Pecchioli, Renzo. *Dal "mito" di Venezia all'"ideologia americana": Itinerari e modelli della storiografia sul repubblicanesimo dell'età moderna*. Venice: Marsilo, 1983.

Penny, Nicholas. "John Ruskin and Tintoretto." *Apollo*, 99 (1974), 268–72.

Perocco, G., and A. Salvadori. *Civiltà di Venezia*. 3 vols. 3rd edn. Venice: La Stamperia di Venezia, 1979.

Pertusi, Agostino. "La presunta concessione di alcune insigne regali al doge di Venezia da parte del papa Alessandro III." *Ateneo Veneto*, n.s. 15 (1977), 133–55.

Phillips, Christi. *The Rossetti Letter*. New York: Pocket Books, 2007.

Phillipson, Nicholas T. *Adam Smith: An Enlightened Life*. New Haven, CT, and London: Yale University Press, 2010.

Pignatti, Terisio. "Le pitture nella chiesa dei Gesuiti a Venezia." In Zanardi, *I Gesuiti e Venezia*, 723–6.

Pirri, Pietro. *L'Interdetto di Venezia del 1606 e i Gesuiti: Silloge di documenti con introduzione*. Rome: Istitutum Storicum, S.I., 1959.

Pope-Hennesy, John. *Italian High Renaissance and Baroque Sculpture*. 4th edn. London: Phaidon, 1996.

— "Portrait of an Art Historian." In *Essays on Italian Sculpture*, 199–208. London: Phaidon, 1968.

Pozza, Marco. "Marco Polo Milion: An Unknown Source Concerning Marco Polo." *Medieval Studies*, 68 (2006), 285–301.

Preto, Paolo. *Peste e società a Venezia 1576*. Vicenza: Neri Pozza, 1978.

Prodi, Paolo, ed. *Disciplina dell'anima, disciplina del corpo e disciplina della società tra medioeveo ed età moderna*. Bologna: Il Mulino, 1984.

— *Ricerca sulla teorica delle arti figurative nella riforma cattolica*. Bologna: Il Mulino, 1984.

Prosperi, Adriano. "Clerics and Laymen in the Work of Carlo Borromeo." In *San Carlo Borromeo: Catholic Reform and Ecclesiastical Politics in the Second Half of the Sixteenth Century*, edited by John M. Headley and John B. Tomaro, 112–38. Washington, DC, and London: Folger Shakespeare Library, 1988.

—, ed. *Dizionario Storico dell'Inquisizione*. 4 vols. Pisa: Scuola Normale Superiore, 2010.

— "L'inquisitore come confessore." In Prodi, *Disciplina*, 187–244.

— "Pio IV, papa." In *Dizionario Storico dell'Inquisizione*, vol. 3, 1212–13.

Pullan, Brian, ed. *Crisis and Change in the Venetian Economy in the Sixteenth and Seventeenth Centuries*. London: Methuen, 1968.

— "The Famine in Venice and the New Poor Law." *BISSSV*, 5–6 (1963–4), 141–203.
— *A History of Early Renaissance Italy from the Mid-Thirteenth to the Mid-Fifteenth Century*, Harmondsworth, UK: Penguin, 1973.
— *The Jews of Europe and the Inquisition of Venice, 1550–1670*. Oxford: Basil Blackwell, 1983.
— "The Occupations and Investments of the Venetian Nobility in the Middle and Late Sixteenth Century." In Hale, *Renaissance Venice*, 379–408.
— "Poverty, Charity and the Reason of State: Some Venetian Examples." *BISSSV*, 2 (1960), 17–60.
— Review of *Industry and Economic Decline*, by Richard T. Rapp. *EcHR*, 2 ser., 30, no.1 (1977), 207–8.
— *Rich and Poor in Renaissance Venice: The Social Institutions of a Catholic State to 1620*. Oxford: Basil Blackwell, 1971.
— "Le Scuole Grandi e le loro opera nel quadro della Controriforma." *SV*, 14 (1972), 83–109.
— "The *Scuole Grandi* of Venice: Some Further Thoughts." In *Christianity and the Renaissance: Image and Religious Imagination in the Quattrocento*, edited by Timothy Verdon and John Henderson, 272–301. Syracuse, NY: Syracuse University Press, 1990.
— "Service to the Venetian State: Aspects of Myth and Reality in the Early Seventeenth Century." *Studi Seicenteschi*, 5 (1964), 110–47.
— *Shakespeare's Venice, 1589? The Warders of the Ghetto*. Centre for Italian Studies, Occasional Papers. London: University College, London, 2002.
— "The Significance of Venice." *Bulletin of the John Rylands University Library of Manchester*, 56 (1974), 443–62.
— "'Three Orders of Inhabitants': Social Hierarchies in the Republic of Venice." In *Orders and Hierarchies in Late Medieval and Renaissance Europe*, edited by Jeffrey Denton, 147–68. Basingstoke, UK: Macmillan, 1999.
— "Town Poor, Country Poor: The Province of Bergamo from the Sixteenth to the Eighteenth Century." In *Medieval and Renaissance Venice: Essays in Honor of Donald E. Queller*, edited by Ellen K. Kittell and Thomas F. Madden, 213–36. Urbana and Chicago: University of Illinois Press, 1999.
— "Wage-Earners and the Venetian Economy, 1550–1630." In *Crisis and Change*, 146–74.
Queller, Donald. *The Venetian Patriciate: Reality versus Myth*. Urbana and Chicago: University of Illinois Press, 1986.
Raines, Dorit. *L'invention du mythe aristocratique: L'image de soi du patriciat vénitien au temps de la Sérenissime*. 2 vols. Venice: Istituto Veneto di Scienze, Lettere ed Arti, 2006.
— "Strategie d'ascesa sociale e giochi di potere a Venezia nel seicento: Le aggregazioni alla nobiltà." *SV*, n.s. 51 (2006), 279–317.

Ranke, Leopold von. *History of the Popes, Their Church and State, and especially Their Conflicts with Protestantism in the Sixteenth and Seventeenth Centuries.* Translated by E. Foster. 3 vols. London: Bell & Daldy, 1866.

Rapp, Richard T. *Industry and Economic Decline in Seventeenth-Century Venice.* Cambridge, MA: Harvard University Press, 1976.

— "Real Estate and Rational Investment in Early Modern Venice." *Journal of European Economic History*, 8 (1979), 269–91.

— "The Unmaking of Mediterranean Trade Hegemony: International Trade Rivalry and the Commercial Revolution." *J. Econ. Hist.* 35, no. 3 (1975), 499–525.

Redondi, Pietro. *Galileo Heretic.* Translated by Raymond Rosenthal. Harmondsworth, UK: Penguin, 1988.

Reeves, Marjorie. *The Influence of Prophecy in the Later Middle Ages: A Study in Joachimism.* Oxford: Oxford University Press, 1969.

— *Joachim of Fiore and the Prophetic Future.* Oxford: Oxford University Press, 1977.

Reinhard, Wolfgang. "Disciplinamento sociale, confessionalizzazione, modernizzazione: Un discorso storiografico." In Prodi, *Disciplina*, 101–23.

— "Reformation, Counter-Reformation and the Early Modern State: A Reassessment." *Catholic Historical Review*, 75 (1989), 383–404.

Renouard, Yves. *The Avignon Papacy, 1305–1403.* Translated by Denis Bethell. London: Faber & Faber, 1970.

— "Mercati e mercanti veneziani alla fine del duecento." In *La civiltà veneziana del secolo di Marco Polo*, 83–108. Florence, 1955.

Reynolds, Sir Joshua. *Discourses on Art.* Edited by Robert R. Wark. New Haven, CT, and London: Yale University Press, 1975.

Rigoni, Chiara. "La bottega dei Caliari a Verona." In *Veronese e Verona: Catalogo della Mostra Veronese e Verona*, edited by Sergio Marinelli, 85–107. Verona: Federigoni, 1988.

Rodolico, Nicolo. *I Ciompi: Una pagina di storia del proletario operaio.* 3rd edn. Florence: Sansoni, 1980.

Romano, Dennis. "Charity and Community in Early Modern Venice." *Journal of Urban History*, 11 (1984), 63–82.

— "The Gondola as a Marker of Station in Venetian Society." *Ren. Studs* 8, no. 4 (1994), 359–74.

— *Housecraft and Statecraft: Domestic Service in Renaissance Venice, 1400–1600.* Baltimore, MD, and London: Johns Hopkins University Press, 1996.

— *The Likeness of Venice: A Life of Doge Francesco Foscari, 1373–1457.* New Haven, CT: Yale University Press, 2007.

— *Patricians and* Popolani: *The Social Foundations of the Venetian Renaissance State.* Baltimore, MD, and London: Johns Hopkins University Press, 1987.

Rosand, David. *Myths of Venice: The Figuration of a State.* Chapel Hill, NC, and London: University of North Carolina Press, 2001.

— *Painting in '500 Venice: Titian, Veronese, Tintoretto*. Revised edn. Cambridge: Cambridge University Press, 1997.

—, ed. *Titian: His World and His Legacy*. New York: Columbia University Press, 1982.

Rösch, Gerhard. "The *Serrata* of the Great Council and Venetian Society, 1286–1323." In Martin and Romano, *Venice Reconsidered*, 67–88.

Roskill, Mark. *What Is Art History?* London: Thames & Hudson, 1976.

Rossato, Valerio. "Religione e moralità in un merciaio veneziano del Cinquecento." *SV*, n.s. 13 (1987), 193–253.

Roth, Cecil. "The Background of Shylock." *Review of English Studies*, 9 (1933), 148–56.

Rubin, Miri. *Corpus Christi: The Eucharist in Late Medieval Culture*. Cambridge: Cambridge University Press, 1991.

— *Mother of God: A History of the Virgin Mary*. New Haven, CT, and London: Yale University Press, 2009.

Rubinstein, Nicolai, ed. *Florentine Studies: Politics and Society in Renaissance Florence*. London: Faber & Faber, 1968.

— *The Government of Florence under the Medici (1434 to 1494)*. Oxford-Warburg Studies. Oxford: Oxford University Press, 1966.

— "Political Ideas in Sienese Art: The Frescoes by Ambrogio Lorenzetti and Taddeo di Bartolo in the Palazzo Pubblico." *JWCI*, 21 (1958), 179–207.

Ruggiero, Guido. "Modernization and the Mythic State in Early Renaissance Venice: The Serrata Revisited." *Viator: Medieval and Renaissance Studies*, 10 (1979), 245–56.

Ruskin, John. *Modern Painters*. Edited by David Barrie. London: André Deutsch, 1987.

— "The Relation between Michael Angelo and Tintoret (1871)." In *Works*, vol. 22, 75–114.

— "St Mark's Rest: The History of Venice, Written for the Help of the Few Travellers Who Still Care for Her Monuments." In *Works*, edited by Cook and Wedderburn, vol. 24, 195–400.

— *The Stones of Venice*. 3 vols. London: Everyman Editions, 1907.

— *The Works of John Ruskin*. Edited by E.T. Cook and Alexander Wedderburn, 39 vols. London and New York: G. Allen, Longmans Green, 1912.

Rutenburg, Viktor. "Arti e corporazioni." In *Storia d'Italia*, vol.5, *Documenti*, 615–42. Turin: Einaudi, 1973.

— *Popolo e movimenti popolari nell'Italia del '300 e '400*. Translated by G. Borchini. Bologna: Il Mulino, 1971.

Ryskamp, Charles, Bernice Davidson, Susan Galassi, Edgard Munhall, and Nadia Tscherny. *Art in the Frick Collection: Paintings, Sculpture, Decorative Arts*. New York: Harry N. Abrams, 1996.

Salingar, Leo. "The Idea of Venice in Shakespeare and Ben Jonson." In Marrapodi et al., *Shakespeare's Italy*, 171–84.

Sangalli, Maurizio. *Cultura, politica e religione nella Repubblica di Venezia tra Cinque e Seicento: Gesuiti e Somaschi a Venezia*. Venice: Istituto Veneto di Scienze, Lettere ed Arti, 1999.

Sbriziolo, Lia. "Per la storia delle confraternite veneziane: Dalle Deliberazioni Miste (1310–1476) del Consiglio dei Dieci; Scolae communes, artigiane e nazionali." *Atti dell'Istituto Veneto di Scienze, Lettere ed Arti*, vol. 126 (*Classe di Scienze Morali e Lettere*), (1967–8), 405–42.

— "Per la storia delle confraternite veneziane: Dalle Deliberazioni Miste del Consiglio dei Dieci; Le Scuole dei Battuti." In *Miscellanea Giles-Gerard Meersseman*, vol. 2, 715–63. Padua: Antenore, 1970.

Scarabello, Giovanni. "Per una storia della prostituzione a Venezia tra il xiii e il xviii secoli." *SV*, n.s. 47 (2004), 15–102.

Schilling, Heinz. "Between the Territorial State and Urban Liberty: Lutherans and Calvinists in the County of Lippe." In *The German People and the Reformation*, edited by R. Po-chia Hsia, 263–83. Ithaca, NY: Cornell University Press, 1988.

— "Chiese confessionali e disciplinamento sociale: Un bilancio provvisorio della ricerca storica." In Prodi, *Disciplina*, 125–60.

— "Civic Republicanism in Late Medieval and Early Modern German Cities." In *Religion, Political Culture*, 3–59.

— "Confessional Europe." In *Visions, Programmes and Outcomes*, vol. 2 of *Handbook of European History, 1400–1600*, edited by Thomas A. Brady, Jr, Heiko A. Oberman, and James D. Tracy, 641–82. Leiden: E.J. Brill, 1995.

— "Confessionalisation in the Empire: Religious and Societal Change in Germany between 1555 and 1620." In *Religion, Political Culture*, 205–45. English translation of "Die Konfessionalisierung im Reich: Religiosen und Gesellschaften Wandel in Deutschland zwischen 1555 und 1620." *Historische Zeitschrift*, 246 (1981), 1–45.

— *Religion, Political Culture and the Emergence of the Early Modern State: Essays in German and Dutch History*. Studies in Medieval and Reformation Thought, vol. 50. Leyden: E.J. Brill, 1992.

Schulz, Juergen. "The Houses of Titian, Aretino and Sansovino." In Rosand, *Titian: His World and His Legacy*, 73–118.

Seidel Menchi, Silvana. "The Inquisitor as Mediator." In *Heresy, Culture and Religion in Early Modern Italy: Contexts and Contestations*, edited by Ronald K. Delph, Michelle M. Fontaine, and John Jeffries Martin, 173–90. Kirksville, MS: Truman State University Press, 2006.

— "Italy." In *The Reformation in National* Context, edited by Bob Scribner, Roy Porter, and Mikulas Teich, 181–201. Cambridge: Cambridge University Press, 1994.

Selfridge-Field, Eleanor. *Venetian Instrumental Music from Gabrieli to Vivaldi*. 3rd edn. Toronto and London: Dover, 1994.

Sella, Domenico. *Crisis and Continuity: The Economy of Spanish Lombardy in the Seventeenth Century*. Cambridge, MA, and London: Harvard University Press, 1979.

— "The Iron Industry in Italy, 1500–1650." In *Schwerpunkte der Eisengewinnung und Eisenverarbeitung in Europa, 1500–1650*, edited by Hermann Kellenbenz, 91–105. Cologne and Vienna: Bohlau, 1974.

—"The Rise and Decline of the Venetian Woollen Industry." In Pullan, *Crisis and Change*, 88–105.

Seneca, Federico. *Il doge Leonardo Donà, la sua vita e la sua preparazione politica prima del dogado*. Padua: Antenore, 1959.

— *Venezia e Papa Giulio II*. Padua: Liviana Editrice, 1962.

Setton, Kenneth M. *The Papacy and the Levant*. 4 vols. Philadelphia: American Philosophical Society, 1976–84.

Shaw, Christine. *Julius II: The Warrior Pope*. Oxford: Basil Blackwell, 1993.

Shaw, James E. *The Justice of Venice: Authorities and Liberties in the Urban Economy, 1550–1700*. Oxford: Oxford University Press for the British Academy, 2006.

Sherman, Allison Morgan. "The Lost Venetian Church of Santa Maria Assunta dei Crociferi: Form, Decoration and Patronage. Unpublished PhD diss., University of St Andrews, 2010.

Signorotto, Gian Vittorio. "Il rientro dei gesuiti a Venezia: La trattativa (1606–1657)." In Zanardi, *I Gesuiti e Venezia*, 385–420.

Sinding-Larsen, Staale. *Christ in the Council Hall: Studies in the Religious Iconography of the Venetian Republic*. Acta ad Archaeologiam et Artium Historiam Pertinentia, vol. 5. Rome: L'Erma di Bretschneider, 1974.

Smith, Adam. *An Inquiry into the Origins and Nature of the Wealth of Nations*. 2 vols. Edited by R.H. Campbell and A.S. Skinner, textual editing by W.B. Todd. The Glasgow Edition of the Works and Correspondence of Adam Smith. Indianapolis, IN: Liberty Fund, 1981.

— *The Theory of Moral Sentiments*. Edited by D.D. Raphael and A.L. Macfie. The Glasgow Edition of the Works and Correspondence of Adam Smith. Indianapolis, IN: Liberty Fund, 1982.

Smith, Robert. "In Search of Carpaccio's African Gondolier." *Italian Studies*, 34 (1979), 45–59.

Southern, R.W. *The Shape and Substance of Academic History*. Inaugural lecture, 2 November 1961. Oxford: Oxford University Press, 1961.

Spufford, Margaret. "Literacy, Trade and Religion in the Commercial Centres of Europe." In *A Miracle Mirrored: The Dutch Republic in European Perspective*, edited by Karel Davids and Jan Lucassien, 229–83. Cambridge: Cambridge University Press, 1995.

Spufford, Peter. *Power and Profit: The Merchant in Medieval Europe*. London: Thames & Hudson, 2002.

Stahl, Alan M. *Zecca: The Mint of Venice in the Middle Ages*. Baltimore, MD, and London: Johns Hopkins University Press, 2000.

Stanley, Joseph Fahey. "From Medieval Corporatism to Civic Humanism: Merchant and Guild Culture in Fourteenth- and Fifteenth-Century Florence." PhD diss., State University of New York, Binghamton, 2011.

Stella, Aldo. *Dall'anabattesimo veneto al "Sozialevangelismus" dei fratelli Hutteriti e all'illuminismo sociniano*. Italia Sacra: Studi e Documenti di Storia Ecclesiastica, 54. Rome: Herder, 1996.

— "Ricerche sul socinianismo: Il processo di Cornelio Sozzini e Claudio Textor (Baniero)." *BISSSV* 3 (1961), 77–120.

Stendhal [Henri Beyle]. *Histoire de la peinture en Italie*. Edited by V. Del Litto. Paris: Gallimard, 1996.

— *Stendhal and the Arts*. Selected and edited by David Wakefield. London: Phaidon, 1973.

Strauss, Gerald. *Nuremberg in the Sixteenth Century*. New York: Wiley, 1966.

Symonds, John Addington. "Como and il Medeghino." In *Sketches in Italy* (Selected from *Sketches in Italy and Greece*, and *Sketches and Studies in Italy*), 209–26. Leipzig: B. Tauchnitz, 1883.

— *Renaissance in Italy*. 7 vols. London: Rivington, 1904.

Sypher, Wylie. *Four Stages of Renaissance Style: Transformations in Art and Literature, 1400–1700*. Garden City, NY: Doubleday, 1956

Tafuri, Manfredo, ed. *"Renovatio urbis": Venezia nell'età di Andrea Gritti (1523–1538)*. Rome: Officina Edizioni, 1984.

— *Venice and the Renaissance*. Translated by Jessica Levine. Cambridge, MA, and London: MIT Press, 1989.

Tassini, Giuseppe. *Curiosità veneziane, ovvero Origini delle denominazioni stradali di Venezia* (1863). Reprinted with an introduction by Lino Moretti, preface by Elio Zorzi. Venice: Filippi, 1990.

Tavuzzi, Michael. *Renaissance Inquisitors and Inquisitional Districts in Northern Italy, 1474–1527*. Vol. 134 of *Studies in the History of the Christian Tradition*. Leiden-Boston: E.J. Brill, 2007.

Tawney, R.H. *Religion and the Rise of Capitalism: A Historical Study*. Harmondsworth, UK: Penguin, 1938.

Tedeschi, John. "The Organisation and Procedures of the Roman Inquisition: A Sketch." In *The Prosecution of Heresy: Collected Studies on the Inquisition in Early Modern Italy*. 127–203. Binghamton, NY: Medieval and Renaissance Texts and Studies, 1991.

Tenenti, Alberto. *Piracy and the Decline of Venice, 1580–1615*. Translated by Janet and Brian Pullan. London: Longmans, 1967.

Tracy, James D., ed. *The Political Economy of Merchant Empires: State Power and World Trade, 1350–1750*. Cambridge: Cambridge University Press, 1991.

—, ed. *The Rise of Merchant Empires: Long-Distance Trade in the Early Modern World, 1350–1750*. Cambridge: Cambridge University Press, 1990.

Tramontin, Silvio. "'Calendarium' veneziano." In Tramontin et al., *Culto dei santi*, 275–327.

— "San Marco." In Tramontin et al., *Culto dei santi*, 41–74.

— "La Visita Apostolica del 1581 a Venezia." *SV*, 9 (1967), 453–525.

Tramontin, Silvio, A. Niero, G. Musolino, and C. Candiani. *Culto dei santi a Venezia*. Collana storica dello "Studium cattolico veneziano," no. 7. Venice: Edizioni Studium Cattolico Veneziano, 1965.

Tretiak, Andrew. "*The Merchant of Venice* and the 'Alien' Question." *Review of English Studies*, 5 (1929), 402–9.

Trevor-Roper, H.R. *Archbishop Laud*. 2nd edn. London: Macmillan, 1965.

— "The General Crisis of the Seventeenth Century." In *Religion, the Reformation and Social Change*, 46–89.

— "The Gentry, 1540–1640." *EcHR*, Supplement 1, 1953.

— *Princes and Artists: Patronage and Ideology at Four Habsburg Courts, 1517–1633*. New York: Thames & Hudson, 1976.

— *Religion, the Reformation and Social Change*. 2nd edn. London: Macmillan, 1972.

— "Religion, the Reformation and Social Change." In *Religion, the Reformation and Social Change*, 1–45.

Trivellato, Francesca. *Fondamenta dei vetrai: Lavoro, tecnologia e mercato a Venezia tra Sei e Settecento*. Rome: Donzelli, 2000.

Tucci, Ugo. "Il libro di Marco Polo tra filosofia e informatica." *SV*, n.s. 43 (2002), 77–94.

Il Tumulto dei Ciompi: Un momento di storia fiorentina ed europea. Florence: Leo S. Olschki, 1981.

Ullmann, Walter. *A History of Political Thought: The Middle Ages*. Harmondsworth, UK: Penguin, 1975.

— *The Origins of the Great Schism: A Study in Fourteenth-Century Ecclesiastical History*. London: Burns, Oates & Washbourne, 1948.

— *Principles of Government and Politics in the Middle Ages*. London: Methuen, 1961.

Van der Wee, Herman. "Structural Changes in European Long-Distance Trade, and Particularly in the Re-export Trade from South to North, 1350–1750." In Tracy, *Rise of Merchant Empires*, 14–33.

Vauchez, André. *Francis of Assisi: The Life and Afterlife of a Medieval Saint*. Translated by Michael F. Cusato. New Haven, CT, and London: Yale University Press, 2012.

— *Les laics au Moyen Age: Pratiques et experiences religieuses*. Paris: Editions du Cerf, 1987.

Vazzoler, Chiara. *The Scuola Grande di San Giovanni Evangelista*. Translated by David Graham. Venice: Marsilio, 2005.

Ventura, Aldo. *Nobiltà e popolo nella società veneta del '400 e '500*. Bari: Laterza, 1964.

Villari, Rosario, ed. *Baroque Personae*. Translated by Lydia G. Cochrane. Chicago and London: Chicago University Press, 1995.

Vio, Ettore, ed. *St Mark's Basilica: The Art and Architecture of Church and State in Venice*. London: Thames & Hudson, 2000.

Vio, Gastone. *Le Scuole Piccole nella Venezia dei Dogi: Note d'archivio per la storia delle confraternite veneziane; Cultura popolare veneta; Collana di studi e di ricerche della cultura popolare veneta realizzata su iniziativa della Regione del Veneto*. Costabissara: A. Colla, 2004.

Viroli, Maurizio. *From Politics to Reason of State: The Acquisition and Transformation of the Language of Politics, 1250–1600*. Cambridge: Cambridge University Press, 1992.

Wallerstein, Immanuel. *Mercantilism and the Consolidation of the European World System, 1600–1750*. Vol. 2 of *The Modern World System*. New York and London: Academic Press, 1980.

Webb, Diana. *Patrons and Defenders: The Saints in the Italian City-States*. London and New York: I.B. Tauris, 1996.

Weber, Max. *The Protestant Ethic and the Spirit of Capitalism*. Translated by Talcott Parsons, revised introduction by Randall Collins. Los Angeles: Roxbury, 1998.

Weissman, Ronald F.E. *Ritual Brotherhood in Renaissance Florence*. London: Academic Press, 1982.

Wheeler, Joseph. "Neighbourhoods and Local Loyalties in Renaissance Venice." In *Mediterranean Urban Culture, 1400–1700*, edited by Alexander Cowan, 31–44. Exeter: Exeter University Press, 2000.

Wierusowski, Helen. "Art and the Commune in the Age of Dante." *Speculum*, 19 (1944), 14–33.

Wilson, Charles. *The Dutch Republic and the Civilisation of the Seventeenth Century*. London: Weidenfeld & Nicholson, 1968.

— *Economic History and the Historian: Collected Essays*. London: Weidenfeld & Nicolson, 1969.

— *England's Apprenticeship, 1603–1763*. London: Longman, 1965.

— *Mercantilism*. Historical Association Pamphlet, General Series, 37. London: Routledge and Kegan Paul, 1958.

— "'Mercantilism': Some Vicissitudes of an Idea." In *Economic History and the Historian*, 62–72.

— "The Other Face of Mercantilism." In *Economic History and the Historian*, 73–93.

— "Taxation and the Decline of Empires, an Unfashionable Theme." In *Economic History and the Historian*, 114–27.

— "Treasure and Trade Balances: The Mercantilist Problem." In *Economic History and the Historian*, 48–61.

Wind, Edgar. "The Crucifixion of Haman." *JWCI*, 1 (1937–8), 245–8.

— *The Religious Symbolism of Michelangelo: The Sistine Ceiling*. Edited by Elizabeth Stears, with essays by John W. O'Malley and Elizabeth Stears. Oxford: Oxford University Press, 2000.

Winston-Allen, Anne. *Stories of the Rose: The Making of the Rosary in the Middle Ages*. University Park: Pennsylvania State University Press, 1997.

Wittkower, Margot, and Rudolf Wittkower. *Born under Saturn: The Character and Conduct of Artists; A Documentary History from Antiquity to the French Revolution*. With an introduction by Jospeh Connors. New York: New York Review of Books, 2007.

Wölfflin, Heinrich. *Principles of Art History: The Problem of the Development of Style in Later Art*. 7th edn. Translated by M.D. Hotlinger. New York: Dover, 1950. From the 1932 edition, by G. Bell & Sons.

Wolters, Wolfgang. *Storia e politica nei dipinti di Palazzo Ducale: Aspetti dell'autocelebrazione della Repubblica di Venezia nel Cinquecento*. Translated by Benedetta Heinemann Campana. Venice: Arsenale Editrice, 1987.

Wootton, David. *Galileo: Watcher of the Skies*. New Haven, CT, and London: Yale University Press, 2010.

— *Paolo Sarpi: Between Renaissance and Enlightenment*. Cambridge: Cambridge University Press, 1983.

Worthen, Thomas. "Tintoretto's Paintings for the Banco del Sacramento in Santa Margherita." *Art Bulletin*, 78, no. 3 (1996), 707–32.

Wright, A.D. *The Early Modern Papacy: From the Council of Trent to the French Revolution, 1564–1789*. London: Longman, 2000.

Wurthmann, William. "The Council of Ten and the *Scuole Grandi* in Early Renaissance Venice." *SV*, n.s. 18 (1989), 15–66.

Wyrobisz, Andrej. "L'attività edilizia a Venezia nel XIV e XV secolo." *SV*, 7 (1965), 307–43.

Yates, Frances. *The Art of Memory*. Harmonsworth, UK: Penguin, 1969.

The Occult Philosophy in the Elizabethan Age. London: Routledge & Kegan Paul, 1979.

Zanardi, Mario, ed. *I Gesuiti e Venezia: Momenti e problemi di storia veneziana della Compagnia di Gesù*. Padua: Gregoriana Libreria Editrice, 1994.

Zannini, Andrea. *Burocrazia e burocrati a Venezia in età moderna: I cittadini originari (sec. xvi–xviii)*. Venice: Istituto Veneto di Scienze, Lettere ed Arti, 1993.

— "Un censimento inedito del primo Seicento e la crisi demografica ed economica di Venezia." *SV*, n.s. 26 (1993), 87–116.

— "Un ceto di funzionari amministrativi: I cittadini originari veneziani, 1569–1730." *SV*, n.s. 23 (1992), 131–45.

Zorzi, Alvise. *Venice 697–1797: A City, a Republic, an Empire*. Translated by Judith Schaubhut Smith. Woodstock, NY, and New York: Overlook Press, 2001.

— *Vita di Marco Polo Veneziano*. Milan: Rusconi, 1982.

Index

Note: In a work dealing with several hundred institutions over four centuries, the constraints of space and sanity are very severe. Accordingly, readers should be aware that all scuole are listed by title, i.e. "scuola del," "scuola di," etc., except for the Scuole del Venerabile, which may be found under "Venerabile, Scuola del," "Venerabile, Scuole del," etc. All churches are listed under loosely standardized titles and include cross-references for as many variants as I have discovered. Figures, tables, and appendices are listed separately and not included in this index.

Abraham, prophet, 40–1
absolutism, 250, 278–80
Agnadello, battle of, 114
Agordino, 132, 143
Aleandro, Girolamo, cardinal, 251
Alexander VI, pope, 101
Alighieri, Dante, 54, 57
alms, almshousing, 9, 253, 261, 262, 268, 278
Ambrose, Saint, 116, 140
Angelo Michele, church of. *See* Sant'Anzolo
Angelo Raffaele, church and parish of, 53, 68, 191
Annales School, 23–4, 310
Antony of Padua, saint, 14, 55, 95, 98, 219
Antwerp, 265
apothecaries, 152
apprentices, apprenticeship, 83, 324
Aretino, Pietro, 117–18, 199–200, 283
Arsenale, 26, 29, 83, 115, 128, 129, 207, 297, 309; iron for, 135–49; trades in, 30, 31, 36, 190, 210, 211. *See also* ironsmiths, guild of
arte dei fabbri. *See* ironsmiths, guild of
Ascension Day, Feast of (Sensa), 46, 158. *See also* mercers
Atlantic, 307
Augustine, saint, Augustinianism, 42, 54, 55, 84, 197, 211
Avanzi, Paolo, and Inquisition, 264–5
ave, 72, 83, 85, 87, 101
Avvogadori di Comun, 82, 187

Ballabio, 139–50
banks, banking, 32, 216, 219
Barbolano, Pietro, doge, 126
Barnabites, Order of, 248

Basaiti, Marco, 88
Bellarmine, Roberto, cardinal, 250
Bellavitis, Anna, 321
Bellini, Gentile, 236
Bellini, Giovanni, 98, 236
Bellini, Jacopo, 96
Beloch, Karl, 308
Belogno, Jacopo, patriarch of Grado, 44
Bembo, Pietro, cardinal, 283
Bergamo, Bergamasco, 139–50, 272
Bernardino da Siena, saint, 15, 80, 96–8, 246
Bertuccio, goldsmith, 44
Bianchi, 52, 76, 89–93, 200
Bisticci, Vespasiano da, 96
Black Death, 15, 79, 81, 83, 86. *See also* plague
Blaise, saint, 207
boatmen, 215
Boccalini, Traiano, 142
Bolognetti, Alberto, papal nunzio, 272
Bon, Bartolomeo, 74, 96
Bonanome, Alessandro, and Inquisition, 265
Bonaparte, Napoleon, 28
Bonaventura, saint, 57, 71, 95, 96
Bontempelli, Bartolomeo, 132, 165, 187, 189
Borgia, Cesare, 147
Bornstein, Daniel, 89, 99
Borromeo, Carlo, cardinal and saint, 132, 149–50, 197, 251, 254, 271, 273, 284
Boschini, Marco, 282, 283
Bossy, John, 249
Botero, Giovanni, 26
Brescia, Bresciano, 139–50, 181, 272
Brown, Peter, 31–43
building trades, 209
bullion, 33
burials, 100, 219. *See also* funerals

Cadore, 25, 66
Caldiera, Giovanni, 101–2
Calle dei Fabbri, 121, 128, 130, 132–40, 186
Calle della Fiubera, 186
Calvin, John, Calvinism, 197
Campagna, Gierolamo, 219
Campo dei Frari, 116
Campo San Polo, 241
Canal Grande, 26, 66, 68, 121, 215, 266
Canale della Misericordia, 66
Canale, Martino da, 31, 36, 55, 72
Canaletto, Antonio, 336
Canareggio, Sestiere di, 58, 61, 69, 84, 95, 201
Carafa, Giampietro, cardinal, 251
Caravia, Alessandro, 19, 200, 261, 262, 275, 283, 287, 293, 320
Carmini, church of. *See* Santa Maria dei Carmini
Carpaccio, Vetor, 80, 81
Casola, Canon Pietro, 139, 201
Castelfranco, Giorgione da, 116
Castello, Sestiere di, 115
Castiglione, Baldassare, 118, 181
charcoal porters, 233
Charity, 37, 61, 86, 88
Charles V, emperor, 118, 147, 148
cheese sellers, 219
Chojnacka, Monica, 322–3
Chojnacki, Stanley, 29
Christian humanism, 200. *See also* humanism
Christopher, saint, 65
Church and State, 25–6, 245, 253
Cima da Conegliano, 311, 314
Cinque Savi alla Mercanzia, 323

Cinque Savi alle Mariegole, 21, 133
cittadini, cittadinanza, 5, 7, 67, 85, 95, 101, 116–17, 319–20
Clark, Kenneth, 334
cloth stretchers, 258–9
colleganza, 33
Collegio delle Arti, 186
Colomban, Francesco, 201
Commynes, Philippe de, 115, 117
Como, Lake, 15, 139–50, 246
Compagnia del Divino Amore, 149, 248
confectioners, 259
Confessional State, 16, 245, 247–52, 272
Contarini, Gasparo, 4–6, 8, 51, 60, 118, 152, 309
Cooper, Tracy, 19
corn chandlers, 221
Corona, Leonardo, 233
Corpus Christi, Feast of, 91
Corpus Domini, convent of, 90, 92, 201
Corte Nova, 69
Corte Prima del Milion, 66
Corte Seconda del Milion, 66
Council of Forty, 32, 187
Council of Ten, 5, 20, 76, 77, 82, 89–92, 101, 249, 270, 309
Council of Trent, 10, 89, 197, 248, 272, 274, 335. *See also* Counter-Reformation
Counter-Reformation, 16, 197, 200, 246, 277, 335
couriers, 219
courts of appeal, 126, 157, 187
Cowan, Alexander, 319
Cracco, Giorgio, 29, 60
Crete, 116
cripples, 81
crusades, 30
cult of the saints, 42, 252

Dandolo, Giovanni, doge, 33
Datini, Francesco, 89
Demetrius, saint, 58
dice playing, 83, 297
Dickens, Charles, 92
Dives and Lazarus, story of, 41
dogaressa, coronation of, 160
doge, office of, 42–3, 81, 162
Dominicans, 26, 90
Dominici, Giovanni, 90, 92
Donà, Leonardo, doge, 251
Donatello, 88, 116
Dorsoduro, Sestiere di, 89, 99, 100. *See also* San Nicolo, Sestiere di
double-entry book keeping, 33
dowries, 30, 48
drapers, 160
ducal palace, 26, 76, 123
ducat, 31, 32
Duerer, Albrecht, 200, 223
Dutch, 307, 326
dyers, 259

earthquake of 1513, 225
England, 246, 307, 326
Enlightenment, 3, 42, 334
Erasmus, Desiderius, Erasmianism, 200, 282
Esecutori contra la Bestemmia, 249
Eucharist. *See* Holy Sacrament
Eugenius IV, pope, 60, 96
evangelicalism, 200, 252, 257
Evelyn, John, 152

Faggiani, Francesco, and Inquisition, 270–81
Falier, Vitale, doge, 43
Fasani, Ranier, 52
Fiammengo, Paolo, 283
fishmongers, 18, 191

Flabianico, Domenico, doge, 126
flagellants, flagellation, 52, 67, 76, 82, 90, 207
Florence, 28, 32, 79, 89, 91, 178
Fogazzaro, Antonio, 140
fondachi, 116
Fondaco dei Tedeschi, 66, 116, 123, 125, 179, 221, 266. *See also* Germany, Germans
Foscari, Elena, 95
Foscari, Francesco, doge, 95, 96
Francis, saint, 54, 57, 96, 99
Franciscans, Franciscanism, 15, 26, 44, 51, 55, 61, 77, 85, 93–8, 102, 201, 251, 253
Frari, church of. *See* Santa Maria Gloriosa dei Frari
fraterna, 33
Frezzaria, 121, 136
funerals, 48, 72, 83, 87, 100, 198
furatole, 120
furriers, 310–11
fustian weavers, 58

gastaldi ducali, 155
gastaldo, office of, 22
Geneva, 254, 265
Genoa, 32, 60
George, saint, 7
Germany, Germans, 142, 205, 249, 251, 259, 260, 266. *See also* Fondaco dei Tedeschi
Gesuati, church of. *See* Santa Maria del Rosario
Gesuiti, church of. *See* Santa Maria Assunta
ghetto, and Jews, 39–40, 116, 124, 128, 326
Gibbon, Edward, 42
Giles of Viterbo. *See* Viterbo, Egidio da
Giuistizia Nova, 35, 58, 119–26, 135, 137, 141
Giustizia Vecchia, 35, 82, 114, 158, 170, 180, 258
Goldoni, Carlo, 123, 335
goldsmiths, 158–9, 160, 192, 207, 209
Grand Canal. *See* Canal Grande
grand chancellor, 155
Greater Council, 160, 162. *See also* Serrata del Maggior Consiglio
Great Schism, 15, 78, 89
Greenblatt, Stephen, 24
Gregory XIII, pope, 271
Gritti, Andrea, doge, 118, 127

Henri, duke of Alençon, 160, 182
Hohenstaufen, 32
Holy Office. *See* Inquisition
Holy Sacrament, 9, 87, 91; cult of, 16, 100, 101, 190, 197, 199, 201, 203, 271, 273, 282, 284. *See also* Venerabile, scuole del
hospitals, 9, 248, 249
house carpenters, 25, 211, 213–14
Huguenots, 264
humanism, 99, 246, 256
Hume, David, 42

Ignatius Loyola, saint, 309
Immaculate Conception, doctrine of, 57
immigrants, 15, 93, 113–19, 135–49
Incurabili, hospital of, 248
India, cape route to, 114
inns, 119–26
Inquisition, 16, 197, 250, 252–71, 278, 283
Inquisitori di Stato, 249
insurance, 33, 208
Interdict crisis, 278, 307

iron, 15, 117, 126–8, 130–41, 134, 142–3
ironsmiths, guild of, 15, 25, 93, 126–39, 146, 186–8

James, Henry, 299
James, saint, the Greater, 51, 219
James, saint, the Lesser, General Epistle of, 14, 39–41, 87, 88, 93, 211
Jesuits, Order of, 248, 251, 257, 309–14
Jews. *See* ghetto, and Jews
Joachim of Fiore, 51–2, 102
John, saint, gospel of, 88
joint-stock companies, 33
Julian the Hospitaller, saint, 72, 233
Julius II, pope, 201

Karlowitz, Treaty of, 307
kiss of peace, 41, 72, 88, 91, 100, 161
Koenigsberger, Helmut, 335

Landriano, battle of, 147
Lane, Frederic C., 3, 29
lavoranti, 93, 258
Lazarus, saint, 94
Le Court, Giusto, 327
Le Roy Ladurie, Emmanuel, 25
League of Cognac, 147
Lecco, 139–50
Leoni, Leone, 24, 148
Lepanto, battle of, 133, 190
Lombardy, 134, 135–50
Lorenzetti, Pietro and Ambrogio, 72
Lotto, Lorenzo, 251, 275
Lucca, Lucchesi, 32, 116
Luther, Martin, Lutheranism, 39, 255, 260, 269, 271

Machiavelli, Nicolo, 147, 271
Madonna dell'Orto, church of. *See* Santa Maria dell'Orto, church of
Magnus, saint, 54, 276
Malombra, Pietro, 225
Mandello, 141–50
Manhattan, 122
Manzoni, Alessandro, 139, 141
Maranini, Giuseppe, 28–30
mariegole. *See* statutes
Mark, saint, 37, 42, 61, 140
Martial, saint, 70
Marvell, Andrew, 326
marzeri. *See* mercers
Masegne, Jacobello and Pierpaolo dale, 242
masons. *See* stonemasons
Matthew, saint, 14, 37–8, 58
Mazza, Damiano, 215
Medeghino, il, Giangiacomo de' Medici, 24, 147–9
Medici family, 24, 149
Medici, Gabriele de', 149
Mendicant Orders, 51
mercantilism, 307
Mercerie, 38, 121, 131, 152, 154, 160, 182, 185, 186, 191, 202, 231, 233, 283, 321. *See also* mercers, guild of
mercers, guild of, 15, 18, 60, 100, 138, 151–88, 214, 322
merchants, mercantile activity, 33, 37–74, 85, 96, 102, 257, 263–9, 321
mercy. *See* Misericordia; works of mercy
Miano, Gierolemo, 248
Michelangelo, artist, 148, 198, 281
Michieli, Andrea di, "il Vicentino," 283
Milan, 139–50
Milizia da Mar, 21, 160
mirror makers, 318–25
Misericordia, 6, 11, 22, 36–74, 75, 82, 84, 236. *See also* Scuola di Santa Maria della Misericordia
Mocenigo, Tomaso, doge, 95, 96

Monte Vecchio. *See* public debt
Morea, war in, 307
Moro, Cristoforo, doge, 95, 96, 98, 101
Moses, prophet, 130
Mueller, Reinhold, 86
Murano, island of, 22, 59, 128
music, 73, 241
Musso, 148–50

"nations," 140–9, 257
nicknames, 117
nobility, sale of, 319
nobles in scuole, 82, 85, 87, 101. *See also* patriciate
Nuremberg, 116

oarmakers, 58
Ochino, Bernardo, 253
Ognissanti, church of, 225
oil decanters, 219
Oio, Antonio Dall', and Inquisition, 256
Ortalli, Francesca, 17, 76, 82, 88
otium and negotium, 66, 85, 225
Ottoman Empire, 114, 197, 279

Padua and Padovano, 55, 72, 124, 308
Paleotti, Gabriele, cardinal, 197
Palma il Giovane, Giacomo, 24, 191, 221, 225, 233, 236, 276, 283, 314
Palmi, Benedetto, 248
Panofsky, Erwin, 24
parish, parishes, 22, 68, 115, 119–26, 145, 189, 247, 261–3
paternoster, 71, 72, 83, 85, 87, 101
patriciate, 4, 5, 28, 35, 67, 95, 115, 154, 178, 250, 279, 319–20
Paulinus, bishop of Nola, 42
pax. *See* kiss of peace
Peace of Lodi, 134
Pellizari, Nicolo di Battista, and Inquisition, 264
Pellizeria, 136, 137
Peranda, Sante, 221, 231
Perugia, 32, 52, 89
Peter, saint, 70
Philip of Courtenay, 44
physicians, 208, 210
Piazza San Marco, 26, 61, 118, 233
Pietà, hospital of, 334
pilgrimage, 82, 139, 267
Pisano, Leonardo, 90
Pitati, Bonifazio de' (Veronese), 117, 221, 233
Pius IV, pope, 148–9
Pius V, pope, 254
plague, 4, 17, 75, 98–101, 198, 208, 307–18. *See also* Black Death
Pojano Maggiore, 117
Polo, Marco, 33, 66, 68
Ponte, Lorenzo Da, 336
Ponte dei Baretteri, 187
poor, poverty, poor relief, 6, 22, 39, 71, 81, 82, 83, 143, 145, 151, 246, 289, 293
popolo, popolani, 3–17, 35, 95, 114, 189, 212, 245–6
pork butchers, 231
Porto, Luigi da, 145
Portuguese, 114
Pozzoserrato, Lodovico, 291
priesthood of all believers, 200, 252, 282
princely courts, 118–19
Procurators of Saint Mark, 6, 183
prostitution, 48, 59, 121
Protestant, Protestantism, 39, 254
Provveditori alle Pompe, 249
Provveditori di Comun, 17, 19, 21, 22, 76–7, 82, 84–5, 93, 114, 187, 221, 258, 316
Provveditori sopra i Monasteri, 249

Provveditori sopra le Scuole Grandi, 249
Pullan, Brian, 6, 51, 57, 61, 76, 166, 177–8, 249
purgatory, 261, 317

quilt makers, 58

Raines, Dorit, 320
Rangone, Tomaso, 286
Ranke, Leopold von, 255
Raphael, artist, 198, 281
Rapp, Richard, 152, 322
Ravenna, 53
Ravi, Pietro Francesco, 323–5
reason of State, 26, 250, 258, 269–71, 278, 279
reciprocity, 11, 250, 258
Reformation, 16
Rialto, 15, 26, 27, 58, 94, 95, 116, 118, 242
Ridolfi, Carlo, 281, 297
Risorgimento, 140
Riva degli Schiavoni, 115
Riva del Carbon, 129
Roch, saint, 51, 219, 268
rosaries, 221
Rossi, Domenico, 311
Rousseau, Jean-Jacques, 329, 335
Rudolf II, emperor, 221
Ruga degli Oresi, 221
Ruskin, John, 19, 26, 86, 216, 280, 293, 299, 334

Sacca della Misericordia, 25
Sack of Rome, 118, 145
Sagornino, Giovanni, 126, 129
San Barnaba, church of, 93, 191
San Bartolomeo, church of, 58, 202, 203, 221, 242, 272, 274–5
San Basso, church of, 190
San Biasio, church of, 86, 204
San Cassian, parish of, 68
San Daniele, church of, 53, 88
San Fantin, church and parish of, 94, 121, 263
San Felice, parish of, 68
San Filippo Giacomo, parish of, 120, 210
San Francesco del Deserto, island of, 96, 99
San Francesco della Vigna, church of, 80, 135
San Gallo, parish of, 121
San Geminiano, church and parish of, 130, 137, 203, 205
San Giacometto. *See* San Giacomo di Rialto
San Giacomo dell'Orio, church and parish of, 68, 93, 276
San Giacomo di Rialto, church of, 216, 219, 339
San Gieremia, church of, 53, 90
San Giobbe, church of, 53, 85, 95, 99, 101
San Giorgio dei Greci, church of, 100, 115
San Giorgio Maggiore, church of, 26
San Giovanni dei Furlani, church of. *See* San Giovanni del Tempio
San Giovanni dei Templari, church of. *See* San Giovanni del Tempio
San Giovanni del Tempio, church of, 80, 99
San Giovanni di Malta, church of. *See* San Giovanni del Tempio
San Giovanni Elemosinario, church of. *See* San Zuan Elemosinario
San Giovanni Grisostomo, church of. *See* San Zuan Grisostomo
San Giovanni in Bragora, church of. *See* San Zuan in Bragora
San Giovanni in Oglio, church of. *See* San Zan Novo

San Giovanni Novo, church of. *See* San Zan Novo
San Giuliano, church of. *See* San Zulian
San Gregorio, church of, 83
San Lio, parish of, 68, 121
San Luca, church and parish of, 121, 136, 203
San Marco, basilica of, 26, 42–4, 60–71, 120, 242. *See also* Piazza San Marco
San Marco, Sestiere di, 94
San Marcuola, church of, 100, 230
San Marzilian, church and parish of, 63, 70
San Matteo, church of, 59
San Matteo, church of (Murano), 59
San Maurizio, church of, 94
San Moise, church and parish of, 53, 82, 121, 263, 318, 327
San Nicolo dei Mendicoli, church and parish of, 73, 100, 191, 205, 210
San Pantalon, parish of, 68
San Paternian, parish of, 121
San Pietro di Castello, church of, 26, 42, 86
San Polo, church and parish of, 65, 68, 202, 209
San Provolo, church and parish of, 121, 203
San Salvador, church and parish of, 73, 93, 94, 137, 154, 203, 212, 231
San Samuele, church of, 206, 220, 260–71, 273
San Silvestro, church and parish of, 191, 207, 209, 215–16, 241, 274–5
San Simeon Grande, church of. *See* San Simeon Profeta
San Simeon Piccolo, church of, 212
San Simeon Profeta, church of, 53
San Simeone e Giuda, church of. *See* San Simeon Piccolo
San Stefano, church and parish of, 74, 121, 197, 198
San Tomà, church and parish of, 68, 260
San Trovaso, parish of, 68
San Vitale, church of, 273
San Zaccaria, church and nunnery of, 53, 73
San Zan Novo, church and parish of, 80, 99, 120
San Zanipolo, church and parish of, 20, 88, 190, 208, 251, 263, 272
San Zuan Elemosinario, church of, 219, 242
San Zuan Grisostomo, church and parish of, 66, 121, 266
San Zuan in Bragora, church of, 204, 335
San Zuan in Oglio. *See* San Zan Novo
San Zulian, church and parish of, 73, 121, 161, 181, 191, 202, 203, 286
Sansovino, Francesco, 58, 68, 69, 96
Sansovino, Jacopo, 96, 118, 233, 283
Sant'Agnese, church of, 212
Sant'Alvise, church of, 95
Sant'Anna, church of, 85, 87
Sant'Anzolo, church and parish of, 80, 121
Sant'Apollinare, church of. *See* Sant'Aponal
Sant'Aponal, church of, 191, 241, 273
Sant'Eufemia, church of (Giudecca), 205
Santa Croce, church of, 87
Santa Croce, Girolamo da, 215
Santa Croce, Sestiere di, 211, 318
Santa Margherita, church and parish of, 68, 191, 314
Santa Maria Assunta, church and locality of, 84, 85, 191, 248, 310, 329
Santa Maria dei Carmini, church of, 81
Santa Maria dei Crociferi, church of. *See* Santa Maria Assunta
Santa Maria dei Miracoli, church of, 139

Santa Maria dei Servi, church of, 86, 96
Santa Maria del Carmine, church of. *See* Santa Maria dei Carmini
Santa Maria del Giglio, church of. *See* Santa Maria Zobenigo
Santa Maria del Rosario, church of, 329
Santa Maria della Celestia, church of, 85
Santa Maria della Fava, church and parish of, 26, 121
Santa Maria della Presentazione, church of (Giudecca), 248
Santa Maria della Salute, church of, 327
Santa Maria dell'Orto, church of, 66, 84, 96, 98, 287, 310
Santa Maria di Nazaret, island of, 96
Santa Maria Formosa, church and parish of, 68, 100, 209, 214, 273, 275
Santa Maria Gloriosa dei Frari, church of, 15, 68, 69, 84, 88, 95, 239–42, 272
Santa Maria Nova, church of, 203
Santa Maria Zobenigo, church and parish of, 121, 327
Santa Marina, church and parish of, 82, 121
Santi Apostoli, church and parish of, 68, 87
Santi Ermagora e Fortunato, church of. *See* San Marcuola
Santi Gervasio e Protasio, church of. *See* San Trovaso
Santi Giovanni e Paolo, church and parish of. *See* San Zanipolo
Sanudo, Marin, 43, 60, 121, 131, 143, 145, 148, 197
Sardi, Giuseppe, 327
Sarpi, Paolo, 132, 251, 255, 278–80
Savi sopra le Tansse, 133
Savoy, Duchy of, 307
Sbriziolo, Lia, 77
Scuola degli Albanesi, 88, 94
Scuola degli Armeni, 94
Scuola degli Ebrei, 116
Scuola degli Schiavoni. *See* Scuola di San Giorgio degli Schiavoni
Scuola dei Milanesi, 88, 94, 116, 139
Scuola del Rosario, 132, 190
Scuola del Volto Santo (dei Lucchesi), 116
Scuola della Beata Vergine dei Zotti, 80
Scuola della Beata Vergine del Terremoto, 203, 275
Scuola della Beata Vergine dell Nattività, 93
Scuola della Beata Vergine della Concettion, dei Ciechi, 82
Scuola della Beata Vergine (San Salvador), 94
Scuola della Beata Vergine (Santa Maria Maggiore), 101
Scuola della Dottrina Cristiana, 251
Scuola della Madonna (San Marzilian), 69
Scuola della Madonna e San Francesco dei Mercanti. *See* Scuola di Santa Maria della Misericordia
Scuola della Misericordia. *See* Scuola di Santa Maria della Misericordia
Scuola della Nattività della Beata Vergine, 191
Scuola della Passione, 236
Scuola della Santissima Croce (San Salvador), 80, 94, 100
Scuola della Santissima Croce (Santa Croce), 87
Scuola di Corpus Domini, 87, 91, 95
Scuola di San Bernardino, 77, 85, 95, 97, 99
Scuola di San Biagio, 23
Scuola di San Cristofalo (dei veluderi), 191, 311
Scuola di San Cristoforo dei Mercanti, 17, 22, 23, 65, 67, 69, 84, 85, 96, 101, 310, 311

Scuola di San Francesco, 80
Scuola di San Giacomo, 93
Scuola di San Gieremia, "della Buona Morte," 94
Scuola di San Giorgio degli Schiavoni, 88, 99
Scuola di San Giovanni Battista, 80
Scuola di San Giovanni Evangelista, 51, 57, 58, 61, 86
Scuola di San Giuliano, 72
Scuola di San Giuseppe, 100, 203
Scuola di San Gottardo, 59
Scuola di San Gregorio, 81
Scuola di San Lorenzo, 191
Scuola di San Lunardo, 94
Scuola di San Marco, 23, 57, 61, 76, 95, 202, 233
Scuola di San Mattia, 192, 221
Scuola di San Nicolo, 94, 191
Scuola di San Nicolo dei Greci, 100, 115
Scuola di San Nicolo di Bari dei Mercanti, 81, 82
Scuola di San Pietro Martire e San Vincenzo Ferrer e Santa Cattarina, 20
Scuola di San Raffaele e Nicheta, 73
Scuola di San Rocco, 21, 51, 57, 100, 233
Scuola di San Rocco e San Nicolo, 99
Scuola di San Rocco e Santa Margherita, 99, 191
Scuola di San Sebastiano (San Giacomo dell'Orio), 100
Scuola di San Sebastiano (San Sebastiano), 100
Scuola di San Stefano, 74
Scuola di San Teodoro, 16, 18, 57, 58, 73, 153–4, 169
Scuola di San Vettor, 78, 89, 191
Scuola di San Zaccaria e San Lizier, 94, 203
Scuola di Sant'Agnese, 68, 83
Scuola di Sant'Alberto, 81
Scuola di Sant'Alvise, 95
Scuola di Sant'Ambrogio, 87
Scuola di Sant'Anna, 87
Scuola di Sant'Antonio, 23, 239–42
Scuola di Sant'Antonio degli Orefici, 207
Scuola di Sant'Orsola, 80, 81
Scuola di Santa Barbara dei Bombardieri, 100
Scuola di Santa Catterina, 203
Scuola di Santa Maria dei Carmini, 57
Scuola di Santa Maria della Carità, 51, 57, 58, 60, 83, 86, 202
Scuola di Santa Maria della Celestia, 68, 80, 83
Scuola di Santa Maria della Misericordia, 35, 48–74, 77, 84, 96, 202, 299, 310
Scuola di Santa Maria della Val Verde. *See* Scuola di Santa Maria della Misericordia
Scuola di Santa Maria della Visitazione, 100
Scuola di Santa Maria e San Cristofalo, 84. *See also* Scuola di Santa Maria della Misericordia
Scuola di Santa Maria e San Francesco. *See* Scuola di Santa Maria della Misericordia
Scuola di Santa Maria e San Giovanni Battista, 77
Scuola di Santa Marina, 80
Scuola di Santi Apostoli, 17, 51, 61, 86–7
Scuola di Santi Cosmo e Damiano, 80
scuole: expenses of, 83; foundations of, 20, 76, 79, 92, 93, 132
Scuole del Santissimo Sacramento. *See* Venerabile, Scuole del
scuole delle arti, 48, 51, 58, 191

Scuole di Sant'Adriano, 316
Scuole Grandi, 6, 21, 51, 65, 75–7, 79, 95, 99, 157, 191, 201, 207, 242, 249, 278, 282. *See also* flagellants, flagellation
scuole piccole, 9, 17, 77, 79, 93, 99, 316
Sebastian, saint, 269
second-hand dealers, 236
Secchini, Francesco, 132, 165, 187, 190, 271
Senate, 160, 272
Sercambi, Giovanni, 89
Sermon on the Mount, 38
Serrata del Maggior Consiglio, 12, 28, 30, 45, 65
Sestieri, 23, 120. *See also* Cannaregio, Sestiere di; Castello, Sestiere di; Dorsoduro, Sestiere di; San Marco, Sestiere di; San Nicolo, Sestiere di; San Polo, Sestiere di; Santa Croce, Sestiere di
Sffoger, Zuan, and Inquisition, 265–9
Sfondrati, Battista, 57
Sforza, Francesco, 147–9
Shakespeare, William, 4, 42, 281, 299
shoemakers, 211, 260
Siena, 72, 89
silk merchants, 160
Sixtus V, pope, 255
Smith, Adam, 3, 11, 33, 42, 269
"social discipline," 247, 279
Somaschi, Order of, 149, 248, 311
Soranzo, Antonio, 90
sovvegni, 10, 89, 100, 189, 190, 206–13, 317
"Spanish" Conspiracy, 252, 279
spice trade, 114
statutes, 13, 18, 27, 58, 87, 92, 94, 177, 211
stonemasons, 25, 117, 139
suffragi, 306–18
sumptuary laws, 320
Swiss Confederation, 142, 147
Symonds, John Addington, 149

Taiamonte, Martino, 23
tailors, 311, 325
Taine, Hippolyte, 299
Tassini, Giuseppe, 90
tax, taxation, taxes, 251, 279
Terraferma. *See* Venice, mainland state
Theatine Order, 149, 251
Theodore, saint, 43, 60, 154
Thiene, Gaetano, cardinal, 248
Thomas Aquinas, saint, 57
Tiepolo, Baiamonte, 92
Tiepolo, Giambattista, 329
Tiepolo, Jacopo, doge, 30
Tiepolo, Lorenzo, doge, 13, 31, 44
Tintoretto, Domenico, 221, 282
Tintoretto, Jacopo, 215, 231, 236, 258, 280–99, 320, 335
Tintoretto, Marco, 283
Tintoretto, Marietta, 283
Titian, 55, 116, 118, 281, 283
Tomaso, silk throwster, and Inquisition, 265
Torre dell'Orologio, 129, 185
traghetti. *See* Venice, ferries
Tramontin, Silvio, 41
transubstantiation, 198
Tre Savi Sopra l'Eresia, 255
Treaty of Bologna, 118
Tremignon, Alessandro, 327
Trevisan, Giovanni, patriarch, 255
Treviso, 52, 154
Tronchetto, 113
Turks. *See* Ottoman Empire

Ullmann, Walter, 280
Ursula, Saint, 81

usurers, usury, 55

Val Sassina, 141–50
Valgrisio, Vincenzo, bookseller, and Inquisition, 264
Valier, Agostino, bishop of Verona, 272, 273
Vassilacchi, Antonio, l'Aliense, 283
Vecellio, Francesco, 233
Venerabile, Scuole del, 9, 73, 74, 76, 89, 189, 190–206, 214, 219, 246, 262, 274, 277, 317
Venerabile, Scuola del, San Bartolomeo, 203
Venerabile, Scuola del, San Benetto, 205
Venerabile, Scuola del, San Biasio, 204
Venerabile, Scuola del, San Geremia, 201
Venerabile, Scuola del, San Lio, 205
Venerabile, Scuola del, San Nicolo dei Mendicoli, 205
Venerabile, Scuola del, San Pantalon, 204
Venerabile, Scuola del, San Paternian, 205
Venerabile, Scuola del, San Pietro di Castello, 201
Venerabile, Scuola del, San Polo, 199
Venerabile, Scuola del, San Provolo, 94
Venerabile, Scuola del, San Silvestro, 205
Venerabile, Scuola del, San Stae, 205
Venerabile, Scuola del, San Zan Novo, 21
Venerabile, Scuola del, Sant'Antonin, 204
Venerabile, Scuola del, Sant'Anzolo, 205
Venerabile, Scuola del, Sant'Eufemia, 205
Venerabile, Scuola del, Santa Margherita, 204
Venerabile, Scuola del, Santa Sofia, 205
Venerabile, Scuola del, Santa Ternità, 201
Venetian dialect, 87
Venice
  commune of, 17
  constitution of, 4–8, 12, 23, 28
  decline of, 12, 17, 307–36
  economy of, 33–6
  ferries in, 19
  interdict in, 251, 278
  mainland state, 15, 98, 102, 114, 122, 135–49, 255; and plague of 1630, 307–18; population of, 144, 307
  markets in, 26, 153, 216
  myth of, 5, 7, 53, 90, 209
  public debt, 30
  Republic of, 3, 114, 118, 139–50, 177
  shipyards of, 30. *See also* Arsenale
  as Signoria, 17, 89
  temporary visitors, 119–26
  workforce, 308
Vermigli, Pietro Martire, 254
Verona, Veronese, 117, 308
Veronese, Paolo Caliari, detto il, 117, 236, 268, 283
Vio, Gastone, 19, 22, 66, 88, 316
Virgin Mary, 42, 55, 61, 65, 71, 75, 80, 89, 93, 196, 204, 252, 316–17
visitation, apostolic, 20, 249, 271–8
Viterbo, Egidio da, 74, 197, 198, 246
Vittoria, Alessandro, 231, 283
Vivaldi, Antonio, 335
Vivarini, Alvise, 88

War of Candia, 4, 307, 308, 319
War of Chioggia, 57
Wars of Religion, 245
widows and orphans, 48
Willaert, Adriaan, 236
wine merchants, 215
women, 22, 73, 80–91, 85, 93, 94, 100, 121, 143, 248, 323
works, 83, 218

works of mercy, 40, 80, 205, 221, 278
Wotton, Sir Henry, 202

Zachary, saint, 94
Zattere, 251
Zechini, Francesco. *See* Secchini, Francesco
Zen, Ranier, 249
Zen, Ranieri, doge, 44
Zitelle. *See* Santa Maria della Presentazione
Zompini, Gaetano, 137
Zonca, Giovanni, and Inquisition, 265–6
Zuccaro, Federico, 299
zuoba grasso, 127
Zwingli, Huldrych, 197, 269

www.ingramcontent.com/pod-product-compliance
Lightning Source LLC
LaVergne TN
LVHW090145080826
844660LV00013B/676/J

* 9 7 8 1 4 4 2 6 4 9 6 8 2 *